The Complete Correspondence
of Friedrich Hölderlin

The Complete Correspondence
of Friedrich Hölderlin

Translated and edited by

CHARLIE LOUTH

Published by State University of New York Press, Albany

EU GPSR Authorised Representative:
Logos Europe, 9 rue Nicolas Poussin, 17000, La Rochelle, France
contact@logoseurope.eu

For information, contact State University of New York Press, Albany, NY
www.sunypress.edu

Library of Congress Cataloging-in-Publication Data

Names: Hölderlin, Friedrich, author. | Louth, Charles, translator and editor.
Title: The complete correspondence of Friedrich Hölderlin / Friedrich Hölderlin, author, and Charles Louth, translator and editor.
Description: Albany : State University of New York Press, [2025]. | Includes bibliographical references and index.
Identifiers: ISBN 9798855804171 (hardcover : alk. paper) | ISBN 9798855804195 (ebook) | ISBN 9798855804188 (pbk. : alk. paper)
Further information is available at the Library of Congress.

CONTENTS

CHRONOLOGY

1770   *20 March* Johann Christian Friedrich Hölderlin born into the "respectability" class in Lauffen am Neckar, north of Stuttgart, in the Duchy of Württemberg. Hegel, Wordsworth, and Beethoven born the same year.

1772   Death of father and birth of sister, Heinrike (Rike). Inherits a substantial sum to which he is never given direct access.

1774   Hölderlin's mother remarries and the family moves to the Schweizerhof in Nürtingen, south of Stuttgart.

1776   Half-brother, Karl Gok, born. Schooling begins in Nürtingen.

1779   Death of stepfather.

1781   Kant's *Critique of Pure Reason* published.

1783   First gets to know Schelling, five years his junior.

1784   Confirmed; enters *Klosterschule* (for pupils destined for the Church) in Denkendorf. First surviving poems from this year. Mother begins her record of "expenses incurred by dear Fritz, not to be deducted [from his inheritance] if he remains obedient."

1785   First surviving letter.

1786   Moves up to *Klosterschule* in Maulbronn.

1787   Writing poems and reading Schiller, Klopstock, Ossian, Young. Letters to Nast.

1788   Kant's *Critique of Practical Reason* published. *June* Hölderlin first sees the Rhine on a journey to Speyer, the first outside Swabia.

Gathers his poems together, and translates first two books of Homer's *Iliad*. In October enters the Stift (seminary) in Tübingen at the same time as Hegel. Meets Neuffer there.

1789 French Revolution. Complaints about life in Stift, which gains a reputation for revolutionary sympathies among its students. Hölderlin breaks off engagement to Louise Nast. First letters to Neuffer.

1790 Along with other students, begins reading Kant; also Leibniz and Herder. Works on his two examination dissertations: "History of the Fine Arts among the Greeks" and "Parallels between Solomon's Proverbs and Hesiod's *Works and Days*." Having passed examinations in philosophy (*September*), gains the title of *Magister* and moves on to the more narrowly theological part of his training. Writing poems influenced by Schiller. Schelling joins the Stift, aged fifteen. Begins complicated relationship with Elise LeBret. Kant's *Critique of Judgement* published.

1791 *April* Journey to Switzerland. First poems published. Reading Rousseau.

1792 Begins work on his novel, *Hyperion*. France declares war on the Austro-Prussian coalition, and French troops occupy Mainz. *October* His sister marries and becomes Heinrike Breunlin.

1793 *21 January* Louis XVI executed. First contact with Sinclair. Reading Plato. Meets Schiller, who recommends him for a post as house tutor in Waltershausen. After taking his final examinations, arrives at Charlotte von Kalb's in Waltershausen at the end of the year.

1794 Teaching Fritz von Kalb 9–11am and 3–5pm, otherwise reading Greek literature, Kant (*Critique of Judgement* especially), Fichte, and working hard on *Hyperion*. Acquaintance with Wilhelmine Marianne Kirms. Execution of Danton (*April*) and Robespierre (*July*). *November* Trip to Jena, where he meets Schiller and Goethe and attends Fichte's lectures. Moves to Weimar with the Kalbs. "Fragment of *Hyperion*" published in Schiller's journal *Neue Thalia*.

1795 *January* Leaves the Kalb household following troubles with Fritz, and with Charlotte von Kalb's blessing returns to Jena and lives next door to Fichte. Goes to his lectures, sees much of Schiller, also Niethammer, reads Goethe's novel *Wilhelm Meister's Apprenticeship*. The publisher Cotta agrees to publish the as-yet-unfinished *Hyperion*. Begins to get to know Sinclair better, and in *April* moves into his "garden-house," where he also meets Böhlendorff. Writes important early essay fragments. *May* Matriculates at the university, meets Novalis, and then suddenly quits Jena and goes home to Nürtingen via Heidelberg, where he meets Ebel. *July* Luise Agnese born (she died in September 1796), daughter of Wilhelmine Kirms and, very likely, Hölderlin. Several important conversations with Schelling in Tübingen and Nürtingen; becomes friends with Landauer in Stuttgart. Arrives in Frankfurt at end of the year, having accepted a new post in *September*. Publication of Schiller's *On Naive and Sentimental Poetry* and *On the Aesthetic Education of Man*.

1796   *January* Takes up job as house tutor in the Gontard household in Frankfurt, teaching in the mornings. Soon falls in love with Susette Gontard. Contact with Sinclair and Schelling. *July* With the family, minus Jakob Gontard, flight from advancing French troops to Kassel, and to Driburg (*August*). *End of September* Returns to Frankfurt. Hegel dedicates his poem "Eleusis" to Hölderlin. Resists mother's urging that he return to Württemberg to a post in a parish. Perhaps writes "Fragment of Philosophical Letters." At about this time "The Oldest Programme for a System of German Idealism" is written, a collaboration between Hölderlin, Hegel, and Schelling.

1797   *January* Hegel joins him in Frankfurt. *April* First volume of *Hyperion* appears. *22 August* Last meeting with Goethe, who advises him to write "little poems." *17 October* Treaty of Campo Formio. Continuing work on *Hyperion*, begins his tragedy *The Death of Empedocles*, many poems.

1798   Life in Frankfurt becomes difficult and unhappy. *End of September* Leaves Frankfurt and moves to nearby Homburg. Sporadic secret meetings and exchangings of letters with Susette. *November* At the Rastatt Congress with Sinclair. Finishes *Hyperion*.

1799   In this year, in Homburg, most of the theoretical essays are written, some for the unrealized journal project (*Iduna*), conceived in *May* and abandoned in the autumn. Some also relating to *Empedocles*, which after going through several versions is also abandoned at the end of the year (or early next). *October* Second volume of *Hyperion* appears. *9 November* Napoleon becomes first consul, and then declares the Revolution over. Last letter to Neuffer.

1800   Probably in this year translations of Pindar's Olympian and Pythian odes, closely connected with the deliberations of the essays. *2 March* Death of brother-in-law C. T. Breunlin. *8 May* Last meeting with Susette. *15 June* Treaty of Marengo, good prospects of peace. *June* Leaves Homburg for Nürtingen, having been away for four and a half years, then to lodge at Landauer's in Stuttgart (*20 June*). Gives private lessons; on the lookout for a new house tutor post. Home to Nürtingen for Christmas. Writing poems, including the first elegies.

1801   *January* Travels to new job in Hauptwil, Switzerland, mostly on foot. *9 February* Peace of Lunéville. *April* Employment in the Gonzenbach household terminated. Back home to Nürtingen. *2 June* Last letter to Schiller. Writing elegies and hymns. Plans for an edition of his poems with Cotta, which lead (only) to the publication of several important poems in journals. *December* Sets off toward Bordeaux, where his last tutorship has been found. By foot to Strasburg where he has to wait for a pass.

1802   *9 January* From Strasburg arrives in Lyon (possibly seeing Napoleon), then continues, still mostly on foot, to Bordeaux, arriving in the Meyer household at the end of the month. Possibly begins translations of Sophocles here (*Oedipus* and *Antigone*). *10 May* Issued with a pass to Strasburg and leaves the Meyers without apparent ill feeling on either side. Goes via Paris and sees some of the art treasures Napoleon fetched out of Italy. *June* Back in Stuttgart in a bad way, shocking those who see him. *22 June* Death of Susette Gontard. Summer in Nürtingen. *October* Attends congress at Regensburg with Sinclair. *November* Reported to have "totalement perdu la raison." Completes Sophocles translations and their "Notes" and looks for a publisher. Poems include "Patmos" and "Celebration of Peace."

1803   *January* Sends "Patmos" to the Landgrave in Homburg, via Sinclair. *June* Wilmans agrees to publish Sophocles translations. Visits

Schelling, who judges his mind "utterly ruined." Late revisions to Sophocles versions, which he sends to Wilmans in *December*; also revises several poems, including the "Night Songs."

1804 *April* Publication of *The Tragedies of Sophocles*. *June* Sinclair fetches him to Homburg via Stuttgart and Würzburg (possible last meeting with Schelling who finds him "in a better state than last year"). Takes lodgings with a French clockmaker, not far from Sinclair's, and receives sinecure as court librarian. Princess Auguste gives him a piano. *Pindar Fragments* perhaps written this year, following the publication of the "Night Songs" in the autumn. "The Archipelago" also published in one of Cotta's journals.

1805 *February* Sinclair arrested and accused of being party to treason against the Elector of Württemberg. Inquiries are also made into Hölderlin's involvement, but he is spared trial by being declared clinically insane. *9 May* Death of Schiller. *July* Sinclair is released without charge. Hölderlin moves to lodge with a saddler. Apparently working on Pindar.

1806 *July* The duchy of Hesse-Homburg absorbed in the new grand duchy of Hesse. *August* Sinclair writes to Hölderlin's mother saying that his madness has attained a "high degree" and he can no longer look after him. Hölderlin forcibly removed to Autenrieth's clinic in Tübingen. In the autumn, publication of the poems "Stuttgart," "The Journey," and "Night" (first strophe of "Bread and Wine"); the latter in particular much admired in Romantic circles (Schlegel, Tieck, and Brentano).

1807 *3 May* Discharged from the clinic as incurable with "at most three years" to live, and taken in by the carpenter Ernst Zimmer and his family. Their house is on the banks of the Neckar in Tübingen, Hölderlin's room forming a sort of tower overlooking the river. In the autumn the poems "The Rhine," "Patmos," and "Remembrance" published in a journal (unknown to Hölderlin).

1808 Hölderlin is given a piano, and later a flute. Musical improvisation is one of his main activities.

1811 Plans an almanac and writes a good deal for it. Begins to be frequently visited by students and others, as a spectacle.

1812   Probably first letters to mother, instigated by Zimmer.

1814   *February* Zimmer reports on a calm period in Hölderlin's life.

1815   Death of Sinclair. Battle of Waterloo.

1820   First moves toward collecting Hölderlin's poems.

1822   *Hyperion* reprinted in one volume.

1823   A notable though passing improvement in Hölderlin's condition. Many outings with the young writer Wilhelm Waiblinger.

1826   Hölderlin's *Poems* appear, edited by Ludwig Uhland and Gustav Schwab (without many of the most important).

1828   Death of Hölderlin's mother, who seems never to have visited him during his time in Tübingen. Dispute over inheritance breaks out between his sister and brother. Hölderlin is eventually awarded over nine thousand florins.

1830   Zimmer fixes the price for Hölderlin's board and lodging at 250 florins, a great deal less than the interest earned by his inheritance.

1831   Publication of an essay by Wilhelm Waiblinger, who had often visited Hölderlin when studying in Tübingen in the early 1820s (sometimes in the company of Eduard Mörike): *Friedrich Hölderlin's Life, Poetry and Madness*, the first biographical account. Death of Hegel.

1832   Death of Goethe.

1838   With the death of Zimmer, responsibility for Hölderlin's care is taken over by his youngest daughter, Lotte (1813–1879).

1839   Death of Neuffer.

1840   Publication of Bettina von Arnim's novel *Die Günderode*, which uses material about Hölderlin from Sinclair.

1841   Many poems signed Scardanelli, with fictitious dates.

1842   Second, expanded edition of Hölderlin's *Poems*, still far from complete. The same is true of the *Collected Works* that appears in two volumes in 1846 with a biographical essay by Christoph Theodor Schwab.

1843 *18 April* A newspaper in Cologne carries an article on Hölderlin, probably written by Gustav Schwab, which ranks him with Goethe and Schiller. Final poems. *7 June* Death of Hölderlin. Neither his sister nor his brother attends his funeral, but about a hundred students do.

INTRODUCTION

all that is good and sacred must be celebrated, and for that reason our correspondence should never remain interrupted for too long.

—Letter 230

Friedrich Hölderlin's first surviving letter, which is also his earliest existent manuscript of any kind, is written in a neat, confident hand on three sides of two small pieces of paper (about 5¼ by 6½ inches) that have been folded twice, down and across the middle. The lines are remarkably level, the writing clear, with minimal corrections. There is a wide and even margin on the left, and on the right the lines stop just short of the paper's edge. It must be a fair copy of a letter done first in draft, and the care that has gone into it is evident.[1] This is in keeping with the content, in which the fifteen-year-old Hölderlin presents himself, to his teacher and spiritual advisor, as someone examining his conscience and striving to live a good Christian life. His earnest desire to give account of his state of mind, in accordance with Pietist principles and practices, is reflected in the handwriting. The balance and repose suggested by the letter itself point to an ideal that the "to and fro" of his feelings, the supposed inconstancy of his "heart" as it negotiates between the demands of his fellow humans and those of God, seem to prevent access to.

It is unusual to be able to comment on the relationship between the form and content of Hölderlin's letters in this way because, as is widely thought, the greater part of the correspondence has not survived. And

---

1. A facsimile of the letter is given in Friedrich Hölderlin, *Sämtliche Werke*, ed. Dietrich Sattler et al., 20 vols. (Frankfurt: Stroemfeld/Roter Stern, 1975–2008), XVIII, 11–14.

what has made it down to us is often not in original manuscripts but in copies made in the nineteenth century by Christoph Theodor Schwab and Gustav Schlesier. Adolf Beck has pointed out that the late discovery of Hölderlin's importance, which became widely clear only on publication of the fourth volume of Norbert von Hellingrath's edition in 1916, meant that he missed out on the positivist phase of scholarship that might have secured the documentary basis, as it did for Goethe and Schiller, during the nineteenth century. The first attempt to gather the whole of Hölderlin's correspondence was not made until 1890, by Carl Litzmann.[2] A handful of letters emerged in the following decades, but Adolf Beck's meticulous research for the letters volumes (1954 and 1958) of the Stuttgart edition only unearthed one unknown letter. And since then just a single further letter has come to light (in 1999).[3] Many letters were destroyed by Hölderlin's half-brother, Karl Gok, including the originals of all the letters Hölderlin sent him. Apart from a clutch of partial drafts the letters to Susette Gontard, Isaak von Sinclair, and Siegfried Schmid, the last of whom said that Hölderlin wrote him "splendid letters," have disappeared without trace. It seems probable that at least some of these would have been of comparable density and acuity to the two famous letters to Casimir Böhlendorff (Letters 238 and 242 in this edition). But despite the likelihood that what we have represents only a "fraction" (Beck) of the letters Hölderlin actually wrote, the "torso of a torso" (Sattler), this is still a full and revealing correspondence, and the best source of knowledge about Hölderlin's life we have. In it we can read the "ebb and flow" of his sensibility, the quality of his engagement with the world, the conditions in which he lived, and, though it can be only a glimpse, gain some sense of his everyday life and character. We can also, of course, witness his development as a poet and thinker, not just in what he tells us about it but in the writing itself.

～

The span of time covered by Hölderlin's letters was one of the great periods of letter writing in Germany and one in which the letter was seized upon

---

2. Carl C. T. Litzmann, *Friedrich Hölderlins Leben: In Briefen von und an Hölderlin* (Berlin: Hertz, 1890).

3. Letter 188 to Ebel (6 July 1799)—discovered by Hermann F. Weiss and first published in *Text* 5 (1999): 121–34.

as a particular conveyance. By then it had developed, thanks in part to its use in the epistolary novel under the influence of Rousseau, into a recognized means of articulating the self, a place where it was possible to expose one's thoughts and feelings and reveal doubts and weaknesses. In a letter from 1795 to his friend Ludwig Neuffer, one of his most important correspondents, Hölderlin apologizes for bothering him with his discontentedness and then adds: "But if I wanted to force myself to abstract from the poor individual I am, I'd write a dissertation and not a letter" (Letter 109). A letter is for grumbling, among other things, but grumbling understood as an aspect of how one really is, something the letter is peculiarly able to relate. The letter is a key mode of friendship, and the good and the bad thing about friendship, Hölderlin continues, is that "one always acts as one is, that one feels the bad days twice over because one can speak of them, as also with the good days." Speaking of one's days, presenting oneself as one is, as a "poor individual," is what the letter is for. There is a fundamental openness about Hölderlin's engagement with others in his letters even though particular circumstances almost always mean that he is also obliged to conceal things, especially when writing to his mother. In this letter to Neuffer, besides voicing his anxieties about the future (he is waiting to hear from Frankfurt about a tutoring position there), regretting his precipitate departure from Jena, and worrying that he may have outstayed his welcome at home, Hölderlin asks his friend to send the piece of cashmere and the measurements for a suit he has left on his table. He then promises to send an elegy he is writing and says he has taken refuge in Kant again, "as always when I'm fed up with myself." He appears to his friend in a state of undress, presenting a patchwork of the pieces that make up his life at that moment. But connecting all these segments is an overriding "tone," what in a later letter to Neuffer (Letter 168) he calls the "tone of my soul." It is this personal tone or note that the letter has to transmit.

There is not much reasoning in this letter—Hölderlin says he is not in the right frame of mind and lacks the time. But many of his letters, including some to Neuffer but notably those to his half-brother, Karl, do contain long passages of exposition in which he unfolds his thoughts. And around 1800 the letter was also a favored vehicle for philosophy and a form Hölderlin chose for several of his actual and projected works. To his "philosophical mentor," Immanuel Niethammer, in February 1796, Hölderlin writes that he and Friedrich Schelling, though not always in agreement, were "at one" in the belief that "new ideas" could best be expressed in the form of letters. It's possible that by new ideas he means not merely fresh ideas but the ideas of the new post-Kantian, Romantic philosophy he was closely involved with. Schelling wrote his "Philosophical Letters on Dogmatism and Criticism" for Niethammer's *Journal* in 1795, and at about the same time Hölderlin decided to convert his novel *Hyperion* into the epistolary form and told Niethammer about his own plans for a series of "philosophical letters," which in pugnacious allusion to Schiller he intended to call *New Letters on the Aesthetic Education of Man*. A significant start on this is probably what survives as a "Fragment of Philosophical Letters."[4] Several of Hölderlin's other essay-drafts, especially those intended for his failed journal project *Iduna*, also take the form of letters. Part of the attraction is the idea of an (implicit or explicit) addressee, someone whose interest and attention is built into the mode of speaking and who can complete the sense. As Hölderlin put it in his late idiom: "Psyche among friends, the formation of thoughts in conversations and letters, is vital for artists" (Letter 242 to Böhlendorff, November 1802). "Psyche" implies something provisional, something evolving, which is peculiar to the letter form. Unlike with a "dissertation," there is room for uncertainty, for changing tack, for hints and jumps in the argument, and for the moment of writing to be part of what is being worked out. Possibly it is this nonsystematic aspect of the letter that Hölderlin has in mind when he tells Niethammer that in his proposed philosophical letters he will "go on from philosophy to poetry and religion." Letters also come with a clear and again intrinsic sense of a particular person developing a point of view, improvising in a way that the situation of the letter facilitates, creating a current of thought that might be drawn off in different directions. To Hegel in January 1795 Hölderlin wrote that he would take "your image and your friendship as the conductor of my thoughts into the outer world of the senses" by sending him letters "which you can judge and correct" (Letter 95). Contemporary philosophy was in large part an investigation of the self, and the letter was particularly apt to explore and extend it and perhaps more importantly to acknowledge its part, including its limitations, in the unfolding of knowledge.

---

4. See Friedrich Hölderlin, *Essays and Letters*, ed. and trans. Jeremy Adler and Charlie Louth (London: Penguin, 2009), 234–39. This is the title given by the Frankfurt edition ("Fragment philosophischer Briefe"); the Stuttgart editors call it "On Religion" ("Über Religion").

Many of Hölderlin's letters are of course to friends. If it is true, as Hölderlin writes to Neuffer in 1796 regretting his absence, that "the written word is to friendship what opaque vessels are to a golden wine" (Letter 124), then letters are engaged in the impossible task of summoning up at a distance something that demands presence, and in doing so with a means that ill suits the task. To Hegel he says similarly that "letter writing can only ever be a makeshift" (Letter 85). But the moment in Hölderlin's correspondence that acknowledges that situation most intensely, words that open a draft to Susette Gontard, do not speak of failure: "Every day I have to invoke the absent divinity again" (Letter 183). A letter is more than the sum of its words. Novalis thought that "every true letter is in its nature poetic," and that seems to hold true for Hölderlin's in that they aim to make the separation that is the premise of any letter resonant.[5] His poems, many of which are themselves addressed to friends or relatives, observe a similar dynamic, one expressed in its purest form in lines 9 to 15 of "Patmos":

> since the peaks of time
> Are heaped around us, and those we love most
> Live nearby, failing fast
> On divided mountains,
> Give us innocent water,
> Oh give us wings, to go across
> In all fidelity, and to return.

The bulk of the surviving letters, well over half, are addressed to Hölderlin's family, to his mother, sister, and brother (and this is without counting the final letters written from Tübingen, all of which are to the family, mostly his mother). The strange cohabitation of the near and the distant that animates "Patmos" is also at the heart of the letters.

~

Hölderlin's parents both belonged to the Swabian "Respectability" or *Ehrbarkeit*, the class that had long filled the ecclesiastical and main secular administrative positions in Württemberg. They represented both these

---

5. Novalis, *Schriften*, ed. Paul Kluckhohn, Richard Samuel, et al., 6 vols. (Stuttgart: Kohlhammer, 1977–99), II, 435.

traditions, since Hölderlin's father, a lawyer by training, had inherited from his father the role of steward and administrator of what had once been a Benedictine convent, and his mother was the daughter of a village pastor. The *Ehrbarkeit* had certain rights that guaranteed them a degree of independence from the power structures of the court, an arrangement dating back to 1514 that had been reaffirmed vis-à-vis the Duke of Württemberg only a few weeks before Hölderlin's birth on 20 March 1770 in the small town of Lauffen am Neckar.

Most of the recollections of childhood in Hölderlin's letters and poems are fond and idyllic, and it was certainly a privileged one in many ways. But it was also marked by death and disruption, and, from early on, the career his mother determined him for, to be ordained in the Lutheran Church and take a living somewhere in Württemberg, meant that he was subjected to a severe and disciplined schooling accompanied by an acute sense of duty and debt. His mother was anxious and frugal, qualities heightened no doubt by the loss of Hölderlin's father to a stroke in July 1772, shortly before the birth of her daughter Heinrike ("Rike"). She remarried in 1774, but this "second father," a wine-merchant from Nürtingen who was soon to become mayor, died in 1779. By then Johanna Christiana Gok had given birth eight times with only three survivors, the youngest of whom was Hölderlin's half-brother Karl, born in 1776. Left a widow, she was well provided for, but seems never to have relaxed. Hölderlin's letters to her, which include one in which he remembers her "daily grief and tears" after the death of his stepfather and ascribes his own "melancholy tendency" to that event (Letter 181), show a clear attachment to her and even a kind of intimacy; there is a strong sense of gratitude, but they are also strained, as if the relationship could never quite fall into the ease he would have liked. Fundamentally the two were at odds, since she wanted him to settle down as a country pastor nearby, whereas it became clearer and clearer to him that such a life would never be compatible with the single-minded pursuit of his poetic ambitions. But though he had no doubt that in order to fulfill them he would have to remain "abroad," that is, outside the confines of Württemberg where the Consistory, or ecclesiastical board, could oblige him to take a benefice, he was continually drawn homeward, so that his life can be described as a series of ventures outward, resulting in various kinds of failure and return and leading in the end to a life "homeless at home" (John Clare) in Tübingen, living in the shadow of the Stift where his theological training had been completed and now so estranged from his family that his mother never visited him.

Hölderlin's first school was the *Lateinschule* in Nürtingen, where the precocious Schelling, though five years younger, overlapped with him and became a friend. Progressing on the long road toward ordination meant passing yearly exams, and Hölderlin received supplementary instruction in Latin and Greek from Nathanael Köstlin, the deacon (*Diakon*) who was the recipient of his first letter and something of a mentor to him at this stage. Hölderlin sent this letter from Denkendorf, about five miles north of Nürtingen, in autumn 1785, by which time he had been studying in the lower convent school there for a year. Having satisfied the requirements, he had, at the age of fourteen, entered into a legal contract that guaranteed him a free education, an excellent one in the humanist tradition, so long as he went on and became a servant of the Lutheran Church. If he did not, the entire cost—tuition, board, and lodging—had in principle to be reimbursed. In practice this seemed rarely to happen, but it remained the case that Hölderlin was bound to the ecclesiastical authorities and into a system, and was continually, at the very least, having to justify himself for straying from the intended path. Most immediately and in the first instance, the sense of duty and obligation was to his mother, and really their whole relationship was colored by the growing disjunction between her expectations and his.

At Denkendorf, as in the upper *Klosterschule* in Maulbronn he moved to two years later, Hölderlin was subject to strict monastic discipline and living conditions quite unlike what he had been used to at home. Pupils wore a black habit, rose at dawn or earlier, washed in water cold from the well, and shared their beds with mice. Though it was no doubt usual to complain, Hölderlin seems to have hated both institutions, which were also corrupt and coarse in various ways. His letters from these years—twenty-four have survived from his going to Denkendorf to his leaving Maulbronn for Tübingen—contain many complaints and mournful self-characterizations. Most are to his friend Immanuel Nast, a clerk in Leonberg whose cousin, Louise Nast, was the daughter of the steward-administrator at Maulbronn. The letters to Nast, while introspective, are also a celebration of their friendship and often have a liveliness and energy that perhaps owe something to the prose of Goethe's hero Werther. Like Werther, Hölderlin was quick to fall in love, and soon after arriving in Maulbronn had begun a relationship with

Louise Nast that ended a few months after he moved on to Tübingen in October 1788. The reasons he gave for breaking off the engagement are revealing and only slightly veiled: in talking of his "vast desire" and "frustrated ambition," he implies that his commitment to writing will make him unfit for married life (Letter 27). His final school report included a mark for *Poësie* in which he is the only student with an "excellent." By then he had indeed written a good deal of verse and gathered some of it in a manuscript known as the "Marbacher Quartheft" as a kind of sum of his achievements so far. This verse was not yet particularly accomplished, but it betrays an absolute seriousness of intent. One poem to which he seems to have attached a special significance, since he reworked it when he arrived in Tübingen, already names his two most important poetic models: Pindar and Klopstock. They were the "highest," most ambitious models available, and never supplanted. But perhaps the best bit of writing from this time, the clearest sense of a deep impression being made, comes in the letter journal he wrote his mother giving an account of a journey made during his final year at Maulbronn. At the invitation of relations in the Rhineland he traveled to Speyer, his first venture beyond the limits of his Swabian homeland, and encountered the Rhine at evening "coming from so far away that the boats were barely visible—and so far across that almost it could be taken for a wall of blue" (Letter 23). The writing seems to breathe.

The Stift in Tübingen, the Lutheran seminary where Hölderlin entered the third stage of his theological training in October 1788, was a prestigious and long-standing institution, though its reputation was flagging a bit by the time Hölderlin got there. It was part of yet slightly apart from the university, and as such it afforded more freedom than had been the case at school. But still there were many constraints, and growing tension with the new political ideals soon to be released by the French Revolution and the new philosophical ideas elaborated by Kant. The *Critique of Pure Reason* had come out in 1781. The *Critique of Practical Reason* (1788) and the *Critique of Judgement* (1790) coincided with Hölderlin's student years, and he was soon reading Kant avidly. Looking back, Hölderlin referred to at least some of his teachers in the Stift as the "Tübingen gravediggers" (Letter 108) and discouraged Hegel from applying for a job there by saying that it "smells like a bier that's already been attacked by the worm" (Letter 128). But it's notable that these dramatically negative remarks are both addressed to Hegel, and in reality the teaching Hölderlin received at the Stift was more open-minded. Several of his teachers, including the theologian whose ideas did most to shape what was taught, Gottlob Christian Storr (1746–1805), were receptive to Kant, even if they also defended their exegetical work against what they saw as the corruptions of the Enlightenment. Storr combined historical criticism of the Bible with a practical faith in the person of Christ, both of which were nourished by Pietism and seem clearly to have marked Hölderlin.[6] Pietism, a significant part of Hölderlin's upbringing and of that of most of his teachers, encouraged a belief in the possibility of a fully realized life here on earth, which sometimes came into conflict with the more conservative or orthodox aspects of Lutheran theology. The motto "Kingdom of God" (*Reich Gottes*) with which Hölderlin and Hegel parted on completing their studies in 1793, standing for faith in immanence as opposed to the consignment of fulfilment to an afterlife, had a Pietist origin.

Hegel, one of four boys from the *Gymnasium* in Stuttgart, entered the Stift at the same time as Hölderlin but they did not become close until 1790, when, as Hölderlin tells his sister in Letter 38, they moved into the same room and were joined by the fifteen-year-old Schelling. His best friend in Tübingen was Neuffer, who had already been at the Stift for two years when Hölderlin arrived. Together with another student, Rudolf Magenau, they formed a poets' club that met weekly in a pub to present and criticize one another's poems. Neuffer was urban, seemed perhaps exotic (his mother was reputed to be Greek), and introduced Hölderlin into the literary world in Tübingen and Stuttgart, leading late in 1791 to his first publication, four poems in the *Swabian Muses' Almanac*, whose editor, Gotthold Stäudlin, was important to Hölderlin both for his literary views (like Hölderlin he favored Schiller and Klopstock) and for his political ones. He was a fearless campaigner for the ideals of the French Revolution and was banned from Württemberg in 1793, eventually drowning himself in the Rhine in 1796. Neuffer may also have had a hand in Hölderlin's acquaintance with Elise LeBret, the daughter of the university's chancellor. Despite Hölderlin's vow to his mother in 1791 "never to marry" (Letter 47), he fell in love with LeBret in 1790 and some sort of relationship lasted until at least 1794. But to signal to his

---

6. For more on Storr, see the late Michael Franz's account in Michael Franz, Ulrich Gaier, Valérie Lawitschka, et al., *Hölderlin Texturen*, 1.2, *"Alle meine Hofnungen"*: *Tübingen, 1788–1793* (Tübingen: Hölderlin-Gesellschaft, 2017), 125–34.

mother that he wished to remain single, however she may have taken it, was tantamount to saying, not for the first time, that he didn't want to become a pastor. After only a year at the Stift, Hölderlin had had serious doubts about continuing and considered switching to Jena to study law. His mother was against it, and in January 1790 he gave in and wrote a conciliatory letter evoking "the joys of a quiet parish" (Letter 33). As he wrote to Neuffer on 28 November 1791, "the reason I'm still in the Stift is that my mother wishes it" (Letter 49). To his sister he had already made plain his heart's desire, "to live one day in peace and seclusion—and to be able to write books without going hungry" (Letter 45). Perhaps occasionally he managed to convince himself that this could be done in a quiet parish, and the formulation, which he knew his mother would also read, is meant not to rule that out, but deep down it was obvious to him that the two were incompatible. His commitment to his writing was, from the beginning, total. In the copy of Stäudlin's *Almanac* he gave to his mother, he made that quite clear, provocatively connecting it to her in his words of dedication: "Allow me, dearest Mother, to dedicate what you will find in here by me to you. They are youthful efforts, juvenilia. They would, even if this kind of poem were better suited to our times, find little favor with our readers, male or female. But perhaps one day I'll manage something better! Then I shall proudly and gratefully say: this I have my mother to thank for—your upbringing, your continuing maternal love, your friendship toward me."[7] The first two years of Hölderlin's studies in Tübingen were devoted mainly to philosophy (logic, metaphysics, and ethics), together with Greek, Hebrew, and Latin and some maths and physics. These were "propaedeutic" studies, preliminary to the three years of theology that were to crown his education. This first phase culminated in the award of the title of *Magister der Philosophie* for which two dissertations or "Specimina" were submitted: "Parallels between Solomon's *Proverbs* and Hesiod's *Works and Days*" and "History of the Fine Arts among the Greeks." In the latter of these, which draws largely on Winckelmann's *History of the Art of Antiquity* (1764), he cites Pindar as "the *summum* of the poetic art." Hölderlin didn't think much of the academic title, as he wrote to his mother in August 1790 (Letter 35). And though he learned things from his teachers that made a lasting

---

7. Hölderlin, *Sämtliche Werke*, ed. Friedrich Beißner and Adolf Beck, 8 vols. (Stuttgart: Kohlhammer, 1943–85), II, 357. All further references to Hölderlin's *Sämtliche Werke* in this introduction are to this edition.

impression on him, his own reading of Plato, Rousseau, and Kant was more important.

Hölderlin followed the French Revolution and subsequent events as closely as he could, though it seems that there was no outright support for it among the students in Tübingen until autumn 1791.[8] Nevertheless, when he set off on a brief walking tour to Switzerland with two medical students at Easter 1791, it was the republic of freedom, as well as the land of sublime and pristine scenery, that he was visiting. The trip took in a visit to Johann Kaspar Lavater, famous as a preacher and physiognomist, in Zürich, who wrote "NB" next to Hölderlin's name in his visitors' book. (What he noticed about him we don't know, but there are many records of Hölderlin's strikingly handsome appearance and aura.) Hölderlin also saw the spectacular Rhine Falls at Schaffhausen, and the Vierwaldstättersee. On his return, the contrast made the confines of the Stift even more palpable. Barely into the second phase of his studies, and quite likely before, Hölderlin had resolved not to "stay in a place where my best energies would go to ruin" and to try his luck "elsewhere" (Letter 51). Though these remarks relate to his intentions if the statutes of the Stift were tightened up, a process that Duke Karl Eugen had begun in response to unrest among the student body, it seems evident that he meant to get out whether the new measures went through or not (and he rightly regarded them as inevitable). In his comments on political events, which often come in letters to his sister, it is clear enough where his sympathies lie: "Pray for the French, the champions of the rights of man" (Letter 53). It's likely that he hoped, in the wake of the National Convention's decree of 19 November 1792 offering "fraternity and assistance to all peoples who wish to recover their liberty," that Württemberg too might become a republic. Though it's also possible that, like some other Swabians, he thought that the privileges the *Ehrbarkeit* had already won were enough. His comments to his mother, always meant to reassure, are not always easy to interpret. In November 1792 he admits that "it's far from impossible that changes may occur in our parts too," without its being clear whether he would welcome them or not. He follows this by saying that in any case people like them have nothing to fear: "So far, wherever in Germany the war has extended, the good citizen has lost little or nothing & gained a great deal" (Letter 57). The word translated as "citizen," *Bürger*, might

---

8. See *Hölderlin Texturen*, 1.2, 340–43.

also mean someone comfortably off such as his mother was, and there is no indication Hölderlin would have been ready to cede any of their established advantages. But his support for the revolutionary armies seems absolute, as is demonstrated by the grisly end of the letter where he celebrates the fact that they have "15 & 16 year-old boys" in their ranks, even going so far as to imagine them happily giving their fellows the right to shoot them down if they gave ground.

On his departure from Tübingen—his release from the "galley of theology," as he put it to his brother (Letter 63)—he received a final report that gives us a glimpse of how he was seen as he left. The original was written in Latin:

> Sound health, above medium height, well-spoken, pleasing gestures, good intellect, refined judgment, reliable memory, easily legible handwriting, good manners, admirably hard-working, abundant powers.
>
> Has carried out his theological studies with great success, delivered a correctly elaborated sermon very decently.
>
> Works intensely at philology, especially Greek, and philosophy, especially Kantian, as well as at the literary arts.[9]

The sermon was one of the requirements he had to fulfil; his text was Romans 5:10. The closing characterization accurately picks out what would remain Hölderlin's key preoccupations—he almost seems to echo it when he writes to his brother-in-law the following year: "I divide myself at the moment, as far as serious study goes, purely between Kant's philosophy and the Greeks, and seek also from time to time to produce something of my own" (Letter 82). Final examinations took place in Stuttgart in December 1793, by which time, via Hegel (who turned it down in favor of a similar job in Bern), Stäudlin, and Schiller, Hölderlin had secured a position as house tutor in Waltershausen and so, as he thought, got closer to realizing what to his mother he called "my Jena plans" (Letter 65).

Having put off for a while the fate of becoming a *Vikar*—something like a curate, usually helping an old or ailing pastor on very little pay while waiting for a parish to become free—Hölderlin hoped to devote himself to his writing and make his way in the literary world, where, having met Schiller in September, he was becoming quite well connected. He also

---

9. Hölderlin, *Sämtliche Werke*, ed. Beißner and Beck, VII/1, 479.

wanted to continue his studies, and that meant primarily philosophy at this stage. Like many others, including older *Stiftler* like Niethammer with whom he was soon in touch again, his heart was set on going to Jena because it was intellectually the most exciting place in Germany at the time: "The center of philosophical idealism and of early Romanticism."[10] Not only was Schiller there but a host of philosophers expounding and developing Kant, the most important of whom, Fichte, was just about to arrive. Among other possibilities, Hölderlin envisaged setting himself up as Niethammer had done, teaching philosophy. Waltershausen turned out not just to be further from Jena than he had been led to believe but altogether a small and remote place. The nearest town, Meiningen, he reckoned to be five hours away. His duties as private tutor, which he took very seriously, at first gave him time to read and write, and there are many references to Kant in the Waltershausen letters, often coupled with "the Greeks." "Practically the only thing I'm reading at the moment is Kant. His magnificent mind reveals itself to me more and more," he writes to his brother in May 1794 (Letter 81). And in July he tells Hegel: "My preoccupations are pretty focused at the moment. Kant and the Greeks are virtually all I read. I am trying to become particularly familiar with the aesthetic part of the critical philosophy" (Letter 85; see also Letter 82). The work of getting into Kant is something he looks back on in a letter to his brother of November 1797: "The man's mind was still remote to me. The whole thing couldn't have been more foreign. But every evening I had overcome new difficulties, which gave me a consciousness of my freedom" (Letter 148). In Waltershausen, to work at Kant did not seem at odds with his poetic ambitions, which were mainly being channeled into his novel *Hyperion*, and the pull of Jena in any case swung the compass point of Hölderlin's mind toward philosophy, which was undergoing a revolution at the time.

To become a house tutor was one of the very few ways open to Hölderlin if he wanted to escape the clutches of the Consistory in Württemberg—"more or less the only refuge" as he later put it to Johann Gottfried Ebel (Letter 104)—but it was a precarious and uncomfortable position. Despite being highly educated and recommended by Schiller, his status was not clearly distinct from that of a servant, and this was the same in all four such posts Hölderlin took. Still, in many ways he

---

10. Gerhard Kurz, foreword to *Hölderlin Texturen, 2, Das "Jenaische Project": Winter-semester 1794/95* (Tübingen: Hölderlin-Gesellschaft, 1995), 5.

was lucky in Waltershausen—the family, as he wrote to his grandmother, were "good people" (Letter 75), and Charlotte von Kalb in particular, whose son Fritz he was teaching, was instrumental in getting Schiller to take an interest in him and also introduced him to other leading writers in Jena and Weimar. When the pedagogical relationship with his pupil finally broke down, she gave him her blessing and enough money to live on in Jena for three months, which he made last a bit more than that (Letter 93). Also in the household was her "lady companion" Wilhelmine Kirms who when Hölderlin mentioned her to his sister on 16 January 1794 had just borrowed from him Kant's latest book, *Religion within the Boundaries of Mere Reason* (Letter 73). It seems almost certain that the baby daughter to whom she gave birth in July 1795 and who died of smallpox the following year was Hölderlin's.

Once in Jena, Hölderlin led a rich and concentrated life that supplied him with crucial experiences and friendships. His first letter from Jena announces: "My head and heart are now full of what I want to carry out in my thinking and writing, and, as is also my duty, in my actions, though this last naturally not on my own. The proximity of truly great minds, and also the proximity of truly great, independent, courageous hearts, casts me down one minute and raises me up the next" (Letter 90). Jena was a ferment of not just philosophical ideas but also political ones, and it drew in students with republican and revolutionary sympathies who thronged to Fichte's lectures. One of them, Isaak von Sinclair, became a great friend. Fichte was, as Hölderlin put it to Neuffer, "the life and soul of Jena": "I've never met a man of such depth and energy of mind" (Letter 90). He represented philosophy come to life, acting in the world. Whereas his predecessor, Reinhold, had devoted his lectures to expounding Kant, Fichte, unusually at the time, presented his own thinking, pretty much as it was being formulated, which also meant as it was shifting and changing course. There is evidence that Hölderlin—who had begun reading Fichte while in Waltershausen, went to his lectures daily once in Jena, and from January 1795 lived next door to him—had some influence on this evolution. In his letter to Hegel of 26 January 1795, which is unfortunately damaged, he identifies a weakness in the argument when he points out that Fichte appears to want to abstract from the "fact of consciousness" in a way comparable to how metaphysicians "have wanted to get beyond the existence of the world" (Letter 95). The letter is torn at the point where Hölderlin seems to suggest, with the words "Fichte confirms my," that in conversation Fichte had acknowledged the justice of his critique.[11] His quarrel with Fichte was also part of a quarrel with philosophy, and his deep involvement with the philosophical thinking of his time in the end led him away from it and toward poetry as a medium better able to overcome, while still acknowledging, the differences and divisions that consciousness encounters even as it is attempting to apprehend the whole. These are among the preoccupations of *Hyperion*, which Hölderlin set about reworking in Jena once more, having published a first fragment in Schiller's *Neue Thalia* in November 1794. This fragment seems to have adjusted Schiller's thinking in what would become his *Letters on the Aesthetic Education of Man* (1795). It was thanks to Schiller that in March 1795 the well-known Tübingen publisher Johann Friedrich Cotta agreed to take the novel on, though it was at most half-written.

Hölderlin matriculated at Jena in May 1795 but then left abruptly at the end of the month, for reasons that have never been elucidated. It will have been a combination of things. Since about Easter he had been sharing "a very pleasant summerhouse overlooking the town" (Letter 99) with Sinclair. The intensity of their friendship, which Hölderlin alludes to in several places, perhaps became more than he could bear at such close quarters (he later often lived in close proximity to him, but never again in the same house). It also seems clear that he was fleeing Schiller, whose presence was likewise too much for him; and perhaps in some sense philosophy, which threatened to impinge fatally on what he was clear was his real domain, "this most innocent of all occupations" as he would later call his writing (Letter 174). Fichte was no longer lecturing, having been forced to retreat to Oßmannstedt in the face of student unrest. Possibly also the fact that Wilhelmine Kirms would shortly give birth played a role, though there is no indication whether Hölderlin knew about this or not. He was also simply out of money.

Hölderlin's last letter from Jena was a fond one to his mother of 22 May 1795. His next, written from home in Nürtingen on 23 July, was an "apologia" to Schiller. All his letters to Schiller obey a similar dynamic, and it is the dynamic of their relationship. They portray it, and also analyze it, but the analysis offers no protection: "I was always tempted to see you, and the only effect of seeing you was to feel that I could be nothing to you" (Letter 103). And later (not, however, in winter): "I believe that it

---

11. See Violetta Waibel in *Hölderlin Texturen* 2, 107–14.

is the property of exceptional people to be able to give without receiving, to be able to 'warm themselves on ice,' [. . .] I am rigid with cold in the winter that surrounds me. The sky above me is like iron, and I am like stone" (Letter 105). Hölderlin's sense of Schiller was of a disablingly abundant source. Although it is likely that Schiller, as suggested above, took him seriously enough to be influenced by his ideas, Hölderlin did not feel, though perhaps did know himself, his equal. He felt like ice. His letters to Schiller contain moments of terrible self-abasement, and they are trapped in a lock of dependence. Even the last, written in June 1801 when he was at the height of his powers as a writer, still seeks Schiller's "approval," and even his "authorization" (Letter 234).[12]

Hölderlin traveled back to Nürtingen via Heidelberg, where he met and made a particularly sympathetic friend, Johann Gottfried Ebel. It was through Ebel that he got his second post as a house tutor, in Frankfurt, but he had to wait several months for the details to fall into place, leaving him with plenty of time to regret having quit Jena: "If only I'd stayed where I was. It the stupidest thing I've ever done to come back home" (Letter 108). What he later referred to as "bad times" (Letter 117)—Magenau, who saw him in the autumn, told Neuffer he was a "living corpse"—lived under mounting pressure from the Consistory, were alleviated by two meetings with Schelling. And he was not without hope, writing to Ebel of an "invisible church militant" formed by the communion of like-minded spirits (Letter 107). He kept working on *Hyperion* and at the end of the year set off for Frankfurt when word finally came.

Frankfurt had no university and was instead a center of commerce, big and brash and unprovincial. It was not a congenial place, but that was offset by the household Hölderlin now found himself part of, which from the start made a good impression on him. Jakob Gontard, the head of the family, was a banker and cloth merchant of Huguenot origin. Hölderlin immediately took to his charge, the eight-year-old Henry, and the feeling was mutual. Three younger daughters were in the care of a governess, Marie Rätzer, a beauty. Even more beautiful was Susette Gontard, who had read the fragment of *Hyperion* when it appeared in Schiller's *Thalia* in 1794 and with whom Hölderlin was soon in love. She came from Hamburg, where her mother was a friend of Klopstock's. After a month

---

12. On Hölderlin's eleven letters to Schiller, see Charlie Louth, "The Question of Influence: Hölderlin's Dealings with Pindar and Schiller," *Modern Language Review* 95, no. 4 (October 2000): 1038–52.

in her house, he sent home for his flute, to accompany her on the piano. There are many reports of her grace and poise, and Hölderlin's letters give ample account. His life and sense of the world underwent a radical adjustment. Rapidly the letters from Frankfurt speak of and with a new ease and confidence. The encounter seems initially to have created a feeling of resignation. In his first letter to Neuffer from Frankfurt, he writes: "I shall probably get even more used to making do with little and to directing my heart to come closer to eternal beauty more by my own efforts and endeavors than by waiting for fate to give me something that resembles it" (Letter 116). This evinces a Kafka-like "there is beauty, but not for me," only the endless laborious approach.[13] But when his love was returned there was no longer any need to make this division between the work and the life. By June he was in a "new world": "Before I may have thought I knew what was good and beautiful, but since I have it before me I have nothing but scorn for all my knowledge" (Letter 124). And by February 1797: "My sense of beauty is now proof against all disruption. . . . I write little and hardly do any philosophy any more. But what I do write has more life and form" (Letter 137). Since his thinking was tending toward the conclusion that beauty, and by extension poetry, was the only way of resolving the contradictions of philosophy, Susette in a sense rendered it superfluous.

Hölderlin did in fact still have philosophical projects, such as those for the "philosophical letters" announced to Niethammer of 24 February 1796, but they remained fragments, and to Hegel, in November, he wrote that "the ethereal spirits with metaphysical wings that accompanied me out of Jena have left me since I arrived in Frankfurt" (Letter 129). This too is a declaration of allegiance to "life and form," to the "shapes of the world" (Letter 137). His writing became ampler, thickened into concreteness, and this can be seen in a poem like "The Oak Trees," probably from 1796, which Hölderlin seems to have recognized as marking a shift when later, in 1800 or 1801, he earmarked it as the opening poem ("proemium") for a collection he was hoping to bring out with Cotta.[14] It was also one of his first poems to use classical meters (hexameters). As soon as he

---

13. "Es gibt unendlich viel Hoffnung, nur nicht für uns": words Kafka reportedly said to Max Brod ("There is an infinite amount of hope, just not for us").

14. See *Hölderlin Texturen* 2, 255. For the poem, see *Sämtliche Werke*, I, 201, and *Selected Poetry*, trans. David Constantine (Hexham: Bloodaxe, 2018), 21.

arrived in Frankfurt Hölderlin was on the lookout for an opportunity for Hegel to come and join him, which he did in January 1797. It was in anticipation of their reunion that Hegel wrote Hölderlin his poem "Eleusis," which is included here as part of the correspondence. Sinclair was also nearby, in Homburg. The letters to his brother, which dominate in the Frankfurt years, take it upon themselves to provide a philosophical education, especially after his plan to help Karl pursue his own studies was blocked by their mother.

At the beginning of July 1796 the revolutionary armies approached Frankfurt, which was soon under siege. The household, minus Jakob Gontard, fled northward, heading for Hamburg but in the event going no further than Kassel and Bad Driburg. This made for a kind of idyll, a pool of intimate seclusion amid the confusions of war. In Kassel they met Wilhelm Heinse (1746–1803), a friend of the Gontards and the author of *Ardinghello and the Fortunate Isles* (*Ardinghello und die glückseligen Inseln*), famous for the sensuality of its evocations and like *Hyperion* an epistolary novel. Hölderlin had read it in Tübingen, and found in Heinse a passionate Hellenist, "a splendid old man" (Letter 137). His importance can be seen in Hölderlin's later dedication to him of the elegy "Bread and Wine." In his company, Hölderlin encountered great art for the first time in the galleries in Kassel—Rembrandt and Rubens among others—including some Greek statues. There seems no doubt that like Goethe's experience in Rome the apprehension of human and artistic beauty had complementary force. The figure of Diotima in *Hyperion* begins to be confirmed and nourished by Susette and in some sense becomes her, which is why later, sending her the second volume of the novel in 1799, he asks her forgiveness for "letting Diotima die" (Letter 200).

Back in Frankfurt, despite having witnessed brutalities on the part of the French armies, Hölderlin's support for the revolution's ideals was still strong. Consoling Ebel, who had gone to Paris to be at the heart of the republic and sent a disillusioned letter, he wrote in January 1797: "I believe in a future revolution of attitudes and ways of seeing things that will make all we have had till now go red with shame. And Germany can perhaps contribute a great deal to this" (Letter 133). Coupled with this was a firm belief in his vocation, which made it easy to fend off various attempts his mother made to bring him home to Swabia. The presence of Hegel did him good, as he told Neuffer (Letter 137), and he was deeply happy with Susette. The so-called "Oldest Programme for a System of German Idealism," a collaboration of some sort between Hölderlin, Hegel, and Schelling, was written (in Hegel's hand) at about this time. It contains an affirmation that seems to issue directly from Hölderlin's life and work: "I am now convinced that the highest act of reason, that in which reason contains all ideas, is an aesthetic act, and *that truth and goodness are only united in beauty*."[15] This echoes thoughts in the last letter of the first volume of *Hyperion*, which appeared in April 1797.

The situation in the Gontard house was bound to break down, and it was exacerbated by the demeaning and trivializing Hölderlin was subject to as the household's "spare wheel" (Letter 149) and by the "thousandfold Thing of human society and activity that devoid of form, soul, or love persecutes and disperses us" (Letter 148). By July 1797 he was "torn apart by love and hate" (Letter 141). Eventually, toward the end of September 1798, after an altercation with his employer, he left and took rooms near Sinclair in Homburg, about eight miles or three hours away.

Painful as the separation from Susette was, Hölderlin must also have felt some relief in Homburg. He was among friends of a very congenial kind, Hegel was not far off, and some contact with Susette was still possible, though always fraught. Mostly, they exchanged letters through a hedge; only very rarely could they risk being seen together. "In Homburg I tried to recover my peace of mind by working constantly, and when I was tired I spent most of my time with Sinklair. He has acted toward me as a true friend" (Letter 170). As he told his sister, to whom he is always most forthcoming about the realia of his life, "I live out toward the fields, have gardens at my window and a hill with oak trees" (Letter 175). Outwardly at least, his life was peaceful and focused, and what is certain is that, with *Hyperion* finished, he moved into a new phase of his work, a very deliberate and purposeful recalibration. Although he now regarded philosophy as a "hospital" for sick poets and set it explicitly against "the sweet land of the Muses" (Letter 168), the two years of this first Homburg period were deeply reflective and produced his most extensive and difficult theoretical investigations. Unlike the earlier philosophical reflections, poetry and poetological concerns are always at the heart of these writings, though often with the broadest ramifications. In particular, there is persistent inquiry into the role poetry plays in the course of history, especially in transitional phases such as the postrevolutionary one in which Hölderlin was living. It is combined with precise attention to the composition of

---

15. *Essays and Letters*, 341–42 (342).

poetic works and in particular the sequence of "tones" that each genre runs through and modulates. This was based in large part on intensive study of Pindar, culminating in a remarkable translation of seven of his Olympian and ten of his Pythian odes. Not intended for publication, and not mentioned in any of Hölderlin's extant letters, but nevertheless written out fair, this translation is a word-for-word transcription of Pindar's Greek into German, a simultaneous decomposition and composition of the text that had far-reaching consequences for Hölderlin's own poetic language. The spirit in which he did it, and the overarching purpose of his work in Homburg, is summed up in a remark made to Neuffer in December 1799: "I find more and more that the true recognition of poetic forms greatly aids and facilitates the expression of poetic life and spirit, and I am amazed that we wander around so helplessly when I look at the sure, thoroughly purposeful and considered progression of ancient works of art" (Letter 204). It is this twin emphasis, on "poetic life and spirit" and on what he would later call the "calculable law" that underlies but cannot on its own guarantee it, that forms the focus not only of Hölderlin's theoretical writing but of the many poems and poetic drafts he wrote in Homburg—mostly Alcaic odes. It was a period of immense industry and advance.

A key letter, one that can be seen to inaugurate this period of intense reflection and poetic activity, is that to Neuffer of 12 November 1798, in which he writes, "Life in poetry is what now occupies my thoughts and senses more than anything else" (Letter 168). What he means by "das Lebendige in der Poësie"—life or liveliness in poetry—becomes indirectly apparent in the course of the letter, and importantly it is a matter both of the poem and of the person. What he says he needs, in both, is more "nuances," "not so much a main tone as a spectrum of diverse tones." The "common and ordinary aspects of real life," which he thinks he has a tendency to shun, need to be worked into his character and into his poems to make them more varied and to resemble the conditions in which in nature a thing has its being: not abstracted or pure but in interdependence with a multitude of other things. "Purity can only be represented in impurity and if you try to render fineness without coarseness it will appear entirely unnatural and incongruous." In tempering and holding back, letting its concerns appear in the company of contradictions and obstacles, a poem actually becomes more powerful, taking on the complexity and even messiness of life itself. This is really the driving insight of all of Hölderlin's work at this point and into the future, the question of manifestation or representation. At its highest pitch, the poem can come close to making the ideal actual, to precisely the extent that it stops short of, or slips back from, its direct expression.

This also has a political aspect, and Hölderlin, already well-informed, gained direct and in some ways sobering knowledge of the political situation when he attended the Congress of Rastatt at the end of November 1798 in the company of Sinclair. The main purpose of the congress was to negotiate compensation for German rulers who had lost territory to the French, but it also provided an opportunity for democrats to get together on the fringe and in particular to discuss plans for a Swabian republic—Württemberg, because of its unusual constitution, seemed one of the most propitious places for radical reform. On his return from Rastatt, Hölderlin wrote to Sinclair, who was still there: "No force is monarchic in heaven and earth. Absolute monarchy will always cancel itself out, because it has no object; in the strict sense it has never even existed. Everything is interconnected, and suffers as soon as it is active, including the purest thought a human being can have" (Letter 172). This goes back to his critique of Fichte's notion of the "absolute I," but more immediately it transfers his thoughts about the workings of poetry to the workings of politics. The ideal poem, like the ideal polity, should be a "living whole," or, as he puts it in his next letter, "a live, intricately articulated, intense whole" (Letter 173).

Hölderlin's thoughts about monarchy were prompted by reading Diogenes Laertius, who was the source for his central undertaking in Homburg, *Der Tod des Empedokles* (*The Death of Empedocles*), an attempt to write a modern tragedy on the classical model that has been considered "among the mountain tops of literature."[16] A plan for this had been drawn up in Frankfurt, and it went through three versions and several theoretical examinations before being abandoned at some unknown point late in 1799 or early in 1800. The attraction of Empedocles as a subject was partly to do with his reputed advocacy of political equality in Agrigento. Empedocles as Hölderlin presents him is at a turning point, a shift in the course of history, and that is how he also saw his own time, as radically unsettled by the French Revolution and thus particularly susceptible to change. The idea of fermentation, a messy, violent process that results in

---

16. George Steiner, *The Death of Tragedy* (London: Faber, 1961), 236. For a complete translation of all the *Empedokles* material, see Friedrich Hölderlin, *The Death of Empedocles: A Mourning-Play*, trans. David Farrell Krell (Albany: SUNY, 2008).

clarity, is one that occurs both in *Empedokles* and in Hölderlin's letters as a metaphor for the times. (It is an image also used by Hegel.)

The *Empedokles* project as a whole was a sustained investigation into the possibility of tragedy, which he thought the "strictest of all poetic forms" (Letter 184) and a particularly potent form of manifestation. One of the most fascinating of all Hölderlin's essay fragments, written it seems as the *Empedokles* material was being left behind as intractable, addresses the connections between tragedy and historical change. It views the transition from one epoch to another as especially fertile because it holds all the possibilities that in a "particular world," a "particular reciprocal relationship," narrow to one reality. "In the state between being and non-being," Hölderlin writes, "the possible everywhere becomes real, and the real becomes ideal, and in the free imitation of art this is a terrible, but divine dream."[17] As he examined Empedocles's transitional world and sought to make the idea of a totality appearing there poetically credible, he was also drawn to the "terrible, but divine dream" that by continuously readjusting and recommencing his drama, by keeping it on the way to itself and in flux, "between being and non-being," he was holding it open to the possible, to the point where it might live up to his ideal of tragedy as a total manifestation. It can thus be argued that the play fails because it attempts the impossible, perhaps contradicting Hölderlin's own insight that a pure totality can never be represented. Later, in 1802, he returned to tragedy in the "mixed" form of a translation, in his radical versions of Sophocles's *Oedipus the King* and *Antigone*.

A further focus of Hölderlin's activity in Homburg, for which many of the essay fragments were envisaged, was his plan to found a literary magazine, a "poetic monthly" he intended to name *Iduna* after the Nordic goddess of rejuvenation (prompted by an essay of Herder's). He approached a publisher in Stuttgart, and hoped to be able to make enough money from it to secure his existence as an independent writer. The project came to nothing, partly perhaps because he was dealing with what Schiller in his letter to Hölderlin of 24 August 1799 called "an insignificant beginner of a publisher" whose priorities were rather different from Hölderlin's own, but more because of the reluctance of Schiller and other established writers to supply material. Schiller wrote

---

17. *Essays and Letters*, 271 and 272. The essay is known both by its opening words, "Das untergehende Vaterland," and by the supplied title "Das Werden im Vergehen" ("The Process of Becoming in Passing Away").

warning him off the endeavor, which may well have been good advice, but Hölderlin detected an element of rivalry: "it seems to me that among these people, whom I can think of as *roughly* my equals, there is a bit of professional envy at work" (Letter 194). He cut his losses and tried instead to get Johann Friedrich Steinkopf, the publisher-bookseller, to bring out a collection of what he had written for the journal, but this too came to nothing. His response was to apply himself even more purposefully to his writing, and to the scrutiny of the workings and structures of poetry, coming to conclusions that as he said were "rather different from others I am aware of" (Letter 217).

On the face of it, much had gone wrong or not been worked through: the journal had failed, *Empedokles* had had to be abandoned, and hardly any of the theoretical writings can be considered complete. It must have been difficult to know whether the work on Pindar was really going anywhere. But it is impossible to date most of the poems precisely, and Hölderlin was either on the point of or actually already embarked on writing some of his best work, such as the great hexameter hymn "The Archipelago," perhaps finished before leaving Homburg in June 1800. Either way, against all appearances and despite the desolation caused by the thwarting of his love for Susette Gontard, this was the period in which Hölderlin "became" the poet he is and definitively brought his writing into the singularity and independence of great work. This can also be seen in his letters. There is nothing in his previous prose quite like the draft for a letter to Susette that was probably written in June 1799 (Letter 183). But the amplitude and authority of the letters to his brother, which form a more accessible pendant to the poetological essays, are also remarkable.

Hölderlin and Susette met for the last time on 8 May 1800. In her last letter to him, handed over at that meeting, she wrote: "Promise me that you will not come back and will go quietly away again from here, for [. . .] in the end we have to be quiet again so let us trustingly go our ways and in our sorrow still feel happiness." Their correspondence, though lacking Hölderlin's actual letters, shows the fact of their love in every word. He had been thinking of leaving Homburg for some time, partly at the prompting of Christian Landauer, a Stuttgart merchant and good friend who was often in Frankfurt, visited Hölderlin, and seems to have been concerned for his well-being. In September 1800, writing to his sister, Hölderlin referred to the "bad malady-ridden year" (Letter 213) he had just got behind him. On 10 June, Hölderlin did return home to Nürtingen, "secure in his poetic vocation and in nothing else," and after little more than a week was off on foot to Stuttgart, where he lived with Landauer as a paying guest, sending his washing home.[18] According to Schwab's brief biographical account, he was a "shadow" of what he had been. But he had many friends in Stuttgart, and made more. Although still beset by illness and bouts of depression, he was now in a very rich vein: the intense work of Homburg, in the congenial surroundings of Landauer's household, released into a steady stream of poetic productivity. Though again precise dating is not possible, he seems above all to have reworked some of his Frankfurt odes into much longer and fuller versions and to have turned to the elegy as the form in which his hopes and fears for the times could be best expressed.

Hölderlin stayed in Stuttgart till the end of the year, giving private lessons, working with great fluency and freedom, and spending time in the company of republicans who had high hopes for reform, or even the "revolution of attitudes and ways of seeing things" he had spoken of to Ebel in 1797. The elegies can all be read as laying down such hopes in the present as a time of transition, with Germany, and specifically Württemberg, as the favored place. Dwelling on the fulfilled life realized in Ancient Greece, and reproducing its lineaments in their form, they seek to imagine, or perhaps even actually create, an equivalent life in the familiar surroundings of home. The elegy "Stuttgart" is based on the grape picking Hölderlin witnessed that autumn, and the maturity it represents both remembers Greek plenitude and beckons forward to a possible fulfilment in the future, while giving us glimpses of its meaning in the present. The work of tending the vines, and the celebration of the vintage, are points of continuity with the past, and Stuttgart is seen in Greek terms: "Glorious she stands with thyrsus held up and the fir tree/High, as far as the clouds, crimsonly blessed by the light."[19] But for the moment these are no more than hopeful signs, and the poem tempers its own exuberance, acknowledging at the end that the time has not yet come.

Although on arrival he wrote to his mother that he envisaged staying some time in Stuttgart, praising the "contentment and calm" of his situation and the ability it gave him to pursue his "true occupation" (Letter 211), Hölderlin seems by the autumn to have become restless and to be

----

18. David Constantine, *Hölderlin* (Oxford: Clarendon Press, 1988), 153.

19. Friedrich Hölderlin, *Poems and Fragments*, trans. Michael Hamburger, 4th bilingual ed. (London: Anvil, 2004), 315.

looking out for opportunities to get away and into greater independence. Probably he was wary of staying too long so close to the Consistory, but to his sister, his main correspondent while in Stuttgart, he wrote on 11 December: "I have in me such a deep and urgent need of peace and quiet" (Letter 220). He hoped to find this in a third post as house tutor, this time in Switzerland; and in January, after spending Christmas at home in Nürtingen, and though his friends begged him to stay, he set out again and journeyed, mostly on foot, down to Lake Constance and across to Hauptwil. Clear details of what happened there are lacking—from now on letters are sparse and they confine themselves to the "absolutely necessary" (Letter 218), as can also be heard in their tone. The letters written from Hauptwil, where he was tutor to two daughters of Anton and Ursula von Gonzenbach, are mostly joyous. On 9 February 1801 the Peace of Lunéville was declared, and the Alps, evocations of which fill the letters and soon also the poetry, seemed to offer a correlative to the happiness and hopes this released: "The clear blue of the sky and the pure sunlight on the Alps close by were all the more welcome to my eyes at that moment since otherwise I should not have known where to look in my joy" (Letter 230). Many of the free-verse hymns, written on the Pindaric model, were begun here, among them "Celebration of Peace" and "The Rhine." From this point on, letters and poems converge ever more, and every word Hölderlin writes bears a weight that it is equal to.

Hölderlin's main mood at this time seems to be elation. But in mid-April he left, for reasons it is impossible to make out with any clarity, apparently without ill feeling on the part of his employer, who supplied him with a warm letter of recommendation. A few remarks in letters suggest a sense of isolation, though often generalized—to his brother he writes that "very often among us human beings the signs and words are still missing" (Letter 231). But to Landauer, who knew about Susette Gontard, he is more forthright: "That I have a heart but can't see what for, have no one to talk to here, no one I can wholly open myself to. [. . .] My dear friend, if you go to Frankfurt, think of me" (Letter 232). Nevertheless, buoyed by the peace (in fact short-lived), the Alpine landscape, and no doubt by a confidence in his poetic nerve, the return home seems to have been made in good or even high spirits. The last elegy, "Homecoming," contains details of his journey, absent from any letter.

Give or take a month or so, Hölderlin returned home at the same time of the year as he had from Homburg, and there must have been a heavy sense of repetition. Although he was often in Stuttgart, he seems not to have tried again to establish himself there, and immediately set about finding some other way of supporting himself "abroad." In June he wrote his last letter to Schiller, saying that in a few weeks he would be obliged to serve as a *Vikar* under a country parson if he didn't find an alternative, and that the requirements of such a post "contrast so greatly with my way of expressing myself that the contradiction would end up making me lose all facility of communication" (Letter 234). He hoped that Schiller might be able to help him establish himself as a lecturer on Greek literature in Jena. Later in the month he wrote about the same "old project" to Niethammer: "I should like to show young people who are interested what the characters of the great works are and explain to them what sort of spirit was capable of organizing the material and releasing the poetic life in it" (Letter 235). Neither Schiller nor Niethammer replied, and so Hölderlin had to fall back on the ever-available possibility of becoming a house tutor again. Through Landauer's connections he was offered a job in Bordeaux in the household of the Hamburg consul, Daniel Christoph Meyer. Also at this time, in August, he received a proposal from Cotta to publish an edition of his poems the following Easter. For unknown reasons this came to nothing, but it is clear enough that in Stuttgart at least Hölderlin's reputation was growing.

Before setting out on yet another winter journey he wrote two letters of farewell on 4 December 1801, one to his brother and one to his friend Böhlendorff. In both, he professed a love for his country and the need to leave it: "I am now full of parting. It's a long time since I have cried. But when I decided I had to leave my country, perhaps for ever, the tears came, and they were bitter. For what do I have in the world that is dearer to me? But they have no use for me" (Letter 238). There is a finality and unalterableness about everything he writes, enactment and statement fall ineluctably together. The letter to Böhlendorff contains famous reflections on the relationship between Greece and Germany, between what is one's own and what is foreign, and between antiquity and modernity, and it seems clear that he sees his need to depart out of Germany in similar terms: "What we are actually born with, the national, will always become less and less of an advantage." Therefore, we need the foreign because it can actually give us, according to Hölderlin's dialectical understanding, an apprehension of what is proper to ourselves. His sense of being "rooted," as he puts it to his brother (Letter 237), transfers to the post-*Empedokles* insight that a modern work cannot resemble an ancient one but must obey its own dynamic: "I have labored at this for a long time and know

now that apart from what must be the supreme thing with the Greeks and with us, that is, living craft and proportion, we cannot properly have anything in common with them" (Letter 238). But: "What is our own has to be learned just as much as what is foreign. For this reason the Greeks are indispensable to us." It seems that he saw the "outside" of France as indispensable in the same way: "I look forward too to seeing the sea, and the sun of Provence." The sobriety of expression is that of one who has come through: "O my friend, the world lies more brightly before me than usual, and is more serious."[20]

He left on about 10 December, on foot as he was for most of the journey, arriving first in Strasbourg, where he was detained until the end of the month before being given permission to continue not via Paris, as he had originally hoped, but via Lyon. It's just possible that the new route was deliberately chosen to coincide with Napoleon's stay in the city. To his mother he wrote from there on 9 January that the "long cold journey" had been "hard and eventful" (Letter 239) but worse was to come. He got to Bordeaux on 28 January 1802 and wrote home of crossing "the snowy hills of the fearful Auvergne, in storms and wilderness, the nights icy-cold and a loaded pistol beside me in the rough beds." And then that tone again, as if distanced from and at the same time entirely centered in himself: "I am now hardened through and through, initiated as you could wish. I think I shall remain so, in the main" (Letter 240). There are just two letters from Bordeaux, and we know very little about his time there. He seems perfectly happy with his situation when he writes to his mother on 16 April, but on 10 May he was issued with a pass to travel back to Strasbourg, which this time he did via Paris. Some details of the journey are held in the second letter to Böhlendorff, now in wholly mythical terms: "The violent element, the fire of the sky, and the quiet of the people, their life in the open and their straitenedness and contentment, stirred me continually, and as one says of heroes I can probably say of myself: that Apollo has struck me" (Letter 242).

Certainly when he arrived back in Stuttgart at about the middle of June he was barely recognizable. According to one account he was "pale as a corpse, emaciated, with hollow wild eyes, long hair and beard, and dressed like a beggar." At some point, it's not known exactly when or how,

---

20. For an excellent concise discussion of this letter, see Joshua Billings, *Genealogy of the Tragic: Greek Tragedy and German Philosophy* (Princeton, NJ: Princeton University Press, 2014), 193–96.

he learned that Susette had died on 22 June, the immediate cause being measles caught from her children. Perhaps in Stuttgart he hoped to regain the stable and productive conditions of the year before at Landauer's. But on receiving this news, probably from Sinclair's letter of 30 June, which had been sent to Landauer for forwarding to Bordeaux, he went to Nürtingen and with only a handful of brief interruptions stayed there for almost two years, until Sinclair fetched him to Homburg in June 1804.

The main interruption was a journey to Regensburg, where at Sinclair's invitation he traveled in late September, staying for at least the first half of October. Sinclair was again on diplomatic business, negotiating for Hesse-Homburg. The four-week permit Hölderlin was issued with on 29 September in Nürtingen tells us he was, at the age of thirty-two, six foot tall, with broad shoulders, brown eyes and beard, reddish cheeks, and discolored teeth. Sinclair wrote the following year that he had "never seen greater powers of mind and spirit" in him than at that time. He was working on his translations of Sophocles and perhaps also began the poem "Patmos." It was probably on his return to Nürtingen, at about the time of the second letter to Böhlendorff, that he inaugurated the extensive manuscript known as the "Homburger Folioheft" that he seems to have designed and composed as a whole, at least at first. The return from Bordeaux is commonly regarded as a caesura in Hölderlin's life and work: "after Bordeaux" there was a clear shift, a major readjustment. The work of the years 1800–1802, between the separation from Susette Gontard and her death, has been seen as constituting a "coherent world."[21] Thereafter, that coherence, "always precarious," begins to strain and fragment, though not at all in a way that could be taken as a falling off or straightforward loss, and the process is of course gradual. It can be seen in the "Homburger Folioheft" itself, which begins with fluent fair copies of the three major elegies "Homecoming," "Bread and Wine," and "Stuttgart," and then moves into complex and often unfinished hymnic writing, some of the most beautiful and intense and also difficult parts of Hölderlin's work. The three elegies, all originally composed well before the "Homburger Folioheft" was begun, represent the (hard-won) "coherent world," and the writing that follows goes beyond that coherence into something more disconcerting, more threatened, and more radical. "May I keep in mind how I have come to where I am now!," he wrote to Böhlendorff in November 1802 as he considered "the philosophic light at my window" and resolved that poetry

---

21. Constantine, *Hölderlin*, 152.

would "take on a quite different character" (Letter 242). The writing out of the three elegies would be the poetic equivalent of that, standing for the work that had brought him to where he was and prepared him for the new work to come. At a later stage, it's not known precisely when, he returned to the fair-copied elegies as well as to other finished poems and revised them into a strange, disruptive and antilyrical idiom.

For the next two years Hölderlin worked with extraordinary intensity and originality, keyed into his times in a way utterly unlike anyone else. He was clearly in full possession of his powers and yet beset by episodes of extreme mental distress amid his more general grieving for Susette. He was isolated, and seems rarely to have sought company. There are very few letters from this period, and although we know of a handful that have been lost, notably to Sinclair, it seems he rarely wrote, even to good friends like Landauer, who on 8 February 1803 gently rebuked him for sending no news. Yet he sent the finished "Patmos" to Sinclair on 13 January 1803 and brought several other poems to completion, including "Remembrance" and "The Ister," and besides them wrote a wealth of shorter poems and drafts for longer ones. In June he made a sudden visit to Schelling, who was at his parents in Murrhardt, northeast of Stuttgart, arriving "straight across the fields." In a letter to Hegel, Schelling, who seems to have been horrified by this visit, wrote that since the "fatal journey" to Bordeaux his mind was "utterly ruined." He judged him just about capable of some sorts of work, "such as translation from the Greek," but concluded that "he neglects his appearances to a disgusting degree and, though what he says does not point so much to madness, he has completely taken on the outward mannerisms of people in this condition."[22] These words have been taken to mean that Schelling thought he was putting it on, adopting an "antic disposition," but the letter as a whole makes it irrefutably clear that he thought no such thing. Either this state did not prevent Hölderlin from working, at whatever cost, or he had more collected periods. Much later, Schelling also wrote that the visit had shown him "how great the power of innate, original grace is."[23] Hölderlin's mother's observations, relayed in lengthy letters to Sinclair, suggest he wore himself out either by writing or by long walks that did nothing to alleviate his state. And yet, the information we have from this

---

22. *Sämtliche Werke*, VII/2, 262 (from Schelling's letter to Hegel of 11 July 1803).

23. *Sämtliche Werke*, VII/2, 253 (from Schelling's letter to Gustav Schwab of 11 February 1847).

time is contradictory. It even seems possible that the story related by both Ernst Zimmer and Wilhelm Waiblinger, according to which Karl Gok (on 28 May 1804) married a woman Hölderlin had been intending to wed himself, has some basis and is to be situated in this period, the woman in question being a second cousin, Marie Eberhardine Blöst (1777–1853).[24]

Hölderlin seems to have had a full version of his translation of *Oedipus the King* and *Antigone* done by the end of 1802, and several of his friends made efforts to find a publisher. In the end it was the Frankfurt bookseller Friedrich Wilmans who took it on, and Hölderlin continued work at it throughout 1803, notably revising the notes and making the language of *Antigone* more "lively" (Letter 244). Wilmans deserves great credit for recognizing the quality of the translation at a time when even friends such as Schelling regarded it as proof of his mental degeneration. When *The Tragedies of Sophocles* came out in April 1804, copies were earmarked to be sent to Hegel, Schelling, and Goethe (among others) but not Schiller. It is now acknowledged as one of the two or three most significant works in the history of translation, and is an extraordinary encounter between two poets across a linguistic and epochal divide. Wilmans was also ready to take on other works and, thus encouraged, Hölderlin prepared "individual lyric poems of some length, 3 or 4 folio pages, each poem to be printed separately because they will deal directly with our country and the times" (Letter 244) and "a few Night Poems for your almanac" (Letter 245). The former are the hymns: a fair copy of "Celebration of Peace" has survived with an introductory note in which Hölderlin defends his idiom: "Should some people find such a language too unconventional, I must confess: I can do no other ["ich kann nicht anders"]. On a fine day almost every kind of song may be heard, and nature, whence it comes, also receives it again."[25] The latter, a group of nine poems (*Nachtgesänge*) including one of his best-known, "Half of Life," were published in Wilmans's annual *Taschenbuch* in 1804.

Sinclair's letter of 30 June 1802, announcing Susette Gontard's death, had already invited Hölderlin to come to him in Homburg, and this plan

---

24. The arguments for this are set out in *Hölderlin Texturen*, 6.1, "*offen die Fenster des Himmels*": *Nürtingen, Homburg, 1802–1806, Lebensstationen und Werke*, ed. Michael Franz, Priscilla A. Hayden-Roy, and Valérie Lawitschka (Tübingen: Hölderlin-Gesellschaft, 2024), 138–52.

25. *Sämtliche Werke*, III, 532.

eventually came about in June 1804 in odd circumstances, Sinclair coming to pick him up at a time of political crisis in Württemberg—his friendship with some of the main reformers would lead, the following year, to his being denounced for involvement in a supposed plot to assassinate the elector of Württemberg. The denunciation, perhaps in fact part of an attempt by the elector of Württemberg to trap the former mayor of Ludwigsburg and leader of the reform party in the Stuttgart parliament Christian Friedrich Baz, resulted in Sinclair's arrest. Hölderlin was among those present at a supper held in Baz's house in Stuttgart in June 1804, on his way to Homburg with Sinclair. There he lived not far from his friend, in the house of a French clockmaker. Sinclair arranged for him to receive two hundred florins from his own salary and a sinecure as court librarian, but was often away, first in Mainz, then in Paris, and then after his arrest on 26 February 1805 in Ludwigsburg until July, when he was acquitted for lack of evidence. The affair caused Hölderlin a great deal of distress as he was implicated, and inquiries were made. A doctor certified that his "madness had gone over into ravings," though it is possible that his condition was exaggerated to protect him. Sinclair had already suggested, in a letter to Hölderlin's mother of 6 August 1804, "that what appears to be a confusion of his mind is not that at all but a carefully considered form of expression he has assumed."[26] But plenty of other accounts allow little doubt about the seriousness of his decline, and in summer 1805 he had to be rehoused, lodging this time with a saddler and fellow Swabian, where he was known for improvising "day and night" on the piano he had been given by Princess Auguste von Hesse-Homburg. Sinclair was away again from September 1805 till the following spring, this time in Berlin. Not long after his return the duchy of Hesse-Homburg was absorbed into the larger unit of Hesse-Darmstadt, and shortly afterward the Holy Roman Empire was dissolved. Sinclair wrote to Hölderlin's mother that under these circumstances it would no longer be possible to keep "my unfortunate friend, whose madness has reached a very high degree," in Homburg, and asked her to arrange to have him picked up. On 11 September 1806 he was forcibly removed—thrust back into the coach when he tried to escape—and taken to a recently opened clinic in Tübingen run by J. H. Ferdinand Autenrieth, a professor of medicine at the university.

---

26. *Sämtliche Werke*, VII/2, 299.

Opinions differ widely on how much Hölderlin wrote while in Homburg. It may have been very little—no letters from him survive at all. Apart from a few notes, there is no firm evidence that he wrote anything in those two years, but the unpublished poetry can rarely be dated with any certainty. The Frankfurt edition of Hölderlin's works assumes that pages of the "Homburger Folioheft" continued to be filled, though we do not know for sure that he even took it with him to Homburg (its name comes from the fact that it was kept there from the middle of the nineteenth century). In July 1805, Johann Isaak Gerning, whom Hölderlin saw a handful of times, reported that "Hölderlin, who is still half crazy, is jabbing away at Pindar."[27] Some have taken this to refer to the *Pindar Fragments*, nine complex texts in which scraps of Pindar transmitted only via the writings of other authors are translated and then drawn out in a lyrical-philosophical meditation. But they survive as fluent fair copies and have points in common with the *Nachtgesänge* and with the notes to the Sophocles tragedies, which were both completed in the winter of 1803–4.

The clinic seems to have done Hölderlin more harm than good; certainly his condition worsened there, and on 3 May 1807 he was released as incurable and given no more than three years to live. In fact he was at the midpoint of his life. He was taken in by a joiner and his wife, Ernst and Marie Zimmer, who lived in a house built into the town walls of Tübingen overlooking the river Neckar. Zimmer had read and liked *Hyperion*, and he and his family looked after its author in an exemplary way until the end of his life. By contrast, his mother seems never to have visited him, never in fact to have seen him again after the departure from Nürtingen in 1804, and his sister and half-brother came only a handful of times. We have a disproportionate amount of information about Hölderlin's last years in Tübingen—Zimmer and his family sent regular reports, and in due course he had many curious visitors who left accounts—but there was little change over the course of the years. "Nothing happens to me," Hölderlin is supposed to have often repeated, although the phrase—*es geschieht mir nichts*—could also mean "nothing *can* happen to me."[28] On first arriving at the Zimmers', it seems that he wrote a great deal, but little or nothing of this has survived. The poet Eduard Mörike, who studied in

---

27. *Sämtliche Werke*, VII/2, 287.

28. *Sämtliche Werke*, VII/3, 69 (from Wilhelm Waiblinger's *Friedrich Hölderlins Leben, Dichtung und Wahnsinn* [1831]).

Tübingen and visited Hölderlin several times from about 1823, reported in 1838 that he had just received a "jumble" of Hölderlin's papers, "mostly illegible"—these have disappeared.[29] What has survived is the sixty-eight brief letters home, almost all to his mother, which seem to have been sent between about 1812 and 1829 at Zimmer's prompting, and around fifty poems largely written in two periods: in the first few years at his own volition—in 1811 he apparently had plans to edit an almanac and prepared a number of poems for it—and then in the final years of his life, 1841–43, perhaps entirely on request ("Shall I write verses about Greece, spring, the spirit of the age?," he asked one visitor in 1843).[30] The typical form of these later verses is two rhyming quatrains evoking in idyllic terms the landscape and the seasons, or sometimes making abstract reflections on life, signed with invented dates ("1648," "1940") and the name Scardanelli. Apart from the first few pieces, there seems to be no connection to Hölderlin's earlier work, they are as if the work of another, but there are moments of great beauty and tranquility, a limpid repose.

As for the letters, they also are radically different from what came before: they no longer seem to seek a connection but rather to ward one off. They breathe estrangement and yet are oddly moving. In a way, they read like an extract or abstract of Hölderlin's earlier letters to his mother, in that the sense of indebtedness and obedience that hampers much of his correspondence with her here appears pure, almost devoid of content: "That I can say so little to entertain you comes from the fact that I occupy myself so much with the sentiments I owe you" (Letter 255). The letters are almost purely formal in that they take their own occasion as their substance. In doing so, they offer a performance of the relationship between mother and son and at the same time a diagnosis. In declaring his filial piety, Hölderlin reveals how rigid the ties between them have become, in what sometimes feels like resistance by overcompliance, especially given the repetitive nature of the letters, something Hölderlin frequently adverts to: "Here I am writing to you again. The repetition of what one has written is not always an unnecessary state of affairs" (Letter 272). He also confesses, in one of the many moments of lucidity, that "I now have no other way of saying" (Letter 300), which is a cruel echo of the

---

29. *Sämtliche Werke*, VII/3, 170. Later he received "a large basket" of manuscripts (VII/3, 312).

30. *Sämtliche Werke*, VII/3, 301.

proud claim in the note to "Celebration of Peace" that "I can do no other." But there is more variety in these letters than is commonly recognized, and some are warmer, such as, for all its brevity, Letter 270. Whether the letters can be regarded as ironic—knowing to that degree—as has recently been claimed, is questionable.[31]

In 1820 first steps were taken toward making an edition of Hölderlin's poems, and *Gedichte* appeared in 1826, edited by Ludwig Uhland and Gustav Schwab. It lacked many of the poems for which Hölderlin is now best-known: even a finished poem like "Patmos," written at the height of his powers, was judged to show that "the clarity of his mind was already significantly impaired" and so excluded. *Hyperion* had been reissued in 1822. A copy of the novel lay open in Hölderlin's room and he often read out from it. Among the many young writers drawn to him was Wilhelm Waiblinger, who gave the first biographical account of Hölderlin's life, published in 1831 after Waiblinger's death. Waiblinger arrived in Tübingen at a time when Hölderlin's condition temporarily improved, to the extent that there were hopes of recovery, and Hölderlin seems to have taken a particular liking to him. They went for walks together, sometimes to a summerhouse Waiblinger was renting on a hill on the outskirts of the town, and Waiblinger noted many snippets of their conversations in his diary. There were lots of other visitors: Hölderlin would receive them with deep bows and extravagant titles such as "Your Excellency" or "Your Majesty."

Hölderlin's mother died in 1828, unleashing a quarrel between his sister and brother over the inheritance that had to be settled in court. Hölderlin was not at her funeral, and his siblings were not at his when he died on 7 June 1843. According to Lotte Zimmer, the daughter who took over the care of Hölderlin after Zimmer's death in 1838 and whom Hölderlin called "Holy Virgin Lotte," he played the piano (or flute) as usual that evening, ate with the family, but was restless once in bed and got up again. She stayed by his side and he died peacefully later that night.

～

---

31. See Giorgio Agamben, *Hölderlin's Madness: Chronicle of a Dwelling Life, 1806–1843*, trans. Alta L. Price (Seagull Books, 2023), 141. See also Paul Raabe, *Die Briefe Hölderlins: Studien zur Entwicklung und Persönlichkeit des Dichters* (Stuttgart: Metzler, 1961), who speaks of "diabolic irony" (189).

Walter Benjamin has written that from about the beginning of the century—certainly from the letters written in Hauptwil—there was for Hölderlin "no linguistic arrangement, even his everyday correspondence, to which he did not bring the masterly, precise technique of his late poems." And more dramatically that in certain letters "the bare rock of language everywhere becomes apparent."[32] The letters are an indispensable part of Hölderlin's work, and, more than that, they are one of the essential correspondences, perhaps in part because of what has been lost. We can regret the many letters we know of and will never be able to read, but what we have is enough to give us the lineaments of a life and the shape of Hölderlin's becoming as a writer, and these emerge cleanly from the material in a way that is not true for writers such as Goethe or Rilke, where the abundance impedes the view of a trajectory. T. S. Eliot thought that "abundance" (alongside "variety" and "complete competence") was one of the qualities needed in the greatest poets, but perhaps the same is not true when it comes to correspondence. If you look at German letters, it is hard to find a correspondence to set beside Hölderlin's—perhaps Heinrich von Kleist's comes closest. Hölderlin was a much more interesting letter writer (because more vulnerable, and because the letter apparently meant more to him as a form) than most of his contemporaries—Hegel or Schelling, say—and for all the differences belongs more in the company of John Keats, whose correspondence, for other reasons, is of about the same extent. We can apprehend it as a vital whole.

This translation does not follow any one German edition of the letters. The definitive work of gathering, dating, editing, and annotating was done by Adolf Beck for the Stuttgart edition of Hölderlin's works. With the exception of the later discovery of one further letter, mentioned above, very little has come to light since to affect his findings, and his commentary is still by far the fullest. Beck also collected all the surviving letters to Hölderlin and published them separately, in volume 7 of the edition. The first edition to insert the letters to Hölderlin among his own letters, as is done here, was Michael Knaupp's (sometimes known as the Munich edition). That is also the course taken by Dietrich Sattler in volume 19 of the Frankfurt edition (2007), who in addition breaks up letters written over several days into segments, each with their own position. Both Knaupp and Sattler occasionally adjust the order established

---

32. Walter Benjamin, *Deutsche Menschen: Eine Folge von Briefen* (Leipzig: Kiepenheuer, 1979), 34–35.

by Beck, but the changes are in the end minimal, and in Sattler's case sometimes contentious. This edition triangulates between these editions and also the Italian edition by Luigi Reitani (in *Prose, teatro e lettere*), but broadly speaking follows Beck except where there is good reason not to, the exception being the placing of the letters to Hölderlin. Including these, and including them in sequence, raises obvious difficulties because they are even more sporadic than Hölderlin's own and precise dating is often difficult—as Beck points out, half of Hölderlin's letters up to 1804 are undated.[33] But though the arrangement must sometimes be approximate, to read the surviving correspondence as a whole allows a lot more context to seep into our understanding of Hölderlin's own letters and helps us see what is distinct about them. The place and date given at the head of each letter are placed in square brackets when Hölderlin (or his correspondent) has not supplied them himself, which, as just noted, he often hasn't. In such cases the dates are to a greater or lesser extent conjectural; any particularly contentious or interesting instances are dealt with in the notes.

Some of Hölderlin's letters survive only as partial transcriptions and/or "regests," brief summaries of content that has not been copied word for word. These were made by the writer Gustav Schlesier (1810–1881), who was intending to write a biography.[34] His summaries are shown as italics in square brackets. The general principle of the translation has been to convey as much as possible of the particularity of the letters, including abbreviations and variant spellings of names, while avoiding unnecessary distractions. Different kinds of emphasis (underlining, Roman script) are all rendered as italics. Variants, of which there are in any case very few, are given only in a couple of interesting cases in the notes. The notes themselves aim to elucidate where necessary rather than provide a running commentary. A special word is needed about Susette Gontard's letters to Hölderlin. These are a famous document in their own right, translated previously into many languages, and several times published separately in German. Partly because they were often written in a hurry and in an agitated state, they are often unusually punctuated, and this is reflected in the English versions here. It is a great bonus for this book that Susette Gontard's letters have been translated by David Constantine,

---

33. *Sämtliche Werke*, VI, 478.

34. Schlesier's notes on Hölderlin have been published: Gustav Schlesier, *Hölderlin-Aufzeichnungen*, ed. Hans Gerhard Steimer (Weimar: Böhlau, 2002).

thus introducing a separate voice for what are by far the most important letters to Hölderlin. My debt to David is much greater, though: he has been through the whole of my translation and helped me sharpen it at many points, for which I am deeply grateful. I should also like to thank the two anonymous readers, who have been exemplary in the care and knowledge they have shown. I have adopted many of their suggestions, and given them all my earnest consideration. Rebecca Colesworthy has been a supportive and sympathetic editor. Thanks also to Penguin for permission to use material originally published in Friedrich Hölderlin, *Essays and Letters*, translated by Jeremy Adler and Charlie Louth (2009), though it has all been revisited. That book contained 120 letters by Hölderlin, this one has all 316, plus the 103 to him (including Hegel's poem "Eleusis"). To Jeremy Adler I am indebted for allowing me, many years ago, to collaborate on the Penguin selection and so for helping to bring this complete edition about.

DENKENDORF AND MAULBRONN, 1785–1788

1. TO NATHANAEL KÖSTLIN

[Denkendorf, November 1785]

Very reverend, learned and ever to be venerated Deacon,

The perpetual great favor and love you have shown me, and something else that will have made no small contribution to it, your judicious Christian way of life, have aroused in me such love and reverence for you that to state plainly the facts of it, I can do no other than look on you as my father. You will, therefore, not take this request amiss. A number of observations, especially since I've been back here from Nürtingen, have caused me to reflect on how to combine prudent behavior, obligingness, and religion. I could never quite manage it; I was always wavering one way or the other. Then I felt many stirrings of goodness which presumably came from my natural sensibility, and were therefore all the more unconstant. It is true, I believed that now I was a real Christian, I was filled with contentment, and nature in particular, in such moments (for this contentment seldom lasted much longer) made an extraordinarily vivid impression on my heart; but I could endure no one around me, always wanted only to be on my own and seemed as it were to despise mankind. And the slightest circumstance started my heart from out of itself, and then I became all the more frivolous. If I set out to live wisely, my heart became unreliable and the smallest of insults seemed to convince it of how very wicked and diabolical human beings were and of the need to be careful of them and to avoid the slightest familiarity with them. If on the other hand I wanted to work against this misanthropic disposition, I strove to be pleasing to my fellow humans, but not to God. So you see, beloved Deacon, I swayed this way and that, and whatever I did went beyond the moderation I aimed for. And today especially (Sunday) I looked back on my comportment hitherto toward God and man and formed the firm resolve to be a Christian and not a vacillating dreamer, prudent and wise without becoming false and misanthropic, obliging toward people without being guided by their truly sinful habits. I know for certain that God will lead my heart with his Holy Spirit. And now I most obediently ask you, beloved Deacon, be you my guide, my father, my friend (which you have long been!), allow that I may inform you of every circumstance that affects my heart and soul, of every broadening of my knowledge: your teachings, your advice and the transmission of your knowledge, these will satisfy all my desires as they pertain to the things of this world. I know for certain that this sincere letter is not a burden to you and that you will look on this confidence as a sign of my reverence and love toward you. Should you find anything to fault in these my convictions, I ask you to make the same known to me. And so I close and remain with the greatest of respect

your most humble servant

Hölderlin

2. TO HIS MOTHER

[Denkendorf, shortly before Christmas 1785]

Dearest Mamma,

If my letter this time is a bit more scrambled than usual then you have to remember that my head is also preoccupied with Christmas tasks, like yours—though they're not quite the same: for me, apart from today's laxative, they are plans for a talk I'm to hold at vespers on St. John the Evangelist's Day, thousands of drafts for poems I want to do during our weeks off (there are four, when you can work on your own things), and must do (NB Latin poems too), whole stacks of letters I need to write, even though the New Year won't help much, e.g., to the

Deacon, to Herr Klemm, Herr Bilfinger, to Altona, and other things of the sort; and for you, all the usual business.

For the Christmas visits this year, I'm inclined to take the liberty of inviting you here because my task for St. John's, as I said, won't really let me get away. My dear brother and sister will be glad about that; but, in confidence, I'm pretty anxious about what I'm going to give them. I'll leave it to you, dearest Mamma, if we can keep things much as they always were between us, take it out of my money and give them something on my behalf. My best wishes to dear Grandmother, and tell her I mean to give her a Christmas present too—I mean to thank dear God with all the joy of Christmas Day that once again he has kept you in such good health over the course of this almost completed year. Despite my diarrhea I'm otherwise very well. Here it's true it's not too late as in your case, but I don't know what else to write apart from to say I am my dearest Mamma's most obedient son

Hölderlin

Here is something to distract you from Christmas occupations: if you don't want to read it yourself then at least get my dear brother and sister to read it out loud to you, you'll like it very much. Just send it back to me as soon as you can. The other parts will follow soon. Please send me back the *bouteille* as well, it was borrowed. Herr Harpprecht from Nellingen visited me yesterday and asked for the 4th part of the *Brittisches Museum*.

3. TO IMMANUEL NAST

[Maulbronn, at the beginning of 1787]

Dear friend,

I left you entirely at peace in myself—I felt so good in the melancholy sensations of parting—and still, when I think back to how we became friends at once, in the first moments—how close and how contented we were together, I'm happy just to have had you these few days;—O my dear Nast, there were times when I'd have given one of my fingers for a friend like you, & even if my thoughts of him had to stretch as far as the Cape—I think I've already gone on at you about this once before—It annoys me that the thought of my gloomy old hours comes to mind so often—and just be glad if I don't write often—you would perhaps see many a complaint slip from me, however much I avoid it. And we humans feel so good when there's something to grumble about.—Many times in my life I've been a fool, but never less than when my heart's desires were not fulfilled—when undeservedly I got to see disapproving faces—

But now I can say in all seriousness—forgive me, I have been a burden to you!—That was a lot of unseemly drivel again! Not so, dear friend?

I wish I could send you the Brutus and Caesar music now, but if one wants something from the Stuttgart *académiciens* it goes at snail's pace, however good their intentions are. In Schiller's honor I mean to learn it on the piano too, as hard as that will be with my plunking. Oh, how often in my thoughts I've clasped him by the hand when he has his Amalia go into raptures over her Karl—! You will think me a fool; but I don't know, is it amour propre, or—or—thoughts like these make me feel content. Good night now, dear friend! One last thing! Hesler sends his regards. You would receive many more compliments if I were to call out to everyone "Today I'm writing to Nast!." Look after yourself. And love your

Hölderlin

4. TO IMMANUEL NAST

Maulbronn, January 1787
4 o'clock in the morning

Dear friend,

How good that you have so much feeling for nature—I always did flatter myself that our hearts beat as one—but now I'm quite certain of it. But you mustn't imagine that you might find the exact image of your heart in me; oh no, dear friend! Neither should you be surprised if with me everything looks so stunted—so contradictory—Let me tell you that I have a disposition from my childhood years—from the way my heart was then—and I still hold to it fondly—a kind of wax-like softness, and that is the reason why in certain moods I can weep about anything—and it is precisely this part of my heart that has been most abused during my time in the *Kloster*—even good old Bilfinger with his larking can call me a fool for a rather enthusiastic outburst—and for that reason I also have a regrettable disposition toward a certain rawness—so that I often lose my temper—without knowing why, and fly out at my brother—when there is hardly the hint of an insult. No, it doesn't beat like yours, my heart—it's much worse—I used to have a better one, but they took it from me—and often I must ask myself how you came to call me your friend. Here not a soul likes me—now I'm beginning to look for friendship among the children—but in truth it's not very satisfactory either.

Bilfinger I can call a friend—but he is too happy a sort to be bothered to look out for me—you will have no trouble understanding me—he is always full of fun—I'm always moping—it's obvious to anyone that leads nowhere. Let me tell you—I'm the only one here who doesn't know a single woman, other than by name, not a single clerk—or whoever else passes as society in Maulbronn.

My flute might be some consolation, but they've spoilt that for me too. Whenever Efferenn and Bilfinger etc. get together for some chamber music, they prefer to leave a gap than call on Hölderlin. You mustn't believe that I sour all pleasures for myself, or don't accept them when they come. Lately, out of sheer discontentment, I followed your aunt, the wife of the assistant into her garden—to her annoyance no doubt. And then the girls in the offices spoke to me for the first time ever as I went past. You should have seen me—I was as happy as a child—just that someone had spoken to me—and yet there wasn't all that much to be happy about.

One more thing I have to say to you—if ever it enters your head again to go off to the Cape, you'll have me as your companion. Word of honor!

Look after yourself in the meantime, dear brother! What a dreary morning!

Yours,

Hölderlin

I'll have to send you a duet—for solo flute I've nothing apart from concertos. The little things I play by ear.

5. TO IMMANUEL NAST

[Maulbronn, January/February 1787]

Dear frend,

Another hour lost to daydreaming! I was among other things with you—I can never do that better than in my empty evenings—when I'm alone in the dark—I was somewhere else too—and the end of it all was—that I felt sorry for myself and for others. For tell me, friend, why must I raise a palisade round my best intentions, let my most innocent actions be interpreted as crimes—that there are such ill-meaning people, among my fellows such wretched types—if friendship didn't from time to time restore me to myself: I'd sometimes have wished myself in any other place rather than among human society.—Look, dear Nast, it's not amour propre and exaggerated sensitivity that makes me so upset—somebody else, whose affairs mean more to me than mine suffered this hurt—oh if only I didn't have to be so sparing in what I can tell you—but I must, I must—perhaps another time—It would have been better to say nothing, you're perhaps fed up with this childish whimpering—and yet I've no idea where to turn but to you. Recently I wanted to write to you, but was plagued with a raging toothache.—If only I could write something really amusing for once. Patience, it will happen!—I hope—or—or—haven't I borne enough already? Did I not learn as a boy what would make me sigh as a man? And as a young man, does it look any better? And this, they say, is the best time of our life! Dear God, am I the only one, is everybody happier than me? And what have I done?

Yes, my friend, precisely what ought to console me weighs heaviest upon me. And then I say to myself—when lust, rancor, aggression rage in you, if you were like so many of those around you—Oh I must stop—Forgive me, dear Nast, you hardly know me—and must almost know me as someone who rails against him who in his great wisdom guides our destinies—but I never want to be taken that way. Another bad night awaits me—if only I were with you. Perhaps you'll charge me with—being in love—Tell me, friend, would I speak this way if I were? or don't you know? Well—I don't know either. And now good night—in the morning I shall come to a judgment on these scrawlings, and perhaps I'll tear them up.

Hölderlin

6. TO IMMANUEL NAST

Maulbronn, 18 February 1787

One question above all! You count yourself among the fraternity of those for whom the art of writing is particularly sacred—Now friend Bilfinger claims to have discovered, in the letter you recently wrote me with flying pen, an ambiguous spelling mistake—he says, that in the—love

your

L Nast—

there is a bit of roguery, and he intends to avenge it in my name (because I'm not really made for vengeance), and look out, do you know what sort of vengeance he has in mind? He will write to you—& love your

B—r.

What Br.—. is supposed to mean I—if you so wish—don't know. But now for serious matters! You ask how I like your *Amadis*—and I say—not at all. And why's that??—Not because Wieland is in any case not my thing, and not—because I'd rather have read a fairy-tale that wasn't interrupted by satire—but—I say this in all soberness—because there are things in it that excitable people such as I am, unfortunately!!!—cannot bear to read. Oh brother! do you think I've read him more than half way? I thank God that my imagination is still untainted, that I feel disgust for a poet who would certainly make any true innocence blush with shame. Admit it to me, dear Nast, don't you feel better in your heart when you hear the great singer of the *Messiah*? or read of our Schubart's raging Ahasuerus? Or the fiery-spirited Schiller?—Convince yourself of this by reading *Fiesko* and *Kabale & Liebe*—In the last of these there is such a lovely girl—think of me when Louise stands there with her gaze lost in the detachment of eternity—and tell me if I'm not right.

Thinking of that passage, whenever I imagine losing a girl one day, and the clod I'd become again, as usually happens in my unhappy hours, I'd only need to read the passage and I'd have air enough to breathe. I can already see you laughing at me, you're thinking: before someone goes on about losing he first needs—to have??—? Think what you like. I can put up with anything.

Would you believe it—my friend Hiemer in the Academy has now left three letters in each of which I ask him for Brutus and Caesar unanswered. Bad, don't you think?

That fellow also has a whole jumble of poems of mine, and if he never sends them back to me I want to see no more of him.

My best regards to your cousin Miss Heinrike Nast. Has she already told you about Maulbronn? I imagine she also met Miss Brecht? Do you know her too??

Hölderlin

I don't know—perhaps there are also spelling mistakes at the end of my letter, like in yours, but—I was in a hurry.

7. TO IMMANUEL NAST

[Maulbronn, beginning of March 1787]

Dear friend,

Just a word or two! A pity it's only a few—I'm in such a good mood at the moment. Just think of that! Something for the annals! I really am content with myself once again—with my fate. You want me to elucidate my mystical letters? I'm jolly glad I did write them so mystically. I'd be even more embarrassed now otherwise. Now I must stop.

Last week I couldn't write because of the *examen solenne*. A feeble excuse!

Bilfinger & Efferenn send greetings! Tell me, dear Nast, you won't take revenge for my silence up till now, will you, and for this scrawl? You'll write me 2–3 good long letters before Easter? 5 weeks to go!

Your

contented

Hölderlin

8. TO IMMANUEL NAST

[Maulbronn, mid-March 1787]

Some news, some good, good news to quicken the heart! I have here Ossian, the bard without peer, Homer's great rival, I have him now in my hands.

You must read him, friend—and your valleys will all become the Cona's valleys—your Engelsberg a mountain of Morven—such a sweet and melancholy sensation will come over you—you must read him—I'm not good at declaiming. The book must come back with me to Nürtingen in the holidays, and then I'll read it until I have it half by heart.

I don't yet know whether I'll be able to visit you, not on the way up at any rate. I don't know what to write at all—the good, blind Ossian is roaming around in my head. My friend the *académicien* has written to me—apologized of course—asked for my forgiveness—but—I wish he'd kept his excuses and deprecations to himself and sent me the music.

If you write to Bilfinger and Efferenn, give them a good fright—for fun—by saying you've heard a rumor about 2 students visiting the offices almost every day—and it's thought to be suspicious—. The lads have ensconced themselves over the road at the curate's, and Bilfinger, the old devil, feels quite at home there. And Efferenn—he only has to hear the pantaleon—and he's not interested in anything else—I reckon that if Lucifer himself were to play the pantaleon over there he'd run after him—but good for him, because (from what people say—Bilfinger —) she's an angel. I don't make many friends here—I'd still rather be on my own—and then I fantasize about this and that, in my head, and it's all so heartfelt that sometimes I'm close to tears when I've imagined that I've lost my girl and am despised and rejected by everybody. Keep well—my friend—the bell's ringing, I have to go to my class.

Yours

Hölderlin (just as contented as you)

9. TO IMMANUEL NAST

Maulbronn, 26 March [1787]

Dear friend,

Nothing but a request from me today, an urgent supplication easily granted. And that is? Well, listen!

Märklin is going to visit me from Leonberg, & think how lovely it would be if—you came with him! Oh my friend! I won't give up—you must, if you want to call yourself my friend—even if only for a few days—I've put everything into it, Bilfinger, Märklin and I all ask you together! Are these three friends worth anything to you? And can you turn down such a request from them? No! I know it for sure—you'll come—& even if there are a few small difficulties to overcome. Look here, dear Nast, if you won't do it as a favor to me, do it as a favor to your other friends who in their & my name also ask you the same thing. But it would truly hurt me if you were able to come, & found things that prevented you—and came up with—excuses. If you knew how what I ask springs from the depths of my heart—how mad with joy the mere promise of your coming would make me—then promise, dear friend, go on—I know you'll gladly grant me a few hours of cheer—But you are a man, & as such won't leave it there, with a mere promise. You know how much of what we desire comes to nothing, & how painful that is! Should this too come to nothing?

I beg you—and if what I beg is granted—to thank you I'll do all that can be done round here within the limits of my sphere of influence—& with that

Yours

Hölderlin

10. TO IMMANUEL NAST

[Maulbronn, mid-April 1787]
5 o'clock in the morning

Dear friend,

At last! And what? Should I be cross with you? But it's done now, and quarrelling over it will only make it worse. No good would have come of it, as far as I can see, if I had convinced myself to have a quarrel with you. Friend Märklin told me you had a fine good time together, and I was very pleased to hear it. Bilfinger and I also paid each other a visit and prospered wonderfully in the other's company. Oh, what a shame that Nast couldn't be with us! You were never serious about it, you rascal! Admit it! And here—I am now content again. I am so much alone, all the time, in peace and quiet—and that suits me—but far, so far, from Bilfinger, more's the pity.—I hardly speak to anyone, but I think all the more often of my dear friends scattered about the world—and it gives me such a feeling of contentment.

Would you mind sending me *Kabale und Liebe*—someone here has asked for it.

And my album—I bet you've forgotten it. Brutus and Caesar you'll have in a fortnight, as truly as I'm your friend. Bilfinger will send you Wieland's *Merkur* today.

Yours

Hölderlin

11. TO HIS MOTHER

[Maulbronn, second half of April 1787]

Dearest Mamma,
You can believe me when I now say that—barring a quite extraordinary turn of events that would seem to make my happiness more complete

elsewhere—it will never again enter my head to deviate from my path—I can see now that as a village pastor one can do as much good in the world and be happier too than if one were I know not what.

Recently a hot air balloon went up, and the parson from Diefenbach came to see it—and with him one of the Camerers, the one in the middle of studying law—he came directly from Poppenweiler and brought me a thousand thousand greetings, saying that the good man greatly desired—to see me again one day. And so now I *must* go, whenever I can. The pastor of Diefenbach was also extremely friendly toward me, he hadn't known until now that one had to get leave—the ones in the year above had come over every week without his having spoken with the Prelate beforehand. I put my sermon somewhere safe to send it to you—but can't find it anywhere at the moment. My hair is beautifully neat. It's in curls again. And why's that? For you!

For here I have no one I wish to please. A thousand kisses to Carl! What's he up to all alone with his dear Mamma? Look after yourselves—I'm in a rush, as you can see.

Your most obedient son

Hölderlin

12. TO HIS MOTHER

[Maulbronn, May/June 1787]

Dearest Mamma,

At the moment I once again have masses to do; and the kind of work that really taxes the mind—so only in passing do I confess that Bilfinger's coffee, and my sugar, are quite used up, and that consequently I have sometimes longed for breakfast—given how early we have to get up—and the constant mental effort required of us—and the other day I once again, with a dreadfully empty stomach, had to force myself to eat a soup that your most ravenous laborer would have balked at—and then I felt so wretched that I could almost have flung the bowl at the wall in anger. So it would be a good, good work for your Friz if you could send him a little coffee.

You will smile at my long-winded petition, but it was just to give you a little sense of what we have to put up with in the *Kloster*. For worries about food are not negligible when they mean yearning for a sip of coffee or just a decent bit of soup, and not being able to get them anywhere, anywhere. And things are not too bad for me; but you should see some of the others, who still have debts to clear from the winter and haven't got two coins to rub together—it's laughable* when people don't go to bed because they're so fed up, and go up and down the dormitory half the night singing:

Rise up, you brothers, gird your loins
The creditor's at the door.
Our debts are growing every day
We have neither peace nor stay
So off to Africa!—(to the Cape)

and so on through most of the night, then they end up laughing at one another and themselves and at last to bed. But you have to admit it's a dismal kind of fun!

And on top of all this, the Prelate, the fêted Weinland, has such unfathomably bizarre mood swings at the moment that he sets about professors, students and the famulus alike, giving them such a telling off that before you know where you are all the professors and students—and students and famulus—are reduced to tears. That's the way of the world! I'm learning, thank God, to come to terms with it more and more. I can firmly assure you, dear Mamma, that I, who was once anything but content, am now no longer to be counted among the discontents! I've written to dear Rike—and comforted her!

I have to say that I shed tears over her letter—and as straight afterward I had to lead the chant I could hardly speak I was so upset. I'd never have believed my love for her was so great! But for sure, she's a fine, wonderful girl, Rike. God will give her a thousand blessings for her tears. You can be proud of such a daughter!

Your

most obedient son

Hölderlin

* forgive me for using such poor paper!

13. TO IMMANUEL NAST

[Maulbronn, summer 1787]

A thousand thanks—dear friend—for your splendid painting—your kind letter!

You should have seen how I reacted to it—I received it at table—and I had the misfortune—that I could not refrain, in particular at the end where you comfort me so nobly with a cheering future, from shedding tears—a few of them fell in my soup—and it was all I could do to conceal them from Bilfinger who was sitting next to me. But he must have noticed something in fact, he winked at me so with his mischievous eyes, and that made everything all right!!!

If only you knew how often I think of you! How often I wish you were with me!

O dear friend and brother! I am such a weak fellow—but I admit it to no one other than you—and isn't that right, it's more pity you have for me than an inclination to laugh at me for weeping over your letter? But dear God, I can't help confessing to you that what I have to put up with is more than what I wrote about the other day! You can take it from me that God has sent me a healthy share of sufferings! I can't tell you any of them—you might get my letter at a moment of good cheer and then I'd have it on my conscience to have spoilt it for you with my lamentations! I know how often I yearn for a brief moment of respite—and how I then try to hang on to it when I have it, and the same thing might easily be true for you—

I can't bear it any longer here! Really not, I must get out—I've told myself I'll either write to my mother in the morning asking her to take me out of the *Kloster* completely, or approach the Prelate to request sick leave for several months because I often cough up blood.—. You see, my friend, I'm gradually calming down.

Don't worry!!! Whatever you do don't trouble yourself over me!!!

Yours,

Hölderlin

For your lovely Apollo a thousand thanks again—it has already brought me many a good moment—I must look at it every day!

14. TO IMMANUEL NAST

[Maulbronn, late October 1787]

Dear Nast,

Back here again now! In the quiet—after so many distractions, back
in the *Kloster*—your letter didn't reach me in Nürtingen—but a
thousand—thousand thanks for it! O, I also have a great great deal to
say to you, friend, but my head is so confused again, so many different
feelings fill my heart. Where I've just been—during the holiday, the
unfulfilled desires—the incomplete moments of happiness—I don't
know, is it imagination or reality—what I see only half pleases me—it's
all so empty around me—and often I reproach myself that I no longer
take part in the fate of my brothers in quite the warm, whole-hearted
way I used to. Oh Nast, my dear brother, tell me, am I the only one to
be so alone, forever miserable with myself?

But no, no! It's just this evening is one of those when I no longer
remember the contented hours that God has already given me on this
dear earth; I'm ungrateful toward him—quite ungrateful! I've such a dear
mother, such a dear, good brother and sister—oh you should have seen
how they all cried when I left! Brother of mine! I can still remember the
feeling (it was nearly midnight) as I set off with heavy heart!

And don't I have you, you—and still I complain?—Yes, when I
no longer have you, then I can complain—. But let's not dwell on that
yet, don't you think, dear Nast? I will be the last person to make your
departure for foreign parts bitter, isn't that so?—? But you'll come here
again first—and I have things to tell you—no, think nothing of it, it's
nothing that important, trifles—perhaps I'll have forgotten by then.

Now let me reply to your dear letter. Just one thing! I confess
I only half believe it, if you hadn't written it I wouldn't believe it at
all—when you say that she still remembers me, your honorable girl—or
did you tell her how unhappy I am, or believe myself to be—and she's
taken pity on me? And she wants to comfort me, together with this
kind sign of her memory, with a compliment? Yes, dear friend, yes,
this compliment did indeed comfort me—That she should remember
me still—God almighty, such a girl!—But silence! Now I must tell
you something that will make you laugh—just think, laugh at me as
much as you like, today I was walking along in my thoughts—and

suddenly my favorite weakness, the shape of my future, flitted before my eyes—and listen, but have a good laugh at me, what came to me was that after finishing university I would become a hermit—& the thought pleased me so much that for a whole hour, I reckon, I was a hermit in my imagination. You see, friend, I'm not ashamed to tell you my fondnesses, & that excuses me to some degree—with you—but otherwise—don't let this letter fall into strange hands—into hostile hands—or else everyone will say—he's a fool!!!

Send your good, honorable girl my best compliments!!!

Ever

yours

Hölderlin

15. TO IMMANUEL NAST

[Maulbronn, November 1787]

Dear and good friend,

Here I am once more at last! But I've a great deal—a great deal to say, and yet only half—because another's dear lips have reserved it for herself—for when you come here—and I'm to tell you to be sure to come soon.—O my friend! From her dear lips you'll learn the source of all my joys, all my sufferings, all my complaints—you'll be able to explain the puzzling moods in which I've often written to you. If you could look into my heart as it is now, dear Nast, how it looks so calm, so bright, so content, you'd be filled with gladness—and tell your splendid girl how I now no longer grumble at him who deals out my fate, who so kindly and wisely distributes days of contentment and days of sorrow.—Oh I was such a fool—thought often, when people hated me, when mockery plagued me—when everything, everything conspired to spoil my every last little—so long yearned for hour of happiness—then, dear friend, I believed that God did not love me, believed—he was angry at my *love*!!! Now you know everything—Nast! But I'll write no more—she shall tell you.

I'd just like to embrace you now—shed tears of joy at your breast—in your little room—I can see it now, that little room of yours—everything there was so sacred—I thought, there you had so often thought of me—& it was all so quiet around us—& I had come straight from Maulbronn—from the parting—the parting—& had just seen your girl, how ever so gently she—I'd better stop, I'm getting too far into description—and writing is such a wretched business—one expresses oneself not half as warmly as one would like to—looks much the same as in the days of my lamenting—when among friends I wanted to be cheerful—and only made a sour, skewy face—To be sure, it's much the same—my Nast! But forgive me—dear friend—forgive me—a whole year I didn't let on—the precious secret you still don't know—you may consider me false—but, God knows—how often I burned with it—how I exerted all my force to keep the confession to myself a little longer—but look, I had to promise her so often and so earnestly not to tell a soul—but lately she asked me in one of our hours of bliss—whether I'd not yet said anything to my Nast—o friend, friend! How happy I was then—"I'll write to him at once," but she wants to tell you herself, the sweetheart—

Here some poems by H— he sends his greetings—and asks why you don't pay him a visit?

And here's my picture!

Bilfinger is so kind at the moment—so good and kind—I can tell you, dear friend—he's like you—kinder than me!

I'm not sure whether it's Hiemer in Stuttgart or you have my Pfeffel—let me know!

And write very soon! Come soon! We'll have paradisial times together! Now good night, dear friend! In the morning perhaps I'll write to you again!

Yours

Hölderlin

16. TO IMMANUEL NAST

[Maulbronn, November 1787]

My dear friend,

Oh, that I can't say anything—I'd call out to you a thousand
times—dearest Nast—and weep tears of joy over the best of
friends—were I with you now. Yes, brother—if I were to roam half the
world—in search of a friend who could be more to me than you—I'd
not find him—given what our friendship is!—I'd not find him. I must
have had a premonition—dear Nast—of the joy this letter of yours
would give me—I had a whole pile of unopened letters before me,
from my mother—my dear brother and sister—from friends—but
you can ask Bilfinger—as if I intended to devour it—I pounced on
yours—tore the letter almost in two as I broke the seal—and found
then a thousand times more than my highest expectations had
expected. Dear, dear friend—how overwhelmingly I felt it then, that
love and friendship are our greatest happiness on this earth! I wanted
to sit down at once and write back—but I couldn't produce a single
word—

But I have so much to say to you, so much—beloved friend!
First of all, Hiemer! Listen to what he wrote me the other
day—"You want poems? Fine, here's one—he's a wild unruly
lad—makes up his own rules—often runs breakneck—so that I was
worried he might bust an arm or a leg—a real Roman in the way he
casts about him with grandeur of mind—and love of country and
freedom—so much so that sadly (!!!) I can't take him into any kind of
society—he's already caused me many a sleepless night, this lad—he
just won't do anything to fit in—" And he goes on like this page after
page! Listen to this—striking a more serious note: "You are my friend,
he wrote, and a loyal one—that I know! You can devote an hour or
two to your H—so, read my work through as if you were a critic—find
fault where there is fault to find—write telling me what you thought
was all right—and get on with it!!! And send it to your beloved Nast
as well—not a soul else—it must be lies what you say about him—or
he's more than I or you—send it to him, ask him to do exactly what
I've asked you—you must all write down your thoughts—but don't
ask Nast in my name, he mustn't know that he's writing down what

he thinks for my sake—do you get that? So that he is all the more severe—all the more unbiassed.—I hope his judgments will be of great use to me —" I didn't think I needed to heed his suggestion—I know, dear friend, you'll write what you think—don't flatter—I'm also going to say his faults to his face—if not, he'd immediately announce an end to our friendship. Make sure you're really severe! Let's make a point of sitting on our critic's tripod—he shall receive blows when he deserves them—that way we'll please him best. The actual costume of his poem—the plan—the particular laws he's devised for himself, I'll send you next time.

But listen to what he says about this hero—

"You will fault me—and rightly—you *must* fault me—for making, of all people, the quick-tempered, cavalier, vindictive Trenk, and whatever other epithets people might give him, quite rightly—for making him the subject of my poem—The reason for it—is that I didn't want to tackle a great hero—which Trenk isn't at all—for what is a first attempt—in short, I beg you to attend more to the poem itself than to its subject."

I'll stop this now—and tell you more about it next time—Just send me your judgments soon—and on every page—he'll love you then above all else—you'll see—But now—my dear Nast—what do you reckon? Shall I stop here?—No! No! I can't, you must know—for long enough I've been wearing a mask over this corner of my heart—You ought to be angry, friend—but you know the reasons for it, and forgive me—.

It's her—you've already guessed—must have guessed it at the first mention of love—for—could there be anyone else here I might be in love with? And even if there were a thousand—I swear to you, brother—so loyal—so tender—so wholly devoted to me and nothing to anyone else—you'd find no one like her—except—you know! You'd be cross, & I'd be unjust—if I'd not written this *except*. But where to begin? Should I recount to you all our days of joy & pain? I will—but won't be able to stop for a good while.

I arrived here—saw her—and she me—We each inquired about the character of the other—as often happens—Louise perhaps only chanced to—both of us asked your good cousin, the son of the famulus—who was here at the time—I won't describe to you the way our love grew—your dear kind cousin brought us together in the very first month of my being here—How my heart thumped

in my breast—how I could scarcely speak a word—how in my
trembling I barely managed to stammer the word Louise—you know
all that—brother of mine—you've felt it yourself. Your cousin soon
left—and—terrible days followed. I had spoken with the beloved
girl in a particular spot—without a prior arrangement I could never
speak to her—there wasn't a soul we could confide in—no other
place was possible—so apart from those few moments—those few
stammering words—we remained apart for almost a month. O Nast!
My brother! Those were terrible days—unspeakable suffering—a
madness I'd never felt before tore at my heart. For—jealousy had
come into the picture—& the object of it was—Bilfinger—he, ignorant
of all, was—also an admirer of Louise's. I learned this—converted
her distance from me into a deliberate avoidance—and at last found
the opportunity to write to her—fearful nonsense, as I can still
remember—was in a rage with Bilfinger the whole time—& neither
did B. know the reason for the incomprehensible enmity, nor did
the good L. what the nonsense was all about. At last—in an hour of
utter fury I spat it all out before B.—he renounced her willingly—for
he had not yet exchanged a single word with her—and that was the
beginning of our friendship. I also soon spoke to L. in the place
where we first came together—she asked me full of dread—what I
meant by my letter. I was bewildered—she even more so—and yet
it was a blessed hour—we parted glad in heart. It was about this
time that you came here—that I became your friend, once I went
straight from being with you to her. I was still plagued by fits of bad
temper—& many tears flowed—over the uncertainty—whether she
really loved me. Only rarely did I make it to her—always in stolen
moments—and this often made the dear girl anxious—she was very
reserved with me—because she didn't know me—and isn't that in itself
an admirable trait in her beauteous soul?—Summer came—and with
it more unhappiness about Louise and me—God in heaven! I can't
bear to think back to those days—Friend, dear friend! Days when
doubts about the controller of my fate swam into my soul—doubts
I prefer not to tell you about. He has forgiven me them, in all his
mercy—I have shown my remorse with many a tear, many a night-
time prayer.—. The distress of my soul was soon noticed—and in the
whole *Kloster* I was soon reputed for being dangerously melancholic.
Louise came to hear of it, and her distress equaled mine. Sleep eluded

me at night—and any kind of work by day—I stifled my feelings for
the most part—when I wrote to you—for I thought—you'd perhaps
laugh at me—so great was my distrust of everybody. Ask me about
the causes of our miseries if you wish—you shall know them all—they
will appear slight to you—when I think it over—I cannot grasp it
myself. No more now of the unhappy days. For a pitiful month I
had one hour of gladness when I wept with my Louise—and for that
hour I gave thanks to God, thanked him at last for everything—for
all the tribulations—all the persecutions—all the tears. The doubts,
the grievances directed toward the Almighty, those you need only
imagine in the first weeks of my troubles, when I was not yet used to
bearing them. Do you still remember, dear Nast, how wrought up I
was—when you left last summer—I could tell, you were astonished—I
parted from you as if it were for ever—dear good friend, I saw you
making speed back to your Leonberg—heard your delighted talk of
joy-filled days and blissful hours—and—I—knew then of nowhere
in the whole wide world where I could find contentment, and there I
was again without you, who had made me forget my miseries—and
I saw how my fate grew ever darker, my soul ever weaker, my body
ever sicklier—(you'll recall that several times I coughed up blood—)
and this was the reason for my leaving you in a way you must have
found so inexplicable. Do you remember, dear friend, how gaily high-
spirited I was when we walked to Oelbronn together? That day I'd
been with her—I saw her go into the garden behind us—leapt over the
wall by the road—& how it was with her you can glean from how I
was—with you—and that's why you all had to wait so long for me to
catch up. In the end I was perfectly content—except when memories
of my distress sometimes cast a cloud over me.—. And now, best of
friends, now I am the happiest man on earth—. Come what may—I
love my Louise for ever—ever; and for ever—ever—my Louise loves
me. O Nast, you don't yet know her as she really is—I've seen her in
the company of others—seen her, without her noticing me, among her
girlfriends—oh! how different she is with me! When with me she begs
God for a happy life together—brother! brother!—when full of these
dreams she takes my hand—"when the time comes when I won't see
you for so long!" I tremble with joy when I think of these moments
of happiness. She confessed to me once, the dear girl, that she used to
be so frivolous—and that she is so different now—so good, so true, so

tender—I'd go on night and day—if I were to set down for you all my heart is full of.—It really is the middle of the night! So you won't be surprised that I'm falling asleep.

Say to your honorable girl all that I should say to her. The thanks for her kind regards to me will be better and warmer from your lips than from my weary pen. Sleep well.

Yours

Hölderlin

17. TO HIS SISTER AND BROTHER

[Maulbronn, New Year 1788]

Dear brother and sister,

I'm sure you will have wished your dear grandmother and dear Mamma lots of good things—and with heartfelt sincerity and gratitude for all the tender attentions and efforts they have devoted to you over the past year—and also, dear brother and sister, you thought of me, didn't you, and wished me something too, for I know you are fond of me and you showed you were when you sent me all those presents recently. And now I too am sending you wishes from the depths of my warm and brotherly heart—I wish you love and obedience to Almighty God—love and obedience toward your dear grandmother and mother, diligence in all things and, if I may ask this—also love for your brother, as you always have loved him and as he loves and always will love you. Dear Heinrike, dear Carl—if I could be with you a few moments now, and kiss you—be always at peace with one another, and when you are contented together, think too of

your

affectionate brother

Hölderlin

18. TO HIS MOTHER

[Maulbronn, early February 1788]

Dearest Mamma,

Something to ask you again! You will know that it's soon the Duke's birthday, which is celebrated here with great pomp. The Prelate and ladies and gentlemen, young ladies and students and clerks gather for music and speeches and the reciting of poems the whole afternoon, and in the evening there are to be illuminations. As everyone else has clubbed together for food and drink—we're also going to sit together: Bilfinger and Efferenn and Hesler and Märklin and I—I'd like to ask you for a few jugs of wine, dear Mamma. Thank you very much for what you sent. As concerns your advice I'm full of admiration for your good sense—when I turn 60 I'll never have as much. A thousand thanks to dear Rike for her letter. I'm so busy right now that I haven't got a moment more to write anything.

Yours

Hölderlin

Next time you'll get quite a few torn garments.

19. TO HIS MOTHER

[mid-February 1788]

Dearest Mamma,

Forgive me for not having written last post-day. You'll probably have realized for yourself that precisely the day I usually write letters was that of the Duke's birthday celebrations. I had the honor to figure as a poet at these festivities.

But as on this occasion I'm sending you something that will perhaps give you more pleasure than my poem, I'll save that until next post-day. You were recently so tenderly concerned—about my health.

Well, I can assure you that over the whole winter I've suffered no pain whatsoever. But in connection with the wine you were even more tenderly, even more maternally concerned—and here, if you promise not to take it as conceitedness on my part, I'm enclosing clear evidence that there is nothing in my character to make you fear anything like that. The letter is from the Reverend Rotaker from Hausen, near Verena. I must tell you the whole story though. Rotaker is poor. Some of the womenfolk here, knowing that, and being keen to help him without his being aware, used me as their go-between. This noble action touched me. Ashamed, I resolved to do the same. But the state of my purse did not permit that pleasure. But—what if I keep him from ill company, I thought, what if I help him with his essays and teach him as much of what I know as I can (as *teaching* will in any case be my main occupation one day)—will that not please our beloved God just as much, I thought, as supplying money or items of clothing?—The letter will tell you the rest. But I must add that Rotaker at the time enjoyed the worst of company—that the Prelate wrote to his father telling him what he had been getting up to and that upon his father's threats and warnings he confessed everything to him, full of remorse, saying that he had changed completely and that he had me to thank for it. But don't let anyone else know of this, dear Mamma! I'd be mocked for it—accused of doing what is my duty purely to satisfy my own pride—I only told you about it because you are such a tender and anxious mother.

A thousand thanks to Karl for what he has sent.—I'd write to him and dear Rike if I didn't have half a dozen other letters to answer. Perhaps you'll already have sent the linen cloth off when this letter gets to you. I must hurry.

Your

most obedient son

Hölderlin

A good friend asks me if I can order him a boxwood flute with horn rings at Wohlhaupter's—would you be so kind as to do it for me? Write to let me know if we're going to the Unterland—If nothing comes of it, I've made my arrangements—I can travel with Renz, Bilfinger and Hiemer in the Unterboihingen coach—but it's not too late, I can always say no.

20. TO HIS MOTHER

[Maulbronn, ~ 11 March 1788]

Dearest Mamma,

So in a week's time we'll be together, whether in Nürtingen or in the
Unterland. I've no need to order anything more now. If we do travel,
I think we'll have a journey like the one we had at Easter once before.
I am prepared for any eventuality. If you let me know, or write, that
you're staying in Nürtingen, I'll take the Unterboihingen coach as far as
Boihingen—and you'll come and meet me there—if on the other hand
you do go to the Unterland, I'll wait for you on the Tuesday after Palm
Sunday in Schwiebertingen, in the Ox. As far as clothing goes, though,
I've prepared myself quite for the journey—I'm not taking any shoes
for example. We've got snow here at the moment, which shouldn't
however be too bad for traveling.

I'm looking forward to soon being in the arms of my family. A
thousand greetings to all.

Your

most obedient son

Hölderlin

21. TO IMMANUEL NAST

[Maulbronn, end of April 1788]

My dear Nast,

I've just laid my Ossian aside to rejoin you. My soul has feasted on the
heroes of the bard, I have sorrowed with him when he sorrowed over
his dying girls.

And so—this put me in the mood to devote a moment or two
entirely to you.

It's a long long time now since we last heard from one
another—and just think, dear friend, for the whole of the holidays I

was barely a mile from you and could not possibly get away—not even for half a day. I sat for the whole four weeks at my aunt's deathbed in Gröningen and learned how to endure suffering—from her! And now, friend, now she is dead!

O Nast! She is said to be exactly like my lamented father, I never knew him, I was three when he died, but he must have been a splendid man if he was like her. When in unspeakable pain she looked up sorrowfully to the heavens, and as the hour of death neared lost the power of speech, and I prayed for her—and then she suddenly woke from her labored breathing and marveled to find herself still with us—o my friend, that taught me so much! And just before setting off back here, when I took my leave from her for evermore, and she said—"If we don't see one another again in this world, we'll meet in the next"—Oh! those are words I'll never forget! The thought of eternity is the supreme and most blessed thought man can have—When as so often I come to my Louise in a downcast mood, and complain about the way people are—and worry about what the future holds—she reminds me then of eternity—and those are blissful hours.

My poems are on their travels at the moment;—if they make it back home without having their heads bloodied—and paternal circumspection doesn't force their Papa Hölderlin to lock them into his desk again for six months (for they're a pretty silly bunch), well yes, if all this doesn't happen, they shall also march on to Leonberg.

At Whitsun, my friend—if your Hölderlin means anything to you—if you want to see him again—(this coming autumn I'll have to go straight home, and then to Tübingen) dear, dear brother, in the name of all those dear to you in Maulbronn, I beg you, come! I beg your honorable girl—just tell her I humbly implore her to tell her Nast he mustn't let his friend hope this way in vain.

Be so kind and send me the Pfeffel, and Brutus and Caesar . . .

Oh if only it was certain you were coming! Just this once don't let my hopes be idle—For I am

your

Hölderlin

22. TO LOUISE NAST

[Maulbronn, end of April 1788]

What curious people we are—my love! I believe this moment with you
was more blessed than any, any other hour spent by your side. I was
inexpressibly happy as I went along the top of the hill and felt your
kiss still on my lips—I looked over the landscape so full of warmth
I could have embraced the whole world—and still, still I feel the same
way!

Your violets stand in front of me, Louise! I mean to keep them as
long as I can.

Because you're reading *Don Carlos* I want to read it too, in the
evening, when I've got my work done.

At the moment I'm writing poems at breakneck speed—I'm to
send a shipment to the good Schubart.

On my walks I'm always turning verses on my slate—and guess
what?—to you, to you! And then I wipe them out again. I'd just done
this when I saw you coming down the hillside.

O love! You think of God and of me in your little room? Stay as
you are, unique as you surely are among hundreds of others.

Is your sister Miss Wilhelmine coming today? Did you send
her the letter, or are you going to wait and give it to her? I hear she's
feeling better. I've got to send Bilfinger a note too—but I can see it's
impossible before tomorrow.

If only I could always remain as contented as I am now. But—my
love for you will endure whatever my mood—and so my situation
could be a lot worse. Be sure to think of me often. You know that I
remain inseparably

yours,

Hölderlin

23. TO HIS MOTHER

[Maulbronn, ~ 10 June 1788]

Dearest Mamma,

Here is part of my travel diary. You'll have to make do with these scribblings, I often wrote them half in my sleep, before I went to bed. I still think with pleasure of the journey, which although it lasted a mere five days took me a good distance. From Mannheim I traveled on yet further to Frankenthal—as you'll hear shortly. And so a thousand thanks, dearest Mamma, for having given me this treat. I promised to note all my expenses—here they are.

Pub in Bruchsaal	43 kr.
Fare over the Rhine	8 kr.
Pub in Rheinhausen	7 kr.
Another fare over the Rhine	24 kr.
Theater in Mannheim	48 kr.
For the wigmaker in Mannheim	24 kr.
In Frankenthal I paid the bill	1 fl. 58 kr.
Tip in Speyer	36 kr.
For the wig-maker in Speyer	24 kr.
For the journey back from Speyer I took a horse	1 fl. 30 kr.
In Bruchsaal a drink for the man	15 kr.
For the horse back down	2 fl.
Sundries	1 fl.
Total	10 fl. 17 kr.

Blum paid in most of the pubs on the journey, as you can see—so I came out of it very well. If only I could tell you everything in person. Tell dear Carl that in the second installment there is lots about big ships, with sails and masts. Something for him to look forward to. Imagine, dearest Mamma, I didn't feel quite well before I set off and took some medicine the evening before—but the journey did me such a power of good that everyone noticed it. I've still got a lot to do. So I close with the assurance that I am

your

most obedient son

Hölderlin

On Monday the 2nd of June I set off. It was a fine invigorating morning. My heart opened at the thoughts of all I would see and hear. Never had I felt better than when, half an hour out from here, I rode down the hill—and beneath me lay Knittlingen, and far in the distance the prosperous lands of the Pfalz. In this bright mood I continued my way through Bretheim, Diedelsheim, Gundelsheim, Heidelsheim, and then I was in Bruchsaal. I had in mind to spend time there on the way back—so just waited in the pub for cousin Blum. I waited until one, no Blum, waited until two, three—still nothing! Now I started to feel annoyed. I hadn't much liked Bruchsaal in any case, with its stupid clerics and holier-than-thou inhabitants—I'd only hired my horse for the one day, it was a long way to Speyer, not much time left, the road unfamiliar. What was I to do?

I sent home the man who had come with me to take the horse back, climbed on my horse and posthaste to Speyer!

After Bruchsaal I was no longer on the high road, but I had a good broad sandy track. I passed mostly through thick, scary woodland, where apart from the road I could hardly see three paces around me. In Württemberg I've never seen such thick woods. Not a ray of sun pierced through. At last I came out into the open again, having passed Forst, Hambrüken and Wiesenthal. An endless plain lay stretching before my eyes. To my right I had the Heidelberg hills and to my left those forming the border with France—I stopped for a long time. The new, unexpected view of such an immense plain moved me. And this plain was such a blessed region. Fields whose fruit were already ripening yellow—meadows where the grass, not yet cut, swayed its head—standing so tall and abundant—and then the beautiful blue vast sky above me—I was so taken by it that I'd perhaps be standing there with my horse still if, straight in front of me, I hadn't noticed the residence of the prince-bishops of Waaghäußel.

I wanted to head straight for it as it was on my route—from there I'd have gone via Lußheim—but I was sent left to Oberhausen, being a quicker way. Of the residence I can therefore say no more than that it lies in the woods with a chapel & several other buildings round it, but nothing else worth mentioning, no gardens, no wilderness as at Hohenheim, or what else I might have expected to find. Only just before Oberhausen did I notice the cathedral of Speyer, though I might have seen it soon after Bruchsaal—as vast as the plain is, this cathedral is immensely tall. I thought I had no more than quarter of an hour to go and was already looking forward to supper in Speyer, but I was utterly wrong. From Oberhausen I came to Rheinhausen. Here I had to cross the Rhine, but had to wait quite a while for the ferrymen to come over from the opposite bank because the crossing usually takes half an hour. But I've never been so happy to wait as then. I hardly noticed the time pass.

Imagine it—a river three times wider than the Neckar at its widest point—this river in the shadow of woods from top to bottom on either bank—and downriver the view stretching so far that it makes your head spin—that was a sight—I'll never forget it, it moved me profoundly—At last the boatmen came over. They cross in boats that are so big they have room for two coaches with their horses and plenty for other people besides. Half an hour later I was on the quayside at Speyer. I asked passersby whereabouts Frau Blum lived—and was pointed in the direction of the Reverend Mayer's house by somebody who knew her. As it was late in the day my little horse had to summon all the strength remaining in its stiff legs—I thought he and I would soon be enjoying supper now and a good night's sleep. And so I went through the gates of Speyer. The endless riding round the streets nearly wore me out, until at last I found Reverend Mayer's house.

Rike & Blum welcomed me with cries of joy, Frau Blum and her daughter, Mrs. Mayer, and Reverend Mayer with great courtesy. Enough for that day!

3rd June

Before my arrival Blum and Rike had already been planning a journey to Heidelberg for this day. So it was agreed that I should send my horse back up with Blum's coachman, who had to go back to Markgröningen again, and travel with them, Blum himself driving—I therefore had to quit my bed at 4 in the morning again—and by 5 I was sitting—to the great relief of my tired limbs—in the cart. We took the boat over the Rhine again—and in a few hours we were in the famous pleasure gardens of Schwetzingen that belong to the Elector Palatine.

Description can do little here. You have to have seen for yourself the splendor of it—the extraordinary beauties of art—the exquisite paintings, the buildings, the fountains etc.—if you want to get an idea of what it's like. But one feature I must mention. In the gardens is a Turkish mosque (temple) that some people would perhaps forget among the many fine things, but it's what I liked best of all. The whole is like Hohenheim and the Solitude taken together—as I see it. From Schwetzingen to Heidelberg we had three hours of dead straight high road—with on both sides ancient, oak-like mulberry trees. At about midday we arrived in Heidelberg. I liked the town a great deal. Its situation is the finest one can imagine. On either side and behind the town rise steep wooded hills, and there stands the ancient, venerable castle—I climbed up there, and made a pilgrimage to the famous Heidelberg barrel, the mascot of so many tipplers, the *bon mot* of so many drinking songs. It really is so big that there's plenty of room to dance around on the top. There are barriers round it, so that one can walk there without danger. But I can assure you that to fall off the top would be as unpleasant as to fall from my window at the *Kloster*. The new bridge is also very remarkable. The same afternoon we traveled on to—Mannheim. We had a marvelous road down by the Neckar. Hardly had we alighted before we were off to see a play. Nothing finer, more elegant, more perfect can be imagined than the National Theatre at Mannheim.—After the play I saw the arsenal too, where cannonballs are heaped up like piles of stones and where for the first time I saw grenades, bombs, cannon etc.—& then the Jesuit church—the most splendid edifice I came across on my journey! The town is almost twice as big as Stuttgart. The prince's palace can be seen from virtually every street. The streets are quite straight—everything is level. All the buildings form a large square. The staple house is so immense that it took me nearly quarter of an hour to walk round it. At supper I found myself sitting next to a Count of Styrom. He is a brother of the bishop in Bruchsaal. I only spent an hour with this man, but I shall revere him to my grave. He is a general, and grew old in the service of his lord, the King of France. He conversed with me as if with his brother—told me of his battles, the perils he had been in, his victories, his defeats—I might almost have forgotten that this man was Count Styrom, and I the student Hölderlin, and could have embraced him, so great was the love the old man inspired in me. He is the person most worthy of admiration among all those I met on my journey.

4th June

The promised further installment.

Wednesday the 4th of June

I remained in Mannheim until 10 o'clock in the morning, during which time I visited the Court Treasurer Dillenius, an uncle of my friend Märklin's, and was received with great courtesy.—I had a quick scout around the most elegant streets of the town, taking in the palace & the fortifications, & wherever I went I found grand houses that filled me with wonder. In the meantime my companions had made themselves ready, I leapt in the chaise, and was sad to part from a place where there was still so much of note to see and I could have acquired so many new impressions. We had to cross five bridges before we got onto the road; the one that crossed the Rhine proper was enormously long, and a bridge of boats. There were large boats firmly anchored, & abreast in a row, and on them stood the bridge. If boats come along, there are machines with which one can open the bridge at various points. But what drew my eyes most of all were the Electoral ships moored by the bank. From the waterline to the deck (so not counting the bottom) they must be about a small story high, but in length at least 24 foot, with the mast soaring a high story above the deck—and a mass of stays (ropes) hung down it, to let the mast down and to raise it, to haul in the sails and let them out. Right in the bows was a cabin with green shutters, and the rest of the ship was painted red and yellow. There were two of them, exactly the same save that the Electress's ship was a little smaller than Theodore's (the Prince-Elector's).

Via the most beautiful avenues we came to Okkersheim where the Electress has her seat. I stopped at the same pub that the great Schiller stayed in for several weeks after he had fled Stuttgart. It was a holy place for me—& it was all I could do to conceal the tears that came to my eyes in my admiration for the great and inspired poet he is. I can't give any particular details about the Electress's summer residence—I saw nothing—but houses and gardens, for I couldn't get Schiller out of my head. Toward noon we arrived in Frankenthal. After lunch we first went to visit the Gegel printing works, then the porcelain factories, where in the store I saw some very fine work—and from there the silk manufactures—which I also liked a good deal—from there to the canal which is a very noteworthy structure. I cannot describe all this because the details are not very clear to me.

The same afternoon we drove back to Speyer—and thus I had seen most of the remarkable towns of the Palatinate in a short space of time. Tomorrow I'll have a look round Speyer.

Thursday 5th June

My first outing in the morning was to the cathedral. This is one of the most remarkable buildings I saw on my journey, and the only one I looked at properly and with the necessary leisure. If you go in at the front by the great majestic door, you see in front of you an empty space that extends quite a long way up to broad raised platforms and is of unusual height, separated from the aisles by magnificent unadorned pillars. On the platforms there stands a great altar all of marble which is so high that further platforms are built into it, and on it stand 5 lit candles in golden candlesticks. (The candles form a pyramid, and the tallest must measure a good yard.) Next to the altar, on either side, stood the stalls and in the two corners next to the stalls two more altars, each as splendid as the first. Right at the back in the choir stood the throne of the bishop of Bruchsaal, of unimaginable splendor, and on each side of the throne the canons' stalls, all gilt. And so, standing down by the great door, consider the entire gigantic edifice as a whole, and imagine—the throne and the splendid stalls shimmering down from the far end—and the marble altar majestic with its candles—and above the immense vaulted roof—I stayed for an hour and could perfectly well have spent an hour there every day since without getting tired of it.

From there I went on to see counselor Boßler's music shop. That was also very nice. But let me pass on to something more interesting.

In the morning I had had a pretty good look round Speyer. So in the afternoon I wanted to get out into the country to take in the surroundings there. In the course of the afternoon I covered virtually the whole district of Speyer without coming across anything that particularly attracted my attention. It was almost evening when I came to the place they call the Gran (where merchandise is unloaded from the boats). The sight that stretched before me brought me back to life, like being reborn. My feelings expanded, my heartbeat quickened, my mind sped into the distance—my eyes were amazed—I did not know what I was looking at, and stood there like a statue.

Imagine the majestic, peaceful Rhine, coming from so far away that the boats were barely visible—and so far across that almost it could be taken for a wall of blue, & on the opposite bank thick, wild woods—& beyond the woods the darkening hills of Heidelberg—& down one side an immense plain—& all so full of the Lord's blessings—& so much going on around me—here boats being unloaded—there others putting out for sea, with the evening wind filling their sails—I went home moved, and thanked God that I could feel where thousands rush by indifferently, either because they are accustomed to the sight or because they have hearts like lard.

I passed the evening very contentedly with a glass of beer—I could tell that everyone would gladly have kept me longer.

Friday 6th June

And so I came back to Maulbronn. Never had it felt so confined, I was ever wishing to see the church here as the cathedral, my walls as palaces, my lakes as the Rhine and my dark dormitory as princely avenues. Just quickly what happened today. Blum & Rike accompanied me in the chaise as far as Oberhausen, from where I took a horse back here. At 12 I was in Bruchsaal, but this time I stopped at our cousin Mrs. Vogt's because I hadn't liked the pub at all and also wanted to see our cousin Miss Nikolai (as was) again. She was very pleased to hear of you again, and was exceptionally courteous and friendly toward me. At 3 o'clock I continued my journey. And so I got here while it was still light, & so this account of my travels comes to an end.

FROM RUDOLF MAGENAU

Tübingen, 10 July 1788

Dear friend!

You ask for my assessment of your poetic fancies, which I am very
glad to have received, & that I'll give you straight off, on the condition
that you take it as no more than a friendly hint, not meant as either
corrections or verdicts. In "The Soul" I noticed that the rather less
usual words have here & there tended to give rise to obscurities, e.g.,
"rain—spotted": yes, if it didn't say "refreshing" right next to it. &
"the river races" is feeble, rather "rages," "hurtles." The line of thought
from a to b is fine and good, but read that part through with an
unbiassed cast of mind, as if it was somebody else's work, and isn't it
so much prose? 1) a *hundred* years is very little for an oak, 2) "its *life*
tops out," life? You ascribe powers of thought to the oak, & then place
it so infinitely far below the soul? "In its *fury*"—"seize,"—"scattering
splinters," seem to me too common for such a hymn, I'd have done
without the Orions, Uranus & Sirius altogether, they contribute
nothing to the beauty of the poem, But as a whole the poem is
excellently conceived, I would just beg you, dear friend, not to spurn
the wholesome pithy expression in favor of a new and shriller one,
& give yourself almost no poetic license. I can well imagine how it
came about. You were writing your verses & declaiming them at once,
& often an expression *à la Schubart* appealed to you because it made
more noise. It used to be much the same with me until one day Conz
asked me mockingly why it was that whenever he read anything of
mine he couldn't help declaiming it! & beware of imitating others, the
best poem loses its value if one fails to remain true to oneself even
in a detail, e.g., *omnipotence!* "the creator's omnipotence" borrows
from Klopstock, "son of night" is from Ossian, You'd hardly believe
how childishly the gentlemen in Berlin make fun of such little things,
but all the same we're not proof against their criticism & so have to
follow the current and cast off these habits in good time. Among
my poems I also have a few that make such grand entrances, I cut
them & worked at them, hard as that was, but I couldn't reject them

outright, I had too much fondness for my children still. Then I also observed that you start off better than toward the end. "Hero" is very nice, only now & then the better idea gets suppressed for the sake of the rhyme.—"Brings"—"Tears from her cheeks *flings*," goes against usage, & I suspect that X provoked Y, & I found a few other cases like that. Why did you not choose elegiac meter, which is really made for expressions of tenderness like this. I had also translated the same poem & several other of Ovid's *Heroides*, sent them as a sample of my art to Städelin, the philosophical hatter, in Memmingen, & never got them back. "The Song of the Swede" is the better of the last two. It just has a few prosaic blotches, e.g., "But I can live no more"—which produces annoyance with the fellow rather than admiration; "sleepers"—that's not how a soldier speaks, he prefers to bed down with the troops, his sword under his head. "A playful roar," cant! "Murder & death!" You'd have done better to have him address his sword as he started up with a furious yell. Like an exacerbated tomcat biting into wood, the Swede (for it looks as if he'll be captured) could have grasped after his out-of-reach sword. Accept this bit of disinterested criticism from me, & take it to your credit if I was a bit too frank. Wholly for your own use I enclose a little piece which naturally with improvements should also go into my little collection. I'd like it back though. Keep the Longinus for another 3 months as far as I'm concerned. I'm very pleased you like it, Ossian is also at your disposal if you don't own it yourself. I'll let you know about the room in a week's time. I look forward, if you come here, to getting to know you properly,—but don't expect too much, & don't dream of an Elysium, I can assure you that I'd give a lot still to have the wealth of learning I used to have in Maulbronn. But enough, *experire et vide!*

I close with this sentence of Eberhard's from his treatise *On the Melodrama* (p. 12), which is also applicable to you:

"It is useless to want to make up for the lack of poetic rhythm with the inner force of the poem, with boldness of imagery & of the transitions: the stronger the inner poetic impulse, the more the shortcomings of the external features will be felt." Adieu, dear Hölderlin.

Your true friend, Magenau

Greetings to Mohr & Bilfinger

24. TO IMMANUEL NAST

[Maulbronn, ~ 6 September 1788]

Dear brother,
In a fortnight I'll be with you! Not a day sooner—or later! I'll ride with
Elsner and get to Höfingen by midday, and from there on to Leonberg.
But the very next day I *must* be off again. You'll come with me (I won't
hear of anything else) all the way to Nürtingen, even if it's only for a
day or two, and then I'll go back to Stuttgart with you where Bilfinger
will be waiting for us, and he'll accompany you back to Leonberg. How
would that suit, dear friend? *I* shall keep my word, even if the emperor
himself tried to hold me back.

So then, at about 2 o'clock in the afternoon in a fortnight I'll
be at yours! Ah, brother, just for the bliss of our first embrace I'd
travel days and days! You cannot possibly love me as much as I
love you—no! impossible! It would be an unforgivable vanity on my
part—if I were to believe it. Let me tell you—my mother & brother &
sister, & heaven knows I love them dearly—I've taken leave of them
a few times now—but it was never so hard as leaving you. We'll go
and see Landbek and Hiemer together—when we're in Stuttgart. Oh
brother, brother, why do I feel so good at the moment?—Because the
day before yesterday I finished something which for the past few weeks
has been making my head glow—

I can see it's no bad thing—that everything I encounter in the
world goes awry for me—I keep myself for myself that way—and feel
more real joys and have no need to be annoyed by so many inanities.

I long to see you & Landbek friends. I'd like to bet you'll be
inseparable! Imagine a handsome—gentle—tender painter of 20, your
height, & that's what he's like. And Hiemer—well, he's a jolly poet,
quite the *bon homme*! And as for me I'm nothing other in God's wide
world than your very own

Hölderlin

TÜBINGEN, 1788–1793

25. TO LOUISE NAST

[Tübingen, December 1788]

Dear, good Louise,

Never yet did I feel all your noble soul is worth, never saw more clearly how far I lag behind you, than in your last dear letter. Oh if only at your feet I could beg forgiveness for the moment of sadness my somber mood must have caused you, if only you could see how unworthy of your so indescribably noble love I feel myself to be in the moments when I realize that my low spirits, so unforgivably, displaced the honor in which I hold you & always shall. Louise! Louise! Dear sweet girl! And you answer with this heavenly kindness? Love me as warmly as ever? Comfort me so tenderly with regard to my situation, which is indeed pretty dismal. Daily, daily, fresh evidence—of how lucky I am to have you—the more often I read your letter, the more I treasure it—not a word of your love escaped me, not a syllable, each of which gave me access to the beauty of your heart. O God, what blissful days they will be when united forever we live each wholly for the other! Louise—how much you'll mean to me then—you will cheer me up in bad times, you will lighten the burdens I have to bear, you will reconcile me to the world when I have been slighted, you will be everything to me, everything—Oh, I'm so happy! From now on I promise you, sweet beloved girl—from now on—if I ever write so bitterly again I'll no longer be your Hölderlin. What a blissful hour I had this afternoon! I was going to read your last letter again—but an older one fell under my hand—& then another—until in the end I'd read them all—including the very first, my sweet! *You have my whole heart*, you wrote then, & o God! I have it still, after all the ordeals you have undergone, after all the tribulations you had to put up with because of me, I still have it, this precious heart, & isn't it so, dear Louise, I shall keep it for ever?—I had to pause, the thought that I have your heart, & the memories of all the joy we can look back on, made me go quite still—the same would have happened to you—thinking of these things.—My dear Rike has now been here for five days. I go out more often than usual. She told me the other day that she had now met Miss Weber at the weekly gathering, & that they had quickly become good friends. Much as I'd like to thank her for concerning herself with our fate in the way she did and for writing to Miss Böhm about Miss Duttenhofer's questionable friendship (for I imagine that's how you heard of it), you know how the world is, it's considered indiscreet if someone like me makes any kind of compliment to persons of your sex who are unknown to him, & then I'd have to find an opportunity to speak to her, & as you know I don't like to do that. But I can't possibly pretend to be nice to Miss Duttenhofer any more—and for that reason prefer not to go there any time soon. The other day I had to accompany my sister—and could hardly wait to get away I felt so uncomfortable. In any case I think Bilfinger's right and that it's not worth bothering about. I don't mind if the girls round here know about it—the ones who've met you cannot fail to think how lucky I am, & that flatters my pride into the bargain. Here's my silhouette! I'd be sorry if the likeness turned out so badly again. Look after yourself, dear Louise! And never forget

your

Hölderlin

FROM LOUISE NAST

[Maulbronn, early January 1789]

O dear Friz! Here I sit and have almost all your letters in front of me, that is my sole pleasure, and then I feel so good and am so happy to be on my own, it's almost 12 already and yet I couldn't stop, oh it's really my favorite reading. You're right, your dear letter caused me much anxiety, I couldn't sleep for nights on end, and yet I love it so much that I wouldn't give it up for all the treasure in the world. Oh to have you is such happiness, and Friz, it's so long until Easter, so long before I see you, so long to be separated from what is everything to me, yet the thought that you are mine and will remain mine, isn't that true, dear Friz? even years of separation will not make you colder toward me, oh no, you will remain the dear Friz you were on your last visit, I still remember every sweet word, they are deeply etched in my heart, you too will be able to recall the blessed joys, sometimes I am lucky enough to be able to dream of them, oh and recently I had a wonderful dream I should not yield up for anything, you were standing up by the way into the *Kloster*, you'll remember it too those times in the past when I saw you so often, you were stretching your arms out toward me in longing, God in heaven what a sight, your black habit all just as before, and oh it was a dream, those happy times have passed, dumb pain has replaced them, and why all this lamenting? my Friz is still mine, he is as true as ever, oh he's still mine, I too will not be separated from you by anything, no misfortune, no stroke of fate, just you and a hut however ramshackle—that would be a kingdom for me, oh with you even thorny paths are strewn with roses. O God, dear Father, at your hand they will also pass, the years of separation, your time always flies quickly away but the years of love will be eternities. In not long a couple of my acquaintance will tie the bond of eternal fidelity, the dear girl is here at the moment, Heinrike, she seems very content, we have already talked a great deal about you, we often recall the happy times in L— and a thousand times I have thanked her for her love, the sweet girl, I just hope she will be happy, she deserves it for what she did for us. Dear Friz, be sure to write often, I'm already looking forward to the next post-day, oh the holidays felt so long, all that time with no letter from my Friz. Goodbye, sleep well, it's already very late, ever

your Louise

Lots of love from my sisters.

<Postscript from Heinrike Nast:>

Remember also Heinrike from Leonberg who at present is with Louise in Maulbronn and sends her compliments.

26. TO LOUISE NAST

[Tübingen, mid-January 1789]

That was a letter I was glad to receive, my love! If only you could have seen the tears of purest joy that came to my eyes at this new sign of your inexpressibly sweet and cheering love, how at that moment I felt so deeply what I have in you, with what serenity and calm my days pass once again. O my darling! Even in separation your love is a blessing, even this longing is a delight for your friend—for every moment tells me that you long for me in just the same way, that these few years are just as long for you as for me. And only eleven more weeks until Easter, my love? It's ridiculous, really, to say only eleven more weeks—but we must comfort ourselves as we may—and then—o Louise! Louise! then—I can't find words for it, all the blissful happiness that awaits me in your arms—writing is only ever writing, & I prefer to leave you to feel how this expectation lifts my heart—And you still remember the sweet words of our last visit? They are deeply etched in your soul? O Louise! They are all I think about in my solitude, my only preoccupation in the blessed hours I can devote to you.

Oh & your dream?—dear, marvelous girl, how can I be so happy? How much happier I'd be if in your arms I could pour my heart out to you and all the joy it's full of. It feels so good when I think of how I often waited so patiently & yet so full of deepest longing at that spot until I saw you, the beloved, at the window, & how the thought delighted me that in the whole dear world you had eyes only for your Hölderlin, that only I dwelt in your breast—Louise! Louise! & when I saw you leaving your house and going toward the cloister—it's all so vivid still—your lovely graceful gait, the loving way you looked up at me—& with the expectation of the happy time to come so plainly expressed in your face—& how heaven and earth fled from us in the quiet and the dusk!—And sweet Heinrike is with you at the moment? May all the friendship she showed us be returned to her a thousand times in her new situation. With her bright and genial soul she is sure to make herself and her husband happy. And you also remember the happy times in Leonberg—do you think still of all the hours of bliss, the hours of passionate and so sweet love? O Louise! Is it no longer possible to be with you, are there no good people to stay with somewhere or other close by? Don't I deserve it still to have that happiness?—All these plans again!—But you will be doing the same, sweet love! The days I spent in Leonberg were too beautiful for me not to dream of them again many a time. Oh even just our parting!—It shed such a sweet melancholy throughout my soul, & accompanied me the whole way back. Only when I saw the hills round Nürtingen, & the wood by Leonberg gradually disappeared in the distance behind me—only then did tears of bitterest pain start in my eyes—for a while I had to stand still.—The rest of my journey was then twice as hard as it had been.—

A thousand compliments to your sisters—and also to Miss Käufel: I wish her a nimble paintbrush for the new year.

Sleep well, dear girl! Love me as you always have done. I am ever

yours,

Hölderlin

FROM LOUISE NAST

[Maulbronn,] 19 January 1789

Dear good—

Oh the sweet words of your dear letter! Ah only eleven weeks to go *and then, then, Friz, all* the happiness in your arms, oh if only you could feel how at this thought my heart beats harder, soon once again in the arms of my Friz, my—oh a delight that cannot be described for lack of words to say it, o God, dear Father, what happiness you give us, what days they will be, dear sweet Friz, when we can be entirely to ourselves, when no destiny, no time, even death cannot divide us and there in those heavenly regions our love will continue for ever, God! how happy I am, dear Friz, my beloved—every little place I can see from my window reminds me of thousands and thousands of blissful moments from those happy times, you, only you, of all mortals dwell in my breast. At any moment I could give them all up for you, oh for you, good, dear heart, what a sweet sacrifice, oh and this longing now, if only—if only you could now rush to this thumping heart, and I could feel yours—a thought that drives tears from me, hot tears, dear heart, and your silhouette how tightly I press it to my heart, no! never was there such a likeness, every trait springs into life, God, and that divine smile, but no I must be silent, or else you'll think I've taken a page out of your book, and yet, my heart, I feel it so strongly, in the end you're a very sweet flatterer even if I know only too well that you're wrong. Heinrike has made a lot of plans with me, here at her house it would be marvelous, she has a truly good man who will soon be on our side, but eleven weeks is time for plenty more ideas, and then to have you again, to close you in my arms as if I never wanted to let you go again, what bliss. Goodbye—of my heart, it is late already, I cannot write you any more, unless everyone is in bed I've not the peace I need. Lots of love from my Rike, she thanks you for your good wishes, they will soon come true, sleep well, sweetheart.

Always

your true—

Louise

Lots of love from Heinrike and my sisters too, also from my friend Commerelle (she wrote to me to say so), you'll remember her from the time in the bower by the beautiful lake, that bower is sacred to me, until summer I'll focus my prayers on it, the beautiful objects of nature are so moving, every blade of grass shows me the wisdom and kindness of the creator

FROM CHRISTIAN LUDWIG NEUFFER

[Stuttgart, 21–24 March 1789]

you were to read the inimitable harmony of his hexameters you would be truly entranced. If I only had the *Messias* with me, I'd lift out a few passages for you; but instead I must console you until such time as you get the opportunity to read it yourself at Schubart's.

I also soon brought the conversation round to you: In the vacation a very good friend of mine, full of enthusiasm for poetry, would be coming here and would satisfy his desire to honor in person the professor he already honors so much in his writings. Those were my words. He knows your name and he is eager to meet you. The description I went on to give of you was true and sincere. I said you were particularly taken with serious and sublime things and something of an enthusiast. For frivolity you had a distinct antipathy and you were a sworn enemy of the epigram. Greek literature was your passion. The boy sounds very promising, was what he said in return, let him come and visit as soon as he's here. And so Stäudlin and Schubart are prepared to meet you, and for neither of them would you be an unexpected visitor.

Stäudlin is away at the moment for his legal work, but he's due to arrive here any day soon. Because I didn't find him in, I took up again my old acquaintance with his sisters, with whom I shall have to resume the office of *lectoris ordinari* again.

And I met some of my old acquaintances, including Haselmeier and friends, engaged in some sharp-witted gambling.

News in brief
Easter next year my poems are to be published.

In the Viennese papers and the Austrian *Avisen* my "Eugen, a vision of war" has been frequently reprinted.

Sunday, 22 March 89

Here, my dear friend, I send one of my earliest pieces, which I came across with some other things. It comes from my period of rapturous love, as you will see amply demonstrated in the content. That you won't mock me for a dreamer, I know, otherwise you'd never have got to see it.

["Um Mitternacht"]

I often have to laugh at my old reveries, especially when I bear in mind that it was all so serious, that it all came so from the depths of my heart. But nevertheless they were blessed times for me, I lived and dwelt wholly in my imagination, and perhaps such sweet days will never return. Oh a faint premonition tells me I was happy then; for like a black storm the future rises up before my eyes; and the awareness that I am in large part to blame for it myself, this tortures me, to the point that often I can bear it no longer. Let me break off here, I need to give my oppressed heart some relief in the open air.

Tuesday, 24 March

Here you'll find something more of my elaborations, to give you plenty to read. How gladly, dear friend, I'd have brought you them myself, or read them aloud!

Last of all I wanted to say that next time I too will send you a poetical letter, for I see yours as a challenge.

Neuffer

FROM LOUISE NAST

[Maulbronn, March/April 1789]
Monday night

This time my sweet dear my letter comes to you not by B. for my Mene lies sick in bed and so good B. receives no letter from her either, and I am writing even if my letter has to travel alone, o my sweetheart it is my greatest joy, it is everything to me to write to you & an even greater one when I receive a letter from you, oh darling, they are everything, everything to me. Ah God, never did I feel our separation like this; oh I often think, I implore, just one moment, just a single moment, to see you and to hold you in my arms, what rapture, God what would become of me if I even thought there might be a possibility that you could leave me, no no. You can't do that, you won't, oh you are mine—wholly mine, oh wholly mine, how happy I am then, forgive me dear dear Friz, forgive me, I often have these moods and they plague me, oh they plague me so, I often have moments of real sadness but the thought that you are mine makes me quite cheerful again. Oh God knows I love my parents a good deal and my brothers and sisters, I'd do anything for them, anything, but it's no sin, no, it's not a sin if I love you more, if I love you more than anything, oh you who are everything to me, for whom there are no secrets in my heart. You're right, sweetheart, there are often anxieties and tears, but they are nothing at all to the joys and worth the trouble however great they might be and if God wills it so & we are happy. How glad I was that your dear good mother, oh can I call her my mother, spoke so well of our situation, you can imagine, my sweetheart, how I felt, oh my hand trembles with joy as I write "my mother," there is something so blessed about it not all people will feel, to call the mother of my only friend in the world, God, to call her my m—'s mother.

Here I sit, dear soul, it is all so still, so eerie, oh and it feels so good when I am quite alone, remote from other people, there's nowhere I'd rather be than when I go for a walk all on my own in the churchyard in the evening and sit down on the graves of the departed and think that you too have perhaps shed many tears, o dear Friz, it feels so good, I prefer to be among the dead than the living, they welcome my tears, these graves, people would laugh at me, and when the dear moon shines down, now bright, now dim, and I think now perhaps my Friz, my one true and loyal friend among the living, perhaps together we are raising our eyes up to you, beauteous light, to praise the greatness of the almighty creator. I feel sorry for my Mine, she is really ill, she's worried sick, she's becoming so distrustful of B., he writes her mostly such short letters, often just a few words, and sometimes cold and forced, explain this to me, dear Friz, if you can, but best keep it to yourself. If you write to B send lots of love, from her, her illness is not serious, reassure him about that, sleep peacefully & well, sweetheart, imagine, it is already past two, I don't know where the time goes, it is so noisy in our house and I always wait until all is quiet so that I can think of you undisturbed, dear Friz, oh days of separation you're stretching into long years, goodbye, ever yours, yes entirely

yours

Louise

27. TO LOUISE NAST

[Tübingen, March/April 1789]

Thanks, a thousand thanks, dear Louise, for your tender, comforting letter! It has made me cheerful again. I believe once more in human happiness. The flowers were a great joy to me. I'm sending you back the ring and the letters. Keep them, Louise, if only as a souvenir of those happy days when we lived only for ourselves, without being troubled by any thoughts of the future and without any cares to disturb our love. And as God is my witness, Louise, I must be frank!—It is and remains my unshakeable resolve not to ask for your hand until I have attained a position worthy of you. Until then I ask you, good, dear Louise, in the name of all I hold dear, not to consider yourself committed by any word you have given but only by the choice of your heart. You will think it impossible, good soul that you are, to love anyone else, as you have so often assured me—but many an amiable young man will seek to win your heart in the interim, many a respectable man will ask for your hand, and I will cheerfully wish you luck if you choose a worthy suitor, and then you will at last understand that you could never have been happy with your grumpy, bad-tempered, ailing friend. Look, Louise, let me confess my weakness to you! The insurmountable melancholy in me—don't mock me for this—is perhaps not *entirely*, but *largely*—frustrated ambition. Once this has been satisfied, but not sooner, I'll be quite carefree, quite cheerful & healthy. You can see now the true reason why I formed the admittedly premature resolve to put our relationship on a new *external* footing. I didn't want to *bind* you because it is uncertain whether this vast desire of mine will ever be fulfilled, whether this—precisely human—ambition will ever be satisfied, and so whether I shall ever be quite carefree, quite cheerful and healthy. And without that you would never be completely happy with me. Our love could remain the same, but my bad moods, my laments about the world, & all the other idiocies that have become *second nature* with me would inevitably hurt you all the more, the more you loved me and however much stronger, when times were good, *my* love for you became. But I will never be disloyal. And neither will you. For it is not disloyal if at the request of your lover, who asks you it out of the conviction that he could never have made you as happy as the more worthy man—if you then choose this more worthy suitor! That is not disloyal! You would still, in making another happy as your husband, remember the friend of your youth, and your former love for him would merely be constrained by the thought that because of his uncontrollable, oppressive weaknesses you would never have been able to be completely happy with him. And so you would certainly never have been disloyal! And I should think that my love is not for this world & be glad of your happiness, should even trust myself to see you at your husband's side—& be friends to you both.

I well know, my love, what you will say in reply. I should perhaps not have written a word of this had I wanted to conceal from you even a single trait of my character. Fare well, dear all-beloved girl! Ever

yours,

Hölderlin

FROM IMMANUEL NAST

Leonberg, 17 April 1789

I don't know whether I should be cross with you, or whether I should ask you to be cross with me. For it's almost unforgivable that we have spent the whole winter like marmots; but I forgive you and you—not so?—do the same?

Here is your album, L. gave it to me when she left here last autumn—You will find a little painting in it. It's the first I've done this year and I decided it would be yours—because I remembered once having promised you a picture of this sort. Whether you come off better or worse this time I leave it to your feelings to decide.

Also enclosed are 2 *silhouettes* for you to have a look at or, if you find them at all true to the *originals*—for your further use. Although W. will be too big to fit into a tobacco-box as you were thinking of doing when I was with you the last time in Maulbronn.

My news I'd much rather give you in person than via this poor pen. But because I'm on my own in the office and for that reason can hardly hope to get away for a few days I'm writing you what I can.

What a stink Christian, the gobbler, would have kicked up at his father's in Stuttgart over your and Louise's stay here if the day after I accompanied you to Vaihingen I hadn't heard about it in Stuttgart and, by writing a letter to my uncle in which I gave a version of events that was the only one I *could*, brought it about that he wrote to give me an assurance that he *wouldn't* write to M.: all this you will know in detail from L.

There is a lot I could tell you about the affairs of my heart but let this suffice for the moment, that B. & I are as good as separated; I do still enjoy her friendship, which sweetens many a bitter hour of this life for me—but *love*, where ever mine & ever *yours* is the watchword, we were forced to drive from our minds as things were going so badly.

That I have not acted rightly I hope not to hear from you, if you reflect even a little bit on my situation, in which I see virtually no prospects of any sort of provision, and on other circumstances. You will easily see that I owed this sacrifice to my reason.

O dear friend!—It was a long hard struggle which cost many tears and many sighs—But I am reconciled by the thought that I have in the future removed myself as an obstacle in the way, I who *perhaps* made my friend, for love of me, turn down the hands of two—*perhaps* honest men.

Burk told me a few days ago that you were still having trouble with your foot—and had to go home before the vacation—It's just a shame that we can't make use of this fine weather to go on the journey we were planning!

Elsner sends not a word about himself—it almost hurts me. It seems that all the friends I had in Maulbronn have completely forgotten me in their Tübingen—!

About 6–8 weeks ago I was in Maulbronn. At half past 12 I arrived at the *Kloster*, and as I heard that Linde & Karl had accompanied Bleibel to Illingen, I just fed my horse, took a little sustenance, and then rode at a trot to the *Pfleghof*—There I came upon them together in *bona caritate* and Karl & Bleibel thought I was a ghost as I stepped *through* the door and greeted them. In Maulbronn I was pretty content.

A fortnight ago I sent Bleibel the area round Illingen and gave him more pleasure thereby than my pride would have allowed me to suppose. Goodbye, dear—cold? friend, remember me to your good mother & your sister and believe that with all the old warm friendship I am still your fond

Immanuel

I await your letter with eager impatience!

And oh, it occurs to me that you promised to communicate your poems to me!

28. TO HIS MOTHER

[Tübingen, April/May 1789]

It pains me greatly, dear Mamma, to see you so saddened and downcast—& because of me and my behavior. For what has happened, I beg you, dearest Mamma, a thousand thousand times for forgiveness, & have also, when I took communion the day before yesterday, implored God for his in the same matter.

As for my present situation, I can assure you that I would spend my days quite at peace & content with my fate if your sadness did not cause me so many troubled hours. I beg you as earnestly as I can, I conjure you by your duties as a mother & as a Christian that, apart from this excessive sadness, you fulfill so conscientiously—be of good cheer, make the most of this lovely spring, take pleasure in the hopeful green that God has once more bestowed on our fields & trees.

I still have quite a few things, e.g., my flute, several books etc. in Nürtingen. Could you be so kind as to send them to me?

That I visited Schubart, & that he welcomed me with great friendship and almost paternal tenderness, you will already know. He made a point of inquiring about my parents and asked me whether I could count on the support that the often considerable needs of a poet required—& when I replied that I could, he urged me with such fervor to thank God for it with all my might that I was deeply moved. Oh it would be a joy to be the friend of such a man. I was with him for a whole morning.

We Nürtingen students would be keen to take part in the May Day festivities, but as the holidays have just ended we don't want to be turned down.

I've got to go to my class; look after yourself, dearest Mamma, & love

your

most obedient son

Hölderlin

29. TO HIS MOTHER

[Tübingen, ~ May 1789]

Dearest Mamma,

Because I didn't write last time I want to do so now. But there is another reason for writing mixed in with it, I may say, and that is—something I've not done now for a long time—to ask you for money. I must confess, I kept certain expenses to myself, for example the hat, so that you would not have to pay out too much, & firmly expecting to be able to pay them from my pocket money, & do without this and that elsewhere, so as not to be a burden to you. Only—how many unplanned expenses I had and how much of the 30 fl. I have left, you know. I spent the last 8 fl. entirely on settling accounts, because you said you would reimburse me for the most unavoidable expenses the very next post-day. But more urgent expenses prevented you from keeping your generous promise. Just imagine, dearest Mamma, how I had to make shift. For the whole week of the fair I shut myself in so as not to be tempted to spend any money or to borrow any, but unavoidable difficulties forced me to borrow a little. So the 3 fl. I received recently were never mine to use, & the other day I had to borrow again from a good friend when Rheinwald visited from Urach & spent the night with me.—I've been candid with you, dear Mamma, don't be cross with me! The thought that you would approve of me was the only thing that stopped me from falling into my old state of dejection. That I've slipped down the class ranking because of the two Stuttgart boys, Hegel & Märklin, also pains me a bit. How lucky some people are not to be put off by such vexations and just to carry on with their studies!—And that I must hear reproaches from a person who was so dear to me about how I have changed, when she herself saw the necessity of it & it cost me no end of conflict with myself, that I have to think that I have caused her this sadness—o dear Mamma, I really haven't deserved this!!—But I do have a good conscience & know how to console myself with my books, & that is a wonderful thing! I would often have erred onto the wrong path, perhaps, if it was not my lot to suffer more than others do.

I know that you are entirely of one mind with me over this; for to suffer I have only to follow your example. It's true that it's also in my nature to take everything too much to heart, but I thank God that it preserves me from frivolity. Don't be indignant about my letter, dearest Mamma, but it would have been quite wrong for me to write less from the heart. Look after yourself, dearest Mamma, and send greetings to dear Carl.

Your

most obedient son

Hölderlin

I pity Bilfinger. Even more his parents. Professor Seiffert is here at the moment.

30. TO CHRISTIAN LUDWIG NEUFFER

[Nürtingen, perhaps September 1789]

Dear friend,

If ever a request from me has meant anything to you, let it be now! Come to me here. I have such great need of you. My mother was firmly expecting you to come with me and has charged me with inviting you again now. Gentner was supposed to do the same. But I think he has forgotten. You can surely spare a few days from your occupations and your pleasures.

My compliments to Dr. Stäudlin. I conveyed his message. Counselor Bilfinger is willing to pass on a part of the divorce proceedings to him.

Have you seen Miss Lebret in the meantime? or spoken to her? Write and tell me.

Please send the enclosed letter to Miss Bardili at the house of Legal Counselor Jäger by the hospital church as soon as possible. Goodbye, dear Neuffer. Be sure to come.

Yours

Hölderlin

31. TO HIS MOTHER

[Tübingen, before 25 November 1789]

permission. And so on that day I'll come back in the chaise. You see, dear Mamma, my physical and mental state has suffered in this situation; you will understand that the unending frustrations, the constraints, the unwholesome air, the bad food may well have weakened my body sooner than would be the case in freer conditions. You know my temperament, which precisely because it is a temperament cannot deny itself, no more than it can fit itself to mistreatment, pressure and contempt. O dearest Mamma, my late father used so often to say that "his years at university were his happiest and best." Shall I one day come to say "my years at university spoilt my life for ever"? If my request is a weakness, then have pity on me. If my request is reasonable & sensible, oh don't let overanxious doubts about the future hold us back from taking a step that in your old age may be a source of so much joy. I have many more reasons I prefer to tell you in person. Till then, look after yourself. Receive me as you always have done, dear Mamma! Rest assured that the moment I see your counterarguments are more telling or that your heart is too set against it I shall remain

your

obedient son

Hölderlin

Here is the little song I promised dear Rike. My best thanks for what you sent. I'll bring my washing with me.

32. TO CHRISTIAN LUDWIG NEUFFER

[Nürtingen, December 1789]

Dear friend,

A long time since I was in touch with you—here I am at last. I'd have written often from Tübingen if it hadn't been for all the unpleasantnesses, the pettinesses and injustices I've had to put up with, which made me feel indifferent even about friendship. And, dear Neuffer, my fate is beginning to seem pretty bizarre, if only because the day before your arrival, of all days, I went and hurt my foot and, since the very next day I was granted leave to travel, I had to go away for four weeks without seeing you. If only you had been in Tübingen none of this would have happened. I'd have had no cause to plead so hard to be allowed to go on leave, wouldn't be a burden to my mother, nor be making life so difficult for myself in my frustration. O dear brother, what a way to find out what you mean to me!—And things are pretty unpoetic in my head at the moment. What I did force onto paper were brief outpourings of my moods, which a few days later I could no longer bear to look at. Immediately after the holidays I wrote a little song to go with that lovely tune. Things looked better then. In a few lucky hours I worked on a hymn to Columbus that will soon be finished, though it's a lot shorter than my others. Shakespeare's going to get a hymn too—what do you think? The other day I came across a marvelous book—a collection of old German legends. Said to be by Bürger. Neuffer, it gave me so much pleasure. There I found Gustavus portrayed with such warmth, such veneration—and such valuable details about his death, that I made a solemn vow to go back to my notes again as soon as I return to Tübingen and in particular to concentrate what little powers I have in the hymn on his death. The judgment of our beloved predecessor on the hymns to Gustavus struck me suddenly as juster than anything I'd ever heard. Stäudlin is really a marvelous man. Once my mother has taken advice from a clear-sighted person or two, and if it turns out according to my desires, I'll soon be following his example of how to earn one's living. I'm telling this to no one but you & should like to have your advice too. And in general, dear Neuffer, I beg you for our friendship's sake, let me hear from you as often & as much as possible. You have total control over my moods & fits of low spirits & whatever you want to call the devils that plague me. Give my greetings to M. Hoffman, & say that soon I'll be sending the guardroom a shipment of potatoes, as promised. Goodbye, beloved friend.

Yours,

Hölderlin

FROM RUDOLF MAGENAU

[Tübingen, December 1789]

Mon Cher!

Dear old friend, I must write you a little letter just to find out for once how things are with you. Heaven bless you.
Amen!
I & and Master *Genius* have in the meantime remembered you 1000 times, & think of it, the other day Neuffer the old poetic comrade came to me, & said he had a fever, his pulse had stopped, and the result was that it went 7 times faster than before. Dear Holz, if you don't come soon then you'd better look out for a miserable poetic epistle from me! How is your foot? In any case
May heaven lead you on your way!
Dear old friend, & get yourself here soon and in good health, goodbye, *datum* at a good hour, forever and without fail

Your

old friend

the faithful Rudolph,

d. = Dec. 1789

M-genau

Vive la Mariage!

T. Neuffer

33. TO HIS MOTHER

[Tübingen, January 1790]

My dearest Mother,

You'll soon guess why I'm writing to you now. I think this letter will not displease you.

I have decided to stick with the situation I'm in for the duration. The thought of being a worry to you, the uncertain future, the deserved reproaches from my dear ones & those I'd not fail to deal out to myself if my hopes came to nothing, the advice of my friends, my reluctance to study jurisprudence, the shenanigans I'd have exposed myself to as a lawyer and, on the other side, the joys of a quiet parish, the hopes of entering into employment sooner rather than later, the idea of being able to withstand inconveniences for four brief years for the sake of my family & to think nothing of the nonsense that goes with it—all this in the end meant that I resolved to bow to you, dear Mamma. Parental advice is always a comfort, after all. Come what may, I've at least that to console me!

Beyond that, I have friends in my seminary I'm hardly likely to find elsewhere. Neuffer loyally does what's required when my low spirits afflict me. And there's little likelihood of that now as long as I'm busy. I hope that everything will sort itself out. So the black coat can be made up. Just send me the cloth here if it's not a nuisance. My round jacket doesn't make me look serious enough. Vischer preached for the first time this evening. Over the next year, God willing, I shall also mount the pulpit. Perhaps by then a cleric's uniform will suit me even better.

Thank you very much for what you sent. I'll see whether next time I can't get an invitation for dear Rike to visit our cousin Frau Schwab. All that's needed is to bring up the subject. Why Miss F. would have liked to enclose her letters with mine I can't imagine. (This meant for Rike!)

That Gentner is better I'm very glad to hear. Bilfinger is unlikely to have a suit to sell. Of late he always wore the same rather inelegant suit.

Here is my dirty washing.

34. TO HIS MOTHER

[Tübingen, second half of June 1790]

Dearest Mamma,

I cannot begin to describe the pleasure your kind letter gave me. What you have sent will be used wisely, and I'll keep a record of the expenditure as it mounts up.

Rümelin is much to be pitied. And I find the way he has been treated, given his position and the fact that he was in the process of making serious amends, severe to say the least. The pressure we're under in the Stift at the moment can hardly be conveyed. But this kind of thing can be easier related when I come to Nürtingen for a short visit in the summer. At any rate I can assure you that with my friends, esp. Neuffer and Magenau, I get on as contentedly as can be. We sit working away at our desks, not because we have to but because the joy of studying grows with each day as I progress. And so we are less exposed to being mishandled than anyone. The three of us also have more to occupy us than anyone else because the Muse looks askance if her sons make their offerings at exclusively philosophical and theological altars. And on top of that I have the work to prepare for my exams. This reminds me, dear Mamma, to ask you not to let me forget to send you by one of the next posts the list of expenses that will fall when I present my candidature at the end of the summer. That's how it's usually done, and I think it's good that way because you have a chance to make your arrangements accordingly.

The letter to dear Rike was sent on to Reutlingen as soon as I received it, as the postboy was just about to leave.

Take good care.

Your

most obedient son

Friz

35. TO HIS MOTHER

[Tübingen, mid-August 1790]

Dearest Mamma,

Thank you very much indeed for what you sent. That I have to make do with the clothes I have is my responsibility. You have so many expenses in relation to me as it is. Let me write down for you the chief costs associated with the exams, as I was told them by Fischer.

To the chest—the fund that fills the purses of the professors themselves—that is for the exam: 30 fl. For the disputation, 30 fl., of which one carolin goes to Professor Bök, who will preside, and the rest to the printer and to the binder. For the classes, some of which cost more this semester because they are held specially for us, again almost 30 fl. The associated costs, for example eating at the inn which is the usual thing every time we defend the theses, as they call them, in the mornings, and which is necessary given that we can't get back in time for our meal at the seminary, these I reckon I can keep down to 11 fl. I would ask you, dear Mamma, to show this letter to a man who has also gone through all this or is otherwise well informed on the matter; he'll be able to convince you that I can't possibly do with less. It's true it's a nuisance, as the whole thing is so pointless. As far as I'm concerned magister and doctor along with all other titles, including *Illustrissimo* and *Magnifico*, can go to the devil.

I'm glad that Camerer was so eager to help me out with the buckles; only I don't see why I shouldn't have gone ahead with the deal. Märklin's buckles had hardly been worn a fortnight. And weigh 8 ounces like my old ones that absolutely had to be recast. I meant to have them cast exactly like Märklin's, and the silversmith wanted 4 fl. Märklin saw some other buckles at the silversmith's that would have been too fancy for me; he wanted those ones, and so offered to sell me his. The silversmith took my buckles for 10 fl. The ones I have now cost M. 16 fl. and for the new ones he now wears he had to pay another 9 fl. on top. And that my new buckles are of good silver I now have ample proof. So I can't see that the deal was in any way a bad one. I was in too much of a hurry the other day to explain in all this detail.

Here comes my dirty washing. I'll write to dear Rike next post-day. My letter to her is in any case only half written. I am

your

obed. son

Friz

36. TO HIS MOTHER

[Tübingen, late August 1790]

Dearest Mamma,

The news of your journey was a great surprise; just as long as it does no harm to your health. I was very glad to hear that you were well received by Scheelhaß. I'll send him copies of the dissertation. Today I'm having it fetched from the printer's to the binder's. To Nürtingen I'll have to send about 14 or 15. The disputation takes place for me next week. Should you manage to get the whole sum together, I would humbly ask you to send me the carolin for Professor Bök. And if you don't consider the money for the meals after defending the theses to be excessive, now would be the time for that too. It's also usual to pay the binder and the printer straight away. But I leave that to you.

Rest assured, dear Mamma, as far as it lies within my capacities I will strive to render joy for all the efforts and inconvenience you suffer for my sake. There is a great deal more I intend to do. As your son, I can say to you without appearing immodest that the constant study of philosophy in particular has become something I virtually cannot do without. If from time to time I suffer little frustrations, I go with all the more commitment and attention to my books. If I'm not rewarded for it, if more than once in my life I may be misunderstood and put down, well—it was not reward I was after! My work was its own reward.—

Tell dear Rike to write again too next time. Here are the slips for dear Karl's album. For my silhouette he should send me a special slip. I have already had the drawing done. A thousand greetings to my dear grandmother.

Your

most obedient son

Hölderlin

Karl must read *Practical Logic* day and night. I read it several years ago on somebody's recommendation and benefited from it immensely. Tell him from me that the effort he puts into it will go over into pleasure before he knows it.

FROM CHRISTIAN LUDWIG NEUFFER

Stuttgart, 24 October 1790

Dear friend,

I hope and desire that my letter will find you in a good and receptive mood, good health etc., I for my part am living here in an active inactivity, which as you will well know always suits me very well. My father has got a room for you at Weber's, and so he's the person you should be in touch with.

Stäudlin, who sends his greetings, wants to ask you in earnest whether you want the Helvétius or not, because otherwise he has an opportunity to sell it to somebody else.

And now a piece of news I've picked up on my travels, viz. that you are in L. St.'s good books, that she often asks me about you, sometimes calling you a nice modest man, and along with her sisters sends you greetings, she is even pestered now and then by Nannette on your account: there must therefore have been a number of secret debates, all of which speak in your favor.

Your stockings are on their way.

Yours,

Neuffer

P.S. Might you be so kind as to make some inquiries to see if you can find out anything about my pipe?

37. TO CHRISTIAN LUDWIG NEUFFER

[Tübingen, 8 November 1790]

Dear friend,

Why I have not written to you for so long I'm sure you'll have no trouble guessing—I'm afraid it's bad conscience.

Video meliora proboque
Deteriora sequor.

But it's not quite as bad as that. At an auction, where admittedly I had no reason to be, I approached her—at first cold looks—then conciliatory ones—then compliments—then memories and apologies—! That's how it was on both sides. I went away happy as a lark, but once I had calmed down resolved as before to maintain my reserve and hitherto have kept to this intention—that is—on average! We can go into more detail another time. I'll never make a stoic. I can see that very well. Perpetual ebb and flow. And if I didn't always find myself something to do—often I force myself to, I'd fall back into my old ways. You see, brother of my heart, "my better self is willing"—and so you'll forgive me, you'll guide me when need be, cheer me up when need be.—I've not yet kept my word as regards books and marrowbones. Leibniz and my Hymn to Truth have been causing havoc these last few days in my capitol. The first has influence on the second. If you think it's worth the trouble I'll set about reworking the Hymn to Immortality. I wish your Maro all the blessings of Apollo! You can honestly say "Vixi" at the end of each day if you spend them the way you described in your letter. Send me your new poems—or fragments or plans for them. That will allow me to while away a pleasant hour or two.

Reuß's poem on Abel's departure has good bits here and there, it seems to me. A thousand greetings to the Stäudlin household. Did you buy the Helvétius?—Kind, Magenau, Breitschwerd, Wieland and many others send warm greetings.

Do you know anything about Stäudlin's almanac, which poems he's putting in it, and who else is contributing? Can't you tell me anything about Schubart?—

Goodbye. In the next half hour His Highness will make his visitation upon us. Goodbye, dear friend!

Yours

Hölderlin

38. TO HIS SISTER

[Tübingen, 16 November 1790]

Good morning, dear Rike,

I won't be able to match up to you this time. My head is so heavy this morning from working into the night that I'll have trouble getting anything down on paper at all, not to speak of writing a letter as full of bright good humor as yours was. It upsets me that you should think the trouble I have writing letters, with my head taken up with study (and here I am in the same old trouble again), has anything to do with you. Dear sister, nothing could be further from the truth.

Today it's the fair. Rather than getting pushed around in the hustle and bustle I'm going for a walk with Hegel, who is in the same room as me. We're going to the chapel at Wurmlingen with the famous view.

How am I getting on in my room? Marvelously, dear Rike. My repetitor is the best man in the world. The room is one of the best, looks east, is very spacious, and only on the second floor. There are seven people from my year. I don't have to tell you that's a lot more agreeable than 6 strangers. And the few others are also good people, among them Breier and Schelling.

My congratulations to dear Carl on mounting the rostrum. That's how Demosthenes and Cicero appeared before their people, only the scene will have been rather more ample. Just let him become a proper man, our dear Carl. He must think and work every minute his constitution allows him to. Rike, it is an amazing thing: *the desire to learn can consume all other desires.* Believe me.

Goodbye. Thanks very much for what you sent. Look after yourself, dear Rike.

Your affectionate brother,

Friz

If you find any more of my papers please send them. There are still a few missing.

39. TO HIS SISTER

[Tübingen, late November 1790]

Dear Rike,

So I make myself ready in my dark little room, sit down at the window, look out toward daybreak where my beloved Nürtingen lies, and write—to bring you good news. For one thing it will count as good news, because you are so fond of me, that notwithstanding my sequestered way of life that I always observe pretty exactly in accordance with the resolution I have often told you of, that despite this I'm also in fine physical form and am rarely to be seen with wrinkles on my brow, for wrinkles are equivalent to tears now that tears no longer come, which they once did so easily. For another, I regard it as good news that I can assure our dear Mamma she doesn't need to be anxious about my funds, not just for the time being but for this winter she will be almost wholly relieved of the bother of sending me anything extra. I have been put forward to give lessons in Latin and Greek to a young nobleman from Berne of the name of von Vellenberg, and will receive 5 fl. a month. He is very nice & of my age. He's studying here under the guidance of a private tutor along with four other noblemen from Switzerland.

So in a sense this compensates our dear Mamma for unexpected expenses in the past. I pity poor Karl that he's finding his status as a clerk is leaving a bitter taste so soon. Tell him that I know of a remedy that will remove all trace of that bitterness. It is—occupying the mind.—Mightn't we, to this end, exchange little essays, Karl and I?—Ask him whether, in hours of respite, he wouldn't fancy addressing the question: *how does one attain true contentment?* I shall also write a little essay on this, and when Karl has sent me his, let him have mine in exchange. Or if he feels more comfortable with another subject, he can choose that, disregarding my suggestion, and I shall take that subject too. It matters a great deal to me that dear Karl should take to this plan. I hope he will. I expect an essay from him soon.

Your

affectionate brother

Friz

During the fair I rarely left my room. And so didn't get to Reutlingen either. But *here* I did speak to Miss Vischer, her sister and her brother-in-law. Last Saturday Kammerer also came over here, & yesterday, that is Monday, he went back again. He sends his best wishes!

40. TO HIS SISTER

[Tübingen, 7 December 1790]

Forgive me, I'm half-asleep. Hardly have time for a few lines. I'm annoyed with myself to be dealing with your dear letter so briefly. You won't hold it against me, Rike! A body needs its sleep.

Tell dear Mamma not to worry, I'll make sure I arrange my teaching job in such a way that it will be more advantageous than not. She wants to know who it was recommended me?—Someone in my year, Klüpfel, put my name forward to the chancellor, in whose gift the appointment was, and the proposal was favorably accepted.

You'll find the beginning of my essay not much to your taste; I deliberately chose to use a number of expressions that only occur in so-called scholarly language, or very rarely elsewhere, in order to make dear Karl familiar with them. I am curious to know what he'll say. My plan is to send him perhaps 2 more letters on the same subject. I couldn't possibly develop the whole essay in one go because I have so little spare time at the moment. And so I've just dealt with the main things.

Goodbye, dear Rike!

Your

affectionate brother

Friz

41. TO HIS SISTER

[Tübingen, mid-December 1790]

Dear Rike,

Your sweet letter didn't end up as short as you thought it would. But admittedly due to a sad piece of news. I feel more sorry for Klein than I can say. Take a few wrong turns, and a man can find himself plunged into misfortune. Here things are calm and peaceful at the moment. Or rather they are with me. You can change a lot in a short space of time. If I had got into the habit sooner of living for myself, I should have avoided many setbacks.

I hope that dear Karl will write me all the more next time since this time he has left me empty-handed.

From Eßlingen I received 7 fl. 20 cr. last week. But I had to use almost 2 fl. of it for a book I bought last summer, and 2 fl. 24 cr. to pay the repetitor Conz for a class of his I went to last summer also. So what dear Mamma sent was still very welcome. I thank her kindly for it. And also for the other things she sent.

How is our cousin Maier doing in Denkendorf? Does he like the convent?

Are you going to stay at home for the whole of the holidays?

I've gathered my washing together. And am sending it now. All the other things I have left here are clean.

Neuffer is now back here again. He sends his regards. I'm very glad to have him back with me again.

I've been meaning for a while to ask after dear grandmother. But kept forgetting to. Tell me how she is.

I am

your

affectionate brother

Friz

Could I ask you for the rapiers I left behind? One of them is borrowed, and I'd like to return it.

42. TO HIS MOTHER

[Tübingen, 7 February 1791]

Dear Mamma,

So far I haven't been able to find silver buckles despite looking everywhere. Nevertheless I won't give up hope, since going by the tone of your remarks it matters to you a great deal. The suspicion that I don't read your letters I hardly deserve. And as for the shortness of my letters, I've seen many people write letters to their parents, far away and doubtless also dear to their sons, and yet on the whole they kept them very short.

For my part, I shall certainly never measure your love by the length of your letters. Dear Karl hasn't written to me for a long time, and doesn't ask why I don't write to him. Am I therefore to believe he loves me less than before? Forgive me, dear Mamma, if it is wrong of me to write this.

You are quite right that the journey to Nürtingen is going to be hard to arrange. I would in any case, even in the afternoon, find it hard to get permission to leave, and have to return the following day. And on top of that I've no idea what I could wear for this ball, where there will be lots of people, probably also quite a few from Tübingen, including some you'd be very unlikely to approve of and perhaps I shouldn't either.—I thought it funny that dear Rike took the tomfoolery I wrote just to finish the page so seriously in her reply. Though it's true I have no money. Had to borrow some. This will hardly surprise you, dear Mamma, if you reckon up the costs each month just for lights, firewood, paper, and then tobacco and occasionally some vegetables when the seminary food would turn my stomach, and perhaps on Sundays a glass of wine and what have you.—Next Sunday I'm preaching again, when with my monitor I have to pay for lunch myself, & it's usual to have some wine and biscuits. Could you be so kind and add a bit extra to the usual next Monday, so that I can pay the taverner? If you still have my last sermon to hand I'd like humbly to ask for it back. I don't have a copy of the version I sent you. Look after yourself, dear Mamma. And despite his little shortcomings, continue to love

your

obedient son

Friz

43. TO HIS MOTHER

[Tübingen, 14 February 1791]

Dearest Mamma,

You have quite put me to shame with your kindness. I am still so far behind you in goodness and you give me so many opportunities to follow your example. Forgive me, dear Mamma, if in my last letter I said anything that may have lacked the respect I owe you as a son.—I am quite serious about not coming to Nürtingen after all. In the short time I have I could rarely spend time with you as I should like, and I won't get permission to come for longer. But if possible I'll come later this month.—Here is the sermon I gave yesterday (on Sunday). This time I was a little more expansive than in my first. I took pleasure in developing a subject it every day becomes more important for me to improve and refine my knowledge of. The part where I say that if we look at the matter closely *there can be no religion at all, no certainty of God and immortality, without belief in Christ,* that's the thought that for some time now has been preoccupying me more than usual. There are many good Christians, I think, who are not fully convinced of this idea. It is not that they don't believe it if it is explained to them, but they never find themselves in situations where they realize the necessity of the *Christian* religion from this point of view. Allow me to tell you, dear Mamma, the steps that have led me to this conclusion. I had been studying the area of philosophy that deals with the *rational proofs* for the existence of God and with those of his qualities we are supposed to recognize in nature, and I had an interest in it I am not ashamed of though for a while it did lead me into thoughts you would perhaps have found unsettling had you known what they were. For I soon came to see that these *rational proofs* for the existence of God, and also for immortality, were so imperfect that a fierce opponent could knock them down completely or at least in their main lines. At this point I came across writings by and about *Spinoza*, a great and noble man from the last century, and yet strictly speaking an *atheist*. I found that if one looks at the matter closely, with *reason, cold* reason untouched by the heart, one is *forced* to accept his ideas in order to explain everything. But I was still left with the faith of my heart, which is so incontestably full of the longing for the eternal, for God. But don't we most doubt precisely what we *desire*? (I say this in my sermon.) Who can help us out of these labyrinths?—Christ. He shows us by his miracles that he is what he says he is, God. He teaches us the existence of divinity and love and wisdom and the omnipotence of God so clearly. And he must know there is a God and what God is, for he is bound up with divinity in the most intimate way. Is God himself.

That is the course my insights into the nature of God have taken over the past year.

All my love to dear Rike and to Karl—tell him to send me something again soon.—I should be very pleased if my dear uncle were to become pastor in Löchgau. Perhaps that's the little place where I might spend a few peaceful years as a curate one day.—A thousand thanks for what you have sent me . . .

I am

your most obedient son

Friz

44. TO HIS SISTER

[Tübingen, March 1791]

Dear Rike,

You have made a good start to the correspondence we've at last taken up again. Mine is a good deal less good. I can only write to you rather

briefly today, for the simple reason that on account of the severe cold
I have stayed in bed longer than usual and now the postboy will soon
be off. Apropos of which, the day before yesterday there was snow
on the Alb, & yesterday such a heavy fall of hail that the hills, despite
being several hours from here, appeared all white in the distance. Your
description of your journey gave me much pleasure, even more the news
that you're intending to visit me in the summer. So my dear little sister
has caught the deacon's eye, has she?—I don't hold it against him at
all. Am more than happy that he should have you if he is a good man
and *you feel inclined toward him*. For I know I can trust you, dear Rike,
to let your affections be governed by *reflection*, and to take account of
feeling and intelligence, not just youth and handsomeness, and also how
fortunate his circumstances are, when you make your choice. Now I do
know a man you've been acquainted with for longer than the deacon,
and who you can consequently be a better judge of; and I certainly won't
think it wrong of you if your heart prefers him whom you know better
until it is clear whether a union with him is possible or not. The good
doctor must surely learn soon whether and in how many years he can
hope to get a post, & until then our dear Mamma will be glad to have
you with her. If a separation proves necessary, no doubt a respectable
party can be found with whom you will be happy.

Please thank dear Mamma most respectfully for what she sent.

Your

affectionate brother

Friz

I'm wearing my magister's robes at the moment.

45. TO HIS SISTER

[Tübingen, end of March 1791]

Dear Rike,

I'm so pleased you liked my letter. I said what I thought. And that is
not always the surest way of pleasing your sex. For look, dear Rike,

if I were to set up an empire, and had the strength and courage in me to guide people's hearts and minds, that would be one of my first laws—that everyone should be as they really are. No one should speak or act differently from how they think or feel in their heart. You wouldn't see any more idle flattery, people would no longer spend half the day together without exchanging a single heartfelt word—we should *be* good and noble because we no longer wished to *appear* good and noble, and only then would there be friends who loved one another until they died, &—as I believe, better marriages & better children too. *Sincerity!* Heaven be praised, sister, that we have inherited from our dear mother a strong disposition toward this marvelous virtue.—

The reasons you gave for not carrying out your intentions are pretty good.

For myself I become less and less concerned about the future, for every day I am more convinced that hardly anyone is in better spirits when things are going well, or on the other hand shows more fortitude when fortune is not so generous, than me. And this is my greatest desire—to live one day in peace and seclusion—and to be able to write books without going hungry.

Don't laugh at me, little sister. Joseph's brothers—without in the least wanting to compare you with them—I say Joseph's brothers back then called him a *dreamer*—and the boy grew up to be a fine man all the same! So I'm not much concerned about myself, as far as future work & future marriage & general living goes, so long as all is well with you, my dear family, and Mamma lives in good health and cheer among us, & you get a husband who is good to you and not too much housework to shoulder, and good old Karl finds the happiness he deserves!

Little sister, *adieu!* Come and see me soon!

Your

affectionate brother

Friz

Now I'm going to get on with the sermon I have to give tomorrow at mid-day. This time I'm minded to speak from the heart, & that will make it easier. Neuffer sends a hearty greeting to the whole household!

46. TO HIS MOTHER

[Tübingen, early April 1791]

Dearest Mamma,

The overcoat has really turned out very well. The buttons can wait until Monday. Dear Rike's coming here with Miss Gok, isn't she?—She is already announced at the Schwabs'. The Privy Counselor, who is leaving again on Wednesday, asked me whether my sister would not soon be here again, and I told him she would be coming on the Thursday of my departure, which was welcome news to him. I must have left my thorn stick in Nürtingen. If you can find it I beg you to send it over as it's an accessory I can't do without. I'm intending to take 3 shirts, 3 handkerchiefs & 3 pairs of stockings (in case they tear), all in a small knapsack. Because there are three of us traveling (me, Hiller, whom you know & Memminger) a man to carry our clothes between our main stopping-places and to show us the way won't cost us much. But if it all turns out too expensive for me I'll take the essential things myself and leave the rest with some women I know of from here in Schaffhausen until my return. Mrs. Ziegler will probably give me a letter to take with me. And if you think it would be proper, I was going to ask you kindly to request Dean Klemm and Deacon Köstlin to give me a few addresses in Zürich or perhaps also Schaffhausen, Konstanz, Winterthur. Tomorrow I'll write to Stäudlin to ask him. I'll go and see the Chancellor about this too. I reckon one must make the most of a journey one may never go on again.

A while ago I borrowed a shirt from Vischer in Nürtingen. If it should be among the clothes you have there at the moment, would you be so kind as to send it to me marked as such.

Look after yourself, dear Mamma.

Your

most obedient son

Friz

47. TO HIS MOTHER

[Tübingen, mid-June 1791]

Dearest Mamma,

I imagine I can now greet besides you—but only in writing, alas—my dear cousins & Rike, who is now the damsel errant just as at Easter I was the knight errant. I should have loved to come to Nürtingen for a few days if I'd had any hopes of obtaining leave of absence.

The piece of news you gave me *reassures* me a good deal—for reasons you will have no difficulty in guessing. Love doesn't tarnish with time! The dear girl still thought of me, as I learned on many occasions—& had I not been guided by the wisdom of my 21 years I might not have resisted many a relapse. I admit the news also set my poor heart pounding for a few moments! But we don't need to go into that. A propos, I must tell you that for a long time now it has been my firm intention never to marry. I mean this quite seriously. My odd character, my moods, my tendency to be full of projects, & (if I am quite honest about it) my ambition—all traits that can never quite be eradicated with impunity—do not put me in hopes of finding happiness in the calm of married life, in some peaceful parish. But that will perhaps change in years to come.

Forgive me for chatting away like this. The wisdom of my 21 years very often deserts me.

I still have 3 guilders left of the money you sent and I'm being very careful with them. Next post-day, when that little amount will probably all be gone, I'll present you with my accounts.

I always take my wine money. So far I've sometimes spent it on an innocent amusement, sometimes on a good book. But this summer it will be kept for necessary expenses only.

I will do all I can to get the grant.

Here's my washing. I'm sorry I had to be reminded a second time about the white scarf.

48. TO HIS MOTHER

[Tübingen, November 1791]

Dear Mamma,

I thank you with all my heart for the kind concern with which you inquire how things are with me. But I am sorry that my letters should be the cause of it. To tell the truth, I am not always well. Despite my best precautions I sometimes have the colic in the morning, and then often headaches in the afternoon. And as a consequence my inner life no longer has its youthful strength. I am without much sadness, and without much mirth. I don't know whether this is the way the character develops in general, that as we approach manhood we forfeit some of the old liveliness, or are my studies or—the convent to blame. But I shouldn't have written that. In the end it's my moods. Hope consoles me with the future, and the present too doesn't leave me devoid of pleasures. I think everything will sort itself out.—Grüzman has obtained leave of absence for four days. The other day I was forgetting that we simply have to be able to present a letter from home. Wouldn't you be so kind as to write specially, in time for the next post—along the lines "You would like to see me for a few days to discuss a complicated matter, and the change would perhaps do my fragile health some good."—

It would also give me great pleasure to be able to talk with you in person again for a while, dear Mamma!—Lots of love to my dear brother and sister!

Your

most obedient son

Friz

Sincerest thanks for what you sent!

49. TO CHRISTIAN LUDWIG NEUFFER

Tübingen, 28 November 1791

My dear Neuffer,

Since getting your last letter I must have said to myself a thousand times how you are just the same as you always were, understanding and good-natured despite my neglect and flightiness. Given the extravagant disorder of our money affairs you could excuse me easily enough for being so slow to pay my debts, but that I have not written a line to tell you which way my little boat was pointing is once again asking a great deal of your patience, since you must have known I had need of your sympathy and that things must be bleak around me and within me, it must have annoyed you that I was too lazy to brighten up my life for an hour and open my heart to you. Neuffer, since I've been back here I feel as if my best energies were left with those I hold dear, I am indescribably stupid and indolent. Rarely are there any *lucida intervalla.* And when I think of how you and Magenau are coming alive, growing in the strength that happiness and love give, of how charged with pride and courage I felt in the heavenly hours I spent with you in Stuttgart, and that I could be a different person altogether if I weren't in a situation which for me could not be worse—then I want to get out.

But that's the way things are. Despite everything I won't give up completely. My girl still has a sweet hold on me even though she keeps me at a distance. But after a fortnight and more languishing, the recompense is right royal. Yesterday was such a day. As each day passes I am more certain of it: love and friendship are the wings with which we shall reach every goal.

I will soon have finished my "Hymn to Humanity." But then it is a work of the lucid intervals, and they are far short of being a clear sky. Otherwise I haven't done much: learned a few things about the rights of man from the great Jean-Jacques, and on clear nights fed my eyes on Orion and Sirius and the twin gods Castor and Pollux, that's all. Seriously, dear Neuffer, I am annoyed with myself for not having woken up to astronomy sooner. This winter I intend to devote myself to it in earnest.

I've done my best with what you asked me to see to. I nearly lost my temper with the landlord of the Eagle. He said he had already delivered instructions to Uhland but would still send you the money if he had been paid after the vacation. I summoned up all my powers of persuasion, and eventually, after much toing and froing, we agreed that if possible he would send you the proportion* of the grant you had promised him this year and wait for a more convenient time. I haven't quite sorted out the business with the coffee yet. I told Frau Sch. that I was to give her in your name 4 florins 42 but she brought me the enclosed bills and claims you owe 14 florins 24. Just tell me what I should do, I won't let the rogues cheat you. But make sure you do it soon, dear friend, while you still remember the details.—*Saltus dithyrambicus!* The Swabian *Almanac* hasn't been reviewed yet. I got a wonderful letter from Magenau yesterday. It made me happy as a child.—If you like, dear Neuffer, we can respond to each other's verses in writing like in our golden days together. If you think it's a good idea you could have a word about it with Magenau when he comes to see you. I'll write to him soon anyway.—The reason I'm still in the Stift is that my mother wishes it. I suppose I can waste a year or two for her sake.

Send me some of your poems soon. There is more in them for our souls than in letters. Isn't that true?

Yours,

Hölderlin

Here are the books for your brother.
All my love and remembrances in Stuttgart.

* or perhaps the 20 florins are the whole grant? To avoid any misunderstanding.

50. TO HIS SISTER

[Tübingen, early December 1791]

Dear Rike,

Give thanks to providence for me! It has averted a great disaster from me and others.

Last Saturday after 9 o'clock in the evening a fire broke out in the convent. It was in the old building in an out-of-the-way room that had not been used for a long time and lay full of straw. In all likelihood a spark from the light of someone going past got in (for the room had no door) and so a cloud of smoke had formed over the convent that alerted the watchman before we knew anything. Suddenly a Frenchman who had no idea how to pronounce our cry of "Feurio" set up a terrible clamor in a room in the old building, where I happened to be paying a visit—we rushed out—and followed him down the stairs, for what he meant we didn't yet know—but no sooner were we at the bottom of the stairs than we could see, at the end of the corridor we had reached, fire leaping from the room.

We sprang into action, the flames had already begun to attack the beams, and through the fire and smoke good old Rotaker & a number of others had already pushed in through before us, they threw a door onto the burning straw and cleared out the rest of the junk in there completely. Naturally we didn't stand around and ran for water to at least help those right in the fire as much as we could. But we had no containers apart from bottles, we cried for help—which came from those in the town who had noticed the fire before us. Now the need for me there was not so great as my own need to pack my things up. I gathered everything in my bedroom together—it's in the new building and gives onto the Proctor's garden—I intended to wrap all the most essential things up in my bedclothes and throw them into the garden. For I thought that in the press I should scarcely be able to get through the main door with luggage, and there was a danger that the fire would spread extremely rapidly. Soon there were calls that it was all over. But the smoke on the floor directly above the fire long remained so thick that they suspected the fire was still burning under the floor and took it up in several places; and when no sign was found, set watchmen the whole night.

I confess I was less frightened than I'd have expected to be by a disaster of this nature; but perhaps that was due to the large number of people who shared the same fate with me. There was not the slightest wailing or cry of fear, apart that is from the enormous shouts of "Feurio" that rang out into the town because of the lack of water.

Thank God it was all right in the end!—

I'm deeply grateful for the latest sending. I couldn't find the little packet from Miss Kühn. And now I have one more thing to ask our dear Mamma; I do it with a heavy heart. The thing is that I haven't yet paid the bookseller the 13 fl. I owe, and there are some books I really need to buy which I can't very well order while I still owe him money. So if dear Mamma could spare the money?—I really am very sorry indeed that almost every half a year I have to be a burden to her in this way. Put in a good word for me too, dear Rike! I haven't got into this debt for frivolous reasons.—Now I must quickly break off.

Your

affectionate brother

Friz

And this news:
Miss Nast in Maulbronn is promised to a brother of her late brother-in-law, as I've heard.

51. TO HIS SISTER

[Tübingen, early March 1792]

Dear Rike,

A thousand thanks for your lovely letter. There was really no need to apologize for writing it in a hurry.

I'm looking forward even more to my Easter holidays now that it has been brought home to me so keenly that the best place to be is with my nearest and dearest. We had quite a hard frost along the way. But the journey did me not the slightest bit of harm. On the contrary I think it has been very good for my health. Christlieb sends his thanks again. If I'm not mistaken, Karl asked me to do something for him. What it was though, I've quite forgotten. I never found that table knife either.

Kamerer could have made the detour. Give me a week and I'll try and write something definite about these statutes of ours. It would be a shame if they were devised so that no reasonable person could subscribe to them without forfeiting his honor, and if we turn out not to be able to oppose them, if that's the case—I'm firmly resolved to find myself somewhere else to go, even if I have to earn my bread in the sweat of my brow. God knows how dear my family is to me and how much I desire to live as they would wish, but I cannot possibly let absurd and pointless laws be imposed on me and stay in a place where my best energies would go to ruin. Providence, I hope, will make sure that in future things will turn out well for me elsewhere, as long as I do what I can to become a man, especially as by the time I can expect to serve as a clergyman the form of government will probably have changed. For if Prince Wilhelm (as a Protestant) comes to the throne, the giving out of clerical positions is a matter of his whims, just as much as secular ones.—I am far from the only one to have come to this decision. The greater part and the best of our repetitors and students at the Stift will leave if this happens. And even if I were the only one—all the same I want to do all I can to save my honor and my energies. I'd give a lot for all this to be empty anxiety—but I fear . . . The latest news doesn't sound good at all. Georgii was the only one to protest against the Duke's interventions but was outvoted, and so the matter is supposed to be going forward very soon. There's no doubt of its importance. We must show our country and the world that we are not made of stuff that will suffer becoming the playthings of arbitrary power. And a good cause can always hope for divine protection.

Farewell, dear Rike. Don't let our dear mother be too anxious! I can't let myself think of that if I want to avoid losing all courage. The battle between a child's love and honor is a hard one, that's certain. Farewell!

Your

affectionate brother

Friz

FROM RUDOLF MAGENAU

Markgröningen, 6 March 1792

My dear Hölderlin,

Thank you for what you kept captive for so long and have now at last released, & here's my hand, the hand of a friend, for your loving remembrance of your friends, who will never forget you as long as the sun revolves through its spheres. I'm mighty glad that your woes in love are at last over, may they remain so for ever. I am very well, my friend, like a fish in fresh spring water, a week ago today I was lying in her arms, sunning myself in the rays of her blue eyes, the warming spring sun, & was for two blessed hours—blessed!—

Often I asked my heart, when I galloped off from this sanctuary again on my snorting stallion, will it last for ever? Oh what a life, in what an ocean of colorful sensations & feelings my little soul splashed about! She loves me, that is all I can tell you, more I hardly know myself, and wish to know no more! I have given her the name *Margot*, because I liked the name so much in Thümmel's *Travels*. *Nonna!* in case you're wondering, oh I had been prepared for it for 2 months, the barometer pointed to—ice-cold! The final touch was Margot's coming here. Neuffer saw in her eyes the first germs of love, he knows her, was the first to give her a kiss. Afterward she stayed with us for another 9 weeks, we spoke daily, *Nonna* noticed it, her plans were deeper than I'd have given her credit for, she investigated, had good words for her, praised her—*Margot* fled the crafty rival, & became mine! This is the record of our love & how it came about. You'll hear more at Easter. Letters have ears. Just this bit more: where Conrad's imperial pride sought in vain to rob love of its triumph, where supreme loyalty bore on heavily burdened shoulders its most beloved thing into the camp, that's where Margot dwells, in quiet and peaceful seclusion, like a valley-rose that delights all the more for never having been sought for in the deserted valley.

I'd have liked to have enclosed something for you, but I find it so hard to get round to copying things out fair, I've written a little thing called *Caverac*, you'll know the ideal of rural intimacy from Thümmel, who is now my bedside reading. Just one strophe for now—

> A rosary of blooming children winds
>   Around your house, and full of cheer
> Love rests softly on a bed of flowers
>   Every night encircled in your arms,
> The happiness your house bestows
> Lacks only this: it cannot last forever.
>
> No stranger dims the sky of all your joy,
>   Even moodiness is never heard of here,

Suspicion's poisonous seed, that only thrives
   On the hostile heath, perishes here of its own accord,
In this better land where only love & truth are found
The weeds die away unrooted in the ground, etc, etc.

That you mean to dedicate a hymn to us is a fine thought, what can I send you from my cabbage patch in return? Can you lend me something? You soar high over the valley where I dally with shepherds. I'll send you my *Caverac*, if, that is, your earnest *genius* won't fling the tiny troglodyte away? Oh why didn't you write to tell me you would be in Stuttgart, I'd have rushed to you on wings of love, we three, you, me & Neuffer, whom the air of the court is making fat, would have set up an academy of the noble sciences in some wine house, Stäudlin would perhaps have taken the *sceptre* of the presiding member. But that's how you are—so near & yet so far. N. wants to become a satirist, bravo, he only needs to make a goat's face as he's so good at doing and he could pass as a satyr himself! I couldn't help having a good laugh when he told me. If he writes satires, I'll write about some aspect of trigonometry, or about eclipses.

Write me a little letter again soon, do, however short, I'm always keen to know how you're both doing, I just hope you've escaped the burning of Troy, that's my fervent wish. Great and marvelous things are going on in the background of the times, & in the end *parturiunt* etc.—.

I'm anxious for creatures like you, here too the idiot always comes off best, *impavidum feriunt ruinae*. But dear reason doesn't let itself be importuned by expressions of authority. I am like a sailor, glad to have the storm behind him & drying his clothes in the sun, but I'm not indifferent, if only it was possible to speak up more loudly and say how useless it all is—but they wouldn't believe it.

Write to me again soon. Give my greetings to all our friends! And you look after yourself & love as a brother

your

fond friend

Magenau

52. TO CHRISTIAN LUDWIG NEUFFER

[Tübingen, second half of April 1792]

If only I were still with you, brother of my soul! But here I am within my dark walls, reckoning up how stripped I am of true joy, wondering at my resignation. You and the graceful figure do appear to me at brighter moments. But these dear guests find no very welcoming host. I'm done with my hopes, as I wanted. Believe me, the lovely flower that blooms for you, the loveliest in the garland of life's joys, will never bloom for me on earth. True, it's bitter to know that such beauty & splendor exists in the world, & to have to tell one's heart in all its pride that it is not for you! But is it not foolish and ungrateful to yearn for everlasting joy if one was lucky enough to experience smaller joys? Dear friend, I have lost all courage, and so it's good not to desire too much. I cling on to anything I have reason to believe may allow me to forget, & feel each time that I am poor in spirit and incapable of being happy like others. A thousand times I think to myself, if I only had you near me things would soon change. You can't imagine how much I miss the marvelous old days we spent here together.—But I won't plague you any further with my moods. You have such a fine life that it is sinful to disrupt it even in this way. Wergo awoke in me memories of my brief joys once more. I derived a childish delight from that dear Greek. Caffro was a great success here. That occasion was also the scene of another disappointment, but too insignificant a one to speak of it further. It's a shabby place sometimes, the human heart!—

In a verse of my Hymn to Freedom I put in a word by mistake that shouldn't be there. It goes:

> For the sake of all the good that fills the soul,
> For the sake of all the power the gods inherit,
> Oh brothers, for the sake of our true love,
> *Brothers!* Kings of all this finitude, awake!

The "brothers!" in the last line makes 2 syllables too many. Ask the good doctor to cross it out. I expect the poem is not yet in press. It matters to me that such a vulgar poetic sin should not appear before the eyes of the public.

When you are among your friends (men and women) think how
happy the poor lad of Tübingen would be if he were also with you, and
give my greetings whenever you can and want to. The music I'll send
as soon as I've copied it out. I'll probably write a pretty stupid letter to
do with it. They'll go together. She may in any case not have got a very
flattering impression of me. I always acted so clumsily. When I think
I neglected to accompany her the day we parted I could kick myself.
But as I said, I'm done with my childish hopes. And so I feel no grief
even if she did burst out laughing about the languishing poet. But
her soul is too gentle and good for that. By God, I shall always honor
her! The nobility and peace in her being contrasts pretty starkly with
the creatures here & elsewhere who always want to draw attention to
themselves and make their witty remarks & have nothing better to do
than laugh.—You see, dear Neuffer, I've learned to write long letters,
haven't I? Why might that be?—Write to me also saying exactly how
you are. Probably that'll then produce the light to offset my dark.

Yours

Hölderlin

Rotaker sends greetings.

FROM RUDOLF MAGENAU

[Markgröningen, 3 June 1792]

Dearest Hölderlin,

A thousand thanks for the letter you have at last sent me after all
this time, & blessings from heaven & all the 9 Muses on your head.
So you are well, I'm glad, may the gods maintain you in this good
mood, & no pain disrupt it. I'm even better, like a god, so freely &
contentedly do I drink from the cup of joy & and its enchanting wine.
I should like, to borrow Goethe's words, to become a May bug to suck
up all the thousand pleasures and delights of this lovely May. Along
this path I went with *Margot* when snow still covered it, & ice. Under

this tree she spoke words of love to me, this bower listened in on our conversations, my friend, May has never flitted past me in such a lovely way, everything, everything has now become precious to me because of Her. You say I am being secretive, oh I do not want to be, least of all toward you, are you not Hölderlin, should I mistrust you? Shame on me if I did! But let what I say be buried in the deepest corner of your heart. On the wrong lips, even the faintest breath can poison the tender plant of love.

I call her Margot, others call her Caroline Olnhausen, from Weinsberg! A happy chance brought her here last winter, I got to know her over 5 weeks, and did not love her. The kindness of her heart, her bashfulness, her bright open mind, the quietness of her being made me fond of her, in the 5th week I confessed everything to her—do you think, she said, you know me wholly now? You might be mistaken, etc. & thereupon the first kiss of unending love! Friz! Since then my heart has deserted me & sighs in the rosy bonds of her love. At the beginning of the summer I visited her at home. I cannot describe to you, I cannot put into words, what clasps my whole being about like a diamond band. I will do everything in my power to keep her true to me. Back then I had a blessed time at the watchtower near Heilbronn, I waltzed with her in my arms, but sadly lost the beat & got out of step. How was I supposed to attend to such things? She was crying when I left, her sister, a dear little woman, was eavesdropping on us as she embraced me. Go then, Margot said, and take my heart with you, if you can murder it you are the wickedest man in the world. I tore myself away, I couldn't endure the scene any longer. So you see, dear friend, that's how things are. Be glad that things stand so well with me, if only I had a crown to give, I'd offer it to this angel in thanks.

You intend to become a novelist. May Thalia guide you safely past the ravines that threaten the inexperienced peregrine through that terrain, and let me say in advance that I approve of your decision. At the next fair a little work of mine is due to appear, with the title*

Wolf of Blankenhorn, & Kunigunde of Sachsenheim.

An Old Swabian Story.

I too have had to struggle to get the demon into 16 sheets. The story has truth in it, but also poetry. It's finished, & now needs some serious filing. The gnome of Sachsenheim also plays a small role in it, & resolves the complications at the end.

I've been waiting on Neuffer for ages, I'd like to read it out to him, & he's the closest I have to a critical friend. It's bad that I lack such people, a lot of good things go unshown because of it. The ode to "Gaul's Freedom" I wanted very much to send to you, but in Neuffer's view it's no good at all in several places. So I need to revise it first. In the meantime here are a few segments:

6.

Did we not suckle too at your sweet breasts
   And ripen into men? Oh speak,
Are you loved only by the dweller on free coasts
   & did not Germany love you too, long since,
O freedom! Were not the first fruits offered
Germany's, its flocks, the acorns from its forests?

7.

And did you not initiate with your holy flame
   The great German *Hermann,*
To be your avenger against the mercenary tribe
   Of Romulus and of Crassus' men?
Who quelled the pride of tyrants more than he?
Who shielded your inheritance more boldly?

8.

Is it not enough that on the banks of the Seine
   The Franks tore the laurels from our grasp,
That tottering with victory and wine
   They proudly looked on us as slaves?
Not enough that they now have the crown
That long long ago upon our head was found?

Where freedom is

18.

The prince has no need of an army of hired men,
   He sleeps softly, guarded by his people,

The inalienable rights of nature protect him,
    Were he to breach them, he overturns his power,
O freedom, to the ear a silver note, & great feeling
For the heart! Your royal goal shines splendid!

19.

The Frank rejoices, and over from the Seine
    His paean sounds, we hear it come,
It rings on down like thunder on the Rhine
    & on the Danube rings and sounds,
Oh wake the sluggard peoples with your noise.
The Franks are free, the golden morning dawns!

I also came up with a few songs in Catullus's manner while I was at it, all of them referring to *Margot*. Here's one to cool you down after the ode above.

All is joyful round about in bush & tree,
All creatures are brought to life by love,
From long winter's dream of death set free
The swallow lifts its feathers up again, the dove,
The quail, make a racket among the seed,
In the shadows, among the blossom branches,
The finch keeps house in the evening quietness,
Twittering with his lively little bride.
All about, wherever my eye settles,
Even in the cracks of barren rocks
On the mountains' remotest peaks
Love has set up its little altars,
Woe to him whom it vouchsafes none of this,
Or who, like me, after worry and strife,
Does not wake one morning to find himself
Lit by *love* and in *Margot's* soft embrace!

Enough of that. Your patience will be done. Look after yourself, give me some news of you some time, & love me with the same love I have for you. God be with you, dear friend!

Grön. 3 June 1792
Magenau

* but this too must remain a secret between the two of us.

53. TO HIS SISTER

[Tübingen, 19/20 June 1792]

Dear Rike,

I don't know what will become of our correspondence in the end. There are always thousands of things going through my head that much to my regret I can't talk to you about. That is the blessing and the curse of solitariness, I think—our minds tend to be wholly taken up with what we are reading or writing. But it really is bad if there's something else we should be attending to and the untimely guests, the thoughts about our reading or writing, take up the place of the thoughts that should be there. —

Everything will soon come to a head now between France and the Austrians. It's true they report in Elben's paper that the French have suffered total defeat—but don't forget the news comes from Koblenz, and we should never quite trust that source whenever the news is favorable for the Austrians. And what makes the news more than likely a lie is that yesterday in the Strasbourg paper news came in dated the 15th of June saying that Lukner and Lafayette, 2 French generals, have enclosed the Austrian army completely and hope to force the Austrians to surrender unconditionally.

So things will soon come to a head. Believe me, dear sister, we'll be in for bad times if the Austrians win. The abuse of princely power will be terrible. Take my word for it and pray for the French, the champions of the rights of man.

Forgive me for going on so. But then I have Miss Stäudlin as an example. I confess that her letter gave me great pleasure.

The moment for taking my month's break will be determined by when Prof. Flatt stops his lectures for a month. In a week's time I'll know that for sure & give you a definite idea then.

My humble thanks for what you have sent. *Adieu*, dear Rike.

Your affectionate brother,

Friz

54. TO HIS SISTER

[Tübingen, late August/early September 1792]

Dear Rike,

All my best wishes of happiness for your future situation!—If you are as happy as you deserve to be & as you will certainly make *him*, all will be well. I have heard all sorts of good things about the man. It was deeply moving to read what you wrote in your letter. Remain as fond of me as ever, my dear Rike, in the contentment & love of your future husband. You have reached your goal. Who knows where the wind may yet blow my little ship? I have the reassurance of knowing that with our dear mother and with you, sister of my heart, I shall always find a safe harbor! Oh, I have been thinking of you a lot lately. Perhaps it wasn't right that I did not stay. But I should in any case have been an insignificant member of the party. Dear Mamma will also be delighted at the step you are taking, for all the anxieties that may assail her tender heart? Heaven knows that it is my sincerest and firmest intention to make up for the pains she has long taken over me by giving her joy as far as that is possible. Oh! I long for the autumn holidays that we shall still be able to spend how happily together! We won't think of the separation until we have to. You will remain as you always were. And distance cannot separate our hearts.

My little favorite, the squirrel, I must admit I'd like to have seen him again too. It pains the heart when anything in nature passes away. I'm going to make him an epitaph, I confess that the death of the good creature has filled me with a childish melancholy. I'm glad that dear Karl has preserved as much as possible of his remains.

I got the parcel only this morning at 10 o'clock, had to go straight to my class, & now after lunch the post is going to go at once. So I can't possibly pack up my dirty washing. I'll almost run out of shirts next week, given the hot weather. Farewell, my dear! A thousand greetings & thanks to you all!

More next time.

Yours

Friz

In a week my washing will follow for *sure*.

55. TO HIS MOTHER

[Tübingen, ~ 10 September 1792]

Dear Mamma,

So you are being given a foretaste of what it will be like without dear
Rike!—Though the part of next year that you'll spend without her
will quickly pass. And then for six months at least you'll have 2 lads
at home—before the older one ventures out into the world a little, &
who knows how soon that knight errant may turn back? I have never
made a secret of how much I like the taste of Mamma's bread, & there's
nothing easier than getting homesick when you're away, especially if
your dear Mamma is so keen to keep you & may hardly let you go.
More than once I've thought of that good man Camerer lately. Though
I'm pretty sure he will take it better and more sensibly than I should
be likely to in his place. I'm delighted to hear that our dear uncle has
recovered. I enclose the letter from my brother-in-law & the draft
of my letter to him. As luck would have it I had no paper to hand
& the letter really had to be written the very next day—otherwise
I wouldn't have made this draft and so would have nothing to send
my dear Mamma now. You'll probably find it pretty unreadable. But I
think on the whole you'll be used to my copperplate. I'll pack up my
washing. There's probably still time for me to send you a pattern for
the waistcoat (a good friend still has to let me have it from home)—if
it's not too much trouble please send it to Rapp in Stuttgart who I'm
told is bound to have something of the sort, & tell him to send the
cloth here directly. Might I ask for my jacket? I'd like to have the collar
altered.
   In all obedience I thank you for the money you sent.

Your

most obedient son

Friz

And here's the cloth I've got here. Single patterns cost 20 cr. apiece. The
others 18 cr.

56. TO CHRISTIAN LUDWIG NEUFFER

[Tübingen, after 14 September 1792]

Here then is the letter. My head and heart are still swimming from the various emotions that happened to crowd around me as I wrote. It's unkind of you to take your revenge at this of all times by not writing now! Recently I was reading the prophet Nahum. He said of the Assyrian strongholds & fortresses that they are like overripe fig trees: if they are shaken, the fruits fall into your mouth. And I was droll enough to take it and apply it to myself. Upon my word, dear Neuffer, I think one shouldn't shake it too much, or else the young tree will stand bare with its branches dry. There is simply nothing that gives me pleasure here at all. There I sit almost every night in our old cell and think back over all the trials the day has brought and am glad that it's over! Because I can't reconcile myself to this nonsense, it doesn't reconcile itself to me either. Good old Autenrieth was the lucky one. It is sad for the living though, when such a good soul departs this life before it is even half done. The seminary only disgusts me more since hearing the mindless & heartless things people say about his death, and about other pieces of news in the world. There is much dwelling here on a dreadful story about Schubart in his grave. You probably know it. Tell me what you've heard. You've no idea with what longing I always look forward to a letter from you. It really would be a joy to get one again. You can imagine that circumstances being what they are I find it hard to think of the gentle, beautiful creature as infrequently as I had resolved. I have just very discreetly asked her for her friendship. More I cannot hope for. My dear Rike wrote to me today saying that she had had a very good time in Stuttgart. The sweet girl has got engaged without any warning. We should be jolly pleased, dear Neuffer, that things are going well for her.—She writes full of enthusiasm for her new friend, Miss Breier. Did you let anything slip out there? She remarked that she is not at all surprised that such a gentle character, coupled with such great intelligence, should captivate someone, man or youth.—But *captivate* is such a harsh word! Do you really think it's applicable to this poor devil?

It will amuse you to hear that I of all people, in this vegetable life I lead, recently came up with the idea of writing a Hymn to Boldness. A psychological conundrum, don't you agree?—It's well into the night already. Sleep well, dear friend! You're probably already in your dreams. So I wish you a more cheerful awakening than I usually have. Write soon, Neuffer! And do your utmost to get me a few words from her too!

Yours

Hölderlin

57. TO HIS MOTHER

[Tübingen, second half of November 1792]

It pleases me more than I can say, dear Mamma, to see how tenderly you respond to the cheerfulness you find in my letters. The heat of youth led me down the path of melancholy. Now that the heat seems to have dissipated a little it is to be hoped my moodiness will also stay away. It is easy to spoil many a good hour with fruitless wishing & dreaming. And if they are not realized, then that's it, the fire's in the roof. But there is one thing left that you won't approve of. I can hardly ever bring myself to go into company I am supposed to regard it as a great honor to be accepted into, so people say, these gatherings with their follies & posturings. But this doesn't mean, dear Mamma, that I don't carry out my visits, as duty dictates. The kind of gatherings I'm speaking of are for the most part made up of younger people.

But to move away from myself and my doings, I wish to ask you, dear Mamma, as your son, not to alarm yourself too much about the war. Why should we torment ourselves with the future? Whatever may come, it will not be as terrible as perhaps you fear. True, it's far from impossible that changes may occur in our parts too. But, thank God, we are not among those from whom one might remove usurped rights or whom one might punish for acts of violence or oppression. So far, wherever in Germany the war has extended, the good citizen has lost little or nothing & gained a great deal. And if it comes to it, it is also sweet and right to sacrifice wealth & blood for one's country and if I were the father of one of the heroes who died in the great victory at Mons, I should begrudge every tear I shed over him. It is stirring and beautiful that in the French army at Mainz, as I know for certain, there stand whole ranks of 15 & 16 year-old boys. If they are asked to justify their youth they say the enemy needs bullets & swords to kill us just as much as for bigger soldiers, & we are as quick in training as anyone & we give our brothers who stand behind us in the ranks the right to shoot down the first of us who retreats in the battle. But the post's about to go. Look after yourself, dear Mamma.

Your

most obedient son

Hölderlin

58. TO CHRISTIAN LUDWIG NEUFFER

[Tübingen, May 1793]

I promised I'd write to you for sure this time, dear Neuffer. I've kept my word. I've become as fond of you again as ever, old friend of my heart! And I thank my lucky stars that they returned you to me at exactly the moment when all my fine hopes were beginning to fade. Our heart cannot sustain its love for humankind if it doesn't have humans to love. How often we told one another that our union was an everlasting one. I'd forgotten all that, fool that I am! In truth, I am a petty man to allow such childish matters to come between us. But in the end it wasn't such a paltry quarrel. You had changed; the affairs of your heart made you so unsettled; you didn't know yourself; how was I to know you, as the one who was my first friend and whose friendship meant more to me than my first love. You had to again become the one you were in the happy time of our shared joys and hopes and occupations, otherwise our friendship was over. But, thank God, I recognize you once more. And I believe we owe it above all to the charity of love. Your interlude with Miss Hafner was worthless. She came to Nürtingen with Rößlin. Sorrow does not trouble her. Let that be a consolation to you. She was having a good time with Rößlin. There was some pretty silly joking going on now and then. All in all I didn't take to her whatsoever. Perhaps she is good-natured. But if so this nature has been miserably ruined by passion and vanity. A little wit and an abundance of sensuality, that's what's going on beneath her attractive surface, nothing more.

Now you are on a better path. Just send some news occasionally from your paradise. In these parts all is without form and void, and dry as in the drought of summer. Selah.

The queen of my heart is still down there with you. I miss the sweet girl very often.

Having Stäudlin here was a feast day for me. Of course there would have been even greater rejoicing if a certain old friend of mine had been able to detach himself for a day from the magic circle in whose thrall he is bound with body and soul.

Si magna licet componere parvis, or the other way round, my wretched finances also keep me in a magic circle, my solitary room. I observe a pretty strict routine. On the stroke of four I'm up and about, make my coffee myself & then to work. And that's how I stay until evening, in my cell; often in the company of the sacred muse, often with my Greeks; but just now back in Kant's school. Goodbye, dear Neuffer! Next time perhaps I'll send you a fragment of my novel to see what you think. If you're curious you can ask the dear doctor in the meantime. I read some of it out to him.

Yours

Hölderlin

59. TO HIS BROTHER

[Tübingen, early July 1793]

Cotta wrote from France, as I have heard from Stuttgart, saying that the French would observe the 14th of July with great pomp and ceremony in every corner of the country as the day of their federal celebration. I'm curious. It hangs on a hair as to whether France will perish or become a great state.

At the moment I have before me 9 sheets of writing that will be my contribution to our future journal. If it comes off, the nine louis d'ors will do me good. [*Unfortunately he will need almost 100 thalers to pay off debts and expenses on his departure. He should inform their mother of this. For some time now he has certainly been living thriftily.*]

60. TO HIS BROTHER

[Tübingen, mid-July 1793]

[*His brother should do everything possible to get away in peace from those pedants. Despite the poor health of his purse he is living heavenly days, only soured by the thought of his approaching departure and the worry over his debts & future situation. He should do everything possible to get the offending sum together. 30 fl. would be needed a few weeks before his departure.*]

FROM CHRISTIAN LUDWIG NEUFFER

Stuttgart, 20 July 1793

Did your guardian spirit not whisper you a friendly greeting this morning? My dear friend, did you not feel a gentle soughing in your ear? I thought of you vividly this morning, and of our friendship which will carry us together toward the fine prospect of our youthful dreams. Now the seeds shall ripen at last, and the husks fall away. Many more flowers bloom on the fields of the Graces, many more golden fruit are enclosed in Urania's heavenly gardens: rich booty for those who seek it.

For as long as the labyrinthine passages of the heart are not uncovered, for as long as there are still innumerable new situations in which human beings can be set against one another, for as long as philosophy and morality still nourish veiled divinities, for as long as nature has not been sensualized in all its forms, the poet is bound to have a rich field for further discoveries if imagination, the heart and his powers of observation do not fail him. I cannot understand the simplistic complaint about not being able to say anything new in our age. Homer and Ossian may perhaps have said the same thing. There are still undiscovered regions in the province of poetry; but hidden paths lead to them, where courage and boldness cast long, brightening rays. Let us discover them by tracks not yet assayed. The wing of inspiration carries you sooner to your goal over the cliffs than anxious fastidiousness. Are we to let ourselves be frightened off by first attempts? Or by a malicious judgment from one of those pseudocritics? Posterity shall be our judge, and if I cannot foretell that of myself with prophetic certainty, I'll strip every string from my lyre and bury it in the rubble of time. The higher ode and the hymn, two of the Muses that have been most neglected in our day, and perhaps throughout all ages! We shall throw ourselves into their arms, tear ourselves away animated by their kisses. What prospects! Let your hymn to Boldness serve as your motto! And let Hope go before me. Her blazing torch will illuminate the night for me and help me avoid the cliffs so many have foundered on. I have composed a hymn to her which has reconciled me to my poetic presentiments. With our masterpieces we shall put our enviers and enemies to shame. We should live together for just one more year, as before. We could make better use of it now. No wretched gossip would divide us. I greatly look forward to embracing you here soon, for I am sure you will keep your promise and come in August. Those days shall be wholly devoted to higher pleasures.

I am enclosing a little poem of mine: my other works you can have a look at in person.

And finally a double request. If you can do without your Hesiod for a while, please send me it. I'll look after it. Send me your hymn to Boldness. I am certain you will do so, because in this instance I have not let you ask in vain either. I will give it to several friends and girlfriends to read who very much desire to see it: one girl especially, whom I shall not name, is keen to have it because Mathison embraced you on account of it, even though it needs no such foil to commend it.

And then I'll place it in Stäudlin's file for his further use.

Goodbye, my friend! And let me look forward to the fulfillment of my wishes soon.

Neuffer

61. TO CHRISTIAN LUDWIG NEUFFER

[Tübingen, 21/23 July 1793]

You are right, my beloved friend, your spirit was with me these last days. Indeed I rarely felt the permanence of your love for me with such certainty and quiet joy. For a while now your spirit has transmitted to me your very nature, I think. I have written to Stäudlin telling him of the many blissful moments I enjoy now. It was because your soul was alive within me. Your calm, the lovely contentment with which you look on the present and the future, on nature and man, I came to feel it all. And the bold hopes with which you look on our splendid goal, they were in me too. It is true I wrote to Stäudlin: Neuffer's quiet flame will be burning more and more brightly when my straw fire will perhaps long have died out; but this thought doesn't always put me off, least of all in the heavenly hours when I return from the quickening embraces of nature or from the grove of plane trees by the Ilissos where, lying among Plato's disciples, I have watched the great man's flights through the obscure distances of the beginning of the world or followed him into the vertiginous depths, into the remotest reaches of the country of the spirit, where the soul of the world sends out its life into the myriad pulses of nature to which the issuing forces, at the end of their immense cycle, return; or when, intoxicated by the Socratic cup, and by Socratic friendship, I have sat at the banquet listening to the sweet and fiery talk of the enthused youths paying tribute to sacred love, with Aristophanes the joker throwing in his flashes of wit until at last the master, divine Socrates himself, with his heavenly wisdom, teaches them all what love is—then, my beloved friend, I admit I am not so despairing and sometimes I think I must be able to instill into my little work some spark of the sweet flame that warms & illuminates me at such moments, into my *Hyperion*, in which at present I live & move, and also manage from time to time to produce something else for the delight of men and women.

I soon found that my hymns win me few hearts among the sex that in the end is more capable of beautiful feelings, & this strengthened my resolve to write a Greek novel. I'll leave it to your noble female friends to judge from the fragment I'm sending to Stäudlin today whether my Hyperion might not one day take his place among the heroes who provide rather better entertainment than all the knights with their adventures and fine phrases. I'm particularly keen to hear the judgment of the person you do not name. I hope what is to come will reconcile her and others to a harsh passage on her sex that Hyperion had to unburden his soul of. Let me know your own judgment too, dear friend. The point of view I should like this fragment of a fragment to be considered from I have set out in the letter to Stäudlin in a rather long-winded fashion. I'd like to be able to tell you the main points now too, but I don't think I'll have time. Let me just say that if this fragment gives more the impression of a mixture of accidental moods than of the considered development of a definite character that is because as yet I have left the motives behind the ideas and sentiments unclear, & this for the reason that I wanted to appeal to the faculty of taste, by depicting ideas and sentiments (for aesthetic pleasure), rather than to the understanding, by presenting a regular psychological development. But of course in the end everything has to be precisely traceable back to the character & the circumstances that influence him. Whether this is the case in my novel the rest will show.

The fragment I have chosen is perhaps the least interesting. The necessary foundations, without which what is to follow can no more be appreciated than the second book without the first (which still awaits completion), these necessary foundations had to find a place somewhere.—What you say so well about the *terra incognita* in the realm of poetry is particularly true of the novel. Plenty of predecessors, but very few who have come upon new, fertile land, & still a measureless expanse to discover and develop! I give you my solemn word, if the complete *Hyperion* isn't three times better than this fragment I'll throw it on the fire without mercy. Altogether, if posterity is not to be my judge, if soon I can't make that claim with prophetic certainty, like you I'll strip every string from my lyre and bury it in the rubble of the times. Your song did me a great deal of good, especially the last strophe. Dear Neuffer, that last strophe is one of those that give us a glimpse behind the veil covering the divinities of philosophy. What I envy you most for, as I think I have often said, is your luminous powers of depiction. I am struggling after the same with all my strength. But this dear guest, your song, would have met an even friendlier countenance if it had come in the company of your hymn. I am tempted to believe that with this hymn you're behaving as many a rogue may have done in wrestling matches. He kept himself back until his opponent entered the ring quite sure of himself, and humiliated the poor lad then all the more with his unexpected victory. Come on then! I'm ready for anything. I've sent my hymn to Stäudlin. The magical light I saw it in when I had finished it, & even more when I read it to you on that unforgettable afternoon, has now dissipated so entirely that only the hope of soon writing a better poem can offer me some consolation for its imperfections.—How do things stand with the journal?—Have you written to Matthison yet?—I haven't. Here's my Hesiod.

Oh how right you are when you say what a fine, productive time it would be if we could live together again like before. I will do all I can to be with you soon. And now goodbye.

Yours,

Hölderlin

The packet for Stäudlin was already made up when your kind letter arrived this morning. Would you mind giving it to him?

62. TO HIS BROTHER

[Tübingen, second half of July 1793]

That Marat, the disgraceful tyrant, has been murdered, you will also have heard by now. In due course holy Nemesis will ensure the other defilers of the people also get what they deserve for their wicked intrigues and inhuman schemes. I feel deeply sorry for Brissot. That good patriot will probably now fall victim to his vile enemies. Enough of politics.

[*He is to thank their mother a thousand times in his name for having received his confession with such forbearance.*]

63. TO HIS BROTHER

[Tübingen, mid-August 1793]

[*Complains about the tiresome amount he has to do.*] Believe me, it is not so bad to be harnessed to the drudgery of a clerk's life, which is after all commendable work, as it is to slave away in the galley of theology.

I'm not surprised that you like Hemsterhuis. Next time I'll send you the second part.

Wouldn't you also like to read that terrifying tutor to despots, Machiavelli? The whole book deals with the problem of how best to subjugate a people. I trust you not to let yourself be corrupted by his terrible principles.

Schiller (author of *Don Carlos*) is to spend next winter in Heilbronn, my dear Matthison is back in these parts again. He has need of a cure in Wildbad.

Do you think I'll be able to get a small group together this winter to teach Greek to? I'd like that a lot.

FROM CHRISTIAN LUDWIG NEUFFER

Stuttgart, 20 August 1793

Are you going to go back on your promise, friend? And not visit me in the autumn? Not give your friends the pleasure of your company? Stäudlin told me you would not be here before the winter. I cannot believe it; there must be some kind of mistake, and neither do I want to see myself cheated of the beautiful hope of soon clasping you to my heart as a brother again, now that you are once again wholly my friend like at the beginning of our friendship. In my reveries I was already wholly in those marvelous autumn days, devoted to friendship and poetry. You won't utterly destroy my dreams, that's what my heart tells me. Let me tell you how I imagined it. I thought that you would bring the greater part of your works with you. In the peaceful morning hours you would read aloud to me; I, in return, would show you my little things, we would assess one another's work, would delight in the increase of our powers, criticize and praise each other and offer one another our hands like brothers, as encouragement to venture on rougher and more daring paths. Would that not be a blissful pleasure? The rest of the day we'd divide up among other kinds of entertainment. A group of us would go out to a village, enjoy the splendors of nature there, settle round a nice little glass of something, and sing a song of joy. So you see, this was what I was dreaming up when Stäudlin's news threatened to destroy it all. If you really have made an irrevocable decision to go to Blaubeuren, surely you will be able to put aside a few days at least for your old friend. Your beloved family will of course be pleased to have you with them, but don't forget that there are also people here who love you. I have many things to say to you that I cannot confide to a letter. One says more in a quarter of an hour than can be written in a whole day. I hope that you will be more and more content with me; for I myself grow more so by the day. A heart animated by the purest love takes greater interest in everything. Often I hardly know myself any more when I compare myself with earlier times. All my undertakings, what I think and what I do, go off better, and every day I summon up greater hopes in myself, whereas before every day brought the loss of a new hope. A new world is unfolding within me, one I hardly suspected before. I should also like to know how you stand with Elise. I dearly wish to find out. I should like to know that all my friends are as happy as I am.

How things will turn out with Stäudlin's journal I don't yet know. He is doing nothing about it and I reckon it's about time he did. I've reminded him about it more than once. You do the same. If nothing comes of it, I see I shall be obliged to send my bits and pieces abroad.

I am impatient to see Voß's and Bürger's almanacs because there are pieces by me in them. And I'm going to get my first review. May God be merciful on the poor sinner I am! I am anxious for my writings because in my own eyes (and, after all, one is usually a little biased toward one's children) they have lost all value. In general that's how things are at the moment. In the beginning the novelty of it seems to shed a shimmering nimbus round them, but soon this magic vanishes. That's what happened with my hymn to Hope: the same thing will happen in future with other writings. On the one hand it humbles me, on the other it's a spur to achieve more in the future.

Goodbye, and let me have a reply soon.

Yours,

Neuffer

64. TO HIS MOTHER

[Tübingen, August 1793]

Dearest Mamma,

Today I wanted to ride to Nürtingen for an hour to thank you
personally for your kindness and motherly concern, so great was the
joy your letter gave me. But my occupations prevent it. Believe me,
dear Mamma, each day I learn to know and honor more the heart and
mind to which in the end I owe everything I am. It is often so clear
and vivid to me, when once again I've read such a wise and affectionate
letter, that few possess the mother I do, and I can tell you that this
is the ancestral pride I have—it means infinitely more to me than if
my mother were Baroness so-and-so.—There is no question of your
diverting even a penny from your housekeeping for me. And even from
the sum that in any case also stands entirely in your charge I shall
only need relatively little, as by then I can count on earning about a
hundred thalers myself. Believe me, dear Mamma, it is certainly no
fantasy to want to choose for myself a place of this sort for a while.
I have several very concrete reasons for doing so. Some of them, if I
remember rightly, I have already set out to you and I'll soon do it in
more detail in person. In any case you won't need to get a lot of money
together in one go. I need nothing more than essential clothing and
some pocket money to pay for the journey and so on. I'm quite certain
that I'll learn more, acquire a better education, with little money than
with plenty. Neither Jena nor Switzerland need fear war. Should the
war come closer to us, which however doesn't look likely to me, it goes
without saying that I shan't leave my family, and I'll stay. I can't see
that I'll need much money for Blaubeuren. For what you have sent I
thank you in all obedience.

The misfortune of Mr. Majer upsets me too. I'm afraid he's
another victim of bad governance. Damned bureaucracy and all that!
You say exactly what I feel, dear Mamma, about how difficult it can
be when your hands are tied. If we have to look on at our brothers'
troubles, and yet for all our efforts can do nothing to help, it is bitter
indeed!—This large topic is usually the theme of my sermons to the

people. You can be sure that I speak from the bottom of my heart. Often I think to myself when I'm back down from the pulpit: "if you have aroused even a spark more human charity and warm and willing sympathy, you're a lucky man." Oh if I can be of no other and more general use in the world I'll still have this, to be able one day to instruct and counsel a congregation with a fraternal heart. All my thanks once again, dear noble Mother!

Your

obedient son

Friz

My foot has healed, but to make the skin tougher I still have a powder to put on it.

I received the letter I'm enclosing from dear Rike yesterday. I've put mine in too.

65. TO HIS MOTHER

[Tübingen, late August or early September 1793]

I deeply regret that my letter caused you concern. You can be assured that I'll do everything to make sure the pleasure I will constantly strive to give you will no longer be as costly as it has been hitherto. I haven't yet written to Uncle Majer. I must admit that I wasn't thinking of my dear sister's circumstances just then and was not at all sure whether you would still be in Blaubeuren during the holidays or not, nor whether from now on you will be staying up there. Please don't touch on any of this, dear Mamma, but just tell dear Rike that I'll write at the beginning of next week and will come and stay with her in the holidays.

If I can get a good post as a house tutor, I'll be happy to hold off with my Jena plans until I've got together perhaps half (at least) of what I need myself from my tutoring—& from my writing. It's true that it's a rather undistinguished role I'll have to play in Nürtingen if, following your kind proposal, I come and stay at home for the time being. However much I may be doing, people will still say he's eating his mother out of house and home and is no more than a good-for-nothing. There is also the danger, if I take too long to get a position, that the Consistory will get me by the scruff of the neck and force me into a curacy with a parson who can't find a curate to come willingly. But I'm going to do everything in my power to apply for jobs as a house tutor. If by Easter your circumstances change, dear Mamma, so that it is perhaps a possibility after all—I'll still be able to make use of your kindness. Dear Karl's letter I was also very glad to get. I'll thank him for it by the next post.—Forgive me then, dear Mamma, if in my last letter I put things too directly, and continue to love as before

your

obedient son

Friz

My bedclothes are pretty dirty.

FROM GOTTHOLD FRIEDRICH STÄUDLIN

Stuttgart, 4 September 1793

[*Begins by praising an accomplished poem. This passage is truly lyrical:*] "By which . . . stand, Waiting wildly in their fearful armor, millennia."—I was much drawn to your novel for its beautiful language and its liveliness of exposition. I shall be able to give you my verdict on the whole plan once I have received more than this fragment. You will greatly oblige me by sending me the beginning as soon as possible.—Do not neglect . . . to insert hidden passages on the spirit of the times into this work!!!—[*He must promise him not to go to Blaubeuren without visiting him first. Neuffer and Stäudlin would come to meet him halfway.*]

66. TO HIS BROTHER

[Tübingen, first half of September 1793]

It was good of you to write to me again, dear Karl. I guessed you would share my joy in the new acquaintance I have made. I too shall never forget how close we were as boys and as we grew up together. And that's what I thought, dear Karl, when you complained about not having any friends. I know it well, this awakening of a youthful heart, I too have lived through the golden days when warm and fraternal feelings bind us to everything and such sympathy with *everything* is not enough, and we need one person, a single friend, to mirror and gladden our souls. To be honest, this lovely period is almost over for me. I no longer attach myself so fondly to *individuals. My* love is for humankind, though not of course in the corrupt, slavish, torpid form that, however restricted our experience, we only too often find it in. But I love the great and beautiful potential even corrupt people have. I love the generations of the centuries to come. For this is my keenest hope, the belief that keeps me strong and active: our grandchildren will be better than we are, freedom will come one day, and virtue will thrive better in the holy warming light of freedom than in the icy zone of despotism. We live in a period when everything is working toward better times. These seeds of enlightenment, these quiet aspirations and efforts of individuals trying to shape the human race, will spread and gain strength and bear splendid fruit. That's it, Karl, that's what my heart yearns for. This is the sacred goal of my aspirations and of all I do—that I might in our age germinate the seeds that will come to ripeness in a future one. And so it is, I think, that I attach myself with slightly less warmth to individual people. I should like my work to have a general effect. The general doesn't exactly permit us to ignore the particular, but once we have made it the object of our efforts and desires the particular does cease to claim all our soul's attention. But still, that doesn't mean I can't be a friend to a friend, perhaps not as *tender* a friend as before, but a true and active friend. Oh and if I find a soul who like me strives for that goal, there is nothing more sacred or dearer to me in the world. And that goal, brother of mine, *the shaping, the improvement of the human race*, the goal that in our life here we will perhaps attain only imperfectly but that the better generations to come will attain the more easily the more we have helped prepare for it in our particular sphere of activity—dear Karl, that goal lives, I know, in your soul too, perhaps just not with the same clarity. If you want me as a friend this goal shall be the bond that from now on will join our hearts together more firmly, more inseparably and more intimately. Oh, there are brothers everywhere, but few are friends of that kind. Goodbye. Give my love to our dear mother.

Yours,

Friz

Matthisson's poems I've lent to someone. Here's something else. *The discussion between Marquis Posa and the King* is my favorite bit. (p. 259).

67. TO HIS MOTHER

[Tübingen, mid-September 1793]

Dear Mamma,

A thousand thanks for your love and kindness again over the last six months!—As much as I'm looking forward to having my dear family around me again soon, time, which has passed away so rapidly and yet often so slowly, does occasionally make me somewhat sober. I am supposed soon now to have been fully educated for my future profession, and yet there is so much left to do. Believe me, dear Mamma, as content as I mostly am nowadays with the world, I am often bitterly discontent with myself. Oh, when I think of the notions I had 6 years or so ago of what I should be at the age I am now! Is it fortune or misfortune that nature has given me this indomitable impulse always to develop my powers more and more?—

Yesterday I wrote to Seits in French-speaking Switzerland to say I am available from this Easter for 2 years. But if I can fix things up in Jena I'll prefer to stay there as a house tutor or whatever else I can manage so as not to be any more trouble to you, dear Mamma, from then on.

My stockings, some of which were in a poor state, I've given to mend here because I didn't want to wear the better ones until I'd received the torn ones back from Nürtingen. I don't think I need any new ones. In the bursary here the other day someone said to me that my brother-in-law & sister are living together like angels. How glad I was, dear Mamma, & what pleasure it will give me to see the good pair's happiness for myself and then also the joy that it will give you—and isn't it so, dear Mamma, this joy will also be partly an expression of the love you bear me?—

Look after yourself until you will be able to welcome in person, amid a thousand joys,

your

obedient son

Friz

Dear Grandmother is quite well again? Send her my regards!

68. TO CHRISTIAN LUDWIG NEUFFER

[Nürtingen, early October 1793]

Dear Neuffer,

Forgive me for taking so long to thank you for satisfying my curiosity. But as I have so often said I don't like writing when I have little or nothing I could tell a friend that truly comes from my heart and mind. And at the moment I'm flat broke, dear Neuffer!—If only we weren't subject to such ups and downs!—or I at least wasn't among the worst in this respect!

But I think things will soon change. A few hours in your company would, I reckon, do a great deal of good. A proper long letter wouldn't hurt either.—I'm counting the minutes until I learn if and when I'm going to be allowed out into the world. I'm doing as much here as I can. But nothing is really thriving. I'm mighty curious to see Bürger's and Voß's almanacs. Couldn't you get hold of them for me this week? I'd send them back the next post-day. Write and tell me about your occupations and amusements, dear friend! I won't be envious, however great the temptation may be as things stand.

You don't happen to know when our exams are due to start? Would you be so kind as to let me know the date for mine? I'm preaching as much as I can in the surrounding villages to get plenty of practice into the time I have left.

Be so kind and ask Stäudlin whether he thinks money for the journey will be a matter of course or whether I should ask specially, should anything come of my position. It would give me great pleasure to read a few words from the dear man too; only so long as it doesn't put him out, it goes without saying. As soon as I have news of my position I'll be with you, dear friends! My only pleasure at the moment is hope and memory.

Write to me as soon as you hear any more about the fate of the deputies Guadet, Vergniaud, Brissot etc. Alas, what is happening to these men often makes me bitter. What would life be without posterity?

Good night, brother of my heart! Let me hear something of you soon.

Yours

Hölderlin

69. TO CHRISTIAN LUDWIG NEUFFER

[Tübingen, ~ 20 October 1793]

Dear Neuffer

You seem to have forgotten me; otherwise you'd have long since comforted me in my monotonous life with a visit or at least a letter. In my head it's turned winter sooner than outside. The days are very short. All the longer the cold nights. Still, I've begun a poem to

—the companion of the heroes
Iron necessity.

Why I'm *writing* and not as I intended coming to Stuttgart for a few days myself is what I really wanted to explain to you.

Things are not going well for this post as house tutor. I still have no definitive answer and so can't get ready for it and kit myself out.

There are various things my mother needs to get for me before I go, and I'm as impatient as her, for the uncertainty of my future situation can't be said to be putting me in a good mood.

Because I want to see about getting some clothes while in Stuttgart I can't come down until I've had a reply. And so I'd ask you, dear friend, to inquire with Stäudlin, on receipt of this letter, to find out whether he has definite news yet and if you learn anything to let me know of it at once by return of post. But even if there's nothing new you could do a great work of charity by writing me a letter again as soon as ever you can and cheering me up for a bit.

A kind word of friendship is something I need now more than ever.

Don't let these hopes be in vain! A thousand remembrances to Stäudlin and other friends!

Yours

Hölderlin

WALTERSHAUSEN, JENA, NÜRTINGEN, 1793–1795

70. TO HIS MOTHER

Coburg, 26th December [1793]

Dearest Mamma,

I arrived here this evening safe and sound. I could not deny my heart its urge briefly to let you know, especially as the bad roads have delayed me somewhat. I only got away from Stuttgart on Friday. In Nuremberg I had to stop until Tuesday. And yesterday evening, on Wednesday, I set off from Erlangen. Despite all that I haven't needed to open my trunk until now.

I leave here tomorrow morning by post chaise, and will be in Waltershausen by midday. The mail coach isn't much good beyond this point.

As far as the separation from my dear family permitted, I had a very good time along the way, especially in Nuremberg and Erlangen. More on that next time.

I am going now with a good heart toward the purpose of my life. Be you of good heart also, dear Mamma. Take my successfully completed journey as an earnest of future good fortune!

A thousand thanks again for all your love and kindness! And to all my nearest and dearest, in Löchgau and Blaubeuren, and to my beloved brother, a thousand remembrances! How often have I not thought of my loved ones and of you, dear Mother, with gratitude and also, of course, with sadness.

I'll write on the next post-day from Waltershausen, and hope soon to receive good and cheerful news from you.

Look after yourself in the meantime, dear Mamma! Ever

your

obedient son

Hölderlin

71. TO GOTTHOLD FRIEDRICH STÄUDLIN AND CHRISTIAN LUDWIG NEUFFER

Waltershausen, 30 December 1793
To be passed on to Neuffer!

Dear friends,

I have now looked around and become acquainted with the house and the people I have to deal with, also outside in my fir woods and my hills round about—as far as that has been possible since last Friday when I arrived in the evening. And so apart from the unrewarding news of my dull journey in the mail coach I can tell you a few other things that have more to do with my present and future existence. But first I must tell you that you should be grateful to me for writing so soon. In doing so, I stir up memories in me I had taken good care to subdue, memories of you and of all that is dear to me, of the whole sweet past, and this hardly lets me pretend to be very cheerful. Of my journey from Stuttgart to Nuremberg I can tell you nothing. I kept my eyes shut most of the time and conjured you and everything else I love up in my mind. In Nuremberg I came back to life. With Ludwig I had a fine old time, quite wild. He won't be able to contribute much to the journal, his *Englische Blätter* give him more than enough to do as it is. He promises to find a publisher for our journal once, as he put it, he's in a position to exhibit a considerable number of collaborators. His mouth is the trumpet of egoism made flesh. Still, as I said, I had a really good time with him. On Tuesday (having got to Nuremberg on Sunday) I rode over to Erlangen and celebrated Christmas there in the University Church, where Prof. Ammon gave a splendid sermon full of beautifully lucid thoughts that earned him at least ten burnings at the stake and ten anathemas. On Wednesday evening I set off from Erlangen again and arrived in Bamberg late, after midnight, on a damn cold and unsafe road—they sent a hussar to meet us on account of bandits in the forest. From Bamberg to Coburg, where I arrived on Thursday evening, I had the marvelous valley the Itz runs through before my eyes the whole day. (In passing—throughout Franconia I was greatly distressed, as you can imagine, to observe nothing but discontentment with the beneficent Prussian government. In the Prussian parts of Franconia 60,000 men are soon to be conscripted, including in the Nuremberg region. For Prussia has an ancient right over the Nuremberg district. In Nuremberg the blacksmiths have done a German version of St. Antoine, put a tax on fruit and meat, and taught the patricians a thing or two about the gallows. In Coburg citizens gave the soldiery a beating during a fire, etc. etc. I departed from Coburg on Friday at 3 in the morning in a post chaise and arrived here in the evening, met Major von Kalb (who served with the French and took part in the American War under Lafayette), a most humane and educated man, a lady friend of Frau von Kalb, who is still in Jena with two other children, my future pupil, a good and handsome boy, but *also the house tutor*, who like everyone else in the house knew nothing of my arrival and despite his tact and intelligence made me feel very embarrassed. Have a word with Schiller about this if you can, dear Doctor! The Major is comforting me as best he can over this tense situation. I'll tell you the rest very soon. A thousand remembrances to all my noble friends! Ever

yours

Hölderlin

The poem to Fate I almost finished during my travels.—My address is: M. H., tutor in the household of Major von Kalb in Waltershausen, near Meiningen.

Compared to the parson and administrator here I'm a mere dwarf in matters of bottlenecks, which you, dear Doctor, took such pleasure in knocking off!!

72. TO HIS MOTHER

Waltershausen, 3 January 1794

Dearest Mamma,

Comfort and happiness from above for the new year! And a thousand thanks for all your love in the last year, and in all the years past!

Tomorrow I shall have been here for a week. And I can truly say that not a day of it has not gone well. Major von Kalb, the most cultivated and obliging man in the world, received me like a friend, and his attitude has not changed. Frau von Kalb is still in Jena. My charge is such a good, bright and handsome boy that one cannot fail to like him. This is what my life is like: in the mornings my coffee is brought up to me in my room between 7 and 8 o'clock and I am left to my own devices until 9 o'clock. From 9 to 11 o'clock I give my lessons. After twelve we have lunch. (N.B. since you pitied me so much because of Saxon cooking I mustn't forget to say that the cook is Viennese and the table full of good things.) After lunch, as also in the evening, I can stay with the Major, go out with the little one, do some work, or do anything else, just as I like. From 3 to 5 o'clock I give lessons again. The rest of the time is my own. They dine in the evenings here too and the excellent beer that is drunk at table makes it easy for me to forget our Neckar wine. And I feel very well on it. My journey here will be paid for, as I came to hear. It is a very beautiful area. The house lies on a hill overlooking the village, and I have one of the most pleasant rooms. And the people here, as far as I have been able to get acquainted with them, are of a very good sort. With the parson especially I'm already on the best of terms. In conditions like these I have no wish to be in a town. I can use the Major's horses whenever I like. He likes his peace and quiet, is rarely away, and never sees many people. "I have spent long enough gadding about the world, by land and sea," he says, "now I'm all the fonder of my wife and child, my garden and my house." Only three years ago he was serving in the French army, and he took part in the American War of Independence under Lafayette. His features have much in common with those of the Court Councilor in Nürtingen (to whom and all his household please send my compliments).

The most enjoyable part of my journey was the time I spent in
Nuremberg. Stäudlin had given me a letter of introduction to Schubart,
secretary of the Prussian legation. With its gothic palaces and busy
inhabitants Nuremberg is a place with a certain dignity and looks
very inviting on the open plain where it lies surrounded by forests of
fir on all sides. In the book club and in a house in the country I met
some very cultivated people. I spent Christmas day most enjoyably in
Erlangen with a compatriot and cousin, the son of the physician Jäger
in Stuttgart. And also heard there a beautifully lucid sermon by Prof.
Ammon. I'll write to Blaubeuren and Löchgau next week. All my love
and remembrances. And a good morning to my dear Karl!

Yours,

Friz

Remember me to all in Nürtingen!
My letter from Coburg you have I hope got by now.
My address is: Mag. Hölderlin, tutor in the household of Major von
Kalb in Waltershausen, near Meiningen.
(paid for as far as Nuremberg)

73. TO HIS SISTER

Waltershausen near Meiningen, 16 January 1794

Forgive me, dear sister, that I have not yet sent you written proof
of my daily thoughts of you, my brother-in-law and your little ones.
But though I have little company here there have been so many
distractions, hundreds, that I could hardly find a quiet moment to
write to our dear mother. I wrote to her first from Coburg, while still
on my travels; and again on the Friday after the new year; but as yet
have had no reply. If tomorrow again brought nothing I'd begin to
get worried. Be so kind and send this letter on to Nürtingen as well.
I'm certain that cheerful news from here will not be unwelcome.—I'm
settling in very well. That my situation cannot therefore be bad you will
see straightaway, since I'm rightly in some discredit with you as far as

the capacity for contentment goes. Even if I had no other pleasure in the world my dear pupil would make up for it. If only I could present him to you, just once a year! His nature lends itself perfectly to an education according to more humane principles. The Major is a very good man, schooled at sea and in battle and in the company of the best minds of our age in Germany, France & America. And yet people say that intellectually he is dwarfed by his wife, who is still in Jena. "You do humanity a service by educating a genuine thinking human being—she wrote to me in a letter that I'll keep—you do humanity a service, and I have the honor of expressing the gratitude it owes you."

(My little one is making such a racket, overjoyed that today I called him a good hard-working boy, that I cannot gather my thoughts at all. I can't do anything about it, dear Rike! I wouldn't want to interrupt him.)

The parson here is a man after my own heart, and if we didn't drink beer here instead of wine there would surely be no more intimate pair on earth than the two of us. True, my dear brother-in-law would be a bit surprised that two so very different creatures get on as they do when I say that he is a great connoisseur of historical documents. But I'm sure he would also take to this gentleman.

The way everyone here has gone out of their way to welcome me and make me feel at home has, it seems to me, had the effect of making me more sociable than I've ever been before. And various amusements are open to me if I want to avail myself of them. I can go hunting with the Major if I want to, but so far have made sure not to shoot any hare. Perhaps I'll come round to it. The countryside round about is splendid. The lady companion of Frau von Kalb, a widow from Lausitz, is a woman of rare intellect and sensibility, she speaks French and English and has just borrowed from me the latest book by Kant. What's more, she has a very interesting figure. But so as not to be anxious, dear Rike, about your susceptible young brother, you should know 1) that I'm a good 10 years more sensible since becoming a tutor and above all 2) that she is spoken for and even more sensible than I am. Forgive this tomfoolery, sister of my heart! Next time I'll write something with more sense to it! Ever yours,

Friz

A thousand greetings to all!
Especially dear Karl.

In your household it goes without saying. I'll write to my brother-in-law soon.

NB: The Major, who has friends in high places in the political world, absolutely assures me that we'll have peace by Easter.

74. TO HIS MOTHER

Waltershausen, 23 January 1794

I really feel *at home* here now, dearest Mother. My health seems to be growing stronger with my way of life here rather than ailing at all. If my job means I have had to put a bit of a stop to my mind's usual nourishment, the body is all the better for it.—Your concerns about the war still seem to me, as before, a little exaggerated. Even if we don't have peace by Easter, as it is very likely we shall, it really doesn't look as if the French are going to advance much beyond their own territory. The Major has already announced to me that the moment they were completely over the Rhine I should have to move together with Fritz to Jena, because if it came to that he too would be a bit anxious.—At the moment I am in charge here in the house. The Major is off traveling, and her ladyship is still in Jena. The letters she writes me evince an intelligence equal to the goodness of her heart. I live quite without the kind of constrictions that etiquette and pride usually place on someone in my position. I've not yet had the chance, given the weather and all I've had to do, to explore the area much. But next Sunday I'm going on a little excursion to Königshofen, a town near Würzburg 2 hours from here, to meet with a couple of friends from home who were at university with me, Troll, a secretary, and Kleinmann, who is tutoring, both of them employed 6 hours away from here at Herr von Wellwart's in Birkenfeld. Swabians soon track one another down wherever they are.—My traveling expenses will probably be paid when Frau von Kalb arrives. I don't like to request anything before then.

I got your lovely letter yesterday, on the 22nd. So it didn't take much more than a week to get here. I'd like to write to Löchgau too, if I still had time enough to. I'd better say now, dear Mamma, that you mustn't take offence if you often have to wait rather a long time for my letters, and if they're often also very hurriedly written. I often only find out that a messenger is going to Meiningen an hour beforehand. No one goes regularly. A thousand greetings to Karl, and to Löchgau and Blaubeuren.

Ever yours,

Friz

75. TO HIS GRANDMOTHER

[Waltershausen, 25 February 1794]

I am better placed to tell you about my situation here, my beloved grandmother, now that the country and its people are more familiar to me. But the first thing I want to say to you is that the love my family bear me, and yours in particular, is never out of my mind. Thousands of times you appear before me and I thank you in spirit for every manifest sign of your kindness and look forward then to the inexpressible joy we'll feel when one day we see one another again. We are quite certain to see each other again, dear beloved grandmother! I want so much to become a grandson worthy of you! All the goodness that I received from you & my dear family in my youth cannot be better returned than by my doing my duty in the sphere of influence that is mine. And everything invites me to do just that. My dear pupil is as fond of me as a father or brother. I never imagined the blessed happiness the job of a teacher can bring. The smallest seed of goodness I sow in him becomes by its great consequences an infinite blessing. This thought strengthens me immeasurably in my endeavors. And my task is facilitated for me on all sides. I live quite without constraint and find obliging friendship wherever I turn. It is true my life is rather solitary, but I find this actually helps the cultivation of my heart and mind. The people whose company I keep are few, but they are sensible, good people. The little place where I'm living for now is rather remote from towns with their novelties and foolishness, but it is very pleasantly situated and the manor stands on one of the most beautiful hills in the valley and the gardens round the house are already a great source of pleasure. If I want to venture further afield, there's Meiningen 5 hours north of here, in Saxony, in the region around Würzburg, 8 hours from here, Schweinfurt, etc. Gotha is about a day's journey away, the other side of the Thuringian mountains, which seen from here give a fine view. At Easter I hope to make a little journey in that direction, and visit Friemar at the same time.

What news I can give of my journey you'll probably have heard already. The parson here is a fine man—the two of us are proper friends together. At the beginning of next week I am due to mount the pulpit again. What little skill I had would be lost again if I didn't practice, and I wouldn't want that to happen.

I hope you are keeping well, and all my dear ones in Löchgau? I am impatient for more news from you. The last letter from my dear mother I received only on the 18th. That was quite a long wait. But the joy was all the greater when at last it arrived. It's a nuisance I already have to close and that I had to write such a hurried letter. I'll make up for it one day when I'm less pressed for time. Send all my love and remembrances to my uncle and aunt, the deacon's wife, my dear cousins and to Louis. Goodbye, dear grandmother. Ever

your

obedient grandson

Hölderlin

Waltershausen
25 Feb. 1794

Lots of love to you, dear Mother, and the dear ones in Blaubeuren, and to dear Karl—to Markgröningen as well! I've addressed the letter to you because I don't have time now to write more. It's really for dear grandmother, as you will see.

76. TO FRIEDRICH SCHILLER

[Waltershausen, ~ 20 March 1794]

In a moment when the presence of a great man gave me unusual seriousness of purpose I promised to do honor to humanity in my present activity, which in its consequences may have such far-reaching effects. I promised this to *you*. I give account of myself here.

To form my pupil into a *human being*, such was and is my aim. Convinced that all humanity that does not also bear the name of reason, or is not in exact relation to it, cannot be so called, it was my belief that I could not develop the most noble faculty in my pupil too soon. It was no longer possible for him to remain in the innocent state of nature, and indeed he was already past this stage. The child could not be watched over, to cut off all influence of society on his wakening powers. So if at this point it was possible to create in him a consciousness of his moral freedom, to make of him a being capable of assuming responsibility for his actions, this was what must happen. Now it is true that for the time being he hardly has anything, it seems to me, in the way of proper cognizance of moral relations in the wider sense, but he does in the narrower sense, and of these friendship seemed to me the only applicable one in this case.

I did not seek to win his favor. I also sought to discourage him from trying to win mine, and here nature did not require any great resistance. For my part I simply followed the promptings of my heart that in good hours led me to feel a properly fraternal bond with the boy's cheerful, lively and apt nature. He understood me, and we became friends. To the authority of this friendship, the most innocent I know of, I sought to connect everything that should and should not be done. But because any authority we might connect human thought and action to sooner or later begins to make for great disadvantages, I gradually ventured to add that everything he did or did not do was not merely to be done or not for his and my sakes, and I am certain that if he has understood me on this point he has understood the summit of all he needs to know.

This is what I base the means to my end on, to a greater or lesser extent. I do not want to burden you with the details. The deep respect for you, with which I grew up, with which I so often fortified or humbled myself, which even now prevents me from any slackness in my education and in that of my pupil, this respect does not permit me to become too talkative.

This respect is endlessly strengthened by your kindness toward me, to which I owe my present situation, favorable in so many ways.

The uncommon energy of mind I admire Frau von Kalb for will, I hope, be a succor to my own mind, all the more so as everything is conspiring to provide the conditions for untroubled hard work. If only I can realize the motherly hopes this noble lady has for me!

She has been here for a week. She asked me to send you her compliments, with the assurance that she will write soon.

She told me that I might have had the good fortune of living near you for a few months. I feel deeply what a chance I have missed. I have never foregone so much by my own doing before. Let me entertain this belief, great and noble man! Being near you would have worked wonders for me. Why is it I must be so poor and take so much interest in the richness of a single mind? I shall never be happy. Still, I must be willing, and I am. It is my will to become a man. Be so good as to turn your attention toward me from time to time. A person's good will is never quite in vain.

I take the liberty of enclosing some verses whose worthlessness in my eyes is not so incontrovertible that I should think it an obvious act of insolence on my part to importune you with them, but of which my estimation is not sufficient either to put me out of the rather apprehensive frame of mind in which I write this down.

Should you deem the verses worthy of appearing in your *Thalia*, that would be to do this relic of my youth a greater honor than I dared hope for.

I am, with the sincerest esteem,

your most devoted admirer,

M. Hölderlin

77. TO CHRISTIAN LUDWIG NEUFFER

[Waltershausen, early April 1794]

Dear friend,

I think that the moment in which I am writing to you now is exactly as it should be for writing to a beloved friend. You have to feel a veritable need to convey your thoughts to a soul who belongs to you for it to be worth the effort of writing.

I did not treat you at all like the brother you are to me in plaguing you—and myself—with doubts and lack of faith because you did not write at once. I knew you, after all. Of course you have something dearer to you than I can be. But that doesn't make you any less mine than you were at first, with all that that implies.

Circumstances of inner and external life, our hearts and minds as well as fate itself, have created a bond between you and me that will hardly break. We got to know one another so completely, in our weaknesses and our virtues, and remained friends all the same. The charm of novelty has long since vanished with us. The beautiful illusion when, in the first hours and days of finding one another one believes one has found *everything*, where in fact one can only find *something*, no longer holds sway between you and me, and yet we have remained friends.

We strove after the same goal, and yet remained friends. We misjudged one another, and yet remained friends. Dear Neuffer, what more do we want in order to believe that our bond will last for ever and that our hearts are not petty?

It's strange; since we found one another I have undergone many inner metamorphoses, many things I was deeply fond of, ideas and individuals that at the time concerned me more than anything, have lost their significance for me, new ideas, new individuals enthused me, but to you my heart has remained loyal. So I can't be as changeable as all that, where once true worth has won my heart. On your side this surprises me less. Your loyal and persistent nature is the root of all your happiness and worth. And for that reason it's clear to me that in the future you will be happier and greater than me.

You are on the right path, dear friend! You leave the minds of others in their dismay and go your own way. There is an art to not giving up one's whole heart to interesting subjects when they would crowd out others one already has in one's heart. You have this art. You close your heart to nothing that is beautiful and good and great, but neither do you give it more space than is consistent with its existing alongside other things. Good for you! I wish I could do the same. A peaceful inner life is after all the supreme good a man can have.

That you also remain true as ever to your Virgil pleases me more than I can say. The spirit of the great Roman will strengthen yours wonderfully. In the struggle with his, your language can only gain more and more strength and agility. The thanks for your struggle will, it's true, be German thanks, that nation of indolent memory! But you will win yourself friends for sure. Moreover, our people seem to me in recent years to have become rather more accustomed to concerning themselves with ideas and subjects that lie beyond the horizon of what is immediately useful. There is now more appreciation of the beautiful and great than ever before. Let the cries of war subside and truth and art will find themselves entering into an exceptional sphere of influence. It's true that one could also make the opposite case.

And what of it if poor devils like us are forgotten or never properly recognized, so long as things improve for mankind as a whole and the sacred principles of right and of purer understanding are properly recognized and never again forgotten.

At the moment I am occupied almost uniquely with my novel. I reckon now to have got more unity into the plan; and I think that as a whole it goes deeper into the being of man. The poem for your Selma I expect to send in a week or so. The post-day crept up on me before I could carry out a little correction to it. I must ask you in advance for your forbearance, dear friend! It will seem unfathomable to you that one could make your Selma such a bad poem, or at least such a middling one. In the meantime here's a little something for you. It's the product of a happy hour when you were in my thoughts. One day you'll get something better. You can even, half to punish me half to thank me, send the little thing to the *Einsiedlerin* or wherever you fancy.—

To Neuffer. In March. 1794.

Still the sweets of spring come back to me,
Still my childish-joyful heart does not grow old,
Still the dew of love runs from my eye,
Still hope's cheer and pain have not gone cold.

Still the heavens' blue and the greening fields
Comfort my eyes with their gentle peace,
Full of tenderness and youth she yields
Me, sweet Nature, the joyful cup of ease.

Be comforted—this life is worth its toil,
As long as God's sunshine keeps us warm
And thoughts of better times delight our soul
And oh! a friend is there to lend his arm.

—— Hölderlin

Thank you so much for helping me out with the money in that brotherly way. Here are the 2 carolins back. Write to me as soon as you can. Goodbye.

I forgot to say anything about Magenau. I can't understand him. But you mustn't discard him completely, dear Neuffer! Perhaps one day you'll discover a better side to him again.

78. TO HIS MOTHER

[Waltershausen, ~ 5 April 1794]

At last, dear Mother, I can satisfy my desire to converse with you again. If all is as well with you and the rest of the dear family as with me, I am very happy. I am in better health than ever, take pleasure in doing what I have to do, and for what little that is I receive a gratitude I could never have expected. My situation is indeed a very favorable one; given the friendship of the good and intelligent people I have for company, the uninterrupted activity, the beneficial joys occupying my heart and mind, the obliging courtesy with which even the smallest convenience I might wish for is arranged, and given the prospects of a situation even more favorable to my development, I would really have to have a great relish for moaning not to assure you now that I am most content.

My time is divided up into my lessons, keeping company with members of the household, and my own work. The teaching is going very well. There is never any question of having to employ brutal methods, not even once: a look of discontentment is sufficient for my dear Friz, and only rarely does he need to be reprimanded with a stern word or two. When we are all sitting together we usually read to one another, taking turns, now the Major, now Frau von Kalb, now me, and then at table or on our walks we often talk about it, seriously or amusingly, as the mood takes us. But if I am rather distracted by something I am working on of my own, as is obvious from the expression on my face, they understand at once what's up, and I don't need to take part in the conversation if I'm not that way inclined. That this suits me down to the ground, you can well imagine. The time left over for my own occupations is now dearer to me than ever, I'll probably be spending next winter in Weimar in the circle of great men this town has in it. There apart from my own pupil I'll also be teaching a son of the Consistorial President *Herder* and will lodge in his house. Frau von Kalb also means to introduce me to Goethe and Wieland—she is an intimate friend of all of them. Next summer I'll travel there and bring young Herder back here, and then with him and my Friz, in the autumn, move to Weimar perhaps for some time, without the parents. I'm also due to make a journey to Nuremberg soon in Frau von Kalb's name, if the person I'm to speak with there hasn't already left.

Today we're having the Duke of Meiningen as a guest and Frau von Kalb says I'm to make his acquaintance. Perhaps this evening I'll be able to add something about him before this letter goes off (at the same time as he does).

Mid-day.

I took the opportunity to slip away for a few moments so as to talk with you again as much as possible. You can imagine what a contrast it is to think back to my mother's hearth—straight after such a parade. The thought of home does me a power of good now, as pleasant as things are among these people. I keep finding that a prophet is worth little in his own country and abroad too much! It often makes me laugh to think how shy and modest I used to be, whereas now, obliged not to be taken for a nitwit, I give myself a certain grace, if only not to dishonor the house. You can mock me for this conversion as much as you like, dear Mother! My Swabian heart will, I hope, even in these circumstances remain what it was.—Just for an hour I'd like to be with you again, just one! And with my Karl and my sister and the other dear ones. To all of them give my love and remembrances.

The Duke of Meiningen is very different from the other people in this region. He is a man of about 30, but still a youth for his joviality and love of talk. He has the common touch. He wears his hair cut short and seems in general to care little for ceremony.—

Next week I shall also write to my brother-in-law. It would be a pity, dearest Mother, if you had to do without his and dear Rike's company at Easter. Tell my Karl to write to me too. I think of him a great deal. I hope that he won't have to keep his promise to take up arms as a volunteer. I have already spoken about him here, of how hard-working he is and of how well-fitted he is to become a man who

will make a difference. I am always thinking about how to find him a
more pleasant position, one more favorable to his development. What
are his plans now? Is he likely to go to Markgröningen?—And now
a commission! It might not be particularly welcome, but I couldn't
really refuse. Frau von Kalb would like to get hold of six jars of cherry
spirit from Swabia. She will send you the money for it as well as for
the transport, but the cherry spirit would have to be of good quality. It
can't be got here. Frau von Kalb means to write to you herself in the
next few days, she says. I'm sorry the paper is already used up.

Goodbye, dearest Mother.

Ever yours

Friz

79. TO CHRISTIAN LUDWIG NEUFFER

[Waltershausen, mid-April 1794]

Here, dear Neuffer, is the child of spring and of friendship, the song for
your Selma. Admittedly such a father and such a mother should beget
an Adonis, as in Bürger's Song of Songs, rather than a poor devil like
this. But on the whole I'm content if only a faint trace of his father and
mother is detectable in him.

I am very curious to read something of yours again.—Schiller is
said to be sick? This news saddened me a great deal. My poem to Fate
will probably appear this summer in the *Thalia*. I dislike it now already.
All I have in view now is my novel. I've firmly resolved to take leave of
art if I end up having to ridicule myself again when it's done. And in
general I am now making my way back from the region of the abstract
in which I had lost myself with my whole being. I only read now, too,
when I am out of sorts. The last thing was Schiller's treatise on Grace
and Dignity. I can't remember having read anything in which the very
best from the realm of thoughts and from the domain of sensibility
and imagination is so beautifully fused in one. If only this great mind
could remain among us for a few decades more!—Look after yourself,
dear friend! A thousand greetings to Stäudlin! Introduce my little song

as tactfully as possible to your Selma, so that she doesn't take offence. And make sure all the other good friends keep me in remembrance when the opportunity arises.

Yours

Hölderlin

The cobbler you had those shoes made for me by is requesting payment from my mother. I would be sorry indeed to be mistaken, but I'm pretty sure I sent him the money before I left. Can you remember?

80. TO HIS MOTHER

Waltershausen, 20 April 1794

Dearest Mother,

I hurry to reassure you that I am well in mind and body and for the time being still firmly settled in Waltershausen. I can't quite understand how it was that my last letter should not yet have arrived when you wrote yours. I should be very sorry if it had got lost and you in the meantime have had to wait for news from me. And I wrote quite a bit in it that I cannot now for want of time repeat. The only thing that honor really requires me to say again is that I have a commission from Frau von Kalb. I am to ask you to purchase 6 jars of cherry spirit for her. She says she will send back the carrier's fee along with the rest as soon as she knows the amount.

If only I could spend a few hours now with my dear ones in Nürtingen! My brother-in-law and dear Rike are probably there too now. A thousand remembrances. In my mind I am often there.

On Easter Monday I preached again. I'm telling you this, dearest Mother, because I know that is such a comfort to you.

My dear Friz was in bed sick for nearly 3 weeks. But now he has almost completely recovered. And his illness, a kind of rheumatism that crept into his joints, has vanished without trace. I was sometimes very worried about him. The bright young soul has all my love and affection.

I've never seen a more beautiful spring anywhere. Are the fields of my homeland also so full of these infinite blessings? That would please me a good deal, the good Swabians deserve it.

I enclose here my reply to the letter I received together with yours. I can't very well contemplate a change in my situation at the moment, and nor do I want to. Make sure you write me a good long letter next time, with news of the dear guests from Blaubeuren. I often wish there was a regular post from here. I am always caught by surprise and then find I can't write what I wanted to.

I've now discovered that worries and moods are good for something after all. Since being free of them I'm beginning to get fat.

I'm very sorry that dear grandmother is unwell. I hope to hear good news about that too next time. Forgive me, dear Mother, that my letter is so slapdash. I'll try to make up for it next time. Ever

yours

Friz

81. TO HIS BROTHER

Waltershausen, near Meiningen, 21 May 1794

Dear brother,

It was good of you to give me a sign of your existence and of your brotherly thoughts again. I have often thought of you since the moment we parted on the heath and found it so hard to take leave of one another.

The distance between us now always seems so vast, and I often say to myself I should make a quick dash over to see you all. But before that happens we'll probably be a good bit older.

I doubt whether I'll be leaving my present situation in a hurry. I have leisure for my personal education, as well as promptings from the world around me, and on good days my other occupations allow me to rest and recuperate. As yet it is uncertain whether I shall spend next winter in Jena as well as Weimar. Both possibilities, as you can imagine, are very agreeable indeed. Here I live very quietly. I remember only few periods of my life spent in such constant and equal composure and calm.

You know, dear brother, how much value there is in not being distracted by anything. You are lucky enough to enjoy this too. Make the most of it. If one has only a single hour over from the rest of the day to devote to the free use of the mind, when one can attend to one's most pressing and noblest needs, that is a great deal and, at the least, enough to gain strength and spirit for the rest of the time.

Brother, hold up your better self and don't let it be pushed down by anything, by anything at all! It is of great importance to me to know the direction your mind is taking. Make sure, dear Karl, you keep me informed as often as you can. Very soon I will give you an account of my own occupations. I am in the middle of working on something now that I don't want to talk about until I've got it clear in my mind.

If you can get hold of the most recent issues of Schiller's *Thalia* or Ewald's *Urania*, or of the Swabian journal *Flora*, look out for my name and think of me. For the most part it's only small things you'll find there. Practically the only thing I'm reading at the moment is Kant. His magnificent mind reveals itself to me more and more.

I am very glad to hear that dear Grandmamma is there with you all. Give her all my heartfelt respects. She's quite better again now, isn't she? That my little niece is thriving so well was also a piece of news I was very pleased to hear.

I'm going to write to Blaubeuren. Frau von Kalb asks dear mother to wait with the cherry spirit until the cherries here are ripe, and then to send it in jars in a small crate. Friz is quite well again and is always a source of great joy. It wouldn't be easy to find a child as good as him.

God preserve you, my dears!

Yours,

Friz

What's our friend Hiemer up to?

FROM CHRISTIAN LUDWIG NEUFFER

Stuttgart, 3 June 1794

I am very keen to see your novel.—Your poem to Gotthold has my unstinting approval. For the little poem for me warm thanks. Carry out your promise one day and dedicate me a longer one. Selma will thank you for hers herself. [*Rosine's father has died; that news will no doubt already have reached him.*]—You yourself, dear friend, were never more productive of hymns than in that phase of philosophical sacerdocy.—[*Would he consider sending something for Conz's Museum for Greek and Roman Literature?*]

82. TO CHRISTIAN MATTHÄUS THEODOR BREUNLIN

Völkershausen, Whitsun [8 June] 1794

You have allowed me, my dear brother-in-law, to send you my news from time to time. I should have done so earlier, I think, had I not always hoped to have occasion to talk to you of something of more interest than just myself.

But given my solitary situation, which I nevertheless find very favorable in many respects, I am now bound after all to confine myself to matters of my own existence.

What news I have is indeed for my interested friends rather good. Each day confirms my belief that fate has not dealt badly with me in placing me in the narrow circle in which I live. It is easier to get one's thoughts and convictions straight when the variety of objects around one is not too great.

Moreover my life is far from a hermit's. As you can see, I am now engaged on a little journey. The whole household is here on a visit to the very numerous and in part interesting von Stein family. The situation of the estate here is the most agreeable in the world, neighboring the Rhön mountains which separate Franconia from the Fulda region.

Tomorrow I shall make a little excursion into the Rhön mountains and across to Fulda that I promise myself many happy hours from. I really must for once enjoy myself and the world in complete independence.

I hope then to be able to carry out my daily tasks all the more efficiently again. My own occupations are now very concentrated, in part because I wish it that way, in part because my time is after all quite limited. I divide myself at the moment, as far as serious study goes, purely between Kant's philosophy and the Greeks, and seek also from time to time to produce something of my own. By lucky chance it has been possible to place my little things in Herder's *Letters for Humanity*, Schiller's *Thalia* and also Ewald's *Urania*. For the most part I am in good company there.

But do not fear that I might thus be tempted, amid these so far fairly insignificant efforts at expressing my thoughts, to neglect the self-cultivation I still have such great need of. Never was this less the case than it is now.

From time to time I really should like to spend a few days in the company of my family. My dear sister and you, my dear brother-in-law, are too vividly present in my mind for me not to wish I were in Blaubeuren very often; and at Easter too I often thought fondly of Nürtingen and the dear visitors there.

I am very keen to have news of how my nephew, with all his promise, is doing. We have another young genius in the house here, one of Major von Kalb's daughters, who often reminds me of dear Christian. Your little one will also by a great joy to you now.—

Please be so kind, dearest brother-in-law, as to inform my mother of my continuing good health because this week and perhaps also the next I'm never going to be able to write. And I hope to receive news of my dear family again soon after my return to Waltershausen. Forgive me, dear brother-in-law, I was obliged to write in this snatched moment, but I didn't like to let it wait any longer. I hope to make up for it another time. My remembrances to all in Blaubeuren! Lots of love to my dear sister and the little ones!—Ever

your

devoted friend and servant

Hölderlin

83. TO HIS MOTHER

Waltershausen, 1 July 1794

Dearest Mother,

I fear that my long silence may have been particularly unwelcome
to you this time. But you will have seen from the letter I wrote my
brother-in-law what part of the reason for that was. Beyond that, I
confess that a section of your letter made it virtually impossible for me
to reply straight after receiving it, although at bottom my decision on
this point was made long ago. I've long understood that it would be
as good as to give up on my education if I were to settle into a secure
domestic arrangement now. Perhaps, as has often happened, you will
urge on me the counterexample of others who would count themselves
lucky to find themselves provided for, as people call it, so soon. But
it is, I believe, neither immodesty nor idle dreaming on my part if I
consider that my nature, in so far as I am acquainted with its needs,
requires *for the moment* a situation in which I have more opportunity
to nourish my heart and mind on a wide variety of subjects without
the constraints of a fixed position in society. Dear Mother, it is a duty
to know one's own peculiar character, be it good or bad, and as far as
possible to maintain oneself in circumstances which are favorable to
it, or to seek them out. Moreover it goes right against my principles
to enter into a position in society by this means. Even if in my case
that would only be a false impression, I will and must avoid it still,
particularly in a matter such as this.

For the reasons I have given, I am certain that you will approve
of my decision, which has been taken after repeated and unprejudiced
reflection, all the more as I can assure you that I shall never choose
a path to my future career that would involve my becoming a burden
to you in any regard, let alone bring dishonor on you. You say that
you pity Miss L. I think however that if she seriously is fond of me
she cannot wish anything that goes against my character. But if it was
only half serious, well she'll be able to console herself and I too must
look to do the same. As much as I wish not to break off a relationship
of this sort, despite the peculiar aspects it always had in my eyes, I
would never venture to ask her straight out to renounce her happiness
for my sake; for that, I hope, is what it will be for her. I leave this to

you, dear Mother, if indeed a decision of some sort—or say what you have perhaps already said, I'm traveling and sending no letters.—Thank goodness I've got that tricky matter off my chest! Believe me, it was hard for my foolish heart to write so reasonably, for when I look at the matter closely I can't deny that I'm upset, not for my sake, but for hers. I must stop. Write soon, dear and cherished Mother. To Frau von Kalb too, if you wish. I haven't even told you anything about my journey. But next post-day I'll write to dear Karl, and will then without fail.

My health is as good as ever. Financially all is well too. The exercise I got in the Rhön mountains and in the country round Fulda did me a power of good. For all that, much as I like roving about the world, I am fond too of my quiet carefree Waltershausen.—A thousand remembrances to dear Grandmother; dear Karl I'll be sure to write to by the next post. His letter gave me immense pleasure, especially what he told me of his reading these days, so well chosen. Hold me in your affections, dearest Mother!

Yours,

Friz

84. TO CHRISTIAN LUDWIG NEUFFER

[Waltershausen, second week of July 1794]

My dear Neuffer,

With every letter from you the mutual communication of our natures and their fluctuating states becomes more indispensable to me. I truly share your pain at the blow that has struck your beloved girl and with her you yourself. You will have felt for the first time all that you are to each other. It is my heart's innermost desire that this fine union should endure in all its rare intimacy. When I imagine to myself that one day I too could be with such a woman, with hearth and home not far from you and your Röschen, I sometimes manage to set a proper limit on my endless longing from one part of the world to another, from one activity to another, or rather, I understand it better, especially as from my present situation I can see so clearly that a confined, quiet scope and sphere of influence, so long as one has become completely familiar with it, keeps our faculties in unremitting activity and, precisely because we are not wearied and distracted by the multifariousness of the world, preserves our strength and purity. And it also conceals many hidden joys that we can never be aware of if we flit by in a hurry. But as the sacred fates determine! We cannot make mountains into valleys, and valleys into mountains. But up on the mountains we can enjoy their high grandeur, the broad sky and the open air, and down in the valleys the peace and the silence and make ourselves all the more familiar there with the lovely and wondrous things we would not have seen from above. Or even better: if something needs doing up in the mountains we'll climb up there, and if we can plant and build in the valley we'll stay down below.

Forgive me, dear Neuffer. But it is not so easy to let go a chance thought if it corresponds in some small way with our own nature, and one ends up chattering.—In response to the passage in your letter where you talk about the unproductiveness of your mind let me copy you out a passage from Herder's *Tithon and Aurora*: "What we call the self's survival is, in finer souls, only the sleep before a new awakening, a slackening of the bow before it is put to use again. Thus the field lies fallow so that it may yield the more abundantly; the tree dies in winter so that it can send out new sap and shoots in the spring. The fates do not abandon a good man as long as he does not abandon himself and give in to self-doubt. The spirit that seemed to have left him returns at the proper time and brings new activity, happiness and joy. *Often a friend is such a spirit!*" Dear Neuffer, if you write to me soon saying I have been something like that to you it will make me very happy.

Your translation of the *Catiline* is of particular interest to me because it is still familiar from last year, when I read it. It is just the thing to be doing at the moment. You are right, translation is like gymnastics, and does the language a lot of good. It becomes nice and supple when it has to adapt to foreign beauty and grandeur, and often to foreign whims too. But though I have a great deal of admiration for your ability to prepare the means to your ends so doggedly, I warn you I'll have a few words to say if you start a new translation once you have finished the two you are on now. Our language is the organ of *our* minds, *our* hearts, the sign of *our* imaginings, *our* ideas; it must

obey *us*. If it has lived too long in foreign service there is, I think,
the danger that it will never again become quite the free and pure
expression of our minds, shaped entirely from within, thus and not
otherwise, that it should be. I would gladly go into this in more detail,
my dear Neuffer, if I wasn't pressed by the post which is about to
go.—This afternoon I was interrupted while writing by Frau von Kalb.
She saw that I was writing to you and asked me to thank you warmly
for your greetings, to tell you that from all that she knew about us she
had more faith in the lastingness of our friendship than in any other,
for once two individuals join hands with the idea of strengthening
and helping one another through partaking of all that concerns the
spirit and the heart, all that raises, expands and magnifies our being,
they are bound together for ever because their love is unending, like
the process of their perfection. That is almost word for word what
she said. And she went on:—to talk of you is also to include Röschen
in the conversation and there should be no division of what is
inseparable—she'd like to meet the person who would not be gladdened
by a love so rare in our day and age and so on. I think that from these
words that I have faithfully relayed to you you can divine a part of her
nature.—My pupil is of a good disposition, honest, cheerful, tractable,
with harmonious and in no way eccentric mental faculties, and pretty
as a picture from head to toe. I would gladly tell you a bit more about
myself, about my novel, my study of Kant's aesthetics, a journey I
recently made over the Rhön hills into the Fulda region and many
other things if I didn't have to stop. Do you happen to know if Stäudlin
has sent my poem to Boldness into the *Urania*? I'd like to know as I
might do something else with it.

Yours,

Hölderlin

Be so kind and send the enclosed letter to Hegel's house and remember
me when you do to Fräulein Hegel. Tell her Hesler sends his regards
too, and that if I hadn't been in such a rush I'd have taken the liberty
of writing to her myself. Ask her if I might do so when I write to her
brother in future.

85. TO GEORG WILHELM FRIEDRICH HEGEL

Waltershausen, near Meiningen, 10 July 1794

My dear friend,

I am certain you will have thought of me from time to time since we parted with the watchword "Kingdom of God!" By that watchword we would, I believe, recognize each other after every possible metamorphosis.

I am certain that whatever may happen to you the passage of time will never wear away that trait in you. And I think that will also be the case with me. It is this trait, after all, that each of us especially loves in the other. And so we are assured of the eternity of our friendship. But still I have often wanted to be near you. You were so often my genial spirit. I have a great deal to thank you for. Only since we parted do I feel it fully. I should like to learn a thing or two more from you, and also let you have something of my own thoughts from time to time.

Letter writing can only ever be a makeshift; but something nevertheless. For that reason we shouldn't abandon it altogether. From time to time we must remind ourselves that we have great claims on each other.

I think you will find that in many respects your surroundings suit you not at all badly. But I have no cause to envy you. My own situation does me just as well. You have got things straighter in your own mind than I have. You welcome having a bit of distraction nearby. I need peace and quiet. There is pleasure here for me too. You find it wherever you go.

From time to time it would be nice to be among your lakes and Alps. The grandeur of nature has an ennobling and strengthening effect on us that we cannot remain immune to. On the other hand I live in the ambit of a rare spirit, of a compass and depth and refinement and elegance that are extraordinary. I doubt very much you'll find a Frau von Kalb in Bern. It would do you a power of good to sun yourself in her light. Were it not for our friendship you'd be a little annoyed that your good fortune has on this occasion gone over to me. And she too must almost think that she has lost out to my blind good luck, after all

I've told her about you. She has many times urged me to write to you. On this occasion too.

Frau von Berlepsch was in Bern, may still be. And Baggesen. Tell me all you can of them in a letter.—So far Stäudlin has only written to me once, Hesler too. I think we're going to have to work very hard if we're to prevent the latter from making us blush with shame. I live in hope of meeting up with him somewhere before long.

Is Mögling in Bern?—Send him my love. You'll be spending many happy hours together.

Write me as much as you can of what you're doing and thinking at the moment, dear friend!—My preoccupations are pretty focused at the moment. Kant and the Greeks are virtually all I read. I am trying to become particularly familiar with the aesthetic part of the critical philosophy. Recently I made a short excursion over the Rhön hills into the Fulda region. It is like being in the Swiss mountains, with the colossal heights and pretty, fertile valleys where, overshadowed by firs, among streams and herds of cattle, the little houses lie dotted about at the foot of the hills. Fulda itself is also in a very lovely setting. The hill-people are, as always, rather curt, and naive. For all that they may well have many good sides that our civilization has erased.

Write to me soon, dear Hegel. I cannot possibly do without communication from you entirely.

Yours,

Hölderlin

14th

In haste I must add that I got the enclosed sheet, in all honesty, only a few days ago. I am very angered by the impertinence of a lawyer from Hildburghausen whom Hesler entrusted the letters to at Easter time and who probably only sent them on to Meiningen a few weeks ago, which is where I got them from, by what occasion I don't know. For that they come from Hildburghausen I conclude from a letter received yesterday from Hesler in which he appears to express a sense of embarrassment, as he ought to have inquired about the matter earlier. As I said, the affair upsets me a great deal, especially as my carelessness

in such matters is something you are all too familiar with from the
past. But this would exceed even my carelessness, and I have given
my word of honor. To put your mind at rest I should add that I know
Hesler's seal, and it was intact on the letter I got from him. Write soon.
I'll be writing to you about Hesler's letters as soon as I can.

86. TO HIS MOTHER

Waltershausen near Meiningen, 30 July 1794

Dearest Mother,

Thinking you'd prefer to have something rather than nothing at all I'm
writing a few lines now in haste so as not to cause you any concern
by keeping quiet all too long. I thought another messenger would be
going to Meiningen this week; but as I've just heard that this won't be
happening until Monday I must use the opportunity I have now as best
I can. Nevertheless, by Monday, unless I'm prevented, I intend to reply
to your two lovely letters in more detail, and probably I'll also have a
letter to enclose from Frau von Kalb who was very pleased to receive
yours and asks me to thank you for it in the meantime.

What tends to trouble my thoughts of my dear family at the
moment is that you will be worrying overmuch about the war. The
French will never seek to penetrate so far into the center of Germany.
And it is certain that no member of our beloved family has any need at
all to fear for their life or for what is needed to sustain it.

Next week I'll probably go off traveling again for a few days.
I have great need of this because in my solitary life I am more or
less forced to work sitting down all the time, and that way a certain
hypochondria easily establishes itself if one doesn't air mind and body
again occasionally.

I've been meaning to write to dear Karl for ages, but always
waited until I was in just the right mood, and so time has passed. The
trip into the Fulda region I made alone, and on foot.

That the letters *you enclose for me* are always dated a good few
months earlier than the letters themselves are actually written, irritates
me. For I know very well that none of these letters gets held up for
a few months anywhere. I cannot stand this falseness, and the letters

themselves are rather empty too. But in the end it's no bad thing for me to get the odd reminder of my old foolishness, which did however have its good sides too, as a warning not to renew it, although in this hermit's life of mine the opportunity is wholly lacking. I can therefore, if necessary, quite well remain faithful.

But please give me lots of news, dear Mother! However much undeserved hurt has been done me in my homeland I still take the keenest interest, more and more, in everything that reaches me from there. And I'm sure I speak more of my friends and acquaintances than they do of me; that I'm not referring here to my dear family goes without saying. The time I've taken to write this I should properly have devoted to my pupil. So you will understand that I can't possibly go on any longer. And so, for now, *Adieu*, and more soon. Lots of love and remembrances to dear Grandmamma, my Karl and all the dear ones.

Ever

yours

Friz

FROM CHRISTIAN LUDWIG NEUFFER

[Stuttgart,] 16 August 1794

Stäudlin sent your hymn to Boldness in to the *Urania* long ago. But I don't know whether it's already been printed.—[*Announces that his beloved Röschen is going toward her grave, the once so blooming girl. He and Stäudlin are very tense.*]

87. TO HIS BROTHER

Waltershausen, 21 August 1794

I have owed you a letter for a long time now, my dear brother. But in the contract between our hearts it is not written that we should exchange many words and write great long letters, but that we should become men and only on this condition acknowledge each other as brothers. We mature into manhood by restless activity, by striving to act out of duty even if it doesn't afford much joy—even if it seems a very slight duty, so long as it *is* duty, we mature into manhood. By renouncing desires, by denying and overcoming the selfish part of our being that always wants to have things nice and comfortable, by patiently biding our time until a wider sphere of influence opens up, and with the conviction that it is also great to limit our energies to a restricted sphere of influence if something comes of it and no wider sphere of influence does open up, amid a calm undisturbed by any human weakness or vanity, which no illusions of grandeur and no supposed humiliation unsettle or confuse, whose only interruption comes from the sorrow and joy provoked by the well-being or sufferings of mankind or from the feeling of our own imperfections, we mature into manhood. And through unremitting efforts to improve and expand our ideas, following the unshakeable maxim that when judging all possible claims and actions, their legitimacy and raison d'être, absolutely no authority is to be acknowledged other than our own, following the sacred, unshakeable maxim not to let our conscience be seduced by pseudophilosophies of any sort, including our own, nor by enlightenment that is clear as mud or the kind of worldly-wise nonsense that defiles so many sacred duties by calling them prejudices, but equally through not letting ourselves be led astray by fools or rascals who by talking of free thinking and the zeal for freedom seek to condemn or ridicule a thinking spirit, a being who feels his worth and rights in the person of humanity,—through all this and much more besides we mature into manhood. We must make great demands of ourselves, brother of mine! Do we want to be like those wretched folk who are so at ease in the consciousness of their little worth? Believe me, I get a strange feeling when I think of the hopes attaching to the coming century and set them beside the stunted, small-minded, coarse, presumptuous, ignorant, lethargic young people there are so many of and who one day are supposed to play their part. The few who are exceptions to this must encourage and support one another. And another thing! At this point in time it is necessary to say: be shrewd, say nothing, however true it is, if you are sure it will achieve nothing. Never sacrifice your conscience to shrewdness. But be shrewd. "Do not cast your pearls before swine" is the golden rule. And whatever you do, never do it in the heat of the moment. Reflect coldly! And then act with fire!—I am certain you are of one mind with me here: brothers must speak to one another in this way. The enclosed letter is from Frau von Kalb to our dear mother. It shows how rarely tutors take proper responsibility for their charges when someone who acts according to his own general convictions and conscience is regarded as something unusual despite the hundreds of mistakes he makes.

Last Sunday I was on the Gleichberg, which dominates the open plain an hour from Römhild. To the east I had the Fichtel hills (on the border between Franconia and Bohemia), to the west the hills of the Rhön that form the border between Franconia and Hesse, to the north the Thuringian forest that forms that between Franconia and Thuringia, and over toward my beloved Swabia, to the south-west, the Steigerwald on the distant horizon. That would be the best way of studying the geography of the two hemispheres, if only it were possible! Let me know all you're doing as well, and tell me about the joys and anxieties of our dear mother, the circumstances our beloved relatives find themselves in, about my acquaintances, about H., B., G. etc., and about anyone you know who might be of the slightest interest to me. Give them all my warmest regards when you see them. —

That Robespierre had to pay with his head seems just to me, and will perhaps bring some good with it. Only let the twin angels of humanity and peace come and the cause of humankind will be sure to thrive! Amen.

Yours,

Friz

88. TO CHRISTIAN LUDWIG NEUFFER

Waltershausen, 25 August 1794

If only I could help you, dear beloved friend! God knows I'd gladly give my life to be able to. My joy is gone from me, amid what surrounds me I am admonished by your grief and I do not know how I could bear it if you at least did not save yourself.

Dear Neuffer, you must and will hold up your spirit, come what may. You belong to humanity, you must not quit it. It's via great joys and great pains that a human being matures into a man. A future such as the hero hopes for in his struggle awaits you. You will not go through life deprived of your feelings, the royal consciousness of having overcome nameless pain will accompany you, you will fight your way up into the realm of the lasting, you will remain among humankind, a human, but one who has known the divine.

Dear and never-to-be-forgotten man, you belong also to me! Of all the things to which my heart has attached itself with hopes of permanence, until now only the union with you has lasted. I don't know a soul in whom I have believed as in you. I was never yet as rich as you. I have never known the happiness of love, and do not know whether I ever shall, but I was often unutterably happy in you and hoped to become ever more so in the same way. Do you know me no longer, am I nothing more to you, brother of my soul? Let us hold out together in this dark zone, let us act and work together, and nourish our hearts on victory alone. I swear to you that apart from humanity itself nothing on earth shall have the right to me that you shall, I shall be yours the way your soul is yours, and if I yield to no mortal I shall and will always do so to you. To conquer worlds, tear down states and build them up again, will never seem as great an achievement to me as overcoming such pain.

Grant me the consolation of my life, and yourself the triumph of triumphs! I will not let you go. I will call this out to you forever and would say it if I came from your dead body and hers: pain can cast me down, but it cannot defeat me as long as the will is strong.

Let her go before you, if that is how it is to be, on the endless path toward perfection! You follow her apace, even if you abide here for years yet. Pain will give your spirit wings, you will keep step with her, you will remain linked together as you are now, and what is linked will come together again one day.

And will you listen to me? I hope you will. The death of her father, the relationship between you that for all its myriad happinesses will also have brought with it hidden grief, this makes me think that what looks like consumption could have been caused by a deeply suffering soul. If so, that reassures me.

I implore you, write to me again by the next post, even if only a few words, to let me know how things stand with her and with you. If nothing changes then nothing can stop me: I'll make haste and come and beg you on bended knee to spare yourself. And even if I'm not successful, still I hope to interrupt your grief with a few days spent together as friends and so to do something, and that alone is ample reason for me to come.

O my Neuffer, if only I were already with you! I have no peace. If only I could be cheered a bit by your next letter. Don't forget that you are the one suffering, and that I am the one to bear it with you. Blessings from above on the saint in her sufferings!

Ever

yours

Hölderlin

In haste I took the first opportunity, & am writing to you via Würzburg. You will also want your letter to get here as soon as possible. So address it to Waltershausen near Neustadt an der Saale, via Würzburg.

89. TO CHRISTIAN LUDWIG NEUFFER

Waltershausen, near Meiningen, 10 October 1794

I was a good few days nearer you than usual, on an estate belonging to the Kalbs in the Steigerwald, in the Bamberg area, and awaited there your last letter that despite all protestations would have determined me to make haste to you and show you that you still have something loyal in the world had this letter not contained such happy, marvelous news. I got it very quickly; before leaving here I had made every arrangement for it to be sent on to me without delay. So it would have been no great sacrifice, dear friend, as I was already almost halfway and nature has equipped me with a sturdy pair of legs. But then your letter arrived and only I can know how glad I was that you didn't need me. It was one of those moments when our joy gives us strength for months. I have a deep and permanent wish in my heart that this fine love may endure, with all the blessings and virtues it brings, with all its blossoms and fruits. When I compare it to the times we live in it always seems to me like a nightingale in autumn.—Believe me, my dear, good friend, the dissimilarity between our situations in this regard, which has more to do with fate than with my own nature, doesn't prevent me from recognizing with joy and respect all the beauty and all the worth of this relationship. I do not say "with respect" idly, for without that which demands respect, without the nobility and steadfastness of a moral being, such a relationship could certainly not exist. And I have something too: the bond with you—it will endure, with its blossoms and fruits, like the ties of your love. I mean this very seriously, dear Neuffer! My conviction, which is confirmed every day, that a friendship such as ours is not to be found on every street corner, ensures that I shall hold onto it for ever. It is almost my only comfort, when I need comfort, that my heart stands in a lasting relationship with *one* being, that I have *one* friend whom I can trust and depend on. That I need this comfort you will not find hard to believe because like me you know how most people are perfectly well disposed toward themselves, but if they could would deal with others pretty much as they do with their pots and pans, or their chairs—they take care not to break them for as long as they're still of use or haven't gone out of fashion. And of course I don't allow myself to be broken, and I only let people use me up to the point where I can make better use of myself. But that's not a great deal.

It is now often the case that I find my official job burdensome. I dare admit that to you. I had been keeping it even from you because to you in particular I have given all too much reason to suppose me discontented with everything that does not have a gold or silver lining, an endless bewailing that the world is not an Arcadia. I'm pretty much beyond such childish weak-heartedness. But I am a human being. After all, I'm bound to hope that conscientious and often very strenuous efforts should have some success. And so it's bound to hurt if they have virtually no success because of the very average talents of my pupil and because of an extremely badly managed upbringing earlier on in his childhood and other things I'll spare you. That it pains me would be of little importance in itself, but that it inevitably disturbs me in my other occupations seems to me less unimportant. I think you would also find it very disagreeable to have half your day go by on lessons from which you gain nothing more than a bit of patience and more often than not have the other half spoilt by the realization that your pupil has gained nothing from it at all.—Still, I try to hold up, as far as possible, and as long as the sun shines in through my windows I mostly get up in a cheerful mood and make what use I can of the early morning, the only hours I actually have any peace and quiet. These were mostly spent this summer on my novel that you will find the first five letters of in the *Thalia* this coming winter. I have now virtually finished the first part. Hardly a line is left from my old drafts. The great transition from youth into the substance of a man, from affect to reason, from the realm of imagination to the realm of truth and freedom always seems to me to merit such a slow treatment. But still, I look forward to the day when I'll have the whole thing in fair because then I'll be able to move straight on to another project that is almost closer yet to my heart, a play on the death of Socrates, done according to the ideals of Greek drama. I've written very little poetry since the spring. The poem to Fate, which I began before I left home, reworked almost completely last winter and sent off in a letter to Schiller sometime around Easter, seems to have found his approval, judging by what he says in his reply to my last letter, when I sent him the Hyperion fragment. He intends to put it in an almanac he is shortly to become the editor of, and I am going to send in a few more things, as he has requested. Whether I'll be able to send you anything for Reinhard's *Almanac* and the *Academy* and Conz's *Museum* will depend on how productive I am. I should not want to disgrace you and it would be very shoddy of me to reward your comradely offer in such a way—so I want to avoid bothering you with things written in haste. Perhaps I'll be able to send you an essay on aesthetic ideas; as it can be considered a commentary on Plato's *Phaedrus*, taking a passage from it as its express starting point, it might interest Conz. In essence it is to contain an analysis of the beautiful and the sublime in which the Kantian analysis will be simplified and also, from another perspective, varied and extended, as Schiller has already done in part in his treatise on "Grace and Dignity," though he has ventured a step less beyond the Kantian borderline than he should have done in my opinion. Don't smile! I may be wrong; but I've checked, and checked again and again at the cost of much effort.—At the moment I'm working on a new version of my poem to the genius of youth.—At the beginning of November I'm probably going off to Jena. People have noticed that my physical self, together with my other faculties, is suffering in my present situation, and in order to preserve me it has been decided to send me there for six months with my charge, who also needs to go for several reasons. I'll see how it goes. I expect little enjoyment from it, and that is not what I'm after; but if

I'm not mistaken it will contribute something to my education. Many thanks for the kind greetings from your noble girl. I return them with all my heart. Your poem was a delight to read, especially the strophe before last, as poetry and as an outpouring of your heart. Frau von Kalb sends you her regards. Yours to her gave her great pleasure, she says. I'm running out of time and must stop sooner than I want to.

Yours,

Hölderlin

Tell me something about Gotthold too. Has Hiller gone to America? Do you think Fräulein Hegel has sent my letter on to her brother? And the other good friends, what are they all doing? You have no idea how welcome bits of news from your parts and circles are to me at the moment.

90. TO CHRISTIAN LUDWIG NEUFFER

Jena,   November 1794

I'm now here, as you can see, dear friend, and I have good reason to be glad of it, not so much because I am here, as because being here confirms me in the belief that we manage to accomplish something from the moment we are not simply carried to our destination but set out to go there on our own two feet, without worrying if we feel the odd sharp stone underfoot. I know very well there are greater destinations, and greater effort, more work and more gain; but of great things in this world we rarely have more than small instances.

My head and heart are now full of what I want to carry out in my thinking and writing, and, as is also my duty, in my actions, though this last naturally not on my own. The proximity of truly great minds, and also the proximity of truly great, independent, courageous hearts, casts me down one minute and raises me up the next. I shall need to work my way out of half-light and slumber, use both gentleness and violence to wake and form my half-developed, half-withered faculties, if I am not to end up taking refuge in a dispirited resignation with only the other dispossessed and helpless people to

console myself with, letting the world take its usual course and looking
on from my peaceful corner at the rise and fall of truth and justice,
the flourishing and fading of art, the life and death of everything
that concerns mankind as humans and, at the most, confronting the
demands of mankind with my negative virtue. I'd rather die than live
like that! And yet I often have virtually no other prospect. Dear old
bosom friend, in such moments I often miss having you close by, with
your comfort and the visible example of your steadfastness. I know
your courage sometimes deserts you too, I know it is the general fate
of those souls who have more than animal needs. Only not to the
same degree. A passage I came across today in the preface to Wieland's
collected works still burns at my heart. There it says: Wieland's muse
arrived at the beginnings of German poetry, and is leaving him in its
decline. Marvelous! Call me a child, but that kind of thing can ruin a
whole week for me. But even if . . . ! If it comes to it we'll break our
miserable instruments and *do* what the artists have *dreamt of.* That's
how I console myself.—Now some news from here. Fichte is now the
life and soul of Jena. And thank God he is. I've never met a man of
such depth and energy of mind. To seek out and determine in the
remotest regions of human knowledge the principles of this knowledge,
and with them the principles of justice, and with equal force of mind
to think out the remotest and boldest conclusions deriving from these
principles, and despite the powers of darkness to write them down and
present them with a fire and a lucidity that without this example would
have seemed to me in my insufficiency impossible to combine,—this,
dear Neuffer, is certainly to say a great deal, but no more than is
fit for a man like him. I go to his lectures every day. Speak to him
sometimes. I've already been at Schiller's too, once or twice, the first
time not altogether successfully. I went in, was greeted warmly, and
barely noticed at the back of the room a stranger whose appearance,
and what little he said at first, did nothing to suggest anything special
about him. Schiller told him my name, and told me his too but I didn't
catch it. Coldly, almost without looking at him, I greeted him and was
totally taken up, inwardly and outwardly, with Schiller. For a long time
the stranger didn't speak a word. Schiller brought in the *Thalia,* which
contains a fragment of my *Hyperion* and my poem to Fate, and handed
it to me. As Schiller then left us for a moment the stranger took the
journal from the table, flicked through the fragment as I stood beside
him, and didn't say a word. I felt myself getting gradually redder and

redder. Had I known what I know now, I'd have gone white as a sheet. He then turned to me, inquired after Frau von Kalb, the area and the neighbors round our village, and I answered all this in monosyllables, in a way I think I rarely do. But luck was simply against me. Schiller came back, we talked about the Weimar theater, the stranger let fall a few words weighty enough to make me suspect something. But I suspected nothing. The artist Meyer from Weimar also joined us. The stranger conversed with him on various subjects. But I suspected nothing. I left, and learned the same evening in the Professors' Club (have you guessed?) that *Goethe* had been at Schiller's that day. Heaven help me to make good my misfortune and my stupid behavior when I get to Weimar. Later on I had supper at Schiller's—he comforted me as much as he could, and with his wit and his conversation, which revealed the full force of his extraordinary mind, made me forget the disaster that had befallen me on the first occasion. I am also at Niethammer's occasionally. I'll tell you more of Jena next time. Make sure you write soon too, dear Neuffer.

Yours,

Hölderlin

My address is:—in Voigt's garden.

91. TO HIS MOTHER

Jena, 17 November 1794

So here I am, dearest Mother, going to classes, visiting Schiller and occasionally a public circle, and otherwise I'm at home buried in work of various kinds. The half of the day I have to sacrifice to my pupil it is true I give up much less readily here, now that much incites me to work of my own, something that could never happen in Waltershausen. The journey here from Franconia I had to make by mail coach, to my annoyance, and so it was impossible to visit Friemar, which lies toward Gotha. But I was told by a pastor from around there who was traveling with us that he knew of people called Heyn in a nearby village, though not in Friemar itself. I'll definitely do the journey back on foot and whatever happens will make sure my route takes me through Friemar. I don't have much to tell you about the journey, except that Schmalkalden, a town in Hesse, is anything but modern in aspect, though there is a great deal of industry there; and that the view you have from the heights of the Thuringian forest is very grand, with a large part of Franconia behind you, with its hills and woods, the great plains of Saxony before your eyes, and the Harz mountains darkly in the distance. One might well envy the happiness of the inhabitants of the valleys in the Thuringian forest, who have the prosperity and uprightness and good health we know from the Black Forest at home, were it not for the thought that amid the tribulations of civilized life we are perhaps of more use and can do more to help. We have to go through the night, and happy he who can lend a hand and has work to do. Gotha is a pretty place, but the people lead a luxurious life there. I don't want to do anyone an injustice though, and freely admit that my judgment is only a hasty one, with very little to go on. Erfurt is enormous, but deserted. Coadjutor Dalberg is the life and soul of this town; otherwise it doesn't seem to have much in the way of a soul; remarkable, though, the number of beautiful faces you see in the street. I won't say anything about Weimar until I've gone over for a visit and with any luck seen more, heard and gained more than on the fleeting journey through. Here I live in a garden, on the outskirts, with a couple of nice rooms, good food (or what passes for good food in Jena), and with the advantage that my landlord is a bookseller and has a large reading club where I can always get the most recent things firsthand for a day or two. But my work usually only lets me make use of this opportunity at table and in the evenings. Fichte's new philosophy now absorbs me entirely. I go to his lectures and nobody else's. Schiller behaves very amiably toward me. And Paulus has also given me a courteous welcome. I've not been to his house yet. With the professors one is not well acquainted with it is better to seek them out when they have decided to give their time to society, that is in the public circles, of which there are plenty here, and where there is quite a good atmosphere, especially as far as men are concerned, for so far as I've got to know the ladies with my own eyes and from what I've heard there's something rather obliging about them that is hardly grace, and something off-putting that is hardly dignity. In any case I attend these circles only very seldom, if I have to and want to. I meet up with Hesler sometimes. The area around Jena is splendid . . .

My address is: to—in Voigt's garden.

FROM FRIEDRICH SCHILLER

[Jena, December 1794]

You spoke to me recently of a small piece of work you had ready and wished to show to me. As I am just in the middle of putting the final touches to the current issue of the *Thalia* and there is still room for a few more sheets, it might not displease you to take up the space. But it would have to be tomorrow or the day after, as the issue will be finished this week.

Sch.

92. TO HIS MOTHER

Jena, 26 December 1794

I truly regret, dear Mother, that this long silence has given you cause to fret. But I console myself with the thought that it was through no fault of mine. I wrote before leaving Waltershausen, apologizing for not having replied sooner to your letter that accompanied the cherry spirit & the stockings, for which much thanks, due to a journey to the region around Bamberg, to one of the Kalbs' estates, and announcing that I should soon be leaving for Jena and that I intended to visit my relatives in Friemar while I was nearby (for I know now for certain that a family of Heyns still lives there, and in some comfort); and you will find that in my last letter, which I wrote to you from here, I referred to that one, which we must conclude has gone missing. I beg you, dear Mother, never to suppose that the cause of an absence of letters from me might be some accident; I promise you by all I hold sacred that I will make a point of getting in touch with you immediately when ever I have need of a mother's sympathy. Given the state of dependence in which I live it may often happen that unforeseen changes in my situation make it impossible to say precisely where you should be writing to me, or even for me to give certain news of myself, and in such cases and others like them I thought it almost better to wait until I could provide firm information. It's a case like that I'm in now, more or less. My employers

suddenly find their sojourn in the country too boring, and since in
any town my pupil is likely to be as well advised as here, so long as it
is a town, the reasons why he was sent here in the first place fall away
and I am obliged, against all expectations, to leave Jena again as soon
as next week. I shall be able to look round Weimar, where Frau von
Kalb, who has come to pick us up, is staying for a few more weeks,
and then probably I'm off to Nuremberg. I regret that your joy at the
lucky stars that seemed to be settling over me is so short-lived; for the
rest, I am resigned to it and glad that I made as good use as possible
of the little time I had here. I have made friends among the professors
here, Schiller showed a particular interest in me. Niethammer too was
extremely good to me. As I leave I'm discovering that a longer stay
would have given me many pleasant and advantageous opportunities.
I confess that for several well-founded reasons I had resolved to quit
my position and to try and see whether I couldn't support myself here.
I explained this to Frau von Kalb who could not but find my reasons
apt and the matter would have been as good as settled had not Schiller
managed to find a happy middle course and persuaded me to agree
that if my concerns, which he too found valid, had not been overcome
by Easter, the relationship should then be dissolved. As these concerns
have chiefly to do with my pupil you will see the wisdom of my not
going into unnecessary detail. Believe me, dear Mother, that youthful
rashness, if it ever did determine my actions, certainly has no part in
them now. It cheers me to think that I shall soon be much closer to
you, and perhaps one day will be able to see my country and family
again for a few days, much sooner than you'd have thought.—I'll
also be sorry to leave my good fellow countrymen behind so soon,
especially Hesler & Camerer from Sundelfingen who is pursuing his
studies in medicine here.—A remarkable trait of my life is that I have
exchanged not a single sweet word with any lady here! And the limited
time at my disposal did not allow me to visit the fine circles people go
to for amusement. Once, because I had to, I was at Madam Paulus's,
but I preferred to stick with the professor because he is indeed an
interesting man from a theological point of view. I say this by way of
countering your dear well-meaning warnings.—I'll write to you again
from Weimar, even before I've received a reply from you. I'm rather
distracted at the moment due to the impending departure. What is
Karl up to? Tell him to forgive me for neglecting our correspondence

so. Does he still think of me often? And how are the other dear ones? Thanks very much to you & Grandmother for the Christmas present. And a Happy New Year to you! A thousand remembrances in Blaubeuren and Löchgau!

Yours

Friz

The cherry spirit brought you great credit. I am to thank you warmly for it and for your letter.

I almost forgot an important point. You ask whether the living in Nekarshausen doesn't tempt me. I confess that it would be very difficult for me to return from my travels, and my occupations and little plans, so soon, and to enter into a situation that, however honorable and pleasant it is, is too incompatible with my present occupations and with the continuation of my studies for it not to cause an unfortunate revolution in my character. Even distant from one another we are close, dear Mother! The comfort that it is true I should find in a living more than in my present situation will suit me all the better when I am thirty. And I shouldn't want to venture on anything that puts me in the position of a petitioner toward people who do not know me and never will. If I was in need of it this last consideration would be of too little importance to hold me back. I'll write to my friend in T. later today. I admit that given the judgment I am bound to make of her I cannot wish to have formed a closer relationship with her, or to form one now. I appreciate that she has many good qualities. But I don't believe that we were suited to one another. And so I am writing *without any kind of motive* except simply because I have often in the interim had occasion to think impartially about her character and her former behavior toward me. Not that it was ever bad, but it was not of the sort to determine me to make an irrevocable choice.

Do look after yourself.

Please be so kind as to seal the enclosed letter. I think it needs no address.

93. TO HIS MOTHER

Jena, 16 January 1795

Don't be surprised, dearest Mother, at my writing to you from
here, when from my last letter you perhaps thought I would be in
Nuremberg by now.

I think you will not be too displeased at this unexpected news
once I have explained myself properly.

I am living here at my own expense and have no need for the
moment to be any sort of burden to you.—For good reasons I have
never been completely open to you about my situation up to now.
I thought I would be able to overcome the difficulties and intense
suffering I have to an unusual degree encountered in my chosen work
by dint of dogged and well-directed efforts, and did not suspect that
it would in the end come to the point where I cannot very well avoid
telling you several things I had kept from you up until now, being
obliged as I am to justify to you the change in my circumstances.
That my pupil, besides having no more than indifferent gifts, was at
the point when I took over his education at an advanced stage of
ignorance, was certainly not welcome but not in itself grounds for
not embarking on his education with all seriousness, and this I did,
as God is my witness and as his parents also acknowledge, with all
conscientiousness and according to my best lights.

But that he was quite insusceptible to all rational instruction with
which I attempted to work upon his uncivilized character, that firm
words were as unsuccessful in inspiring respect as kind ones were in
eliciting a devotion to goodness, was, I admit, a bitter discovery for
me. I sought the cause of this almost unrelieved stubbornness in the
beatings that to all appearances had been practiced on him to excess
prior to my arrival. Often it seemed that I had woken him from his
sleep, he was open, sensible, and not a trace of his brutishness seemed
to remain. And on such days he made inconceivably rapid progress
in his studies. I was idolized, as if I had performed miracles with the
child, the good old pastor in Waltershausen shook me warmly by the
hand and confessed to me that after all the attempts he had made
himself with the child he had given up hope and had been put to
shame by me, and even the less educated members of the household

and the people in the village could feel the happy transformation the child had undergone. That cheered me and gave me courage. But just as quickly and without warning he fell back again into extreme apathy and lethargy. His father, though with too much consideration for my feelings, had drawn my attention to a vice the child had occasionally shown traces of. His disposition and state of mind gradually made me even more attentive and unfortunately I discovered, partly due to his own admission, more than I had feared. I cannot possibly express myself to you more clearly. I hardly left him for a moment, watched over him anxiously day and night. Body and soul seemed to recover, and I regained hope. But in the end he found ways of escaping my vigilance, and his obduracy, the consequence of this vice, grew, especially toward the end of the summer, to such a degree that it virtually robbed me of my own good health and of all good spirits, and so also prevented my mental powers from functioning properly. I made every effort to help, but in vain. On several occasions I frankly declared the chagrin that all these failed initiatives were causing me, asked for advice, for support. They consoled me and asked me to persist for as long as I could. As some compensation for so many bitterly wasted hours, and also to give the lad some diversion and more exercise by sending him to dancing lessons and the like, we were dispatched to Jena. By dint of indescribable efforts, almost constant surveillance during the nights, the most forceful pleas and admonishments, together with a proper severity I managed for a time to reduce the evil, and once again there were corresponding improvements in his moral education as well as in his studies. But it didn't last long, the total impossibility of having a real influence on the child, and of helping him, began to make inroads into my state of health and my well-being. The anxious staying up at night muddled my head and rendered me virtually incapable of doing my work by day. Meanwhile Frau von Kalb arrived. The noble woman was greatly distraught with the child, and also with my situation. She and Schiller asked me to give it one last try. The Major also sought to console me, and himself, and wrote asking me to keep at it for as long as I could. We left for Weimar and as there the vice increased with every day despite the endeavors of the doctors and my own continuing exertions, whereas my health, my courage, my spirits decreased commensurately, as was unavoidable, Frau von Kalb declared that she could no longer bear to see me suffer, she didn't want me to be worn down for no purpose, and advised me to go to Jena and maintain myself here for as long as I could, promising me to use all her influence to assist my future happiness and providing me with three months' money. Given the reduced circumstances in which I live I think I'll get by quite well with 7 carolins until Easter. Schiller is being very kind and looking after me. If by Easter I finish a piece of work I began several years ago I won't need to be dependent on you then either. I am now in a period that is probably of decisive importance for the whole of my future life. Herder too, whom I visited once in Weimar, shows great interest in me, so Frau von Kalb says in a letter I've just received, and he has asked her to tell me I should visit him whenever I'm in Weimar. And this will happen fairly often; I had to promise Frau von Kalb that when I took my leave. She intends to remain in Weimar and has only taken on a day tutor for her son. Precisely because she was staying in Weimar, she no longer had much need of a resident tutor. She means to write to you any day. I also spoke to the great Goethe when I was there. To meet and talk with such men sets all one's faculties into activity.—My plan now is to carry on attending lectures here until the coming autumn and then to either give classes here or look round for a new job as a tutor in Switzerland or somewhere, or perhaps to become the traveling companion to some young man. Of course all these things do not depend entirely on me. But in so far as they do, I am trying to ensure my success by working hard and keeping my strength up, and for the rest I hope the fates, and people generally, will be well disposed toward me. Help me preserve my spirits by following the course of events with kindness and sympathy. Dearest Mother, don't let any unfounded anxiety disrupt the hopes you will certainly have for me, for what mother can leave off expecting something of her son? Grant me the uninterrupted use of my energies, something I have now almost for the first time since my boyhood. Believe me, the motives that have led me to prefer the frugal meal I take once a day to a well-laden table and even, for the moment, to my hearth and home, are not childish ones. And so I feel now as I write a new surge of energy and courage within me. Only one thing, dear God, just one thing I'd like to arrive at, and that is that my mother should be able to say from the bottom of her heart: all the efforts and worries expended on him were not in vain!—I hope all is well with you. Give my love to all the family. From now on I'll write more often again. In my recent unsettled situation it was almost impossible. Write to me as soon as you can. I long for a letter from

you. And the heartfelt joy I'll get from it you will grant me, I'm sure.
All my good wishes.

Yours,

Friz

I was provided with new clothes before I came here. I'm paying 5
thalers for my lodgings until Easter. 14 groschen a week for food. A jug
of beer costs me 3 cr. a day and breakfast about 6 cr. I'm living—*next
to Fichte's house*, that's the address you can give for my lodgings, they
don't have a name.

94. TO CHRISTIAN LUDWIG NEUFFER

Jena, 19 January 1795

I have lots to write to you, dear Neuffer!—First of all I must tell
you that I have left my former situation and am now living here
independently. You will well understand that I fairly had to pluck
up my courage before taking this step. I know that you'll give it
your blessing. I would scarcely have done it had the just desire to
make a serious go of my life not been compounded by the particular
circumstances of my former arrangements. Before my departure from
Waltershausen I wrote to you saying how much my tutoring work
was disrupting me in my personal development. I suffered more, dear
Neuffer, than I liked to say. I saw how the child got worse day by day,
and could do nothing to help, very likely even a more accomplished
tutor could have done nothing. We came here, I virtually gave up all
thought of benefiting from being in this place, with the sole purpose of
making one final attempt to save my pupil. I risked my health through
continually staying up at night, for his vice made that necessary and
I also wanted to make up in part for the wasted day. Often I seemed
to be succeeding, but there only followed even sorrier relapses, and
I also began to suffer from headaches to an alarming extent from
being up all night and probably also from the frustration of it. Your
letter was a nice surprise in those unhappy days and did me a power
of good despite the contrast between your congratulations and my

feelings at the time. Seeing Schiller also helped me keep my spirits up. At the end of December Frau von Kalb arrived to fetch us because she had suddenly decided to move to a town and so no longer found it necessary to keep us here in Jena. We left for Weimar, and I should have made more of many precious hours if my health and state of mind had not been so damaged.

I was at Herder's, and the warmth and generosity he showed me made an unforgettable impression on me. His style and manner are present in his conversation too. But I sensed a simplicity about him also and an easy nature that one would hardly guess in the author of the *History of Mankind*, it seems to me. I expect I shall visit him again quite often. I also made Goethe's acquaintance. My heart was pounding as I went in through his door, you can imagine what it was like. I didn't actually meet him at his house, but later at Frau von Kalb's. Calm, with majesty in his eyes, and love too, extremely simple in his conversation, though now and then it's spiced with a sharp jab at the folly around him and an equally sharp look on his face, and then again with a flash of his genius that is far from diminished—that's how I found him. People said he was proud; but if you understand by that a condescending and off-putting attitude toward people like us, it was a lie. Sometimes it is like having a father in front of you, full of affection. Just yesterday I spoke to him here at the Club. I also had some good conversations in Weimar and here with the painter Meyer, his constant companion, a simple honest Swiss and rigorous in his art.—Have you read Goethe's new novel, *Wilhelm Meister*?—Only Goethe could have written it. What you'll like best is the serenade beneath Marianne's window and the conversation about poets.—But I'm forgetting my own story. On leaving Jena I had already made it clear to Frau von Kalb, and she had told Schiller, that I would like to stay. Frau von Kalb and Schiller pressed me to give it one final go, there now being doctors on the case, in such terms that I really had no choice. But when things got no better in Weimar, and since the need for a tutor isn't so great anyway as the boy can have tuition there out of house, and in any case the help and attention I can give is not nearly adequate given present circumstances, Frau von Kalb offered of her own accord to put an end to my misery and I took her at her word, but she didn't want me to leave so suddenly. I put it to her that for my health I had to get peace and quiet as soon as possible and that I also wanted to go back to Fichte's lectures, and in the end she gave in, provided me with money for another quarter, promises to do everything to make an extended stay here possible, asked me to make sure to come and visit several times a month and showed as we parted all her magnanimity and, I do believe, her sincere affection toward me.—I wanted to account for my decision to you, hence all the detail. I now work all day long for myself. Just go to Fichte's lecture in the evenings and, as often as I can, to Schiller's. He is very attentive and loyal toward me. What will come of it I don't know myself. The only thing missing here is you, dear Neuffer! When shall we see each other again? Believe me, I often feel that nothing means as unalterably much to me as you. What you are to me I'll never find anywhere else. And if ever in my life I've spoken from the bottom of my heart, it's now. I'd often like to be with you too to cheer you up as best I could. That this noble love should have such clouded days! Send love to your Röschen, tell her I mean to have a proper celebration the day I hear of her complete recovery. Whatever happens, don't let your old spirit slip, dear Neuffer! I worry about that often. But you were always the one who set such a good example. You will find part of your *Aeneid* in the latest *Thalia*. Schiller's new journal, the *Horae*, will be the foremost journal of its kind in Germany. Whatever you do, don't give up what you wrote to me about serious satire. Schiller too says that now is the time to put the public into thorough indignation if there is to be any effect. He spoke sympathetically of your tireless work on your *Aeneid*. And showed me the Nisus and Euryalus episode in Conz's journal. Don't let Voß put you off. Come out into the open, and let people marvel at the man who dared compete with Voß. All the better for you! Will you send me some poems for Schiller's future almanac? I can't understand what he's done with the ones I gave him in Swabia on your behalf, but think he must be saving them for the almanac. He told me to send you his regards.

Yesterday I also met Woltmann, who is the recently appointed professor of history here and, as you will remember, has had a few poems in Bürger's almanac. He is a slight, dainty figure—quite in the Göttingen style.—Niethammer too, who is very friendly toward me, sends his regards.

You ask how things stand with my Tübingen affairs. Much the same. I said to you before I left, if I remember rightly, that I had passed many happy hours with her, and, it's true, bitter ones too; but that having got to know her better would never have desired a closer union. I wrote to her again not long ago, but only the sort of letter you might write to anybody. God, what blessed days they were when without knowing the girl I transposed my ideal into her and lamented my unworthiness. If only we could remain forever young. Tell me why you asked in the first place. The girls and women here leave me cold as ice. In Waltershausen I had a friend in the house I was sorry to lose, a young widow from Dresden who is now a governess in Meiningen. She is an extremely intelligent, dependable and good woman, made very unhappy by a bad mother. It will interest you to hear more about her and her story some other time.

A visit this afternoon got in the way of writing to you and now I must hurry. Write when you can, and this time as soon as you receive my letter. Even more than usual, I long for a few lines from you. Keep a part of your heart for me! I'll never be able to do without it, not in my whole life.

Ever yours,

Hölderlin

One more thing. Do you think you could visit my mother and, if you should find that she is not quite content with the change in my situation, reassure her? I intend to do everything not to be a burden to her and accordingly am living very thriftily, have only *one* pretty middling meal a day and over a mug of beer think of our Neckar wine and the lovely hours that blessed it. Farewell, dear friend.

95. TO GEORG WILHELM FRIEDRICH HEGEL

Jena, 26 January 1795

Your letter was a happy welcoming for me on my second arrival in Jena. At the end of December I had departed for Weimar together with Frau von Kalb and my pupil after spending 2 months with him here on my own, and did not imagine myself I might be back again so soon. The many and various miseries I was exposed to in the business of tutoring—which were due to the particular circumstances surrounding my pupil—my weakened health and the need, which was only increased by my stay here, to concentrate on myself for at least a certain period, induced me even before departing from Jena to set before Frau von Kalb my desire to leave her employment. I was persuaded by her and Schiller to have one more try but couldn't keep it up for more than a fortnight, in part because it cost me almost all my rest at night, and so I went back to Jena with perfect peace of mind to an independence that, really, I am enjoying for the first time in my life and that I hope will bear some fruit. My work is now almost entirely directed at reshaping the raw materials of my novel. The fragment in the *Thalia* is one of these rough-hewn blocks. I expect to have it finished by Easter, prefer to keep quiet about it till then. I've sent a reworked version of "The Genius of Boldness," which you will perhaps remember, in to the *Thalia*, together with a few other poems. Schiller does a lot for me and has encouraged me to write for his new journal, the *Horae*, as well as his planned *Muses' Almanac*.

I have spoken to Goethe, dear friend! It is the finest pleasure in life to find so much humanity with so much greatness. He talked with me so gently and amiably that I can really say my heart laughed, and laughs still when I think of it. Herder was also very warm toward me, took me by the hand, but was a bit more the man of the world; he often spoke every bit as allegorically as you also, knowing him, would expect him to. I shall probably see them again from time to time. Major and Frau von Kalb are likely to stay in Weimar (which is also why the boy no longer needed me, enabling my earlier departure) and the friendship between us, especially with Frau von Kalb, will mean I can visit them fairly often.

Fichte's speculative pages—*Foundations of a Total Theory of Knowledge*—and also his published *Lectures on the Vocation of the Scholar* will interest you greatly. At first I heavily suspected him of dogmatism. He really does seem, that would be my conjecture, to have stood, still stands, at a parting of the ways—he seeks to get beyond the fact of consciousness *theoretically*, a great many of his remarks show that, and this is just as certainly transcendent, and even more strikingly so, as when the metaphysicians we've had up till now have wanted to get beyond the existence of the world—his absolute *I* (= Spinoza's substance) contains all reality; it is everything, & outside it there is nothing; therefore for this absolute *I* there is no object, for otherwise all reality would not be in it; but a consciousness without an object is not conceivable, and if I myself am this object then as such I am necessarily limited, even if only in time, and therefore not absolute; therefore no consciousness is conceivable in the absolute *I*, as an absolute *I* I have no consciousness, and in so far as I have no consciousness I am (for myself) nothing, therefore the absolute *I* is (for me) nothing.

These are the thoughts I wrote down while still in Waltershausen, when I read the first parts, immediately after reading Spinoza; Fichte confirms my

[*page torn off*]

His examination of the reciprocal determination of the *I* and the *Not-I* (in his language) is certainly curious; also the idea of striving etc. I must break off, and must ask you to regard all that as as good as not written. That you're getting to grips with the concepts of religion is certainly good and important in many respects. The concept of providence I imagine you're dealing with in exact parallel to Kant's teleology; the way in which he connects the mechanism of nature (and so also of destiny) with its purposiveness really seems to me to contain the whole spirit of his system. Of course it is the way he solves all antinomies. In regard of the antinomies Fichte has a very curious thought, but I'd prefer to write to you about it on another occasion. For a long time now I've been thinking about the ideal education of the people, and because you are in the middle of dealing with a part of that, religion, perhaps I'll choose your image and your friendship as the conductor of my thoughts into the outer world of the senses and write *in good time* what I would perhaps have written later in letters to you which you can judge and correct.

[*page torn*]

FROM CHRISTIAN LUDWIG NEUFFER

Stuttgart, 26 January 1795

I have read your *Hyperion* in the *Thalia*. Dear Hölderlin! It was as if I had you standing before me. I found you entire in your work, in your feelings and maxims.

FROM CHRISTIAN LUDWIG NEUFFER

Stuttgart, 5 February 1795

A few days ago I was at Consistorial Councilor Griesinger's. He told me Schiller had been put forward for a Chair in Literature at Tübingen, with favorable terms and conditions. Abel in Tübingen had written to him with the proposal. If he were to accept the offer and his health permitted him to give lectures, the matter was settled. [*He has, as H. had asked him to, informed his mother of his change in situation and received the assurance that she would support H. as far as it lay in her power.*]

FROM HIS BROTHER

Nürtingen, 6 February 1795

That you enjoy the company of the great Schiller is enviable. [*Speaks also of the chair Schiller has been offered in Tübingen.*]

96. TO HIS MOTHER

Jena, 22 February 1795

Dearest Mother,

Accept the profoundest thanks of my heart for your rare and constant kindness. Your last letter gave me one of the loveliest hours of my life. Your heart, which will ever remain exemplary for me, is so unmistakably there in every line, and it will be the finest reward for me if one day I am able to delight this heart with fruits worthy of the care they have received. I can easily believe that the rash remarks in my letter before last must have been disagreeable to you. Forgive me, and put it down to my dejected state at the time. Believe me, dearest Mother, that in many respects it was all for the best that I didn't let myself be won over by Frau von Kalb, as almost happened, and stayed. Even the times we're going through, which made you wish that I had continued in my employment, are among the reasons that justify my change in circumstances. And for the moment my prospects could not be better. — — — Schiller has taken me under his wing, really like a father, so that recently I had to confess to the great man that I didn't know what I had done to deserve so much attention from him. He is editing a new journal, with other contributors among whom I could not *now* consider myself worthy to appear without the greatest presumption. He is being paid 5 louis d'or a sheet. Now the other day he asked me how things stood with my plans to stay here. I told him I had received a very kind letter from you that led me to hope I might well be able to stay until the autumn. Then he said to me: "We'll have to see how we can arrange for you to be as little burden on your family as possible," carried on talking in a general way and at last asked me whether I might not want to work up this and that for the *Horen* (his journal), *from 4 sheets I could comfortably live for six months.* Now all depends on whether I manage to submit something good enough, but if I do I'd have a decent income by the end of the next half year, perhaps even sooner. The book I've been working on so far is advancing well. That he might accept that would admittedly be too much to hope for. It's doubtful as it's growing into 2 volumes and he won't want to take a fragment, and also since he can't very well take the whole thing because in his last journal, where he was not so exacting, a fragment of it already appeared, and so a part of the work would have to be served up by him a second time. At his request I will in fact let him have the work, of which the first volume will be finished after Easter. In the meantime I've had a friend inquire with a publisher as to the terms on which he'd be inclined to take on the manuscript. I made it a condition that I should be paid on receipt of the manuscript and not when the book was published, for otherwise I should only get the money by the end of the next half year. I expect an answer soon. I would also be inclined to take a new house tutoring position with Counselor Brun in Copenhagen that would allow me to make a journey to Italy and Switzerland, if, while my name is being put forward here, someone else has not got in ahead of me and you, dearest Mother, have no objection. In any case I assure you that any good position as a tutor that comes up I will never turn down. The hopes that may perhaps come to fulfillment in Jena will not be spoilt by a temporary absence. And anyway these hopes are not something I have set my heart on as much as all that. It would also do me good to be able to return to my homeland, to a post that was not unsuited to my nature.—O my Mother, you ask whether I am fond of you, if only you could look into my heart! I am certain that this profound attachment to you will last for as long as I love what is good. Many are the evenings, when I'm resting from my work, that I fondly think to myself: if only you were sitting round the table now with your family! The pleasure of seeing you all again!—You ask how far Nuremberg might be from Jena, and Jena from Waltershausen and from Weimar. Jena is about sixty hours away from Nuremberg, thirty from Waltershausen, and it's four hours to Weimar. Next week I mean to make the journey there on foot if nothing gets in the way. For the time being the weather has prevented me. I am now, thank God, in better health than I've been for a long time. I always wrapped myself up well during the cold, so as not to use so much wood. It's rather expensive here, and mostly fir. These are fine-weather days. My savings should last until well after Easter. If by then I've had nothing from the bookseller I'd ask you, dearest Mother, if it's not too much trouble, to send me seven to ten carolins. At the same time I give you my word of honor that after that I won't rob you of a penny more; that come what may, because I consider it my duty, I won't take the money without the assurance that I regard it as *a part of what I shall receive from you one day*; I can also assure you that I'll let you know as soon as I can expect to obtain money from the bookseller after Easter, which will mean that for a good while I won't be obliged to bother you; and that I should not have asked for so much if I didn't have a small debt still to settle in Meiningen.

I know of a really good opportunity for you to send me the money without paying carriage. I'll write to you about that next time. Write to me too again soon, dearest Mother. It is always a feast day for me when I receive a letter from you. I thank dear Karl a thousand times for his New Year wishes. If he could just add a line or two to your letters from time to time I'd like that very much. And the next time you write say something in particular about my dear Rike. Do you think she is as fond of me as she used to be? Is dear Grandmother staying with you much longer? I very much hope so. A thousand remembrances to you and all the dear ones, also to my friends in Nürtingen.—Kammerer from Sundelfingen lives opposite me. We sometimes sit for an hour together of an evening.—The little thing I wrote in Schiller's *Thalia* often earns me a friendly greeting or a courteous invitation. I'm always pleased when someone quite unknown to me asks my name and begs the wordsmith to come for coffee, which I then enjoy to the full. Don't take this for immodesty, dearest Mother!

It's just a way of saying that things are going well with me. All the same, I can't give up my secluded life and don't want to either. That's enough chitchat for now. Goodbye! Keep me always kindly in your thoughts, dearest Mother. Ever

your

grateful son

Hölderlin

[*Encloses a letter for his mother from Frau von Kalb.*]

FROM HIS SISTER

Blaubeuren, 1 March 1795

[*Describes the personality of her one-and-a-half-year-old daughter.*]
She often gazes at your dear portrait, and encourages anyone else who is in the room to do the same.

97. TO HIS MOTHER

Jena, 12 March 1795

I'm going to be hard put, dearest Mother, to keep my letter as short as I fear I am obliged to; but it would be just as difficult for me not to reply to your dear, good letter at once, however little time I have left to do it. You are worried about me, beloved Mother, and I have only one concern, which is to sweeten your days, as truly as you and your kindness are unique in this world. The foremost of my desires is to repay this kindness; will I ever be able to? From now on, I have solemnly sworn never to tire in my progress toward all that is purely good and true, and in this progress there is one help of which I am sure. You know it. It is my firm and earnest belief, as it is yours: the father of spirits and nature denies no honest labor his aid. If we strain and strive for what a divine instinct in the depths of our heart is pushing us toward, then anything can be ours! Even the resistance we meet is an instrument of eternal wisdom, to give us solidity and strength in what is good.—I am living very quietly, exactly as I wish. A visit to Schiller's, who never fails to heap me with friendship and the kindness of a father, gives me more pleasure and fortification than any other company. He has written to Cotta in Tübingen on my behalf to inquire whether he would publish my little book, and I expect an answer any day. I am also perfectly content with the other aspects of my way of life. I'm finding that one can be very happy in constricted circumstances. And I can assure you, dearest Mother, that in my work I always make sure to keep plenty of energy and good spirits over for the next day. Nor is the thought of establishing myself here something I'm pursuing to the exclusion of all else. Believe me, it would cost me a great struggle if I were to choose a situation that would oblige me to pass a large part of my future life without your company, dearest Mother, far from all the rest of my dear family. And after all we live, as my Karl wrote, not to shine, we live to do good.—How glad I was to get the letters! My brother is a noble man. O my Mother! if you had only this pure-intentioned enterprising youth for a son, you would be richer than thousands of others. What a joy it will be for my heart to see him again! I must write him a proper letter. I've owed him one for a long time. You will allow me to address my next to him. I want to write to dear Rike too. Today was one of the best days I've had, when I received all your lovely letters! My sister had my own interests at heart when she counseled me to stick to my dear homeland. And I don't think I'll stay away for ever.—Whether Schiller has accepted the offer or not I don't know myself. He didn't pronounce on it clearly and I couldn't very well ask him straight out. But I think it likely that he'll stay here because he has just rented a new house.—If I am to accept a tutoring position it will have to be a very good one. Niethammer has also, since his arrival in Jena, been a house tutor for a while in Gotha, and he was received all the more warmly on his return.

Take care of yourself, best of mothers! A thousand greetings and remembrances to all! Ever

your

obedient son

Friz

98. TO HIS BROTHER

Jena, 13 April 1795

I have owed you a letter for a long time now, dear brother. But the joy
you gave me with the full and varied utterances of your pure kindred
heart can never be repaid in words. Altogether I do not know what I
have done to deserve the love I receive from you all.

The kindness of our dear mother puts me so endlessly to shame.
Even if she was not my mother, and if it was not I that experienced
this kindness, I would still be infinitely glad that a soul like hers exists
on earth. Oh Karl, how much easier our responsibility is made us. We
would have to lack feeling hearts for the sympathy of a mother like her
not to give us infinite sustenance in our intellectual development.—I
think you are on the right path, dear brother. Your heart is full of the
unselfish sense of duty, your mind unfolds this sense with the help of
other noble minds whose writings are your companions, the feeling
of your heart is becoming an unerring principle, clarified by your
thinking, which does not kill it—thought secures it and makes it firm.
On this concept of duty, i.e., on the principle: a human being should
always act in such a way that the conviction that forms the basis of
his action could be a valid law for everyone, and he should act in this
way solely because he ought to, because it is the sacred unalterable law
of his being (as everyone can ascertain by checking with unbiased eye
his conscience, the feeling of the law that manifests itself with each
individual action)—on this sacred moral law then you ground the
judgment of your rights. To approach ever closer to this sacred law
is your final purpose, the aim of all your striving, and you have this
aim in common with all that can be called human. Now whatever is
necessary as a means to this supreme end, whatever is indispensable for
your never completed process of moral perfection, all that you have a
right to. And here of course the most indispensable thing of all is free
will (How could we do a good thing without wanting to? Whatever
occurs by compulsion is not the action of a good will and thus not
good in the proper sense, useful perhaps, but not good, legal perhaps,
but not moral). And so not one of your energies may be restricted in
a way that would make it at all unfit for your purpose, and the same
goes for the products of your energies, and each time you resist such
a restriction of your energies or their products you assert a right,

whether in words or in deeds. Naturally therefore, every human being has *in this sense* equal rights; we cannot dispute the entitlement of anyone, as long as he is a human being, to use his energies or their products if it would prevent him from coming nearer to his aim of the greatest possible moral perfection. —

But since this aim is impossible in this world, since it cannot be attained within time and we can only approach it in infinite progression, we have need of a belief in an *infinite* extent of time because the *infinite* progress in good is an uncontestable requirement of our law; but this infinite extent of time is inconceivable without faith in a Lord of nature whose will is the same as the command of the moral law within us, and who must therefore want us to endure infinitely because he wants us to make infinite progress in good and, as the Lord of nature, also has the power to realize that which he wants. Of course this is to speak of him in human terms, for the will and the act of the infinite being are one. And so the sacred law within us is the basis for the rational belief in God and immortality, and also, in so far as they are not dependent on us, in the wise governing of our destinies. Just as certainly as the supreme aim is the greatest possible moral perfection, just as we must needs take this purpose for the supreme one, equally we need to have faith that when our capacity of will is exceeded, whatever course things take they still work toward that supreme purpose, i.e., that they are bound into this purpose by a wise and holy being whose power goes beyond ours. I see that there is a lot more I could say, but I'll break off here because I should also like to convey to you, as far as can be done in a few words, a chief characteristic of Fichte's philosophy. "There is in human beings a striving toward the infinite, an activity which refuses to let any limit become permanent and makes stasis a sheer impossibility, always endeavoring to go beyond itself, to become more free and independent—this activity, which according to its drive is infinite, is limited. This activity, *according to its drive* infinite and *without limits*, is necessary to the nature of a conscious being (of an *I*, as Fichte puts it), but the *limitation* of this activity is also necessary to a conscious being, for if this activity had no limits, nothing in which it fell short, it would be everything, and outside it there would be nothing; if therefore our activity did not come up against any resistance from without there would be nothing outside ourselves, we would have no knowledge of anything, we would

have no consciousness. If nothing was *against* us, there would be
no objects for us. But however necessary limitation, resistance and
the suffering brought about by resistance are for consciousness, the
striving toward the infinite, an activity that according to its instinct is
boundless, is equally necessary in the conscious being, for if we did not
strive to be infinite, free of all limits, we would not feel that something
is set against this striving and so in turn we would not feel anything
different from ourselves, we would have no knowledge of anything, we
would have no consciousness."—I have expressed myself as clearly as I
could in the brief space available. At the beginning of the winter, before
I had worked my way into it, the whole thing sometimes gave me a bit
of a headache, especially as my study of Kant's philosophy had given
me the habit of testing everything before accepting it.—Niethammer
has also asked me to contribute to his *Philosophical Journal* and so
I've got a good bit of work ahead of me this summer. Schiller has got
Cotta in Tübingen to take on the little work of mine I have mentioned
before. How much he will pay me is, according to Schiller's wishes, to
be decided when Cotta comes over here, which is due to happen in
about a fortnight. I hope not to have to be such a trouble to our dear
mother in future. I thank her for what she has sent with my whole
heart. I shall never forget that in my present situation I was given so
much kind support.

Schiller is likely to stay here. I'll probably present myself
for examination here in the autumn if I stay. Only if I fulfill that
requirement will I be permitted to hold lectures. I am not concerned
about the title of professor, and very few professors here receive any
salary worth the name. Many have none at all.—I have a bit more to
relate about a little journey I made—I badly needed to stretch my legs
after the constant sitting during the winter and happened to have a
few French thalers spare. But I'll save it for a letter to dear Rike.—I'll
be very happy to have the fine waistcoat promised me. Perhaps though
dear mother will not be offended if I confess I still have some unused
cloth for a waistcoat in my trunk (a present I brought with me from
Waltershausen). On the other hand I'm in great need of a pair of
trousers. That was rather indiscreet of me, Karl, wasn't it? I shall have
to write to dear Rike next Wednesday, there's not time enough today.

Goodbye, all my love to everyone.

99. TO HIS SISTER

Jena, 20 April 1795

Dear sister,

Thank you so much for your sympathy, for continuing to keep me in your thoughts. You will have no trouble in believing that, being far away, one misses a great deal if, as in my case, home has been made so indispensable by so much love and kindness. And I could hardly bring myself to stay away for so long without the compensation of receiving a greeting or a letter from time to time. That aside, I am very well and I think my sojourn here will certainly not be without benefit. It would be my own fault if it had no purpose for me.—Over the winter I got a bit weary of sitting inside, I thought it necessary to revive my strength somewhat again and I managed to do so by going a little journey on foot that took me to Halle, Dessau and Leipzig. With a few thalers and a pair of good strong legs you couldn't possibly do more than I found on this trip. It's true that the region is completely flat, mostly sandy and compared to our home country pretty infertile. But it had its points of interest nonetheless: the battle-field at Roßbach that I passed on my way to Halle, and the one at Lüzen where the great Gustavus Adolphus fell—it was an odd feeling to stand by the pitiful stone that is meant to honor him!—& the area round Dessau has been greatly improved by the tasteful parks the Prince has laid out everywhere.

In Halle the orphanage and educational institute was the most remarkable thing. The simplicity of the exterior gave me great pleasure. As to the spirit in which the education is administered there I can only judge by what I saw with my own eyes, when I was present at a public examination of the orphans and other pupils.

There reigned entirely the petty, antic, pedantic and yet childish manner of the pedagogues who carried on their noise for quite a while. It is admittedly hard to find the words to handle and instruct a child in ways worthy of humanity and likely to make a noble manly spirit out of him and not an egoistical, bland, work-shy weakling, that is, employing pure concepts and strict but fair demands while not forgetting that one is dealing with a child. But it really is too bad to be childish in the essentials and pedantic in the nonessentials, to present petty concepts in such a way that the child doesn't understand a word amidst all the solemn bombast, and to deliver themselves of their wretched demands as if the salvation of the world hung on them.

The first thing I did in Dessau was to visit the new churchyard. There is really a good deal of humanity and beauty in the idea that has been realized there. The fine portal immediately gave me unusual pleasure, with the figure of Hope up on the cupola—touchingly well-executed almost throughout—leaning on her anchor, and on either side of the entrance two youths with extinguished torches standing in niches. Then one proceeds via an avenue that passes between the graves standing among flowers and bushes, and round the wall are freshly dug graves with those already harboring someone sealed with white marble slabs whose simple heartfelt inscriptions are mostly very different from our Gothic gravestones. The building that is now the main school in Dessau was of interest to me because the Prince had it fitted out for this purpose and his son lives next door in a house that seems very humble next to the palace. The town is lovely.

The gardens of the Luisium & Wörlitz where I spent a splendid day I'll describe to you another time because I have according to my bad old habit begun this letter too late.

In Leipzig I made the interesting acquaintance of Prof. Heydenreich and of the bookseller Göschen. I was received very well by both of them; and in general there is nothing to compare with the fine manners of Leipzig people from what I've seen so far.

I did the whole journey in 7 days and can now feel that it did my health a power of good.

I'd happily have swapped it for a visit to see you, dear Rike! And my esteemed brother-in-law to whom I present my compliments and will soon be writing an endlessly long metaphysical letter. I'm sure you would have let me have the pleasure of being with you and your dear guests over Easter. A thousand greetings to our beloved mother! If only I could be worthy of all the kindness she never fails to show me; everywhere that I am still known, send my remembrances. Give Demoiselle Fehleisen my hearty thanks for her kind greeting.—I hope your dear little ones are thriving. Goodbye, dear sister! This letter doesn't count. This summer I'll be sure to write more often and God willing we'll see one another in the autumn for a few days at least; I have convinced myself that I can go a long way on very little.

Yours

Friz

I have changed lodgings and am living in a very pleasant summerhouse overlooking the town. But write to me   at Schilling's,   by the bridge gate.

100. TO CHRISTIAN LUDWIG NEUFFER

Jena, 28 April 1795

Dear Neuffer,

I'd been hoping to find a good moment in which to impart myself to you once again entirely, together with all the little occurrences that keep me in motion. But really I think I'll have to reserve that pleasure for the day we see one another again. And I'd have written earlier if I hadn't broken the happy monotony of my life by going on a pleasant journey. In the latter part of the winter I was slightly unwell due to lack of exercise, perhaps also because I was not yet quite strong enough for the diet of nectar and ambrosia to be found in Jena; I remedied this by doing a walk via Halle to Dessau, and from there back via Leipzig. I'm not the one to bother you with travel descriptions, I never really had any patience for that genre, probably because I have no gift for it, I'm mostly content with the total impression and even when something does strike me I prefer not to risk a verdict on it in passing. People of my sort especially, who every day God sends see through a different pair of glasses (come from who knows where), are not to be trusted. I had a good time with Heydenreich and Göschen. Heydenreich seems to be a refined and clever man, with all the experience in the world. Göschen, who has a rare cultivation of understanding and taste for someone in his position, has managed to preserve an even rarer warmth and naturalness.

Now I'm enjoying the spring. I'm living in a house in a garden, on a hill above the town from where I can survey the whole of the splendid Saale valley. It resembles our Neckar valley in Tübingen except that the Jena hills are grander and stranger. I hardly ever come out and see people. I still go to Schiller's, where more often than not I meet Goethe now, who has been staying here for quite some time. Schiller sends his regards and asks for some poems for his almanac. He says you can just send them to me. I'm absolutely delighted you're more yourself again, your last letter put the one before quite to shame; the pleasure you got from what Heyne said I feel as if it were my own—we'll stubbornly persevere, won't we, dear Neuffer, we'll not let ourselves be driven off the path our natures singled out for us by any adversity in the world. I understand now that you like translating so much. Schiller has got me to translate Ovid's Phaethon into stanzas for his almanac, and I've never got up from any other piece of work in such good spirits. There is less passion involved than in a production of one's own, and yet the music of the versification occupies the whole person, not to speak of the other attractions such work has.—Cotta in Tübingen has paid me 100 fl. for the first volume of my novel. I didn't like to ask more, so as not to appear to be acting the Jew. Schiller found the publisher for me. Don't be scandalized by my little book. I'm writing it to the end because I've begun it and it's better than nothing at all, and comfort myself with the hope that I'll soon save my credit with something else.

This summer at least I'll be living in total peace and independence. But the way people are, they always lack something, and what I miss—is you, and perhaps someone like your Röschen. It's curious—probably I'll never fall in love except in my dreams. Hasn't that been my case so far? And since I've had eyes to see with I don't fall in love at all any more. It's not that I want to renounce my past acquaintances—and by the way, you were going to write to me one day about Miss Lebret: why don't you?—But compare that to your love with its joys and pains and pity me! Is your sweet good girl quite well again now? You must spend heavenly days together. In the end it's the only thing there is in the way of happiness on earth, the happiness of loving in mutual respect, having put one another to the test. I think you will find me purer and more understanding when once again we're together and you talk to me into the night again about your Röschen.

God preserve the two of you as you are!—How are you otherwise, dear Neuffer? We don't go into enough detail in what we tell each other about ourselves. But I think that's the way it always is with letter writing. Next autumn I'm coming for sure, even if it's only for a few days. I need to warm myself again with you and my dear family.—Dear brother, I had all kinds of things to write to you, but I've got into a tone I'm going to find it hard to get out of for today. All I'd do is repeat myself, and perhaps get a bit too sentimental. More soon!

Yours,

Hölderlin

101. TO CHRISTIAN LUDWIG NEUFFER

Jena, 8 May 1795

I will try and see, poor dear brother, whether I can pull myself together in my pain sufficiently to spare you in yours. I confess, it overwhelms me too, and I do not know what to say to you when I see in my mind's eye the noble irreplaceable being who lived for you and have to say to myself: this is death! O my friend, I cannot comprehend this nameless thing that delights us for a while and then rends our heart, my thoughts fail at the way things pass, where our heart, the best thing we have, the only one still worth listening to, begs for survival in the midst of all its pain—may the God I prayed to as a child forgive me for it: I cannot conceive of death in his world!—Neuffer, you should be sacrosanct in your grief, the sorry confusion I find myself in about everything, which the pain of what has happened to you has brought home to me for the first time or—I myself don't know which it is—perhaps brought about, I ought not to mention this confusion to you. I am a miserable consoler. I grope around in the world like a blind man and should be showing my brother a light in his suffering, to gladden him in his darkness. Your beloved had a better lesson to give you, didn't she, dear friend? You will find her again, will you not? Oh, what if we were only here to dream awhile and then to become the dream of another—don't hate me for these wretched words, you have always remained true to nature, your pure, untroubled mind will

give you comfort, the sacred girl will not be lost to you, and that you
no longer hear the dear words in which her noble spirit revealed itself
to you, and that she no longer stands before you in her unchanging
loveliness—brother, can your heart bear the words of comfort with
which I would so gladly soothe my own—her spirit will greet you
in every virtue, every truth, you will recognize her in every instance
of grandeur and beauty with which, despite all, the world delights us
from time to time. How weak I must seem to you. I look at your letter
again, which will for ever be sacred to me, and I find you telling me
that she will accompany you your whole life long, that her constant
presence will keep you in the elevation and purity in which you always
have lived with her—how glad I am the dear blessed girl will have this
eternal springtime at her grave, the springtime of your heart! For it is
my hope for you and the blessings that her memory will recompense
you with: the best part of your heart will never age; every day you will
be able to look forward to having become more worthy of her and
more like her.

The love between you was unique, a wonder in the present
heartless and diminished world. Is it not a love for eternity? Believe
me, my beloved friend, in the future you will sometimes say, when
I feel keenly all you are to me and tell you that only you can make
me forget the meagerness of life, you will say to me then: I have her
to thank for it, she helped me up out of the indifference life bestows,
in her more appeared to me than most people even believe possible,
more than thousands of people can be, she gave me belief in myself,
she went before me in life and in death, and I struggle my way after
her through the night.—Dear brother, I am by your side, I follow the
same path, I share your pain and want also to share its fruits; you
are right, our life must be a melody over her grave, a better melody
than anything our poor lyres can give her.—The wonder of it! My
pain was truly inexpressible, I had nothing but tears and had to do a
violence to myself even to write you these few poor words, and the
best consolation came from your letter again—if only mine could be
of some help to you! Oh if only we could be more to one another in
general! Being far from you now increases the pain threefold. I wrote
to you recently that I wanted to come in the autumn. If possible I'll
come sooner. If you were here there would be no reason not to stay.
But as it is I'll never manage it. The two of us now wander about the
world so depleted, neither of us has anything but what we are to one

another, except for the possibility of a better world in and above us, dear Neuffer, and we are supposed to live in this way, only half for one another? I'll come soon, and you can take me to her grave. Dear God, I didn't think to see you again in such conditions.—Couldn't you come and fetch me, dear brother, or visit me even earlier? It would definitely do you good. You would find friends everywhere here. Do it, if it's at all possible. I'll write to you when the post next goes. If you can bring yourself to, do the same yourself soon. Many here suffer with you and with me. We must suffer as she would have done in our place. Preserve yourself for the world and for me. Farewell, good and noble friend.

Yours,

H.

FROM HIS SISTER

Blaubeuren, 9 May 1795

We missed you, dear brother, and only your dear portrait that, as our good grandmother also judges, does fall some way short as a likeness, made up for it a little.

102. TO HIS MOTHER

Jena, 22 May 1795

Today I felt keenly, dearest Mother, that your kind letters have become something I cannot do without. I don't know whether the interval that has passed since I last saw your handwriting just seems so unusually long this time, or whether you have really left me waiting rather longer than normal; for a week now I've been trying to assuage my worries about whether you are in good health, or whether perhaps something in my last letter could have displeased you, with the hope that surely today a letter would arrive. But I hoped in vain. Forgive me, dearest Mother, for saying this. I know for certain now that I'll never take so long to reply to your dear letters as has often been the case. I take it as a just punishment.—Is it perhaps the journey to Blaubeuren that has prevented you from writing? If only that were the reason!

I've been living, since I last gave you news of myself, as I always have done since being here, content with my seclusion and occasionally cheerful when I have cause to think that something in my work has turned out well. But you soon find out how amateur you still are in many matters and it's good that you do, it keeps you engaged. And I'm healthier too than my way of life here would seem to make possible.

Now on to the main point!—This week a house tutoring job was offered me by a man from Frankfurt I was put in touch with by someone studying here who is just back from his holidays in those parts. The man from Frankfurt has been charged with finding a tutor by a Dutch merchant living in Offenbach, an hour from Frankfurt. He is full of praise for the merchant's home, writes that there are 4 sons to instruct and keep an eye on, the previous tutor got a thousand florins, the new one is not likely to receive less, all expenses are paid and I can count on considerate treatment. For the time being they just wanted to inquire whether I might be disposed to take the post in order then to agree the specific conditions afterward. Because the matter can in any case be gone back on and I had to give an answer yesterday, I've said yes for the moment and am waiting for more detail and above all for your decision. This summer I should be able to live here comfortably without being more of a burden to you than I am at present, Cotta in Tübingen is due to pay me 100 fl. by September for an insignificant manuscript of mine he has agreed to publish; but whether the same would be true for the following winter I am unable to say with any certainty because I cannot judge the success of my book. If a more favorable prospect than such a thousand-florin-tutoring post presents itself I'll be free to take it. Be so kind, dearest Mother, as to write to me about this soon without any consideration for what you may take to be my own inclinations. I can assure you that I simply desire to do what is most sensible. I have so often had occasion in the past to feel how salutary it was for me to follow your motherly advice. I shouldn't want to be without it now.—And no doubt you wouldn't take it amiss, dearest Mother, were I to make the journey via my homeland. It wouldn't be such a big detour. I'd walk 8 hours a day; would pace myself, as I have learned to do. The joy of seeing one another again would be worth a few days' travel. I've dreamt of your welcome a thousand times! One learns a great, great deal abroad, dearest Mother! One learns to respect one's homeland. I'm often like a child when I tell my friend about my home, how good it has always been there, my mother and grandmother—and my brother and sister. All my love to all the dear ones. Write soon. I always think the beginning of next week will bring me a letter from you. Perhaps when it comes it will already contain a hint of what you might think about this change in my situation.

Ever yours,

Friz

103. TO FRIEDRICH SCHILLER

Nürtingen near Stuttgart, 23 July 1795

I well knew I would not be able to remove myself from your proximity without doing my innermost self sensible harm. Now I feel it more keenly every day.

It is odd that one can thrive under the influence of a great mind even without its working on one through conversation, merely through its proximity, and that with every intervening mile one feels more deprived. Despite all the motives I had I would hardly have persuaded myself to go were it not precisely this proximity that in other respects had so often unsettled me. I was always tempted to see you, and the only effect of seeing you was to feel that I could be nothing to you. I can see that the pain I so often carried within me was the necessary atonement for my proud demands. Because I wanted to be so much to you I was forced to tell myself that I was nothing to you. But being only too well aware of what I wanted, I do not reproach myself for this in the slightest. If it had been vanity seeking its gratification in this way, begging a friendly glance from a great man recognized as such in order to use this undeserved gift as consolation for its own shortcomings, not caring much who the man was so long as he did the job of flattering its petty desires, if my heart had debased itself to such an insulting courtiership, then indeed I should hold myself in the deepest contempt. But I am glad to be able to say with absolute certainty that there were many happy hours when, in as far as I am able to measure it, I had a pure sense of the worth of the mind I admire so much, and that my striving to mean much to it was at bottom nothing but the just desire to approach in one's whole person the good, the beautiful and the true, whether it is unattainable or attainable; and if one is reluctant to rely entirely on oneself to judge in this matter, that is certainly human and natural.

It is odd that I have given you this apologia. But precisely because this attachment really is sacred to me I try to separate it in my consciousness from all that could degrade it by any apparent kinship, and why should I not write to you about it as it appears to me since after all it belongs to you? I'd just like to visit you once a month, and enrich myself for years. And what of you I brought with me I try to use thriftily and profitably. I am living very solitarily and think it does me good. I enclose some poems by my friend Neuffer. He will take the liberty of offering you another one he still wants to rework.

If you permit, I will also send a few more poems soon.

As for the enclosed it often depressed me that the first piece of work I have undertaken at your direct behest did not turn out better. With everlasting respect I remain

your admirer,

M. Hölderlin

104. TO JOHANN GOTTFRIED EBEL

Nürtingen, 2 September 1795

My esteemed friend,

You gave me great pleasure by writing to me so kindly. The good fortune of living among people who share with me my needs and convictions becomes a rarer thing with each day; all the more reason to thank the person who makes me believe he finds in me a part of his own being.

You are so kind as to inquire after the rest of my journey. For the most part it was very entertaining, for it was for the most part an echo of what you had communicated to me during the good hours we spent together.

I can tell you I have small hope of finding elsewhere days like those I look forward to spending in your company, and from no other possible situation do I expect the benefit for my inmost being that I would have to thank the rare people for that your friendship and my own willingness will perhaps bring me into contact with. So you can see that I had every reason to keep myself free all this time.—The cruel failure of my efforts would perhaps have determined me not to get involved with education again in a hurry, did I not believe that it is impermissible and inappropriate to trace everything back to oneself, & that in the world as it is private tutoring is more or less the only refuge where one can escape with one's hopes and efforts for the education of mankind. Such was the extent to which people and nature were against me in my previous situation!

You need not fear therefore, my dear friend, that I shall expect wonders of myself or of the child! I know too well how many special disadvantages attend every particular method of education, and how very often with me the execution lags behind the project, to expect wonders of myself. And I know too well that nature only evolves by stages and that it has distributed the degree and the content of its forces among all individuals, to expect wonders of the child.—I believe that the impatience with which one rushes to one's goal is the rock that often precisely the best people founder on. The same goes for education. It would be so nice to complete one's work of creation in six days; the child is often required to satisfy needs it doesn't yet have, and to listen to and grasp rational things before it has reason, and then, since they fail to reach their object by the proper course, this makes the teachers tyrannical and unjust, and makes teacher and pupil equally miserable.

I am certain that here as in everything justice is the first law to be followed and I am much inclined to think that here as in everything a thoroughgoing justness, consistent in the last detail, is also the most astute way to proceed.

On these grounds I would not demand rational behavior of my charge (rational in the strict sense) before he had reason, before he had arrived at a consciousness or a feeling of his higher and highest needs. But not to demand reason of him before he has it is not to demand *anything at all* from him until he has given me the right to consider him a rational being. For what I would *demand* of him I would only demand for the sake of *reason*, or however else one wants to call or represent the highest principle out of which a person should act. (For no doubt you will agree with me that it is only sensible, in demanding something of a child, to appeal to the principle of action not as it is represented in some philosophical system but as it can be represented to the child according to his years and his individual character.)

Rousseau is right: *la première et plus importante éducation est de rendre un enfant propre à être élevé.*

I must lead the child out of his state of innocent but limited instinct, out of the state of nature, onto the path where he moves toward civilization, I must waken his humanity, his higher needs, and only then place in his hands the means whereby he must seek to satisfy these higher needs, and once these higher needs are wakened in him I can and must *demand* of him that he keep these needs forever alive and that he forever strive to satisfy them. But Rousseau is wrong in patiently waiting for humanity to awaken in the child and in so doing contenting himself for the most part with a negative education, only fending off the bad impressions and not attending to good ones. Rousseau felt the injustice of those who wanted to expel the child from his paradise, from his happy animal state, if not with the flaming sword then with the cane, and ended up, if, that is, I understand him rightly, at the opposite extreme. If the child were surrounded by another world than the one we have at present, then Rousseau's method might be more adequate. This other better world is what I must surround the child with, not impose it on him; without all pretension, in the way nature meets him, I must conduct toward him those objects that are great and beautiful enough to awaken in him his higher needs, the striving for better, or if you like his reason. I believe that the history of better times can form this world for the child if it is dealt with *selectively* and *vividly,* as it is appropriate for the child in general and for the particular individual I have before me; an example might be Roman history in the lively detail of Livy and Plutarch. But I would never ask the child whether he had remembered what had been said, for the point is not history itself but its influence on the heart, and as soon as the child began to consider history as a memory exercise or as an intelligence test the intended effect would be lost.

As I say, I should not like to *demand* anything from my pupil at this stage, and yet it does seem necessary to give him some instruction that he might be less receptive to later on, and because of this I would have to solicit the drives that are already present and sufficient for this purpose, such as the drive to imitate and the drive to be curious etc. I can't think there are many children who don't wonder what may lie behind the next hill. So long as geography is not, as it usually is, reduced to something dead and papery; so long as the maps are enlivened with suitably adapted travel accounts, this subject can be communicated to the child, I believe, without demanding too much or imposing too many constraints. If the child can come to notice day by day that arithmetic is part and parcel of many useful activities he will very likely take pleasure in doing it, and I confess that I set great store by this element of teaching because as with mathematics in general it gives better than anything else an idea of strict order. To teach a child a language systematically will be very difficult if it is to occur before the child is even capable of working toward a freely chosen goal, given that constraints and unjustified demands cannot well be avoided in this case. Yet it is possible to become fairly familiar with a language through conversation. This would probably work best with French.—Constraint I would only use when the law of reason must always lay claim to it: if someone wanted to do illicit violence to himself or others.

I should not have troubled you with these remarks if I did not hold it necessary to acquaint you and your worthy friends above all else with my conception of this occupation. And yet for this purpose I have said far too little. Words so rarely give evidence of our intentions. But still let me say that I expect my interest in the children to be as pure and loyal as that shown by their own noble parents. I should also not be lacking in vigor and energy if only I might be granted a few hours each day to devote to the peaceful cultivation of my own personal needs. In this way, and in the company of the educated and accomplished people who would receive me in their home, I would maintain my strength and fortify my spirits for my pupils. —

Should you be looking for a tutor for the other family I would suggest a young scholar who is presently living in Switzerland and whom I can imagine so well in such a post that to my mind he would virtually be ideal. I suspect that he would be available.—Be so kind as to give my regards to your esteemed friends. With true respect,

Yours,

M. Fr. Hölderlin

105. TO FRIEDRICH SCHILLER

Nürtingen near Stuttgart, 4 September 1795

You will forgive me, estimable Court Counselor, for the lateness and inadequacy of the contributions you have allowed me to make. Illness and discontentment have prevented me from carrying out what I intended. Perhaps you will not be vexed if I send you this a little later. After all I belong to you—at least as a *res nullius*; and likewise the unripe fruits I offer.

Dissatisfaction with myself and my circumstances has driven me into the realm of the abstract. I am attempting to work out for myself the idea of an infinite progress in philosophy by showing that the unremitting demand that must be made of any system, the union of subject and object in an absolute I—or whatever one wants to call it—though possible aesthetically, in an act of intellectual intuition, is theoretically possible only through endless approximation, like the approximation of a square to a circle; and that in order to arrive at a system of thought immortality is just as necessary as it is for a system of action. In this way I believe I will be able to prove how far the skeptics are right, and how far they are not.

I often feel like an exile when I think back to the hours when you imparted yourself to me without ever becoming frustrated by the tarnished, uneven mirror that you often found it impossible to recognize your expression in.

I believe that it is the property of exceptional people to be able to give without receiving, to be able to "warm themselves on ice."

All too often I sense that there is nothing exceptional about me. I am rigid with cold in the winter that surrounds me. The sky above me is like iron, and I am like stone.

In October I will probably take up a post as private tutor in Frankfurt.

I could excuse my chitchat, perhaps, by saying that I consider it virtually a duty to give you some account of myself, but that would be to go against my heart. Almost the only pride, the only consolation I have is to be able to write to you and to tell you something of myself.

Ever your admirer,

Hölderlin

106. TO CHRISTIAN LUDWIG NEUFFER

[Nürtingen, October 1795]

You put me to shame, dear friend! I was expecting a reproach for my lethargy, for managing to write to you, as ever, so rarely, and found this proof of your sympathy, of your lively remembrance of me.

The situation you have told me about would be very welcome in more than one respect. The people I should live among, the occupations I should find there, would certainly be advantageous to me.

How far my pedagogical ideas and capacities will suffice for this post I cannot decide until I am acquainted with the detail of the education the young man is to enjoy.

Perhaps for the moment you could ask whether further arrangements could be put off until I have a response from Frankfurt to the inquiry I have had to make there. That I am obliged to do this you'll see from the enclosed letter.

I'll do my best to give firmer news as to how things stand as soon as I can. I must confess that I should be very reluctant to renounce this fine prospect.

The relationship that led me to turn down the offer that was made to me this summer in Stuttgart, this bizarre relationship you know well, would I think not trouble me this time. The last letter I sent to Tübingen, which was certainly honest and truthful in every respect, has not yet received a reply, and I wrote it several days before my departure for the Unterland. How good that would be if a kind god freed my heart!

How are things with you, dear friend? In my own quiet I often wish you the calm and ability to work you need to thrive.

Have you read Schiller's poem in the *Horen*? Tell me how you judge it in general. Don't spare me. The intoxication in which I spoke of it was not yet a proper judgment. That seems to me to be precisely the role of taste, to investigate in retrospect the involuntary sensation one experiences before a piece of art and confirm it or, finding it fortuitous, reject it.

With my speculative *pro* and *contra* I think I'm getting ever closer to my goal.

I have made as good use as possible of my happy unbusy life.—We are like young colts. When we set out together we flew on wings or thought we did and now at times it's almost necessary to use spurs and the whip. It's true that for fodder we don't get much more than straw.—But let's keep our spirits up and hope for the best.

Goodbye, dear Neuffer! Write again soon. May I ask you to send my compliments to Prof. Ströhlin?

Yours

Hölderlin

107. TO JOHANN GOTTFRIED EBEL

[Nürtingen,] 9 November 1795

My esteemed friend,

I have put off writing to you from one week to the next. If I wanted to write the truth, I was obliged to tell you about the difficult situation I find myself in, and that could not very well happen without a touch of indiscretion. As I am now driven by necessity I console myself with your kind request that I should let you know if I were forced to change my circumstances. You are probably unaware how much we Württemberg theologians are at the beck and call of our Consistory; among other things these gentlemen are also free to determine our place of residence. Because I am not at the moment employed in a public occupation, and particularly with the Christmas holidays getting closer, I can expect to be sent to work with a pastor any day if before then or at the latest immediately afterward I do not enter into some other legitimate engagement. Now it is true I have recently been offered another job as tutor in Stuttgart; but you yourself can judge how much self-denial it would cost me to relinquish the hopes you have entitled me to.

I admit that it is not without a certain resignation that I make this avowal to you. However great the temptation of soon being with you and your noble friends, or at least of being able to assure myself it will happen, it goes right against my way of thinking to show signs of impatience toward a friend who is quite rightly hesitating in his choice, and even more to seem to wish that he should renounce other more substantial considerations in my favor.

I heartily beseech you, dear friend, to believe what I say to you until you have the opportunity to convince yourself of it properly. If you can offer some comfort to me please do so as soon as you can!

I would also deeply regret not seeing my friend Sinclair. You will share my conviction that the precocious maturity of mind and even more the incorruptible purity of soul that inhabit this man are a rare find in this world.

It would be so good for me to find sustenance for my inner life again. It's not that the soil here at home is poor, but it is unploughed, and the piles of stones that weigh down on it prevent the sky from acting upon it, and so I mostly walk among thistles and daisies.

My best wishes to you! Give my regards to the noble household that will perhaps take me in.

If I don't see you soon, be so kind as to tell me more about your literary work and other things that engage you in heart and mind. Even if I can give you nothing in return but the proof that I have understood you, surely it won't have been in vain. You know that spirits must communicate with each other everywhere there is the slightest stirring of living breath, combine with everything that does not have to be expelled, so that out of this union, out of this invisible church militant the great child of time, the day of days may proceed that the man closest to my soul (an apostle whom his present imitators understand as little as they do themselves) calls *the coming of the Lord*. I'd better stop, otherwise I'll never stop at all.

Your sincere friend,

Hölderlin

Give my love to Sinclair if you happen to speak to him before the letter I have only half finished today reaches him in Homburg.

108. TO GEORG WILHELM FRIEDRICH HEGEL

Stuttgart, 25 November 1795

You do me an injustice, dear friend, if you put my silence down
to neglectfulness on my part. I am being held up by the people in
Frankfurt, because of the war, they say. I have waited from one week to
the next to give you definite news and even now have none, either as
regards your affairs or my own.

In any case it looks as if I shall have to do without you in
Frankfurt because the child is only 4 years old and you don't seem
much inclined to take on a burden like that.—You ask my advice about
the repetitorship? You intend to let yourself be determined by my
decision? Hegel, now you're doing yourself an injustice. First of all I
have no pretensions of that kind and am simply unfit for such a post,
as for any position where one has to deal with a variety of characters,
a variety of situations, and then alas I have quite particular reasons
due to my former foolishness in Tübingen. But for you it would be
something like a duty in that you could perform in Tübingen the role
of a waker of the dead. It is true that the Tübingen gravediggers would
do their utmost against you. When I think that your work might be
in vain then it really seems to me you would be betraying yourself
by taking on that wretched lot. But whether you would have a better
sphere of action where you are in Switzerland or at home in Swabia is
certainly a difficult question. Perhaps you could get a travel grant once
you were here, which would be no bad thing. If I don't find a suitable
private tutorship soon I'll become an egoist again, look for no official
occupation for the moment and take up going hungry.

Renz will probably become a repetitor from what I hear. The two
of you could have a fine time together. Just don't neglect your literary
occupations. I was thinking that a paraphrase of the Pauline epistles
according to your conceptions would be well worth undertaking.

More next time. I'd like our correspondence to come to an end,
for a while at least. If we cannot talk there's very little advantage in it
for you, at least in what I write.

Goodbye.

Yours,

Hölderlin

Fichte is in Jena again and this winter is lecturing on natural law. Sinclair is now in Homburg at his parents'. He sends his best wishes and holds you in high regard, as ever. Remember me to Mögling.

109. TO CHRISTIAN LUDWIG NEUFFER

[Nürtingen, early December 1795]

Dear friend,

I should very much have liked to write to you too when I addressed the letter I'd expressly promised Seits to your house. But I lacked the time. And I find myself as empty as a pot since being back here again, and prefer in that case to keep quiet. The uncertainty of my position, my loneliness and the thought that gradually I may be becoming a tiresome guest, oppresses me and so I can hardly make any use of my time.

And on top of that I am not yet quite well.

I don't know what I'll do if I don't receive a letter from Frankfurt by Sunday. For I doubt the gentlemen in Stuttgart will leave me in peace, and from what I gathered from you the position in Ströhlin's household is unlikely to come to anything.

If only I'd stayed where I was. It the stupidest thing I've ever done to come back home. Now I find there are hundreds of difficulties in going back to Jena; they could not touch me as long as I remained, now I'd have to hear all kinds of things if I were to return.

Have you been filing away at your poems in the meantime? I wish I had your patience. Never in my life have I been so *impatiens limae* as now. But if there's no one to speak to, if you only have your own eyes to hold your efforts up to, no wonder. In the end you get worn down. You don't feel what's good any more and you overlook what's bad.

I'm ashamed to be plaguing you with my discontent like this. But if I wanted to force myself to abstract from the poor individual I am, I'd write a dissertation and not a letter. That's the good and the bad thing about friendship, that one always acts as one is, that one feels the bad days twice over because one can speak of them, as also with the good days.

May I ask you to send me by return of post the cashmere, the sample for my suit, and also the paper I wrote the requirements of Herr Stähle down on and that I must have left on your table. Should the sample and the paper have been mislaid, be so kind as to try to get hold of the one from Landauer and the other from the tailor again.

Farewell!

If possible I'll send you the promised elegy in a few weeks. For now I've taken refuge in Kant again, as always when I'm fed up with myself.

Yours

Hölderlin

110. TO JOHANN GOTTFRIED EBEL

Nürtingen, 7 December 1795

My esteemed friend,

I gratefully accept your kind invitation. I hope to be able further to convince you and your worthy friends how much I appreciate that what I desired has been made possible.

I hope to be able to set off next week. I have been a little unwell recently, but still the signs are that it won't last more than another week at most.

It is very good of you to go to the trouble of looking for lodgings for me. Should it be possible to live somewhere near you, that would be a great pleasure, or perhaps I could win your company at table. Should you trouble yourself with this matter too, and perhaps make arrangements, I would ask that you attend only to the midday meal. If it is purely a matter of my own choice, I do not eat in the evenings.

Assure your friends in advance that they will notice enough dross, natural and unnatural, original and incidental, in me, flaws caused by many a bad situation, but that I have courage and strength of will enough to be improved, among other things by their example or displeasure. It was my firm intention, before I had any hope of being tried and tested in this way, to spell out everything that I am fighting against in me and that I would particularly fight against as a tutor, but it occurred to me on the other hand that to risk such a frank confession would look like trying to make one's vices into virtues and turning one's weakness into an advantage.

It is with reluctance that I break off so soon. But at the moment I am too distracted and pressed upon by other occupations to be able to talk to you peacefully any longer, and I will of course make up for it. Believe me, I know how lucky I am soon to be able to enrich myself in your company and that of your friends.

Goodbye for the time being. Assure your worthy friends of all that you can read in my soul.

Your true friend,

Hölderlin

Would you be so kind and send this letter to Sinclair?

111. TO CHRISTIAN LUDWIG NEUFFER

[Nürtingen, after 7 December 1795]

My dear Neuffer,

I'm leaving for Frankfurt next week. I did not myself think the parting would come so soon. Let's not say anything about that.

Now I am as bombarded and distracted with things to do as you.—Can I ask you to send me the slip of paper from the tailor this time. I must have the clothes by the end of the week and haven't yet been able to send him the lining material. Be so good as to ask him to go ahead and cut them out. I'm going to be in trouble otherwise. Ask Landauer to give him the cloth for the suit at once.

Landauer should also get me a fur coat. The measurements won't be needed for that, I assume. The shoes should be ready.

It's wretched to have to be writing such things to you now; I'll probably stop in Stuttgart for a day, and then we'll be able to talk heart to heart. Let me know which days the mail coach for Heilbronn goes.

Please don't be annoyed by these irritating little chores I'm giving you.
I must close.

Yours

Hölderlin

112. TO FRIEDRICH IMMANUEL NIETHAMMER

Löchgau, 22 December 1795

My esteemed friend,

There was always so much I should have wished to say to you and I
have never said any of it. I hoped to be able to write you many things
and have as yet written you nothing. But what you know without my
having to say or write it is how much I esteem the qualities of the man
who, as my teacher, only ever called himself my friend, and how much
pleasure it gives me that these qualities are day by day more generally
and more justly recognized.

Your kindness toward me lets me hope that the request I am
making to you will not be in vain.

My friend and cousin, Majer from Löchgau, finds it suits his
purposes better to switch from Tübingen, where he has spent a year at
the Stift, to the fortunes of Jena.

Your teaching, your sympathy would give him infinite security
and encouragement in his future development.

He will not be unreceptive to what you could be to him; he has
talent and his will to succeed will help him over even the thornier
parts of study.

Do not deny him the kind welcome many have already benefitted
from, and take as recompense my everlasting thanks and the success
that your support for him will bring. For if I know anything it is that
acts of the mind can never be repaid. I envy him your presence; I often
feel a homesickness for Jena.

I would gladly make up for my absence by writing to you
often—your kindness would give me every cause—but it is hard for

me to communicate when I have not yet got things straight in my own mind, at least to some degree, and so I am obliged to remain solitary against my will.

I am now on my way to a house tutoring job in Frankfurt (at the banker Gontard's) and if I can find enough quiet and time there perhaps I'll soon give myself the pleasure of being put right by you on certain things.

Schelling, as you will know, has rather abandoned his first convictions. He charged me this week to send you all his compliments.—

Everywhere, among all that know you, I encountered the respect that is due to you and great delight in your success, and I was urged to assure you of this whenever I could.

It is a great advantage for my cousin that it is just this respect that he already shares with me.

He is all the happier to be your pupil and to live in your company.

I am sorry to close, but I am in rather a hurry.

Yours truly,

M. Hölderlin

FRANKFURT, 1796–1798

113. TO HIS MOTHER

Frankfurt, 30 December 1795

Dearest Mother,

I cannot yet tell you anything about my situation here. Be content for the moment that I can reassure you of my safe arrival; I am in better health than when I left you, even if the journey was more arduous and lengthy this time than usual.

Only now do I feel the value of the happy peaceful days I spent in your company. Often in my thoughts I am still with you, and with my Karl—what I received from the hearts of my loved ones I cannot thank you for and cannot return, nor can I give it to myself and shall not find it anywhere else.

My Karl must bear his loneliness as I shall also bear mine. It is after all better to be on your own in the clerk's office than among the insignificant din of people who mean nothing to you.

Our cousin adapted very well to being away from home. He was mostly cheerful and calm, sensible too, took things one at a time, as I did. Last Tuesday, the day after our arrival, he set off. The parting was hard for both of us. My best wishes and hopes go with him.

I'll write later this week to my dear sister and to my Karl, and then I'll perhaps be able to say more about myself.

I could write every day from here. The post goes every day.

Make sure you tell me exactly how you are. Only be in good spirits, dearest Mother! Otherwise I'll reproach myself with the thought that if you were happier with me you would feel the unpleasantnesses of life less. If only your health would become robust again soon. I hope the journey to Blaubeuren will help with that.

Has Karl's future not been decided yet?

I'm greatly looking forward to hearing something directly from him very soon.

Now I must also, according to my promise, write to my uncle. You can imagine how avidly the good people will be waiting for news.

Look after yourself! I comfort myself with the thought that I can write again soon. It's cold comfort, it's true! I need to be of good courage and try to give it to myself as best I can. But I feel that I am no longer as strong as 2 years ago. In those days I still hoped to get something back from the world in return for the loss of those who are closer to my heart.

Be sure to look after yourself. Farewell, dear Karl!

Yours

Friz

My address for now is

to M. Hölderlin

in Frankfurt am Main.

to be handed in at the *City of Mainz.*

114. TO JOHANN FRIEDRICH LUDWIG MAJER

Frankfurt, 31 December 1795

Esteemed Uncle!

It gives me endless pleasure to be able to send you something in return for your kindness and your sympathy—good news; and I know what that will mean to you.

Despite the arduousness and slowness of the journey we arrived here last Monday happy and in good health.

I can inform you that my friend bore the bitter separation with a courage I admire in him because I know his nature and his love for his family, and because my own heart tells me how much he has lost.

The day after we arrived, in the morning, he set off again.

It was a sad hour for both of us. But I had the comfort that my friend, at least so far as it depends on him, would continue his journey as happily as he started it, *as something he in every respect wishes to do.* That we were among other things also thrifty with our money may be proved by saying that my dear cousin got this far with 2 carolins and a little bit more. In this way he removed any opportunity for me to be able to give him a proof of my readiness to help him out.

What also reassures me about his journey is that he left with the best of weather, in a closed mail coach and with only a single very well-mannered man, a Frankfurt artisan, for company, and so he should by now have arrived in Eisenach, from where he only has two more short days of travel. His utterances during the journey, in the moments when without a hint of constraint we opened ourselves to one another, the communication of his convictions and desires, confirmed me all the more in the glad hopes I already had in him before.

Of myself I cannot yet say anything definite. Today I am to be closer acquainted with the people I'll be living with.

Yesterday in the evening my future pupil visited me and for the moment I have every cause to believe that he will in no small measure make up for the sorry time that my former pupil gave me. Please be so kind as to inform my mother of this. I had already sealed my letter to her before the little fellow's visit.

A thousand greetings and remembrances to the whole beloved circle of my family, and in particular hope and comfort to the two venerable mothers in your household. Ever

your devoted

M. H.

115. TO HIS BROTHER

Frankfurt am Main, 11 January 1796

I cannot write to you now as I should wish, dear Karl. I should not like to leave it a day longer without giving news of my situation, and yet do not have a moment right now in which I could impart my innermost self to you without distraction. And of that, of me, in the true sense, you need no news for now; for in this regard nothing has changed and in the main, as I see it, nothing is likely to change; but round about me much *has* occurred, the newest thing being that I have now entered on my employment, that as far as I can judge, admittedly not yet firmly and irrevocably, I have the best of people for friends and, in the children of these people, pupils such as one would be unlikely to find again if one is looking for lack of inhibition, pure nature without crudeness, and that in all respects I have nothing to object to in this my employment and 400 fl. a year without anything to pay.

Some other time perhaps, I'll give you an account of some very interesting people I have met, particularly during my stay in Homburg with Sinclair who sends his compliments, of many pleasures, many remarks made to me, and in general of the various life I have led here so far.

I think of you in quiet moments, I feel that we are becoming closer and closer friends. Dear brother, friendship is a big word and contains a great deal in it.

What is our dear mother up to? I'm pleased at how well things have turned out because I think that it will help to put her in good spirits.—I'd really like to write to my dear sister too, but today I have not a moment more left. She mustn't think it a lack of fraternal love, which she will certainly always have found plenty of in me. I have quite a few letters to write over the coming days, and the one to my sister will be the first. Should any letters have arrived for me, or if they ever do, be so kind as to forward them to me as soon as possible. Be sure to send parcels unfranked.

I'm still living in the *City of Mainz*, an inn, because my room in Gontard's house has not yet quite been set in order. Address letters to me there.

Goodbye, dear brother! Let's stay true to one another.

Yours

Hölderlin

116. TO CHRISTIAN LUDWIG NEUFFER

Frankfurt am Main, 15 January 1796

Dear friend,

Without waiting until now I could not well have written to you without distraction and even now you will find signs of a lack of settledness, of the wavering divided attention, that inevitably comes from a situation like mine. I know very well it's high time I stopped letting myself be thrown by novelty in this way; but once again I have found that, careful as I am, the unknown very readily comes to mean more to me than it is really capable of, that at every new acquaintance I come away with some kind of illusion, that I never learn to understand people without sacrificing some golden childish intimations.

I know that I lose nothing in your eyes by making this humiliating confession.

For all that, do not think that my new situation is not such as to allow one to be more or less content with it.

I'm living, as far as I can tell, among very kind and really, relatively speaking, rare people; there could perhaps be more to them, without my having to take back what I've just said.

I'm sure you will understand me if I say that at a certain level our hearts must always remain poor. I shall probably get even more used to making do with little and to directing my heart to come closer to eternal beauty more by my own efforts and endeavors than by waiting for fate to give me something that resembles it. You are probably right with what you have loyally taught me more than once, that we shouldn't for this reason dismiss the pleasant and cheerful moments of life, that laughter too, though certainly not happiness of a high order, is good for us; but no doubt you also see that it cannot easily be learned; it is a natural gift, one that I certainly shouldn't reject if I had it.—

I needed, dear Neuffer, to let you know what was on my mind at the moment, and so you will not be cross that I haven't talked about anything else.

The conditions on which I entered into this arrangement are advantageous enough. I can live with complete independence, need to devote to my pupil, who with his pure and free lack of inhibition has already won my heart entirely, the mornings only, and receive 400 fl. a year without having to pay for anything.

I haven't yet been able to arrange anything definite for Seits. At least, Dr. Ebel has so far not answered my inquiries in a way that would decide for or against our friend's interests, which are also mine. Ebel intends, as he told me today, to write to Seits himself in the next few days. Good-bye.

Yours

Hölderlin

Greet all my friends for me. Counselor Jung sends his greetings.

117. TO HIS BROTHER

[Frankfurt,] 11 February 1796

Dear brother,

I thank you with all my heart for your brotherly interest—and also our dear mother's—in my fate. You saw how I was in bad times and had patience with me; I wish you could now share this happier period with me too.

And it was time for me to rejuvenate myself a little again; I should have become an old man before half my days were done. My being has now shed a few surplus pounds' weight at least and moves more freely and nimbly, as it seems to me.

Deus nobis haec otia fecit. You will let me enjoy it, dear Karl, and won't go and think that my new good fortune means my *old love* will rust. But good fortune is what you will call my situation when you see and hear about it for yourself, and that, at least as far as the cost of the journey and board and lodging in Frankfurt are concerned, I can bring about very soon and very easily.

I'll discuss further plans with you when I've had more of a chance to make inquiries in this regard. I was in Homburg again, at Sinklär's urgent request. He is probably going to join the court in Berlin to serve there as a diplomat and work his way up from the bottom, but considers this only as a not inexpedient preliminary to better days. He sends his warm greetings.

I feel sorry for you, dear Karl, that your in part really stupid situation inevitably puts you in bad moods. Lose yourself in ideas: that is admittedly advice easily given and not much comfort, but still it is certainly worthy of you and of me. Believe, my Karl, that I will do all I can for you, and remember that in these parts you have people who appreciate you. Don't let yourself be worn down.—I am now working exclusively on the philosophical letters the plan for which you know, so that I can send them to Prof. Niethammer who has reminded me of my promise and asked me for essays in the letter you sent on to me.

Is there any news about my novel? Hasn't Schiller sent me anything yet?

Be so kind as to send me my flute, safely packaged. It must still be in Nürtingen.

What is good old Fripon up to? The creature is peculiarly close to my heart, which comes from the fact that he cheered me at times when I was sorrowing over human beings. It is a truly comforting feeling to sense the affinity that connects us with the vastness and serenity of nature and to understand it as far as that is possible. In the summer I'll probably get down to some botany. I'll tell you another time about my educational tasks and their delights.

A thousand thanks to our dear Mother again for the kind maternal things she said. Write to me about her too, about her health and about her state of mind.

Yours

Friz

118. TO FRIEDRICH IMMANUEL NIETHAMMER

Frankfurt am Main, 24 February 1796

My esteemed friend,

I have put off writing to you from one day to the next. And I would probably have waited yet longer before writing the letter I owe you if you had not reminded me of my promise. You do this so gently that it puts me quite to shame. You inquire how I feel in my new situation and whether I will soon have the essays ready that I promised to write for you when still in Jena.

The new conditions in which I now live are the best possible. I have plenty of free time for my own work, and philosophy is once again almost my only occupation. I am busy with Kant and Reinhold and in this element hope to collect and strengthen my mind again that became distracted and weakened by fruitless efforts that you were witness to.

But the echoes of Jena still ring too powerfully within me, and memory still has too great a hold, for the present to have a healing effect on me. Various different lines are intertwined in my head and I am unable to untangle them. I am not yet collected enough for the kind of continuous, concentrated work required for the philosophical task I have set myself.

I miss having you to talk to. Even now you are still my philosophical mentor, and your advice to beware of abstractions is as precious to me today as it was before, when I let myself get caught up in them whenever I was at odds with myself. Philosophy is a tyrant, and I suffer its rule rather than submitting to it voluntarily.

In the philosophical letters I want to find the principle that will explain to my satisfaction the divisions in which we think and exist, but which is also capable of making the conflict disappear, the conflict between the subject and the object, between our selves and the world, and between reason and revelation,—theoretically, through intellectual intuition, without our practical reason having to intervene. To do this we need an aesthetic sense, and I shall call my philosophical letters *New Letters on the Aesthetic Education of Man*. And in them I will go on from philosophy to poetry and religion.

I saw Schelling before I left and he is glad to be collaborating on your journal and to have you introduce him to the academic world. We did not always agree in what we said to each other but we were at one in the opinion that new ideas can be presented most clearly in the form of letters. With his new convictions he has, as you will know, taken a better route, before going to the end of the one that was not so good. Let me know what you think of his most recent things.

Remember me to all who still have fond memories of me and maintain the friendship that has been so precious to me. It would be a fine reward for me soon to offer you fruits that I will be able to say your care and attention have helped to bring to maturity.

Yours,

Hölderlin

119. TO CHRISTIAN LUDWIG NEUFFER

Frankfurt, March 1796

Dear friend,

It doesn't surprise me that you haven't written for so long. I know how it goes: one wants to tell one's friend something that won't have to be taken back a week later, and yet the perpetual ebb and flow rocks us back and forth and what is true at one moment we can in all honesty no longer say of ourselves an hour later, and in the time the letter we wrote takes to arrive the sorrow we were complaining of has turned into joy, or the joy we were telling of has turned into sorrow, and so it is more or less with most of the utterances of our hearts and minds. The moments when we find something permanent in ourselves are so quickly destroyed, the permanent itself becomes a shadow and only returns to us, full of life again, in its own time, like spring and autumn. That at least is why I am reluctant to write.

You seek counsel for your heart from me, dear Neuffer! You must have foreseen that I wasn't the man to give it. If I were wise enough not to pay attention to the mighty voice of nature, I might be able to send you a precocious well-intentioned sermon; and if I were foolish enough to speak up for the heedless pull of the heart I might be doing you an even bigger favor. But I am, sadly or thankfully, neither of these things.

I have nothing to say to you other than what I've said before: if you find that the sweet creature is made for you, and only you, that is, she is, among all that loves, closest to your true self, then scorn all prudence and go for it in the sacred name of Nature, for which our human affairs, the trappings of the social world, have as little validity as our rules about properness and decency do for children.

If on the other hand it's merely a crutch for your abandoned heart, if it's merely the poverty of the life you have suffered from fate that causes you to place such great value on this person, if it is more a child of necessity, wrested from you by chance circumstances rather than a pure unadulterated expression of your inner being, then indeed I should mourn for you if despite this you were to risk *yourself*, the future flowers and fruits of your mind, your ever youthful and calm cheerfulness, the domestic joys that perhaps awaited you elsewhere, and perhaps a great deal else.

My dear old friend, don't let this muddle you! Remember that in these matters no one in the end has anything to say, and so that fundamentally I have not said anything either.

With me things are going as well as they possibly can. I live without a care, and the same is true of the gods themselves.

Schiller was not wrong not to take Phaethon, and it would have been even better if he hadn't pestered me with the stupid problem in the first place; but that he didn't take the poem to Nature was in my view not right. For all that, it doesn't signify much whether one poem more or less by us appears in Schiller's *Almanac*. In the end we become what we are meant to become, and so your misfortune will bother you no more than mine.

Be happy, dear Neuffer, and take it with due patience if great joy is mingled with great pain!—

For the news about Miss Lebret, much thanks; I should in any case have ill deserved it had she not thought well of me.

Yours

Hölderlin

120. TO HIS BROTHER

Frankfurt, March 1796

Things are still going well with me; I'm in good health and have no cares and that is all one needs, at least to carry out the day's work untroubled.

You say you want to occupy yourself with aesthetics. Don't you think that the *definition* of concepts must precede their *union*, and that for this reason the subordinate *parts* of knowledge, e.g., the theory of right (in the pure sense), moral philosophy etc. must be studied before approaching the *cacumina rerum*? Don't you think that in order to get to know the neediness of knowledge and so to sense something higher above it, one must first have perceived this neediness? It's true it is also possible to start from the top—to the extent that the pure ideal of all thought and action, unrepresentable and unattainable beauty, must be present to us everywhere, one has to—but it can only be recognized in all its completeness and clarity when one has found one's way through the labyrinth of knowledge and only then, having keenly missed one's homeland, arrived in the quiet land of beauty.
[But he just wants to give him something to reflect on. Not wishing to be thought an authority on this subject, he frankly confesses to not having thought it over fully as yet.

He had a visit from a member of the Breunlin family who was on his way to Wetzlar.]

121. TO JOHANN FRIEDRICH COTTA

Frankfurt, 15 May 1796

Your kind letter has decided me to take up *Hyperion* once more and to compress the whole thing into one volume; since I sent you the manuscript this desire had risen up in me more than once; the delay in printing it and what you said about the extent of the work were therefore by no means out of place; naturally now though I must also shorten the beginning, which you already have, to achieve proper proportions between the parts; and so I must ask you to send me back the manuscript as soon as possible because the draft that I had is partly lost. I'll be sure to send it back to you in a few weeks' time, and in about 2 months the rest will follow. The number of sheets will now of course necessarily go up by a considerable amount. But my arrangement with you was not reckoned according to sheets and in my present circumstances I can manage with the 100 guilders we agreed. If in recognition of the new labor you wanted to do something to please me and printed the book on writing paper and in a clean Roman font, I should be extremely grateful to you. I have the secure hope that the thing won't remain entirely on the shelf and that it may be well received by the public if the individual judgments I have heard about a fragment of the book that made its way into the *Thalia* are anything to go by. Be so kind as to deduct from the whole what I owe you for the parts of the Plutarch I have received as well as the carolin you gave me last summer and to send me this sum to the address you have in Nürtingen. I remain with the deepest respect

your devoted servant

M. Hölderlin

122. TO HIS BROTHER

Frankfurt, 2 June 1796

Dear brother,

Your last letter gave me endless joy. Goethe says somewhere: "Love and pleasure are the wings of great doings."—And so it is with truth: whoever loves it will find it. Whoever's heart rises above the anxious, selfish field of vision that is what most people grow up in and that, alas, we encounter again almost everywhere on the patch of earth that is vouchsafed us for our rest and peregrinations, whoever's feelings are not narrowly fenced in, his mind certainly won't be either in any real sense.

Your strivings and tusslings make your mind ever stronger and more nimble, dear Karl! You seem to me to be going more profoundly into things and taking more than just *one* direction.

For this is what true thoroughness is: complete cognizance of the parts, which we must ground and comprehend together as One, and, penetrating to the utmost point of knowledge, deep cognizance of what does the grounding and comprehending. Reason, we can say, *lays the ground*, and understanding *comprehends*. Reason lays the ground with its principles, the *laws* of *acting* and *thinking*, in so far as they are related purely to the *general* conflict in the human being, that is, to the *conflict between the striving for the absolute and the striving for limitation*. But reason's principles in turn are themselves grounded by reason, in that it relates them to the ideal, the highest ground of all; and the *Ought*, which is contained in the principles of reason, is in this way dependent on (ideal) being. Now if the principles of reason, which *firmly* command that the conflict of that general, self-opposed striving be *unified* (according to the ideal of beauty), if these principles in general are exercised on this conflict, then every unifying of the conflict must produce a result, and these results of the general unifying of the conflict are then the general concepts of the understanding, e.g., the concepts of substance and accident, of action and reaction, duty and right etc. These concepts are then to the understanding precisely what the ideal is to reason: just as reason forms its laws according to the ideal, so the understanding its maxims according to these concepts. These maxims contain the criteria and conditions under which any action or object is subject to those general concepts. E.g., I have the right to appropriate a thing that does not dispose of a free will. General concept: *right*. Condition: the thing does not dispose of a free will. The action subject to the general concept: the appropriation of a thing.

I'm writing all this for you the way one puts a quick drawing or something into a letter, to entertain you for a quarter of an hour or so.

That your fate often lies heavily on you I can well believe, dear brother. Be a man and overcome it. The servitude that presses against our hearts and minds on all sides in early youth and in adulthood, the abuse and suffocation of our noblest powers, also gives us a marvelous feeling of self-achievement if in spite of it all we carry out our better aims. I will do what I can to help too. Another employment I cannot and do not want to find you. What you need now is simply time of your own; you must be able to live for yourself before you can live for others. It is this consideration that leads me to suggest, contrary to things I've said in the past and having thought about it more fully, that you go to a university. If my precarious fate maintains me in my present situation I can quite easily do without 200 fl. toward the end of next winter. I'll send you that and you'll go to Jena and can, I think, reckon on the same sum from me every year, probably even a bit more, and the little bit extra you're bound to need our dear mother will not refuse you. Whatever you do don't thank me, I am following my convictions, and the fulfillment of such a behest admits of no other reward than that of attaining our goal. And what doubt could there be about that, dear brother!

Unfortunately I've got little or nothing to write to you about *important* acquaintances in the sense you mean.

Let the world go its way; if it can't be stopped we'll go ours.

I hope to get more done this summer than I have so far. The urge to produce something out of ourselves that will remain when we quit this life is the only thing in the end that attaches us to it.

I admit that we often long to pass out of this middle state of life and death over into the infinite being of the world in all its beauty, into the arms of eternally youthful Nature, which is where we began. But everything takes its steady course, and why should we pitch ourselves too soon where our desires take us?

Don't let's be put to shame by the sun, after all. It rises over good and bad—and we can also dwell a while among mankind and its doings, within our own limits and weaknesses.—I'll try to do something for your friend H. if I can. Sinklär, whom I've just visited again, sends his best wishes. He sorrows, as we do.

Fichte has published a *Natural Right*, I've just got it this minute from the bookseller and so cannot yet make a judgment on it. But all the same I think I can advise you with good grounds to purchase it.

All my love to our dear mother and the rest of the family and friends.

Farewell, dear Karl.

Yours,

Hölderlin

Cotta is keeping me waiting which is annoying. With any luck he'll have sent the money, or will do soon, even though they're only starting now with the printing of my book.

123. TO HIS BROTHER

Frankfurt[, June/July 1796]

Your happiness, my Karl, comes from what you are to yourself, and I wish you could see the truth of this as I do. You would be less aware of the lack that surrounds you from outside. Look—that's why most people find wondrously beautiful things everywhere, wondrously great and delightful things, because they measure all they encounter against their own inner poverty and limitations, because they are anything but spoilt in themselves. Because they are bored to tears with themselves, everything appears so amusing to them and because they feel they're not really worth the trouble of being favored by fortune they are so utterly grateful toward it, and in their courtesy call wise and just fate *merciful*.

(While we're on this topic, I'd like to know what mercy actually is.)—But if you are already a great deal to yourself, you need for that very reason to take proper care of your heart and your mind. The enjoyment of truth and of friendship! If only I could provide you with it in the fullness and strength and purity you deserve! But one person is not everything, and I am in any case like an old plant that once fell into the road with its earth and bits of pot and lost its shoots and damaged its roots, and has now been painstakingly put in fresh soil again and just saved from drying out by careful nursing, but is still withered and disfigured here and there and will remain so. And for that reason I'll be sure, as long as I live, to do everything in my power, as far as it depends on me and you may have need of me, to make your life agreeable to you in other respects, that is, to make it suited to the needs of your noble being.

I cannot possibly believe that our dear mother will fail to approve the solid reasons I shall set out to her and refuse to give you her permission and blessing for a journey to Jena.

You will find the truth there and at least one person you can call wholly your friend, that's my hope! I'd like to hear your plans for your studies from you yourself before I make my own suggestions, in order to keep them entirely calibrated to your proper character and desires. One can chatter about anything in a general way, but to be useful we must, in our dealings with one another, pay attention to what each one is and has in particular.

When the time comes you will not lack prospects. Whatever subject you tackle I am certain that you will do much better than average in it, and men who are better than average in financial administration and the judiciary and jurisprudence are precisely because of their rarity much sought after everywhere now in academia or the administrative world.

In any case you can become a private tutor as well as I, and be happy, and mock at all the shoddiness of the political and religious life of Württemberg and Germany and Europe, as well as I.

10 June [July]

That's as far as I'd got with my letter. Now I find myself dramatically interrupted. The Imperial army is now engaged in a retreat from Wetzlar, and so the Frankfurt region is soon set to form one of the main scenes of the war. Therefore I leave today with the whole family for Hamburg where relatives of the household live. Herr Gontard is staying here alone. There will be momentous events. It is said the French are in Württemberg. I hope that this will not cause much real trouble at least to those whose lives touch me closest. Be a man, brother! I do not fear what there is to fear, I fear only fear itself. Tell our dear Mother that. Do your best to calm her! Were I not of use in this way, carrying out my duties, I'd come to join you. Courage and good sense is what we all need now. Heatedness and anxiety are no longer valid currency.

Look after yourselves, all you dear ones!

Yours

Friz

124. TO CHRISTIAN LUDWIG NEUFFER

Frankfurt[, June/July 1796]

If only I had you with me, dear friend, so that we could delight our hearts again together. The written word is to friendship what opaque vessels are to a golden wine. Just enough shimmers through to distinguish it from water but it is much preferable to see it in a crystal glass.

I should like to know how things are with you at the moment. I would like them to be as they are for me. I am in a new world. Before I may have thought I knew what was good and beautiful, but since I have it before me I have nothing but scorn for all my knowledge. Dear friend, there is a being in the world on which my mind can dwell for thousands of years, and will do, without ever forgetting how inept all our thinking and understanding is when faced with nature. Loveliness and majesty, and peacefulness and life, & spirit and soul and form is a blessed unity in this being. You can take my word for it that anything comparable has seldom been intimated in this world, and will hardly be found here again. You well know how I used to be, how the commonplace left me cold, you know how I lived without faith, how chary my heart had become, and how miserable I was for that reason. Could I have become what I am now, happy as an eagle, if this, this one thing, had not appeared before me and rejuvenated, strengthened, heightened, magnified my life, which no longer meant anything to me, with its spring light? I have moments when I find all my old worries as completely foolish and incomprehensible as children would.

And it is really often impossible to think of anything mortal in her presence and that is why so little can be said about her.

Perhaps now and then I will succeed in catching a part of her nature in a happy turn of phrase and if I do it will not remain unknown to you. But it will need to be a solemn, completely undisturbed hour if I am to write about her. —

That I now spend more time writing than ever you can imagine. You'll be seeing something by me again soon.

What you sent me has reaped you a splendid reward. She read it, liked it, wept over your laments.

Oh be happy, dear Neuffer! Without joy eternal beauty cannot flourish within us as it should. Great pain and great pleasure are the best shapers of a man. But to live like a cobbler, who sits on his stool day after day doing what he could do in his sleep, that fetches the spirit to the grave before its time.

I cannot write now. I'll have to wait until I feel less happy and youthful. All the best to you, true, proven and always beloved friend. If only I could press you to my heart. That would be the true language for us two now.

Yours,

Hölderlin

10th June [July]

I'm leaving for Hamburg later today because of the war . . . Goodbye, my dear Neuffer! Time presses. I'll write again soon if I can.

125. TO FRIEDRICH SCHILLER

Kassel, 24 July 1796

I take the liberty, esteemed Counselor, of sending you a short contribution for the coming anthology. I should rather have brought it and enjoyed being near you again. Your health is better, as I hear, and that is an extra spur for me to make a pilgrimage to you and see you. But before then I must be patient for at least a few months more. I am now in flight with the family with whom I have been living very happily since last winter in Frankfurt. The people I am with are truly of a rare sort, and I value them all the more because I found them at just the right time, several bitter experiences really having made me mistrustful of relationships of all kinds.

I wanted once again to appear to you in all my neediness, wanted to ask your opinion on many matters that are preoccupying me at the moment, and wanted by some roundabout route to capture a few friendly words from you, but I am forced to break off.

Would you be so kind as to give my regards to your wife?

Yours ever,

M. Hölderlin

126. TO HIS BROTHER

Kassel, 6 August 1796

I hope, dear Karl, that the post will now make it possible to give you some news once again and also to receive word from you. For you can easily imagine that in all sorts of ways I have a great need to know exactly what the particular circumstances of the great events that have taken place at home are, and especially all that concerns my dear family.

I should probably torment myself with disquieting probabilities more than I do, were my imagination not becoming more acquainted with the war here in the Rhine country too.

I pity our good mother with all my heart, and am concerned for her as I know how much she suffers under such circumstances, being sensitive and modest as she is.

You, Karl, will be strengthened in your inmost soul by the proximity of such an extraordinary spectacle as the one granted by the giant strides of the Republicans.

It is altogether easier to be told about the Greek thunderbolts that thousands of years ago sent the Persians hurtling out of Attica across the Hellespont and down into barbarian Susa than it is to see such a pitiless storm passing over your own house.

It is true you don't witness this new drama without paying for it. But so far, I reckon, you've come off not too badly. Just today I read in the paper that General Saint-Cyr is pursuing the Austrians through Tübingen, Reutlingen and Blaubeuren, and this made me worried about our dear sister and her household. I am also anxious because of Condé's monstrous lot, who contaminate the land and wreak so much havoc among you. Make sure you write by return when you receive this letter, dear Karl. In my own situation nothing is wanting apart from peace of mind about my family. For three weeks and three days now I've been living very happily here in Kassel. We traveled via Hanau and Fulda—quite close by the thundering of the French cannon but still safely enough. I wrote to you on the day of my departure saying we were going to Hamburg, but this place is of such interest to Mme. Gontard, in so many regards, that once we'd arrived here she decided to stay for some time. (She sends her greetings to our dear mother and you and advises you to look on your situation as cheerfully as possible.) We also have Herr Heinse, the famous author of *Ardinghello*, living with us here. He is really a thoroughly excellent man. There's nothing finer than the kind of bright serenity this man has in his old age.

These past few days we've had spectacles of our own here too, only more peaceful ones than yours. The King of Prussia was visiting the local Landgrave and was received with great pomp and ceremony.

The natural surroundings here are grand and attractive. And the art is a pleasure too: the *Augarten* here and the *Weisser Stein* have parks that are among the foremost in Germany. We have also got to know some good artists.

The picture gallery and several statues in the museum have given me days of real happiness.

In the next weeks we're setting off into Westphalia, to Driburg (a spa not far from Paderborn). I enclose the address where you can safely send me a letter. If peace comes we'll be in Frankfurt at the beginning of winter.

Goodbye, dear Karl. Don't give up on any of your hopes, which you are quite right to have. Write to me soon and at length and in detail and always from the heart.

Send my love to our good mother and all the dear family over and over again and assure them I am with them in my heart.

Yours,

Friz

FROM GEORG WILHELM FRIEDRICH HEGEL

[Tschugg, August 1796]

Eleusis

To Hölderlin. August 1796

Around me, in me, peace and calm—The tireless care
that keeps them busy sleeps and people give
me freedom, leisure—thank you, Night, for you
have set me free!—the moon attires
the uncertain boundaries of the distant hills
in a pale and misty gauze; the bright strip of the lake
sends out a companionable gleam—
the day's tiresome din is left behind by memory
as if a year of days lay from here to now;
your image, dear beloved friend, appears before me,
the pleasures of days gone by; but soon they yield
to sweeter hopes of seeing you again—
Already I paint the scene before my eyes,
the long-desired and fiery embrace, and then
the second scene, a questioning, each looking out
more covertly to see what change in bearing

or frame of mind in all this time the other
might show—the bliss of certainty, to find
the old alliance's loyalty yet firmer, riper,
the alliance, left unsealed by any oath,
to only live for truth and freedom, never making peace
with a rule of law that fixes opinion and feeling.
And now desire negotiates with dull reality,
desire that carried me lightly to you over mountains rivers,
— but then their altercation's revealed in a sigh, and with it
the sweet imaginings' dream disperses.
My eye looks up to heaven's highest vaulting,
to you, o shining star of Night!
oblivion of all desires, all hopes,
streams down from your eternity;
[my senses drift in contemplation,
what was my own all vanishes,
I give myself up to immensity,
I am in it, am all, am only it.
The returning thought is shy,
it dreads infinity, and in amazement
it cannot grasp the depth of what it sees.
Imagination brings eternity closer to
the mind, and marries it with form—] Welcome,
you mighty spirits, high shadows
from whose foreheads perfection shines!
I am not scared—I feel it as the upper air I dwell in too,
the solemnity, the brilliance, that streams around you.
Ha! if now the very doors of your sanctuary sprang open,
O Ceres, you who hold the throne in Eleusis! Drunk
with inspiration I should now feel
a trembling at your nearness,
would understand your revelations,
I'd be able to interpret the images' high meaning,
hear the hymns at the gods' table,
their council's great decrees.—
But your halls have fallen silent, Goddess!
The circle of the gods has fled back to Olympus
abandoning the desecrated altars,
and fleeing humanity's defiled grave,

the spirit of innocence that first drew them here! —
The wisdom of your priests is still, no tone of the sacred rites
has made it down to us—and all in vain
the seeker's curiosity strains—not love—
for wisdom (they possess that, the searchers, yet hold
you in contempt)—to master which they dig down into words
in which your weighty meaning might be stamped!
In vain! They snatched no more than dust and ashes
in which your life will never return to them.
But under mold and lifeless stuff the eternal-dead
were not dismayed! They keep to themselves. All for nothing:
no sign remained of rituals, of your form no trace!
The abundance of the holy teachings, the depths
of unutterable feeling were far too sacrosanct
for the son of the rites to honor a brittle sign
of their presence. Thought is not enough to catch the soul
that outside time and space, divining boundlessness,
absorbed, forgets itself and now awakes again
to consciousness. Whoever wished to speak of this,
were it with angels' tongues, he'd feel the poverty
of words, the horror of having made the sacred small,
so small in word and thought that speech appears
like sin, and trembling makes him shut his mouth.
What the initiate forbade himself, a law of wisdom
forbade the poorer spirits: not to tell the world
what he had seen in holy night, and heard and felt —
so that their noise and mischief should not disturb him
in his better worship, that their hollow scrabbled words
should not rile him against holiness itself,
that it not be trodden in the dirt, and even
that it not be entrusted to memory, so not
to be sold as the sophist's toy, a ware
exchanged for obols, to become
the mantle of a charlatan, or even
the rod to curb a happy child, becoming
in the end so empty that only in the echo
from strangers' tongues did its life have any root.
Your sons, o Goddess, did not trade your honor

at market or on the street, true misers they conserved it
in the inner sanctuary of their hearts —
and so you did not live upon their lips,
their life was how they honored you, you live on in their acts.
And this night too I sensed you, sacred godhead,
your children's lives often reveal you to me also,
I intuit you as the soul that animates their actions!
You are the high sense, the true faith—which,
divine itself, when all goes under, does not sway.

127. TO HIS BROTHER

Frankfurt, 13 October 1796

I am now a good bit closer to you again than I have been for a while,
and feel it. My last letter you received from Kassel. From there we
traveled into the German Boeotia, to Westphalia, through wild and
lovely regions, over the Weser, over bare hills and through muddy,
indescribably poor villages on even muddier and poorer bumpy roads.
This is my brief and faithful account of the journey.

In our spa town we lived very peacefully, made no further
acquaintances and did not need to since we lived among glorious hills
and woods and were our own best company. Heinse traveled with
us the whole time. I used the baths a little and drank the delicious,
fortifying and purifying mineral water and felt uncommonly well
from it, still do. It will give you particular pleasure to hear that we
were staying only about half an hour from the valley where Arminius
defeated the legions of Varus. Standing on the spot I thought of the
beautiful May afternoon when we sat on a rock in the woods near
Hahrd and read *Hermanns Schlacht* together over a jug of cider. What
glorious walks we had together, dear Karl! We shall, I hope, have even
lovelier walks when we see each other again. I should like to hear our
dear mother's considered opinion on the proposal I made this summer
to improve your situation.

We mustn't rush her. I'm sure she will tell us the precise
economic reasons for her decision if she is not of our opinion.

You *must* study philosophy, even if you only have enough money to buy a lamp and oil and the only time you can find is from midnight to cockcrow. Let me at least repeat that—and I know you think the same.

If it comes to it you can do without professors and universities, but, dear brother, I should like you to have the chance of satisfying your most noble needs without having too hard a time of it.

It would give me so much pleasure to see combined in you one day, as is proper, the thinker and the administrator.

If Jena doesn't come off, you must at least come to Frankfurt. I want you to have a thoroughly good time with me here. Before the Christmas holidays (for at that time the roads will be completely calm), so before the Christmas holidays I'll send you the money for the journey and you can buy yourself a warm coat, get on the mail coach, stay here a few days, go and visit dear Sinklair in Homburg and then back to the office full of energy, without it costing you anything.

This only for if you don't go to Jena!

I'm very well. You will find I'm in less of a revolutionary frame of mind when you see me again. I am in good health too. I'm sending you a piece of cassimere for a waistcoat. The fair here is very empty this year. I hope that Württemberg and my dear family are safe now from new troubles. I don't like to say much about the political misery. For a while I have been very quiet about everything going on in our country.

Remember me to everybody—our dear mother and sister and grandmother, and all the others in Löchgau and Blaubeuren.

If mother doesn't mind I should like her to write a few words as well the next time. I long to see something from her too. I trust she's well and holds nothing against me?

128. TO GEORG WILHELM FRIEDRICH HEGEL

Frankfurt, 24 October 1796

Dearest Hegel,

Things are finally on the move again.

You remember that at the beginning of the summer I mentioned an extremely advantageous position and said my greatest wish, for you and for me, was that you should come here to live with these good people in question.

The disruptions of the war were probably the main reason why I received no answer for so long. Also I was in Kassel and Westphalia throughout the summer and thus quite unable to give you any news about the matter.

The day before yesterday Herr Gogel came round quite unexpectedly and told me that if you were still free and interested in the post he would be glad to have you. Your main task would be to see to the education of two good boys of 9 or 10; you would be able to live in his household without any constraints, would have, which is important, your own room, with the boys in the neighboring one, and would be perfectly content with the financial conditions. He said it would be better not to write too many good things about him and his family because raised expectations are always disappointed, but if you wanted to come his door stood open to you any day.

Now the footnotes! You are very unlikely to get less than 400 fl. Your traveling expenses will be paid, as mine were, you can probably count on 10 carolins. Every fair you'll receive a very substantial present. And everything will be paid for, apart from little things like the hairdresser's, the barber's and so on. You will have very good Rhine wine or French wine to drink at table. You will be living in one of the finest houses in Frankfurt, on one of the most beautiful squares in Frankfurt.

You will find Herr and Frau Gogel to be unpretentious, easy, sensible people who, though you might expect them to be gregarious and sociable given their wealth and conviviality, in fact live largely amongst themselves because, especially Frau Gogel, they prefer not to get involved with and sullied by the *Frankfurt society people* who with their stiffness and poverty of heart and spirit would spoil their domestic happiness.

Believe me, that says it all. But last of all, dear friend, let me put this to you.—A man who despite a variety of changes of situation and character has remained true to you in heart and mind and spirit and will be your friend more fully and warmly than ever and gladly and willingly share in every concern of your being and every aspect of your life, who in his happy situation lacks nothing but you, this man will be living just round the corner from you if you come.

Really, my friend, I need you and think you will also be able to make use of me.

If one day we are on the point of splitting wood for a living or dealing in boot polish and pomade, then let us wonder whether it might not be better to become a repetitor in Tübingen. For me, through the whole of Württemberg and the Palatinate, the seminary smells like a bier that's already been attacked by the worm. Seriously, dear friend, you have no right to be so willful and put your spirit through such an unpleasant ordeal.

As proof that you can rely on what I've said to you about the financial arrangements you should know that all the businessmen here have almost exactly the same observance in this regard. You can be quite certain of the main sum. That I have from a good source. I have told Herr Gogel that I'll ask you to write to me expressing as far as you see fit your thoughts on this situation and your particular desires in a letter I will give him to read. So you can clarify anything further this way or, if you prefer, just come. Only let's try to make sure things move on now as quickly as possible. Though Herr Gogel did say that if need be he could wait a few months more. There are lots of other things I'd like to say but your coming here will have to be the preface to a long long, interesting and *unlearned* book by the two of us.

Yours,

Hölderlin

FROM GEORG WILHELM FRIEDRICH HEGEL

Tschugg near Erlach,   November 1796

Dearest Hölderlin,

What a joy it is to hear something of you again; your unchanging friendship for me speaks from every line of your letter; I cannot tell you how much pleasure it has given me, and even more the hope of seeing you soon in the flesh and embracing you.

Without dwelling any longer on this pleasant thought, let me come on at once to the main thing. Your very desire to see me in the situation you write to me about guarantees that this arrangement cannot be other than advantageous to me; and so I shall respond to your summons without hesitation and renounce all other prospects that were opening up for me. With pleasure I shall become part of the excellent family in which I have every reason to hope that the interest I'll take in the education of my pupils-to-be will lead to a happy outcome. To fill their heads with words and concepts can usually be achieved all right, but a house tutor can have but little influence on the more essential task of forming their characters unless the parents' attitude is in harmony with his efforts.—Although it is often only prudent to ascertain in advance the precise financial and other conditions pertaining in the household, I think that in this case I can do without such caution and leave it to you to make sure all is as it should be, especially as you will know best what is usual in Frankfurt in this regard, and what the relation is between the costs of living and the pay.

Service in the house and free laundry I assume I can also expect.

I shall refrain from asking you for explanations as regards Herr Gogel's wishes concerning the teaching and the particular supervision of his children; the teaching will at this age largely consist of such knowledge as is fitting for all cultivated people—as far as behavior goes, I shall be best placed to find out about the greater or lesser leeway that Herr Gogel wishes to allow for youthful vivacity on the spot, and can communicate with him more fully about it there than would be possible in letters.

As for the journey, I anticipate that the expenses will not be above 10 carolins, and should like you to have a provisional word about that with Herr Gogel now and, as seems to you more proper, request him to send me via you a bill of exchange,—or to reimburse me when I arrive in Frankfurt.

Sorry as I am not to be able to set off at once, it really is impossible for me to leave the household I'm part of at the moment before the end of the year;—and to arrive in Frankfurt sooner than the middle of January. As you have begun to get involved in this matter for me, I must further ask you to transmit the gist of my letter to Herr Gogel and to assure him of the high esteem in which I hold him. He will surely see for himself that a part of what you may have said to him to instill the confidence he is showing me is more to be put down to your friendship for me, or that a friend is not always the best judge of another. Reassure him therefore that I shall make every effort to be worthy of your recommendation.—

The great part my longing to see you has played in my rapid decision, how much the image of our reunion and of the joyful prospect of being with you in the future will hover before my eyes in the interim—nothing of that—goodbye—

Yours

Hegel

129. TO GEORG WILHELM FRIEDRICH HEGEL

Frankfurt, 20 November 1796

Dearest Hegel,

The whole thing is settled. You will receive, as I thought, 400 fl., with free laundry and service in the house, and Herr Gogel will reimburse your traveling expenses when you get here or if necessary send you a bill of exchange in Bern. These are his own words that I've had from him this instant.

If you did want a bill of exchange in Bern, to avoid any possible difficulties, write to me by return and I'll make sure to take care of it promptly without putting you out at all.

That you're not coming till the middle of January Herr Gogel is bearing with more patience than I am; I wish it was New Year's Eve today. Herr Gogel has read your letter and as I expected was very content with it. If you haven't changed you will find in his character and way of expressing himself a great deal in common with your own habits.

The substance and form of the teaching will as is natural be left to you. Your expertise in French Herr G. takes as a rare and important bonus.

His boys, there are two of them, are good, he says, one of his 2 girls, who you will only teach the odd thing to from time to time, is a bit stubborn. But that shouldn't put you off too much. She'll probably be able to remember that Germany is in Europe for you. You won't have anything against a quarter of an hour's talk with a nice little thing like her.

Even though teaching children is often a bit of a burden you'll be better off occupying yourself with the boys than with Church and State as they are at the moment. And for things we cannot be expected to teach like handwriting, arithmetic, drawing, dancing or fencing, masters are usually engaged who can be completely entrusted with the children, so that you will be able to have plenty of rest.

We will share all our troubles and joys like brothers, old friend of my heart! It is a good thing the evil spirits I brought with me from Franconia and the ethereal spirits with metaphysical wings that accompanied me out of Jena have left me since I arrived in Frankfurt. It will mean I'll be some use to you still. I can see that your situation has made you lose a little of your accustomed cheerfulness too. You wait. By next spring you'll be your old self again. What you say about leading and guiding, my dear, cherished friend, pained me. You have so often been my mentor when my disposition turned me into a simpleton, and you will have to be again many a time.

You will find friends here of a sort you don't meet every day.

Last week I visited Sinklair in Homburg. He is also delighted you're coming. I tell you, my dear friend, you need nothing more than your house and mine for your time here to be full of happiness. The day we see one another again will give us a new lease of life. I will come to meet you in Darmstadt if only I can arrange it. Then I'll take you round to my house first and have my fill of seeing you again and then I'll bring you to the good Gogel's house.

The day before yesterday I dreamt of you, you were still making all kinds of circuitous journeys round Switzerland, which was driving me mad. Afterward the dream gave me great pleasure.

Goodbye, dear Hegel. Write to me again soon. If only you had already left the district of Bern!

Yours,

Hölderlin

130. TO FRIEDRICH SCHILLER

Frankfurt, 20 November 1796

Esteemed Sir,

It often saddens me that I can no longer speak to you from my heart as before I could, but your total silence toward me quite takes my courage away and I always have to have at least some small pretext if I am to bring myself to mention my name to you again.

The pretext on this occasion is the request that you be so kind as to let me have back the unhappy verses that there was no space for in your *Almanac* this year, so that I can go through them again; for the manuscript I sent you from Kassel was the only one I had.

I hope you will also consider it worth your while to enclose your judgment on them, for in this regard too anything is easier to bear than your muteness.

I still remember very clearly every slightest sign of your interest in me. You also wrote me once, when I was still living in Franconia, a few words that I always repeat to myself when I feel misunderstood.

Have you changed your opinion of me? Have you given me up?

Forgive me these questions. An attachment to you that I often fought against in vain when it grew into a passion, an attachment that still continues, forces me to ask such questions.

I should reproach myself for it, were you not the only man to whom I have lost my freedom in this way.

I know I shall not rest until by some achievement and success I once again catch a sign of your pleasure in me.

Do not, because I say nothing of my occupations, believe that I have been idle. But it is hard to hold out against the dejection that comes from losing the kind of favor I used to enjoy or dreamed I did.

I am embarrassed and scrupulous over every word I say to you, and yet otherwise, when I find myself in other people's presence, I have more or less got over youthful anxiety.

Just say a friendly word, and you will see that it transforms me.

Your unfeigned admirer,

Hölderlin

131. TO HIS MOTHER

Frankfurt, 20 November 1796

Dearest Mother,

I'm writing to you on this occasion because first of all I owe you a justification for the decision I have taken, on well-considered grounds, as regards the teaching post. Let me assure you that it costs me no less self-denial than it does you and my Karl for me to have to renounce your daily presence and affectionate company. My situation is a very happy one, but where in the world would one not miss one's mother and a brother like mine and all one's family? So you will have no trouble believing that it is no easy thing for me not to avail myself of this invitation from my good compatriots, which is so favorable and does me such honor. But for one thing it would be ungrateful of me to leave a household whom I have not yet been able to pay back a tenth part of the beautiful friendship that is extended to me every day, and to leave my pupil, with all his promise, at precisely the point when he is beginning to get a proper understanding of my teaching and of my heart. For whether anyone else would be quite what I can be to him is not certain. Nature has fashioned this child in almost exactly the way that I, as far as I can tell, left her hands. I recognize myself in him in a thousand particularities that form part of myself, and the child too divines a kindred spirit in me and this precisely makes my job of education so much easier, this precisely seems to me, more and more, to be the indispensable condition for any successful education.

Beyond that, I fear that my health, on which my mind and my character have so often proved to be dependent, might easily, in a situation such as the one proposed, lose once more the equilibrium it had found. You know, dearest Mother, how I suffered in body, and largely for that reason also in mind, during the summer I spent in Nürtingen. I am now fully recovered. But would things stay that way in such a busy job, and would I be able to supply the effort and energy it requires for long? I am no schoolmaster, and to educate 40 boys according to pure principles and with sustained and invigorating zeal is truly a gigantic task, particularly when family upbringing and other institutions so very often work against it.

For another thing, the occupations that by nature and habit have become an indispensable need and without which no happiness on earth can have any savor for me, these cheerful and certainly innocent occupations would have to fall away almost entirely unless I wanted to turn every midnight into daytime, and that I cannot and must not do if I don't want to be done for within a year.

That makes, I reckon, three solid reasons. I could add more to them, but I don't think it necessary since I know how very much you yourself share the sentiments I have just expressed.

Let's do all we can to make up for not taking this opportunity to live closer together by coming on visits and sending plenty of good news. You have often said yourself, as I well know, that you would never actually advise me to take up such a position.

Thank everybody in my name most warmly for thinking of me! Tell them that I know how to value and seek always to deserve the memory of my compatriots.

Dear Karl I shall if possible write to separately tomorrow, in reply to the first of his two kind letters.

You, dearest Mother, I thank from the bottom of my heart for your long generous letter. What you tell me of our financial situation I accept with modesty and conviction. I know very well that you will continue to do what you can for our Karl, who promises so much for our country and for ourselves, and I vouch to do the same. You will be glad to hear the news that one of my most precious friends from university, M. Hegel from Stuttgart, will probably be coming to Frankfurt at the beginning of next year, by my intermission, to take up a post as house tutor in one of the best families here. If only I could also have my Karl nearby for a while. But I shouldn't be saying that to you.

Keep in good health, whatever happens, and enjoy your happiness and that of your children with an untroubled heart.

Give everyone my love. What is my dear sister up to and her family? It gives me endless joy that all my dear ones have come through the ravages of the war unharmed. Goodbye, dearest Mother!

Yours

Friz

132. TO HIS BROTHER

Frankfurt,   November 1796

Dear Karl,

This time I can only echo the first of your dear letters and say for the time being a hearty Yes! to all that you have said; and must leave it till another time to go into more detail with you about the necessary formation of your mind and an appropriate situation to favor it, together with the direction it should take.

In setting out your ideas you have very nicely and quite rightly combined the fire of youthful activity that tends toward infinity and the limitation of the same in a free domestic life. The whole wisdom of life consists in our not extending ourselves too much and not concentrating ourselves too much, and the person who has the breadth of mind and yet the simplicity of heart to cultivate his own land and bring up his children, that is, the sort of person you may very well become, seems to me, from all I have thought and experienced, the happiest and most human, and so the most accomplished person of all. You are sure to find a situation soon in which you will have a few hours in the day to raise your spirit out of the wearying unproductiveness in which it is admittedly kept by most established occupations.

So let us make the best of it until better times, which you will then use with twice as much energy and felicity because you will have learned to value them from doing without. And there is another thing that should console you, that is, the incontrovertible truth that any uncommon mind is bound to find the sphere he is confined to, whatever it may be, too narrow from time to time. I say from time to time, for such a person, on reflection, will realize that an infinite field of action is likely to be even less favorable to the development of the spirit than a limited one.

So far you have wrestled with your situation like a noble champion. Do so a while longer and the worst phase will be over.

About the suggestion of making a journey to Frankfurt you say nothing at all.

About Fichte's *Natural Right* I'll write to you next time. I'd like to say something thorough and complete and don't have time to do that now.

My *Hyperion* will probably appear by Easter next year all in one go. Various chance occurrences have delayed it.

Be so kind, dear Karl, and send me the two Swabian almanacs that have my earlier poems in, I'd like to rework them and have no manuscript of them.

Goodbye, my Karl! Make do with this for now.

Yours

Friz

FROM FRIEDRICH SCHILLER

Jena, 24 November 1796

I have in no way forgotten you, dear friend, as you think: only distractions and occupations, alongside my usual aversion to letter writing, have delayed my reply to your amiable letters for so long.

Your most recent poems arrived several weeks too late for the almanac, otherwise I would surely have made use of one or another of them. On the other hand I hope that you will play all the greater part in the next issue. As I lack the leisure today to go through the pieces you sent last I'll keep them here for the time being in order to add my comments to them.

It would give me great pleasure if in the next almanac I could present several mature and lasting fruits of your talent. Summon up, I beg you, all your power and all your vigilance, select a felicitous poetic subject, carry it carefully and nurturingly in your heart, so that it can take shape, and in the finest moments of existence let it peacefully ripen into perfection. Avoid as far as possible philosophical subjects, they are the least thankful of all, and in fruitless wrestling with them even the best energies are often consumed, stick closer to the world of the senses and you'll run less of a risk of losing your sobriety in enthusiasm, or of straying into a contrived expression.

I'd also like to warn you against a characteristic vice of German poets, which is long-windedness, often stifling even the most felicitous thought through endless elaboration in a flood of strophes. This does no small harm to your poem to *Diotima*. A few significant traits bound up in a simple whole would have made it into a fine poem. For that reason I recommend you above all to employ a prudent economy, a careful selection of what is significant and clear and simple expressions of the same. But how can I specify all the things I'd like to see? You have Moses and the prophets; go by the best models and from them yourself derive the rules that otherwise would be only words.

Forgive me for these exhortations, these warnings. The sympathy of friendship has inspired both.

Take good care of yourself and let me hear from you regularly.

Yours sincerely

Schiller

133. TO JOHANN GOTTFRIED EBEL

Frankfurt, 10 January 1797

My dear friend,
The only reason I have hesitated so long before answering your first letter is that I felt how full an answer it needed, and because no moment when I had the time to write to you was rich enough to say to you all that I wished.

Dear Ebel, it is splendid to be as hurt and disappointed as you are. Not everybody has such a concern for truth and justice that he even sees them when they are not there, and if the observing mind is swayed by the heart like this then probably the heart is too noble for the century it belongs to. It is almost not possible to look with the naked eye at reality, soiled as it is, without falling ill; the eyes do well, for as long as they can, to shut themselves against the motes and the smoke and dust blowing up, and it can also be a fine instinct in a human being to look cheerfully on things that do not directly concern him. But you hold out despite it all and I admire you just as much for still wanting to see now as for not seeing in quite the same way before.

I know, it is infinitely painful to take our leave of a place where we have seen all the fruits and flowers of humanity rise up in our hopes again. But we have ourselves and a few others, and it is also good to find a world in ourselves and a few others.

As for the general situation, I have one consolation, which is that all fermentation and dissolution must necessarily lead either to annihilation or to new organization. But there is no such thing as annihilation, and so the youth of the world must come back again, out of our decomposition. One can say with some certainty that the world never looked so motley as now. It is an immense multifariousness of contradictions and contrasts. Old and new! Civilization and barbarity! Malice and passion! Selfishness in sheep's clothing, selfishness in wolf's clothing! Superstition and unbelief! Servitude and despotism! Unreasoned wisdom—unwise reason! Feeling without thinking—thinking without feeling! History, experience, tradition, without philosophy—philosophy without experience! Energy without principles—principles without energy! Discipline without humanity—humanity without discipline! Feigned obligingness—shameless impertinence! Precocious young boys—silly old men!—This litany could be continued from sunrise to midnight without having named more than a thousandth part of the chaos that is humanity. But that's how it should be! This characteristic of the better-known part of the human race must certainly be seen as a harbinger of extraordinary things. I believe in a future revolution of attitudes and ways of seeing things that will make all we have had till now go red with shame. And Germany can perhaps contribute a great deal to this. The more quietly a state grows, the more splendid it will be when it reaches its maturity. Germany is quiet, modest, there is a lot of thinking going on, a lot of work, and great movements are afoot in the hearts of its young people that do not spill into fine phrases as elsewhere. A lot of development, and what is infinitely more: workable material!—Good-naturedness and industry, hearts of children and minds of men are the elements that an excellent people is formed from. Where are these things to be found in greater measure than among the Germans? It's true that vile mimicry has done a lot of damage, but the more philosophical they become, the more self-sufficient. You say yourself, my dear friend, that from now on we should live for the mother country. Will you do so soon? Come! Come here! I won't understand you if you don't come. You are a poor man in Paris. Here your heart is very, very rich, richer than perhaps you realized yourself, and I think your spirit will not want either. You have friends here, you have even more than that. I did not know that you were so difficult and hard to satisfy. Now I do. I do not measure people with a small stick and am certain I know your innermost self, my dear Ebel, and am bound to say I do not understand how you could be discontented with people, or at least with one good soul in particular,—she herself said to me recently she knew no one more perfect than Ebel, and she had tears in her eyes; but I shouldn't really be revealing this.—In other respects too you will feel quite at home again in our circle. Since I started this letter Hegel has arrived. You will definitely grow fond of him.

Herr and Frau Gontard send you their regards. And Henry too! Good wishes. Come soon.

Hölderlin

Hegel had entered into employment here with Gogel before your last letter arrived. But I'll look for someone else who might suit you.

134. TO HIS BROTHER

Frankfurt, 10 January 1797

Dear Karl,

Your and our dear mother's letters were well worth the long wait. Every syllable in them was a pleasure.

That your situation has taken such a favorable turn gives me particular pleasure. I really do believe that B. is a man who will appreciate you for what you are and whom you will appreciate. And you know enough of him to be able to hope if not to enrich, then certainly to enliven your mind in intelligent conversations with him. He is a mathematician, and it will do you good, having completed your studies in natural right, to go on to mathematics which as you will find is the only science to compare with the *possible* scientific perfection of natural right. I often occupy myself with this splendid discipline at the moment, and find, to repeat my point, that it—along with jurisprudence as it may and must become—is the only science with this degree of purity and perfection in the whole domain of human knowledge. Face to face, there is a great deal I want to go through with you about natural right and about the parallel I have just drawn. But what lies closest to my heart at the moment is the hope of seeing you again. I'm very grateful to you, dear Karl, for doing as I ask and coming. You won't regret it. It will be a great liberation for you to venture at last beyond the borders of the society and the country you've lived in hitherto. For someone who has lived in the seclusion you have, a journey to Frankfurt will be as substantial a pleasure as for many others a journey through half of Europe might be. All my joys, all that is youthful in my heart, I shall press on you for yours. You will find me in a more healthy and orderly state of mind. For your accommodation all has been arranged. How do you intend to make the journey? To make things easier I'm sending you four carolins. If it's not enough, just tell me so. For the return journey I can also provide something if need be.

Give dear Mother a thousand thanks for her kind letter. Next time I'll write to her, and to our dear sister too. For now I have almost half a dozen letters more to dispatch. Nothing for the moment about what I'm working on! Allow me that obstinacy, dear Karl. I do mean to satisfy your brotherly interest in the end.

Be so kind, dear Karl, and write back to me very soon—if I'm only writing so briefly this time it's because I have no choice.

Yours

Friz

135. TO HIS MOTHER

[Frankfurt,] 30 January 1797

Dearest Mother,

Your kindness makes me happy and unhappy at once. I should return it by the complete satisfaction of your motherly wishes, and I could do that only in a fashion that sooner or later would be bound to be disagreeable to you. If you judged my character as I am obliged to judge it myself you would resign yourself to the fact that, though I accept with sincere gratitude the honor shown me by the offer in question, I can make no use of an opportunity that I should certainly have grasped if my way of thinking and feeling was different from what it is.

Dear Mother! They are seeking someone fit for the job. Am I really that, if I'm to be honest?

Is the age and disposition in which I'm living fit for any kind of fixed domestic setting? How great are the needs I still have to develop and to make a difference, and how could I possibly satisfy them in a situation such as my future one would be? How many demands I make of people in general, how infinitely many would I make of the being who should be the exclusive and durable focus of my attention? One needs to be older, needs to have been made more content by all kinds of experiments and experiences, to be able to say to oneself: Here I want to stop and come to rest!

Please don't think that these are whimsical or fanciful ideas, as people back home generally tend to treat such pronouncements. It is not lack of understanding that bids me follow nature in this matter and, in that regard, maintain my freedom for as long as I can; precisely because I understand myself and others who resemble me in this way better than is usually the case, precisely for that reason I am determined to follow nature.

A time will come for that to change. A husband at peace with the world is a fine thing; only, one mustn't tell someone to go into harbor when he has barely got half his voyage behind him.

And then I also feel myself better suited to be a teacher than a preacher. I would find it difficult to fall in, as I should have to, with the discourse that has been introduced in our parishes and is now absolutely required, whereas on the other hand a function like the one I am engaged in at the moment, even if it became more extensive, I believe I could fulfill quite well. And teaching, as I see it, is more likely to have an effect in our present time than preaching. I think I already said something about this in my last letter, and in conversation too if I remember rightly.

And you won't hold it against me if I confess that I consider my present situation to be the most appropriate for my nature and its needs. My dear brother will tell you when he gets back whether or not it is easy to leave people as good as those I am living with, and to give up the kind of cultivated company I enjoy every day. Herr and Frau Gontard feel as I do how much it must mean to your motherly heart to have me close. We spoke about your dear letter together with great sympathy. Be assured that we understand you completely, dearest Mother!

But you lose nothing at all if I stay here. Given how far away the place you found for me is, I'd have visited you once a year. That I can and will do from here too.

I'd have given you my news every week. That I can and will do from this day on from here too.

You would have taken pleasure in my financial situation. That you can also do now, and more so!

It's also a long time since I spent the winter in such good health and in this regard I've had due warning not to change my situation unless I have to. I'm in too much of a rush to be able to set out in detail all that might assuage and cheer you as to my decision. Do not let it cause you to give up your interest in my well-being, dearest Mother. You can be full of good hopes for my future as well as yours, for I think they will be fulfilled!

Tomorrow I'll write to my dear sister and to Karl and send him the bit of money for the journey at the same time.

Ever

your loyal son

Hölderlin

136. TO HIS BROTHER

Frankfurt, 4 February 1797

It upsets me now from time to time when I think how I have disrupted the nice plans our dear mother and you had made. But it must make you realize immediately that it is my *innermost being* that drives me to renounce the position that has been offered me this time, given I have all the loyal fondness for you, my dears, to fight against and yet do not let myself succumb to it.

In my last letter I didn't like to touch on the point on which you especially sought to reassure me because I had reason to suppose that it might have to pass into the hands of strangers. But you see yourself, dear brother, how oppressive it would be for hearts like yours and mine to venture into such an intimate union with a person whom, were it not for a vacant parish or some such, we'd perhaps never have set eyes on in our lives, or even if we did come across her would probably never have regarded as the one and only person with whom we wanted to enter into a bond until the end of our days. Such a relationship, in my opinion, must not even be *occasioned* by any other consideration. On both sides there must not be a stirring of even the slightest desire to please one another just because it would be nice and convenient. What's more, since it had been *stated* that only somebody who would marry the girl would get the post, it would be illogical to request a further statement that the position would be attributed only according to one's fitness for it and for no other reason. And only such a statement could convince me to take up such an office, were there not other reasons determining me not to do so at all for the time being. These other reasons I gave in my last letter.

[Sends him the money for the journey to Frankfurt.]

137. TO CHRISTIAN LUDWIG NEUFFER

Frankfurt, 16 February 1797

My dear friend,

I have sailed round a world of joys since we last wrote. I should have liked to have written to you during that time if I had ever stood still and looked back. I was carried along on a wave—my whole being was always too much involved in life to reflect on itself.

And it's still like that! I am still as happy as at that first moment. It is an unending, joyous, sacred friendship with a being who has strayed into this poor unspirited and orderless century. My sense of beauty is now proof against all disruption. It orients itself for ever by this madonna. My intelligence schools itself on her, and my contradictory soul is soothed and brightened every day by her self-sufficient peacefulness. I tell you, my dear Neuffer, I am on the way to becoming quite a good boy. And in other aspects too I am also a bit more content with myself. I write little and hardly do any philosophy any more. But what I do write has more life and form. My imagination is more open to the shapes of the world, my heart is full of desires. And if holy fate allows me to maintain this happy life I hope to do more in the future than I have so far.

I can well imagine, dear friend, that you will be eager to hear me speak of my happiness in more detail. But I mustn't! I have often wept and raged at a world in which the best thing of all cannot even speak its name on a piece of paper sent to a friend. I enclose a poem to her that I wrote at the end of last winter.

Over the summer I lived in Kassel and in a spa town in Westphalia, in the area where ancient Arminius fought his battle, mostly in the company of Heinse whom you will know as the author of *Ardinghello*. He is a splendid old man. I have never encountered such a boundless cultivation of mind together with such childlike simplicity.

The first volume of my *Hyperion* will appear by next Easter. Circumstances have delayed its publication so long.

Being forced to quit Frankfurt and the distractions of the journey prevented me from being able to send in anything in time for Schiller's *Almanac*. Next year I hope to appear along with you once again, dear friend. The song I found in there by you obviously had a lot of work put into it. Write and tell me all about what you're working on, your tastes and moods. Let's correspond more often again. To have Hegel here with me is doing me a power of good. I like calm, rational people because you can orient yourself so well by them whenever you can't make out how you stand with yourself and the world.

My dear Neuffer, I wanted to write you so much but the poor moments I have to do it are so little in which to convey to you what lives and moves within me. And it is always the death of our quiet happiness to want to put it into language. I prefer to wander in joyful, lovely peace like a child, without counting up what I have and am, for what I have cannot be grasped entire by any thought. If I could just show you her picture words would no longer be necessary. She is beautiful as an angel. A face full of tenderness, spirit and serene loveliness! Oh, the manifesting of this modest quiet soul is so inexhaustibly rich that I could spend a thousand years in blissful contemplation of her, oblivious of myself and everything. Majesty and delicacy, cheerfulness and gravity, and sweet play and sovereign sorrow and life and spirit, everything in and about her is united into one divine whole. Good night, dear friend. "Whom the gods love receives great joy and great sorrow." To navigate a stream needs no skill. But when our hearts and fates cast us down to the bottom of the sea and fling us up into the sky, that forms the helmsman.

Yours,

Hölderlin

138. TO HIS SISTER

Frankfurt a. M., 17 February 1797

Dearest sister,

Your letter gave me great pleasure. I think it wouldn't be bad to multiply the fine enjoyment it produced as often as possible and so I promise to answer every one of your letters with the utmost scrupulousness, even if one comes every day. That seems unlikely to happen, but from now on I count on getting 2 a month. Your pieces of news were all of interest to me. That Camerer often thinks of me pleases me very much. He is one of the few people who really know me; this was easy for him, for he saw me in Jena almost every day with both body and soul in full undress. The time we spent together then has endeared him to me for ever, and for that reason I am delighted that he is living in Blaubeuren and among your acquaintances. I reckon your friend has chosen in him the only man suited to her. A woman of lively spirit finds best counsel in a peaceful steady man like Kammerer.

There are times now when I should like to have your outcrops and woods and hills and that Blau valley of yours around me instead of the avenues I have here; of course you would have to be there too.

It would fill you with delight to see how well I am and how I'm beginning to resemble more and more what you think I should be, more content with myself and more balanced.

Wouldn't it have been possible for our Karl to come and visit me in the company of your dear husband? You really should try out your powers of persuasion on him. If it's not possible for him to make what would be an amicable and wholesome journey now, perhaps a more favorable occasion can be found. I cannot take the risk of coming to see you so soon if I want to avoid being suspected of homesickness.

I think the reasons I gave will be enough to convince you that I was right to answer that proposition about the living in the way I did. I should be very sorry indeed if my family did not approve of my not seeking my happiness along that route for now and probably not in future either.

Send my love to your dear children who I hope are in good health. I think Christian will give you ever more pleasure as his mind develops all its promise. I'd like to see the little queen among her dolls one day!

Write to me again soon, dearest sister.

Your

loyal brother

Friz

FROM CHRISTIAN LUDWIG NEUFFER

Stuttgart, 18 April 1797

[Intends in the autumn to come to Frankfurt with Landauer for the fair.] Give my greetings to Hegel and if your brother is still with you, also to him. *[Thanks him for the beautiful poem he had sent him, which bears the traces of the love he has heard about in every lineament.—He is also collaborating on Lang's almanac. He did it out of friendship for the editor.]* If you have seen it you will find in the last issue among other things several of your poems, ones you sent me once to be printed somewhere. He was insistent that I should request you to do him the honor of sending in a contribution. If you have anything of the kind you'd be willing to let him have, give him a mite or two. He will receive it with deep gratitude. Might I not for example slip in the song you sent me in your last letter?

139. TO HIS SISTER

Frankfurt,   April 1797

Dearest sister,

I can imagine that you accompanied our brother here in spirit; I wish you could really have come.

His visit gave me some very happy days. When he arrived I was much the less composed of the two of us; the coach had made the poor lad quite subdued. But he soon warmed up. The very next day I took him over to Homburg, to Sinclair's, a first-rate young man who is my friend in the truest sense of the word. The next day we went up into the hills around Homburg, and from the tops we could see the royal Rhine stretching for miles and its smaller brother the Main and the endless green plains that lie between the two rivers, and Frankfurt with the lovely little villages and woods that lie scattered around it, and Mainz, which stands prouder, and the marvelous regions in the distance, the mountains and forests of Franconia, the Spessart and the Rhön mountains on one side, and on the other the Hunsrück and further up the ranges of the Bergstraße and those of Alsace and behind us the highest tops in the area around Bonn etc.

Then we went down to Mainz; the center of the town had little of interest to us; the great fortifications couldn't be visited without coming up against the military; the churches have been destroyed or turned into magazines, there are not very many interesting people there any more, but Karl was pleased to get to know one of my acquaintances, Prof. Vogt, who from all he had to undergo because of his distant involvement in the revolution in Mainz, but even more because of his pure simplicity and his mind and his learning, is truly a remarkable man in my eyes.

Karl himself will tell you something about the Mainz region. It will certainly come from the heart! Afterward we spent a few days here together, went on small outings, and should probably have stayed together for a few days more if the republicans hadn't put a spoke in our wheel. One morning we saw a small part of the Imperial forces in retreat. A single trait of this physiognomy was enough for us. We decided that our parting should take place the following afternoon. I accompanied our good brother an hour along his way, and that's how we left one another, very briskly and very sadly.

Two days after Karl's departure the French cavalry was already at the town gates, and almost at the same moment a courier from Bonaparte to General Hoche came through here and filled the whole place with jubilation at the peace. It was a very curious situation.—The French at the gates refused to pay any attention to the news of peace (they wanted to follow their orders, and also do a little plundering in the Frankfurt fair). General Hoche, whom the courier was seeking, had not yet arrived and so for a whole morning we were unsure how things would turn out, for the imperial garrison would not have held out against a serious attack. But the generals on either side did eventually agree to an armistice; the French withdrew to the other side of the Nied, a few hours distant from here, and we are now living quite peacefully again.

Next week we are probably moving to a house in the country outside town that Herr Gontard has rented. The house itself is beautifully made and is surrounded by green, with a garden set among meadows. There are chestnut trees round about it and poplars and abundant orchards and a splendid view into the hills. I can see that the older I get the more of a big child I am when spring comes. I intend to enjoy it to the utmost, with all my heart. Make the most of it yourself, dear sister! We must do and receive as much good as possible before we get old.

If you come across a book with the title *Hyperion*, do me the pleasure of reading it when you have the opportunity. It is a part of me and for that reason will no doubt help you pass the time. By rights I should send it to you, but dear Mother has already sent the copies I ordered to me here direct, and I forgot to mention anything about it to Cotta.

Here is a little something from the fair. I hope you like it!

What are your dear children up to? They will be a great delight to me when I am under your roof once again.

Carry on sending me your cheerful bits of news. That's what I like best, to see as if with my own eyes how you are doing. The more trivialities the better!

Generalities are all very well in textbooks, but in our letters we should talk to one another as foolishly as we like, about ourselves and about matters important and unimportant.—You wouldn't believe how much joy it gives me to think of your contented domestic life! It's no bad thing to want to strain upward and outward in one's youth; but in maturity life inclines again to what is human and tranquil.

Take care of yourself, my dear! Warm greetings to your husband and to your children; and to all my acquaintances.

Yours

Friz

140. TO FRIEDRICH SCHILLER

Frankfurt, 20 June 1797

My letter and what it contains would not have been so late if I had been more certain of the reception you would deign to give me. I have sufficient courage and independence of mind to free myself from the influence of other masters and critics, and so to go my own way with the necessary calm, but my dependence on you cannot be overcome. And because I feel how much difference a word from you makes to me, I often try to forget you so as not to become anxious as I work. For I am certain that precisely this anxiousness and inhibition is the death of art, and for that reason can well understand why it is harder to bring nature to its proper expression at a period where there are already masterpieces on every side than at a period where the artist is virtually alone with the living world. He is too familiar with this world, not different enough from it, to have to resist its authority or give in to it. But this bad dilemma is almost unavoidable as soon as the mature genius of a master, with more force and clarity than nature, but also, precisely because of this, more subjugatingly and positively, begins to bear on the younger artist. Child no longer plays with child, we no longer have the primal equilibrium that existed between the first artist and the world, now the boy has men to deal with, and he will scarcely become familiar enough with them to forget their superiority. And if he feels this he is forced to become willful or submissive. Or is he not? At any rate I should not want to react like those weak-minded gentlemen who in such cases, as you know, tend to take the path of the mathematicians and by infinite reduction make infinity and finitude one and the same. Even if one could forgive this disgraceful practice that is committed against the best of things, it's such a poor consolation: $0 = 0$!

I take the liberty of enclosing the first volume of my *Hyperion*. You took an interest in the book when, affected by an unfavorable state of mind and almost completely unmerited slights, it was quite disfigured, and so brittle and needy I cannot bear to think of it. I have begun it again with a clearer, more open mind and happier in myself, and I ask you to be so kind as to have a read of it when you can and to let me know by one means or another what you think. I feel that it was unwise to issue the first volume without the second because it is part of a whole and does not stand well on its own.

I hope the enclosed poems might be judged worthy of a place in your *Muses' Almanac.*—I must admit that I have too much of a stake in them to be able to wait patiently until the publication of the *Muses' Almanac* to know my fate and so I beg you to do one more thing: to address me a few lines saying what you have seen fit to include. If you permit me to, I'll send on reworked versions of one or two of the poems that came too late last year.

I must appear rather needy to you, speaking this way, but I am not ashamed of needing encouragement from a noble mind. I can assure you that I am not one to console myself with vain gratifications and that otherwise I am very quiet about my doings and aspirations. I remain with deep respect

Your humble servant,

M. Hölderlin

141. TO CHRISTIAN LUDWIG NEUFFER

Frankfurt, 10 July 1797

My dear Neuffer,

It is a long time since I last wrote. And it is often impossible. I am about to tell you how things are and they have already changed. Fate drives us forward and round in a circle and we have no more time to stop a while with a friend than someone whose horses have bolted. But the pleasure is then the greater when we do pause again and try to tell an intimate friend what we are about, and in so doing learn it again for ourselves.—I often miss you, dear Neuffer. Philosophy, politics, and so on—we can talk about them with all sorts. But the people we can reveal our weakest side to, and our strongest, are few and far between. I have almost completely forgotten what it is to open myself to a friend in total confidence. I would like to sit with you and warm myself first on your loyalty a while—then I could speak to you out of my heart.—Oh dear friend, I say less and less, and gradually a burden heaps up on me that will all but crush me in the end, or at least give my mind a definitively somber cast. And that precisely is what makes me unhappy: my eyes have lost the clarity they once had. To tell the truth I think I was more balanced than I am now, with a better judgment of myself and others, when I was 22 and still lived with you, my dear Neuffer. Oh give me back my youth! I am torn apart by love and hate.

But vague utterances of this kind are only going to frustrate you. And for that reason I would do better to keep quiet.

You too have been happier than you are. But you have peace and quiet. And without that life is no better than death. That's what I want too, dear friend, peace and quiet.

You say that for some time now you have left your harp hanging on the wall, as you put it. That's all right too, if you can do it without pangs of conscience. And your sense of yourself reposes on other appropriate activities, so you are not reduced to nothing if you are not a poet. For me, every other possibility, anything else I could do, is ruined, and nothing delights me except when from time to time I allow myself, in the heat of the moment, to be pleased by a few lines written down in the excitement of invention. But you yourself know how fleeting that pleasure is. My official duties, it's in their nature, have too intangible an effect for me to be able to feel my strength in them.

Won't you write and tell me what sort of reception the first volume of my *Hyperion* is enjoying among you and your friends, and what your own particular judgment is?

The poem "To Diotima" I sent you last time is already intended for Schiller, so I can't very well let it appear in Lang's almanac. And since the version you have is the final one and I don't have a copy myself, I trust you won't mind if I ask you to copy it out and send it to me as soon as ever possible, otherwise it might be too late to get it in. I'd be very pleased if you put something of your own in with it.

Goodbye, my dear Neuffer!

Yours ever,

Hölderlin

142. TO HIS MOTHER

Frankfurt, 10 July 1797

Dearest mother,

I was waiting for a letter from you with the same disquiet as that which my silence caused you. Sometimes I was worried, sometimes I hoped in vain, and I was on the point of writing to ask what I had done to offend you and my dear sister that I received no reply to my well-meaning letters—but your dear letter was ample recompense. I am now very curious to know what my dear sister will say in hers. The letter you announced has not yet come.

Karl had already written to me about the nuisance looking for a new house to rent is causing you. I'm surprised that you are obliged to move out, as unless I'm mistaken you made it a condition of the sale of the house that you could continue to live in a certain number of rooms for rent for as long as it was convenient to you. And then I am also surprised that you don't prefer to leave ill-fated Nürtingen for good and rent a place in Blaubeuren or Löchgau or somewhere in the vicinity. The inconvenience of such a change is as nothing compared with the favorable influence that a new place, chosen according to your own lights, would have been bound to have on your body and on your spirits.

Unless I'm very much mistaken, dearest Mother, you still have plenty of health and energy in you which could easily be activated by a bit of good cheer and fresh air and the opportunity to contemplate the innocent life of nature. Or my advice would be for you to busy your mind, as much as possible once your tasks are done, by reading, because its natural tendency otherwise is to create work and worries for itself where another person would perhaps be more settled. If you're disinclined to do that, dearest Mother, then write me nice long letters very often and I will respond in kind. That would also perhaps give your heart and mind a cheerful occupation from time to time.

Your children are now all on their own two feet, in good health, all of them in situations one certainly can't call oppressive if one knows something of the world and is familiar with what oppressiveness can mean, you are loved and honored by all of them, from other relationships, for example with the Nürtingen folk, you can liberate yourself whenever you wish, you are not short of means to render life easy and pleasant just so long as you don't *sacrifice yourself for your children* and for *their* sake, out of a virtue I cannot pardon you for, *curtail your precious life through cares that could easily be avoided.* If I'd managed to work my way through life and carried out my responsibilities as valiantly as you have I should want to arrange myself a more comfortable old age than you are! I know, dearest Mother, that not everything can be avoided and that your delicate disposition does not find it easy to harden itself off, but you mustn't allow yourself to enter into a secret union with pain or let it hold too much sway in your heart.—If it can be done I'll come to visit you with my pupil for a few days at the end of the summer. If there isn't enough room in the house then there's no reason why we shouldn't lodge in the inn, should it be necessary. But I can't promise anything for certain. I feel very sorry for the good people in Löchgau! I should have written to my uncle long since but I don't honestly know what I can say about my cousin. His illness will perhaps do some good. All my love to Blaubeuren! And all my warmest wishes to my grandmother for more robust good health! Ever

yours

Friz

I congratulate my good acquaintances on their teaching posts. I wish I could convince myself to take something of the sort. It gives you hearth and home.

143. TO HIS BROTHER

Frankfurt[, ~August 1797]

Dear Karl,

Your concerns were quite unfounded. I haven't got your letter to hand, and there's not time enough to look for it, otherwise I would painstakingly dispel every one of your doubts.

You ask me about my state of mind, about my occupations. The first is a weave of light and shadow, as in everything, except that with me the masses they form are often weightier and in greater contrast. My occupations on the contrary are much as they were. I write, teach my charges and from time to time read a book. And I don't like to stray from my timetable. Anyone who has never been deprived of it, as I have, has no idea of the value of a day spent steadily working, at peace with oneself. For most people life is too drowsy. For me it is often too lively, small as the circle is in which I move. Only a few years ago I could not understand how any situation that hems in our powers could be called favorable in any respect. Now sometimes I feel what happiness lies in it when I compare it with other situations that often take us too far away from ourselves and are to us what rapeseed is to fields, sucking too much strength out of us and rendering us useless for what comes after.

Let your life go on being as insignificant as it is! It will gain significance enough in due course. I wanted to spin you all sorts of arguments. But the night is too beautiful. The sky and the air embrace me like a cradle song, and it's best to be still.

My *Hyperion* has already earned me great praise. I'm looking forward to having got right to the end of it. I have made a very detailed plan for a tragedy, and the subject of it engrosses me.

A poem of mine with the title "The Traveler" is in the latest issue of the *Horae*, where you can read it. You'll also find something by me in Schiller's next almanac.

The day's business has made me a bit tired, dear Karl. You won't mind then letting me off saying more this time. I'll write again soon, with more life, and more warmth! As ever,

yours,

Friz

144. TO HIS MOTHER

[Frankfurt, ~ August 1797]

Dearest Mother,

I'm glad you've been given a reason to write to me. I was just about to reply to your letter from before and am now doubly in your debt. I particularly share your joy at the words of praise Blum has for our Karl. I am certain that all my brother's mind and natural character need in order to appear in their best light is an adequate sphere of influence. You can safely trust my judgment if I tell you that he is no ordinary human being and that with a little more pluck and patience, which he'll have no trouble in developing, he can work his way up to a level that not everyone in his circumstances is able to reach.

You inquire as to my employment, my acquaintances, my hopes. For all the difficulties that inevitably build up in a situation such as mine, I am not for the time being looking for anything else. And I well know that any other position I might enter into would not meet with your full approval, and quite rightly given your opinion of me at present! For any function *I could and should want to look for* requires a maturity I do not yet have. The most recent news I can give you as far as my acquaintances go is that my relationship with Schiller, which for a while seemed to have abated a little, has sprung back to life more warmly than ever thanks to some very pleasant remarks on his side. My hopes are very unspecific, and I wish for no other. Freedom and quiet are all I want and need, and I hope to find them.—I regret, dearest Mother, that I'm not for now going to be able to make the journey home that would have given so much joy to you and to me. I don't know yet, but it may turn out that I have to go to Geneva this coming Easter with my pupil so that he can improve his French, and because I should then come via Württemberg it is easier to renounce a journey in the autumn. In this hope I reckon I should pay heed to the financial arguments and deny myself the pleasure it would give for the moment, but only in order to defer it. I shall write to my dear sister. The sad fate of the good Fehleisen I'd heard about already. I pity his family terribly.—I wish you could be spared the kind of inconvenience caused by having to move house! Peace and quiet is what you need, nothing else!—I am very happy to do as you ask. I have so many letters to write and so beg you to excuse me for now. A thousand fond greetings to my dear grandmother from her oldest grandson! Ever

yours,

Friz

145. TO FRIEDRICH SCHILLER

[Frankfurt, mid-August 1797]

I shall never be able to forget the nobility of your letter. It has given me a new lease of life. I have a deep sense of how accurately you have judged my truest needs, and I am all the more willing to follow your advice because I had already begun to go in the direction you point me in.

I now consider the metaphysical mood as a certain virginity of the mind and believe that being shy of experience, however unnatural it is in itself, is as a phase in life perfectly natural and for a time just as beneficial as any other avoidance of particular circumstances because it contains our strength and preserves it, restrains the prodigality of our youthful life until it grows to an abundance that propels it into the diversity of different objects. I also think a more general activity of the mind, and of the life, precedes the more particular actions and conceptions not just in the nature and substance of things but actually in *time* too, in the historical development of human nature—the idea comes before the concept, and the tendency before the (particular, regular) act. I regard reason as the beginning of understanding, and when the will delays and resists becoming a useful intention I find that just as characteristic of human nature in general as it is characteristic of Hamlet that he finds it so hard to do *something* with the *sole* purpose of revenging his father.

I have always had the habit of letting my unnecessary trains of thought run away with me when I write to you, but somehow I need a preamble of that kind before addressing you more properly and directly, and you understand the reason for it and pardon it.

You will wonder how the new translation of *Kabale und Liebe* the English translator is sending you comes to pass through my hands.

A friend of mine, Mögling, secretary of legation in Stuttgart, visited me on his way back from London where he had spent some time accompanying the Prince of Württemberg, and knowing I have the honor of being acquainted with you he gave me the duty, or really, he wanted to let me have the pleasure, of sending it on to you. The publisher of the book, who was the one who passed it on to my friend, sends you his compliments as well and expresses the wish to receive your most recent works as soon as they appear since he has undertaken to make all your writings available in translation. Should it be tiresome for you to follow this request yourself, I should count it an honor to enter into correspondence with the publisher as you see fit.

Accept my heartfelt thanks for kindly finding room for "The Traveler" in the *Horae*. Be assured that I know what an honor this is. I am also very pleased that you think my poem "To the Ether" worthy of your almanac. Since you permit it, I am sending you the poem to "Those Who Think They Know Best." I have toned it down and refined it as best I could. I have tried to introduce a more definite note, in so far as the character of the poem allowed it. I enclose another poem. It is a reworked and shortened version of the song to "Diotima" you already have. I cherish the hope it might find a place in your almanac in this form.

You say I should be nearer to you, then you would be able to make yourself properly understood. Such words from you mean so much to me!

But will you believe me when I say I cannot afford to let myself be near you? Really, you animate me too much when I am with you. I can still clearly remember how your presence always put me into a pitch of excitement that made it impossible for me to form any thoughts for the whole of the following day. While I was before you my heart was almost too small, and once I had left you I could no longer contain it. Before you I am like a seedling that has just been planted out. It needs to be protected from the midday sun. That might make you laugh but it is the truth.

Hölderlin

146. TO HIS BROTHER

[Frankfurt, ~ 20 September 1797]

[Sends the letters in which the children thank Karl again for the presents he sent them. The letters had been lying around for a while; today they added new ones.]

The fine autumn days are doing me a power of good. I'm still living alone with my pupil in the garden. The family has moved to the city for the fair. The pure, fresh air and the lovely light that is peculiar to this time of year, and the peaceful earth with its darker green, with its dying green too, and with the fruits of its trees gleaming through the leaves, the clouds, the mists, the greater purity of the night skies—all this is closer to my heart than any other period of nature. There is a tender, quiet spirit to this season.

Neuffer did visit me. We spent a few very happy days together. His open-heartedness and cheerful mood are the perfect remedy for the rest of us.

I know how to value, dear Karl, the industry you show in your particular occupation. It's not just *what* we do but *how* we do it, not the substance & the situation but the treatment of the substance & situation that determines the value of human energy. In every human activity there is a perfection, dealing with files included. Of course fish need water and birds need air, and among humans too each has his own element. Only it isn't necessarily the case that the most homogeneous will be the most appropriate. An idealizing mind will do better to create its element in the empirical, the earthly, the limited. If he manages to do this, he, and only he, will be the perfect human being.

147. TO HIS SISTER

[Frankfurt, late September 1797]

Dear sister,

For a long time I'd been counting on spending part of the autumn with you, in your house, among your children and friends, and especially also with your husband, whom I have for some time been longing to become better acquainted with again. I'm greatly looking forward to renewing my relations with him as if from the beginning when once I am with you. I esteem and comprehend people of his character more and more. I should like from time to time to be able to go to him and learn from his repose and his good knowledge of human nature.

You, my dear, are now a true mother, an expectant mother, and I share in your happiness and your concerns. I know of nothing more admirable than a woman in your condition, and it humbles me a good deal when I think of you as you are now. That in the end is really what a contribution to the world looks like. That is the most devout offering a living being can make to Nature. I am glad, dear Rike, that you have already gone through this noble experience so successfully because it allows me to hope that your health, which I cherish so much, will suffer from it as little as I wish.

How lovely it would have been if I could have visited you! But it couldn't be done because I'm due to go on a journey at Easter. By then I'll be with you for sure and then all the happy moments will go into fulfillment that I sometimes entertain myself with. Then we shall go round together in your craggy country and remember our old contented days, then we'll drive over together to Ulm and Elchingen and the ecclesiastical gentlemen there whose ugly visages make such a contrast with the beauty of the region, to Wiblingen and its old nuns, and to Asch and to that little place down by the Blau where once after a boat trip I ate some very good fish and so on.

Forgive me, my dear, for not being able to send you anything yet from the fair here. I haven't yet been at all. You mustn't be scandalized at the bits and bobs I send to show my devotion. What are your dear children up to? My greetings and remembrances to everyone.

Yours

Friz

FROM SIEGFRIED SCHMID

Mannheim, 19 October 1797

[Since that revolution of spirit of which he had told him that it let him see the only thing that could still satisfy him and made him truly

acquainted with himself for the first time, the need for love for a human person had stirred in him with renewed force. But he found no woman he could have loved as he wished; no friend after his own heart.] I spend two hours with you in Frankfurt, and the particular effect of it you perhaps noticed yourself during our conversation. [*Even now he has sensations of such a peculiar kind that he had put his pen aside for a while and was intending to abandon the letter he had begun because it sounded dithyrambic enough as it was.*]

Our acquaintance is too new and too brief to be able to found a solid friendship on it. (Don't laugh!) I hope we shall get to know one another better and become really good friends. When I am in Basel and somewhat calmer, let's speak about the literary, or if you prefer the artistic part of our Frankfurt conversation at rather greater length. Tomorrow I set off from here. [*Going to Basel. Address:*] c/o . . . Iselin in Basel.

148. TO HIS BROTHER

Frankfurt, 2 November 1797

My dear brother,

It means immeasurably much to me to find my being taken up so productively and so sympathetically into a soul such as yours. Nothing calms and soothes me more than a drop of pure, unfeigned love, just as on the contrary people's coldness and hidden desire to dominate always, whatever I do to avoid it, work me up and provoke an excessive tension and unrest in my inner life. Dear Karl, everything we do prospers so well when it happens with a sustained soul and we are enlivened by the quiet, durable fire that more and more I am coming to discern particularly, as their chief characteristic, in ancient works of art of all kinds. But who can maintain a fine bearing if he has to work his way through a crowd where he is pushed and shoved in all directions? And who can keep his heart within the proper confines if the world rains down blows upon him? The more we are attacked by nothingness, which yawns around us like a chasm, or by the thousandfold Thing of human society and activity that devoid of form, soul, or love persecutes and disperses us, the more passionate and intense and violent our resistance *must* become. Or is that *not* so? That is precisely what you are now experiencing for yourself, dear brother. The affliction and neediness from without turn the fullness of your heart into neediness and affliction. You do not know where to go with your love, and your richness forces you to go begging. Isn't the purest part of us rendered impure in this way, through fate, and aren't we bound to spoil in all innocence? What remedy can there be for this? To be active, to be able to tire oneself out over something or other, helps a good deal. That way we at least have a hint of perfection in our sights that our eyes can feed on from one day to the next. It was with this attitude that I used to read Kant. The man's mind was still remote to me. The whole thing couldn't have been more foreign. But every evening I had overcome new difficulties, which gave me a consciousness of my freedom. And the consciousness of our freedom, of our activity, whatever it exercises itself on, is deeply related to the feeling of a higher, divine freedom that is also the feeling of the highest thing of all, of perfection. And in the object itself, however fragmentary it may be, there is a hint of perfection from the moment any sort of order is brought into it. Otherwise how would many a beautiful feminine soul find a world in a well-tidied room?

The poem "To the Ether" signed D. in Schiller's new *Almanac* is by me. Perhaps you'll come across it and it will give your heart some fulfillment.—Why don't you go one day to Vaihingen to visit Conz who's a deacon there? You certainly won't regret meeting him and I think he will like you very much as well. Assure him that I hold him in remembrance and thank him in my name for the treasured greetings he sent me by Neuffer, and for the kind response to my *Hyperion*. Tell him I was just waiting for the second volume to appear before sending him the whole thing and asking him about several points with regard to the little book that are very close to my heart.—I find myself pretty much in opposition to the prevailing taste of the day but do not intend to leave off from my own obstinate course in the future, and hope to fight my way through. I am of one mind with Klopstock:

> The poets who only play,
> They cannot know what they or their readers are,
> The proper reader is no child,
> He wants to feel the heart he has, not play with it.

Heinze, the author of *Ardinghello*, spoke very encouragingly of *Hyperion* at Dr. Sömmering's.

The other parts of your letter that need answering I'll answer *scrupulously* next time and soon. Only I've got so much to write now. Don't feel you would be under any obligation. That would be very small-minded of me and you would have to mean a lot less to me. I shall certainly remain loyal to you. For we are brothers, even if not in name.

Yours,

Hölderlin

FROM SIEGFRIED SCHMID

[Basel, early November 1797]

Even his more lively depictions pass over me in such cold and grandly ringing words. "Song and Kiss" I except from this. "Lindor and Mirtha," "Light and Shadow" by Sophie *Mereau* I like very much; on the other hand, in the Matthisson-like Fried. Brun I can hear nothing but a wearying echo. The elegies by K. have some good bits; but what would be needed to give charm to the whole is lacking. I wonder whether Schiller himself regarded the remaining bunch of poems as a *Mantissa*?—Presumably not, and for that reason I'll read them through again at some point and see whether I should have been ill-humored had I answered the question in the affirmative.

You will be kind enough to let me have your assessment of the productions in this *Muses' Almanac* as well?

What is superior to genuine Greekness, to the golden mean?—The perfection of the inner ideal that can never be represented?—Or do we want to set up outside ourselves anything more excellent (more humanly noble) than the Greeks? That we cannot do. We should deceive ourselves in the attempt and become *inhuman*. We shall establish similar and yet differently modulated works, and therefore become true artists creating for eternity. Have I understood you correctly?

The elaboration of a tragedy shall be an occupation for spare moments this winter. May the gods give me strength! *Dextrae Deus adsit!*

What do you think about Goethe's *Hermann und Dorothea*? I'm due to receive it any day.

I'm going to write down for you here a lament and consolation I urged upon myself last summer, the latter of which—heaven knows for what reason!—for a while now I have often not been able to draw on very effectively.

Dull and all too pitiful is how human life appears to me,
   Cast in the ocean's floods teeming with bustling life.
All are driving and pushing so busily, running one into the other,
   Oh this industrious crowd, is it so different from plants?
Proper to them, so fate ordains, is to vegetate peacefully.
   Only to vegetate though, people do bustle and rush.
Truly you'd like to curse life itself; for nothing but sameness
   Is what one finds in this press, nothing that looks much like life.
If a lament were to slip from your somber lips, no friend would
    hear it,
   If remote from the gods, hours pass away into sighs,
O then you have never had the chance of seeing the work of the artist
   Who with his spirited power made us superior life;
Or perhaps you did get to see it and it struck home, you dissembler,
   Life seeming still as it was when you began to lament.
O then do not imagine yourself to be inhabited by one of the spirits.
   He'd tell you otherwise, world would appear in new light!
Everything is life if the invisible god inspires us, and felt on the pulse.
   Gently it touches us, soft; holy and healing its power.
That's why only a few of us feel it; for gently touched by the fineness
   Which at innumerable points joins Nature and Spirit as one,
So that an urge to create emerges in the mighty weavings of heaven,
   That is not given to all; darlings though feel it and act.

I've started reading *Hyperion*,—friend! my friend!—Sinclair saw in the book the personification of a moral system. God forbid! What will all the others see in it!

S. Schmid

149. TO HIS MOTHER

Frankfurt,   November 1797

Dearest mother,

Don't be surprised that I have taken so long to reply. There are certain kinds of moods that make it necessary to be silent. If I had written in moments when I felt that in the many and various distractions that my employment exposes me to it was almost impossible to salvage my character and the better part of my energies, if I had written then and said that favorable as my situation appears, it is in many respects quite unfavorable to my true interest and I must look to finding a quieter way of life even if from the outside it seems less pleasant, rather than persisting in what has the appearance of a perfectly pleasant situation if it does not allow me a sense of self and repose and the undisturbed activity of my soul—if I had written all this, how would you have received it? What would you have replied? And yet I had well-founded reasons to write in this way; on the other hand it would have gone right against my inclinations to cause you upset, as it inevitably would, in this way and to appear to you as the discontent, unstable, impatient, imprudent person of old. I could hardly do any other than put off writing if I didn't want to tell you something to keep up appearances that had nothing to do with my heart, and you know that sort of utterance is not our way.

You ask what my feelings are now, in the present moment, as I write? If I am to be frank with you I am bound to say that I am in conflict with myself. On the one hand the rational concerns for my character that amid the many contradictory impressions I undergo hardly manages to maintain itself and the most justified needs of my spirit seem to require me to quit a situation in which there are always two parties forming for and against me, of which one makes me almost exalted and the other very often despondent, miserable and sometimes rather bitter. That was what happened to me constantly over the whole two years, it was inevitable, and I saw it coming clear as day in the first few months. No doubt the best thing would have been to stay at a distance, in peace and quiet, keeping relations with both parties as general as possible. But this is all very well if one has one's own lodgings and no particular circumstances that force one to come frequently into contact. You can imagine that in my position—in so far as one wants to maintain it—it is not always possible to follow one's judgment. So I really had no choice but to expose myself to the encounters of all kinds that to a certain degree anyone will be subject to who tries their hand at my job here and is not ready to reduce himself to zero. Now let me repeat that I am on the one hand utterly convinced that my character and energies are bound to suffer one way or another if I am obliged to continue my experiences of the last two years any longer, and so it would seem to be my duty to choose some other less distracting arrangement. I should for example experience far fewer clashes of the kind I have mentioned were I, like Neuffer in Stuttgart, here or in Mannheim or some other large town, to give lessons in a number of different houses, and it is quite commonly the case here that a house tutor changes his situation in this way. I should also gain more time for myself, and the income would be enough to keep me going.—But on the other hand I feel too that it is always difficult to maintain ourselves in a certain degree of well-being and strength and that a situation one is already familiar with and has already learned to cope with somewhat is always, in general, to be preferred to an unknown one where one has to start putting things in place all over again. And then the people with whom I live are not such that I could bring myself to leave acrimoniously, and to get away in a gentle fashion is going to be very difficult; I don't at least see for the moment how it could be done. And then I'd be unwilling to abandon my children, partly because I really am fond of them and partly because gradually I have become used to them. And then a change in my situation would disrupt my occupations, which I am very reluctant to interrupt just now. Above all however what holds me back is that I fear to upset you. So for the time being there is nothing to do but employ all art and prudence not to let the society in which I live have too destructive an effect on me, and to fall back, quietly and firmly, on my own resources. Above all I must bear and keep in mind that life is a school and that the peaceful, truly happy moments are only moments. Perhaps things will also calm down now in our household; the whole of this year we have had almost constant visits, celebrations and God knows what else, and on these occasions the insignificant person I am always comes off worst of all because in Frankfurt more than elsewhere the tutor is always a kind of spare wheel but has to be there for form's sake. Amen! I don't know how many pages my lamentation has gone on for again. One has to remember that the honor of belonging to the more cultivated classes always has to be paid for with a bit of suffering. Only the ploughman is truly happy. But don't let yourself be upset by all this, dearest Mother! So long as you don't have to worry that my true nature is suffering from this fate! And that I shall never allow to happen. I didn't think I should keep wholly silent. In order to be able to judge me now and in the future you need to know the essentials of my circumstances.

I'm sending you and dear grandmother these scarves that I hope correspond to the indications you kindly gave. The net is for my dear sister to do up her hair in. They are much worn here. The way to put them on will presumably also be known in Blaubeuren. Tell her she must make do with it until I've found something more substantial. For my brother-in-law I permit myself to enclose some pieces of English leather for boots. The uppers are made of ordinary leather. I hope he won't find this ridiculous of me.

Dear Karl I'll write to directly in Gröningen. My dear sister I'll write to later this week. This long letter to you, dearest mother, has swallowed up all my time.

A thousand remembrances to all.

Your

devoted son

Hölderlin

150. TO HIS BROTHER

[Frankfurt, ~ November 1797]

My days now tend to be so full that it is more or less excusable that I have neglected to send off the letter I wrote you, dear Karl, for so long. Be so kind as to write to our dear mother saying that I have got my situation quite in order again and that I am living peacefully and am in better health than over the summer; but I beg you, dear brother, to do so at once. I should not now like to think our good mother worried about me a moment longer, for given her character that was probably the effect of my last letter. Goodbye, Karl! Send me some good news soon.

FROM HIS BROTHER

[Mark]Gröningen, 1 January 1798

[*The last letter he received via Enzweihingen where it must have got held up for a while. He is glad to see from it that H. is content again, more so than might have been concluded from the remarks in a letter to his mother. That letter had given their mother a real fright. H. seems there to have complained about certain pressures he is exposed to stemming from the conventions in his otherwise so excellent employment.*]

I have on several occasions been led to compare your character with Rousseau's, and I think you will yourself have to allow a fundamental resemblance between yours and that of our favorite writer. The love for the still grandeur of nature, for the unadulterated truth, and for true freedom that animated that great man is precisely what typifies your own character too, but the sensitivity, the natural consequence of having a heart made for feeling, which soured so many hours of that good man's life, is also yours, and sadly it will also continue to give rise to many a troubled moment and only the company of good respectable people and the enjoyment of the joys of nature and art will be able to reduce the sum of the same.—

How are things going with the drama you began working on?
[*Sends greetings to Sinclair.*]

151. TO HIS MOTHER

[Frankfurt, early January 1798]

Dear Mother,

I deeply regret having given you cause for concern about me. For that reason I should, for one thing, very much have liked you to have taken my last letter for what it really was, which is to say a dispassionate depiction of a house tutor's life as it is more or less everywhere; and, for another, for you to have looked on what I said bearing in mind that it was necessary for me to tell you the truth about my situation, because in the case of a change in circumstances you would otherwise have found my measures groundless. You cannot possibly wish *anyone* to stay in an employment *unconditionally*.

You can in any case be assured that I shall never, *unless I am forced to*, leave a position that I have come to understand and, as far as possible, accommodated myself to. But above all I regret, dearest Mother, that the news I gave via dear Karl to say that all was well, straight after your letter before last, has, it seems, not yet reached you. Probably the letter to my brother was delayed because I sent him a packet that had to go by the slow mail coach. That was also the reason why I have taken so long to write. There was so much I wanted to say that I could never find the right moment, and as I thought I had reassured you via dear Karl I reckoned there could be no harm in waiting until I had a good hour of free time.

My dear sister's happiness is worth infinitely much to me, and I esteem just as highly the great honor, so new to me, of being asked by such worthy parents to be the godfather, the special lifelong friend, of their child.

Make the most of the joy your innocent grandson and the domestic happiness of an estimable daughter cannot fail to give your heart, and don't let your peace be disturbed by thoughts of your son who lives abroad and must continue to do so until his own nature and external circumstances permit him also to make himself at home somewhere in heart and mind.

Please let this year be a year of peacefulness for you. You have done your part in the world. You can be content. You have also gone through so much, especially in recent times, such that you can believe and feel vividly within yourself that both in particular and in general a good, all-preserving spirit lives and reigns infinitely amid the storms, a spirit of peace and order that admits of struggle, suffering and death only so as always to conduct everything through the dissonances of life toward higher harmonies. That is also my heart's belief, and in this faith, this sense I wish you a good and happy year. Take good care of yourself! Don't hold my long silence against me.

Your

loyal son

Friz

152. TO CHRISTIAN MATTHÄUS THEODOR BREUNLIN

Frankfurt am Main, 10 January 1798

My dear brother-in-law,

I cannot say enough how much of an honor I consider it to be linked to you now by a new and beautiful bond. Believe me, it means a great deal to me to be able to call myself the godfather of your dear child. You give me a particular right to take part in spirit in your cares and joys as a father, and for me it is a new reason to love life that you have fastened my attention on an innocent creature in this way who is now growing into his fate and the living world. And I regard his christening as an earnest of our belief in the child's future human dignity, of our hope that this holy undeveloped life will proceed into a sense of itself and of other creatures, into the feeling of the living God in whom we live and have our being, into the true Christian feeling that we and the Father are one, and with these thoughts in mind I should have liked, along with the others, to have held the dear child in my arms.

The brave mother will now be able to take pleasure in things too. She so deserves her happiness. I should dearly like to be able to show her how much I love and value her. I now have one more thing prompting me to make a visit to my dear family, and as soon as I can combine it with other matters I am obliged to consider I shall not fail to let myself have this wish.

And then to enjoy your company, dearest brother-in-law, will be to fulfill many of my hopes. I have learned enough respect for fate for a deeply experienced mind to be the only school I should still like to take lessons in. I feel more and more how inseparably our life and our activity are connected with the forces that stir around us, and so it is natural that I hold it by no means sufficient to draw on one's own resources and to cast one's particularity, however universally valid it may be, blindly among the world's objects. Were you to make up for the loss of your personal company with a letter from time to time I should regard it as a privilege.

I have not yet received your letter before last. Allow me, as a sign of my joy, to enclose this little thing for the baby. Count on me for all matters that require accord with you and devotion to your family.

My dear sister I'll write to myself when I next have a quiet moment. Kiss the dear child in my name, and the others as well.

Your

devoted brother-in-law

M. Hölderlin

153. TO HIS BROTHER

Frankfurt, 12 February, posted 14 March 1798

My dear brother,

It is a proof to me of your good character that amid all your affairs you always manage, as I can see, to gain in genuine inner life. On the other hand the example you set confirms my favorable opinion of mechanical work: it is not as deadening as an activity where, in the object and its treatment, there is more scope for choice. It does not tear one apart, as an occupation that engages us in mind and soul does, and leaves us less passionate, in that passion largely seems to stem from the uncertainty we find ourselves in when an indefinite object of attention prevents us from going in any definite direction. If I only know what actually has to be done I do it perfectly calmly. But if I have no exact and reliable understanding of the matter in hand I have no idea what force and how much of it is appropriate and then find myself doing too much for fear of doing too little, or too little for fear of doing too much, i.e., acting out of passion. Dear Karl, it is often more desirable to be occupied merely at a superficial level of our being than constantly to expose one's entire soul, whether in love or in work, to the destructiveness of reality. But it is hard to convince ourselves of this in the period of youthful awakening, when all our energies strive toward deeds and pleasures, and it is probably quite natural that we willingly sacrifice ourselves, that we give up our initial peace for the fortunes of the world and the uncertain fame of posterity. But we mustn't be too hasty, we mustn't be too quick to swap our beautiful, vital nature, the native delight of our hearts, for conflict and ambition and cares, for

unless it is diseased the apple does not fall from the branch until it is
ripe.

Dear Karl, I speak like someone who has suffered shipwreck.
Such a person is all too likely to advise staying in harbor until the
best season for the voyage comes round. I obviously set out too early
on, aimed too soon at something great, and shall probably have to pay
for it as long as I live. It's unlikely I shall wholly succeed in anything
because I did not let my natural disposition mature in peace and quiet,
free from presumption and cares.

I'm writing all this more for my own sake, because my heart is
full of it. You don't have much need of this sermon.

Shakespeare has taken hold of you entirely—I can well believe
it. You too would like to write something of that sort, dear Karl, and
I would too. It is no small ambition. You would like to because you
would like to have an influence on your nation; I should like to for
that reason too, but even more to satisfy my soul, which thirsts for
perfection, in the production of such a great work of art.

If you seriously want to have an effect on the German character
as a writer, and plough up and sow this vast fallow field, my advice
to you would be to do it rather by writing speeches than in poetical
works. You would reach your goal more quickly and surely. I have often
been surprised that our best minds didn't come on the idea more often
of writing a powerful speech, e.g., on the lack of *feeling for nature* in
scholars and civil servants, on religious slavery etc. You are particularly
concerned with political and moral matters in our country, e.g., guilds,
civic rights, communal rights etc. Such subjects are certainly not too
slight, and with your local knowledge they are just right for you, at
least for a start. However, I don't mean to talk you into or out of
anything with all this.

I hope soon to see you and have a talk. If only it can be done I
intend to come home in March. I need peace and quiet, dear brother!
I'll find it in your company and once I'm with the family again. Oh
Karl, all I want is peace and quiet. Don't think I'm cowardly or slack.
My heart, which has been shaken so often and so variously for years
now, only needs to gather its strength before I embark once again on a
fresh piece of work.

Do you know the root of all my trouble? I want to live for the
art that is my heart's desire, and am forced to shift for a living in the
world, making me often so weary, weary of life. And why? Because art

may feed the masters, but not those learning their trade. But only to you do I say this kind of thing. It's weak of me, isn't it, not to wrest for myself like a hero, against the odds, the freedom I need? But you see, dear Karl, then I'm at war once again, and that's not good for art either. But it's too bad. I wouldn't be the first to come to grief who was born to be a poet. We don't live in a climate for poets. That is why of ten such plants hardly a single one thrives.

Among my little pieces of work there is not one that was not interrupted by some deep unhappiness while I was writing it. You may say I shouldn't pay any attention to what makes me unhappy, but I say to you I should have to have the kind of frivolity that would soon lose me all the love of the people I live among.—

What is going on then in your world of politics? I haven't been able to find the parliamentary writings yet. I lent them to someone and can't remember who. Forgive me, dear brother. I'll happily make up for it one way or another.

The letters you were asked to get from me must be in safekeeping in Nürtingen. I have none here. I know my own heart and am sure that things had to happen the way they did. So many days in the best part of my life were spent in misery because I had to endure disregard and disdain as long as I was not her only suitor. Later I found favor with her and responded in kind, but it was not hard to see that my original, deeper attachment had been extinguished by the unmerited suffering I had put up with. By the end of my third year in Tübingen it was over. The rest was superficial, and I have paid for it enough that I continued to go through the motions during the last two years in Tübingen. I have paid for it more than enough through the irresponsibility that crept into my character because of it and that I freed myself from again only after unspeakably painful experiences. That is the whole truth, dear Karl. If you have to speak about me, deal with it as best you can. I wouldn't want to cause any distress to the good soul for anything.

Your affairs I hope we'll soon be able to have a good talk about together. In any case it pleases me very much that you are turning yourself so rapidly into an accomplished administrator.

The hope is that the Cisrhenanians will very soon be republican in a more vital and real sense. In particular, the military despotism in Mainz, which threatened to stifle every stirring of liberty there, will soon, they say, be reined in.

Goodbye for now, dear Karl.

Ever yours,

Friz

154. TO HIS MOTHER

Frankfurt, 10 March 1798

Dearest Mother,

All kinds of things to do prevent me from writing more often. A letter written in a spare minute is hardly worth the cost of sending it and even more than complete silence appears cold and neglectful, and as I say I very often lack the repose and the time for a letter in which I can give you a clearer sense of the enduring presence of the sentiments I bear you as your son.

It is true that it is to my own detriment. And it means that I have all the more often to do without your dear letters that in the truest sense are frequently so very beneficial to my whole being. But perhaps I shall soon have the pleasure of your actual company for a time. The journey to Switzerland I was to make with my pupil seems unlikely to take place. Nothing is said about it at least any longer, and the troubles in those parts are in any case a sufficient reason not to undertake it.

But I have provisionally spoken of being keen to visit my family and no objection has been made. The costs of the journey, which as far as possible I shall spare you & myself, should not be too high compared with what I should gain for my heart and my health.

It is true that if my time in Frankfurt should not last much longer it would be imprudent to run down the little money I have saved up, because a change in my situation would inevitably be bound up with certain expenses.

I am now in better health again than a while ago when I suffered badly from nervous headaches. Spring does everyone good, and it would be a real blessing to me to be able to enjoy it in peace with my relatives and friends.

It must have given you great joy to spend time with your little grandchildren in Blaubeuren. It is a lovely place and you must warn my dear sister for me that she'll have to put me up for a few days if my little journey comes off. My visit couldn't last more than a fortnight altogether because the journey itself takes almost a fortnight and I can't very well be away for more than a month. Whether I'll bring my pupil with me or not is not yet settled. I should also have written to Blaubeuren again long ago if so much didn't get in the way.

Wouldn't I be a nuisance to you if I moved in with you for a few days? You haven't yet told me whereabouts I should have to look for your new dwelling. I am in any case eager to know where I should be imagining you.

I'll find out today how the hairnet is to be worn and then add the instructions for my sister. I'd forgotten all about it, I'd have attended to it long ago otherwise. —

I've just had a chance to ask. The part that can be tightened goes at the back of the neck; the rest of the opening is pulled right over the hair down to the ears; and above the forehead it comes to about 2 fingers back from the hairline. At the back, the hair, plaited or not, is tucked up and the net goes over it like a nightcap so that when it is pulled tight and knotted over the forehead no wisps come out at the back or sides. And then a ribbon is tied over the string that pulls the net tight, and on top of the head, a little to one side, a bow. But I shall probably have to put the hairnet on my dear sister myself.—I'll write again soon, dearest Mother. I have far too much to do at the moment. Look after yourself.

Yours

Friz

155. TO CHRISTIAN LUDWIG NEUFFER

Frankfurt, in March 1798

My dear Neuffer,

I have the pleasure of putting you in touch with an interesting young man who is returning from a journey through Germany to his Swiss homeland and will not reckon the hours he spends in your company to be wasted. This is Herr Schinz, a student of theology from Zürich. He will tell you tales of Father Klopstok, of Jena, Göttingen, Dresden, Berlin etc. In return, be so kind as to take him to meet the artists in Stuttgart and others you think will be interesting from a literary or political point of view or because of their relations in society. Forgive me my long silence—illness, occupations, distractions—which I hope to make up for as I'm coming in a few weeks myself.

Yours

Hölderlin

156. TO HIS MOTHER

Frankfurt, 7 April 1798

Dearest Mother,

You will be surprised perhaps to receive a letter rather than a visit. But the things that prevented me from bringing my pupil also prevented me from coming myself, for I cannot very well part with him without going against my maxims and my disposition. And even if my constant attention may not be crucial for him at the moment, I should not be completely tranquil to be away from him because it is always possible that he would let things slip in my absence.

That I didn't write sooner is due to the indecision I found myself in as to my journey.

Perhaps a more opportune moment to see my family again will soon present itself. I am accustomed to renouncing desires that cannot be realized, and so as the circumstances seemed to demand it I was able to give up this project even though I had been entertaining myself with it over the winter.

You will be having a very contented time over Easter. And it gives me pleasure to think of you all. If only the worries caused by the troubles in Württemberg don't unsettle you too much. But I think all will be well. If only our Württemberg deputies in Rastatt showed somewhat more courage and spirit, and less pettiness and incapacity, especially those who make the decisions. But the Lord gives to his beloved in their sleep. The troubles won't get all that bad. And if the peasants get out of hand and threaten order, as you fear, they'll soon find a way of curbing them.

As far as my future arrangements are concerned there is no need to be anxious, Mother dear! I shall *certainly never again* be obliged to be a burden to you. Only I must ask you to consider that at the present time it is no longer reasonable to regard, out of a certain fondness or tender concern, this or that arrangement as exclusively honorable, realistic or suitable. Had my education served only for me to earn my living in the pulpit, which I have no wish to mount because it has been desecrated in too outrageous a manner, had I applied the energies of my youth to no other end, then perhaps I should soon be in a sorry pass as far as earning my bread goes. But I think things will not turn out as badly as all that.

My brother-in-law, my dear sister and Karl I'll write to later in the week, when I've had a chance to look round the fair a bit. And then you too shall receive a letter, dearest Mother, that is less rushed than this one. This time I shall look out something for you at the fair that I like myself; for you don't really tell me what pleases you best.

Much love and remembrances to all!

Yours

Friz

157. TO HIS SISTER

[Frankfurt, mid-April 1798]

Dearest sister,

I'd have written sooner if I hadn't hoped to speak to you from one week to the next. Sadly this has come to nothing and I would probably have foreseen that my situation would prevent it if my desire to see you all again hadn't blinded me. A principal reason is that I cannot afford to leave myself completely without money, so as not to be fettered to my employment by this bond and to have a little saved up that would do at least for a start in case of a change of circumstance. As there were yet other reasons, e.g., that I couldn't leave my pupil here, nor, without difficulties, take him with me, I at last decided to renounce a pleasure the prospect of which had sometimes cheered me over the winter.

The longer we are separated, dearest sister, the happier will be the time when we are once again closer to one another, and the lovely hope abides of always finding one another as we are and in good health.

You will be glad to be able to enjoy the spring in peace and quiet, amid your family and in the company of good friends. Your happiness is genuine; you live in a sphere where there are not many wealthy people, not much nobility, let alone aristocrats; and only in a society where the golden mean dwells are happiness and peace and true feeling and pure sense to be found, it seems to me. Here for example you see, apart from a few genuine people, nothing but monstrous caricatures. With most of them their wealth has the effect of new wine on peasants; for they are just as silly, giddy, coarse and exuberant. But that is also good in its way; one learns to keep *silent* among people like this, and that is something.

I'm sending you a very chic fan from the fair here, it's decorated with little phials of scent. Because I am too thrifty to send you something substantial I'm obliged to send you something foolish: both mean the same.

Give your dear husband my apologies for not yet having written; I'd like to find an hour for him when I can really focus, and that's not often the case when I have time off.

Send my love to your dear children. Christian will have really grown up now. Heinrike, Miss My-bride-to-be, will find me single still after her confirmation. The little one is strong and healthy I trust?

Goodbye, dear sister. Remembrances to my friends.

Yours

Friz

158. TO HIS MOTHER

[Frankfurt, mid-April 1798]

Dearest Mother,

You will come off a little worse than the other two today. Confident of your understanding, I have already written to them and unless I wait for the next post that means I have almost no time left. I thanked you my heart brimming with joy for your dear affectionate letter. You have already given me so much, give me so much still with your mother's love; if only I could also contribute more to brighten your life that is so dear to me.

I am most anxious that moving house might have been too much for you. Remember, dearest Mother, how many houses I've moved in and out of in my life, and believe me when I say that every change, even if it is insignificant, brings suffering unless one looks on it with a certain equanimity and strength. More and more I see now how much we can brighten and lighten anything that may befall us by thinking about it in a particular way. In thousands of instances it is right to say that he who doesn't want to suffer never does. Admittedly it takes some work before one learns to regard external occurrences with a bit more indifference and finds one's way to a state of good humor and interest that can always be relied upon. But once one has got that far one has as much as a person can wish for.—

What is our dear Grandma up to? These fine days you should take walks together as often as you can.

You ask me for one of my works? Thank you very much for taking an interest in my scribblings. Next time I'll enclose something.

Tell me also, dearest Mother, what I can send you from the fair. I don't know much about that sort of thing. But please do let me know of something. Otherwise I'll deliberately spend more and end up buying more than I should.

Take care of yourself.

Yours

Friz

159. TO CHRISTIAN LUDWIG NEUFFER

Frankfurt, June 1798

I do not like to leave you in doubt about me a moment longer, my dear Neuffer, and for that reason am writing these few words in great haste before the post goes in order to reply to your last letter at once.

Heigelin told me you had told him to take my contribution to your almanac with him on his way back, and it's because I was expecting him any day that I put off my reply for so long. Various sufferings have also made me indolent. Forgive me, dear friend, and for old times' sake don't let me lose your affection, for I need it greatly.

The enclosed letter I wrote you long ago. I could not very well write to Frau Mereau because there are rumors of my having had a love affair with her or who knows who in Jena.—Oh, dear Neuffer, there are so few people who still believe in me and their hard judgments will probably pursue me until I'm gone, at least from Germany. Make do with these little verses. If at all possible I'll send you a longer poem as well. I was also approached, before I knew that I could be of service to you, by other people asking for poems and had to keep my word as I had promised them.

Ever and with all my heart

yours

Hölderlin

Be so kind as to write to me again soon and let me see something of your work; it was a strange piece of fantasy on your part to think that your almanac did not have my approval. Only its contents can determine my verdict, & I know already that I'll like what is by you.

160. TO FRIEDRICH SCHILLER

Frankfurt, 30 June 1798

Do not consider it an immodesty that I am sending you a few poems again; even though I myself do not deem my hopes for your approval to be justified.

However much I am oppressed on many sides, however much my own unbiased judgment robs me of my assurance, I cannot bring myself to separate myself, out of fear of censure, from the man whose singular mind I feel so deeply and whose power would perhaps have taken my courage away long ago were it not just as great a pleasure to know you as it is a source of anguish.

You see right into a person's soul. Therefore it would be pointless and idle not to be candid toward you. You know yourself that every great man deprives those who are not great of their composure, and that only among men who are equal do equilibrium and easiness prevail. For this reason I can admit to you that I am sometimes in a secret struggle with your genius to salvage my freedom from it, and that the fear of being completely ruled by you has often prevented me from approaching you with serenity. But I can never remove myself entirely from your sphere; I should hardly forgive myself such a defection. And it's good that way too. As long as I am in some sort of relationship to you it is not possible for me to become an ordinary person, and if the transition from the ordinary to the excellent is even worse than ordinariness itself, I, in this case, will choose the worse course.

Your unfeigned admirer,

Hölderlin

161. TO HIS MOTHER

Frankfurt, 4 July 1798

Dearest Mother,

I suspect you are now in Gröningen and so am addressing the letters to dear Karl. You can imagine how much it affects me that his work has been made more difficult by the disagreeable consequences of ill health, and I am very glad for him that you are lending him your company for a while.

You are quite right to take umbrage a little at the scarcity of my letters, and quite seriously I will attend to it that in future I no longer let myself be impeded so often in such a pleasant duty by all the occupations and interruptions. I owe you so very much—how could I do otherwise than to multiply the small pleasure I can give by sending you letters as often as possible? There is just one thing I must ask, dearest Mother, and that is that you should not be surprised if you don't always find the tone of my letters equally lively. For while it is in our power to think and act rationally when we wish to it is not in our power to convey our emotions. You will know from your own heart that it is sometimes more weary and taciturn, sometimes more lively and disposed to warmer utterance, and you would consider it an unjust reproach to be called neglectful or unloving because your heart is not always fully awake. And believe me, I am often glad if I manage to be more reserved and matter-of-fact, for that way one is better fitted for the world.—

Write to me again as soon as you can to tell me how Karl is doing; if he doesn't have plenty of time and inclination, he needn't write to me himself. His letters give me endless joy but I will happily do without them if this joy comes at a cost to him. Once he is in good health again my demands will be stricter.

Whatever you do don't be too anxious about the state of my dear brother, and hope as I do that his natural vigor will soon come to his aid. My compliments to the District Administrator and his family.

Your

obedient son

H.

All my thanks to dear Grandmother and you for the lovely presents!

162. TO HIS SISTER

Frankfurt, 4 July 1798

Dearest sister,

I have all kinds of things to thank you for: the present you sent, your long letter and all that it contains. After I'd received it and read it I went for a walk and took it with me, wanting to read it again, but

I kept it in my pocket because I knew it by heart, and besides was thinking too hard of you and your loyal affection for me to read it again with composure. Dear sister, the advantage of the various experiences I have had is that I appreciate all the better every sign of sympathy. We are like the herds I have often observed in the fields, the way they move closer together and stand huddled in rain and bad weather. The older and more silent one becomes in the world, the more firmly and gladly one holds on to those who have proved their worth. And it's bound to be that way, for we properly understand and appreciate what we have only when we see how slight many other things are.

Don't mention those trinkets, my dear Rike, they are just to show you I am thinking of you and to express my desire to pay you some greater service. Please accept it for what it is, a harmless pleasure that I treat myself to by wondering which of these things would suit you and so allowing myself to be with you and your family in my thoughts.

You talk of thanks, but the debt of thanks I owe you reaches so far back now. Believe me, someone who lives without hearth and home and often among strangers learns to appreciate it when a friend or his mother or sister welcomes him into their house, and he never forgets it. How many generous and joyful days have I not spent under your roof?—Dear sister, you yourself can have no idea what a house like yours is worth, where the humane spirit of your dear husband and a heart like yours reign. You are happy, and would feel it even more sharply if you saw how joyless and desolate the world of show and grandeur is, not only for us but for those who live in it and seem to prosper there, when all the while a hidden discontent they do not fully understand themselves gnaws at their souls. The more horses a man sets before his carriage, the more rooms he shuts himself up in, the more servants he has surrounding him, the more he covers himself with gold and silver—the deeper he digs his own grave, where he lies more dead than alive and the others don't notice him any longer, no more than he does them, despite all the fuss they make on both sides. The only person this sorry comedy can delight is the one who looks on and deceives himself. If only I too could stop and stare at the splendor of the world! I'd be happier, and perhaps a perfectly tolerable young man! But the only way to impress me is by character and by genius, and since these are such rare things in the world I have unfortunately only rarely shown it the proper humility. Well, I'm humbler now, having suffered a bit more, but that's not the right way.

I must break off, the post is going. Give my remembrances to your dear husband. My love to all the children, and to each as it pleases them best. As soon as Miss My-bride-to-be starts scribbling we'll have to set in train a tender correspondence between us. —

All my kind regards to Dr. Veiel. I'm delighted at his good taste, and if he's happy into the bargain, even more so.

Yours,

Friz

163. TO HIS BROTHER

Frankfurt, 4 July 1798

You've learned the habit of putting off writing from me, dear Karl, but I'll set you a good example and write another letter before getting a reply to the one I sent you at about Easter time. Our dear mother writes saying you're a bit unwell and have a great deal of work. So I can very easily imagine how hard it is to get round to writing a letter. Life is sometimes so disruptive and debilitating that, for all the energy of youth, often one barely has thoughts and patience enough left over for what is necessary, and no period is worse in every respect than a young man's transition to maturity. I think that at no other time in our lives do other people and our own natures cause us so much trouble, and this period really is that of sweat and anger and sleeplessness and anxiety and storminess, the bitterest of our lives, just as the period that follows on May is the most unsettled in the year.

But as with all other things that mature, human beings ferment, and the task of philosophy is simply to ensure that the period of fermentation is as harmless, as tolerable and as brief as possible.—Swim through, brave swimmer, and just keep your head above water! Sweet brother, I have also suffered much, very much, and more than I ever told you or anyone else, because not everything can be told, and even now I still suffer a great deal, and nonetheless I think the best of me has not yet perished. My character Alabanda says in the second volume: "What lives, is indestructible, *even in its deepest form of subjection remains free*, remains whole, and if you tear it down to its base, and if you smash it to the marrow, yet it remains at bottom unwounded, and its being flits triumphantly from out of your hands etc." This is true of more or less any human being, and most of all of the truest and best. And Hyperion says: "Everywhere there remains a joy for us. True pain inspirits. Whoever treads on his misery stands higher. And it is a marvelous thing that only in our sufferings do we fully feel the soul's freedom." Farewell, dear beloved brother. Write to me soon. Remember that I am loyal to you, as you are to me! Oh, only remain the person you are, for our country's sake and for mine!

H.

There are letters too from the children.

164. TO CHRISTIAN LUDWIG NEUFFER

Frankfurt, August 1798

I am pleased, my dear Neuffer, that you are content with my bits and pieces. One day, when the fates, whom I love even in unhappiness, will perhaps repay my love with some tranquility and good spirits, I will make sure you also profit from it. You must know that you, who were the first properly to teach me the joy of true friendship, will and must receive from me everything that men can demand of one another, spirit and action and affectionate devotion. Dear Neuffer, do you honor the times of our shared intimacy as I do?—I believe that people who have loved one another as we have are for that very reason capable of all that is great and beautiful and are bound to achieve it if only they understand one another properly and have the courage to work their way through the dross that hinders them. I know very well I have achieved nothing yet, and perhaps I never shall. But why should that affect my faith in myself? Does it make it a vain illusion? I think not. I shall say I have not understood myself properly if I do not succeed in anything excellent in this world. To understand ourselves, that's what saves us. If we err in ourselves, in our θειον or whatever you want to

call it, then all art and labor is in vain. That's why it's so important
to stick together and tell each other what is in our minds. If out of
petty rivalry etc. we separate and become isolated it's our own greatest
loss—the voice of a friend is indispensable if we are to be at one with
ourselves again whenever, because of the stupidities of ordinary people
and the selfish pride of those who have already achieved something, we
are at odds with our own soul, our own best life.

Here are a few more little poems.

I didn't have enough time for what I promised you in my last
letter.

Yours,

Hölderlin

FROM HIS SISTER

Blaubeuren, 13 August 1798

My Friz is full of joy whenever he catches sight of your portrait and
already knows exactly where it hangs when I ask him about his uncle.

FROM SIEGFRIED SCHMID

[Basel, late summer 1798]

and now let's wait and see how it fares in the world. I didn't send
Schiller anything for the *Muses' Almanac* despite the heap of little
things I have ready here. I didn't feel like it.

For most of the summer I've been idling around, lots of walks. I
am curious as to when it will come to an end; various different subjects
have occurred to me from time to time that I wanted to work up; but
I've let the thoughts flit by and am still not doing anything.

Give me the pleasure soon of your splendid mind, and take me in
your arms as I do you.

Siegfried Schmid

165. TO HIS MOTHER

Frankfurt, 1 September 1798

Dearest Mother,

You can imagine how much pleasure all the lovely letters together you sent recently were bound to give me. In particular I must thank you for your kind invitation. You well know that my profit would always be more than yours if I were able to live once again among my dear family and in your affectionate company, dearest Mother. So you can work out whose side the denial is greater on. But I have learned so well to bow to necessity that on this occasion too I am resolved to put off the visit I was planning. My dear pupil suffered greatly the whole summer from the ague and so I was obliged to be more sparing than usual with my lessons and now must make use of all the time available to catch up with what we missed. The occupations that are more properly my own have also suffered somewhat because I hardly left him all day long while he was ill, and his illness, despite not being very perilous, still meant that my heart and mind were not free. And so for myself I am also obliged to stay here. I think, dearest Mother, that sooner or later the chance will come for us to spend good and happy times together.

Believe me, I share in spirit your gladness in having your dear visitors with you, and so I do not come away empty-handed either.—

I am surprised that in Tübingen the librarian Schott has been promoted to a chair; it is more or less a requirement in such a post for the holder to have made himself a reputation abroad since otherwise the faculty won't be much visited by people from outside, something that for the education of the students and also for the financial situation of the university cannot well be done without. For precisely this reason I'm surprised that Schelling was overlooked. Age is irrelevant; and as his fame is now new and would be bound to increase a good deal if he were called upon to exert all his force and vigilance, he would have been likely to bring no small honor on the university. I have sometimes quarreled with him over his opinions; but I have always found that even when his claims are wayward they come from an uncommonly sharp and thorough mind. But I'll keep this for a letter to my brother-in-law in which I shall try to put the case for the young philosopher.

The Harter story is frightful.

Many remembrances to my grandmother and to Blaubeuren. As ever

your

loyal son

Friz

FROM SIEGFRIED SCHMID

Basel, 23 September 1798

Two lovely letters, my dear Hölderlin, apart from the disgruntledness that had to be vented. You're right, beloved friend, it's all natural, the barbarity and its effects on *us*; but still there is something I was going to say to you about that, an insight that came to me some time ago now and lets me be as cheerful and carefree as a god.
[*gap of indeterminate length*]

deeply thought and with sharp distinctions, about lyric and epic poetry; it all comes down to how they are applied, in order to condemn this or that. But friend, even if from amongst the latest productions many do not hold up against such principles (I mean in general, without

HOMBURG, 1798–1800

FROM HENRI GONTARD

Frankfurt am Main, 27 September 1798

Dear Hölder,

I can hardly bear it that you have left. I was at Herr Hegel's today, he said you had been thinking about it for a long time, when I was going back again I met Herr Hänisch who came round the day of your departure, looking for a book; he found it, I was in my mother's room then, he asked Jette where you were, Jette said you had left, he too wanted to go and see Herr Hegel and ask about you, he accompanied me and asked why you had gone away and said it pained him a good deal. Father asked at table where you were, I said you'd gone away and that you sent him your compliments. Mother is well and sends you her greetings many times and says you must think of us very often, she has had my bed put in the balcony room and wants to go through with us everything you've taught us once again. Come back to us soon, my Holder; who else is there to teach us. Here is some more tobacco for you and Herr Hegel sends you the 6th part of Posselt's *Annals*.

Goodbye, dear Hölder.

I am

your Henri

FROM SUSETTE GONTARD

[Frankfurt, ~ 25 September–5 October 1798]

My love, I must write to you. My heart cannot bear my silence toward you any longer, let me speak my heart before you just once more and then, if you think it better, gladly, gladly I will be quiet.

Since you went, how barren and empty in and around me everything is, as though my life had lost all meaning, only in my pain do I feel myself to be alive. — —

And how I love this pain! When it leaves me and there is numbness in me again, longingly I seek after my pain, only my tears over our fate can give me any pleasure. — — — And they flow in abundance when every evening, to shorten the day, already at nine, at the same time as the children, I lie down to sleep when all is quiet and no one can see me. Often then I have asked myself must this pure beloved love of ours in future dispel and vanish like smoke and nowhere leave any lasting trace?—Then a desire came into me through written words to raise it a monument, for you, so that time would have mercy on it and leave it unaltered and never to be erased. How I should like to depict and fathom this noble love of our hearts in its smallest nuances, in shining colors, could I only find the solitude and the quiet! but continually torn and troubled as I am I can feel this love only in fragments, seek after it constantly, and yet in me it is whole!—

I still feel best in the open and constantly I long to be out there in the fields and to see our beloved hill, the Feldberg, that is like a wall and a gentle obstacle to prevent you from cruelly going further away. But when I come home again it is not as it once was, such happiness I once had coming home when you were near, now it is as if I return to be shut up in a great box, back then my children came down to me from being with you, how that gave me strength in my frequent sadnesses, when a soft blush, a deeper seriousness, a tear in the eye, showed me your influence on them, now they no longer have that meaning for me and often I have to correct my feelings toward them. — — —

I had written this far in the 1st week since you went away and my heart has been fighting with my reason whether I should actually send you these lines or not. my heart has won for in case all other dealings with you are severed I must seek a means of letting you know, I could not bear the thought that still living as close as we do and after such intimacy we would not wish to hear or know anything about one another, I could not reconcile such self-denial with my loving feelings and I almost believe you would be bound to expect to hear from me and if I kept silent you would have cause to accuse me of having no such feelings. I felt sure you couldn't write first because I was always against it. These thoughts decided me, don't take it amiss that I have written to you and tell you of my unhappiness, if unhappiness were not also proof of my love you would not hear of it, I assure you.   Then *Henry* had your letter, which greatly lifted my spirits, always before my eyes I had only your new freedom and independence, your domestic life your quiet rooms and the green trees at your window but your letter, that dear comfort, I kept scarcely a quarter of an hour, till H.—. very conscientiously demanded it back, to disclose it, and I wasn't given it again I don't know all the things that were forbidden H.—. on this occasion but afterward I found him very much altered, he scarcely dared say your name. You came to F. . . and I didn't see you, not even at a distance, and that was hard for me! All the time I had been reckoning on Saturday but I must have had a feeling about you because on the evening you went past around half past 8 I opened the window and thought I might catch sight of you by the big streetlamp. A little while later when I wanted to send *Henry* to H.—. he said he wasn't allowed anymore, I told him very seriously that if he raised no objection to this prohibition and didn't feel very sorry about it he must have an ungrateful heart but it did no good, he said he had to do as he was told.

Now that all our means of communication have been severed and I am very outraged by it I rest my hopes on the man you sent from the inn to us.

If you agree and *Sinclair* is coming this way you can ask him, if it would work and won't put you in a wrong light with him, to visit me and through him send me *Hipperion* if you already have a copy, it isn't possible for me to go and buy it. In that way I shall have news of you again, how happy that will make me if you are doing well!—

I have already noticed that I am being treated with great courtesy, every day new gifts, treats and excursions, but accepting the smallest favor from him who had no mercy on the heart of my heart would be like taking poison so long as this heart still feels, for who after the fall of her friend could enjoy the good life (as they call it) and still uphold any sense of herself and her feelings so having this sense I am glad to live more simply than before, by choice restricting my needs, this pride and this feeling are dearer to me than all earthly possessions. God and my love preserve me in it!   I am almost always alone with the children, seek to be as useful to them as I can.

Often I have regretted that when it came to your leaving I advised you to go at once, I still cannot understand what feeling drove me to beg you so urgently to go, but I think it was fear of the whole sensation of our love that became too loud in me at this violent sundering and the violence I felt made me there and then too acquiescent, I thought afterward how much more we might have arranged for the future, if only our separation had not taken that hostile tone no one would have been able to forbid you entering our house but now, oh my kind friend, tell me how it can be done that we see each other again however distantly.—That, to renounce it utterly, I cannot do. It will always be my dearest hope. — — Give thought to it!

I shan't be able to write to you often, I shall trust this way only once, via S. . . you'll receive a few lines back. I also think that in future it won't work so often with the theater, people would soon notice because they're not used to seeing me at bad plays and we don't want to be watched, also it would upset me too much to know that you were coming in bad weather, So, if you agree, we'll make this arrangement, you come on the 1st Thursday of every month and if the weather is bad then on the 1st fine theater day following and I'll fit in with that.

All those words for an arrangement! And there is so much I wanted to say to you but the real thing I cannot express, it lies buried deep in my heart, only tears of sorrow can say it and quieten it. As you see, I cannot find the words. — — I am so altered, this terrible blow of fate has turned me completely in upon myself, a deep and holy seriousness inhabits my whole being, but often I feel so numb, I can't think, if I try to read, my thoughts stand still, they will not go on, I can do only the most necessary things, my patience is a wonder to me. Otherwise I am in good health, but my courage fails me, I can't bestir myself, I feel rather lamed, all I want to do is sit there, and also I want to dream! but even my imagination often refuses to serve me, oh for sure it will be better once I know that I shall be certain of having news of you and that I shall always have a visible point, a day of hope, ahead of me, for only hope keeps us alive. — — This remains certain: that I shall never change. — — —

I wrote so far on Wednesday.

Friday morning, half past 9.

Since I saw you yesterday the one thing alive in me is the
desire to speak to you, if you will risk it, if you are not bound by any
promise, come this afternoon at a quarter past 3, come in without
precaution at the back door that is always open run lightly and swiftly
up the stairs as you used to, the door to my room on the landing will
already be open for you, at that time the children will be having their
lessons in the blue room at the back and if you keep to the wall they
won't see you, *Wilhelmine* will stay with *M* in the living room and
we can hope for an hour of peace and quiet, to talk, but if you think
it foolhardy or have any other grounds against it I promise to honor
them and for certain in all things I shall be unchanged, and then we'll
keep to the old arrangement, you can always do that, you will always
find me.

even if anyone should see you that doesn't matter at all, It can't seem
odd if two people who lived under the same roof for 3 years spend half
an hour together, rather the opposite.

166. TO HIS MOTHER

Homburg vor der Höhe, 10 October 1798

Dearest Mother,

Your pure good will toward me, which I felt once again in your last
letter and which gave me such pleasure, also your partly justified
concern for my health, give me grounds to hope that you will not
disapprove of the change in my situation which I have been building
up to for quite some time.

First of all I must demonstrate to you how stable and appropriate
in every respect my present situation is, and when I then go on to
name the reasons that inevitably caused me to leave my previous post,
despite having stayed put for a long time and with much patience, you
will find more cause for contentment than for discontentment in this
letter.

Through my work as a writer and by being thrifty with my
salary I have in the last one and a half years of my time in Frankfurt
got together 500 florins. With five hundred guilders I think one can

be quite free of financial worries for at least a year anywhere in the world, so long as it is not as dear as Frankfurt. So I had every right to restore the health and energies I had necessarily forfeited to the strenuous combination of my official duties and my own work by seeking out a more peaceful way of life, something that my savings, though not without considerable effort on my part, had made possible.—In addition, my friend, the governmental Counselor von Sinclair in Homburg, who had long since been privy to my situation in Frankfurt, urged me to move over into his house in Homburg, take board and lodging with him for a small fee, and *get on with my work and so finally begin to establish for myself a position in society*. I made many objections to this, among other things that I risked falling into a state of dependence on him that would be unfitting between friends. To remove this objection he found me board and lodging somewhere else where conditions are extremely pleasant and I live in good health and free from disturbance and pay 70 florins a year for the rooms, service and laundry. For lunch, which is really unusually well prepared for the price, I pay 16 groschen a day. In the evening I have long been accustomed to drink only tea with a piece of fruit. (As I have brought far more clothes with me than I need, though admittedly they were all required in Frankfurt, you can see how far my savings will get me.)

The members of Sinclair's family are all excellent people who always treated me with courtesy and kindness on my earlier visits and, now that I'm actually here, are so generous in their sympathy and encouragement that I have more reason to keep myself to myself for the sake of my work and to preserve my freedom than fear I might lead too solitary a life. My book has had a certain amount of success at court and the wish has been expressed to make my acquaintance. The Landgrave's family is made up of genuinely noble men and women whose attitudes and way of life set them quite apart from others of their class. But I take care to keep my distance so as to protect my freedom; I pay my respects and leave it at that. You understand that I am only telling you this because you might be pleased to hear it and it could be useful to me in an emergency. But the crucial thing is the intelligent, rational, warm companionship of Sinclair. With such a man every hour brings joy and enrichment for the soul. You can imagine the good influence this is having on my work and my character. So as not to go on too long I'll save for another occasion much else that will convince you how well fitted this place and my present situation are to my most real needs. It was simply necessary, after all this time, to adopt a more independent situation to prepare for my future profession, and judge for yourself whether the place I have chosen for this purpose could be more suitable.—For all that, I admit I should very much have liked to remain in my previous situation a little longer, for one thing because it was terribly hard to part from my dear pupils, who were doing so well, and also because I was well aware that any change in my situation, however necessary and favorable, would upset you. And I should certainly not have shrunk from the effort it would have taken to carry on my own work alongside my lessons, although I must say that I was so involved with the children that it was simply not possible for me to take my teaching lightly in any way. The fondness they had for me, and the success of all my efforts, often cheered me and did make my life easier. But the discourteous pride, the deliberate, daily belittling of all learning and culture, the opinions expressed about house tutors—that they were only servants, that they couldn't expect any special treatment because they were paid for what they did etc., and many other casual remarks of that nature let drop in my presence because it's the fashion in Frankfurt—that hurt me, however hard I tried to rise above it, more and more, and sometimes left me in a state of contained anger that never does body or soul any good. Believe me, I was patient! If ever you believed a word of mine, believe this! You will think it exaggerated if I tell you that nowadays it is simply impossible to hold out for long in such conditions; but if you could see in what degree *the rich businessmen in Frankfurt, in particular, are incensed by present events,* and how they make everyone who depends on them pay for their resentment, you would be able to understand what I am saying.—I don't want to speak about the matter any more, or any more clearly, because I am really very reluctant to speak ill of people.—It was really these almost daily injuries to my feelings that made my professional tasks and other occupations unutterably more difficult and would have rendered me quite useless for both had I not sought to counter what I suffered with the most strenuous efforts. However that could only last for a while. The whole of last summer I was almost completely idle once I had finished with the children because most of the time I was too poorly or too tired for anything else.—I am ashamed to talk about myself in this tone, and do so only for your sake, only to convince you of the necessity of a change.—Eventually I had to make the painful decision to part from the dear children, which I had put off for so long and with God knows how much toiling and anxiety. My self-respect, too, prevented me from continuing to appear before my friends in such a miserable state. I announced to Herr Gontard that my future development demanded that I make myself independent for a time, I avoided all further explanations, and we parted on polite terms. There are lots of things I'd like to tell you about good little Henry, but I have to banish virtually all thoughts of him from my mind if I am to prevent my feelings from getting the better of me. He is a marvelous boy, full of unusual talents, a boy after my heart in so many respects. He will never forget me, just as I shall never forget him. And I think I have laid good firm foundations in him he will be able to build on in the future. I'm glad I am only three hours away from him so that I can at least find out how he's getting on from time to time.—I must break off here to get the letter to the post in time. Give me the pleasure of one of your kind letters soon. Remember me in Blaubeuren. I mean to write to them very soon. All my love to dear Karl: a long letter will go off to him this week too if possible. How is grandmother? Give her my warmest compliments. I am, as ever, with childlike devotion

Yours,

Friz

My address.
M. Hölderlin, c/o Herr Wagner, glazier in Homburg vor der Höhe.

FROM SUSETTE GONTARD

[Frankfurt, perhaps 31 October 1798]

Tomorrow after 10 o'clock I will be expecting you. Beg with me the guardian spirit of our love for one quiet hour. — —
If it should be impossible, you know the sign, then after 3 o'clock. I long for the hour!—sleep easy and may my image hover round you. Have courage, I am prepared for every eventuality and feel sure everything will go well. Tomorrow you will also have a long letter from

me and surely you will bring me too something lovely, I feel the joy of
it already—

167. TO HIS MOTHER

Homburg vor der Höhe, 12 November 1798

Dearest Mother,

I am so grateful that you have taken the news of the change in my
situation with this kind trust and confidence in me. Since I've been
here I've been living peacefully in the daily company of my friend
Sinklair. Now he is going to travel to Rastadt on business of the
Landgrave. He has suggested I might keep him company on the
journey and during his time in Rastadt, and as thanks to the generous
provisions of my friend I can do so at almost no cost and can continue
my occupations at least for a part of the day quite undisturbed in
Rastadt too, I considered it unreasonable to neglect this opportunity
to add to my education and have decided to set off with him for 4
weeks today or tomorrow. If the weather and the roads permit, perhaps
I'll make a trip from Rastadt to Nürtingen & Blaubeuren in order to
spend a few days with my dear mother and the rest of the family again,
which I have done without for so long. But if I find that it's too far and
the traveling expenses exceed the current state of my finances, I shall
at least arrange to meet dear Karl in Neuenbürg which will not be too
far for either of us. He should be able, in this case, to take a few days
off from his affairs, and the District Administrator will, if I ask him
expressly, gladly consent to it. It will of course be very hard for me
not to see Nürtingen and Blaubeuren too.—I'll write to you too from
Rastadt, and to my dear sister and Karl. Be so kind as to pass on my
apologies to my dear correspondents in the meantime.

Sinklair sends his regards. He was pleased to hear that you trust
him to look out for me and says he will be sure to do so. It's really
quite funny that Sinklair's mother has appointed me the attentive
companion to her son, just as you have made the Counselor my
mentor. And there can be few friends who hold such sway over one
another even as they yield.

Send my remembrances to dear Grandmother. It gives me a good deal of pleasure that you don't have to do without this beloved company over the winter. And send my love to everyone.

Your

obedient son

Hölderlin

168. TO CHRISTIAN LUDWIG NEUFFER

Homburg vor der Höhe, 12 November 1798

My dearest Neuffer,

I have changed my situation since I last wrote to you and intend to live here in Homburg for a while from my own means. I have been here for just over a month and have spent the time peacefully, at work on my tragedy, with Sinklair for company, enjoying the beautiful autumn days. I was so torn by various sufferings that I probably have the good gods to thank for the blessing of my present peace and quiet.

I am very eager to have news of you and to receive your almanac; but I'll almost certainly have to wait unless I come and fetch it from you myself, not because I think you neglectful, but because your letters will only find me here again in 4 weeks' time.

My friend Sinklair, you see, is going to Rastadt on business to do with the court he works for and has suggested that I accompany him, on very favorable conditions. Thanks to Sinklair's generosity I can do this almost without touching my meager savings and also without significantly interrupting my work, and so it would have been odd of me not to agree.

We are setting off later today or tomorrow.

Perhaps I'll make a trip from Rastatt into Württemberg. If this doesn't prove possible I'll write to you from Rastatt asking you, if you're not prevented by other circumstances, to be in Neuenbürg on a certain date, and I'll come there too so as to see you face to face again. I should love to be able to speak with you again about all the things that interest us both.—Life in poetry is what now occupies my thoughts and senses more than anything else. I feel so keenly how far I still am from arriving at it but all the same my whole soul strives for it, and often it all comes home to me so palpably that I cry like a child when I everywhere feel how my work is lacking in this or that respect and yet I cannot extricate myself from the poetic labyrinth I'm wandering about in. Oh, in my early youth the world frightened my spirit back into itself and I'm still suffering from the effects. True, there is a hospital where poets afflicted as I am may find honorable refuge—philosophy. But I cannot relinquish my first love, the hopes of my youth, and I'd rather die without achieving anything than abandon the sweet land of the Muses, which only chance has cast me from. If you have any good advice, to put me on the right path as quickly as possible, let me know. I lack not so much strength as lightness, not so much ideas as nuances, not so much a main tone as a spectrum of diverse tones, not so much light as shadow, and all this for one reason: I shun the common and ordinary aspects of real life too much. I'm a real pedant, if you like. And yet unless I'm mistaken pedants are usually so cold and loveless, and my heart is always so eager to unite with everybody and everything beneath the moon. I almost think I am pedantic out of sheer love, I'm not shy because I'm afraid that reality might disturb my selfishness but because I'm afraid reality will disturb the intense, ready sympathy with which I commit myself to other things; I am afraid the warm life in me will be chilled by the icy-cold happenings of everyday life, and this fear comes from having always reacted more sensitively than others to anything destructive I encountered, and this sensitivity seems to have its origin in the fact that, relative to the experiences I had to go through, I wasn't of a sufficiently strong constitution, I was not indestructible enough. I can see that. Is being able to see it of any good to me? To this extent, I think: since I am more liable to be destroyed than many other people I must try to extract some advantage from the things that have a destructive effect on me. I mustn't take them for what they are in themselves, but only in as far as they can be of use to my own truest life. I must when I come across them make it a principle to take them as indispensable material without which my innermost will never come to full expression. I must take them up into myself so that when the opportunity arises (as an artist, if that's what I want and am to become) I can place them as shadow next to my light, reproduce them as subordinate tones among which the tone of my soul will spring forth with all the more life. Purity can only be represented in impurity and if you try to render fineness without coarseness it will appear entirely unnatural and incongruous, and this for the good reason that fineness itself, when it occurs, bears the color of the fate in which it arose; and beauty, when it appears in reality, necessarily assumes a form from the circumstances in which it emerges that is not natural to it and that only becomes its natural form when it is taken together with the very conditions that of necessity gave it the form it has. So for example the character of Brutus is a highly unnatural, nonsensical character unless he is seen amid the circumstances that forced his *gentle* spirit to adopt this *stern* form. Nothing fine, then, can be represented without coarseness; and for this reason I shall always tell myself, when I encounter coarseness in the world: you need it just as much as a potter does clay, therefore embrace it and don't reject it or shrink from it. That's my conclusion.

Wanting to ask you for advice and thus to give you a very clear picture of my faults, which of course you're already acquainted with to a point, and at the same time wanting to become more conscious of them myself, I've gone further than I meant to, and so that you can understand my fretful ponderings properly I'll admit that for some days now my work's been at a standstill, and when that happens I always fall into reasoning. Perhaps these brief thoughts will stimulate you to further reflection about art and artists, and particularly about my main poetic faults and what can be done about them, and perhaps sometime you'll be so kind as to let me know what you think. —

Good wishes, my dear Neuffer! I'll write again as soon as I'm in Rastadt.

Yours,

Hölderlin

FROM ISAAK VON SINCLAIR

[Rastatt,] November 1798

[On a trip to Swabia Muhrbeck made the acquaintance of Zwilling and was delighted with him.]

169. TO HIS MOTHER

Rastadt, 28 November 1798

Dearest Mother,

I arrived here a week ago and since then have made many interesting acquaintances. And even the unknown throng of foreigners one has the opportunity to see is varied enough in their faces and dialects and habits for one to accustom the eye to be more and more at home in the world.

I am often together with my fellow countryman, the secretary of legation Gutscher—he treats me with a good deal of respect and I am glad to find in him such a sensible and attentive diplomat.

I was very sorry indeed that last week the weather was so bad that a journey to Württemberg on foot was all but impossible. As I am now due to leave here again at the end of the week I am obliged to renounce my intentions once again, and you can imagine how hard for me that is. But next spring, when I'm done with a piece of work I'm in the middle of, I'll deny myself no longer and come to live for a few weeks with you and my dear family.

I hope then to be all the happier in your company. At the moment I am swaying between past and future; that is, the dejection that still clings to me a little from the past sometimes prevents me from looking into the future as hopefully as I'd like, and the future is still further away than I can see, and I have not yet got on far enough toward my present goal to be able to forget a humiliating past.—

What I am working on now will be my final attempt, dearest Mother, to give myself a sense of worth on my own path, as you call it; if it doesn't come off, I shall calmly and modestly seek to be of use to society in the simplest post I can find, I shall take the strivings of my youth for what they so often are, for a fortuitous exuberance, for an overreaching inclination to remove myself from the sphere that is ordained for me by my natural abilities and the circumstances in which I have grown up.

Be so kind as to address your next letter to Homburg again, like the last time. Continue, dearest Mother, to put me right and to cheer me with your advice and an affectionate word or two, as you have until now. My remembrances to dear Grandmother and to all.

Your

obedient son

Hölderlin

PS

I am very sorry, dearest Mother, that you were so unsettled by what I proposed; but you can see yourself that I am hardly to blame because I had heard nothing about the insecurity of the roads in Württemberg. Please, I beg you, don't worry about me and make your life as cheerful for yourself as possible, as you have so much cause, in yourself and in the end also in external circumstances, to allay the sorrow of life with joy. It also casts me down; I always think that I can't be much good at all since other parents often have such high ideas of their children.

170. TO HIS BROTHER

Rastadt, 28 November 1798

My dear Karl,

We should have become strangers to one another if the similarity of our attitudes and our nature had not made us infinitely and lastingly close, for this time we really have left our friendship without nourishment for longer than at any other period. But the gods, though they do not need a sacrifice, demand it nonetheless as a tribute. And so we too must again begin to make sacrifice from time to time to the divinity between us: the easy, pure sacrifice of speaking to one another about it, of celebrating what eternally unites us in the sweet letters that we only exchange so seldom because they come from the heart and not, as so often happens, from the pen. A living flower takes longer to grow than a flower made of taffeta, and a living word must also mature in our hearts before it can appear, and cannot be produced in profusion like the things that one shakes from one's sleeves. It's not that our letters are so extraordinary in their thoughts and wit and in the diversity of their ideas and subjects, but they have something that can be called the sign of all living utterance, which is that they say more than they seem to, because in them a heart stirs that in life in general can never say all that it wants to say. Dear brother, when will people recognize that the highest power is in its expression also the most modest and that the divine, when it makes itself manifest, can never be without a certain sadness and humility? Of course at the moment of decisive conflict things are rather different! But as you can see that's not what we're talking about. I don't need to tell you how much my heart has been shaken by the changes in my life during the silence between us. That I am living in Homburg, and why, you will have seen from the letter I wrote to our dear mother. Karl, how often I'd have liked to write to you in the last days in Frankfurt, but I concealed my suffering from myself, and there were times when if I had tried to utter it I would have wept out my soul. In Homburg I tried to recover my peace of mind by working constantly, and when I was tired I spent most of my time with Sinklair. He has acted toward me as a true friend. It was at his suggestion that I accompanied him here. There are all sorts of people here. Only it's a pity that diplomatic *sagesse* keeps everybody's faces expressionless, and their minds too, so that little open social interchange goes on. Nevertheless, despite the prudence common to all, the differences between the French, the Austrians, the Swabians, the Hanoverians and the Saxons and so on are still pretty obvious.

I should very much like to have spoken with you, dear Karl. I did have the plan of at least getting you to come as far as Neuenbürg or Pforzheim to meet there, but the time I had in mind has been marred by bad weather, and this week I mean to go back to Homburg. Next spring, when I've finished what I'm working on, nothing will keep me from following the bidding of my heart and spending a few weeks with you all. That then I'll have a few more miles to walk doesn't matter, especially in the fine days in May. Let the glad, good, pure spirit of life be with us both until then and protect and sustain us! —

The real gain my stay here has brought me is meeting a few young men full of spirit and pure endeavor: *Morbek*, a Pomeranian, a restless soul who is now traveling, drawing inspiration from people and nature for a bold philosophical work he is still jotting down notes for; *Horn*, secretary of the Prussian legation, a man of genuine culture with profound sentiments and great curiosity together with fine manners and conviviality, a thinker with a proper sense of beauty and art; *von Pommer-Esche*, a Swede—all calm and kindness, unpretentious and happy in himself, accomplished in all kinds of disciplines and languages, proud and manly but completely good-natured, figure and countenance intact in their beauty; then also a splendid old man, Councilor *Schenk* from Düsseldorf, an intimate friend of Jacobi's, a pure, cheerful, noble character, lucid and full of ideas—he speaks, often like a very young man, with sheer joyful enthusiasm, especially when talking about his beloved Jacobi, and casts such a friendly eye over us younger ones that together we make up a completely harmonious family.

Let me soon have news of you again, dear brother. I got R. to tell me a lot about you, and afterward on his return to Württemberg he also wrote to say he'd visited you as I had asked him to and told me how you were. You'll write to me soon, won't you? Address your letter to M. Hölderlin, c/o Wagner, glazier in Homburg vor der Höhe.

There are hopes here again, more than before, that peace will come soon. I speak to our countryman, Herr Gutscher, secretary of legation, nearly every day. He is a sensible man.

And now good night, dear Karl!

Yours,

Hölderlin

FROM HIS BROTHER

[Markgröningen, early December 1798]

that this was unlikely to be your actual intention and that in the course of time you would be bound to give more from your abundance of riches.—He charged me with many warm greetings for you.

Conz is a dear fellow, and his undemanding peacefulness, the sure sign of a noble character, must surely make friends even of people not yet well acquainted with him.

I am sorry that I was only able to speak to him briefly and amid the noise of a dance in Vaihingen I was present at, but one day soon I shall go over to Ludwigsburg to visit him—

In the letter our dear mother sent me to enclose for you you'll
see that you are offered a house tutoring job in Heilbronn. Did I not
delight as I do in the independence in which you are currently living,
and not hope myself soon to move closer to you through a change
in my situation, the desire to be near you would almost compel me
to wish that you might take up this post. But your peace and quiet is
more important to me than the satisfaction of my wishes, and for that
reason not a word more on this proposal.—

But now, dear chap, you'll have had enough of my talk which as
you'll have noticed was mostly written down during the night when I
was granted an hour or two of peace to lift myself out of the dust of
my files and give myself up to thoughts of you, dear brother.

You look after yourself and let me see something of you again
soon; give our dear friend *Sinclair* greetings from me, and commend
me to his wider circle of friends.

Ever yours,

Carl

FROM SUSETTE GONTARD

[Frankfurt, perhaps 5 and 6 December 1798]

In the evening

My letter gave you sorrow, my love, and your letter beyond expression
gladdened me and made me so happy, it showed so much love. Oh
how my heart answered in every chord when I read it, how warmly my
feelings joined with yours! And you, could you perhaps have doubted
my love, could my cold hard letter have distressed you? how wrong you
would be! if you could only see my pain and tears at such a thought.
Then you would not think it, but very likely that is not what tormented
you, you are very likely fearful that my heart is dying in me and then
I will not be able to love you anymore.   I can't conceive what
effect my words had on you, I saw your tears, they fell burning on my
heart, I could not halt them — — — numbed and speechless I sat
the whole evening and found this moment of relief for the oppression

of my heart, because I am alone. Oh if only I could come to you and comfort you, you are the soul of me, I have nothing secret from you, nor could my heart die, the love in it being so abundant, so when I am silent and hard do not doubt me, in my depths it is burning and like you I must shield myself from passion, grief does eat at me a little but the sweet healing melancholy comes down from heaven in time and pours her blessing into my heart and I shall never lose faith in the powers of Nature even should I feel death within me I would say, she will wake me again she will give me back all my feelings that I have faithfully harbored and which are mine and which only the force of fate has taken from me and she, Nature, will be victorious, out of death she prepares me a lovelier life, for the seed of love lies deep and ineradicable in my being, I speak from experience for I know how always with a greater liveliness my heart has lifted out from under every weight.   Oh my dearest, I don't know whether my tone is the right one, it's certain I had nothing to *tell* you, but much, so much, to say to you, but what oppresses me is nothing other than that I can't be with you. if only I could give you certainty, but I am afraid my passionate language will not persuade you—oh let it! and in your love be happy again! It still gladdens me this evening that I did nevertheless see you again and oh God how terrible if you had left in that mood, truly I could offer up prayers of thanks to the spirit of love for invisibly guiding me and with those thoughts I shall go to sleep and wish blessings upon you. — — —

In the morning

I slept well, my darling, and again I must tell you how much joy your letter gave me and I thank you for the quiet bliss you have made for me, oh don't read my letter anymore if it has saddened you and hold to the one before it which you liked so much, yesterday I could not help thinking a great deal more about passion, — — — Probably *the passion that is the highest love* will never find *its satisfaction on earth* — — — — feel this as I do: to seek it would be foolish. — — — *To die together* — — — — Hush, it sounds like romantic folly but is nonetheless so true. — — — — is love's satisfaction. — — But we have sacred duties toward this world. What we are left with is our most blessed faith in one another and in love's all-powerful being that will for ever invisibly lead us and bind us ever closer. — — —

A quiet devotion, trust in the heart, in the triumph of the truth and supreme value of what we have given ourselves to. And could we really go under and cease to be? — — — But then everything would lose its equilibrium and the world would become a chaos were it not upheld by the same spirit of love and harmony that upholds us, if it lives in the world eternally, why then and how should it forsake us, like as we are to the world, how should it be otherwise in us, as in great things so in small, why then should we not have faith? We having daily proofs of Nature who in her splendor gives life to us also, who shows us only love, should we have conflict and discord in our lives when everything calls us to the stillness of beauty? — — — Oh my love, surely not! we cannot become unhappy since that soul lives in us. And I know that pain will only make us better and bind us ever more intimately.

So don't be still grieving that you made me sad, believe me that is over with now if you are at peace again, and I have felt strong. I must also tell you that my trust in you is boundless, as you are, however you manage things, I approve of it and have no need to say so, I don't even ask why you didn't come last week, yesterday you didn't say that you would call again, that you would come this morning, even though in my letter I had suggested it. I assure you that it didn't disconcert me in the least, so happy your letter had made me, and all I thought was it is certainly for love and I wondered no further and having this faith in love we must respect what we can't explain. Oh my love, my dearest, be at peace again, be cheerful and bring me the uniquely blessed feeling that you are content and give me peace of mind too, then for sure then I will be happy. — — —

171. TO HIS MOTHER

Homburg vor der Höhe, 11 December 1798

Dear Mother,

Your kind letter no longer found me in Rastadt and was sent on to me here. It gave me a great deal of pleasure to see that I am still held in fond memory among my relatives, your kindly thoughtfulness and sympathy especially, dearest Mother, stirred me intensely, and you can imagine how that in itself made me feel drawn toward you. In order to be able to think things over calmly I was obliged to put off my decision about the proposed post as private tutor until the next day, and even then I was unwilling to trust my judgment at first and wanted to let a few more days go by so as to be able to give you an answer that had been properly considered.

Probably the most valid argument I can put forward is that in a year's time I shall hardly have any trouble, should nothing else present itself before then, in finding a similar post, since private tutors who are worth their salt are very hard to come by at present, and many resolve to find some other way of getting by rather than entering into what in our day and age is such a difficult situation and exposing themselves to all the misunderstandings which are now so much a part of this equivocal calling. For a well-defined office, where a man has a mechanical employment set him in advance, is something quite different and can be much more readily executed in tranquility than educating children, which is something that has no end; and sharing day-to-day life in one household, where, mutually, any pretensions have to be reduced to a minimum if one is to avoid ending up a burden on each other, is so difficult and, as I said, the frame of mind common to almost all those who take on private tutors nowadays is even with the best will in the world and the greatest tact on both sides so hard to cope with that a young man really does best not to venture on this difficult task so long as some other situation is open to him which he doesn't need to be ashamed of and will allow him to make ends meet. But as everything can be learned, and I feel I now have a fair idea of how to manage a peaceful life as a tutor in most households, I have less cause to fear this position than others who have no experience of it and are less practiced and forbearing—only in such a situation I always forfeit in liveliness of mind what I acquire in reserve and patience. For this reason I think it is my duty to spare myself in this regard for as long as I can without causing distress to others, in order to spend a year with all my living powers devoted to the higher and purer occupations God principally intended me for.—This last remark may surprise you, and you will want to know what these occupations are.—From what of my work has come your way up until now you will hardly be able to guess what the business is I most call my own, and yet even in those insignificant pieces I have, from a distance, among those who can hear me, begun to *prepare* the deeper opinion of my heart which I shall perhaps be unable to express fully for a long time yet. At the moment it is not possible to say everything straight out to people because they are too dull and concerned with themselves to abandon the thoughtlessness and irreligiousness they live in like a plague-ridden city and escape to the mountain-tops, where the air is purer and the sun and the stars are closer and we can look down with tranquility on the turmoil of the world below, that is, where we raise ourselves up to a feeling of the godhead and contemplate all that was and is and will be out of this feeling.

Dearest Mother, you have sometimes written to me on the subject of religion as if you did not know what to make of my religious feeling. Oh if only I could at one stroke reveal my innermost thoughts to you.—Just let me say this: there is not a living note in your soul which does not find an answering tone in mine. Have faith in me. Do not doubt what is sacred within me and I will open myself to you the more. Oh mother, there is something between you and me that divides our souls. I don't know what to call it—does one of us have too little respect for the other, or what is it? I say this to you from the bottom of my heart. Even if you cannot put into words all that you are to me it lives in me all the same and on every occasion I have a strange sense that secretly you rule over me and that, with an indelibly faithful attentiveness, my soul is anxious for yours. Can I tell you something? If I have often lacked orientation in my thoughts and drifted around restlessly in the world, it was only because I thought you had no joy in me. But it's that you don't trust yourself, isn't it, you are afraid you will make your sons soft and too headstrong, you are afraid your motherly nature might get the better of you and that your sons would then be left helpless, without direction, and for that reason you have too little confidence in us, and out of love deny yourself the pleasure which is proper to parents when they are older, and prefer to expect less of us so as not to expect too much? —

I wanted to tell you the reasons I had for turning down the post that has been offered me, and I am glad that it has given me the opportunity to speak from the heart again. That is a pleasure we so rarely have in this world that it could easily be forgotten.

I wrote to our dear Karl from Rastadt. Now I won't leave it any longer and will write to Blaubeuren too. It troubles me that my dear brother, who deserves to be so happy, does not feel that the situation he is in suits him. Can't you write to me, dearest Mother, and tell me what the unpleasantness is he has to put up with?—It is nice that our dear relatives can find some consolation for the death of the good pastor in the happy state of my dear cousin Karoline. Wish her warmly all the joy she deserves from me. And write to them thanking them sincerely for having thought of me with the job; but I couldn't get away for at least six months and Herr von Gemmingen probably wouldn't want to do without a teacher for his children for so long. If things were different I should have considered myself lucky to enter into relations with Herr von Gemmingen. All my best wishes to dear grandmother and to everybody!

Yours,

Friz

All my regards and congratulations to my old friend Gentner.

172. TO ISAAK VON SINCLAIR

Homburg vor der Höhe, 24 December 1798

My dear friend,

The reason I have not written to you for so long is that I would only have put half my mind to it, for until now I have been taken up more than usual by my work, which had become dearer to me because of the interruption. As you well know, I have no trouble abandoning things when you are with me in person, but I take a bit longer about it if presence, which has power over everything, is not there making its agreeable pressure felt.

Thank you very much for your letters. Pommer-Esche's visit gave me enormous pleasure because it was of real benefit to me to see the man again, so pure in his kind, and to take his form and being into me where it will now lodge all the more firmly. Then it also meant much to me to have news of you all again. I have greatly gained in faith and courage since I've been back from Rastadt. You yourself I see more clearly and sharply now that I can think of you together with my new friends, and you know how much it strengthens relationships such as ours if we understand each other and have a clear image of each other

in our minds. Once the foundations have been laid, as with us, and one
has got a deep, complete feeling of what the other must by his nature
remain true to, whatever transformations he might undergo, then love
does not need to shy away from judgment, and in this case one can
certainly say that faith grows with understanding. And then of course
it's true that my soul rejoices all on its own that, despite all the apostles
of meagerness, there is more than *one* person in whom nature has
expressed herself in her fine abundance and that I can now, besides your
own spirit, call others to witness against this doubting heart of mine that
sometimes threatens to take sides with the unbelieving mob and deny
the god within. Tell them, your friends and mine, that I often think of
them, whenever it seems to me that apart from myself and a few solitary
beings whom I carry in my heart there is nothing more than my four
walls; and tell them that they are to me like a melody in which one
seeks refuge when the bad demon threatens to take over. It is the whole
truth, all this, but I don't like speaking in such general terms about a few
excellent people, and I know very well I would have to write to each of
them separately if I wanted to do justice to my feelings.

These past few days I've been reading your Diogenes Laertius.
And I've experienced something I've come across before, which is that
the transient and changeful nature of human thoughts and systems
has struck me as almost more tragic than the destinies that ordinarily
we regard as the only real ones; and I think this is natural, for if man
is dependent on outside influence even in his most proper and freest
activity, in independent thought, and if even here he is always affected
by circumstances and by the climate, as is incontrovertibly the case,
then where is his dominion? But then it is a good thing, and even
the first condition of all life and of all forms of organization, that no
force is monarchic in heaven and earth. Absolute monarchy will always
cancel itself out, because it has no object; in the strict sense it has
never even existed. Everything is interconnected, and suffers as soon
as it is active, including the purest thought a human being can have.
And properly speaking an *a priori* philosophy, entirely independent
of all experience, is just as much a nonsense as a positive revelation
where the revealer does the whole thing and he to whom the revelation
is made is not even allowed to move in order to receive it, because
otherwise he would have contributed something of his own.

Anything made, every product, is the result of the subjective and
the objective, of the individual and the whole, and the fact that the

share the individual has in a given product can never be completely separated from the share the whole has in it shows once again how intimately every individual part is bound up with the whole and that together they make up *one* living whole that, *individualized through and through as it is, consists of parts that are entirely independent* but *at the same time intimately and indissolubly interconnected.* Of course, from any one *finite perspective one of the independent forces in the whole will be the dominant one,* but it can only be regarded as temporarily dominant, a matter of degree.

173. TO HIS BROTHER

[Homburg, New Year's Eve, 1798]

If your fate doesn't take a turn for the better sooner or later I give you my most sacred word as a brother that I will be at your side with all I have and can. In the meantime I beg you, dear brother, to look on your situation as cheerfully as possible. Grant me the satisfaction of having gone through many bitter experiences not only in my name but in yours too, and grasp what I have to say to you with a clear, keen mind and believe that it comes from my love for you: the world will destroy us utterly if we let every affront penetrate into our hearts, and the best will quite simply come to grief one way or another unless they manage, in good time, to react to everything that is done to them in neediness and paucity of spirit and heart with calm understanding and not with the goodness of their souls—for even if hurt the soul remains, as it must, magnanimous, and does people's paltry insults the honor of taking them seriously. Believe me, who am certainly not speaking here out of self-importance but out of a profound sense of my deficiencies based on many unhappy memories, believe me, calm understanding is the holy aegis that preserves the heart from poisoned arrows in the war of the world. And I believe, a fact that comforts me a good deal, that this calm understanding, more than any other virtue of the soul, can be acquired by realizing its value and working at it with willingness and perseverance. When I think back over the years half of which I've wasted in sorrow and misguidedness but that you, dear Karl, still have ahead of you, I often feel there are so many things I'd like to write down for you in blood. It is a curious sensation to have fought one's way through with hard effort and only by the skin of one's teeth and to think that others one cares about are not likely to find it any easier. In general we tend to fear fate far less for ourselves than for those who are close to our hearts. —

The bell is just striking twelve, and the year 1799 is beginning. A happy year to you, dearest brother, and to all the family! And then a great happy new century for Germany and the world!

I'll go to bed on that.

1 January 1799

Today I had put my usual occupations to one side and in my leisure fell into all sorts of thoughts about the interest the Germans currently have in speculative philosophy and in reading matter of a political nature and also, but in smaller measure, in poetry. Perhaps you have read a humorous little essay in the *Allgemeine Zeitung* on Germany's band of poets. This was what first set me off, and since you and I rarely philosophize nowadays there may be some point in writing these thoughts of mine down for you.

The beneficial influence philosophical and political reading matter is having on the development of our nation is beyond dispute, and perhaps the German national character, if, that is, I have derived it correctly out of my very incomplete experience, was more in need of precisely that double influence than of any other. For I believe that the most habitual virtues and flaws of the Germans can be reduced to a rather narrow-minded domestic coziness. They are always *glebae addicti*, most of them are in one way or another, literally or figuratively, bound to the sod, and if it goes on like this they will end up, like the good-hearted Dutch painter, sinking under the weight of their cherished (moral and physical) acquisitions and inheritances. Everyone only feels at home where he was born, and only rarely do his interest and ways of thinking give him the ability or inclination to go beyond it. This is the reason for that lack of elasticity, of drive, of a diverse unfolding of the energies, and for the dull, dismissive shyness or the fearful, submissive, blind devotion with which they react to anything that lies outside their own anxiously narrow sphere; the reason too for the lack of a sense of shared honor and shared property, which it is true is very widespread among the modern nations but in my opinion is to be found to an eminent degree among the Germans. And just as one cannot be content shut away in one's room unless one also lives out in the open, so too the individual, particular life cannot subsist without a sense of the universal and an open view onto the world, and at the moment it seems that among the Germans both have perished equally. And it really does show how wrong the apostles of restriction are that among the ancients, where everyone belonged with sense and spirit to the world that surrounded them, there is far more intensity to be found in particular characters and relations than among us Germans for example, and the affected talk of heartless cosmopolitanism and inflated metaphysics can probably not be more truly refuted than by such a noble pair as Thales and Solon, who traveled through Greece, Egypt and Asia together to acquaint themselves with the constitutions and philosophers of the world, and were thus *generalized* in more than one respect but at the same time close friends and more human and even naive in their relations than all the people who seek to persuade us that we should keep our eyes shut and not open our hearts to the world (which always deserves it) if we are to maintain our naturalness.

Now, as the Germans for the most part found themselves in this state of anxious narrow-mindedness they could come under no more salutary influence than that of the new philosophy, which takes the universality of interest to an extreme and discovers the infinite striving in the human breast. And even if it does orient itself too one-sidedly toward the great autonomy of human nature, still it is the only possible philosophy *for our time.*

Kant is the Moses of our nation, leading it out of its Egyptian lethargy into the open, lonely wilderness of his speculation and bringing the energetic law down from the holy mountain. Of course they are still dancing round their golden calves and hungering for their fleshpots, and he would probably have to take them out into some quite literal desert for them to relinquish their servitude to the belly and their dead customs and opinions, which have lost all heart and meaning and under which their better, living nature sighs inaudibly, as if in a deep dungeon. In another way, political reading must have just as beneficial an effect, especially if the phenomena of our times are presented with vigor and authority. Man's horizon expands, and if we attend to the affairs of the world daily our interest and involvement in it arises and grows as well, and the sense of the general and the transcendence of our own narrow milieu are certainly encouraged just as much by witnessing the widespread variety of human society and its momentous fates as by the philosophical imperative to generalize our interest and points of view. Just as the soldier feels bolder and more powerful when he is working within an army, and really is, people's energy and liveliness in general increases to the precise degree that the zone of life expands in which they feel themselves to be acting and suffering alongside other people (as long as the sphere doesn't extend so far that the individual loses himself in the whole). For all that, the interest in philosophy and politics, even if it were more general and serious than it is, falls far short of being sufficient for the education of the nation, and it would be a good thing if there were at last an end to the boundless misconceptions that lead to art, and especially poetry, being devalued by those who practice and enjoy it. So much has already been said about the influence of the arts on the education of man, but it always came out as if it wasn't meant to be taken seriously, and that was quite natural, because they didn't reflect on what the true nature of art, and especially poetry, is. They confined themselves to its unassuming external aspect, which is certainly bound up with what it is but is far from making up the whole of its character; they took it to be playful because it appears in the modest form of play, of a game, and so rationally no other effect could be expected of it than that produced by play, that is, diversion, almost the exact opposite of the effect it has when it occurs in its true nature. Then, a person becomes collected, gains focus, and it gives him repose, not empty but living repose, where all the faculties are alert and only seem not to be active because of their intent harmony. It brings people together and joins them, but not as play does, where they are only united in that everybody forgets themselves and the vital particularity of each is held back.

You will forgive me, dear brother, for writing such a slow and disconnected letter. Few can find the transition from one mood to another more difficult than I; particularly hard is to move from reasoning to poetry and the other way round. Also these last few days I've been so preoccupied by a letter from our dear mother in which she expressed her joy at my religious life and asked me among other things to write a poem for our dear grandmother's 72nd birthday, together with much else in what was an inexpressibly moving letter, that I spent most of the time when I might perhaps have written to you thinking of her and the rest of you dear ones. On the very evening I received the letter I started a poem for our dear grandmother and almost finished it that night. I thought it would give her and mother pleasure if I sent a letter and the poem straight off the next day. But the tones I produced resonated so powerfully within me, the transformations of mind and soul I have undergone since my youth, the past and present of my life, became so pressing as I worked that afterward I couldn't get to sleep and in the morning had trouble collecting myself again. That's how I am. You will wonder, when you come to see the verses, which are poetically so slight, how they could have had such a curious effect on me. But I have said hardly anything of what I felt as I wrote them. It seems to happen quite often that I proffer my keenest, most vital soul in utterly flat words, so that no one knows what they really mean apart from me.

Now let's see whether I can get a bit further with what I was trying to say before about poetry. I was saying that poetry unites people differently from the way play does; that is, if it is genuine and has a genuine effect, it unites them with all their manifold suffering and happiness and aspiration and hope and fear, with all their opinions and errors, all their virtues and ideas, with all about them that is great and small more and more to form a live, intricately articulated, intense whole, for this is what poetry itself should be, and the effect is like the cause. Don't you agree, dear brother, that the Germans could do with a panacea of this kind, even after the philosophico-political cure? Apart from anything else, the disadvantage intrinsic to a political and philosophical education is that it may well connect people to the fundamental, incontrovertibly necessary conditions of law and duty, but how close are we then to the harmony of humankind? A landscape drawn according to the optical rules, with foreground, middle distance and background, is a long way from equaling the living work of nature. But even the best among the Germans are mostly still of the opinion that if the world were only nice and symmetrical all would be right with it. O Greece, with your genius, your piety, what has become of you? Even I, with all my good intentions, only stumble behind these people, the only humans the world has known, vainly feeling my way with my thoughts and actions, and I am often all the more clumsy and muddled in what I do and say precisely because I stand there in the modern water like geese with their flat feet and beat my wings helplessly at the Greek sky. Don't be offended by the comparison. It is awkward, but true, and between us such things can pass, in any case it's only really meant for me.

For your encouraging remarks on my little poems and many other sympathetic and fortifying words in your letter I am very grateful. We must hold firm together in all our need and our spirit. Above all let us adopt, with all love and seriousness, the great words: *homo sum, nihil humani a me alienum puto.* That does not mean we should be irresponsible, but simply true to ourselves and clear-sighted and tolerant in our dealings with the world, and then we must make sure not to let any idle aspersions of affectation, exaggeration, ambition, oddness etc. put us off from fighting with all our energies and concentrating all our rigor and tenderness on bringing all that is human in us and in others into ever freer and more intimate relation, whether in figurative representation or in the real world. And if the realm of darkness irrupts with violence *then* we shall throw our pen under the table and go, in God's name, where the necessity is greatest and we are most needed. Goodbye.

Yours,

Friz

174. TO HIS MOTHER

Homburg, January 1799

My dear Mother,

I'm ashamed to have left your lovely letter, which has given me so many hours and moments of pleasure, without an answer for so long. On the very evening I received it I wrote down most of what I enclose for my dear beloved grandmother, and I thanked you in my heart for having reminded me of her birthday, which is sacred to me. The letter to you was to have been written the following day and it would have been a real joy for me if I could have expressed immediately what I felt on receiving yours. But I was prevented from doing so in all kinds of ways. There was probably time enough, but I like to write to you with an untroubled soul. What unsettled me and robbed me of a more tranquil frame of mind was without importance. I say that so as not to worry you. I happened to read some harsh statements that were an assault on my spirits because they went right against my most heartfelt convictions, that was the main thing that disrupted me in the peacefulness of my life. Of course it's not good that I am so fragile and indeed I wish for nothing more than a firm, constant mind. The knowledge of my weakness in this respect humbles me more than anything else: for all my honest efforts and consciousness of what would be better and happier I am still as thin-skinned as ever. I have wasted half my youth in sufferings and errors that had this as their one source. Now I think I am more patient and don't take against people, and if I'm not mistaken I am less temperamental in my dealings with others than before, but my inner tranquility and calm concentration can still be destroyed by impressions that perhaps wouldn't trouble a man of firmer constitution for a moment. Admittedly it is natural that every passing dissonance affects me more deeply now, when I've just escaped hundreds of anxieties and disturbances and am wanting to collect and soothe myself in the harmony of goodness, truth and beauty. I promise you, and myself, to keep on working at it so that I learn to accept on the spur of the moment what I can so easily reconcile when my mind is at rest. I know no greater happiness than to work away modestly and in hope. But that can't happen if one's sensibility is easily hurt.—I also try to strengthen my body with gentle exercise and a routine because I see that sometimes it has to do with that. It's not that I'm not in good health—I'm in better health now than usual and no longer have headaches and stomach pains—but I do find that my nerves are too sensitive. I say all this in particular because you inquire with such tenderness and sympathy how I am.—That you have reacted to what I said about religion with such great joy shows me so clearly that your character finds repose only in the highest sphere. My dear Mother, I can well believe that it must be a relief and cheering for you to think of me as having the best feelings a human soul can have and to be able to hold on to that knowledge amid the doubts and anxieties with which even the best must regard each other, and the more so the closer they are, for in the end we hardly know ourselves and shall never know another person even as well as that. I reserve the right to deliver you a complete profession of faith at more leisure, and I wish I could express my heart's opinion to everyone with the candor and purity I do to you. But the scribes and Pharisees of our time, who have made out of the dear holy Bible a cold prattle that kills heart and spirit, I certainly don't want them as witnesses of my intense, living faith. I know very well how they came to their views, and because God forgives them for giving Christ a worse death than the Jews, making his Word into a letter and him, that lives, into an empty idol, because God forgives them this, I forgive them too. Only I don't care to lay myself and my heart bare where it will be misunderstood, and for that reason keep quiet before those who are theologians by *profession* (that is, who are not such freely and in their hearts but under duress and because of their office) just as readily as before those who want to have nothing to do with it all because for them religion, which after all is the first and last need of mankind, has been spoilt in childhood by the dead letter and the terrifying *command** to believe. My dear Mother, if there are harsh words in these lines they are certainly not written out of pride or hate but only because I could find no other way of making myself clear with the necessary brevity. The way things are now, particularly with regard to religion, this all had to come about, and the state of religion was almost as it is now when Christ appeared in the world. But just as winter is followed by spring, so the spiritual death of man has always been followed by new life, and the holy always remains holy, whether people respect it or not. And there will be many who are more religious in their hearts than they are willing or able to say, and perhaps many of our preachers, who simply can't find the words, say more, too, in their sermons than others suspect because the words they use are so ordinary and have been misused in hundreds of ways. Make do with this unfeigned expression of my thoughts for the moment, until I can find an hour when I can write with all my soul.—I quite agree with you, dear Mother, that it will be good for me in future to seek out the most modest position I can, and especially for this reason: that the perhaps unfortunate penchant for poetry, which from the beginning I always made honest efforts to oppose by concentrating on occupations thought to be more serious, is still in me and, to go by all that I have learned about myself, will remain so for as long as I live. I cannot say whether I'm deluding myself or whether it is a true impulse of nature. But this much I do now know, I have brought acute disquiet and discontentedness on myself in part by devoting excessive attention and effort to activities that seem to be less well suited to my nature, such as philosophy. And I did it with a good will because I wanted to avoid the reputation of an empty poet. For a long time I didn't understand why the study of philosophy, which usually rewards

---

*Faith can never be bidden, no more than love can. It must be voluntary and spontaneous. True, Christ says: he that does not believe shall be damned, that is, as I understand the Bible, severely judged, and that's natural enough, for the man who is merely good out of a sense of duty and the law can never be forgiven, because he restricts himself to works, but that doesn't mean that faith should be imposed on him.

the assiduous hard work it requires with tranquility, only made me more and more restless and even passionate the more completely I surrendered myself to it. And I now explain this to myself as coming from my distancing myself more than was necessary from my proper inclination, and my heart would sigh during this unnatural work for the occupation it loved best like Swiss herdsmen in the army longing for their valleys and their cattle. Don't think this fanciful. For why is it that I am peaceful and good as a child when I'm working undisturbed in sweet leisure at this most innocent of all occupations, which, it is true, and quite rightly, only earns proper respect when it is practiced with mastery? Part of the reason why I am a long way from that is perhaps because from boyhood on I never dared work at it as hard as at many other things, which I perhaps devoted myself to in a rather meek and overscrupulous manner to conform to my circumstances and what people expected. And yet every art requires a man's whole life and everything an apprentice learns must be learned in relation to his art if he wants to develop his disposition to it and not end up stifling it.

You see, my dear Mother, that I am making you my intimate, and I have no fear of your misunderstanding these honest confessions. There are so few people to whom I can open my heart. Why then shouldn't I exercise my filial right and comfort myself by telling you my deepest concerns? And do not think I have some ulterior motive. I can only write to you with complete truthfulness, and so you will just have to have me as I am. What I really wanted to say was that part of the reason why I should do well to look for a very simple position for the future is that any other would be hard to reconcile with my favorite occupation. There are men, who must have been stronger than I am, that have tried to be men of affairs or scholars in office while remaining poets. But it is always the case that in the end they sacrificed one occupation to the other and that was never good, whether they neglected the job for the sake of their art or their art for the sake of their job. For if a man sacrificed his job he was acting dishonorably toward others, and if he sacrificed his art he was sinning against his god-given, natural gift, and that is at least as great a sin as sinning against one's body. Good old Gellert, whom you mention in your kind letter, would have done better not to become professor in Leipzig. If his art didn't suffer, his body must have done. So if I do have to accept a post, as is probably inevitable, I think a living in a village (right away from the city and the high dignitaries of the Church) will be the best thing for me. And why not in the region where you and the family are, rather than among strangers?

But in any case I prefer to wait a few years yet, and when I've come to the end of the book I'm writing now and my money what I'll do is become a private tutor again. The Swedish secretary of legation von Pommer-Esche, whose acquaintance I made, as you know, in Rastadt and who recently visited me here on his way back, offered as he left to arrange a private tutorship for me in his part of the country (in Swedish Pomerania, in the Wismar region). His father, who if I'm not mistaken is governor in Stralsund, generally finds posts of that kind for his acquaintances. I didn't want to refuse outright, so as to have somewhere to go if need be, especially as he says he will find me a post where I would accompany a young man to the university. An increased knowledge of the world (knowledge of the German people, particularly for someone who wants to become a German writer, is as vital as knowledge of the soil is for the gardener) is the only recompense I can hope for from this laborious employment, and that it is in such a distant, unfamiliar place, which in any case would not be so noticeable at a university town, seems to me an advantage rather than a disadvantage for the few years when I cannot yet count on a peaceful life near my family. But for the moment I am undecided, and perhaps in the meantime more favorable opportunities of this nature will present themselves. I shall only take up such a post at all if certain fixed conditions are met to protect me as far as possible from annoyance and embarrassment. And if I come to the recognition that such an existence is necessary for me a while longer, and inevitable, I shall probably summon up the patience and discretion required. As a curate I would be dependent on my pastor, and as I have no experience of this situation it would probably be no easier, and moreover I should have to live largely at your expense which I do not want to do. You have done so much for me already and dear Karl has more need of your help.

I'm writing all this to you, dear Mother, because I know very well how much you wish to know where you stand with me, and if you should find that my life is not an easy one at the moment you won't take it too much to heart because you know better than anyone that with our youth what we call happiness generally tends to fade. I at least prefer not to ask any more of the world than that I may not find it too difficult to keep true to my heart and mind in whatever circumstances I have yet to encounter in life. You and the rest of the family I should in any case dearly like to see again before I move on from my present residence which it is true will be a wrench to leave.

I was so pleased with your lovely presents that I could think of nothing better in my joy than to run to the good people whose house I live in and announce that I too had got a Christmas present. Thank you very much, and dear grandmother too. I'm just sorry that my finances no longer allow me, as in Frankfurt, to give you proof of my feelings for you in this way. Please give my apologies to my dear sister too, for contenting myself for now with good intentions. Anyway she knows my fondness for her and her whole household too well to need any sign to prove it. The letter you sent me from her was a gift in itself. I should really have written to her long before now, but as I was making the journey to Rastadt I hoped to see her in person, and I've had so much to do since then making up for lost time that very soon I'm going to have to sit down for a few days to answer all the letters I owe, and when I do she shall be among the first.

My best wishes to you, dear Mother, ask my dear grandmother to take the enclosed page as a small part of the joyful and earnest feelings with which I celebrated her esteemed birthday in my heart.

Remember me to all the family.

Your loyal son,

Friz

FROM SUSETTE GONTARD

[Frankfurt, January 1799]

Dearest, we shan't see each other tomorrow, we must be patient and wait for better times. The long dreaded visitors have arrived. It hurts me beyond expression that I can't tell you face to face how much I love you. Love me likewise for ever, faithfully, truly, warmly, and let implacable fate steal nothing from me! — —

All the storms of heaven have come over me again. The evening after I last saw you our coach broke down, I bruised my arm and had to stay indoors a long time. The next day I learned that my brother out hunting had been shot in the leg. And both your letters got into the wrong hands, they were soon restored to me however and the only consequence was that I had to wait a week till the usual meeting which having to stay in because of my accident did make easier to bear.

Don't ever think, my darling, that the way our love is fated to be will ever revolt me or weigh me utterly down,   Often, it is true, I weep bitter bitter tears but these tears are my salvation, so long as you live I will not go under. if I felt nothing anymore, if love had vanished out of me, and what would a life without love be to me, I should sink down into darkness and death. so long as you love me I cannot become a worse person, you sustain me and lead me on the way of beauty, have faith in me and build solidly on my heart.   Farewell for now, dear heart, my precious love, and think as I do that our dearest innermost being will remain unchangeably itself, unchangeably its own.

Next month you will surely risk it again, you may be able to find out from *H* . . whether I am on my own again.

FROM ISAAK VON SINCLAIR

Rastadt, 8 February 1799

[*Muhrbeck is back from his journey. Shortly, perhaps in a week's time, both will also come to Homburg.*]

That you write nothing about *Agis* & that you have only written to me once at all leads me to suspect you have been working hard at it, and that much enjoyment is in store for us when we get to hear what you, far away from us but thinking of us from time to time, have written.

175. TO HIS SISTER

[Homburg, late February/early March 1799]

Dearest sister,

I have almost forfeited the right to be remembered by you, so long has been my silence. But it is often the case that one fails to write out of a great need to write. When that happens I always want to wait for an opportune moment when I can write from the heart, and so doing I miss the point when I'd have perhaps not written without distraction from other thoughts and occupations but still enough of a letter for you to recognize my unchanging love for you.

I have become a hermit again for a time, as you know, and I think you approve of this because you know me well enough to reckon that I am not doing it without good reason and that I am not letting this leisure turn into idleness, nor am I making a convenient arrangement for myself at others' expense. Believe me, dearest, there is nothing capricious about what determines my occupations and my situation here. It is my nature and my fate, and these are the only powers one must never deny obedience to, and I hope that these convictions will one day make me more than worthy of your steady and loyal affection.

You in any case are more fortunate than the man who perhaps only at the end of his efforts will be able to say with certainty: I am content. You live from one day to the next in the satisfaction of your best desires, and your domestic happiness probably has only just the amount of care required to make you all the more sensible, every day, of what is yours. But each is allotted his own, and I respect and honor what you are and have the more readily because I lack it myself. In many disconsolate moments I have already longed to be with you, in order to let your joy cheer me up and to receive in your love for me something of what you have within and around you. I had imagined a properly peaceful reunion for myself. But the tempestuous times that are perhaps no longer far from our country come between our dear desires, and we should perhaps see one another again amid much unrest were I to return to my dear family in the next while. The new war and all the rest causes me so much anxiety for my family that I prefer not to speak of it. What comforts me about your situation is that you are not alone and can lean on the clear-sightedness and steadiness of your inestimable husband in emergencies, which let's hope won't arise.

What are your dear children up to? I'll hardly recognize them any more. Three years is such a lot at that age, growing every day in body and soul as they do. And little Friz, whom I've not yet seen at all, will seem to have been in the world for a good long time already. Send them all my love, each according to what sense they have of me.

How are my friends Veiel and Kammerer & my other acquaintances?

My company here is limited for the most part to just two friends, but they provide such rich entertainment, because of their wit and the unusual degree of knowledge and experience they have acquired in sorrow and joy, that we are often obliged to avoid one another so as not to let our conversations dominate over everything and our minds become too preoccupied, because each one of us needs more or less all his attention, undispersed and unenthused by other ideas and interests, for his work. One of these friends is Sinklair whom you will already know of from my letters to our dear mother; the other, Professor Morbek from Greifswald who is now traveling around and as a favor to Sinklair and myself is stopping here for a few months. Otherwise the exceptional beauties of the region here are my only pleasure; the little town is on the slopes of some hills, and woods and tasteful parks lie all around it; I live out toward the fields, have gardens at my window and a hill with oak trees, and am a short walk away from a lovely meadowed valley. That's where I go when I am weary of my work, climb up the hill and sit in the sun, and look out over Frankfurt in the nether distance, and these innocent moments give me strength & courage again to live and to write. Dear sister, it is as good as if one had been to church, to have felt the light and the air and the beauty of the earth with a pure heart and open eyes.

  Good-bye! You write soon now too. My compliments to all. Ever

your

loyal brother

Hölderlin

I had written this letter a while ago, and it only remained unsent because I wanted to add a bit more to it, from which I was prevented by my occupations and illness (a gallstone colic that has now passed).

176. TO HIS MOTHER

Homburg vor der Höhe[, early March 1799]

Dearest Mother,

I can only write you only a few words this time. I have so much to do.

  I was deeply shaken to hear of the accident that could have had such serious consequences for you and my dear grandmother. May every misfortune pass over you that way!

  It is probable that the war that is just breaking out again will not leave Württemberg untouched, although I know from a good source that the French will respect the neutrality of the states of the Empire, of Württemberg too therefore, for as long as possible, because Prussia is using all its influence to ensure it and the French have reason to avoid a war with that power. Should the French be successful there will perhaps be changes in our mother country.

My dear Mother, I beg you with all my truest filial devotion: summon up everything that is noble in your exemplary soul and all the faith that raises us above the earth to look on our times as calmly as possible, and to bear anything untoward that happens to you with the tranquil mind of a Christian. I should lose all my resolve were I to think that the present anxieties might overwhelm your spirits. Remember that I have no father going courageously ahead of me in life, and give me, in the beautiful shape of calm endurance, an example of such courage. I also need it if I am not to become faint-hearted in my own work and cause. If certain possible events occur I shall exert all my energies to prevent anything from happening to you, and not perhaps without effect. But all this is still a long way away. —

FROM SUSETTE GONTARD

[Frankfurt, after 4 March 1799]

My love, I should be only too glad to tell you how I spent the sad days of our separation if recalling that time were not so painful for me. These last few days I have been alone again and it is already somewhat better, the worst was I could never be sure of even fifteen minutes to myself and even when I was alone I had to forcibly suppress my feelings so that tears in my eyes would not betray me and give rise to tiresome questions. But the first solitary hours were terrible for me, I wanted to give myself up entirely to my feelings again but could not permit myself even that, my longing for you became so great I was at a loss what to do and a violent struggle started in me. With all my powers I sought to summon the dream-image of you, that had formed and was fading within me, back into my imagination in living colors, but this was denied me, I felt at once the desire and the impossibility, of course I thought of your letters, your books, your hair, but I didn't want such aids, wholly from within myself I wanted to renew you in me but my foolish heart was soon ashamed and apologetic in the presence of reason, a few days later I got out all the dear things of yours, and letters, from earlier days, which back then, when I still had you, had not meant much to me and which had quite gone from my memory, what a treasure trove of loving words, what a comfort, what a lovely image of you I found in them, how they tempted sweet tears of tenderness into my eyes and strengthened my heart and how I cling to them now in every anxious hour. But, alas, that is the past—What is the present?—What is the future? — — — — Now with every passing day I ask myself: "How should a person whom love has raised to a life of nobleness and beauty now in isolation in herself and by her own means abide?"—Always I wish to dream, but dreaming is the way of self-destruction. Self-destruction, cowardice! — — — Feeling!—In these impoverished times that are the death of everything still my heart has warm and lively feelings, longs for reality, for response to love, for mutual exchange, consonance, harmony, bliss! am I to blame it? But every feeling in me recalls my whole longing mixed with a thousand torments.   Even through my deepest thinking I can find nothing worthwhile but relations in love at its most intense, for what can be our guide through this ambivalent life and death if not the voice of our better being which we entrust to a like and loving soul, this voice which we cannot always hear from within our selves? We are bound strongly and unchangeably in what is beautiful and good, beyond all thinking, in faith and hope. But this relationship in love exists in the real world which involves us not only through the spirit. the senses (not sensuality) belong there too, a love which we removed entirely from reality, could only feel in the spirit, could not nourish or give hope to anymore, would in the end become dream and fantasy or vanish, it would still exist but we should no longer know it and its beneficent effect on our being would cease. Since I have all this clearly before my eyes and it is so hard to find a way out of the numbness, Should I deceive myself further and lull myself to sleep, — — Should I dream? Should I stunt my heart, should I think differently? — — Why do I ask these things, my darling? "Don't I still have you?" Oh because since the day of our separation there is a fear in me that the time will come when all relations between us will cease, because I have no certainty about the future, about the future course of your life, I tremble to think of the upheavals that may be approaching us and may tear us apart for ever. How often I blame you and myself that we so proudly made all relations between us impossible, relying only on ourselves, and now must go as beggars to Fate and through a thousand detours seek for a thread that will lead us to be together. What will become of us if we should be lost to one another? — — — —

Nor could I ever be at peace if I must think I had taken you completely away from reality, if you wished to make do with my shadows, that because of me you will perhaps fail in your vocation, if I heard nothing from you about it anymore and was relieved that I didn't. If we are to be sacrificed to Fate then promise me you will free yourself from me and live wholly in a way that might yet make you happy so that you may fulfill your duties to this world as you think best and do not let my image hinder you, only this promise will give me peace, and satisfaction with myself. — — — Never will you be loved by anyone as I love you, nor will you ever love anyone as you love me (forgive me this selfish wish) but do not stunt your heart or do it violence, I must not wish to jealously destroy what I can't have. Dearest, do not think that I am speaking on my own behalf, it is very different for me, in part I have accomplished what was required of me, I've enough to do in the world, through you more has come to me than I had any right to expect, my time was already over but it is now that you should be beginning to live, to act, to have an effect, don't let me be any hindrance and don't dream away your life in hopeless love.   Nature who gave you all your noble energies high intelligence and deep feelings determined you to be a noble, excellent and happy man and to show it in all your actions.   But there is still a light of hope for our beloved love, let us tend it and sustain it as long as ever we can. One hour filled with the bliss of seeing one another again, and hope in the heart, are enough to keep our love alive for months. But let us not shut our eyes and allow Fate to surprise us or we shall not be able to do what is most necessary and best. Reassure me if you can about the future.   My brother (now quite recovered) is coming in the middle of May, unless disturbances caused by the war make it quite impossible, and during that time I don't yet see how we shall be able to have any dealings with one another because I can't know when I will be on my own and it would make me constantly tense and worried, if you could think of a way of being in touch by letter, not too risky, not making me anxious, that would be a great blessing since it is necessary for my peace of mind to learn of the life you lead.   When I am on my own again (for under no circumstances will I agree to go traveling unless during a brief period when in any case we could not

see each other) let us do again what we have done so far. You spoke
of one and a half years, I tremble when I think that more than half a
year has gone by already, how will it, how might it, be? what do you
think would be best for you?—If you would tell me how it looks to
you. in my mind I see only blackness and the most terrible thing
would be if under this hard fate even our gentle love were suffocated,
if the inevitable end were the numbing of our hearts, our lives were
lost and still, beyond consolation, we knew it.   Forgive me, my
dearest, that I drag you with me into these black thoughts, all should
be sweet for you, I wish I could give you the heavens, put out of your
way everything that might trouble you; but feeling the holiness of our
love I cannot deceive you, I owe you an account of every feeling in me,
you know that I am easily cast down, perhaps better things will come
and how we shall thank fate for every flower we find together.   If
only it weren't so difficult for me to write to you. Whenever I take up
my pen a world opens before me, full of thoughts and feelings, I want
to say everything at once and can't bring any order into it, I am afraid
of writing nonsense, then my words are again too prosaic and if my
imagination joins in then I think what I have written was not so true,
in the end I want to tear it all up again.   I think you understand me
better than I do myself and even feel the things I don't say. — — —

　　But I must say something about the children, you already know
that in my eyes they have lost a great deal since you stopped being
their teacher and having an influence on them and they no longer
seem to me to promise so much. It is very difficult for me to work
against all the skewed impressions they receive and often I have to
let things go and then, for my own comfort, I put my faith in their
developing and not yet addled reason which will itself lead them back
from all the errors they may get into and I often think if their moral
education became too refined they would then perhaps never feel at
home in their world and that their upbringing must accommodate itself
somewhat to our situation. What annoys me most about *Henry* is that
because he suddenly felt himself free he likes to be lord and master, he
is loud-mouthed, relishes the coarsely physical things and is besides in
his work rather idle and careless, he has to be constantly chivvied and
all ambition seems to have deserted him. I wish for his own good he
would get away from here, it is not at all the right place for him, he is
waited on and flattered far too much and hears too little of the truth
quietly spoken. I should like to know what you think! — —

The two older girls have also got somewhat coarser but are still good children, I put my hope more in little Male because in her later upbringing we shall be able to see what mistakes we made, but again I censure myself for nourishing my partiality, she really is an affectionate and lovable child, these last 2 weeks she has been running around again and that gives me such joy.   We have also taken on Herr Hadermann, a very tedious religious man who likes the sound of his own voice, my patience gives out if I have to listen to him for more than ten minutes. They will get learning enough but I am often very fearful concerning the formation of their characters and for their unique inner qualities. My counterinfluence would still not be strong enough even if I were always in a position to decide what is best for them and even this I find almost impossible.

And now I must tell you how I propose spending my future time. It was perhaps a good thing this winter that I wasn't much on my own for I often have days when I lose all equilibrium, at the very thought of you I am in tears, I have to force myself and seek company if I am to hold on, throughout the winter I was a burden to myself, I flitted around, but now that has to change, I couldn't even read any serious book because my head felt tired all the time.   I will see if I recover my love of music, spring will keep me sweetly busy in the garden (though first I will have to get used to it again) and your beloved *Hyperion* will enliven my mind—oh how I look forward to that!—You promised to prescribe me other remedies too! You'll keep that promise, won't you?—You also asked me to put some of my thoughts and ideas into words. Dearest, all my utterance belongs only to you. My mind, my soul are mirrored in you, you give what can be given more beautifully than I ever could and the pleasure I have in the praise that belongs to you more than satisfies my amour propre.

177. TO SUSETTE GONTARD

[Homburg, Spring 1799]

That the glory of spring still gives joy to me too, darling, fills me with unutterable gratitude,

FROM SIEGFRIED SCHMID

Basel, 29 March 1799

[*On H.'s pain:*] But you should not rage at the world in your sorrow,
artist; but rejoicing in your inner creator leave it as it is, ever
unchanging and always different; and yet collapse it and raise it up
again divinely transformed in all its parts through your tones, or brush,
or anyhow you like.

[*On the drama he is working on at the moment.*]

How true, dearest friend, that the poet's soul—and more strongly
so than any other—must preserve all elements of humanity within
itself. . . . All-roundness is the character of the great, true and most
enduring poets.

[*Cotta has told him he is ready to take on the publication of his
poems. For the time being however he wants to see what will come of a
proposal in Berlin.—Perhaps also, in time for the autumn fair, he will
have a collection of short poems printed with at least part of a larger
poem that is split into several books.*

*Despite how he is living in Basel, at the bidding of chance, the very
thought of house tutoring makes him sick. He is very curious to see how
he'll get through.*

His father has written to him warmly of H.'s visit.] Now, to all
appearances, the noise of war will ruin our plans of spending some
companionable time together. [*He would invite him otherwise to go with
him to French-speaking Switzerland for a few months.*]

Look here, I am so impatient and eager to take part in a
campaign or two that I have just written in all earnestness to *Sinclair*
to find out how my desires can best be realized. The elevating nature
of war and the multifarious situations in which it puts us have much
attraction; and the contemplation of the shoddiness of human life,
where the whole of existence is reduced to the random organization
of certain machines (of a more or less spiritual or earthly kind), [*is
something he wants to indulge in for a while, in constant alternation
between pleasure and frustration*].

I am looking forward like a real child to seeing your picture. Be
sure to send me it soon; accompanied by a few marvelous notes from
your soul.

FROM SUSETTE GONTARD

[Frankfurt, 12 March–4 April 1799]

Tuesday 12 March

Your letter yesterday and the wish it contained made me think I should also write you a sort of diary, if only I could manage to! I am so rarely left in peace and if I have to do it in secret there's a sort of fear in me which prevents me from finding the right words, I am so often snatched away from my thoughts and that puts me in a bad temper, but I will try and I'll take advantage of every minute of quiet, but you mustn't expect it to be very coherent.

Yesterday, after you left, I felt so completely the mixture of pain and joy and anxious presentiments about the future, I at once took up your letter, but could read only words, my heart was beating violently, I could not make out their sense, I had to save it for a quieter time. I went out into the open air, to be restored to myself. In the afternoon the sun shone so sweetly into my room and soothed me just as though counseling me to be still and then I was patient and could read your letter word by word, I sent the children into the garden and so remained alone with you. It was an hour of happiness!—Nor did my grateful heart mind the tears your letter brought to my eyes, all I heard in me was, He is alive, is near, truly loves me, today is a happy day!

— — — — — —

When later the anxious future threatened to trouble me, I scolded myself, saying, People in their childish religion would hold it a sin to lose faith like this and not to count on their God. Why after all should not some secret and unknown power be a friend, a comforter and a guide to us, why should we despair? — — — And is it right only to imagine *the blackest things*? — — May it not still turn out better than we think?—Or do we have an understanding so far-sighted that we can know all our fate in advance?—Does not often some small chance occurrence determine happiness or unhappiness?—We are after all subject to chance in this world, why then should chance not make us happy? We were fated to find one another and have often and passionately rejoiced over that. Should we not then find one another again and rejoice again? — — — —

Afternoon

That word I wrote—chance—I can't get it out of my head, I
don't like it, it sounds so small and cold, and yet I can't find any other.
Could we not also say that the secret connections of things make up
something for us that we call chance but which is a necessity? Because
of our short-sightedness we can't see anything of it in advance and
are astonished when an outcome is not what we expected. But natural
laws go their constant ways, unfathomable to us and for that very
reason a comfort because even things we had no inkling of and did not
remotely hope for may happen to us.

This morning I came across a lovely passage in a little French
novel which touched my heart and for that reason I will copy it out
for you. "Religion would certainly have originated in unhappiness had
gentler souls not found it in gratitude." — — — — — — —

14th March

My love, I have found the picture! After our first separation I did
not want to withdraw myself from all the pain of it, the sorrow was
dear to me and welcome, two days after you left I went into your room
again, wanted to weep to my heart's content and gather up a few dear
traces of you, I opened your desk and found a few pieces of paper still
in there, a bit of sealing wax, a small white button, a piece of hard
black bread, for a long time I carried all those things around with
me like relics. The lock of one of the drawers in the chest had stuck,
I couldn't unlock it, I went out and met *Henry* by the door, he said
sorrowfully to me "you've lost a lot from this room, first your mother
and now your Hölder as well! It must be an unbearable place for
you!" — — — That hit me hard, but at once the thought of your life
comforted me and brought something that was sweet into my grieving
soul, and I went on my way. — — A few days later I had the drawer
opened and found that picture and oh how it fills me with grief! In
my innocence I was drawing a tomb at the time when I gave you the
picture and we were looking through all those engravings together,
such bliss such hope were in me then and seemed to me they would
last for ever. And now are we to think it is finished? — — — — — I
don't know whether I should give you the picture back or not, all these

thoughts would very likely seize hold of you and shake you as they did me in the quiet of yesterday evening. — — — — —

19th March

I've been out again once or twice with the children and it has always given me strength and lifted my spirit, once in the mild light of the sun I saw my beloved *Homburg* up there on the hillside, what a blessing went from my eyes to that tranquil place and the room I don't know in which you are living now, how my thoughts hurried away to you and surely touched you, for I thought that on such lovely spring days you must also have me always on your mind and feel me closer as I do you. — — But how my thoughts also terrified me, oh soon I shall also have to part from that beloved place, my eyes will no longer turn that way so gladly, I shall look away, so everything vanishes.—I shall not even be able to imagine where you live. See, my love, in that sense you are much better off than I am, you will always know where you can find me, you are familiar with all the little things around me whereas when I shall think of you your image will appear in an impenetrable fog and only for moments, unless you sometimes give me a picture of your surroundings and also of the people with whom you come into contact. Always do that when you can. I wish nothing so much for you as that always wherever you may be you will find a friend with whom your heart will not need to be dumb and in whose company your soul will find nourishment and free exchange for, my dearest, you are too rich in gifts and always too abundant to be there just for yourself and to rest only on yourself, you have a need to communicate and to speak from your best being, when sometimes you are so bad-tempered the only thing wrong is that you are not being understood and then you can't see your own self and you doubt yourself. but in that exigency you are soon in danger of choosing the wrong people and that is all I wish to warn you about, please don't take it ill, I mean well, believe me.

You wanted to hear from me as well how I occupy myself all day long, the account will be very simple.   I'm almost always in my own quiet room and there I work and sew and knit, the children when they are not having lessons in the room next door are noisily all around me but quite soon this does not disturb me in my thoughts which are often with you or rather are always in some connection with you, often I write you entire letters but then there's such a mêlée in my head nobody would be able to follow it on paper, I often feel driven toward my desk but I am afraid and must wait for a moment of strength and often my whole being shuts down and I can't bring forth a single word, and so I am not able to write as often as I would wish, for really there is a deep pleasure in it and afterward I am much quieter and for days then everything is easier.   Being with other people matters so little to me but loneliness is often such a burden that I prefer the most banal conversation but it is only a deception and in the end always I admit to myself that I am heartily glad to be alone and without constraint again.   With my reading I am still not doing very well! It seems to me that for serious thinking you need a completely tranquil spirit and a way of being that is steady and without worries, at present I'm more in need of being rocked to sleep and so an interestingly written novel suits me better than the finest writings of our times. (reading through this I remember that you call your beloved *Hipperion* a novel too but I always think of it as a beautiful poem.)

Even things I don't esteem enough to be prompted into thinking by them, things I read solely for entertainment and to pass the time, they suit me better, so now and again I even come to the novels of M. la Fontaine, if I don't like a passage I fling the book in the corner and don't think ill of myself. — — Leafing through good books when you are not in the mood and not reading with proper attention, I think sacrilegious, they belong to people who can wholly feel and understand them.

I had written thus far and was interrupted. Since then I couldn't come back to it.

26th March

I have got through the holidays, and as always I am glad of that, things are quieter around me, on Sunday morning I went to our church once again, naturally the sermon could not hold my attention and all I thought about was you and conjured up your image, and I was trying to make a plan to see you in future when we have left the town and I think I've hit on the best way and will tell it you at the end of my letter. In the afternoon we went out into our garden with a few not very interesting people, the air was so sweet and clear as it is in my spirit when some happiness is still lingering there or some well-founded hope has animated me, but on this occasion it was only like that outside me. — — Every time I go out I automatically look toward the side window and I'm always glad if it is shut then it doesn't give me false hopes. There were a few people from Hamburg visiting us too, they are here for the fair, and they began talking about my brother, they said he would very likely go from here to Piedmont for his health and leave his wife here. I wonder does he mean I should go with him? — — If I couldn't see you after all and didn't know how to have news of you I would think of something, but if I went away and fate separated us and the thread between was entirely severed I should be inconsolable, I'd regret every step I took. Thoughts of traveling often put me in a quandary and yet not for anything should I wish to hurt my dear *Henry*. that is the only reason I might go away from here where I'd rather be than anywhere in the world if you weren't with me. and the pain I

[*Page or double page missing*]

for that reward I'll gladly wait a long time if then I can occasionally hear from somebody that you are well. Don't think me mistrustful, I'm certainly not. But, my love, you know that against mistrust one can never take enough precautions.   If we are to see each other in the future and not, for want of a message, miss the meeting, I must tell you a definite day from which I'll begin counting, and that will be the day you will come, once a year, you will surely always be so present to me that your appearance that day will not be a shock. — — — — —

Sunday 31st 9 in the evening

I am all alone and cannot go to bed without saying good night to you, heart's love, my dearest, if you could feel now how passionately I feel you, how our love's holiest moments are present in my soul, how happy I should be if I could know that!—Sleep quiet and sweetly, picture me near you! — — —

2nd April in the evening

I am quite calm again, alone, and would so like to speak to you, only I don't know where to start, there is so much I'd have to say for which the words are so hard to find The more one has to say the less one *can* say, I feel that again and think "hush, that's not true." So I *will* tell you!—In the 3 weeks we haven't seen each other I have lived a very quiet and domestic life, never at all in company, I was nearly always quietly at my work and (since you like to know every little circumstance) my favorite occupation was making up a dress that I had from my dear brother, exactly to your taste, lilac and white, he gave it me on the day you were last here with me and so it is a sweet reminder, I shall love wearing it.

I also showed my little Male how to knit and had much pleasure watching her busy little fingers.

I counted every hour of every day until our meeting and was angry with the heavens when it turned cold, not a wink of sunlight escapes me, though I know even in bad weather you will come, I can't bear to think of you walking in the rain or the freezing cold and have to shut it out or I'd suffer more on your account than you likely do yourself, don't take it the wrong way, my dearest, that I write to you in such a childish fashion, I should love to say things to you and yet not arouse in you and in me all the feelings whose tone I am always too close to and so often it's better if I sound frivolous. There, after all I've said a lot! — — — Wilhelmine is just bringing me my soup, I shall think of you till sleep closes my eyes.

4th April

Now I will tell you how I think this summer we can manage to be our own letter carriers for to entrust them to anyone else would really be quite a risky decision and anyway we both feel rather averse to it.   So you come on the first Thursday of the month if the weather is fine and if you can't then on the next or the next but only ever a Thursday so that we won't be confused by the weather, so then you can leave H . . . in the morning and when it is striking 10 o'clock in the town you appear at the low hedge by the poplars and at that time I'll be upstairs at my window and we can see one another, for a sign rest your stick on your shoulder, I'll hold a white cloth and if then after a few minutes I close the window that's a sign that I'm coming down but if I don't, I daren't risk it, if I come you walk to the end of the drive not far from the little arbor because behind the garden we can't reach one another because of the ditch and we're more likely to be seen but the arbor will hide me and you will be able to see in both directions that nobody is coming and that we'll get enough time to exchange our letters through the hedge. Next day when you are going back you can risk it again at the same time if it hasn't worked

the first or if there are things in the letters we have to answer.   I
don't need to tell you how unpleasant I find it to make such covert and
complicated plans, your delicate feelings recoil at them, that is certain,
and you suffer as I do but you can't think ill of me for it because I do
it only in the noble intention of preventing the ruin of the loveliest and
best thing human beings have. — — If the weather is fine we shall
probably be out there by 2nd May or the 9th for sure (my brother is
coming on the 15th) if you shouldn't see me at the window it would be
a sign that unforeseen circumstances have kept us in town and then on
the Friday at 10 o'clock you would come to the familiar corner.

You're coming today! I am so glad the weather is clear, I'm sure I
shall have an uneasy evening because I know you will be in town and I
can't decide to go to the theater because you think that exposes us and
you are right.

178. TO HIS MOTHER

[Homburg, ~ 25 March 1799]

Dearest Mother,

I am terribly sorry that you were unsettled by my silence. The last letter
I received from you is from 17th February. And I have gone some
way toward excusing myself in the letter you will now have received.
Sometimes, lost in the thoughts that my work sets off in me, the days
escape me, and also, recently, I have been less able to withdraw from
the company of my friends which has filled my hours of leisure, and I
always find it so difficult to keep up with my letter writing in any case,
so that it is certainly forgivable by and large if often, despite the pangs
of conscience I sometimes feel, I put off writing to you from one day
to the next.

Only believe, dearest Mother, that I am far from taking my
relationship with you lightly and that it often gives me plenty of trouble
when I try to combine my life plan with all your wishes and yet often
find that I might have caused you less concern and more happiness
on an ordinary path than on the one I am following now, which for
me too is in the end the less comfortable one but better suited to my
nature. I thank you with all my heart for your kind invitation, and one

day the time will come when at last I can make use of it. For now you will acknowledge yourself that a simple visit, given my present situation of having to devote all my available time to my work, would be too costly. I should at least like to remain here until I've finished my book, which may well take a good six months. What I embark on next will partly depend on the success or nonsuccess of my book, partly also on other circumstances. Now while I reckon I can if need be manage until then on the money I still have saved up, I must admit that because of the enormous rise in the price of wood and my three weeks of illness, when though I was not obliged to visit the doctor more than once I found myself unable to eat my normal food, my funds are now somewhat lower than I had expected they would be by now. I therefore take the liberty of making use of your kind and noble motherly offer to the extent that I reserve the right to write to you toward the middle of the summer to say whether I need the hundred guilders or not, though I can assure you in all purity and earnestness that *for my own peace of mind* I shall only accept the money as a *loan*. I owe it to you & to my brother and sister to act in this way. The times being as they are I should not want to reduce your income by a penny, even if it could be done under some legal title, for as long as I can still make my way in the world. So if in a year's time I send you the interest on the loan in cash or in kind you must not regard it as coldness on my part; it will only be a sign that what I am now in irrevocable seriousness setting myself as a condition was not idle words, and I am telling you in advance, dear mother, that it would cause me real disquiet if you sent me the money without the express assurance that you had marked it down in your papers as capital. I should have no compunction, if you were not happy about this way of doing things, in borrowing the money from another source, with your knowledge, as I am sure of receiving sufficient money for my book to be able to pay off such a sum. In Frankfurt I sometimes helped out a good friend of mine for a while, also others, and so I'm sure I could ask the favor to be returned one of these days.

And lastly I'm going to copy out for you a passage from the Jena literary magazine where I am mentioned. Although I have hitherto avoided boasting to you about my little reputation as a writer, in the present circumstances I should not let pass any opportunity to give you cause to hope that what I am working on at the moment will find a favorable reception, and it would be childish to deprive you of however small a joy just to avoid the suspicion of vanity. Here is what the magazine I mentioned says about the almanac Neuffer is the editor of and which out of friendship I contributed a few little things to:

"The contents of the almanac we should almost like to confine to the contributions by Hölderlin. The editor's (Neuffer) are endless versifying etc. Among the others, the little pieces by Hillmar and Siegmar show themselves to some advantage, as do the intimate elegiac lines by Reinhard (the French ambassador) to his wife on his departure from Germany. The prose essays are of no interest. But Hölderlin's few contributions are full of spirit and inner life, and we are glad to print a couple of them here to prove it."

Then a couple of my poems are quoted; in one of them I had alluded to what I am working on now; the reviewer comes back to this at the end:

"These lines allow one to conclude that Hölderlin has in mind a poem on a larger scale, for which we warmly wish him the best possible conditions, as what we have seen of his poetic abilities so far, along with the elevating feeling uttered in the poem we have quoted, give hopes of a successful execution."

But I must ask you, dearest Mother, for Neuffer's sake, not to pass this on to anyone. If you wish to show it to Karl, I cannot prevent it. My brother-in-law in Blaubeuren probably reads this paper himself.—I am very eager indeed to receive a letter again from my good sister. Karl owes me one; I shall write to him again one day soon nevertheless, because my last was much too short. It gives me endless pleasure that he makes himself so worthy of your affection and admiration. I also have great esteem for the fact that someone of such intelligence and genuine inner cultivation also shows such patience and skill in his administrative work. Don't worry about him! He will go a long way. For in the end necessity itself demands that truly exceptional and useful people like him will always be sought after.

The good health I'm enjoying at the moment contributes a good deal to my happiness, and my friends are mighty glad to see it. "Ah, now I can see joy in those eyes again!," my noble friend Morbek cried the other day when he saw me. It really was a disagreeable state I was in. To sit there so vacant and dull all day was all the harder for me because for the most part I only kept myself cheerful by having something to do.

With the spring I have become young again and look into life with new courage and new energy. Never again shall I become proud, impatient or immodest toward the guider of my fate.

Sleep well, dearest Mother. My room is getting too cold with the night air and I shall go to bed.

I'm really looking forward to May. The days here are almost all quite chilly still.—And by the way it's peaceful here. These parts, from what I can make out, need fear nothing more from the war. I am so pleased that so far my dear family has been spared.

Your

loyal son

Friz

18 April 1799

That is what I had written a few weeks ago now. But among other things I was interrupted by the news of the war—I wanted to wait and see what would happen so as to perhaps say something about it to you. Admittedly it was also that I was ill, as you will see from the letter to my dear sister, and that I wanted to make use of the time when I was without pain for my work. Now I am completely well again and feel it with gratitude and joy, and am taking proper care of my health, as I feel bound to say for your peace of mind.

Dearest Mother, I cannot very well come to Württemberg this spring as in the winter I was not able to devote all my time to my work and my studies, and it is of great importance to me that I should make the best use of my independence. So I shall save my money and my time as best I can for now and instead grant myself the pleasure of coming once I'm done. Look after yourself. Remember me to dear Grandmother. My love to Karl.

Your

loyal son

Friz

FROM SUSETTE GONTARD

[Frankfurt, 9 May 1799]

Thursday morning 9th

I must say a few more words to you, my love. Late yesterday
evening we came out here, I thought I saw you at the window in
the Weidenhof. — — my eyes are fixed with longing on the allée of
poplars, — — If you will only come!—Now let us wait two months, in
July you could surely risk coming to the hedge. we might be able to see
each other and should know we are both well, if it were at all possible
I'd also come down, if I don't appear it would be because we'd gone on
an outing. — — —

I must also reassure you and say that since if you came into town
there were several things I wanted to tell you, they were not at all
important and lastly that nobody noticed you.

Farewell now dear heart, and be always sure of my tenderest
feelings for you—

FROM SIEGFRIED SCHMID

Basel, 13 May 1799

Here, beloved friend, I send you a kind of legacy, with the request that
you take care of bringing it to publication. Some people at least will
then put together from all these little traits a picture of your friend
that will not leave him entirely transitory and forgotten up here if he is
destined to go early to the shades.

It gives one the feeling of immortality to be *wholly* recognized by
an uncommon soul, and without vanity to be often reminded that one
is different from the masses. The only thing that can make a hero feel
more immortal is when he thinks that through being bruited abroad
his name will be spoken by perhaps many thousands of people. That is
how I feel thanks to your last letter.

22 May

I suddenly have the opportunity to send you the manuscript, but hardly the time to read back over what I have just written to you.

You look after the publication of what will perhaps even be *posthuma*. If you get a honorarium for it, I imagine I'll be able to make use of it in my new circumstances, and you can send it to me. The positions taken up by the armies have thus far not allowed me to make my intended journey; you will naturally receive news as soon as I get away from here.

Many greetings to Sinklair.

Adieu, dear Hölderlin. I've had a pretty good think about most of what very soon awaits me, & about the extremest possibility most of all, that's the way I am. If it turns out differently we shall perhaps embrace one another again soon as firmly and gladly as ever.

Siegfr. Schmid

179. TO CHRISTIAN LUDWIG NEUFFER

Homburg, 4 June 1799

Dear Neuffer,

You can certainly count on a few contributions from me, and, in accordance with your wishes, I will also let you have you some prose pieces. Perhaps I'll also be able to send you a few things by people I know here or am in correspondence with. I wish your second son all the life and all the strength and grace I should wish him if he were my own.

I intend to edit a monthly poetry journal. As I already have most of the material for the first year, at least what of it will be written by me, and given my present mode of life will be able to devote myself entirely to the enterprise, I have hopes of carrying it through. And as I am not yet engaged in a firm contract with anyone, would you please ask Herr Steinkopf whether he wouldn't consider it worth his while to take it on. At least half of the journal will contain actual poetry, the rest made up of essays to do with the history and criticism of art. The first numbers will contain a tragedy, the *Death of Empedocles*, which I have finished apart from the last act and, also by me, lyrical and elegiac poems. The essays will contain: (1) Characteristic traits from the lives of poets ancient and modern, the circumstances they developed in, and especially the artistic character peculiar to each. On Homer, Sappho, Aeschylus, Sophocles, Horace, Rousseau (as author of the *Nouvelle Héloïse*), Shakespeare etc. (2) The setting out of the peculiar beauty of their works, or of individual parts of them. On the *Iliad*, particularly the character of Achilles, on Aeschylus's *Prometheus*, on Sophocles's *Antigone* and *Oedipus*, on selected odes by Horace, on the *Héloïse*, on Shakespeare's *Antony and Cleopatra*, on the characters of Brutus and Cassius in his *Julius Caesar*, on *Macbeth* and so on. All these essays will as far as possible be written in a lively manner likely to be of general interest, mostly in the form of letters. (3) Theoretical essays, presented in popular fashion, on declamation, language, on the essence and the different kinds of poetry, and also on the beautiful in general. For all these essays, particularly for the last, I can with good conscience promise new or at least not yet worn-out perspectives, and I think I have a few truths to say that could be useful for art and pleasant to the soul. (4) There will also be reviews of particularly interesting new poetic works. I hope to obtain contributions from Heinse, author of *Ardinghello*, Heydenreich, Bouterwek, Matthisson, Conz, Siegfried Schmid, and also from you if you can spare anything.

The overall tone probably means it would be suitable for the publisher, if he sees fit, to give it the title *Aesthetic Journal for Ladies*. As to its spirit I think I'm justified in saying that it should do more for moral development and genuine recreation than many other publications.

Every month an issue of 4 folio pages, not too closely printed, would appear in octavo format. The publisher could terminate the contract whenever he wanted, only not less than 3 months before a fair.

The question of remuneration I leave to his judgment and sense of fairness. I would only add that I will live entirely for and from the enterprise, and that in any case my frugal existence doesn't require the kind of salary the great men who edited the *Horae* need. I will exert all my courage and industry and all my energies to make this journal viable and commendable, and I will make sure that if possible at least one substantial poetic work, e.g., a tragedy or a novel etc., will appear complete every year.

Should Herr Steinkopf decide to join me in this venture I would gladly promise to set aside the requests I have received for contributions to other journals and deliver at least 4 folio pages a year for his calendar for ladies free of charge.

I would also give him the option of publishing after a certain lapse of time the essays in the journal by me separately, on the conditions that go with the second edition of a book.

I confess it would give me particular pleasure to enter into this relation with Herr Steinkopf, him being your friend and an acquaintance of mine, and even though I must not assume he has the trust in me such a decision requires, still I wanted to let him know of my plan. If he finds it to his advantage it will have been appropriate for me to have made him the proposal, given that I am already in contact with him. If it's not for him then it is no different than if I had not mentioned it. Give him my compliments, and let him have a read of this letter.

Forgive me for making you the middleman. I should not have done so if I could not say of myself that you would find me ready to do anything to be of service to you. In any case I'll send you the promised essays. The prose pieces will probably contain something generally accessible, simple and not too dry, about the lives and characters of Thales and Solon and Plato. I should find it quite difficult to provide a genuinely moral essay for the calendar for ladies without revealing either too much of my deepest feelings and convictions or too little.

Please give me some news and an answer to this letter as soon as ever you can.

Yours,

H.

180. TO HIS BROTHER

Homburg, 4 June 1799

My dear brother,

Your sympathy and loyalness are a great strength to me, and what you are in yourself, your diligence, the skillful way you have of dividing your mind and energy between your professional affairs and your more general development, your braveness and your modesty, are a constant source of joy. Dear Karl, nothing cheers me more than to be able to say to another human being: I have faith in you. And though the coarseness and inadequacy to be found in people often upsets me more than it should, I am also perhaps happier than others when I encounter goodness, truthfulness and purity in life, and for that reason I have no right to accuse nature of anything: it has sharpened my sense of what is lacking in order to help me recognize excellence with more and deeper joy. Once I have managed to learn to see and feel in what is lacking precisely the particular, specific lack, the lack at that moment, rather than the vague pain it often causes me, and so also to recognize in better things the particular beauty, what is characteristically good about them, rather than remaining content with a general sensation, once I've achieved this, my mind will be calmer and my work will *progress more steadily.* For if we only experience infinitely what is lacking we will naturally tend to want to remedy it infinitely and so in some cases our energies will be wasted in an indefinite and unproductively fatiguing struggle because we have no definite knowledge of what is lacking and how the lack, the precise lack, is to be put right and supplied. As long as there are no hitches in my work it goes very well, but a small mistake that I feel too keenly to perceive with clarity is sometimes enough to make me unnecessarily overwrought. And the same is true in my ordinary life, in my dealings with people, I'm still such a child. This sensitivity is certainly not a bad thing in itself but in my case it has not yet developed into a more definite capacity of feeling, and this is probably due among other things to the fact that I have felt too much inadequacy and not enough excellence in the conditions and characters I have come across.—You will find that at the moment those of a more humane constitution, those spirits whom nature seems to have most definitely formed for humanity, are always the unhappier ones, precisely because they are rarer now than in other times and places. The barbarians around us destroy our best energies before they can become fully formed and only the resolute and clear-sighted recognition of this fate can save us, or at least prevent us from perishing in ignominy. We must seek out perfection, make common cause with it as much as we can, derive sustenance and wholeness from our sense of it and so gain the strength to perceive what is crude and askew and malformed not just with pain but as what it is, what constitutes its character and peculiar flaw. In any case, so long as people don't directly encroach on us and disturb us it is not so very hard to live with them in peace. The trouble *lies not so much in their being what they are as in their considering what they are to be the only possible mode, refusing to countenance anything else.* I am against selfishness, despotism and misanthropy, but otherwise I am coming to like people more and more because in all aspects of their activity and characters I see, more and more, the same basic character, the same fate. And indeed, this striving, this giving up of a certain present for something uncertain, different, better and yet better again I see as the original ground of everything the people around me work at and do. Why don't they live like the deer in the forest, content with little, limited to the ground, the food at their feet, where the connection with nature is like that of the baby to its mother's breast? Then there would be no anxiety, no toil, no complaint, little illness, little conflict, there would be no sleepless nights etc. But this would be as unnatural for man as the arts he teaches the animals are to them. To push life onward, to accelerate nature's endless process of perfection, to complete what he has before him, and to idealize—that will always be the instinct that best characterizes and distinguishes man, and all his arts and works and errors and tribulations stem from it. Why do we have gardens and fields? Because mankind wanted a better world than the one it inherited. Why do we have trade, ships, cities, states, with all their turmoil and their good and bad? Because mankind wanted a better world than the one it inherited. Why do we have science, art, religion? Because mankind wanted a better world than the one it inherited. Even when they chafe against one another in a headstrong way it is because the present is not satisfactory, because they want things different, and so they fling themselves sooner into nature's grave, and accelerate the march of the world.

What is greatest and what is smallest, best and worst in mankind, grows from one root, and all in all everything is good and everybody fulfills in his own way, some more beautifully, some more wildly, his purpose as a human being, namely that of multiplying, quickening, separating, mixing, dividing and binding the life of nature. It might be thought that this original urge, the urge to idealize or encourage, to rework, develop and perfect nature, no longer animates most people in their occupations nowadays, and that they do what they do out of habit, in imitation, in obedience to convention, out of the necessity into which their forefathers have brought them through industry and invention. But in order to carry on as their forefathers began, along the road of luxury, art, science etc., those that come after have to have precisely the urge in them that inspired their forefathers, in order to learn they need to be constituted as the masters were, but the epigones feel this impulse more faintly and it is only in the hearts and minds of original characters, of independent thinkers, of inventors, that it attains its full vitality. You can see, dear Karl, that I have presented you with the paradox that the artistic and creative impulse with all its modifications and varieties is actually a service human beings render unto nature. But we have long been in agreement that all the meandering rivers of human activity flow into the ocean of nature, just as they begin from it. To show people this path, which they mostly go down blindly, sometimes crossly and reluctantly and all too often in base and vile fashion, to show it to them so that they may go down it with eyes wide open, joyfully and nobly, that is the job of philosophy, art and religion, which themselves proceed from this creative impulse. Philosophy brings the impulse into consciousness, shows it its infinite object in the ideal and so strengthens and clarifies it. Art presents the impulse with its infinite object in a living image, in a higher world of representation. And religion teaches it to sense and believe this higher world precisely where it looks for and wishes to create it, i.e., in nature, both in its own human nature and in the surrounding world, as a latent disposition, as a spirit to be unfolded.

Philosophy and art and religion, the vestals of nature, thus affect man above all, are primarily there for him, and only by giving his concrete activity, which directly affects nature, proper direction and strength and joy do they also have an effect on nature, an effect that is concrete, though indirect. And another effect they have, particularly religion, is that man, to whom nature offers itself as the material of his activity and whom it contains, as a powerful motor, in its infinite system, does not think himself the lord and master of nature and

in all his arts and activity preserves a modesty and piety toward its
spirit—the same spirit he carries within him and has all about him
and that gives him material and energy. For human art and activity,
however much it has already achieved and can achieve, cannot produce
life, cannot itself create the raw material it transforms and works on; it
can develop creative energy, but the energy itself is eternal and not the
work of human hands.

Thus for human activity and nature. I wish I could present it
to you as it is in my mind and before my eyes too when I look at
the people around me, each in his particular world, for it consoles
me and gives me peace of mind and reconciles me in particular
with the diversity of human occupations, and I get great pleasure
from all the industry and feel a deeper sympathy for the doings and
sufferings of mankind. It is quite something you are attempting, my
dear brother, if you want to draw up the system of an aesthetic church
and to my mind you shouldn't be surprised if the execution of it
throws up difficulties that seem almost insurmountable. To set out in
philosophical terms the components of the ideal and their internal
relations alone would be hard enough, and the philosophical exposition
of the *ideal of all human society*, the aesthetic church, may well, if
executed in its entirety, be even harder. Just give it your best try—it
is best to aim high, and whatever happens you will reap this benefit
from it: you will find it easier to gain a clear idea of all other social
conditions, both as they are and in potential.

I got so drawn into our favorite realms of thought that I have no
time left to say much more about you and about myself.

In any case it is too early yet to tell you anything more definite
about myself and how I intend to live my life in the years to come
and when I might be able to visit you, my dear family. Oh what good
people they are, I cried, tears of joy in my eyes, when I read your three
letters.

To end with I'll copy out a passage from my tragedy, *The Death of
Empedocles*, so that you can see roughly the spirit and tone of the work
I'm devoting my slow love and toil to at the moment:

There were times of ecstasy, the soul in me
Was woken like Endymion by the gods
And from its child's sleep it opened out

A living thing and sensed the spirits of life
That always live in youth—O lovely sun!
I was not taught by men, my own heart drove me
Undying in its love for those undying,
To you, to you, nothing was more like God,
Your quiet light. And just as you do not
Hold back your light from life and, unconcerned,
Discharge your golden fullness, I, with you,
Was glad to grant my soul's best part to mortals,
And open, without fear, my heart
Gave itself like you to the somber earth
And all its fates to dedicate all life
To it in youthful joy until the end.
I said so often in our quiet hours,
We made together a covenant of death.
The trees were swayed then in a different way,
And the tender sound of streams in the hills came close —
The joys of all the earth were true, as warm
And full they ripen out of toil and love:
You gave them all to me. And often when
I sat up on the quiet hillside and thought
In wonder on the wandering fates of man
Too deeply drawn into your endless changing,
And sensed that soon my life would start to fade,
The ether breathed on me as it does on you
Soothing me and closing the wounds of love,
And, as cloud gives way to lightning or the sun
In the upper blue my cares dissolved to air.

Goodbye now, my dear Karl. Write to me as soon as your affairs and
the circumstances permit.

Yours,

Hölderlin

FROM SIEGFRIED SCHMID

Zürich, 12 June 1799

[*Has really carried out his intention and joined the Coburg Regiment of Dragoons in the army of Archduke Karl as a cadet.*] In a few days' time I shall be equipped and officially a member of the regiment. Given how things are, I hope that I shall be considered as rather more than a usual cadet.

[*He hopes that what may turn out to be his* posthuma, *which he gave to a Frankfurt man to deliver, has been received. He has asked H. to take on the trouble of getting it all published.*

He has sent his drama to Heinrich Frölich in Berlin.]

I also enclose a little song composed on my way here, if you might be willing to have it printed with the rest.

FROM JOHANN FRIEDRICH STEINKOPF

Stuttgart, 13 June 1799

[*On 4th June Hölderlin had laid out his plan in a letter to Neuffer and asked Neuffer to communicate this letter to Steinkopf. Steinkopf is writing to Hölderlin in immediate reply. They knew one another personally from a few hours they had spent together when they met in Frankfurt.*

St. finds the idea excellent and goes into it at once. It is, he says, a properly detailed plan. He at once makes a few suggestions of his own. The first of these is to add to the expression aesthetic *that of a* humanist *journal.*]

As to the contributors the important thing would be their number and even more their names, in so far as they had acquired one through their merits. Herder, Schiller, Goethe, von Humboldt, Thümmel, Fichte, Schelling, names like these would be desirable in every respect and surely the editor should be able to get hold of at least some of them.

[*These were his chief observations on the journal, which really did need to be* humanist *in the main and which should therefore aim at cultivating both aesthetic and moral sense. They could not well make a start on it before the following year.*]

I ask you now for a prompt reply, and above all that you write at once to all your friends and especially to a few men of reputation, such as Schiller, Goethe etc., asking them for their support, even if only occasional. The success of the announcement will in large part depend on having such names.

[*Thanks him for the kind attention he is giving to the almanac. The essay on* Solon *would probably suit the journal better. Neuffer asks him in the enclosure for a very short narrative or novel about Emilie, who must be given the character of an exemplary and noble-minded girl. The rest he leaves entirely for H. to decide. If he had a longer poem, or wanted to write one, of particular interest to the* female sex, *he'd be very pleased to have it. He also hopes that H. will not submit much to other magazines, at least this time.*]

181. TO HIS MOTHER

Homburg vor der Höhe, 18 June 1799

Dearest Mother,

If I had nothing else to raise my spirits and fill me with gratitude and faith, a heart such as yours, this kindness and love, would be enough. Believe me, dear, honored mother, you are holy to me in this pure sympathy of yours, and I would be a man stripped of his senses not to know it and value it. No, the religious spirit that reigns between mother and son will never die out between us! Oh what good people they are, I was moved to say to myself, and wept with joy when I read the three lovely letters from you and from Rike and Karl.

Don't think it impatience and feebleness on my part, which sort so ill with my years and my sex,—if I complained and spoke of desolate hours. It was less my own pain that often prevented me from finding solace in these moments than the sadness that sometimes overcame me in my total solitude when I thought of our present world and of the rare and good people in it and how they suffer precisely because they are better and more excellent. And probably it is *necessary* that I feel this from time to time, for this is what drives me to my purest activity. It is a wonderful thing that no one gets anywhere if he looks on everything with indifference, and at the same time doesn't achieve or further anything either if he despairs, that if he wants to live and be active therefore he has to combine both in his heart, sorrow and hope, joy and pain. And this, I believe, is also what it is to be a Christian. And that is how you meant it too.

How grateful I am to you, too, for your words on my dear departed father. What a good and noble man! Believe me, this is not the first time I have been put in mind of his serenity of soul, and of how I should like to resemble him. It is not you either, dearest Mother, who have given me this melancholy tendency that I cannot quite pronounce myself free of. I have a pretty clear perspective on my whole life, almost back into my earliest youth, and I know very well at what point my mind took on this disposition. You will perhaps hardly believe it, but I still remember all too clearly. When my second father died, whose love for me is so unforgettable, when, with unfathomable pain, I felt myself an orphan and saw your daily grief and tears, that was when my soul first altered into this seriousness that has never entirely left me and could only ever grow with the years. But in the depths of my being I also have a serenity, a faith, that often still breaks into true, full joy, only it is not so easy to find words for this as for pain. It gave me great pleasure that you encouraged me to enjoy my youth. I tend to imagine myself a bit younger than I am, and, for all my seriousness and circumspection, probably am often still a little boy, too good-natured sometimes with other people, and the result is always oversensitivity and distrust. Comfort yourself, dearest Mother, with the thought that I am honest and serious enough to see my faults, something that always leads to more sense.

I have a pleasant piece of news to tell you. I have come to an agreement with the bookseller Steinkopf in Stuttgart to edit a journal of which he will be the publisher. It will appear once a month, most of the essays in it will be by me, the others by writers I shall count it an honor to figure alongside. This will earn me about 500 fl. a year, and so from next year my existence will be assured in a respectable manner for some time. As I have already got quite a long way forward in my work you need not fear, dearest Mother, that this occupation will be too much of a burden for me. In the letter in which he pronounces himself inclined to take it on, Steinkopf has requested that I should first set out for him the commercial conditions and tell him how much I would ask for looking after the journal and supplying my essays. I shall expressly stipulate that I am paid at least a hundred guilders at the beginning of the year and so on every six months until the end, and that way, being provided for for quite a while, I see no reason why I should find myself in the position of having to abuse your kindness. In my next letter I'll give you the definite and more detailed facts about the journal. I take the liberty of accepting the 100 fl. in the way you have judged appropriate, and in my thoughts and deeds I'll never forget it.

You will not find it hard to imagine, dear Mother, how much I want to see you and all the rest of the family again, and if it were not too great a disruption of my affairs and of the few savings I have I'd come up to see you for a few weeks in the autumn. I fear however that for the moment I won't have enough time, and you will not be surprised if in this I keep to my own rules and resolutions as strictly as if I was bound to someone else. If I didn't do this, my present independence would do me more harm than good, and in the end I would find fitting into any sort of order irksome. —

Forgive me for breaking off suddenly, but it is already quite late and I don't like to expose myself to these cool evenings. My health has really become more precious to me having been deprived of it for a while at such an unfortunate time and needing it as I do. All my love and respects to my dear grandmother. I'll write to my dear sister later this week. I don't want to leave her waiting for a letter any longer.

Yours,

Friz

Hang on to the money for another month or so. If you don't mind I'll write to you for it as soon as I foresee having need of it. At the moment sending cash at least won't be safe.

182. TO JOHANN FRIEDRICH STEINKOPF

Homburg vor der Höhe, 18 June 1799

[Now sets out the idea of the project at greater length. Here among other things he says:

True popularity dwells less in the everyday nature of the material than in the liveliness and intelligibility of the exposition.

The main aim he proposes is to reconcile the conflicting elements of the ideal, the original-natural, the purely lively on the one hand, and of the real, the cultural, the theoretical, the artificial on the other.] I know very well that the same thing has recently been attempted, and produced a sensation but no fundamental effect; but having looked at this very thoroughly and exactly it appears to me that whether through passion or through ignorance one main point was missing, viz. the proper impartiality: there is the usual exaggeration, the usual reaching for extremes, with incomprehensibility and giving offence to those at the opposite extreme the result. This last experience has however also produced a purer conviction, and I believe that I am not the only one to see things in this way.

So the union and reconciliation of theory with life, of art and taste with genius, of the heart with the understanding, of the real with the ideal, of the cultural (in the broadest sense of the word) with nature—this will be the most general character, the spirit, of the journal.

[*The poetry will not merely be a passionate, rapturous, capricious explosion, and not a forced, cold feat of artifice, but will proceed at once from life and from the ordering understanding, from sentiment and from conviction.*

Essays on poetry in general, on language, declamation, poetic genres, on genius, feeling, imagination etc. on particular poems and their authors] (by giving a sense of the man, his life, his own nature and the nature that surrounded him, they make sure that the poem receives its due as a product of nature).

[*He proposes the title* Iduna, *because he seems to remember a journal's having used that name before. But leaves that up to the publisher.*]

I shall give you news of the success of my efforts to secure a number of collaborators who will serve to recommend the journal in the way you wish as soon as I know where I stand, and at the same time send you the prospectus, which will necessarily depend on this, for you to examine. I can assure you in the meantime that I shall do all I can to approach many different people with all expediency, and not let my good will be put off by any difficulty it might encounter if we turn to men of reputation and expose ourselves to an unsatisfactory response.

Meanwhile I will devote all my time and all my powers to it, and also above all to giving my tragedy the proper pleasurableness and finish, which because of the peculiarity of its subject matter it can less afford to do without than other works.

[He intends to deliver 3 folio pages for each monthly issue at 1 carolin each. That makes 36 carolins, and as he needs at least 50 carolins a year, he would ask for the rest to be paid to him as editor.

At the beginning of next month he will send Neuffer "Emilie" and a few other poems and some by a young poet whose products are not without talent and felicity.]

183. TO SUSETTE GONTARD

[Homburg, ~ late June 1799]

Every day I have to invoke the absent divinity again. When I think of great men at the great moments of history, how they caught at the things around them like holy fire and transformed everything dead and wooden, the world's straw, into flame that flew up with them to the heavens; and then of myself, how I often go about like a poor glimmering lamp that would dearly beg a drop of oil to shine into the night a bit longer—then, I tell you, a curious shudder runs through my whole body, and softly I call out to myself the terrible words: more dead than alive.

Do you know the reason for all this? People are frightened of one another, they are afraid that one's genius will consume another's, and so they are willing to grant each other food and drink, but no nourishment for the soul, and they cannot bear it when anything they say or do is taken up in someone else's mind and transformed into flame. The fools! As if anything that people could say to each other were more than firewood, which only becomes fire again when it is caught by the fire of the spirit, just as it issued from life and from fire. And if they will only not begrudge each other mutual nourishment they will both have life and light, and neither will consume the other.

Do you remember our untroubled hours when we were with each other, and we alone? That was triumph! Both so free and proud and alert and open and bright in soul and heart and eye and countenance, and both in such blessed peace with each other. I sensed it and said it then: one could travel the whole world and not find anything to match it. And every day I feel it more keenly.

Yesterday afternoon Morbek came to my room and said, "The French have been beaten in Italy again." "So long as things are right with us," I said to him, "things are right enough with the world," and he fell about my neck and we kissed each other's deeply moved and joyful souls on the lips and our eyes met, full of tears. Then he went. There are still such moments. But can that replace a world? And that's what will make me faithful to you for ever. Many people are excellent in one way or another. But a nature like yours, where everything is joined in intimate, indelible, living union, this is the pearl of time, and whoever has recognized it and seen how its heavenly innate unique happiness is also its deep unhappiness, he is likewise for ever happy and for ever unhappy.

184. TO CHRISTIAN LUDWIG NEUFFER

Homburg vor der Höhe, 3 July 1799

I haven't quite kept my word, my dear friend, and am sending what I promised you a week later than I had intended. I was obliged to go away for a few days when among other things I spoke to our friend Jung, who is in particularly good spirits at the moment. He wants to give me his Ossian for the journal. Some passages would make perfect text to be accompanied by a commentary.

I'm going to take the opportunity, in case it might be of interest to you, to say a few words about the method and manner in which I have written *Emilie*. You can well imagine that given the haste with which I had to set to work I could not express the poetic genre, which I have had in mind for some time, quite as I wanted to and as would be necessary to make palpable the advantages that it probably has, especially with subjects that are not properly heroic. It is not at all the impression of the new that is important to me; but more and more I feel and see how much we are caught between two extremes: having no rules at all, and blind subjection to old forms and the constraint and wrong application that go with it. Do not think, dear Neuffer, that I arbitrarily set and devise myself my own particular form. I examine the feeling that leads me to this or that form and make sure that the one I have chosen doesn't contradict the ideal and in particular the subject that it treats. Of course it is then true that I can be right on a general level but for that reason lose my way in the actual execution, because I simply follow my idea and have no concrete pattern to go by. But there is no alternative: as soon as we deal with any subject that is even a little bit modern it is my conviction that we must abandon the old classical forms, which are so intimately fitted to their subject matter that they are no good for any other. Now it's true we're accustomed to seeing a love story, for example, *that is no more than that*, being presented in the form of a tragedy, though among the ancients this form, in its inner progression and its heroic dialogue, is quite unsuited to a true love story. If the heroic dialogue is retained it is always as if the lovers were quarrelling. If it is abandoned, then the tone contradicts the fundamental form of tragedy, which of course is not retained at all strictly but for that very reason loses, among us moderns, its peculiar poetic value, its meaning. But then all they want is moving or shattering passages and situations—neither writers nor the public bother much about the meaning and impression of the whole. And so the strictest of all poetic forms, *whose whole purpose is to proceed through a series of harmonic changes without any ornament in almost exclusively major tones each of which is an independent whole*, and which in this proud renunciation of all accidentals presents the ideal of a living whole as briefly and at the same time as completely and richly as possible, and thus more clearly but also more seriously than any other known poetic form—the venerable tragic form has been debased into a means of providing the odd occasion for saying something flashy or tender. But what headway could they expect to make with it if they did not choose the subject matter it was intended for and coupled with which alone it maintained its life and sense? It had died, like all other forms when they have lost the living soul for which they served as the organic frame and out of which they were originally bodied forth, like, for example, the republican form in our Free Cities, which is now dead and meaningless because the people in them are not such that they *need* it, to put it mildly.

Just as the tragic subjects are made to proceed through a series of harmonic changes in exclusively major *independent* tones, and to present with all possible sparing of accidentals a whole that is full of powerful, meaningful parts, the *sentimental* subjects, e.g., love, are wholly suited to proceed through a series of harmonic changes not in major, proud, firm tones and with decisive renunciation of accidentals but with *a tender shying away from accidentals,* and in deep, full, elegiacally meaningful tones that convey a great deal in the longing and hope they express, and to present the ideal of a living whole not with this concerted power of the parts and this irresistible progress, this rapid concision, but as if on wings, like Psyche and Cupid, and with *intimate* concision, and the only question is what form this can be managed in with the most ease and naturalness and effect, so that the beautiful spirit of love will have its own poetic figure and mode.

Forgive me if I'm boring you with this uncertain train of thought. I'm living so much on my own that at the moment I often like to spend a leisurely hour conversing with an impartial friend in writing about matters that concern me, and as you can see it makes me chattier than is perhaps agreeable to my correspondent. Admittedly I have said very little to you indeed and had more of a conversation with myself than with you.

It gives me great pleasure that you are devoting yourself to poetry more and more. The age has cast such a heavy burden of impressions on us that only, as I feel more clearly every day, by dint of working hard and long, right into our old age, making ever-renewed serious attempts and experiments can we perhaps in the end produce what nature has primarily destined us for and that in other circumstances would perhaps have matured sooner but hardly with such perfection. If responsibilities that are truly sacred to both of us impose themselves we shall be making a fine sacrifice to necessity if, at least for a while, we renounce our love for the Muses.

It must have been a happy evening for you when your comedy was performed and you were conscious of yourself, amid the hilarity of the spectators, as the initial moving force behind it. Has it been published and do you think I'll be able to buy it in Frankfurt?

I wish your journal many happy collaborators. Should you be discontented with a number of contributions and prefer to have the gap filled by me, I'd willingly devote you another week, *only in an emergency of course,* otherwise this would be a presumptuous thing for me to say. I'll send you a few more of my poems later with contributions from another young poet. Bölendorf's, which I enclose, should be of some interest to your readers and you can always make a selection if you see fit.

Be so good and make sure that the intervals that have been left between the iambic stanzas in the manuscript of *Emilie* are printed properly.

Don't take exception to the title; we'll soon have too many prefaces, more prefaces than poems, and if I can as it were replace such a preface with a few words and indicate to the reader that this is only a moment in Emilie's life and that the poet is obliged in general to concentrate all biography as far as possible into a significant moment—why not?

Though I wrote this exercise very quickly I can assure you that I have said very little that lacks dramatic or general poetic purpose.

Good night, dear friend. Remember me to Herr Steinkopf and all my other friends and acquaintances in Stuttgart, and do me a favor and write me something about them too and let me have another letter soon.

Hölderlin

FROM JOHANN FRIEDRICH STEINKOPF

Stuttgart, 5 July 1799

[*Is essentially in complete agreement.*]
And so I ask you to write at once to Schiller, von Humboldt, Goethe, Schlegel in Jena, Thümmel, Matthisson, Herder, Pfeffel, Schelling, Sophie Mereau, Falk in Weimar, Meisner in Prague and Lafontaine in Berlin, the last two for stories, to ask them for contributions. . . . Schiller's name and participation, in particular, is *crucial.* If these men only send in something from time to time that would be sufficient, the main thing is to have their names, and unless we get a good number of them I think it very unlikely that the enterprise will have quite the success we desire in terms of sales. I therefore ask you, my friend, not to spare any effort in this regard, and if you don't get a prompt reply, to write again.

[*Wants to see a draft of the prospectus soon. It would be necessary to distribute it in early September. He wants to be able to incorporate it in the* Taschenbuch für Frauenzimmer.

Neuffer says he has not yet received from him what was promised. He requests it, as the printing of the almanac has already begun.] Your essays and poems in the new almanac for the year 1800 will make an immense difference in promoting *Iduna.*

185. TO FRIEDRICH SCHILLER

[Homburg,] 5 July 1799

Only the generosity you have always shown me, esteemed Sir, and the deep devotion toward you, which grows in me day by day, can give me the assurance to burden you with an immodest request, and I should certainly refrain from doing this if I could foresee with certitude that it would cause you displeasure. Perhaps I am blinded by my desire and by the knowledge of how important the satisfaction of this request would be for me. I have therefore every cause to ask for your forgiveness should it really prove a bother to you.

Were I so worthy of your protection that I did not need it I should not ask you for it, or if I needed it so much that I was not worthy of it at all I should not ask you for it either. But I believe I need and am worthy of it just enough to make asking for it excusable.

I have in mind gradually to publish the literary and poetic essays I am in the middle of working on in a humanist journal, and would prefer to wait and see whether I do not at last produce something whose value and success I could be surer of, if only circumstances allowed me the untroubled independence such a thing would require. As it is I am obliged to offer samples that perhaps promise more than they achieve, and in view of my readers cannot do without the authority of a well-established man of reputation if I am to avoid failure, knowing myself and the times as I do.

For this reason I take the liberty of asking you for a few small contributions, if you should not find it below your dignity to give me this public sign of your favor and kindness.

Believe me, esteemed Sir, my admiration for you is too sincere for me not to feel afflicted by this indiscretion. And now that the perilous plea has been uttered I cannot make up for it, as I should like to think I could, by once again expressing, more freely and with less inhibition, the gratitude I felt toward you and could not express when years ago I saw you for the first time, a gratitude that your unforgettable company and every sign of your presence in the world have only made more profound as time goes on.

If there is some goal of merit I might attain in the future, only then shall I be able to thank you properly, for only thanks from someone who has become worthy of you to a higher degree can give you pleasure, and then perhaps I could also justify my immodest request.

Be so kind, even if you should deem my project not worth your emphatic support, as to reply to me nonetheless, however briefly, for if you say nothing I shall take the blame for my indiscretion onto myself, a blame that might well turn out to be more severe than any you would utter against me.

Should you wish, I could send you the manuscript of the first issue for you to inspect.

I am with unfeigned esteem

your

M. Hölderlin

My publisher joins his request to mine.
Allow me to add my address:

at the glazier Wagner's

in

Homburg near Frankfurt.

FROM SUSETTE GONTARD

[Frankfurt, ~ 3–6 July 1799]

could makes me very glad and I shan't let it show how important the carrying out of this plan, that is not yet quite certain, is to me. The second Thursday of August you would very probably find me back here again. After that my brother wants to take a little trip up the Rhine with us as far as Coblenz, and from there we'll go with his wife as far as Ems where she is to take the waters, and he advises me also to have a course of Piedmont water, this whole journey would certainly not last longer than four weeks, and then I shall try to give you a little journal of it—only think what might be in it!—and just as you always like to share everything with me, how glad I shall be in this way to avoid the social occasions that are often so wearisome to me and live just for myself with my dear brother and his wife.   Being away from here always gives me pain of course because I think of here as the fixed point of our union.

I should also love to say something to you about your future course in life, you asked me to, but how difficult it is in every respect for me to advise you and won't my choice for you always be too timid, a faithful and experienced male friend can do more in this matter. I know you can't take any step that my soul doesn't approve of and although perhaps having been spoilt and made too tender-hearted by being near you I might struggle against them, my better convictions must prevail and should you launch on a career that would bring you fame and would be useful to the world all my tears on your account would surely become tears of joy but I should still need to hear from you and my hopes must not be disappointed, take advice for your future with your true friends and men of experience and if then no *secure* way opens to you, you'll do better to remain as you are and make your own way than again risk being overwhelmed and flung back by fate, you would not be strong enough to bear it and for the world, and for posterity which living quietly you also live for, you would be utterly lost. No you mustn't do that. You mustn't gamble with your own self, your noble nature, the mirror of all that is beautiful, must not be broken in you, and you owe it to the world to give forth the things that in higher forms, transfigured, appear to you and to watch particularly over the preservation of yourself. *There are not many like you! — —* And what does not have an effect now remains secure for future times. Could you not also in the future perhaps have young people come to you for teaching, forgive me this suggestion if it's not to your liking. but I know you did once think of giving such lectures and that surely wouldn't be difficult for you.   All I ask is that you never act in the wrong idea that you must bring honor to me, as though everything you do and achieve without its being known is not just as dear to me.

As though you must more loudly justify my love for you. Your love honors me enough and will always be enough for me and for the thing that people call honor I have no desire, great men honor you I find you in all depictions of nobility of character and don't need the world's wretched testimony as well, only today I was reading Tasso and found aspects of you there quite unmistakably. read it again yourself.

3 July

A few more moments on my own I can give to you, my companion has gone visiting the neighbors, and this evening S . . . is coming out to us, I pray heaven she won't hinder me on Thursday morning. Often the thought that I might not be able to get to you crosses my mind like a shock. I put my trust in the guardian angel of love for has not everything worked as we wished since our separation. It will go well in the future too. Also I must ask you to be there on the 1st Thursday in August and if by then our journey isn't finished, which is very unlikely, you'd come again on the following Thursday wouldn't you, but if we come home earlier we should want to be away again because of the baths. and I can't postpone it. My brother wrote yesterday that we could travel on the 12th.

Thursday morning

How I should love to spend a while longer quietly conversing with you but the thought, Someone is coming! spoils everything in me, and is also the reason I have written nowhere near as much to you as I should have wished, I had so many things more to answer in your precious letter. Be cheerful, my love, and trust people a bit more than you do, they are surely sometimes better than we think, and because we always measure them against the highest and the best that we recognize in one another, they are also bound to go down too far in our estimation. let compassion and never hatred and revulsion dwell in you. Forgive me that I touch on this subject again it was always as though I had forgotten it and still had to speak of it. Farewell! Farewell!

— —

Our journey is definite we can leave on the 12th.

186. TO JOHANN WOLFGANG GOETHE (?)

[Homburg, early July 1799]

I do not know, esteemed Sir, whether you still remember my name well enough to make it unexceptionable to be reading a letter and what is more a plea from me.

Your qualities and your renown would do so much to further the matter I am approaching you about, and the memory of a few unforgettable hours that your good dispositions granted me years ago also gives me so much confidence, that I put my request to you not quite without hope of a favorable reply. I have in mind (together with a number of writers) to edit a humanist journal that would be primarily poetic in its fundamental character, both in practice and in theory, which last aim it would pursue by containing essays of a general nature on the ideals shared by all the arts, on what is proper and peculiar to poetic compositions and to poetic speech, but then also addressing various masterpieces by ancient and more recent writers and seeking to show how each of these works is an ideal, systematic, characteristic whole that has issued out of the living soul of the poet and the living world around him and through his art has formed an organization of its own, a nature within nature.

[*But then the discursive essays would also take in art and the creative impulse and the character of the journal in general would be that of* humanism.]

I only wanted to describe roughly the spirit and character of the journal, in the hope that at least in its tendency it will not be something you would not countenance.

How important it is for me to win the honor of your support, and how much the project and the public would gain from it—let my very temerity be proof of that. Without it I certainly should not venture to make this request, since a negative answer from you or total silence would carry too much weight for me to be able to remain indifferent. I will do everything I can, through the greatest possible maturity of my own contributions and through the kind sympathy of writers of merit I flatter myself will give the journal the worth it needs,

187. TO FRIEDRICH WILHELM JOSEPH SCHELLING

[Homburg, early July 1799]

My dear friend,

Since we last met I have followed your affairs and your fame with so much loyalty and concern that I think I can allow myself to remind you of my existence once again.

If during this time I have given you no sign of life it was mostly because one day I hoped to approach you, who have continued to mean so much to me, in some more important regard or at least having accomplished something that might recall our friendship in a more fitting manner.

Now a request drives me to you sooner than that and even in this form you will not fail to recognize me. I have made use of the solitude in which I have been living here since last year to work without distraction and with all my concentrated and independent powers on something that will perhaps be more mature than has been the case hitherto, and although I have mostly lived for poetry, even so necessity and inclination have not allowed me to stray so far from theoretical concerns that I have not sought to develop my convictions into greater firmness and completeness and, as far as possible, to put them into application and reaction with the world past and present. For a large part my thoughts and my studies were restricted to what I was mostly working on, poetry, in so far as it is a living art and comes at the same time from genius and experience and reflection and is ideal and systematic and individual. This led me into thoughts about culture and the creative impulse in general, about its ground and its purpose, how far it works ideally and how far actively, and then again how far, as art and creative impulse, it is conscious of its ground and its own essence, beginning from an ideal, and how far it is instinctive, though obeying the laws of its material etc.; and when I came to the end of my investigations I believed I had established the standpoint of so-called humanism in a more solid and comprehensive form than any I had come across before (by attending to the unifying and communal aspects of human natures and the directions they take rather than to what differentiates them, though that too requires just as much attention, it's true). All this material led me to conceive the idea of a humanist journal which would for the most part be devoted to the practice of poetry, but would then also include theoretical approaches, from historical and philosophical perspectives, and finally would pursue such approaches to subjects other than poetry, from the standpoint of humanism.

Forgive me this laborious preamble, dear friend, but my respect for you prevented me from announcing my project to you *ex abrupto* and I felt I was bound to account in some fashion for what I have been doing, particularly as I might easily fear that what I have produced so far may no longer inspire in you the degree of faith you seemed to have in my philosophical and poetic abilities before, now that I should be able to give you proof of them.

It will be easy for you, who penetrate and encompass human nature and its elements with a breadth and skill that are only too rare, to put yourself in my more limited position and with your name and your participation sanction an undertaking whose aim is to *bring people closer together without frivolity or syncretism*. It will do this by treating of and arguing for, though not too strictly, the particular energies and directions and relations in their nature. But while maintaining due respect for each one of these energies, directions and relations it will attempt to make the intimate and necessary connections between them clear and apprehensible, and to show how every one of them only needs to be considered in its excellence and purity in order to see that it is far from contradicting any other, so long as it is also pure, but that each one already contains within itself an openness to reciprocal interaction and harmonic exchange. And likewise the soul within the organic structure, being common to all members and particular to each, leaves not a single one of them in isolation—the soul cannot exist without the organs, nor the organs without the soul, and both, if they do occur separately and so in an aorgic state, will tend to become organic, and already contain the creative impulse within them. As a metaphor I think it makes sense to say that. It was not meant to mean any more than this: spirit that has no substance cannot exist without experience, and experience that has no soul cannot exist without spirit, and they carry within them the necessity of taking on form and constituting themselves through judgment and art, of ordering themselves into an animate, harmonically changing whole; and finally organic art and the creative impulse it issues from cannot exist either, are not even conceivable, without their inner element, natural disposition and spirit, *and* their outer element, experience and historical learning.

All I wanted was to give you a general idea of the journal's character, to touch on what one might call its spirit. I will try to make the style and tone as accessible as possible.

I didn't think it was quite proper to go into more detail about the plan I have been obliged to draw up or the material I have ready, however much at the same time I was tempted to demonstrate to you, as far as can be done before the fact, that my project is not ill-founded or rash and has perhaps more chance of success than what I have produced before; and that from what I know and sense of your mind and ways of thinking I shall not be going against you, not in the general tendency at any rate.

I shall wait for your reply, which I shall attach much hope to, and your thoughts on the matter, before, should you ask me to, going into more length about the spirit and composition of the journal such as I have been able to plan it in my own mind, together with the possible materials for inclusion and those already written.

In any case, friend of my youth, you will forgive me for turning to you with the old familiarity and expressing the wish that with your participation and companionship in this enterprise you might help keep my courage up, which due to my situation and other circumstances has suffered various shocks since we last met—I should be able to admit that to you. For my part, with the greatest possible maturity of my own contributions and the kind participation of the established writers I flatter myself on getting, I will do everything to give the journal the quality it requires for you to be able to answer to your conscience and your public should you, at the least, put your name to it and, if you are able or willing to do no more, contribute once or twice a year. —

The bookseller Steinkopf in Stuttgart, who has shown willingness and understanding toward me in this matter and who perhaps precisely because he is a beginner is seeing to his side of things with great persistency and loyalty, promises to pay every contributor, and I have made it a condition that everyone should be sent *at least* one carolin a folio page. Although I intend to live almost exclusively from and for the journal, nevertheless I thought I should ask no more for myself, seeing that I haven't had much success as a writer so far and my frugal way of life doesn't require any more income than that. But I have left it

to his good sense to show his appreciation and, in whatever degree he
sees fit, make an exception for the various contributors.—Forgive me
for going into that too. But as it is part of it, let the nature of the thing
take the blame for not being able to exist without such a pendant.

Be so kind, my dear Schelling, as to at least give me an answer
soon, and know that I have always honored and respected you, and do
so more and more.

Yours,

Hölderlin

PS. My publisher makes a point of joining his request to mine.
My address is: at the glazier Wagner's in Homburg near Frankfurt.

188. TO JOHANN GOTTFRIED EBEL

[Homburg,] 6 July 1799

My dear friend,

Since we last met I have followed you and your affairs with such
enduring concern that I think I can allow myself to remind you of my
existence once again.

If during this time I have given you no sign of life it was mostly
because one day I hoped to approach you, who have continued to
mean so much to me, in some more important regard or at least
having accomplished something that might recall our friendship in a
more fitting manner.

Now a request drives me to you sooner than that and even
in this form you will not fail to recognize me. I have made use of
the solitude in which I have been living here since last year to work
without distraction and with all my concentrated and independent
powers on something that will perhaps be *more mature than the little
things I have produced as a writer hitherto,* and *although I have mostly
lived for poetry,* even so necessity and inclination have not allowed me
to stray so far from serious thoughts that I have not sought to develop

my convictions into greater definiteness and completeness and, as far as possible, to put them into application and reaction with the world past and present.

For the most part my thoughts were restricted to what I was mostly working on, *poetry,* in so far as it is a living art and comes at the same time from genius and experience and reflection and is ideal and systematic and concretely individual.

This led me into thoughts about art and culture and the creative impulse in general, about its ground and the directions it takes, its produced forms, and how it works instinctively, often correctly, often on diverse wrong paths, running wild and into caricature, but then also more reflectedly and surely and purely proceeding from the ideal, but in all this as art and creative impulse, always in its origin out of the genuinely human striving, shared by all individuals, to organize, to idealize; to cultivate, to arrange and to adorn the elements of their own nature and of that which surrounds them. To promote life, to quicken the action of the world, indirectly or directly. *In this character shared by all humans and in the view of human life as bearing that shared character more purely or more impurely, in fine essential directions and forms as well as in unfine and inessential ones,* I believed I was bound to establish what up until now has been understood, in a more or less defined way, under humanism, and I also believed I could regard poetry, and the view of it as a naturally derived art product, as a branch of humanism.

In this way the material I am working on has given me cause to conceive the idea of a humanist journal that would basically be concerned with the practice of poetry, but would also treat of art theoretically in that it would show how a work of art is organized, into a particular character as well as into an ideal meaning, and show the harmonic exchange of its tones, in general as well as with regard to its particular subject matter, and would also consider the work of art as proceeding from nature and life, arising from the soul and the peculiar character of the poet and the world that surrounds him, whereby a masterpiece would have the fixed and nominal aspects removed as regards its qualities, and the odd, unpleasantly strange aspects removed as regards its accidental characteristics, so that in that in which it is eternal, and in that in which it bears the trace of its time and its creator, people could more easily become familiar with it and also, in their own structures and arrangements and ways of organizing themselves, feel closer to the artist and the work of art.

Finally and in general—observing and reasoning from the standpoint of humanism, and concerning the characters and customs and opinions and forms of human life as proceeding from a common, shared source, the organizing creative impulse and its ground, human nature in its diverse and intent organicity, distinguishing however between the fine and the misconceived, the pure and the errant—the journal should be: instructive and entertaining.

Forgive me this laborious preamble, dear friend, but my respect for you prevented me from announcing my project to you straight off; no more did I think it proper to give you the particulars of the plan, in as far as I have been able to draw it up for myself, and the material I have ready; all I wanted was to give a general idea of the journal's character, to touch on what one might call its spirit, and as far as can be done before the fact demonstrate to you that my project is not ill-founded or rash and perhaps more apt to succeed than what I have produced before; and that from what I know and divine of your mind and ways of thinking I shall not be going against you, not in the general tendency at any rate.

For you, who encompass and penetrate human nature with a rare breadth and skill, together with the various characters and directions it takes and the customs and opinions and forms it can express itself in, and who have such a multifarious, active, open world, both big and small, to observe and reflect upon, it will not be hard, after more serious preoccupations, to put yourself in this position too and with your name and your participation favor an undertaking whose aim is to *bring people closer together without frivolity or syncretism. And it will do this by combining the various forms of their living and doing in one spirit and putting them into harmonic exchange, so as to quietly animate them, to shift them away a little from their limitations, to lessen their fearful egoism, which always gets stuck in one point, and to bring the soul of society into more rapid circulation.*

In any case, my unforgettable friend, you will forgive me for turning to you with the old familiarity and expressing this wish to you. Your depiction of the mountain inhabitants of Switzerland has made me particularly keen to have contributions from you.

May I ask you to send my compliments to Herr von Humboldt, who I read is at present in Paris, and ask him in my name whether he might not sanction and support my efforts by taking part also and sending frequent, or should this not be possible, just a few contributions. Only the kind participation of other writers of merit, and the consciousness of my best intentions, permit me to approach men of reputation with this request.

I should have taken the liberty of approaching him in writing myself; but as I do not have the honor of being so closely acquainted with him I thought I needed your advocacy.—Perhaps at least you know where he is staying exactly, and would be so kind as to let me know.

For my part, with the greatest possible maturity of my own contributions and with a lively and generally comprehensible tone and exposition, I will do everything to give the journal the quality and felicity it requires for you and him not to find it beneath your dignity to have taken part in it.—

The bookseller *Steinkopf* in Stuttgart, who has pronounced himself willing to publish it and is accommodating toward me in this matter and who perhaps precisely because he is a beginner is seeing to his side of things with great persistency and loyalty, promises to send every contributor *at least* one carolin a folio page. Although I intend to live almost exclusively from and for the journal, nevertheless I thought I should ask no more for myself, seeing that I haven't had much success as a writer so far and my frugal way of life doesn't require any more income than that. But I have left it to his good sense to show his appreciation and, in whatever degree he sees fit, make an exception for the various contributors.—Forgive me for going into that too. But as it is part of it, let the nature of the thing take the blame for not being able to exist without such a pendant.

Be so kind, my dear Ebel, as to at least give me an answer soon, and know that I have always honored and respected you, and do so more and more.

Yours,

Hölderlin

My address is: at the glazier Wagner's in Homburg near Frankfurt.

189. TO HIS MOTHER

Homburg, 8 July 1799

Dearest Mother,

Your kind letters are always cause for a sort of celebration when I
receive them, and every time I feel as if I was at home, with you, and
the motherly love you show me makes you so present, together with
the country I know and my dear relatives, so close and true, that
being far away is made much easier. You can be quite reassured about
my health. For a good while now I've felt perfectly well, and a joyful
gratitude for being vouchsafed this, not something we can bestow on
ourselves, guides me in my work and in my hours of rest.

You shouldn't have been disquieted by those verses, dearest
Mother! It didn't mean any more than how much I want one day
to have the peace and quiet to carry out what nature seems to have
destined me for. And in general, my dear Mother, I must ask you
not to take everything you read of mine as strictly literal in meaning.
To express his little world the poet must imitate creation, where not
everything is perfect and where God sends rain on good and evil and
on the just and the unjust. The poet must often say something untrue
and contradictory which then of course resolves itself into *truth* and
harmony in the greater whole, where it is said as something *transitory
and perishable*. And just as the rainbow only shows its beauty after a
storm, so in the poem truth and harmony emerge with even greater
beauty and pleasure from falsehood and from error and suffering.—I
know and am very grateful, my noble, good mother, that you do all
you can to encourage me, and I promise you your blessing shall not be
without fruit.

As for the journey you so kindly invite me to make, you will see
from the letter to my dear sister how very tempted I am to make use
of your kind permission and whether or not it will be possible for me
to fulfill this desire.

I have not yet had the opportunity to find out exactly the best
way of getting the money to me in complete security, so please wait
for my next letter before sending it off. I don't need any more for the

moment, even if other things permit me to travel up to see you for a few weeks in the early autumn. Accept my heartfelt thanks again. It was an endless source of joy to hear you say you could now leave off worrying and put your mind to rest in so many regards.

Don't let my indisposition get in the way of any of the joys that at your age you have so fully earned, when you have done so much for us and undergone so many things in life. For I am healthy now, dear attentive mother, and have all the more reason to hope I shall remain so since I shall be able to live for a while in such tranquility and without any great strain or violent interruption. Pass on my affection to Karl too, when he's there. My best regards to all the family! How much I would like to be part of the joyfulness your dear guests will feel, but the latest preparations for the journal, which I mustn't put off if I am to settle the matter soon, mean that I can't very well get away now.

A thousand respects to my dear grandmother. As ever

your much indebted son,

Hölderlin

190. TO HIS SISTER

[Homburg, July 1799]

My dear sister,

I would not forgive myself for having taken so long to thank you for your last, kind letter if in the meantime I hadn't had so many other letters to write which couldn't be put off without causing me difficulties. And it isn't so much that I lacked the time, for an hour or two is easily found, but if I have been busy writing in a tone that between us is foreign (however much it is often a real need for me) it is not easy to find my way back into the mood I like to write to you in and to find words more fit for a brother and sister than those which are appropriate for conversing with people less familiar to us.

For me it is a constant source of joy that the lovely affection we have for one another has not lessened, and that we still mean the same to each other as we always did, and I believe nothing from our youth survives with such persistent liveliness as the love between brothers and sisters and other relatives and am so glad to let myself be guided by it, as a cherished remnant of my past, when I sense that so much in and around me is different now than before. However much my conscience pushes me forward I cannot help often thinking with gratitude, and often with longing, of the days of my youth: in childhood we can still live more by our hearts than by the light of understanding, and our sense of the beauty of ourselves and the world is still whole enough for us not to be obliged to derive almost our only satisfaction from hard work at what we have chosen to do.

But when I feel we cannot remain young for ever I often think, and I like the thought, that everything has its time, and at bottom summer is as beautiful as spring, or rather neither one nor the other is completely beautiful—beauty consists more in all seasons and periods of life together in their sequence than in any one on its own. And it is the same with our days. No one day satisfies us entirely, none is wholly beautiful, and each has if not its evil then at least its imperfection, but add them all up and you get a sum of joy and life. —

Dear Rike, I have just read through your letter again and am almost ashamed now at the generalities I have come up with in reply to the kind words that flow from your heart.

If I manage to advance my present occupations enough to be able to take a few weeks off in the autumn, and if I can find a reasonable way of returning where I am now without drawing too much attention to myself in Württemberg, I think I really will follow my heart and come to rest and live once again in the company of you and your dear husband, and with your children and all the rest of the dear family.

If only I could be the bearer of as much joy as I shall receive. But that's silly. We have not changed and shall be seeing one another again, and that is enough. And you will allow me to live in your happy household as if I belonged to it too.—When and where shall I be the one to invite you to stay with me, dear Rike? My own arrangements are ample for me. A couple of nice little rooms, one of which, where I spend most of my time, I've decorated with maps of the four quarters of the globe, a big table of my own in the dining room that also serves as the bedroom, and a chest of drawers there too, and here in the study a desk where I keep my money safe and another table with books and papers on it, and another little table by the window, near the trees, where I like being best and get on with my work. And I have chairs too, for a couple of good friends, plenty of clothes brought with me from Frankfurt, cheap but healthy food, a garden with a summerhouse the owner lets me use, lovely walks round about, and I pay my bills in a straightforward and orderly way and soon perhaps I'll be my own master with an annual income of 500 florins, I'll tell you more about that next time. That would be enough for the time being. And who knows where my writing will lead me in the future? I might make my fortune. Then I'll set myself up in style and invite you to stay.

Forgive me this nonsense, Rike. The way I am means I can only really be spoken about half in jest and half in earnest. But I promise you never to fritter away my days unthinkingly and, so long as it suits my requirements and I am suitable for it, to accept with joy any good situation in society that might present itself, and to establish myself in it. For the moment I think I can wait a bit, since I would have to live without my own home and without an official post of my own anyway, and am not a total burden on our good mother.

It was only very reluctantly, given all the kindness mother showed me during my time at university, that I came to confess to her that despite my expectations I hadn't quite managed to make do this year with what I brought with me from Frankfurt, since I could not foresee my illness and the change in diet it necessitated for almost three months, nor the hard winter and several other expenses. But I have repeatedly and expressly insisted that she make careful note of the 100 florins she intends to send me and also of anything else I may be obliged to ask her for in an emergency, and in this way simply let me have some of my inheritance in advance, should the circumstances require it. And I nevertheless regard it as very generous of our dear mother and of all my beloved family that they favor me with so much confidence, especially as in many respects dear Karl now has greater claims to make on our mother's support than I do.

I now enjoy a constant state of health which means I am in good spirits and busier and calmer again, and you won't find it odd, dear Rike, if I admit to you in saying this how much the way I feel and my mental powers depend on my body. But precisely what made my illness so hard to put up with was that it was intrinsically connected with my state of mind, to the extent that the tiniest disagreeable thought would often set it off again whereas the illness itself wore out my poor head and made it fit for nothing. My strength of will and my patience were only enough to prevent me from becoming grumpy and a burden to others. I'm sorry to be talking to you about this again.

The air up here in the hills is a good bit sharper than in Frankfurt or at home. That is the only thing I have against the area and the town itself. The heavens forgive me for it. And the summer is now all the more pleasant.

You can see I'm becoming almost too tender writing to my tenderhearted sister. But there's no harm in that, as long as it's not the only thing I am. I often say to a wild friend I have here: we must be solid and loyal and unrelenting in what we see to be true and good, but to be nothing but iron and steel is not right, especially not for poets.

Every person has something that gives him joy, and who would want to do without it entirely? Mine now is the fine weather, the bright sunshine and the green earth, and I cannot reproach myself for this joy, whatever it is, I have no other now at hand, and even if I did I would never leave off this one or forget it, for it does no one any harm and does not age, and the spirit finds so much meaning in it. And one day, when I'm a grey-haired boy, spring and the morning and the light of evening day by day will make me a little younger until I feel the end and go and sit outside in the open and from there go away—to everlasting youth.

Give my love to your dear children. You were so very right, dear Rike, they would be the best consolers for me if I made a sour face and behaved as if there were nothing but misery and discord and coldness and wrong in the world, as if life were not alive, and as if I and other living beings had no heart and no soul.

Goodbye, dearest! Send my regards to your esteemed husband and tell him he is often in my thoughts and how much I admire him.

Ever your affectionate brother,

Hölderlin

FROM CHRISTIAN LUDWIG NEUFFER AND JOHANN FRIEDRICH STEINKOPF

Stuttgart, 9 July 1799

I remember once talking with Schiller about the forms of poetry. At that time he rejected Greek meters. He thought them unsuitable for the spirit and tones of our language; rhyme was characteristic of us, he said. No sooner have we abandoned it than we stray around in a foreign territory and embark on an adventure. And how quickly he took this judgment back again. Perhaps it was Goethe's elegies that adjusted his taste.—

[*On Emilie's letters. They please him very much. But he doesn't think that they will have a great success with readers.—Steinkopf wishes for another little, light story by him for the almanac, so that the readership can see that he can also cater for them in this way.—He plans to throw all his energies into the journal.—Thanks him for sending the poems by Böhlendorff, some of which he will include. Awaits H.'s own poems and those of a younger poet he had announced.—The other day there was a dinner at Steinkopf's. Märklin, Süßkind and Pfister were there too. They had spoken about him a good deal and wished he was there.—The Batavian envoy, a friend of the Muses and himself a poet, who had given him some poems for the almanac, sends Höld. his greetings. N. is now reading Tacitus with him.*

Steinkopf dispatched this letter and wrote on the last page (10 July) about Emilie, *reiterating the desire to receive another little essay by him for the almanac, in prose or verse, but as simple as may be, and especially with a little more story to it, roughly in the style of Voß's* Luise *or Goethe's* Hermann.]

FROM KARL PHILIPP CONZ

Ludwigsburg, 19 July 1799

My dearest friend,

[*Replies to the friendly letter H. had recently surprised him with. He is entirely at his disposition with contributions to his journal, as far as his capacities allow. He has a certain number of things in the drawer, including some longer poems; and could probably also furnish one or two aesthetic essays, e.g., on Shakespeare, Sophocles, Euripides, Klopstock, Goethe.*

In the meantime, he thanks him for his continuing expressions of friendship toward him.] Believe me, I too have often lived with you, notwithstanding the distance that lies between us, and drawn sustenance from your mind and often gone back to the at least for me happier days we spent together in close communion on the banks of the Neckar, protected by better Muses than the seminary could offer.

191. TO CHRISTIAN LUDWIG NEUFFER

[Homburg, second half of July 1799]

I'm sending you some poems, dear Neuffer! I hope they might please you. As I cannot well interrupt the piece of work I am engaged on at the moment for very long, I have given you what I had to hand that seemed to me not out of the question for your almanac. If some of them are perhaps not popular enough, they are perhaps worth something for more serious readers and will conciliate them, who are sadly often as disposed to condemn our more pleasant productions as those of opposed taste make it their business to reject everything that is not pure amusement. What's more, I'll also send you a *story*, as soon as I know that the journal project is not heading for failure. You can see for yourself that in the opposite case I should have no choice but to save my time and my productions for another plan.

Send my compliments to friend Steinkopf. In any case I shall be glad to have become better acquainted, thanks to my project, with this noble man. Thank him for his last letter, which was very friendly; I should answer it now along with yours—but as I have not yet written the letter to Matthison I was to enclose I shall have to put it off until the next post.

I look forward to perhaps getting to see the little epos you are working on soon.

I had a good time with Landauer. Give him my greetings and thank him again in my name for his friendship.

If in a leisurely hour you feel like writing me something again that might give me cheer it will not be for nothing. A moment of happiness is of such benefit for my work.

Send greetings to all my friends and ask them to think of me from time to time. I had been meaning to ask you whether the poem "Do you know the hand" etc that I read in this year's almanac was by Bilfinger. It is definitely not without taste and poetic faculty.

And now, good night, dear friend. Remember me particularly to the noble friend with whom you are reading Tacitus. I shall never forget the hours I spent in his company in Frankfurt.

Hölderlin

I have tried to get a bit more simplicity and harmony into one of Emerich's poems. His poems contain as you will find a number of excellent thoughts. But on the one hand the tones do not vary enough, on the other they do not unify enough into a characteristic whole, and he can of course be forgiven for it, for it is more or less the fate of several well-reputed poets of our times. If he can manage to organize the abundance of force and substance that, from what I know of him, will always be his, he could become an excellent poet. Bölendorf is a Courlander on his travels who stayed here for a while but has now set off for the Jena region with the intention of becoming better acquainted with the great writers there.

The other poems by Emerich you will have time to make the necessary changes to.

FROM FRIEDRICH WILHELM JOSEPH SCHELLING

Jena, 12 August 1799

Since we last quitted one another in Frankfurt etc.—[*He would be delighted to take part as far as possible but had nothing to offer for the winter apart from a few lectures on the organic relationship between the sexes and on the philosophy of art.—He should put Schlegel down as a contributor, although as he is himself the editor of a journal he couldn't promise anything.—He is sure that Sophie Mereau would provide contributions, and he had spoken to her as well.*

He begs him to refrain from using the word humanism, *which Herder had brought into such discredit.*]

I am now in a situation and a state of mind that allow me to write very little that could even begin to match up to *your* letter.—Perhaps my fate will clarify itself more rapidly than I can hope for at present—and then I hope to be able to encounter you as a different person.

I embrace you. Your loyal friend,

Schelling

192. TO JOHANN FRIEDRICH STEINKOPF

Homburg vor der Höhe, 23 August 1799

The only reason I took so long to send you the promised letter is that I hoped from day to day to be able to give you a complete list of contributors. The ones I can now name with certainty are these:

Konz
Jung (author of a translation of Ossian)
Sophie Mereau
Heinze (author of *Ardinghello*)
Prof. Neeb (author of several interesting philosophical writings)
Prof. Schelling
Prof. Schlegel

I hope soon to receive answers from Ebel and Humboldt in Paris. And I also believe that Lafontaine will be with us. Matthison you'll already have heard from as I hear he is staying in Stuttgart. I doubt whether Schiller will take part. Incidentally, a great deal will depend on the character and content of the first number, as to whether he and others might still be persuaded to take part.

[*For that reason, he wishes to make the philosophical-poetic character of the journal unmistakably clear.*]

Please be so kind as to let me know your decision as rapidly as is possible so that I don't have to leave my colleagues in uncertainty for long and can put the plans for my life and work in the right direction. I'll send you the announcement, should you find that things as they stand are looking good, immediately on receipt of your letter.

As you have made a point of showing me your confidence and kindness by suggesting that you might in due course be able to publish my productions on their own, you will no doubt prefer that these writings are not merely ephemeral in value.

Would you perhaps like to ask Herr Haug for a contribution or two? Or shall I do it, if you think it a good idea? Remember me to him, as also to Herr Matthison if you speak to him.

I enclose a manuscript by a young poet who, as you will see, has distinguished himself in Schiller's almanac and whom I know that Schiller also thinks highly of himself. Would you like to publish it perhaps?

FROM FRIEDRICH SCHILLER

Jena, 24 [August] 1799

Gladly, my good friend, would I fulfill your desire for contributions to your journal if I weren't so short of time and so tightly bound up in my current piece of work that I shall be leaving even my own *Muses' Almanac* without contributions this year or at least only furnish it with any very frugally, and in the future I may give it up entirely because I must renounce any occupation that is not compatible with my absolute independence. The experiences I have had as the editor of periodicals over the last 16 years, in which time I have captained no fewer than 5 different vessels on the rocky sea of literature, offer so little comfort that as a sincere friend I cannot advise you to embark on anything of the sort. Rather I come back to my old advice that you should quietly and independently *concentrate* on a particular sphere of activity. And even as regards the lucrative aspect we poets can often not avoid, the path of periodical works is only seemingly attractive, and with an insignificant beginner of a publisher, without certain reserves of his own capital to allow him to weather a small knock, it's absolutely not to be ventured on.

How very much I'd like to be able not just to give you my advice but also make it easier for you to follow it. If you want to make me more familiar with your present situation I might be better placed to suggest something that corresponds to your wishes.

Farewell and be assured of my loyal devotion.

Yours,

Schiller

193. TO HIS MOTHER

Homburg, 27 August 1799

Dearest Mother,

It's been ten days again now that I've waited for a letter from you, and always in vain. This is the fourth I've written since the beginning of July without having received news from you in reply to any of them. I have been searching for every possible reason to fathom this utter and enduring silence on the part of my dear family; but I cannot find one that fully explains it, if, that is, neither your nor my letters have gone astray. But I have during this time received other letters from Stuttgart, and Sinclair likewise; and for that reason I am bound to think that the post is functioning reliably.

May I ask you, dearest mother, to send me the money now? I had not reckoned with our correspondence being interrupted for 2 months, else I'd have taken precautions to allow me to do without the money for longer. I have paid my rent in advance for this quarter, and made some other expenses that I could have put off, and so now I find myself in some difficulty if it should still take some time for the money from you to arrive.

But above all I ask you, as assuredly as I strive to become more deserving every day of the kindness you have always shown me, not to leave me in this anxiety as to how things stand with you any longer. It is preventing me from getting on with my daily work with the undivided energy I need.

In the past I have sometimes received your reply to a letter of mine within a week; and if you receive this one and I again have to wait longer than a week and a half without a letter in return I really don't know what I shall do to free myself of this constant anxiety. I have also written urgently to Karl, telling him to give me news of you, in case you don't get this letter either. I just hope all is well!

As ever

your

loyal son

Friz

194. TO SUSETTE GONTARD

[Homburg, late August or early September 1799]

Dearest,

Only the uncertainty of my position prevented me from writing before now. The project of the journal which not without good reason I wrote to you about with so much confidence looks to me as if it is going to fail. I had placed so much hope in it as a way of supporting me in my work and allowing me to continue to live close to you. Not only have these hopes and efforts been in vain, but have now ended in many bitter experiences. I had drawn up a viable and modest plan—my publisher wanted things more ambitious: he requested me to secure the collaboration of a host of famous writers he considered to be my friends, and although such a course seemed to me fraught with problems still I was fool enough to let myself be persuaded so as not to appear headstrong, and my old acquiescent heart has got me into frustrations that unfortunately I must write to you about because in all probability my future, and so in a way the life I live for you, depends on it. Not only men whom I was more an admirer of than friend, friends too, darling, even those who could hardly refuse to participate without real ingratitude, have so far left me without response, and I have now been living for a good 8 weeks in this state of hope and expectancy on which my existence more or less depends. What the reason for this turn of events can be, God knows. Are people so very ashamed of being associated with me?

That this cannot well be the case, rationally speaking, is proved to me by your fine judgment and the judgment of a few friends who have duly joined me in my venture with true loyalty, e.g., Jung, in Mainz, whose letter I enclose for you. It was the *famous*, whose participation was supposed to vouch for so slight and obscure a thing as me, who offered no help, and why should they? After all, anybody who makes a name for himself in the world will seem to detract from their own—they will then be the uncontested idols no longer. In short, it seems to me that among these people, whom I can think of as *roughly* my equals, there is a bit of professional envy at work. But knowing this doesn't get me anywhere. I've wasted almost 2 months on preparations for the journal, and probably the best thing I can do now to avoid being led by the nose any longer is to write to my publisher asking him if he wouldn't prefer to take the writings I had intended for the journal on their own, which even if he did would admittedly fall short of securing my existence.

And so what I have in mind is to use all the time I have left on my tragedy, which may take about another three months, and then I shall have to go home or to a place where I can support myself by giving lectures, which is not feasible here, or by some other occupation that will allow me to continue my work.

Forgive me this direct language, dearest. It would only have been more difficult to tell you what I needed to say, my love, if I'd let the movement of my heart toward you voice itself, and it's scarcely possible the way things are with me to preserve the necessary courage without losing for a few moments the tender tones of our innermost life. That's precisely the reason why up till now I haven't written

195. TO HIS MOTHER

Homburg, 3 September 1799

A thousand thanks, dearest Mother, for the joy your lovely letter has brought me now that I have news of my dear family again and no longer have to live in uncertainty about you, my beloved Mother.

I think, from what I understand about the ways of the post and from what I have been able to find out from the postmaster here this evening, that we have no need to worry about the money. It seems quite possible that the last time the mail coach arrived in Frankfurt was the 20th of August and that since then it has stopped somewhere on the way, perhaps in Heidelberg. But I think the postmaster in Stuttgart will have received news of the coach by the normal post, so it should be possible for him to inform you where the money is.

You should be able to make an inquiry, in a preliminary way, without seeming to be demanding an explanation; I'll see what I can find out tomorrow in Frankfurt, via my landlord who is going there, as to whether the mail coach has been in Frankfurt since the 20th of August, though I doubt it has. In any case, I'll write to you again tomorrow or the day after, partly also because that way you are all the more sure to get at least one letter from me; and as I shall perhaps be able to tell you more about the matter in my next letter, please wait a few days before writing to the postmaster in Stuttgart. The proof of postage is valid for a whole three months, and I hear that he would be bound to reimburse you if the money were lost. And he would be quite sure to find out where and by whom it was lost; but I am really not very worried about this possibility.

For the time being my heartfelt thanks, dearest Mother, for this generous support of yours, and I hope not to put you to such considerable expense again for a long time. I can well imagine how little you can afford to be without in present circumstances. Thus far I have not needed to restrict my habitual way of life and with the sizeable sum you have sent me I hope to make do until the prospect of a secure livelihood presents itself.

As to the publication of my journal, nothing is yet decided; Schiller wrote to me recently saying that he could not wholly recommend such an undertaking to me, meaning as it would that my work would be too dependent on it; but he asked me to give him more detail about my situation and *perhaps he would be able to suggest something that corresponded more to my wishes.* That's how things stand with me, my dear, beloved mother.—Sinklair, who came round this evening, thanks you warmly for the trust you have put in him; it is certain that in an emergency I can count on him;—and my good landlord, too, when he heard that my money had not arrived, at once and of his own accord offered to help me out if I needed him. The good people take the best care of me and are selflessly devoted to me.

How I pity my good brother-in-law, & my dear sister! So my worries were not altogether groundless! I hope the best for the noble man & my sister & for all of us.

Yours

Friz

I hope, dearest Mother, that things will stay fairly quiet for you in Nürtingen. Only the situation in Blaubeuren unsettles me a little. But so far everything has always been all right. Here in Homburg & round about all is calm.

196. TO HIS MOTHER

Homburg, 4 September 1799

Dearest Mother,

I have just received the money and your dear letter of 15th August. This generous help and the mother's blessing that accompany it will not fail to bear fruit; and I cannot thank you better than by saying that I shall use what I have received to carry on living a while in daily labor, in particular to give the work I am presently engaged on the perfection that lies in my power; and if this time I do not yet earn the attention of my German country so that people seek out my place of birth and inquire who my mother is, still I intend, God willing, to do so in future. For that is in the end the only, and also the sweetest, reward for all the sacrifices and all the pains without which the writer will come to nothing: for him to pass himself and the name of his family on to his people and into posterity. And these are not empty words, dear Mother!

And please don't be concerned for my health! I know very well, the mind takes strength from the body, but it gives it strength too, and a single hour of rest after work one is content with makes up for perhaps a week of frustration. And furthermore I am particularly well at the moment and thank the heavens for it, which despite many ordeals have preserved the strength of my youth thus far.

If only my good sister could stop worrying and her dear husband were in good health! Or if only I could think that he's not in danger! Please write assuring them of my heartfelt sympathies. If I had grounds to hope that words of mine might give the noble man some cheer, I should gladly write to him at length in the next few days. I have in any case often done so in my thoughts.

You are probably right that a few words from my brother Karl are enough in themselves to give me pleasure. As interested as I am in every advance his intellectual development makes and every one of his convictions and newly acquired pieces of knowledge, I have too much respect for the heart, and especially my brother's heart, not to be content with what comes from it. But he will get round to writing rather more often when he is a bit older, frugal letter writer that he is. You remember very well how it was with me before. Without being untender toward one's family, one is rather more content with oneself at that age. But once one has lived here and there in the cold world, then one comes to have a real need of the loyal sympathies that hold between parents and children and brother and sisters. That at least is my experience.

I am glad that Miss Lebret has chosen such a good husband as Ostertag. She will be happier with him than she would have been with me. We weren't really suited to one another, and the sad thing about such youthful relationships is that one only comes to know one another when the attachment has already been formed. Clear as this was to me during my last stay in Württemberg, I was, as you know yourself, firmly resolved not to break off lightly. But she saw the necessity of it herself, and she must have recalled that even in Tübingen she had given me plenty of proof that she had difficulty really understanding what sort of person I was, and that even back then both of us carried on the relationship more out of mutual convenience than out of true harmony. Furthermore, it didn't really fit with my life plans and the circumstances in which we live for me to get engaged so soon. From what I now know of myself and *our times* I consider it necessary to renounce such happiness for who knows how long, and experience has taught me that a bachelor's life can be led *with dignity* too. Even if I became a parson I should prefer, unless it was quite against your own wishes, to remain unmarried, and if you could be persuaded to move in with me, or I at least lived somewhere near you, that would be enough.—

I hope, dearest Mother, that the war won't trouble you and the rest of the dear family, at least not at close quarters. I know all too well how our poor country is burdened by taxes etc, and I always think of you, for even if your income is by no means small it is always hard to cover, besides the costs of housekeeping, so many extra expenses simply from the interest on your capital, and it is cold comfort that half the world has to suffer in this and other ways at the moment. I hope for peace with all my heart, and believe it to be necessary and salutary and of incalculable importance for all sorts of reasons. And perhaps it's not so far off as it seems. But that is just a supposition of mine.—In the present circumstances a journey to Württemberg is hardly advisable. How much I long to see you, dearest Mother, and all the dear family again after all this time, you can well imagine. But perhaps more propitious times will come round soon. I wanted to say too that I cannot think that you need to worry about the Consistory. They probably know I am working here on my own account and see fit to leave me in peace, as they will have been able to ascertain that I am not wasting my time.—A thousand remembrances to my dear Grandmother.

Yours

Friz

FROM SUSETTE GONTARD

[Frankfurt, ~ 8 August–5 September 1799]

Around the 8th

How hard it becomes again to break the silence!—And yet my feeling is always that only by writing could I find peace and contentment, how it torments me when often for days on end I go around without ever finding a quiet time to write if I could beg one thing of heaven in my present situation it would surely be just to have every day one hour solely to myself which I would then dedicate with all my heart to you, dearest.   You won't believe how oppressive it is to be so shut in with the whole weight of my feelings and not able to confide them even to the pen.   So I have been hither and thither always on the move till now and had so much to say to you. I must talk to you about the last time I saw you. That morning I was undecided whether, without a letter, I should come down to you or not, whether I shouldn't rather leave you in the illusion that we hadn't come back. and wait for you then the following Thursday. I was very tired and weak and very afraid this might mislead you, on the other hand I feared you might hear of our return and would not understand my not coming so I risked it.   But how shall I describe to you the unnameable mood I fell into that evening? I thought that before my eyes I could see your shape in the allée. Was it you really?—or not? — — I wasn't on my own S. . . . were with me. It struck me like a bolt of lightning I went warm, and cold, and soon the others noticed that I wanted to be alone and left, It seemed to me then that it was really you and some anxiety was driving you to me, you had to come to me, I went to the window and stood there, my eyes fixed on the place, and the illusion came on me again, I saw your face through the bushes, then you were leaning against a tree and peeping out, I knew it to be a trick of the imagination and persuaded myself the earlier event had been the same. Then sorrow seized my heart with a cold hand and threatened to squeeze the life out of it, my thoughts froze, it was as if I had gone to embrace you and you had become a shadow and this beloved shadow would still have been able to comfort me and when my senses asked for this it too vanished from me and a nothingness, if that is conceivable, remained.

Out of this dumb sorrow I had to tear myself and then out of the depths of me came a groaning a whimpering a torrent of tears which for a long time were so violent I could not halt them. and since then I have felt such a heavy sadness, and as though in your heart you had something against me, and I can think of nothing else, Over the memory of my journey it is as if a dark veil has been drawn and it will be hard for me to write you anything about it. Oh God! never appear to me again like that! Oh never doubt my love! — — — — — — It is you I love, you alone, and will in all eternity. — — — — — —

10th

In the midst of this indescribable sorrow I was intruded on, I ascribed the mood to my suddenly being alone after long and enjoyable distractions and now being without my brother and his wife, but my state doubtless told too much of the truth and betrayed another cause, because my sadness lasted, after a few days the matter was addressed more closely, the idea that certain relations were continuing and that they were the particular cause was reinforced. I had trouble keeping as close as possible to the truth, and meanwhile I also learned that your first visit to the house was no secret, I admitted it and said you had not been here in the house again. and I would certainly never do anything that might harm myself and the whole family. And everything concluded quite calmly, and has had no bad effect. But now I must confess to you that the future frightens me I see no solution and without you I can resolve nothing. Can we in the future when I am back in the town live without hearing from one another? — — If I make that sacrifice will I ever feel at ease about you? will not a thousand unhappy fantasies torment me just as much as other troubles?—and even if I do nothing at all won't the same suspicion still rest on me and so I shall be forced to suffer and with no recompense for it?

I get confused in my thinking so tell me what you think and don't let the heavy burden of deciding rest on me alone, what you think best is my will too, and if you also believe it is best in reality to make a complete separation between us I won't misconstrue your motives, *the invisible relations will continue and life is short.* I feel cold! — Because it's short, waste it? — — Oh tell me where shall we find each other again? — — — My dearest, my beloved heart and soul! — — — Where shall I find quiet? — — — — Let me strictly recognize my duty and forget myself and however hard it is, help me carry it out, but I still don't know what that duty is. Self-preservation, without that I can't do anything, and self-forgetting contradict one another, for everything I might do against my love, it seems to me now it would undo me, destroy me. What a difficult art love is! who understands it? who can choose not to follow it? — — — Bring all your reasoning powers together and speak persuasively to me, for I feel it is necessary and who else can I ask but you who are my only friend. — — — —

8 in the evening the 15th

I am alone! — — Now I should like to tell you about our journey, but what seems to me more necessary always presses upon me, my heart needs to breathe in the beautiful quiet of the evening.—How low in spirits I am, always close to tears, I long for an answer from your kindred soul, all so lovely, so harmonious and yet for me so dead where the sign of your existence is missing, the certainty that now your heart is speaking to mine. Oh happy beloved heavenly love once felt what an emptiness separation leaves in the heart that nothing can fill and everything makes more felt. After all I have to confess to you that I can't go through the winter hearing nothing from you, I can't do it, so I have thought that if you remain in these parts you could every two months on the particular Thursday being *very* careful appear under the window at 9 in the evening and I will see then that you are still here and in good health. *How much even just that would be for my heart!* and I would probably be able to throw you a note down but probably go without letters from you because for now I don't think it's advisable that you come into the house, I shall search in your writings to know how you are and for sure will know you in them. tell me what address I can order your journal through. if it has already been produced.   Next spring we shall be out here again and the first song of the new larks will be the sign of our closer union. I am writing in the dark, the sun and its beams of light have sunk away from me. so many things will be dark till *our* sun shines again, but it will, it will come again, won't it? — — — — — Oh, Mother Nature, be kind, teach me to have faith and soothe this heart of mine! — —

18th

I will give you a brief survey of my little journey because I want to make use of this moment on my own, it will be brief because I'm really not in the mood for narrating and you must forgive me the wooden language I only want to give you an idea so that your imagination will have a place to rest.   We set off a week later and only gave ourselves 10 days, we left here early in the morning, my sister-in-law, the youngest *Brentano* girl and myself, nobody accompanying us except our Jacob, in Giessen we met Director Tischbein who is visiting a sister there and was expecting us. an elderly man turned grey by many events, 20 years he has been abroad and being back now his homeland rejuvenates him, and even in his praise of Italy again and again you hear the German, so for example often when traveling he will say, Such beautiful green trees are not to be found in Italy! This man a long time ago was a great painter, he neglected his art and his own interest to study the ancient works of the Greeks, their poets and especially Homer inspired him to do that, if you heard him speak you would know how passionately and truthfully he understood him, and you'd be delighted to see that enthusiasm and warmth of feeling are still there at his age. And he recognized me at once and showed me a great deal of respect. You will soon see his works, more on him another time. (I shall see your own observations on *Homer*, shan't I? —) We stayed 3 days in Cassel, the first night I woke early, since my traveling-companions were still asleep I took your beloved poems out of my folder and they were my morning prayers, they enveloped my loving spirit in a softly stirring melancholy and embraced me close against your heart, so I went boldly forth into life again, the lovely sun rose over Cassel and I rejoiced to see all my beloved places again. — — — —

As we were sitting at table an old and dear friend from Hamburg surprised us, he had come to meet his children and in the evening they all arrived and joined us, We had 3 happy days together. but I was never on my own. — — — —

We parted from the Hamburg people to continue our journey to Gotha, Tischbein also remained behind. after 2 days traveling we arrived there, it was raining heavily, we saw very little, the next morning we went on to Weimar and reached there at 4 in the afternoon, we intended to go straight from there to Wieland's estate to join *la Roche* and her granddaughter but heard that they were all in town, we wrote a note to announce our arrival and at once *Sophie Brentano* came to invite us all to her house where all Weimar's notable men of letters were gathered, we quickly got dressed and went with her, old *la Roche* was very friendly toward us very informal jolly and extremely lively introduced us to the company, Wieland, Herder! (Goethe wasn't there) and several other less significant men. My sister-in-law at once captured W. . . in conversation, I had messages for Herder from Tischbein and so the first half hour passed. Over tea W. . .'s conversation continued, I joined in with only a few words when I was sure of what I wanted to say, when we were leaving W. . . took me warmly by the hand and said, the few words you have spoken make me want to see you more often. That pleased me for your sake, and on the way back I thought only of you, next day Wieland asked *Sophie* which of us two she would choose to be with after he had particularly praised my sister-in-law. she chose me, and W. gave her a short answer ("For that, my girl, someone should kiss your hand") forgive me my vanity that I pass this on to you, I'm only telling it to you and if it's wrong I can't conceal from you that it made me proud. The following morning we went on to Jena, with a letter of introduction to Mme. *Merau*, we went straight to her and asked her by a note to Schiller to beg him to grant us an hour of his time, she at once dashed all our hopes, he lives very privately and seldom receives visits from strangers, The others willingly gave up the idea of seeing him but *Sophie* and I were determined to venture anything to get to him.

23rd

I must again make use of my time the others have gone out, I wanted to write a great deal and then unfortunately along comes a bee and stings me in the right hand, it really does make me cross that whenever I try to write so many things get in my way. and surely I must love you a great deal that I manage to write as much as I do. I will finish the account of my journey now in a few words.

In the afternoon *Sophie* and I went again to Mme. *Merau* to hear his reply, our request was granted, for 4 o'clock. so at that time accompanied by a servant we made our way through the town gate to where he lives in a garden. How fearfully our hearts were beating and how peculiarly sad my mood was I cannot tell you, I felt too keenly at that moment how short a time I had in the half an hour given me to see the man about whom I have such large ideas, to whom my feelings could certainly speak, and the impossibility of revealing that connection to him by my look, In this beautiful soul I did not want to be mirrored as something small and yet I could only make a humble appearance. I didn't have the courage to say a word and begged *Sophie* to do all the talking. We were announced and waited in the doorway of the garden, saw his noble form at the end of a long allée, his wife was with him and two lively boys were leaping about in the grass. We apologized for the intrusion he led us into a shady arbor, we sat by his wife, and he remained standing before us, majestically, he spoke a good deal with the granddaughter of *la Roche*, about her and Wieland and I had time to observe him closely. We were in a great hurry because of them waiting for us, his dear kind wife said she would accompany us back, we said no she mustn't, but he said it will do my wife no harm, and I — — — he added quietly, but then bethought himself and went back to the house, we went with his wife as far as the city gate, as we were saying goodbye to her his oldest son arrived, sent after us with the servant who conducted us to our lodgings where the post horses stood already in harness waiting, we reached Weimar that evening. From there in one day via Fulda to Frankfurt, enjoying the scenery.

Nothing came of our journey to Ems, we might go next Friday via Mainz and Coblenz and back through the spas, but we would be home here again on Monday.

My brother is staying till the end of October. I'll go back to town after the Fair. If you intend a journey or have any other plans which it would be necessary for me to know about it would in that case be possible to get a letter to me by somebody, but it would always have to be on the morning after the particular Thursday between 10 and 11 so that I could be on the lookout and if you miss a meeting to say why, but only in an emergency

Thursday 5th September

I think you may find these pages more than a bit dismal, my dearest, so I must add that now I am feeling much more cheerful again and when I see you how my whole being changes! — — — Oh hold me always in your love! And if our love remained for ever unrewarded it is in itself, biding quiet in us, still so beautiful that it will for ever be the dearest thing we have, our own, is that not so, my sweet friend? and so it is for you, and the meetings of our souls are constant and eternal! — — —

197. TO FRIEDRICH SCHILLER

[Homburg, first half of September 1799]

I cannot say enough to thank you, esteemed Sir, for the generosity with which you answered my unseemly request, and I can assure you that the kind words you had for me enrich me as much in real terms as any other help I could wish for. The blessing of a great man is the best help for those who can recognize or sense it, that at least is what I had most need of from you. I have long made the mistake of always wanting to *earn* the right to your company and kind sympathy. For that reason I withdrew from your presence and promised myself that I would only approach you again when I could make more justifiable claims on the attention you honored me with, and through this false pride I have forfeited the beneficial influence of your instruction and encouragement which I was in less of a position to do without than others because my courage and my convictions are only too easily confused and weakened by the unfavorable effects of everyday life.

The valuable advice you gave me some time ago and repeated in your last letter I have not let go by completely unheeded and I am concentrating everything on developing the precise tone that without being whimsical seemed to lie closest to my natural unaffected disposition. I have made it my maxim to first become proficient in any one kind of writing, and to gain character in it, before I attempt to acquire a flexibility that can belong only to someone who has already achieved a firm standpoint. I thought I could execute the precise tone I wanted to make my own most completely and naturally in the tragic form and have ventured on a tragedy, the *Death of Empedocles*, and this is the work I have been devoting most of my time to during my stay here.—I must admit that I cannot make this confession without feeling slightly ashamed of it, above all to you. To mention just one point, since I have come to a somewhat more thorough recognition of the beauty of the tragic form, the composition of the *Robbers*, in its essentials, and particularly the scene by the Danube as the poem's center, has revealed itself to me with such grandeur and depth and with such immutable truth that I took this insight as an achievement in itself, and have long wanted to ask your permission to put my thoughts into writing. And that is how you once began, noble master! I have also studied your *Fiesko* and there again it is the inner structure, the whole living shape—which as I see it is the most enduring aspect of the work—that I admired above all, even more than the characters, which while larger than life are so true to it, and the brilliant situations and the magical colorful play of the language. The other plays I still have to attend to, and it will not be easy for me to keep my wits about me when I come to read *Don Carlos*, which for so long was the magical cloud the good god of my youth enveloped me in so that I did not see too early on the pettiness and barbarity of the world that surrounded me.

Forgive me, esteemed Sir, if you should find these utterances, which at least have the virtue of literal truthfulness, not quite seemly. But I should have to say nothing at all to you, or else restrict myself to remarks of a very general nature, which indeed is what I ordinarily do when I write to you, even if occasionally I permit myself to make an exception.

You allow me to tell you something more precise about my situation. It is such that I probably cannot continue in it, without considerable inconvenience, for more than a few months. With my little bit of writing and my life as a private tutor I had put together enough wealth to be able to hope I might live independently at least long enough to get my tragedy to a certain stage of completion. But ill health, which lasted almost all the winter and part of the summer too, forced me for one thing to change my frugal way of life and for another also took up more of my time and energies than my plans allowed for.

who for their part have too many concerns of their own to contribute regularly, even if they are more my equals than your esteemed self and could more readily and acceptably be invited into my company.

FROM SIEGFRIED SCHMID

Kappel in the Toggenburg, 10 September 1799

To allow us to rest a little we've been moved up here into the valley along the Thur.
[*He is living in the present and confining himself to that, just as the others are who serve alongside him and in all their lives have never felt the infinite poetic power and never will.*]
Why don't you try something similar, my dear friend? This as it seems to me is the source of your complaints, which are distressing and whose nature is too well-known to me for me to think they have the slightest resemblance with the usual kind. You cannot overestimate the deep impression it made on me when you told me that the gulf between you and your family gets greater every year. Oh come out here, dearest friend, out into life, plunge into it from whatever side you will and live with everyday people as one of the most everyday of all; that, it is true, you will never be able to do; but for that very reason force yourself to as far as you can, the divine can after all never become mere earthliness, it is precisely because it is so extreme, so as not to fly out beyond the earthly altogether, to keep oneself receptive for the most ordinary natural phenomenon as well as for the greatest.
[*Sends him 2 poems: "On the lake"—"The happiness of being blinded by love."*
With Zwilling he spent a few pleasant days;] I am to send you his greetings.

If anything important happens in the intellectual world, let me know of it. Has Schiller's *Wallenstein* appeared? What are people saying about it?

In the last engagements our regiment has not suffered much. We have no plains on which to go into action. As far as I know anything about operations, inexperienced as I am, things are going to hot up by the time you receive this letter.

[H., as soon as he can, should let him know the details about the publication of his poems as he has things in mind for some copies.]

FROM JOHANN FRIEDRICH STEINKOPF

Stuttgart, 18 September 1799

[Their letters crossed. By now he would doubtless have the reply to the letter of 23rd August. In his next letter he awaits instructions as to Schmid's manuscript.

In his last letter he has already answered much of what was in his from the 12th.

Schiller's nonparticipation is of course much to be regretted. Still, that on its own does not frighten him off.

He now makes it clear that he requires more consideration for the readership and less speculation. He had spoken with Schelling during his last sojourn in Jena after the Leipzig Easter fair about this matter, and back then Schelling had said himself that a particularly cherishable kind of journal is one that contains nourishment of various kinds, both heavier and lighter (so long as none of it is bad).]

Your taste, my dear friend, is certainly apt to provide the man or woman of education with true edification, if only, to speak frankly, you would make it slightly more popular—this is what a heavyweight in the field of the arts said about you not long ago concerning your *Hyperion,* which we happened to be speaking of, along with many very just words of praise.

[To produce the journal at indeterminate intervals would not be feasible.

A question: given the inconvenience of being far away, especially at the present moment of time, would he not consider selecting a coeditor on the spot, who at the same time would greatly lighten the burden of

the editing and correspondence work? St. suggests Haug as a possibility,
without wishing to sway things.

But if circumstances should conspire to prevent the journal from
coming together, he would with pleasure accept his second proposal of
publishing individual volumes of H.'s own writings. To be able to judge
whether the essays he had written to him about were better suited for a
journal than for a book of their own, please could he let him have a look
at a few of them.]

FROM FRIEDRICH MUHRBECK

Jena, September 1799

Dear beloved friend,

With a frivolity that flies round my eyes like chaff an eagerness
for true seriousness has penetrated more deeply than ever into
Böhlendorff. He is freer in appearance and expression—and longs for
firm independence.—This winter he intends to stay here and attend
Schelling's lectures—he will show him that his seriousness still lacks
roots.—Enough.

I've almost said all too much about Böhlendorff. Keep it to yourself.
Your advice I passed on to him as well as I could; he thanked you
sincerely—and asseverated that he had long told himself the same—and
did now with greater seriousness and longed for peaceful circumstances
in which to achieve it.

I should almost like to take back my advice that you should think of
coming to Jena, as Schelling has announced *principes rationes phil.*
artis and Schlegel also several lectures in aesthetics. You would have
to give the winter over to the attempt. Schlegel would not otherwise
be the least danger to you—he lectures like he writes, half reason, half
wit—without firmness and without feeling or life. You will be bound to
think my advice against coming rather hasty. Whether you will find an
audience now I don't know. Next summer a firmer exposition following
on Schelling's lectures might perhaps be very welcome.—I'll write you
more about him when I've spoken with him more—about whether he

might be intending to try out something similar himself. They say he wants to go to Vienna to study medicine.—

I was at Schelling's for the second time, I couldn't make myself understood and anyhow had only gone with the intention of showing him—that I

FROM FRIEDRICH MUHRBECK

[Jena, September 1799]

The profoundest respect took hold of me again in his lectures on transcendental philosophy—his firmness, which in some parts I regard as perfectly accomplished, forced it from me—and the joy of finding such a complete correspondence with my own thoughts was immense—I was so pleased to feel the movements of thought in a wholesome body—his eye was so steady—and so chaste.—His thinking during the three hours I sat in on went like this: he came on to deal with history, distinguishing 3 periods, in the 1st) blind fate—2) traces of providence (so that the intelligence of nature appeared to man in his actions)—3) "then God will be here."—And how he said this—so steadily—so coldly, as was proper from a lectern, and so seriously.—The monastic air of the lecture hall could not restrain my tears—my chest swelled mightily—I'd have been fully justified in throwing myself into his arms and giving him my hand in alliance.

FROM SUSETTE GONTARD

[Frankfurt, October 1799]

I feel it to be a proof of your love, my dearest, that you come nevertheless to collect a few words from me but now how it grieves me that I know you to be so close and must go without receiving anything from your hands, there was no possibility of going out into the garden because by ill luck the apples are just being picked and also because of the weather I would have had no excuse. Last time I could only be in the room downstairs without giving offence (because the following day we had company and I could busy myself naturally there). But that works only very rarely. Forgive me this cold language and don't, I beg you, think that it is a coldness in me. I only think that if I allow myself any joy it is politic as well as being my duty not to offend anyone.

But should it be urgently necessary for me to have your letter then call tomorrow between 10 and 11, ask for me and say that it is to be handed to me and I will come down (but don't get the wrong door). But if my anxious forebodings should by then be unfounded show yourself on the corner at 10 and that will be the sign that I am to expect nothing else. Your beloved *Hipperion*, that must by now be out, as soon as I can read it at leisure I will deviously get myself a copy.

In the great upheavals in Hamburg's commercial world my brother has not lost out and it has perhaps helped him toward his goal of one day living with us.

I am in very good health and looking forward to the quiet winter and shall spend the evenings when I am alone reading your essays, poems and letters that are so dear to me, they will call forth many loving and strengthening tears in me that spring only from the treasury of faithful and noble love and bring blessings over the dry life of everyday. so I shall continue on my quiet course and become ever better.

Be active too, for yourself and don't let the daily worry over your future existence prematurely lame and suffocate your best energies, what you do I will approve of, that is certain. — — As things were and are with us so they will be for ever. farewell! farewell!

In November you can come again, according to arrangements and circumstances

A thousand sweet names, and words!

— —

198. TO HIS MOTHER

Homburg, 8 October 1799

Dearest Mother,

I would have written sooner, had I not wished to give you more detailed news of my present situation. For that reason I wanted to wait for several letters that will have an influence on my future existence. But so far all I can say with certainty is that things are at last settled with my bookseller for the journal, that it will go ahead, and that I have promised to supply him several sheets a month for which he will pay me a carolin each, and that, if after a while he feels disposed to print and publish my contributions for the journal separately, he will pay me a further 11 florins a sheet. I have however, on Schiller's advice, decided against the actual editing and all the administration of the journal, because the correspondence with others involved in it etc. would take up too much time for me to be able to get on with what I should really like to write with proper calm and attention. Altogether the laborious business of the correspondence and the gathering of contributions, & other things connected with the administration of the journal, would have earned me too little in proportion to the time it would have cost me. But since the income I now have for the contributions to the journal is not going to be quite enough to live on properly, I have written to Schiller *at his own behest*, asking him to find me if possible some little job not far from him that would not occupy me completely and would give a little supplementary income to my earnings as a writer. I expect a reply any day. If Schiller could find a way of meeting my request it would suit me all the better because his company is so beneficial to me in many respects. But if nothing comes of it, which of course I hope won't be the case, I don't know if I might not go to Stuttgart and give private tuition there to a small number of young people, which, from what I have been able to ascertain, would not be impossible. If however I receive from Schiller the response I wish for, I shall take the liberty, dearest Mother, before I leave for Saxony, of spending some time with you and the rest of the family. If that were to happen this winter it wouldn't get in the way of your own plans. My honorable brother-in-law and my dear sister will also take me in no doubt for a few weeks, and then I have several other friends and acquaintances with whom I can and indeed must stay for a while.

Don't send the money you spoke of. I have done my accounts and have in the meantime received a few small sums and so don't need any more for now. In *unforeseen emergencies* I can draw on Sinklair without any difficulty; he in any case doesn't want me to go from here, and for that reason will gladly do something for me should it be necessary. So I ask you again please not to send anything. Thanks once again, with all my heart, for what I have received. I haven't yet thanked you for the gloves that gave me so much pleasure and to which I attach particular importance as a sign of your kindness. It was *certainly* not an inattention of the heart, but just of the head.

I am very eager to have more recent news from you, especially on how my dear brother-in-law is faring with his health. Perhaps my good sister might be able to write to me again soon.

The post is leaving soon. I had to rush because of it. Remember me to my dear grandmother and all the beloved family.

As ever

your

appreciative son

Friz

FROM CASIMIR ULRICH BÖHLENDORFF

Jena, 24 October 1799

[*Was on the Schwarzburg with Muhrbeck.*]
How do things stand with the January issue of your journal? I'd like to see it come together nice and quickly, so as to find your *Empedocles* in it which I'm looking forward to with real yearning, as to the second part of *Hyperion* which I can hardly wait for. I have given it to several young men here and witnessed with delight the enthusiasm that filled their breasts and the way their minds came to full consciousness.—Goethe is working on an Achilleis, and on a poem on the nature of things, and is making a careful study of Schelling's natural philosophy.

I had in mind to ask you to come here and lecture this winter. For Schlegel's lectures remain unattended and a good intellect will find an open field on which to act. [*But the kind of scholars here and the way they consort would frighten him off.*

Hölderlin and Sinklair should send him his Italian Letters, *which they still have not given back to him.*]

Gries has translated the first five cantos of Tasso *really outstandingly*. The poet's spirit seems to float in the German verse.

We had a very contented time together. In future he will perhaps participate in your journal; but this winter he just has too much to do.

FROM SUSETTE GONTARD

[Frankfurt, 31 October 1799]

My feeling that you would mistake today's date was correct, for today is only the last of the month.—Now I am well again, but I was sick, my love, on the day you went by again last I got some sort of feverish cold and such a bad headache that I had to keep quite still for some days, I took my usual remedy (an emetic) and also kaolin, but it still lasted more than a fortnight, but I thanked heaven that I was still able to expect you and only wanted to be well again by then. I can't tell you how much I thought of you and felt myself to be with you. when in the evenings I was quiet and on my own, (for I couldn't bear to have anyone around me.) My imagination, livelier than normal, pictured our past so beautifully, in particular those blessed hours of our love at the beginning in all its newness, when you said once, Oh if this happiness would last even half a year!

— —

So many and such heavenly-sweet feelings came over me then, I was afterward full of longing and I thought that if only you were here I would surely get well again. I racked my brains over whether it wouldn't be possible in the real world in a good and natural way to be with you again and then when I fell asleep I dreamed I might find you in one sort of society or another, on a walk, I saw you nonchalantly climbing our stairs as formerly you did and I opened the door to you, we were together, quite without fear with untroubled hearts and my eyes rested in yours and were glad and when I awoke there was such a gentle agitation around my heart and truly for a few hours I was strengthened. but afterward I was all at a loss. I felt very keenly that without you my life is wilting and slowly dying and at the same time I know for certain that any step I might take to see you in a secret and anxious fashion, with all the consequences it could have, would eat at my health and my peace of mind just as much. I shall perhaps have to believe in miracles because I can't see how else we shall be together

and every day this is my most passionate wish, but without fear.
careless as in the beginning of our love.

Especially these last few days I have felt much better since now I
am on my own again. also I am back in my old room and here I can
more easily find a quiet hour in which to write, I have more order
around me, also I've put lots of flowers for myself by the window and
they alone can lift my spirits now for even your beloved poems and
letters I dare scarcely touch they trouble me so.

I have such a need to know something definite about your
situation but today again I don't know how I can receive anything
from your hands, if you should think it right and necessary to try
tomorrow in the way we agreed last signal it by not appearing at 10.
Next Thursday evening I could come to the bottom window (Because
we do the washing in those rooms) at half past 8 the staff leave and
I can come and look. What I thought is that when I see you I will
go downstairs and you will be very very careful. if I don't come it's
impossible and then the only way is you send somebody to me with
the letters.

I would like to say something to you about your future situation
if only I had better insight into your present thinking. If fate does
call you onward in some honorable way then follow if you must but
I will advise you and warn you in one thing. Don't go back to where
you fled from with your feelings torn to pieces into my arms. — — I
must admit to you that it rather alarmed me when you wrote that in
a certain case you would follow Schiller's advice and decision. Will he
not seek to have you close to him? — — — — — Will you not be
seduced by such a flattering summons?—If that were to happen, oh
give thought to love and its countless torments! —

— — — — — — — — — — — — — — — — — — — —

Oh my beloved boy, my heart's own, how I wish I could be with
you just once more!—forgive me, dearest, that I say it so forthrightly, but
when I feel you and have seen your image I feel it into the very heart
of my heart, often my own self astonishes me that I have advanced so
far into the years of reason and yet seem to me so young, then I think
too, better a sacrifice to love than to live on loveless. Who knows what
might come, the ways of fate we know are obscure. — — — But let us
never be remiss toward love and toward one another let us always be
truthful. Senseless words! for if we were otherwise, we should of course

no longer love. Trusting in love that nature in her kindness put into our hearts to ripen there into her highest purpose a mystery still to us here in our short-sightedness but feeling ourselves made nobler for something that matters and striving for that. incapable of giving nourishment to any unworthy feeling. And surely in this faith safeguarded against the bad infections of the world.

I must also tell you that on your account since the last time I wrote of it I have had no such experience again. and that my illness was just a cold.

And by way of a warning, opposite us now some annoying strangers are living and almost every day are in and out of the house. They're on the third floor draw the curtains in the evenings. but be careful during the day.

And now farewell, heart's love, in a week you will probably come again, but not if the weather is bad Farewell. sleep well, my dearest. — —

199. TO FRANZ WILHELM JUNG

[Homburg, October/November 1799]

[*Is in a very oppressed state: his publisher is on account of the war and for other reasons again unable to come to a decision.*] I am just waiting for a letter from Schiller that will decide whether I head for Saxony or home. I cannot say how reluctant I am to leave these parts etc.

200. TO SUSETTE GONTARD

[Homburg, early November 1799]

Here is *Hyperion*, darling, *our Hyperion*. It is the fruit of the days when our souls were at one and will give you some joy in spite of all. Forgive me for letting Diotima die. You remember, we could never quite agree about that, before. I thought that the disposition of the whole made it necessary. My darling, everything that is said about her and about us, all the scattered remarks about the life of our life, take them as thanks, which are often all the truer the more ineptly they are expressed. If I could have formed myself as an artist at your feet, gradually, in peace and freedom, I'm sure I should have quickly become what amid the suffering, in its dreams and in broad daylight, and often in silent despair, my heart longs for.

That we were not to have the happiness we could give each other is reason enough for all the tears we have wept during the last years, but to think we shall perhaps both perish in our prime for want of one another, that is criminal. And that is what makes me so quiet sometimes, because I have to guard against thoughts of that kind. Your illness, your letter—however much I seek to blind myself to it, it was again so obvious to me, unavoidable, that you are always suffering, all the time,—and all I can do is cry about it!—Tell me, what is better, to keep quiet what we have in our hearts or to tell it to one another? I have always played the coward so as to spare you,—have always pretended to be ready to resign myself to everything as if I were meant to be a plaything for people and the circumstances and had no solid heart of my own that beats with loyalty and freedom for what is right and for what it has best in the world, light of my life, have often denied myself and held back from my love, which is what I cherish most, sometimes not even allowed myself to think of you, all to get through life and this fate of ours as gently as possible, for your sake.—You too, you who are so peaceful, have always struggled to be calm, have borne it with heroic strength and kept quiet about what cannot be altered, have hidden and buried your heart's everlasting decision within yourself, and for that reason things often go dark around us and we no longer know who we are and what we have, hardly even know one another. This endless fighting and contradiction within, it will kill you in the end, and if no god can assuage it I have no choice but to grieve away over what has happened to us, or to take nothing into account but you and look together with you for a way of putting an end to the conflict.

I have already had the thought that we might be able to live from renunciation, as if it might perhaps give us strength if once and for all we said goodbye to hope,

FROM SUSETTE GONTARD

[Frankfurt, 2–7 November 1799]

Saturday

I can say only a few words, my dearest, about the one thing that since I saw your beloved face waking and dreaming like a soft sweet melody still lingers in me. — — — That evening when my loving words passed into your soul and I could picture so vividly the benign fire they lit in your angel eyes, how contented I felt then and light around my heart. My lips, so long shut to singing, began of their own accord to murmur old songs they had loved best and it was a long while before I noticed and smiled. — — — — Oh you happy happy birds! I thought then — — — Such well-being I felt, beyond expression, when I heard the voice of Nature in me, how that moved me, how I thanked her! — — — — — —

Monday

Imagine! Yesterday evening I heard from S. . . the completely unexpected news that Z. . . from Bern (who five years ago made a copy of your Fragment for me) had just visited her. This intruded violently into my peaceful mood and at once I worried that his appearance might distress you in some way and I became very uneasy. But I beseech you, my one and only love, don't let it cause you any anxiety, that would be quite unnecessary, I assure you once again. He was never more to me than a brother and friend! and never can be any more than that. But you know me and have a thousand proofs of my heart's devotion to you and you know that if we are remiss toward love it is ourselves we wound most. Trust wholly in me and don't let these words mislead into thinking they were needed, I was not speaking to your heart. — — — — —

I saw him again on Sunday evening he got a distant relative of ours, B. . . to introduce him to me as an old friend. I found him very changed, he said himself that he had paid his country its due of his energies and would now leave that concern to others, he would probably stay here a while. but no doubt travel to Hamburg first.

If this does not trouble you, in one respect I shall be glad to have somebody near me again with whom I can talk freely and openly, How glad I shall be to speak about you with him and how much that will ease my heart. I shall never treat him *distantly*—for more than one reason that would not be wise—but I shall face him in all the feeling and pride of my love which he will certainly respect.

Wednesday

The skies are so clear today, you will surely come tomorrow, oh if only I get news of you. Good news! How dark the future is to me but come what may I shall never leave you, you will always find me again — — — —

Thursday—11 o'clock

Oh, how I thank you, my dear love, you are there — — I was fearful you might be ill because I knew for certain the bad weather would not stop you giving me the joy of hearing from you. I pray heaven for a favorable minute, what you tell me will be good, you looked cheerful, if you could see my emotion and feel it in the beating of my heart, how much that presentiment gladdens me! — — — — But you, dearest, my news will not trouble you?—Oh don't let it! — — — Who knows how it might turn out, what good it might do, if I disclose to a trusted friend the whole truth of the pain I have living so far away from and yet so near to you. — — — — — — You can be certain that always as you would approve I shall say only the most necessary things and our dearest love will remain a sacred secret known only to us. You can count on my utmost delicacy. So don't let anything trouble you, The truth is I wouldn't be telling you so much, I feel I am offending our love, if I didn't know you so well and how easily your imagination leads you astray so that you see things not as they really are, and that is why I speak of them, don't look for any other reason.

You had a book in your hand, how happy that makes me already!   I can't at present say anything about our future arrangement to hear from one another except that it remains the same, if your news changes nothing then you will always find me — — And always yours. so long as I live, my never forgotten beloved! — — — — —

I can't write anymore, my eyes are too much affected by my emotion. a few more words this afternoon perhaps.—

Oh that wasn't the last time I will see you! I can't, I won't let myself think it. Oh let me have hope — — — let me banish such thoughts. — — Heavens, what weather, how unsettled it makes me, don't go if it continues like this, you might get ill. Oh take care of yourself, my dearest. When will I be able to hear from you again, if only it were evening already and I had in my safe hands what will give me such joy. What we have to suffer is indescribable but why we suffer it is also *indescribable.*

I wondered before you came whether in future, (if possible,) in the winter months you might be at the corner by 11 rather than 10 or, if you'd prefer, not until 3 because I think today you really hurried and I don't like you leaving home in the dark. I want to say so much more to you but then at once I feel so sad and don't know what to do with myself afterward. but this to finish: I am fully back in good health. Farewell, farewell. *I will always be true to you.*

FROM JOHANN GOTTFRIED EBEL

[Paris,] November 1799

[*His excuse for his long silence is the turbulent situation he finds himself in at the moment.*] My soul, [*he adds,*] was too violently swept up in certain ideas and feelings over the summer for me to be the person I was before, and it is entirely to this mood that you should put down the neglect I have shown, which I do not forgive myself for. I have at last worked my way out of this state of mind up into life again, and I hasten to reply to your letter.

Herr von Humboldt [. . .] no longer here.

[*Ebel himself goes into the program of the planned journal with great interest.*] Only as I must pursue my studies to earn a living, and am making efforts alongside to get on with the work I have begun, I am for the moment unable to supply what you require. But rest assured that as soon as circumstances permit I shall try to send you bits and pieces. I shall be speaking with some good minds, perhaps I shall be so fortunate as to muster another collaborator for you.

You are living in Homburg and have detached yourself from the Gontards—this was unknown to me until I received your letter. It seems you thought I was already apprised of this, since you say nothing about it all. I hope that you are reaping greater inner delight in your situation of independence in the lap of the Muses than I am in the dirty reality of the human world here. Here one sometimes draws the breath of life in the galleries showing the products of artistic genius, but not among the living. Although at the cost of much pain, one does learn a *lot* here about human nature. With unchanging sentiments of friendship and esteem

ever yours

Dr. Ebel

Give Herr Sinklair hearty greetings from me.

201. TO HIS MOTHER

Homburg, 16 November 1799

Dearest Mother,

I could well imagine that this time you would be obliged to put off writing for a while, and reconciled myself to it the more readily because I thought of your dear guests and then the journey, which is bound to be good for your health and well-being. How gladly I'd be part of the happy circle in which you are living, and contribute something from my side to the pleasure being with your family gives you. But I think I shall be obeying your own view of things if I postpone my visit at least until our part of the world and the roads generally are rather quieter again. These last days I have been very concerned for our relatives in Löchgau because I guessed that some of the fighting must have occurred at the place itself or very nearby. Now they will be in peace again, at least for a while.

Here we no longer encounter the war except in the papers, and the people of Homburg have earned it: this is the first winter in many years they will spend without foreign boarders and lodgers and without the disruption of war and military charges. I am often amazed that this region, which has been virtually a constant scene of war, more or less, is despite that recovering so quickly and that the people are for the most part able to continue to run their households and their lives as usual.

To come to my own affairs, I'm afraid I cannot yet tell you anything more precise about my prospects, and really this displeases me more for your sake than for mine, for if it weren't for the inevitable disadvantage of my present way of life—that it won't immediately satisfy my material needs—I should be content with it for ever. I am deeply conscious that the cause I live for is a noble one and, once it is brought to its proper expressiveness and formal perfection, one that is beneficial to mankind. And with this determination and purpose I live at peace in my occupations, and although I am often reminded (as inevitably happens) that people would perhaps respect me more if they could make out that I held a decent office in society, that's easily borne, because I understand it, and I make up for it in my delight in the truth and beauty of what I have secretly devoted myself to since I was a boy and have returned to from the experiences and lessons of life with all the more resolve. And even if my inner self never attains a clear and full language—and a lot of it depends on luck—at least I know what I have wanted; and I have wanted more than might be supposed from my slight achievements so far and can also hope, from the odd thing I come to hear, that even in inept execution what I do will be taken up and approved by an intuitive soul now and again, and so my existence will definitely not fail to leave some trace on earth.

I make these confessions to you, dear Mother, because it is important to me for my own peace of mind to show myself to you in my present way of life in as sincere and unbiased fashion as I can, the more especially as you have helped me this far with your kind support.

I thank you dearly for what you have sent. Neuffer will probably have kept it back until now because of the unsafe roads. I shall be able to put most of it on one side, and use it partly for the coming journey. It does something to set my mind to rest over all I am costing you that I could not live as a curate either without some help, and that I have at least persevered a reasonable length of time in the, in this regard, more advantageous life of a private tutor.

How it gladdens me that you can in every respect be so content with our Karl. And how much I value his concentrating and applying his energies so manfully in the situation he finds himself in. I honor from the bottom of my heart anyone who makes himself useful to the world in this way, and it only makes me sorry when occasionally I see that in the main people are not so well disposed the other way round, being less inclined to acknowledge someone who because of the nature of his occupation and way of working is in some degree distanced from any particular sphere of activity, and can only survive by having the courage to affirm his own nature, understanding and assuming his fate as others do theirs. And it is the comfort and rule of my life that in the real world no one can be everything and is forced to become one particular thing, and, together with the merits of his position and peculiar way of life, bear the disadvantages that necessarily go with it.

Mother, I thank you a thousand times for showing such sympathy for me in this regard even though I have not arrived at anything yet, but you and the rest of the family will surely think it to my credit that I am unable to be indifferent about the judgment you form of me.

I also beg you not to be put off if sometimes in my letters I slip into lengthy reasonings. From what I can gather of the more general moods and opinions of people today, there seems to be developing, as a reaction against the great, violent upheavals of our time, a way of thinking that is very unlikely to animate and awaken the faculties and in fact ends up oppressing and numbing the living soul, without which there can be no joy and no proper value in the world at all. Exaggeration is never good, and it is no good either when people are frightened of everything that is not already familiar and settled, with the result that they hold all striving toward anything nearer perfection than what we already have to be bad and harmful. Precisely this seems to me the general attitude nowadays, and it is a great weight on my mind because it reaches into the small things in life as well as the greater things, and because no man can free himself from the influence of others, be it harmful or beneficial.

And if on a particular day I am more caught up in feelings of this kind than usual it is only natural that this should show through in my utterances when I come to speak with those close to my heart.

But so as not to go on too long now I will just add that I hope to be able to say something more certain about the visit I have been intending for so long, and also about my future existence, in a month's time.

As always, dearest Mother, I am

your grateful son,

H.

I have just learned that the French Directory has been dismissed, the Council of Elders sent to St. Cloud, and Bonaparte made a sort of dictator.

202. TO HIS SISTER

Homburg, 16 November 1799

Beloved sister,

I could hardly allow myself the joy that your dear letter gave me. It is so needful for me to keep with equanimity to my path, and your generous, kind invitation was not made to remind me of the circumstances that limit my desires.—You are quite right, dear Rike, that it's high time we saw each other again, and how much my heart's disposition resembles yours in this will be clear enough to you from how often I go on to you about my hopes of being able to visit you one day. If so far I have always found obstacles that prevent it, I only bowed to them with such patience because I needed to learn to bow to many things I should have wished otherwise. I had the firm intention of coming last winter, and in fact only accepted my friend Sinclair's proposal because from Rastatt I planned to make a visit home. But the poor weather and the doctor with whom I was already forced to have some dealings in Rastatt, obliged me to spend the time I had allowed myself in the town and mostly indoors, and when I was well again it seemed to me too late and I thought I had no choice but to hurry back to my work. My mind works so slowly that I sometimes take days and weeks for things that others have done at once, and so I need a lot of time and have to use it sparingly, almost fearfully.—

You say I could just as well carry on with my work at your house. At first I certainly couldn't, sweet Rike! I have too little control over a joy such as this would be, and should not be able to keep my thoughts together as I need to. So I had come to the conclusion that once my journal was just about under way I could take a few weeks off with a good conscience, or, in the case that I was obliged by a letter from Schiller to quit my present arrangements, that I would visit my dear family then. But for as long as I have no prospect of a definite job, I cannot permit myself, as I see it, to leave the work that is in part to provide my living, at least not until it is properly under way. I have received no further letter from Schiller.

That your dear children are thriving gives me great pleasure. Such a good mother as you are deserves no less.—I must, somewhat simply, confess that it often annoys me that I am no longer the wealthy man in

Frankfurt, able to send a little surprise to my niece and nephew from time to time.

Mere greetings are not much of a language, especially for little Friz, who for the moment is better at looking and touching than speaking. But when I come I'll bring something proper with me, tell them that.

My friend Veiel I wish all happiness in his new life.

What pleases me most of all is that the worries for your dear husband no longer weigh on your heart. Remember me to him and assure him of my continued admiration and respect.

Keep me in your affections, dear Rike!

Your

loyal brother

H.

203. TO JOHANN GOTTFRIED EBEL

[Homburg, ~ mid-November 1799]

My dear friend,

However much I am obliged to you for your kind promise of future participation in my literary enterprise the real pleasure your letter gave me was quite a different one. I felt more strongly than I can say, as I read it, how much you meant to me from the first moment, and how much I have done without since I last saw you.

The more I come to understand and tolerate and love people in their various sufferings, the more deeply and unforgettably the outstanding ones among them press themselves into my mind. And I must confess that I know few people with whom I can follow my soul with such assuredness as I can whenever I think of and talk about you, something that happens often. If only we were closer to one another—for my sake, for you do not need me, or less than I do you, and I don't know if I would mean as much to you as I once seemed to. Many experiences, that given my disposition were almost inevitable, have pretty much undermined my confidence in all that used to be my chief source of hope and joy, the ideal image of man and his life and being; and the ever-changing conditions of the world, great and small, in which I belong frighten me still, now that I am somewhat freer again, to a degree that I can only admit to you, because you understand me. Habit is such a powerful goddess that probably no one can abandon her with impunity. The agreement with others that we achieve so easily when we keep to what we already have, this consonance of opinions and customs, appears to us in its true significance only when we have to do without it, and our hearts may well never find the same peace again once we have given up the old ties, for in the end the forging of new ones is something we have little control over, especially as concerns the finer and higher sort. It is true that people who have raised themselves into a new world of rightness and goodness then hold together all the more closely and enduringly.

How much I should have liked to give you a full account of my departure from the household that meant, and still means, so much to both of us. But then I should have had to tell you infinitely more than I can say! I should have preferred to ask you a favor, and should still like to. Our noble friend, whom I have always seen come through her many ordeals in greater affirmation of her best life, even finer and more delicate despite the bitter anomalies of her situation, nonetheless seems to me, if her sadness is not to be the end of her, in great need of a firm, clear word that would secure her inner worth and her own path through life for the future. And it has become virtually impossible for me to communicate with her with the necessary calm. It would be a great service to me, dear Ebel, if you could do this one day. Our own thoughts or a book or whatever else helps to give us direction do some good, but a word from a genuine friend who knows the situation and the person concerned strikes home more truly and has more effect.

Your judgment on Paris affected me deeply. It would have unsettled me less if it had not come from you but someone without such a wide perspective and without your clear unprejudiced eye. I can understand how a powerful fate, capable of shaping so splendidly men and women who are firmly grounded in themselves, simply ends up tearing the weak apart, and I can understand it the more readily when I see that even the greatest owe this greatness not just to their own natures but also to the place in which they had the fortune to come into active and living relation with their times, but I do not understand why many great and pure forms do so little to help and heal in general and in particular, and this it is above all that often makes me so still and humble before the omnipotence of necessity, which rules over all. If necessity decisively and constantly outweighs the ability of pure and independent minds to have an effect then either collectively or individually the end will be a tragic and fatal one for the people who live in that time and place. We are fortunate then, if we still have some other source of hope. How do you find the new generation, I wonder, in the world you live in?

FROM PRINCESS AUGUSTE OF HESSE-HOMBURG

[Homburg, after 28 November 1799]

The feelings of gratitude prompted by receiving your gifts compel me to send you these lines, and the wish accompanies them not to be unworthy of your flattering song: but that I am not.—

Your career has begun, begun so beautifully and assuredly that it has no need of encouragement; only, my true joy in your victories and advances will always accompany it.

Auguste—

204. TO CHRISTIAN LUDWIG NEUFFER

Homburg, 4 December 1799

My dear friend,

First of all let me express to you my sympathy for the death of your good mother, which I was left to learn from your poem. You knew the respect I had for this unusual woman, and for that reason it was almost wrong of you not to write and tell me about it. But I know very well myself that in many cases it does a man more good to keep silent than to speak of his suffering to others.

You must also be assured that I feel for you in the inconvenient change in your job, and I regret it all the more since I'd have liked to see you able to enjoy the success of your poetic work in peace. It is almost as if no happiness costs more dear than being a writer, especially a poet. You ask my advice, dear Neuffer! How I'd like to say something reliable, and how I'd like to find you a solution myself. But you don't need me to tell you how much I for my part need advice and the help of a friend. I confess that little by little I am finding out that nowadays it is almost impossible to live from writing alone if you don't want to be too much at the service of others and sacrifice your reputation for the sake of your livelihood. And for this reason I am undecided whether sooner or later I should become a curate or rather a preceptor or private tutor again. I almost think this last alternative the best. And even if some less modest post should present itself I don't know if I would take the opportunity since I should be unwilling to sacrifice either my writing to an office or an office to my writing, and for that reason I should like to choose a post that did not require too much energy and time. If you manage to find something better for yourself I shall be very pleased for you, and I don't know, perhaps with your connections in Stuttgart you can arrange something suitable, for example a journey at the Consistory's expense. That would certainly correspond to you and your plans in every respect.

If anything occurs to me that seems to suit you, or if any opportunity shows itself that I find fits in with your wishes, I'll certainly let you know.

About your most recent poems I'll say no more than that they distinguish themselves through the faithful, unadorned representation of the inward or outward life they address. And you know yourself how much that means. Especially "The Dream" seems to achieve a combination of the ideal-poetic and simplicity. The alterations in the hymn to "Calm" pleased me particularly in the clarity they maintain alongside their significance. If only I lived closer to you so that we could talk some sense together from time to time about our noble art. For, in confidence, I find more and more that the true recognition of poetic forms greatly aids and facilitates the *expression* of poetic life and spirit, and I am amazed that we wander around so helplessly when I look at the sure, thoroughly purposeful and considered progression of ancient works of art. And I have to confess that I was a bit angry about the pretty unthinking remarks about poetry you made once last summer (the occasion was *Emilie*). Do not misunderstand me, dear Neuffer! It was not because of *Emilie*, which was dashed off without

much thought because I had to and as a favor, it was for the sake
of the art that you disparaged in what you said to me. Think me
an unfeeling theorist if you like. I know my own mind, and I agree
with you entirely when you say our dull aesthetic compendiums are
a patchwork of one-sided conceptions you'd like to throw in the fire.
Only let a god give me enough time and equanimity to execute what I
see and feel. —

The esteem I have for the progress of your journal and how my
own literary affairs stand you can gather, if you like to, from the letter
to our friend Steinkopf. I must break off, it's getting late. I hope things
will be well with you soon. Console yourself with the Muses and, if it
can do any good, with the faithfulness of

your sincere friend,

H.

Please could you send me the 100 florins as a bill as soon as ever
possible.

FROM SUSETTE GONTARD

[Frankfurt, before 5 December 1799]

I can't tell you enough, my dearest, how much happiness your latest
letters gave me, they were a rich compensation for the anxious time I
had getting them, I can't describe the fear that took hold of me when I
couldn't catch sight of you anywhere from the window below, I thought
the bright moonlight must have given you away and when I went
spying out from one window to the next and you didn't show yourself
I had such a violent trembling in my knees that I could scarcely keep
upright, it was terrible for me to remain in that uncertainty and I was
thinking all the time somebody or other would come in behind me
into the room and I would give myself away too and then finally thank
goodness you came. I hurried with my treasures to my own quiet room
but there for palpitations and breathlessness I could not read a word, I
began at the end or the beginning but that evening couldn't understand
what they meant, then a few days later when I was calmer they rejoiced

and strengthened my heart and my quiet thanks blessed you and flew across to you.

My fear has now almost decided me this winter not to try again in that fashion to have news of you, especially since in a few months it will be *the beginning of spring,* if there is something you must tell me it is still less risky if you send a parcel of old books addressed to me with an envelope in among them as we agreed before *so that I can know when.*

You wish me to tell you how content I am with my social life. Well I must be honest and say that really I have none and that because of feeling unwell I hardly left the house half a dozen times all summer long. even my brother and his wife were not much with me, they both found in the neighborhood little love affairs to pass the time, spoilt by the stupidities modish in Hamburg nowadays in that respect as in many others they were out of tune with me and I was often left sitting there on my own with love of a different order in my heart furious that it should count for nothing while vanity and triviality make their way in the world.

But it is easy for people to let be what at bottom they don't care about, it's only what they might envy that they wish to interfere with and only the life aroused by true love will be tormented on account of that love.   I feel more and more that I don't fit into worldly circumstances and do better living alone in the quietness of my soul.

On the same morning that you came by again a few hours later Z. . . called, dressed for traveling, and asked did I have anything to send to *Hamburg.* He has arrived there since and will probably stay a few months for business reasons to have closer dealings with his brother who is in America.

Now I really must tell you where my aversion to your being in Jena comes from so that you won't get me wrong for I had not the least inkling of what you wrote to me about nor has anyone said anything to me. The root of the matter is that *Weimar* is only half a day's journey from *Jena.* By chance this summer I was in a lady's room that, not lived in, had been cleared for occupancy by Frau *la Roche* and her granddaughter, I think this room can't be unknown to you. Now some time ago I heard for certain that Schiller will move to Weimar, into that house, this winter, you couldn't avoid visiting him, it might not be pleasant for you and what I would feel about it I knew from my violently beating heart when I happened to spend a few hours there.   I didn't write to you about it at the time because I hadn't then realized what you had in mind and it wasn't relevant. But now I think I owe it to you and to myself to confess this weakness. I know very well that before the high ideal of Love such weaknesses are out of place and deserve condemnation, but before Love as human beings feel it—*some* indulgence—you understand me! — — — —

FROM SIEGFRIED SCHMID

Tuttlingen, in the region of Schaffhausen, 19 December 1799

[*Asks why he has received no news from him?*
Sends him some poems: "Forebodings"—"The language of love"
What has become of his poems?]
We are not yet in winter quarters and moving round quite a bit.

FROM JOHANN FRIEDRICH STEINKOPF

Stuttgart, 12 January 1800

[*H. will have received his two letters. Today via Landauer he is sending him back the two manuscripts by Schmid and Prof. Jung.*

He has asked Landauer, who told him he would be sure to speak to H. himself, to steer the subject matter onto his coming here, which everyone desires, and hopes to see Landauer return with a favorable reply.

Perhaps H. will also give Landauer a manuscript or two.]

205. TO HIS MOTHER

Homburg, 29 January [1800]

Dearest Mother,

. . .

I am now *certain* to receive about 400 fl. from my bookseller in quarterly payments. [*Moreover he has arranged things in Stuttgart so that he can stay there without being obliged to carry out any theological function as soon as the time seems right.*] . . . If therefore I keep my journal going for a few years, which I shall certainly try to do for my reputation's sake, and if I earn a bit more by giving private lessons here or in Stuttgart, I'll be able to reckon with an income that will almost be sufficient. It seems to me sensible, unless I am forced to do otherwise, to interrupt the present form of my occupations and studies as little as possible with a new mode of life and work, as I am only now more or less in harness and after many distractions and troubles have at last gained some steadiness in what I am doing. So the arguments that present themselves to me at the moment are against embarking on such a course, which in any case I should hardly want *you* to carry the burden of.—The point is, if it turned out not to work it would almost be too great an ordeal for the peace of mind that means so much to me and for the patience I have for relations with other people, for, as I say, I sense that I need to grow a bit stronger before I can expose myself to that kind of humiliation, which at least for a time would rid me of the desire and the proper energy to do anything useful in human affairs. And I can admit it to you, dearest Mother: it is precisely on this that my physical and mental well-being, if I can put it that way, largely rests. The other reason is that I am now more or less safe for a little while and the thing must be to carry on pursuing a career that whatever happens cannot end so very badly for me, until some definite success results, and now of all times it hardly seems possible to me to combine my present occupations, which require such a concentrated and undivided frame of mind, with a post where I would have to get used to my surroundings and settle into my work all over again.

If you allow me to add that I won't be worse off than many others if in the future I take up a position with somewhat less in the way of funds, then it seems to me well worth the trouble to supplement my income a little in the meantime if it is not quite sufficient, when need arises, especially since if I remain in good health I do not intend in any future position to give up my writing entirely, which though it may never make me rich will not be completely thankless in the end either.

In any case I leave the matter up to you and my dear brother-in-law, having given my opinion as far as the short time allowed it; especially as I am not, as you are, in a position to judge whether the exact circumstances will allow me to secure my existence without taking up a substantial post. If I discount the expenses caused by my ill health last year I find that I can more or less manage with 500 fl., and I could probably earn that much in Stuttgart or here.—You will not blame me for looking on the matter so one-sidedly; as far as higher motives and points of view are concerned, I believe I can claim with a good conscience that in my present occupation I am doing at least as much service and good to people as I would in a parish, even if appearances would seem to suggest the opposite. This is based not just on my own judgment but on the express and earnest gratitude I have received for some of my publications from persons whose opinions command respect.

In the meantime my departure from here depends above all on the next letter from my bookseller. As it is a matter of expediency you will understand me when I say that whether I stay here or move to Stuttgart hangs on where I find it easier to make a living. In any case I'll carry on here until Easter, because I cannot possibly interrupt my work before then. In about a fortnight I should be able to give you certain news. If Sinclair, who is probably leaving for Swabia later this week to visit a friend in the imperial army, comes to Blaubeuren as he intends to, please don't mention anything to him about my probable departure unless he brings it up himself first. Until I am quite decided myself I prefer not to say anything to him because he doesn't really want me to go and I should like to think the whole matter over and settle it coolly. To quit this place would by the way cost me a great deal, and only the prospect of returning to my beloved homeland and my loved ones, whom I would miss wherever I was, could make it easier. I have got to know good people here, some of them excellent, and enjoy more attention and sympathy than a stranger can expect who has nothing to give but an honest opinion now and then.—There's no need to be anxious about my health, dearest Mother. For a good while now I have enjoyed this most precious possession without interruption and it gives me the more pleasure because I always feared that the bad cramp-like condition might become permanent. This has made me well acquainted with the local doctor, a man who is always cheerful and dependable, someone who for a moment or two at least can make you feel better simply by showing his kind, healthy face. He is your man for all hypochondriacs.—The Gontard you tell me about in your letter who recently died is an uncle of the family I was with. Dear Henry is now in an educational institute in Hanau. The only reason I write so seldom of him is that I can never think of the marvelous boy without sadness. It is a very good thing for him to be out of Frankfurt, where each day corrupted his truly noble character, or at least distorted it.—I have received the money from Neuffer and thank you again for it very much. If I do leave, and if it can be done without inconveniencing you, I would ask for a little bit more, not so much because of the traveling costs, which will not be great, but because I still have a debt to settle with the bookseller in Frankfurt. Thank my dear sister on my behalf for her lovely letter. I would answer it today myself if the same thing weren't happening to me as did to her: my good friend the stove is getting too cold, and so I'd better behave myself, and spare and nurse my thirty-year-old body. The waistcoat will suit me well and keep me warm.

All my love and remembrances. As ever,

your loyal son,

Hölderlin

FROM SUSETTE GONTARD

[Frankfurt, 31 January–6 February 1800]

Friday 30 January

I must think now of getting a letter ready for you in case you come next Thursday or there'll be no time or peace and quiet, if only I could know whether you have been back home or still are. I'd be very glad if you and your dear ones have had this joy.—

A week ago we had compatriots of yours dining with us, I felt certain they must have seen you and for that reason I felt very at ease in their company, I liked their accent too and I kept thinking if they were alone with me they would speak of you, how I should have liked that with people who know you and esteem you as I do. In my thoughts I was often with you and I felt that you thinking of me in your family circle would not be an intrusion and would nurture the gentle feelings of love for them because you are more than formerly in need of sympathy and are yourself more forbearing.

I wonder have you come to an agreement with them about your future and found something suitable? There are many things I should so like to know but I shall have to be patient! I was very pleased at the end to work out with them that it was no further from our house to theirs than it is from here to our beloved Cassel and that seemed to me last time no more than an outing! You'll never go further away from me than that, will you? — — — Never *quite* away? — — — You might go there again and again and come back again to me. You can imagine how glad I should be to see you in a place that is right for you, but choose cautiously and be sure not to snatch at one that isn't right, I shan't in the next few days hear anything from you unless you will decide to send me a parcel, if you think that necessary there's nothing to stop you, it will surely work, if you appear yourself I'll take that as the sign that I needn't worry and shall wait and I shall feel a bit better when I think that news of you means I am distant from you and shan't be quite so full of impatient longing for such news as I usually am. I shall see you! and you are nearby, I can and must be content with no more than that.

Also I must tell you that from now on I shan't throw my letters down, I had a feeling (perhaps quite without foundation) that people are getting suspicious so if next month the weather is at all good and dry so that it would be natural for me to go out, please can you appear at 10 o'clock and then I'll come to the usual place at 11 that same day. but if that can't be done without arousing suspicion, you will only see me. it matters a great deal to me that I hear from you because at the end of March my brother will be here again and I'll be less often without company. He and his wife will be spending the summer with us again. so if you want to send me something do it before then. It may also be that the war will bring disturbances and prevent me from taking a walk then send me something in any case as arranged I'll give the man a book to take back to you and so that each knows that what was sent has been received, can you show yourself for a moment on the corner again, at 11, and by the way I advise you not to linger there because a sick neighbor lives above and he is bored. if I can't come out I'll hang a cloth from the window.

And now just a few words about me and how I have been spending my life. I am in *good health* and the solitary peace and quiet in my cozy room was very good for me, I do love sitting there among my flowers and working, nobody passes my silent window to disturb me only now and then a sparrow comes to peck bread from the sill and the clouds go by, often I follow them when in the evening some rays of the setting sun shine through the clump of trees at the back, and all is well in me. The gentle melancholy and sadness in my spirit, that doubtless will never fade away, nor should it, attunes me more receptively to every little joy, I feel it more gratefully, my heart will never be an arrogant thing, the tears of pity and goodwill are always closer to me, so I wish to remain, so you are too. — — —

Also this winter I was a bit more sociable and sometimes in our old circles the long solitariness and the novelty meant that I had more enjoyment there than formerly and people were glad to see me again, several times I was told that I looked much better and was more cheerful and so you can surely believe it when I tell you that I am quite restored to health. If I only knew the same of you! — — —

Thursday

You really did come!—I didn't dare hope, have you not been away at all?

You didn't deprive yourself of a pleasure for my sake, did you?—My dear kind love, I wish you could have pleasure and that I could give it you. — — I don't know I am so full of fear I always think we may be found out and the difficulties that already can hardly be overcome are increasing, if just this time you receive my words then I would gladly go without, I know you love me, as I do you, and no one can take that from me.

Did you not look rather pale? You haven't been ill, have you? You will preserve yourself I know for my sake — — — And won't deny yourself any joy that comes your way, you don't seek it, but nor will you unkindly spurn it either, promise me, my dearest? — —

If you come tomorrow I will be able to be calm. I'm sure of that and have reason enough to be glad.

Farewell, farewell near or far away you are always with me. And so woven into me that nothing can separate you from me, we are together wherever we are, and soon I hope to see you again.

Tell me very clearly how you are.—And for my sake look after yourself.

Z. . . . is still in Hamburg and I don't know when he will come back and whether he will stay here, but I think probably if he can he will stop here a while.

I have read your beloved poems, all of them, with more joy than I can say! I've put all your letters together like a book and if I should ever not hear from you for a long while I will read in them and think, And so it is *still*! You do the same, and believe that in our innermost lives the things that bind us together will last as long as we ourselves last and I can never give up the belief that we shall find one another again in the world and again be joyful. Only be happy (as we mean it) and believe that what you begin will be dear to me, so long as it succeeds. But don't choose something that doesn't suit you. If you could feel how the loveliest image of you often lives and blooms in me then you would also feel that everything, everything around me must give way to it. and how every whisper of a feeling in me awakes the vast one and only feeling that I have for you and gives me up to you entirely! — — — So do not shun your heart, and believe as I do that we are eternally *ours* and only ours.

FROM FRIEDRICH EMERICH

Mainz, 13 Ventos 8 [4 March 1800]

[*writes with delight about the 2nd part of Hyperion which he has now read. The verdict on the Germans, though, filled him with indignation.—Is waiting, like Böhlendorff, for a third part.*]

FROM SUSETTE GONTARD

[Frankfurt, 5 March 1800]

He will move into your rooms upstairs sit at your desk, I shall be glad to go up there again and see with quiet delight how your previous lodging is honored now by his presence, I should never have allowed anybody else in there and nor, I think, would you? He will sometimes see secret tears in my eyes when I go to him, his feeling heart will understand me and I shall find peace in his soul.

How I am looking forward to tomorrow! I shall hear from you again, Whatever it is, all will be well, you will surely act as is best for me, I put my trust in fate, I believe things will go well for you. I shall again have nourishment for a long while. but you will have to be patient again because next month you will very likely not hear anything from me I don't know how I should manage it Because my relatives are coming just at that time and there might easily be another change in the family it is probably better for you not to come at all but since I can't know what your future course will be I'll let you decide and if it is by any means possible I'll do exactly what you ask.

But we probably won't have anything from one another until we're living out of town again, the 1st Thursday in May falls on the 1st and if I remember rightly by that time last year we weren't out there yet and here if I went for a walk on my own the others would notice So it would probably be safer if for now you reckoned on the 2nd or 3rd Thursday, Not long ago it occurred to me could we not in the future get news of one another through Herr Landauer, he is your friend and last time I saw him he was especially courteous and nice to me. But it would have to be done with extreme caution and obliqueness so that he himself wouldn't arouse suspicion.   It's just an idea and if you don't think it a good one we won't discuss it further, meanwhile through him indirectly you can always have news of me from time to time. He will probably be here for the next Fair, but if you happen to see him perhaps you can make him feel that he might just mention you by name to me. I can't tell you how eager I am to know what your plans for your future are. if only the hours of waiting were already over!   I can't write any more, farewell, farewell, you are an abiding presence in me and there you will remain so long as I myself remain. — —

206. TO FRIEDRICH EMERICH

[Homburg, perhaps March 1800]

You've reproached me for my silence like a true friend, dear brother, and I beg you once and for all never to misinterpret it. For as long as my interest in my friends and in everything else that touches on me is not less keen than is the case now I shall probably be obliged to appear a bit detached, out of a natural instinct to preserve my sense of self. You wouldn't believe how much trouble I've had with this, and what an old problem it is. Every relationship with other people and other objects immediately takes hold of all my thoughts, so much so that, once I've let some particular interest come to light and be articulated, I then have great difficulty leaving it behind again and moving on to something else. If you write to me, it resonates on and on until by a trick or by violence I manage to devote myself to something else, and if I write to you it's even worse. That's the kind of toiling Swabian I am.

So you have made a courageous start by publishing your poems. With your firmness of mind you've got more right than others to conduct the poetic game a bit like a game of chance for the time being and to cast the dice in the name of genius. By that I don't at all mean that you haven't used your powers of reflection too, your artistic sense, which you hardly seem to do justice to given the faithful and ingenuous way it serves you, like an honest shield-bearer in battle. I'm sure you will have been aided by your well-founded judgment and taste, but for all that you're not completely certain of things. And who is among our poets, old or young? And whom would one thank for it, given the way matters now stand? We cold Northerners like to maintain ourselves in doubt and passion, to prevent us from organizing ourselves into snails' lives out of sheer love of order and security.

But seriously, Emerich, you must, if some grander career is not to be yours, make a serious go of poetry. You seem to me to have in plenty the poetic trinity—a tender sensibility and force and spirit—together with the ethereal element and the earthly one, to be able to fix this noble life in such a noble art and to transmit it undamaged to posterity. And that is why I honor the free, unprejudiced, thorough-going artistic understanding more and more, because I take it to be the holy aegis that protects the genius from transiency.

I must give you the impression of being a true penitent. But in my defense I can say that for all the apparent carelessness with which my works have been written hitherto I went about them very deliberately and that the fault lies not so much with me as in the one-sidedness of our modern-day taste if I appear to be angry and for that reason to have proceeded in a somewhat revolutionary way. But it was probably good as a beginning, and as I said you can better make such a beginning than I. I had the luck to see where I was, and so was able to choose my subject matter and arrange it accordingly.

FROM HIS BROTHER

[Mark]Gröningen, 8 March 1800

[On behalf of his mother and sister imparts the painful news that his brother-in-law, Prof. Bräunlen, has been taken from them.—Requests him to come home to comfort his sister; he himself is putting off his journey to Blaubeuren for the time being, in order to travel there with him if he comes soon.]

FROM SUSETTE GONTARD

[Frankfurt, 15 March 1800]

My mother-in-law died yesterday. I can't tell you any more now, farewell, farewell and preserve yourself — —

207. TO HIS SISTER

Homburg, 19 March [1800]

My dear Rike,

I'd have written to you before now had I not preferred to wait for a moment when I could think about the loss of your husband, unforgettable to me, with some calm and with a quieter mind.

I knew him, and know how much that was truly elevated and eternal resided in his heart, and for precisely that reason I can easily imagine that he was able to die with serenity; to a soul such as his, accustomed to look on human life and its sufferings and vicissitudes with a higher eye, and always to attend more to what is permanent, to the foundations of our being and life, to a mind like his, death must appear more as a brief farewell than as a long separation, & this must also have made the parting from you, my sweet Rike, and from all those near to him a little easier. I am comforted by the thought which is always the best comfort for me, that is, that God is everywhere and that through him and in him we are all now and forever joined.

What gives my heart sorrow above all is to know you, beloved sister, no longer escorted by this noble companion of your life, and that your dear children now only have their mother, one, it's true, wholly made to compensate this loss and to be everything to their youthful needs, but to whom, suffering as she will be, this precious care cannot but be hard to bear. Dearest sister, preserve yourself, for all our sakes, for whom you are so truly valuable! Trust to your good nature, remember that you have so many fortunate gifts that are wholly fitted to help you endure the vicissitudes of life more easily and without harm! How often have I envied you your beautiful calm and patience the many times I have found the going hard, and how much I always strive to learn for myself what is native to you! The company and support of our good mother will be consolation enough to you. A heart that has been through what hers has assuages by its very presence, and it must be a fortifying thought for you to be to your children what she was to us in our childhood, since we have her to thank above all for the best we possess. And you have other good people around you, and the blessings of heaven that protect us on all sides will not fail you, pure soul that you are!

If I can do anything to help you, you only need to say. Just as soon as my affairs allow—they are rather more pressing at the moment—nothing will prevent me from coming and I think, dear Rike, that I shall be of some use to you because I have learned to bear much in this world and after many kinds of experiences my fondness for you and the rest of the family has only become more profound and everlasting. You have in me a loyal lifelong friend for you and your children, that you can believe. Look, good, beloved sister—it is in my eyes an inestimable fortune, and one all too rare, that there is such a genuine harmony and respect and joy among us brothers and sisters, and that we have the mother we do!

Take care of your health, dear Rike, and enjoy life. We should not begrudge those who leave us for peace and new youthfulness; but this life is also good, God is here too, and my belief is that here too things will get better and better. There are many other things I'd like to say to comfort you; I have so often experienced how an appeal come from the sanctuary of our soul can gladden us in deep distress and give us new life, new fervent hope. One thought I have especially often is that the living God who is in us and around us, from the beginning and into all eternity, is more powerful than death can ever be, and the feeling of this immortality often cheers me on my own behalf and on behalf of all those alive and those who have died in our sight. And it is my certain belief that in the end all things are good, and all sorrow is just the path to true and sacred joy.

Let me break off here, my beloved sister! I'll write again soon! To our dear mother too, and our brother. So long as I don't lose you, you dear ones! Preserve yourselves for me and for each other!

Your

ever-loyal brother

Hölderlin

FROM SUSETTE GONTARD

[Frankfurt, 7 May 1800]

Will you come tomorrow? dearest, I believe you will and yet I don't like to rely on it, my longing might then be too violent if I weren't to see you anymore.   Your decision to live a useful life in the circle of your family comes as if spoken out of my own soul and now, in the circumstances, it is your proper course to be all you can be to your dear sister, it will be a blessing to have around you again someone who loves you deeply and whom you can trust, and why should I not be gladdened by it?—I shall always hear of you, I shall see you again as soon as that is possible for you. we shouldn't have been able to have news of one another as often as we have till now, certainly not every month and I already had in mind to tell you that we might exchange our letters just every half a year via the letter carrier but always for one another whenever we have a moment that feels happy to write to one another. and say all manner of things just as they occur to us. speak from the heart and *breathe* at times when the breast is crammed so tight. Let that be our arrangement now. You come when you can and I will wait for you without anxiety. You will come to me one day for sure. I shall see you again! No one shall take from me that certainty.   I will bear your look and the clasp of your hand with fortitude, so I'll not be too weakened, after so long a separation, going again into a separation, to endure it. And give you the courage for it.

A few words now about my life lately. I am very well and have at present a lot of things to do and that distracts me enjoyably and in a rewarding fashion gives my energies the outlet they need. As you know, we have become the owners of the garden on the Main, it was always my wish, as you know, to plant some trees, to set something up entirely as I choose, and to cultivate some land. I very much like being out there, as you always said I would, I get everything laid out simply, to my taste, 25 acres of fruitful ground are under my supervision, that gives me pleasure enough and the sort of activity I love. I've got a year to set it up, there's time in hand since we're still living here, and so everything has to be ready by next summer.

We only came out here yesterday and my brother isn't coming till Saturday, Z. . . is still in Hamburg and we hear nothing of him.   When you think of me in the future always picture me in some occupation that I enjoy. And I shall think of you that you are doing something that rewards your kind heart, and so we shall think of one another with cheerfulness. And bravely, with the rapid passage of time, hasten toward reunion, whenever that might be, ask of fate that the happy moment might come soon, and put your trust in the secret powers that guide our footsteps. All I ask of you is that in none of life's relationships will you let yourself be uneasy on account of ours, and let me always be your confidante, you will never lose by it for your happiness is mine.

When you next appear in town and see a white cloth at my window don't send your letters and come again next morning and if you see nothing send them at once and then come back once again for the sign.

Thursday morning

Will you come now! — — — All around here is dumb and empty without you and I am so full of fear, these powerful feelings going out in waves toward you, how will I close them and keep them in my bosom again?—if you don't come! — — — —

And if you do come! it is so hard to keep any balance. and not to let the feelings be too alive. Promise me that you will not come back and will go quietly away again from here, for if I don't know that, I shall be at the window till morning so very tense and unquiet and in the end we have to be quiet again so let us trustingly go our ways and in our sorrow still feel happiness and wish that it will endure a long long time for us because in it we feel fully ennobled and strengthened in our souls

Farewell! Farewell! Love's blessing
go with you. — — —

208. TO HIS MOTHER

Homburg, 23 May 1800

Dearest Mother,

I was almost quite ready for my departure when I received your letter. Though the news that was the cause of your anxieties had also made me somewhat doubtful about my decision. I inquired in Frankfurt whether the mail coach was still going and was told it was. I think that in a few weeks' time, at least as far as my journey is concerned, things will be no more difficult than they are now, and as anyway I probably wouldn't be able to move into my lodgings immediately I intend as a compromise to put off my departure until you send me word that my lodgings in Stuttgart are at least fit for me to move in when I arrive. As I am bound to lose some time for my own occupations, it is anyway vital that I begin working again as soon as possible once in Stuttgart.

For the rest, please don't go to any more trouble and cost over the furniture than you absolutely have to. It only recently occurred to me that sooner or later a suitable post abroad might turn up for me, and that seems to me a reason, along with other things, not to settle myself in for a proper long stay. The bookcase is just what I need. If I could always be as sure of my health as I am now, I think I could say I would be able to carry on my work as a writer uninterruptedly enough to live from it. But on the other hand it is no bad thing not to depend on it exclusively, and so I will simply resolve to take on the additional occupations that are open to me in Stuttgart. Having said that, when I listen to the judgments of men and friends on me and what I do, I can't help asking sometimes, in all humility (though it could easily be misinterpreted), why I have to make shift in this way in the workaday world. But so long as I see no other path open to me I'll consider the one I must take the allotted one and adapt to it as best I can.

A few days ago something happened that will give you as much joy as it gave me. A merchant from Frankfurt, whom I saw just once when I was there, has without saying why made me the present of a book which is more than a mere courtesy as its value cannot be much less than 100 fl. I shall pay this worthy man a visit before long and thank him as he deserves.

Could you be so kind and write to Landauer, asking him to send me 6 carolins via Herr Kling or whoever else he prefers?* I wouldn't put you to this bother if I didn't need your credit, and as you will presumably be writing to Landauer anyway I thought it better than writing to him directly. The money is only in case of need.

I wish you could be at peace with me at last. It hurts me more than I can say always to be causing you trouble and anxiety, especially as simply being so far away means you cannot wholly share the little bit of recognition I have so far received in the world, and so have to remain almost without recompense.

I hope that this time things will not go too badly in our parts. All my love to my dear sister and to all!

I'm in a hurry because the post's going.

Ever and from my heart,

your grateful son,

Hölderlin

* I'll write to him myself too.

STUTTGART, HAUPTWIL, NÜRTINGEN, BORDEAUX, HOMBURG, 1800–1806

209. TO HIS MOTHER

[Stuttgart, end of June 1800]

Dearest Mother,

Thank you very much for your kind letter and the good wishes it contains. I will endeavor to do everything on my part to make myself worthy of a rapid and lasting fulfillment of them.

You will not believe with what feelings of gratitude and respect toward my loved ones I made my way here. The sympathy and encouragement of loyal, well-meaning souls is in the stage of life I am at now a greater gift than anything one might otherwise have cause to appreciate.

My lodgings and the welcome I received in my friend's house were all I could wish for.

Altogether my old acquaintances have been so well disposed toward me that I have every hope of living here in peace and quiet for a time and of being able to do my day's work with less interruption than hitherto.

I consider it a piece of luck already to have had a respectable and pleasing offer of giving lessons in philosophy to a young man who works at the Chancellery, for which I shall be paid one carolin a month.

Otherwise I have had to spend a certain amount to get myself fully established in my living arrangements here. In particular I have reluctantly decided to order myself a desk that also serves as a chest of drawers that, as a decent piece of furniture, did seem necessary—Landauer advised it too—because I can't very well maintain order among my papers on the little table, and, as you'll see yourself, can't keep my clothes and linen etc. in the trunk all the time without inconvenience either.

I don't need to pay for the desk immediately, so you won't be bothered with any new expenses for the moment. But if it were possible to help me out with a few carolins more sometime and so secure my position completely I should accept it with heartfelt thanks and probably not pester you again, dearest Mother, for another year. Have patience with me now above all! I shall not be found wanting for industry and good courage and the proper degree of thriftiness, not now or ever.

It really saddens me that for the moment I always have to take more than I can give, when I should like to be nothing but a source of joy to others and especially my family.

Give all my love to my dear sister. Recently I began a little poem to her as I was going along: I'll send it her soon if it can give her a moment's pleasure. The Landauers send you and Rike their respects. It is still my hope that we'll have peace shortly and be freed of the unrest of war.

I have found quite a quantity of clean linen in my trunk, so you mustn't be surprised if you find the dirty washing short of this and that. Please could you mend the trousers and have the short ones dyed. In my next letter I'll let you know how many shirts and so on I still have here, so that you can see what's missing.

Give the dear children a kiss in my name.

Ever your grateful son,

Hölderlin

The bookcase & curtain have turned out exactly as I wished. I've received all my things safely.

210. TO HIS MOTHER

[Stuttgart, after 15 July 1800]

Dearest Mother,

Just a few words to thank you with all my heart and above all to assure you that a reminder from you will never again meet with an oversensitive reception, as was sometimes the case in the past.

As my mother you are after all my natural and eternal friend, and what is more venerable and beneficent to the heart than when a loyal disposition such as yours assumes on our behalf the worries and unavoidable difficulties of life.

Only believe that when I looked at you sometimes without saying a word and noticed the age coming into the face I so often see before my eyes, I thought in my heart, that is how one person sacrifices herself to another, & yes, you have devoted to me in particular much love and much of your strength that has been used up in anxiousness and efforts for me. And if I rarely say anything of this sort to you it's only because I prefer to keep such thoughts to myself in order, if possible, to manifest them in a life that is worthy of you.—

Now for a time you can, I hope, stop worrying about my needs. I have a few carolins due to me from my publisher, and so along with what you have kindly sent it will be possible for me to pay for the desk and manage the housekeeping for a little while. I've also received a new request for some lessons from the registrar Gutscher whom I got to know in Rastatt.

Registrar Frisch is probably intending to pay me every quarter, for I haven't received anything from him yet, but I know I can count on his generosity whatever the case.

The letter from Karl is addressed specifically to you and I beg your forgiveness for again forgetting to send it last time. I had too much to do at the time.

My love to all!

As soon as my affairs permit I'll take the liberty of making you a visit.

Your

loyal son

Hölderlin

211. TO HIS MOTHER

[Stuttgart, late July 1800]

Dearest Mother,

As at the moment I am very busy trying to get a few things finished before my visit to Reutlingen you will have to make do with just a few words this time. My fondest thanks for your kind letters! Yesterday I also received the last one you wrote to me in Homburg.

When I think how much stronger and better I feel since moving here and how my present situation daily takes on a form more certainly suited to my vocation and to making a living, I feel a contentment and calm I have long lacked, and I hope it will remain that way and that this condition will maintain in me a steady and cheerful thankfulness toward my dear family and my friends. I now have three offers to give lessons, all very agreeable.

My spare time I spend in good and sympathetic society, and my true occupation, as it seems to me, is now also coming from the heart more easily and purely.

Our good Karl, excellent man that he is, will surely not have to remain in uncertainty about his situation much longer.

[*Is glad that his mother has not recently been alarmed by any military presence in Nürtingen. He hopes that in general it will pass over fairly lightly for people in those parts.*] There is much talk of an imminent and proper peace. [*He intends to spend Sunday night at his mother's. Landauer will come with him.*]

Your

grateful and loyal son

Hölderlin

212. TO HIS BROTHER

[Stuttgart, ~ August 1800]

Dearest Karl,

Bookkeeper Frisch has so far not returned home from the Chancellery; but I should still be able to ask him after supper and then write you a reply before the courier goes.

I think that with so many opportunities for a decent position you cannot fail to find one.

Have you quite recovered now? Be so kind as to tell me a bit about how you are in your next letter.

In this fine and splendid time, and given the peace and freedom I now enjoy, I would be able to say that I am truly alive were it not for the old sufferings that still,

213. TO HIS SISTER

[Stuttgart, ~ September 1800]

Dearest sister,

I don't seem to be keeping the promise I gave you very conscientiously. But if it had been possible I should certainly have written at least once a week since then. The bad malady-ridden year I've now got through has made me rather slower in my work, and I often have to spend many a good hour thinking things over in an idling sort of way, so cannot afford to be interrupted more often than necessity demands. And because of the novelty of my situation necessity has made itself felt more often than will be the case in future. Also I am gradually feeling more strength again to do what out of love and duty I labor and work on all day long, and so in future can more easily and more frequently find an hour to give up to you.

That you too feel better is one reason why I am more in spirits than usual.

That your heart in its loss begins to feel stronger now *you* have grown stronger again is something I can well understand, dearest Rike.

Only live as peacefully as you can, and bring to mind all that you still have in as favorable and modest a light as possible, and don't let yourself be put off by the fortuitous and rapidly passing moments of sadness that each day holds. You can see yourself how much we mean to one another, for example, and yet if we saw each other every day there would be times now and then when we did not quite get on. So it is with everything. The good things in life often seem unpalatable for the simple reason that they often have, as they must, a rough shell, but because of it we are able to have the kernel in the end.

Give my love to our dear mother; Karl visited me recently before leaving for his new post, which really does seem to be an advantageous one, and he was full of praise and gratitude for the kindness with which she had helped him out of his difficulties. We, her sons, are her great debtors.

Give my love to your dear children. And especially to our esteemed grandmother and, if they are still with you, our other honored relatives.

You can see, dear Rike, that I am pressed for time again.

Here is my dirty linen, and I take the liberty of asking for a little coffee.

Your loyal brother,

H.

214. TO THE DUKE OF WÜRTTEMBERG

Stuttgart, . . . September 1800

[The stipendiary Mag. Hölderlin humbly begs authorization to reside here for some time as a tutor. Having been given permission by the Duke to remain abroad as a tutor since 1794, he has now returned to his own country on account of continual ill health. He has recovered to a certain extent and intends to stay with his friend Landauer as the educator of his children.]

FROM KARL PHILIPP CONZ

Ludwigsburg, 4 October 1800

[*On the second part of* Hyperion *which he has just received from the bookbinder's and read.*]

215. TO HIS SISTER

[Stuttgart, late October 1800]

Dear Rike,

I am prevented from coming tomorrow; but hope that makes it all the more likely I'll see you and the family the Sunday after next.

The beautiful autumn we're having is doing my health a great deal of good and I feel renewed and alive in the world, and gradually a new hope that I may do what I have set out to do among men a while longer revives and increases within me.

You too, dear Rike, are, I hear, firmer on God's ground again. We are bound to have many more fine days together, especially when the peace which, so a French officer told me today, is supposed to have been decided, has at last come.

We have heavy billeting here. At least you and the family are so far undisturbed by this situation.

My love to our mothers, and to your children.

Yours,

H.

216. TO HIS SISTER

[Stuttgart, mid-November 1800]

Dearest Rike,

I thank you and our good mothers again from my heart for the happy moments I spent amongst you. Such days of rest are our life's reward on earth.

Your letter moved me deeply; but a beneficent calm spread over me at the thought that I am bound together in this way with you, good sister, and the rest of the family, in what is truest and most holy. This maintains my heart, which in the end only too often loses its voice in too much loneliness and dwindles even from ourselves. And what is all wisdom without this childlike voice of piety within us?

I'll make the visit to your friend tomorrow. Today I'm a bit too tired.

May I advise you to go out often into the open this fine autumn, and recover peace and health beneath the lovely blue sky?

I know from my own experience how much this helps, and you will not want for company.

Your dear children are a good for me. How much more so they must be for you. Rarely does one find such happily born and well brought up creatures, & you know yourself what a beautiful and noble purpose it is to govern such a richness and succor their natural growth.

Give them my love, and to our esteemed mothers.

Your loyal brother,

H.

FROM JOHANN BERNHARD VERMEHREN

Jena, 28 November 1800

Your humanism, which finds expression with great *liveliness* at every point in your work, makes me hope for forgiveness if, perhaps quite unknown to you as I am, I turn to you directly, in all candor, in the hope of seeing your kindness fulfill a desire that lies very close to my heart. There is a deep sorrow on the German Parnassus that *Voß* and *Schiller* have ceased to publish their almanacs.—From the sweet lips of one of the nine sisters I received in a blissful dream the task of transforming this sorrow, as far as it is in my powers, into joy.—In accordance with this task, which I shall endeavor to carry out with all conscientiousness, you can be certain that it cannot in any wise be my intention to swell the countless numbers of almanacs with a new one that did not surpass the rest in its inner purport. My desire and goal is to create a collection of poems that wound together in a single beautiful garland will bestow eternally flowering laurels on our German genius and bear the stamp of immortality on them; but how shall I elevate this desire into a deed, how shall I reach this goal if I do not boldly turn to the established and proven men who are alone capable of setting the crown on my undertaking?—Seen from *this* point of view, you will forgive me my humble request that you honor me with a few contributions from *your* hand. And if I should only have the good fortune of being able to place the name *Hölderlin* under *one* poem, my heart would overflow with gratitude toward you, and the Muses would bow down to you tenderly because you had brought the offerings dedicated to them closer to divine perfection.—That I am inviting you into a company that is not unworthy of you may be shown by the names: *Goethe, Schiller, Voß, Matthisson, Kosegarten, Klopstock, Sophie Mereau,* who have made firm promises to contribute. I could name for you a whole series of poets that Germany counts among its best, but what is the need, since you are not accustomed to act under the impulse of others but from your *own*?—If I might count on contributions from your kind self, you would oblige me greatly by informing me of it in a few words at your earliest convenience.—If you permit it, I shall then remind you in February or March of your amiable promise because I need to have the manuscript settled by the end of March, as the almanac is due to come out for 1802. Most respectfully I sign myself

your humble servant

Johann Bernhard Vermehren

217. TO GOTTLIEB ERNST AUGUST MEHMEL

[Stuttgart, November/December 1800]

Please accept my warmest thanks, esteemed Sir, for the sincere efforts with which you are concerned to uphold a better literature, and rest assured that I will take up your kind invitation with the best energies I have.

The rules I commit myself to in so doing correspond so purely and exactly with my own thoughts that I have every reason to hope it will not be too hard for me to obey them. I believe I have grasped their spirit and on the whole have nothing to add to them. If you want to give me a position involving the judgment of poetical works I think I will perhaps be suitable as for several years now my reflections and observations have been almost exclusively devoted to this subject.

The intense study of the Greeks has helped me in this and served instead of the company of friends to save me from becoming too sure of myself or too uncertain in the solitude of my meditations. And the results I have got from this study are rather different from others I am aware of. As you know, there has often been a complete failure to recognize the strictness with which the ancient writers distinguished between the different kinds of poetry, or where this has been acknowledged it is only the externals that have been attended to, and in general their art has been held to be a nicely calculated amusement rather than a sacred propriety with which they *had* to proceed in dealings with the gods. What was most spiritual, for them, had also to be supremely *characteristic*. And likewise its *representation*. Thus the formal strictness and precision of their poetic works, thus the noble forcefulness with which they observed this strictness in subordinate genres, and thus the tact with which they avoided the main characteristic traits in higher genres, precisely because the supremely characteristic contains nothing foreign to it, nothing extraneous, and therefore no trace of coercion. So they presented the divine in human form, but always avoiding actual human proportions; quite naturally, because poetry, which in its whole nature, in its inspiration as in its modesty and sobriety, is a joyous service rendered unto the gods, was never to make men into gods or gods into men, never to commit impure *idolatry*, but only to bring the gods and humankind closer together. Tragedy shows this *per contrarium*. God and man appear one, then comes a fate that arouses every element of humility and pride in man and in the end leaves behind as human property adoration of the gods on the one hand and a purified soul on the other. It is according to these aesthetic convictions, which follow on from your pronouncements and the words *want, ought* and *can* and are probably timely, that I would seek to criticize works of poetry, with unshakeable fairness and attentiveness and sparing as far as possible the writer's person, also bearing in mind,

218. TO HIS SISTER

[Stuttgart, Autumn 1800]

My dear Rike,

I will write only what is absolutely necessary again. If it suits you, my dears, I'll perhaps come and see you later in the week, for a few hours at least, and talk with you at greater length.

Landauer seems very much to want me to stay and has taken steps to find me perhaps a few more lessons, making roughly 3 louis d'or a month. Whether I'll manage as well on that as we all hope is then the question. I've heard nothing from Switzerland as yet. The advice of my family, in so far as it can be impartial and not seek counsel from the heart, will be welcome to me, because I should like to do what is to be done in total agreement. Heaven knows that all I ask is what is *necessary*, and that to necessity I am ready to submit in all its forms. But once, as far as possible, we've recognized what this is, we want to be as confident and joyful in our minds as we can, in this as in all other cases.

Only let faith, hope and charity never fade from my heart, and I will go wherever I must and at the last am sure to say: I have lived! And if it is not pride or delusion, I think I can say that little by little, through the ordeals of my life, I have become more solid and stronger in those respects.

Mrs. Landauer sends her regards. She says the bonnets will probably not cost as much as all that.

My love to everybody.

Your loyal brother,

Friz

219. TO HIS SISTER

[Stuttgart, beginning of December 1800]

[Writes that he is in negotiations with a family in Switzerland about a post as house tutor. Judging by the son of the family, whose acquaintance he had made a few days ago, they must be good and and cultivated people. He already knows roughly where the place is situated and it suits him very well. The salary is to be 30 louis. In a few weeks' time the matter will be settled.]

220. TO HIS SISTER

[Stuttgart, 11 December 1800]

Dear Rike,

It was wrong of me not to announce the unexpected visitor, and I apologize to you and to him. But the day I should have done it, last Saturday, was so full of happenings that had you seen me and known what was going on in my head you would have found the distractedness which, to be honest, made me quite forget, fairly natural.

My friends pressed me almost unmercifully to stay, various good teaching opportunities were offered me the same day, and besides all this, amid all the errands I had to do, and in inner and outer turmoil, I was to give a final answer to the stranger, who I really became fond of and with whom I then had so much to talk about concerning him and his family and myself and my future situation. I confess, Rike, that I find it easier and easier to reconcile my decision with the feelings of my heart, however much it went against them at first. I have in

me such a deep and urgent need of peace and quiet—more than you
can guess, or than I want you to. And if I can find this in my future
employment I shall be keeping my heart all the fuller in warmth and
loyalty toward my relatives and friends, whom I shall never forget.
I cannot bear the thought that I too, like so many others, in the
critical period of life when even more than in our youth a numbing
restlessness gathers round our inward being, that I, to survive, should
become so cold and unfeeling and withdrawn. And often I really do
feel like ice, and inevitably must if I don't find some quieter and more
restful place where everything that affects me touches me less nearly,
and precisely for that reason upsets me less. For me and, as I believe,
for you and the rest of the family too, this is the main argument, and
much else being equal it has determined my decision. Of course there
is a lot more to be said. I'll explain myself as much as you like when
we see one another.—We shall always have each other, my dear sister,
and all my family and friends close to my heart. I should very much
like to be able to speak to Karl before I go. Write to him urgently. I
haven't had a proper talk with him for a long time. And it would go
very much against my heart to have to say goodbye to him in writing.
Tell him I'd be pleased if he can find time to come.

I intend to spend at least part of Christmas with you and our
dear mother, and to set off from Nürtingen, but dispatching my
luggage, or at least the main things I'll need, from here, if mother has
no objection. I have very little more expenditure to make here. A pair
of boots I think I need, that's all. If our dear mother can come up with
a few louis d'or for the journey I'd prefer that to borrowing them here.
I have been promised that the traveling expenses will be reimbursed,
and probably generously enough to allow me to return whatever money
I take with me and use the rest to cover any expenses for a while.
Chiefly because of my lessons I'll stay on here until the holidays.—I'll
write again by the next post, and not in such a rush as today. Forgive
me the haste. Today is Landauer's birthday, and that has meant that I've
been interrupted on and off the whole morning and am now expected
at table. In Landauer you will find the man to be a brother to you in
my place while I'm away. Believe me, what we mean to one another
and what all our dear ones mean to me is unalterable.

Yours,

Hölderlin

FROM KARL PHILIPP CONZ

Ludwigsburg, 14 December 1800

[Has, according to H.'s wishes, written some weeks ago via Kerner to Reinhard in Berne about a position as house tutor he is looking for. The reply has now arrived. R. indicates a tutoring position available in Trogen, in the canton of Appenzell, in the house of a wealthy manufacturer whose wife is a daughter of Salomon Geßner's.—His excellent poem (Archipelagus) he will have received back via Haug.]

221. TO HIS SISTER

[Stuttgart, ~ 18 December 1800]

My dear Rike,

I dislike it myself that I have now kept you waiting for a letter several times. When I sent my washing, packing my bags really did prevent me from writing, and yesterday I had just gone out when our Nürtingen friends came to visit, and afterward for all my enquiring I couldn't find them anywhere to pass on at least a few words for you.

For the holidays I'll be sure to come. Only I can't say exactly when as I still have a few things to sort out before I leave. On the persistent entreaties of my friends I've promised to come back here for at least a day's visit afterward.

The money our kind mother sent me arrived at just the right moment. I have a few more earnings to come in, but also one or two necessary items of expenditure, and I didn't know whether the earnings would be sufficient. So I have all I need for my departure which as you can imagine is a great benefit. And by the way I'll spend not a penny of it more than I have to. Thank her on my behalf, from the bottom of my heart.

As for the bill for board and lodging I'll have a word with Landauer so that if need be that payment can be put off until Easter.

Luckily there is so much going on in my head at the moment that I am not so affected by the separation from my friends here. A few quiet days with you, dearest ones, will be a blessing for me as I set off on my travels for the third time.

You can see for yourself, Rike, that my future situation is the happiest thing that could happen to me for the time being.

And I should be able to visit you every year. In haste.

Yours

Hölderlin

FROM ANTON VON GONZENBACH

Hauptwil, 18 December 1800

[*Offers him the position tutoring his younger daughters that H. himself has already told his son Emanuel he wishes to accept.*]

222. TO HIS MOTHER

[Stuttgart, just before Christmas 1800]

[*He has changed his plans, is coming to Nürtingen, but to return to Stuttgart and travel on from there a few days later with his things by mail coach.—He encloses the letter from Hauptwil he has just received today.*]

223. TO HIS BROTHER

[Nürtingen, late December 1800/early January 1801]

My dear Karl,

I got your letter on the way here from Stuttgart. Landauer sent it on after me and so it reached me among the various thoughts provoked by leaving Stuttgart and being on the open road with the open world around me. I felt the unending vitality that full of loving trust conducts us through all periods of our existence, sometimes quietly urging, sometimes in its full affirming force, I felt this spirit of youth and wisdom once again just as it must manifest itself if we are to recognize it, and the good and loyal words you wrote to wish me goodbye only served to make this mood yet purer and finer. How much I said to you in reply there and then in my mind as I went on my way. Yes, there is no reason not to say it, I was full of a great sense of comfort for both of us, and this voice of our guardian spirit is still fresh in my mind.

I will write to you again from Stuttgart. I intend to spend a few more days there. Till then make do with these hastily written words and receive into your heart as we part the silent and unutterable joy of *my* heart—and let it endure until it is no longer the solitary joy of a friend and brother but—but what, you ask?

This, dear Karl, that our time is at hand, that the peace that is forming *now* will bring us what peace and only peace could bring; for it will bring much that many hope for, but it will also bring what few intimate.

Not that any one form, any one opinion or assertion will triumph, I don't think that has much to do with what peace will give us. What I mean is that selfishness in all its guises will give way to the holy rule of love and kindness, a common spirit will settle over every last thing, and in such a climate, blessed with this new peace, the German heart will open for the first time and silently as the growth of nature unfold its hidden ramifying powers, this is what I see and believe, and this is what more than anything lets me look forward with good spirits into the second half of my life.—So continue to be glad in your innocent and modest way of life, my good Karl. You are preserved, saved up; the storm has passed over you, be glad that you heard it from a distance in a place of safety and have kept your soul pure and loving and fearless for the better times that will come, and believe me, on your safe path you will attain the higher purpose in life that is meant for you. You can no more forget it than I can forget you. Let us write often, and try to visit one another as often as possible too. After all I'm only three days' journey away from the family. And even if it were further, Karl, you know how strongly love and faith bind us together.

Ever yours,

Friz

224. TO HIS FAMILY

[Stuttgart, beginning of January 1801]

Not a word of all that you said to me in the goodness of your loyal hearts, my dear ones, shall be in vain, and none of the kindnesses your love has shown me.

I have arrived here safely, a bit tired, as always happens when the heart is full and stirred and our thoughts are working more busily and we nevertheless have to pursue our ordinary course here on earth. But if only I could always walk on so between heaven and earth for the rest of my life, equal in humility and faith, and earn that way the sweet sleep and rest we hope for.

From now on I will never let discontent gain the upper hand within me. But pride too shall bend before what is above and around us. It is certain, I cannot believe it to be otherwise, if I do what I have to do I too shall fulfill my purpose in life on this earth as far as humanly possible and be content yet despite the ordeals of my youth.

I hope to be in as good health at the end of the coming journey as I am now. Circumstances oblige me to stop here until Saturday.

Landauer, good friend that he is, intends to accompany me with my other friends as far as Tübingen, which will give me a good start for the rest of the journey. He says you can arrange to have the pieces of furniture collected here whenever you like, straightaway or later.

If he finds a good buyer he says he will dispose of the writing table.

I shall probably be able to write once more before I leave. It is a real need for me, my dear family, to express to you, as often as I can, what is in my heart.

Believe me, my esteemed Mother, and you my dear, good sister and brother, the sincerity, the innocence, the purity of heart that I have experienced in each of you from boyhood, like a voice from the heavens, before I even knew what it was, and that I now recognize and honor as the ground of all that is good and true and godlike,—this, this is what would remain unforgettable to me in you, even if I were ever able to forget all the other kindnesses your hearts have blessed me with.

Give my love to all my friends.

Yours,

Hölderlin

225. TO ANTON VON GONZENBACH

[Stuttgart, ~ 6 January 1801]

Allow me, before I can do it in person, to express my sincere thanks for your kind offer of a situation and a function that will be so good and valuable for me. I am bound to respect all you have done to oblige me; I for my part can only promise you good will and attentiveness toward what will be my duties in your house, together with candor and loyalty. And when you say that you attach importance to what it will be my job to achieve, you will certainly also be aware how much value and goodness there is for me in living in the sphere of a family who knows how to be content with itself and exercises daily the most difficult and loveliest of virtues, that of being happy. Even if I were only an observer among you, such an image of peace would be enough for me. I beg you not to take these words as idly spoken.

As in your kindness you have confidence in my capacities as a tutor in general I expect that the particular things I shall have to take account of can wait until we meet and talk.

I hope to set off on   January.

Be so kind as to offer my respects to your esteemed family. I thank your son again and will no doubt often have cause to thank him for having made the separation from my friends and family at home easier by his presence and courtesy and for rendering it so desirable for me to earn the chance to live among a family that he represents so well. In loyalty and truth I am

your obliged

M. Hölderlin

226. TO HIS SISTER

[Stuttgart, ~ 9 January 1801]

My dear Rike,

One last time then from here.

I am ready for my journey. Everything is packed and in order. Yesterday I wrote to Hauptwil, and my only concern is not to let my friends notice any traces of sadness in me.

I shall only be able to enjoy your dear unforgettable words properly once I have the peace and quiet of Hauptwil.

I'll write from Constance, even if only a few words, just so that you will know I'm safe. We two understand each other so well that even the simplest and briefest of words say what is needed and replace the best and deepest utterance of our loyalty to one another.

You know that one is often calm and quiet even though the heart is full. That is how it is with me now. I could not find words for all that I should be saying to you every day and hour, my dearest, and so it is better for me to give up the attempt and right up until the end keep to this dry and unmomentous way of saying goodbye.

Take good care of yourselves, and remain content and joyful in spirit, in the spirit that even in the most painful hours of parting makes us feel entire the happiness of our kindred hearts.

The clear sky can also serve us as a reminder of each other, if things stay as they are, and be a comfort to us. I shall not try now to express my thanks for all that you are to me and all you have done for me but preserve it in my soul, alive and true.

Goodbye, sister and friend. Kiss your children for me. Have your joy in them as I do too. And let our dear mother and our good brother, since I am far away and your heart is rich and abundant enough, partake in my name of the love that sweetens and lightens their life and yours and gives us strength for all the good in life.

Yours ever,

Friz

227. TO HIS FAMILY

Constance, Wednesday evening [14 January 1801]

[It is a little over a week since he said goodbye to them.—He was accompanied by his friends as far as Tübingen. From there he went most of the way on foot—via Ebingen and then the high road to

Sigmaringen—a shorter way than via Schaffhausen. From there he rode to the lake in a carriage in 12 hrs., where he was ferried across and then went on to Constance in 2 hrs.—He'll arrive in Hauptwil tomorrow (5 hrs. from Constance).]

FROM SIEGFRIED SCHMID

Friedberg, 15 January 1801

[Has finished his drama not long ago (the earlier one he sent to Berlin he has no news of at all) and is going to have it printed at his own expense. It will be ready in 4 weeks. But now he is dreading the misery of reviews, especially from the Literatur-Zeitung *in Jena since Schlegel's departure. Asks whether H. would not be willing to take on a review of the play, which he would send him immediately. Schmid has a friend through whom it could be sent to Jena.]* Or if you didn't want to take this task on yourself perhaps you are in contact with Huber and could get him to do it. He could probably be expected to produce a thorough assessment. *[He hopes that a review will appear in time for the fair.]*

FROM JOHANN GOTTLIEB SÜSKIND

Tübingen, 22 January 1801

Sooner, my dear friend, than you might have been expecting I can fulfill your wish that I send you the review of your *Hyperion*. It has just appeared, and as our friend Schoell has offered to look after any errands for you I'm taking this opportunity and dispatching it to you at once. You will probably be content with it. The just and humane cast of mind of its author seems to me unmistakeable, you don't need to send it back to me, keep it as your own property.—

    [Calls himself a friend of H.'s youth & saw him just before he left.]

228. TO HIS MOTHER

Hauptwil, near Constance, 24 January 1801

Dear Mother,

Please accept the good news I am able to give you of my situation here as a first form of thanks for all the kind and loyal care you have shown me, especially during the time I spent at home.

I can really say, and I have been convinced of this throughout the 10 days I have been here, that the large family I am living with consists of people among whom one can only live in contentment, with the soul at rest—there is so much cheerful innocence among the children and such common sense, such fine goodness, among the older members. The master of the house in particular I hold to be a good and admirable man who seems especially knowledgeable and wide in experience for someone of his class, while preserving a simplicity that interests me greatly. He brings to bear a quiet, undemanding, but very real presence on his children (of whom the oldest is married and also lives in the house).

On this occasion I won't go into any further descriptions; suffice it to say that as things are I am contented and my work is on a good footing and going well, and I hope that in years to come people will be as contented with me as they are now, and you, who are dearest to me, will always hear good report of me and one day be able to stop worrying about me at last. I am also in the best of health. How pleased I shall be to hear something from you again soon and feel the nearness of your love. You are so good to me. I am very glad that last year I lived not far from you all for a proper length of time. I had become so estranged from other people and with you I felt once again, and perhaps for the first time with any clarity, that with you, for as long as I live, there remains a refuge for my heart and a lasting joy that no one can take from me. Next time I will write to my dear sister and to Karl separately. The letter I sent from Constance you will probably have received by now. I shall be able to settle at least part of what I owe you with my next letter. Herr Gonzenbach has already instructed me to name my traveling expenses, and as soon as the opportunity arises I shall present him with what I have worked out.

I am obliged to end here. I am expected and the letter must be off by this evening.

Maintain your love for me, dear Mother, and make the most of the peaceful times that will now come. And it is proper for you to spend the years of maturity you now enjoy more in pleasure and calm and serenity than you have done till now. You have done so much for us! And you know yourself that not everyone is blessed in having such a mother, such a daughter and such grandchildren before her eyes every day.

And your absent sons are devoted enough to you to live in such a way as withstands your strictest judgment.

Give my regards to my venerable grandmother.

Ever your loyal son,

Hölderlin

My address is: c/o Herr Anton Gonzenbach in Hauptwil, near Constance.

I have successfully delivered Fräulein Schwab's letter. They had fond memories of her there.

FROM SIEGFRIED SCHMID

Friedberg, near Frankfurt am Main, 3 February 1801

Those were once again exquisite words full of spirit, welling out of the holy depths where eternally youthful life stirs,—and life is what they have found, quivering still and re-echoing with them.

More soon, when I send you the poem. It needs to be printed quickly, among other things because of the business of the professorship. An acquaintance of mine here said: let's print it and share out the costs. In order to clutch something back from the claws of the bookseller, we have set up a subscription among our friends. I am of course not expecting you to recruit subscribers or anything like that; but I am enclosing a few notices so that if you wanted to make any of your acquaintances from your parts aware of it, they could get hold of copies from my brother in Basel at the subscription price. My brother's address is: Ludwig Schmid, c/o Herr Fürstenberger and son.

Think of those far from you when you look cheerfully on the glaciers in your region and the seven peaks in the Toggenburg. I came through that region as a soldier and often looked up at them with feelings of wonder.

Yours,

S. S.

229. TO CHRISTIAN LANDAUER

[Hauptwil, February 1801]

My dear Landauer,

I wanted to leave writing to you until I had collected myself here and looked around a bit, and I think I can say that I hope to hold my own in the present situation.

The contact with you and the other friends has brought me real gains, something I always lacked and will try to make the most of. With you I learned for the first time a proper peace, the peace that comes from relying on the ground of people's hearts after having got to know them by genuine signs. And then one is also more firmly and truly attached to life and to those that matter.

I can make good use of this with the people I'm living among now. They are, in my coolest judgment, exactly what I hoped for, the kind of well-founded people who take an interest in things outside their sphere just to the degree that their hearts are not weakened by it and their sympathy and sociableness remain unforced and true.

That is precisely the reason I will never forget you all, and during the best hours I spend in company here I am reminded of you.

Really I should like to send each of you a personal greeting and say to each how true it is that a lovely echo of our time together in Stuttgart stays with me, and particularly during the journey was my accompaniment morning and evening.

I am still greatly struck by the Alps which are a few hours distant from here, nothing has ever made such an impression on me before. I stand before them and they are like a wondrous legend from the heroic youth of our mother earth and remind me of the old creative chaos as they look down in their calm and above their snow in the brighter blue the sun and the stars shine down day and night.

And now, at the beginning of spring, you can well imagine the good all the elements are doing me and how I feed my eyes on the hills and streams and lakes round here, this being the first spring in three years I can enjoy with a free soul and open senses.

My dear friend, I have long harbored delusions that have been a burden to me and to others and a disgrace in the eyes of the Lord of life and my guardian spirit. I always thought that in order to live at peace with the world, to love other people and to look on the holiness of nature with true eyes, I had to submit, and in order to be something to anyone else give up my own freedom. At last I feel the truth: only where the strength is whole can love be. This truth has come upon me unawares in moments when I looked around me completely pure and free again. The more certain a person is in himself and the more collected in the best of his life, and the more easily he raises himself up out of subordinate moods into the true individual one again, the brighter and more encompassing his eye will be, and he will have a heart for everything that is easy and difficult and great and dear to him in the world.

I would of course have begun by speaking of the peace but the first pages of this letter were written I think a fortnight ago. What pleases me most about it is that with it the disproportionate role political alliances and misalliances have played is over and a good beginning has been made toward the simplicity that is proper to them. In the end it's true, the less people know and experience of the state, whatever form it takes, the freer they are.

It is everywhere a necessary evil to have compulsory laws and their executors. With the end of war and revolution I think that inner Boreas, the spirit of envy, will also cease, and let us hope a lovelier form of sociability than the merely solid and bourgeois will unfold!

Forgive me, dear Landauer, if I'm boring you going on like this in my thoughts. But to you I can surely speak as if I were speaking to myself.

Make sure you keep me in good remembrance with the ladies if you want to do me a service. You'll laugh at me, but I must thank you especially for the golden hours of music. The genial tones repose within me and will often stir again whenever I'm at peace with myself and it's quiet round about.

Remember me to all the friends. I think they know and feel that I'm true to them. With each in turn I hold conversations; no one that was dear to me has faded from my mind's eye. Goodbye.

Yours,

H.

FROM SIEGFRIED SCHMID

Friedberg, 22 February 1801

[*Sends him his poem:* The Heroine. *This seems to be the drama mentioned above. H. is to spell out his thoughts on it very soon.*] I am also very pleased that you want as far as possible to comply with the language of journalism.

230. TO HIS SISTER

Hauptwil, near St. Gallen, 23 February 1801

My dear sister,

I am writing to you and the rest of the dear family on the day when among us here all is full of the news of the negotiated peace, and knowing me as you do I do not need to tell you what my feelings are. And this morning, when the head of the household greeted me with the news, I hardly knew what to say. But the clear blue of the sky and the pure sunlight on the Alps close by were all the more welcome to my eyes at that moment since otherwise I should not have known where to look in my joy.

I think all will now be well in the world. Whether I consider the recent or the distant past, everything seems to be leading up to an exceptional period, days of beautiful humanity, days of certain, fearless goodness and ways of thinking that are lucid and holy and exalted and simple all at once.

This and the grandeur of nature in these parts wonderfully lifts and fills my soul. You would be as struck as I am by these shining eternal mountains, and if the God of glory has a throne on earth it is above these splendid peaks.

I can only stand there like a child and wonder and rejoice in silence when I'm out on the nearest hill and down from the ether come the heights stepping closer and closer into the friendly valley whose slopes are thick with the evergreen of fir woods and whose floor is seamed through with lakes and streams, & that's where I live, in a garden, where under my window willows and poplars stand by a clear water I love to listen to at night when all is quiet and beneath the serene starry sky I write and think.

You see, Rike, I look on my stay here as a man who has gone through a good deal in his youth and is now content and untroubled enough to give thanks from the bottom of his heart for what is there. And the more at peace I am, the more brightly and animatedly the memories of you dear ones far away quicken within me, and yes, I shall say it, since I feel it so vividly, should yet happier days be in store for me you and all we love will only be more unforgettable. In the meantime I shall rely on living with a good conscience and doing my duty; for the rest, let God decide. And if the only happiness the future held for me were to be able to see you and mother and our brother and your children again from time to time, and be a guest at your table, that would be enough.

That our mother in her kindness intends to dispense me once again from repaying what I owe her goes against our agreement. She must at least allow me to thank her in some other way than in these words, which come so easily.

Keep in good health and please persuade our dear mother and grandmother to go out for a walk in the country from time to time in the spring, so that it becomes a habit. I have great faith in this and believe it makes for a long life and strengthens the mind.

Give Karl my apologies for not having written yet. But he knows as well as I do that we are always close and belong to one another for ever. Still, all that is good and sacred must be celebrated, and for that reason our correspondence should never remain interrupted for too long. But then the letters to you are meant for him as well, as for all the dear family.

Goodbye, and write again soon.

Yours,

H.

FROM JOHANN BERNHARD VERMEHREN

Jena, 27 February 1801

[Inviting him to take part in his almanac, which he is editing because Schiller and Voß have abandoned theirs.—But he must ask to receive the contribution by the beginning of April.]

231. TO HIS BROTHER

[Hauptwil, ~ mid-March 1801]

My dear Karl,

I feel we no longer love one another as before and have not done for a long time, and this is my fault. *I was the first to introduce the cold tone.* At the beginning of my time in Homburg, do you remember the letters you wrote me then? But an unbelief in eternal love took hold of me. And I was to slip into the terrible superstitious error of believing in what is indeed a *sign* of the soul and of love, but if taken to be more than that is the death of them. Believe me when I tell you I struggled until I was almost dead with exhaustion to keep hold of the higher life in faith and in sight—I underwent sufferings that, *so it seems,* are more overwhelming than anything a man can withstand with all his force of endurance.—I mean every word of this.—And finally, my heart torn at from every side but still holding firm, I had to go and let my thoughts get caught up in bad doubts over a question whose answer is so straightforward when our minds are clear: what is more important, temporality or eternal life? Only too great a lack of esteem for all that has to be could have led me into an even greater error, which was, to a disproportionate degree and with a quite superstitious seriousness, to have regard for and attach importance to all things external, to everything that does not lie in the domain of the heart. But I carried on until I had learned the truth. And having learned it I tore myself from my mistakes to say this: that all is lost if unity and holy, general love are lost, which make the love of a brother so easy. There is only one quarrel in the world: what is more important, the whole or the particular? And whenever it is put to the test this quarrel cancels itself out in action, since the person who acts truly out of a sense of the whole is of his own accord more ordained to peace and more disposed to attend to the particular because his human sense, precisely what most belongs to him, becomes just as unlikely to let him fall into pure generality as into egoism or whatever you want to call it.

A Deo principium. Whoever understands this and keeps to it, by the life of life, he is free and strong and full of joy, and the opposite is always a chimera and as such melts into nothing.

So let that hold for us too in this renewal of friendship which is anything but empty ceremony or whim: *a Deo principium.*

I still think the way we used to, but now apply it more concretely. All is an infinite unity, but in this totality there is one supreme unifying *unity* that *in itself is not an I*, and this, to us, is God.

I speak as if I wanted to prove something to someone who did not believe, and my heart is always so full of the life of those who love what is holy. Tell me what this means. You can see into my heart. Is there *still* unbelief? Unbelief in a lovely understanding where one does speak, and with all the clarity that comes from joy, but where one takes the friendship of the other as a fact and rejoices in him in every syllable, but without being insistent? Yes, it is unbelief, but not in the other's heart, which belongs to the whole and so also to me. As if the two of us didn't have to love each other, just as we love something higher that in order to be expressed and honored needs two brothers and more, needs brothers and sisters, a whole world of human beings. Brother of mine! The good do not abandon one another. They cannot as long as they are good and the whole in which they are comprised is good. Only often the means are missing for the different parts to communicate, very often among us human beings the signs and words are still missing. And so you see we have to remind one another, make up for what has been neglected, by speaking, by speaking out to say what we are to each other and what for. The misuse of words, falsifying them or not keeping them, is very wrong, but so certainly is not using them enough. And with this letter I do not mean any more than that we should begin again, as if from the start. In the future, whenever we feel how cold our words are when we speak, the more we will try to put our souls and our loyalness to one another into them, the more all that is good will come to life within us. And then the moments when we finally succeed in coming out with something proper and right, when as brother to brother, as man to man, as human soul to human soul we are present in living witness to something sacred and joyful, those moments will be worth all our hopes and any measure of success.

Here in this innocence of life, here under the silver Alps, I shall at last breathe more easily and freely again. I am chiefly occupied in studying religion. You, with your youthful energy and solitude, with that glorious feeling on which, as on a rock, everything divine is founded, the feeling of carrying out your duty, you will also stand truly beside me. A single word spoken from the untrammeled soul is so much, and you know how much. Above all I ask you, you above all, to tell me your heart's opinion on anything that touches on the subject, and to listen to what I have to say to you as a brother so as to be able to say, with the authority only a brother can have: this or that was not for me. Firm faith, inviolable honesty and pure, free openness, let us live by them!

What would life be without flowers like these? But bound together in such truth, in a bond that reaches to the heavens, we also see with the eyes of a higher being, and in the clear element that the spirit receives and creates we move with much more lightness and power and find then our place in the world. And those who are not yet born, they will feel it in times to come too.

These golden hopes are still with me, my dear Karl, as they are also with you.

Goodbye. And write soon. You will feel a sense of joy already. I know, and you must know it too: in the coming years we shall mean a great deal to one another.

Your brother

Hölderlin

232. TO CHRISTIAN LANDAUER

[Hauptwil, toward the end of March 1801]

I have just received your second letter, my good and loyal friend, and in your gentle rebuke I feel keenly what you are to me and always will be.

I haven't yet worked out when the post goes from here. Altogether my head has been a bit confused over the last few weeks.

Oh you know it, you understand me perfectly when I say that the longer I have kept it from myself the more suddenly it comes over me, this, that I have a heart but can't see what for, have no one to talk to here, no one I can wholly open myself to.

Tell me, is it a blessing or a curse, this loneliness that is part of my nature and that, however carefully I seek out situations meant in every respect to help me out, I am all the more irresistibly driven back into?—If only I could spend a day with you all, reach you my hands.—My dear friend, if you go to Frankfurt, think of me. Will you? I hope I shall always be worthy of my friends.

Yours,

H.

FROM ANTON VON GONZENBACH

Hauptwil, 11 April 1801

You will recall, my greatly esteemed Sir—and friend—that both my son and I had spoken to you of two young boys from my *famille* who were to come and live with me and who were in fact the chief object of my tutoring plans—. As now, through unforeseen events, in all probability these boys' fate will be determined otherwise, and therefore the chief part of that on which my intentions bore falls away, you will not misconstrue me if in order not to put you in an awkward or disadvantageous situation I hereby inform you of this in good time, and with utmost courtesy beg you to be so good as to be guided by these circumstances and to take your measures accordingly; that is, as incommodes you the least, since my only wish is that the course you take should entirely suit your convenience in all respects.—I regret with all my heart that fate should be dividing us again so soon, but as the twists of the same do not lie in our power I hope you will not hold the necessity of doing this against me, but even from afar will honor me with the continuance of your estimable friendship, just as my own will remain devoted to you for as long as I live.—

With the sincere sentiments of unalterable respect,

Yours obediently,

v. Gonzenbach

233. TO AN UNKNOWN ADDRESSEE

[Nürtingen, perhaps April 1801]

I regretted, my honorable friend, not meeting you the other day, as I [. . .] you

FROM JOHANN BERNHARD VERMEHREN

Jena, 4 May 1801

[*Expresses his thanks for the poems he has received from Höld.*]—Of the elegies only the first 4 will go into the almanac; the rest will follow as a continuation in next year's. . . . I have no links with Tieck. But as you would like to see the *Archipelago* in his *Poetic Journal* I will find out via Fr. Schlegel, with whom I am in close contact, whether it might fit with his intentions to include longer poems by unassociated contributors.—[*Asks him for contributions to his almanac in future also.*] Always crown my work the way you have crowned it this time!

FROM SIEGFRIED SCHMID

Friedberg, 8 May 1801

I have been blessed by more of the fine hours occasioned by the outpourings into a fraternal soul of your high anger and deepest love than usual lately, and they came in a period when I needed them more than otherwise, (given the delicatesse in friendship of the children of this world, to say this is probably very offensive.)

Truly your galvanizing tones, your invisible, holy music plucked me every time out of a fatal indolence in which for some while I have been vegetating as peacefully as a rich farmer who has come to the conclusion that in all the world he needs to worry about nothing more than finding the most comfortable spot where in summer a cool breeze will blow over him and in winter he can be sure of avoiding it. I let everything take its course, and troubled myself little about the secret spirit of the world and what it might want to make known through me. Of course I sometimes took exception to myself in this state, and condemned myself and despaired as to whether the holy spirit of the universe had ever dwelt in me; or took it to have left me, and thought then to complete this annihilation myself. Then came, as I said, your marvelous gifts, and refreshed me like blossoms and fruits of the Orient in this midnight waste.

Yes, we shall stay true to one another, dearest friend, we shall recognize one another whatever shape we appear in: for we met in the highest regions and for that reason we can see one another—ever the same—even in the most banal, where a thick veil shrouds us from the masses such that those who are so visible to their kin are utterly invisible to them.

You end your lovely last letter in holy fervor; but seem to lament that such passions are little more than a game. But are they really anything else, and for those initiated into the ways of art should they ever be anything at all different? Is that not a chief criterion here, and are they not, the sublime artists, precisely because of this privilege, comparable to the great gods? They are swept along in their images by that high passion that you got into for the sake of what is supreme, and by all passions, like no one else on earth, and yet they are not subjugated by them, it was—just a game. The supreme position to be in! Human divinity!

The professorship has still not been decided. It tempts me now no more than it did before. I've spoken with Sinclair several times. He must understand *his* obstinate metaphysics of art better than I do! Good for him, if he's satisfied with it. And that does seem to be the case.

Adieu! Beloved friend. Don't be put off by my cold letter. I cannot write anything else for now.

Yours,

Siegfr. Schmid

FROM CHARLOTTE VON KALB

Mainz, 15 May [1801]

It's a year now I've been in this region—on the Neckar & Rhein I lived in Wimpfen near *Heilbronn*—Heidelberg, *Offenbach*, all places you have been to ——— At the beginning of *June* I'm going to *Wiesbaden*.—In July I shall prob. be in Mannheim—later in the autumn in all likelihood back in Franconia.—If a journey brings you to these parts I want at least to let you know that I am here.—To write you a letter full of deep thoughts would be impossible after such long separation & silence.—We knew one another—as far as time & opportunity & our development allowed it—Restless—thinking beings become in 6 years something quite different so quick are the changes—outward ones in younger years—just as quick the changes in judgment, thinking & sentiment in later more mature years.—I have also developed in heart & soul, only nowadays the pressures of fate have made me more liberated.—. No word more on that—It is a curious thing that with purest egotism the soul finally says to itself—you have nothing more to lose—but unfortunately you have plenty more to suffer!—Last autumn I read your *novel*—and with great enjoyment.—I shall go back to it soon.—Send me a reply soon, perhaps I'll be able to put a *more significant* question to you. As I could be away on travels address your letter or rather put it in an envelope for *Mademoiselle Remy*, c/o Fr. v. *Kalb* in Mainz, to be handed to Herr Clausius in the Große Bleiche district. That's the best way to keep the letter safe for me.—

With thoughts & sentiments and the desire to hear something of how you are & what you are doing—

Ch. v Kalb née

M. v. Ostheim

234. TO FRIEDRICH SCHILLER

Nürtingen near Stuttgart, 2 June 1801

For a long time I have held hopes of finding the occasion to remind you of my existence again, honored Sir, and I just wanted to bring to completion the work on some papers before showing them to you. You must almost have given me up, and I thought it would be not unpleasant for you to see that I have not quite been overwhelmed by the pressure of circumstances and that to an extent at least I live and try to develop further in a manner worthy of your old generosity toward me. But now I am obliged to write sooner than I originally intended. My wish one day to live near you, in Jena, has become a virtual necessity and as I have weighed up the pros and cons the only thing left for me to do is to apply for your authorization of this course, since I can do nothing without your approval.

My experience so far has shown me that it is not possible for me to sustain a completely independent existence while working with complete independence.

For that reason, with only rare interruptions, I have mostly lived as a tutor, and though on the whole I have done what was required of me I have repeatedly had to suffer the dissatisfaction of others when I have been inept, or their oppressive compassion if for once I seemed to be having some success. In such situations I very often thanked you from the bottom of my heart for having given me by your companionship a joy that no unhappy hour has yet been able to extinguish in me. But nevertheless my patience gradually turned into something of a passion, and I always found myself, when in doubt, taking the course that was more likely to lead to my sacrificing the true aims of my life to the needs of others. Now I am aware, and am quite lucid about it, that it is not impossible to come to terms with being prevented from living out one's personal vocation, but false resignation is just as liable to come to a bad end as too great a rashness. This is particularly apparent to me now, when, unless something else turns up, in a few weeks I shall be obliged to go and act as a curate to some clergyman in the country. It is not that I do not acknowledge the possible worth and particular joys this sphere may have. But I can see that the type of work and the whole style that have now become part and parcel of this kind of post contrast so greatly with my way of expressing myself that the contradiction would end up making me lose all facility of communication.

For years almost my sole preoccupation has been with Greek literature. Once I had embarked on this study it was not possible for me to stop until it had given me back the freedom that at the beginning it can so easily take away, and I believe I am in a position to be of particular use to younger people who are interested by freeing them from servitude to the Greek letter and helping them understand that the great firmness these writers have is a consequence of their abundance of spirit.

I have also been prompted to form particular ideas about the necessary equivalence of supreme principles and pure methods that are necessarily different, which put into full context and presented with proper borderlines might be apt to shed some light on the cultural sphere and on those areas that are excluded from it.

I beg you, esteemed Sir, to read these self-laudatory words that the circumstances force from me with your customary kindness, and above all not to think that in telling you about myself so directly and at such length I might have unlearned the modesty proper toward someone greater than myself.

I only wanted to put to you candidly the reasons that convince me that it would make quite good sense for me to go to Jena and try to devote the larger part of my time to giving lectures there, which, as I understand it, I am permitted to do.

I do not really expect a large number of people to attend, but as many as usually come to lectures of this kind. I hope also that I should not be getting in the way of anybody else.

Should you advise against it, that will help me settle into some other course, and I shall see how to keep myself going.

You will not disdain to brighten up my life and its development a little by taking an interest in it, because after all I am not otherwise so vain as to seek to give it a significance it does not have.

You are the joy of a whole nation, probably something you rarely see. Perhaps it might not seem completely without value for you then to see a new pleasure in life unfold in one who honors you unconditionally, and to know yourself the origin of it.

I should forget a lot, a very great deal, the moment I were to see you again and greet you with the awe I felt when I met you for the first time.

Yours truly,

Hölderlin

235. TO IMMANUEL NIETHAMMER

Nürtingen, near Stuttgart, 23 June 1801

My esteemed friend,

I have plucked up the courage to break the silence that has established itself between us since you found it necessary to stop writing to me. I hesitate to remind you of myself again, for the reason that drives me to do so is so out of the ordinary that it might surprise you. But I am confident that you will not hold the pleasure I have in communicating with you against me, and the more so when I think of the sympathy with which you watched over me in days gone by, and of the friendship I used to enjoy.

The need to write to you has become irrefutable, for I have now reached the point where I require your advice, which you never refused me when I asked for it in the past.

The last few years I have lived in conditions that were not appropriate to my life plan and in which I only rarely felt the happiness of being content with my state.

I did not want to enter a clerical office, and now, at the age of 31, it makes me uncomfortable to consider the prospect of having to depend on a pastor, as his curate. Work as a tutor, which presented itself as a possibility and that I have indeed practiced, appeared to me to be worthwhile only for the reason that everyday life with the children entrusted to my care made it possible to nurture their intellectual development from within and, through the daily instruction

I gave them, to awaken in them the consciousness that one day they would have to continue along the path of education on their own. But the changeful conditions in which the life of a private tutor unfolds did not correspond to either my nature or my life plan, and so it was always my endeavor to follow this with a period of independence in which it was possible to employ myself according to my own lights. And so I lived for almost two years in Homburg in the company of my friend Sinclair, and there was able to work entirely in my own way and pursue literary studies.

Recently I have returned home to Swabia from Switzerland, where I spent a not very happy time as a tutor. And here an old plan I had all but abandoned has lodged itself in my mind again, so firmly that every day I reflect on how it might best be realized. In my life I have only too often had the experience of seeing my plans and desires, however closely they corresponded to my nature, far exceed reality and end up squashed by the circumstances that fate had ordained my life to adopt. I want to change my situation and am resolved not to continue any longer my present life as a freelance writer. I have in mind to go to Jena and should like to make myself useful there by giving lectures in the field of Greek literature, which in the past few years has formed the greater part of my occupations. I should like to show young people who are interested what the characters of the great works are and explain to them what sort of spirit was capable of organizing the material and releasing the poetic life in it. Such an activity now suits my purpose entirely, and I expect from it a turn for the better in my life.

What I intend will not have anything to do with the kind of questions a mere etymological or linguistic erudition might raise. I also hope not to clash with Counselor Schütz and Professor Tennemann, as I have heard that both these gentlemen are giving lectures on subjects in Greek literature.

I have already written to Counselor Schiller and put to him the grounds that prompt me to change the situation of my life. I know you are friendly with him and so I hope it is not presumptuous of me to ask you to have a talk with him about my plan, including whether it is possible to assure my existence and give my activities stability in a position at the university.

It would be a great help to me if you could make some comment on this important decision soon. Your advice, whatever it is, will be dear to me in any case.

Be assured that the memory of your friendship is always a comfort to me, and let me tell you that the expectation of soon living near you again fills me with joy.

Ever yours,

Fr. Hölderlin

Fondest good wishes to Schelling.

FROM WILHELM FRIEDRICH ELSÄSSER

Stuttgart, 26 June 1801

Dear friend, forgive me that your *Agis* arrives so late. I had clean forgotten about it & was reminded of it by chance the other day.

FROM SIEGFRIED SCHMID

Friedberg near Frankfurt a. M., 6 July 1801

There lives here a lawyer, Bartz, who has acquaintances in Jena. He is the one who gave me the idea of asking you to do a review, to prevent the blind from recounting idiotic things about color in the magazine. Now, the editor has transmitted the following to him: "The review could not very well be taken because all contributors were determined in advance. If however it was by a recognizable name (and your name had indeed been mentioned), someone who had already made his mark in the field, they would consider it an honor if he wished to become a contributing editor. They were obliged to take these measures because otherwise they would be buried in reviews from all quarters." Are the good people fishing for compliments or is this a narrow-minded policy? Do you want now to send the review to Huber; or have a word with him about the matter? I don't know where it is I heard that you had dealings with him. And he is, as I understand, employed in this department. . . . Please let me know if you do anything in this affair.

What you say about the actions of heroes and artists is very apt, and about the felicitous disproportionate distribution of faculties.

FROM SIEGFRIED SCHMID

Friedberg near Frankfurt a. M., 31 July 1801

Did you receive my last letter together with the review? What did you decide?

You usually send, I think, something in to several almanacs. Do you get paid a fee? . . . Won't you put me in touch with one or two of the editors? I have several things I'd like to place! Or why don't you edit a journal yourself.

FROM LUDWIG FERDINAND HUBER

Stuttgart, 6 August 1801

[*He announces that Cotta is willing to take on the publication of his poems for Easter 1802 and will pay him after the printing 1 old louis d'or per sheet and once 500 copies have been sold another 1 louis d'or per sheet.—Cotta would like him to give Huber some favorite poem of his for the* Damenkalender. *This would serve as an advance recommendation of the project. They must however ask that the poem be sent over as soon as possible because the* Damenkalender *would be ready in the next few days.*]

FROM CHRISTIAN LANDAUER

Stuttgart, 22 October 1801

I am writing just a few words, my dear friend, to say that yesterday Prof. Ströhlin was at my house and invites you to come here because he needs urgently to speak with you. He has received letters from Bordeaux whose content will satisfy you entirely as for the time being you are dispensed from preaching and will get 25 louis d'ors for the journey along with the assurance that your annual salary will come to 50 louis d'ors. So do come over tomorrow, Ströhlin is very keen that you should lose no time, and be sure to arrange things, dear Hölderlin, so that you can stay here for a while. Ströhlin also told me a few days ago that you had promised him a sermon but not yet sent it, which surprised him.

Your umbrella is not to be found anywhere. I await you with open arms.

Yours,

C. Landauer

236. TO THE FAMILY

[Stuttgart, ~ October/November 1801]

My dear family,

This time I have so much to thank you for that it would be better to say nothing at all than the little I should confine myself to now. Know that to be certain of hearts like yours, to have been convinced of your sympathy and loyalty on so many occasions and to grow in that conviction—this is a happiness in my life that is worth speaking about and more so than many other things I have to do without and do without willingly. And if my situation should change, I ask you to look at it from the best point of view. I should have an existence free from anxiety together with an occupation that has become a habit with me, and with any luck I shall find good people. I must enter into the life of dependence in one form or another, and educating children is an especially happy business now, because it is so innocent.

Yours,

Friz

237. TO HIS BROTHER

Nürtingen, 4 December 1801

My dear Karl,

I come to take my leave. But let us not complain—in cases like this I always prefer to keep the mind content and in honor of God pass over sadness to focus on what is good.

This much I can confess: that in all my life I have never been so firmly rooted to my home country, never in my life have I valued being with my friends and relations so much, and felt so great a reluctance to leave them.

But I have the sense that it is better for me to be out of the country, and you, dear Karl, know very well yourself that for the one as for the other, to stay put or to travel abroad, we need God's protection if we are to survive. For you, it is above all keeping busy that maintains you in your way of life. Otherwise things would become too narrow for you. What I need, essentially, is to manage to do what I have set out to achieve. Otherwise I would be swept away into distraction.

The main thing is that the old love between us two brothers should not fail. It is a sacred happiness when despite different ways of life human beings are held together by bonds such as the one between us. That is the greater meaning that everywhere spurs us on and saves us. And men in particular do not need to resemble one another in their souls for there to be love between them. But without this openness of heart there can be no happiness for them. O Karl, forgive me, so that things can be pure between us.

Goodbye then. Things will go well for you at home since you are so well founded in what you do. Think of me sometimes.

Yours,

Hölderlin

238. TO CASIMIR ULRICH BÖHLENDORFF

Nürtingen, near Stuttgart, 4 December 1801

My dear Böhlendorff,

Your kind words and your presence in them gave me much pleasure.

Your *Fernando* has done me a great deal of good, I breathe more easily. The progress of my friends seems to me such a good sign. We share the same fate. If one of us advances then the other will not be far behind.

Dear Böhlendorff, you have gained so much in precision and supple efficiency and lost nothing in warmth; on the contrary, like a good blade, the elasticity of your mind has proven to be all the stronger in the school of constraint. This is what I congratulate you for above all. Nothing is harder for us to learn than the free use of what we are born with. And it is my belief that clarity of exposition is originally as natural to us as heavenly fire is to the Greeks. For precisely that reason the Greeks are more likely to be *surpassed* in fine passion, which is what you have managed to keep, than in the presence of spirit and faculty for exposition we find in Homer.

It sounds paradoxical. But I put it to you again, for you to verify and make use of as you wish: in the process of civilization what we are actually born with, the national, will always become less and less of an advantage. For that reason the Greeks are not such masters of sacred pathos, because it was native to them; on the other hand they are exceptional in their faculty for exposition, from Homer onward, because this extraordinary man had the feeling necessary to capture the *Junonian sobriety* of the occident for his Apollonian realm, and so truly to appropriate the foreign.

With us it is the other way round. That is also why it is so dangerous to derive our aesthetic rules from the sole source of Greek excellence. I have labored at this for a long time and know now that apart from what must be the supreme thing with the Greeks and with us, that is, living craft and proportion, we cannot properly have anything *in common* with them.

But what is our own has to be learned just as much as what is foreign. For this reason the Greeks are indispensable to us. Only it is precisely in what is proper to us, in the national, that we shall never match them because as I said, the *free* use of what is our *own* is hardest of all.

And it seems to me that your good genius has prompted you to give the dramatic form a more epic treatment. Taken as a whole, it is a *genuine* modern tragedy. For that is the tragic with us, to depart from the realm of the living in total silence packed up in some kind of container, not to atone for the flames we have been unable to control by being consumed in fire.

And in truth our innermost soul is moved as much by one as by the other. It is not such an imposing fate, but a deeper one, and a noble soul accompanies with fear and pity someone dying in that way too, and holds the spirit up amid the fury. Jupiter in his splendor will always be the last thought when a mortal perishes—whether he dies according to ancient destiny or according to ours—if the poet has presented this death as he should and as you clearly intended to and on the whole and particularly in several masterly touches have done:

> A narrow path leads to a somber valley,
> Where treachery has forced him into refuge

and other places.—You are on the right path, keep to it. But I want to study your *Fernando* properly and take it to heart, and then perhaps say something more interesting to you about it. It can never be enough!

As to myself and what has happened to me up until now, how far I have remained and become worthy of you and my friends, and what I am working on and, such as it is, will soon produce, I'll tell you all about that in my next letter which will come to you from the vicinity of your Spain, that is from Bordeaux, where I set off next week to be a private tutor and preacher in a German Protestant household. I shall have to keep a hold of my wits in France, in Paris; and I look forward too to seeing the sea, and the sun of Provence.

O my friend, the world lies more brightly before me than usual, and is more serious. Yes, it pleases me the way things are, pleases me like in summer when "with a calm hand the holy father of old shakes lightning like blessings from the reddening clouds." For among all that I can see of God this sign has become my chosen one. Before, I could shout for joy about a new truth, a better view of what is above and around us; now I fear that I might not end up like old Tantalus who got more of the gods than he could stomach.

But I do what I can as well as I can, and think, when I see that I on my path must go where all the others go too, that it is godforsaken and madness to look for a path out of all danger—there exists no plant to remedy death.

And so, goodbye, dear Böhlendorff, for the time being. I am now full of parting. It's a long time since I have cried. But when I decided I had to leave my country, perhaps for ever, the tears came, and they were bitter. For what do I have in the world that is dearer to me? But they have no use for me. I will always be German and cannot do otherwise, even if the needs of my heart should drive me to Tahiti for nourishment.

Send greetings to Muhrbeck. How is he? He will be preserved, I'm sure. We shall not lose him. Forgive me the ingratitude. I had recognized you, I saw you, but through tinted glasses. There is so much I have to say to you, my good friends! It must be the same with you. Where will you live in future, my Böhlendorff? But those are just worries. If you write to me address the letter to Landauer, merchant in Stuttgart. He will make sure it gets to me. Send me your address too.

Yours,

H.

239. TO HIS MOTHER

Lyon, 9 January 1802

My dear Mother,

You will be surprised to receive a letter from me in Lyon at this stage. I was obliged to stop in Strasbourg longer than I expected for my passport, and the long journey here from Strasbourg was made even longer by flooding and other unavoidable circumstances that held me up.

The journey so far has been hard and eventful but it has also given me many pure moments of joy. I cannot help admitting I thought of you all sometimes and also of him who is a source of courage to me and has preserved me up until now and will continue to accompany me.

I know, a solitary occupation tends to make it harder to come to terms with the wide world; I think though that God and an honest heart help us to get by, and modesty toward other people.

I am still tired, dear Mother, from the long cold journey, and things are so lively here now that only by holding in intimate remembrance those who know us and can be said to be fond of us can we find our bearings again.

Tomorrow I set off for Bordeaux and should get there quickly as the roads are better now and the rivers are no longer in flood.

I forgot to say that it was the authorities in Strasbourg who advised me, as a foreigner, to take the route via Lyon. So I shall not see Paris. And I am content that way.

I look forward to starting my proper job soon.

I will write you and the rest of the dear family a lot more from Bordeaux, when things are calmer.

Give my love to everyone.

Karl will be in Nürtingen by now. Think of me sometimes when in the evenings you are all sitting together. Ask my dear sister to remember the best hours we had together and to mention their uncle to the children sometimes.

I cannot thank you enough for all the kindness and support and sympathy.

I hope you are well.

Your loyal son,

Hölderlin

240. TO HIS MOTHER

Bordeaux, 28 January 1802

I'm here at last, dear Mother, have had a good welcoming, am in good health and will not forget the thanks I owe the Lord of life and death.—I can only write a few words for the moment; I arrived this morning, and my attention is too much taken up with my new situation for me to be able to tell you with the necessary calm some of the interesting things about the journey I now have behind me.

Moreover, so much has happened to me that I can scarcely begin to talk about it yet.

These last few days I have been walking in nothing but fine spring weather, but not long before, high up in the snowy hills of the fearful Auvergne, in storms and wilderness, the nights icy-cold and a loaded pistol beside me in the rough beds—I prayed a prayer then that was the best of my whole life and that I shall never forget.

I am preserved—give thanks, as I do.

My dears, once I was out of danger I greeted you like someone reborn and reproached myself immediately for not having made special mention of my dear grandmother in the last letter from Lyon, I spoke to you, dear Mother, saw my sister before me, and in my head, full of joy, began to write Karl a hopeful, solemn letter.

I am now hardened through and through, initiated as you could wish. I think I shall remain so, in the main. Fearing nothing and enduring a good deal. What good a safe refreshing sleep will do me. My accommodation is almost too grand. I would be happy with secure simplicity. My work will I hope go well. I want to devote myself to it entirely, and make a good start. Take care of yourselves. With all my heart and sincerity,

Yours,

H.

PS. My letter has been delayed a few days. I have begun to get acquainted and to assume my duties, and could not have made a better start. "You will be happy here," the Consul said to me when he received me. I think he was right.

241. TO HIS MOTHER

Bordeaux, Good Friday 1802

My dear Mother,

Do not misunderstand me if I express more the necessary composure at the loss of our now blessed grandmother than the grief that the love in our hearts feels. I find that without a certain firmness of mind it is difficult to get by, I do not want to give counsel to my family but for my part I must preserve and maintain my soul, which has already undergone so many ordeals, and the good and tender words that, as you know, come off my tongue so easily, I must be sparing with them for now, it is not right for me to upset you and myself even more. The new and pure life, which, as I believe, the departed enjoy after death and that is also the reward for those who, like our dear grandmother, lived their life in holy simplicity, this youth in heaven that is now hers, that for so long her soul longed for, this peace and joy after suffering, will also be your reward, dear Mother, dear Sister; and probably a noble death, a safe passage from life into life, awaits my brother and me also as, I believe, it does all those we hold dear.

In the meantime may a true and constant spirit be with us, and heaven on high grant that we not be idle, and be measured in what we do, and carry out the role we have chosen with felicity!

Things here could hardly be better! And I hope gradually to come to deserve all that my situation gives me and when one day I come home again not to be completely unworthy of the truly excellent people I am obliged to in this place.

Think of me often, my dear ones, but do not let it disrupt your own concerns. For my brother I wish that he may continue to prosper in his sphere, in his affairs, as he has done up till now.

The little children will be giving you a great deal of pleasure, and you are fortunate to be surrounded in that way, by living images of hope, as I am by my pupils. Send my love to my friends, and tell them I'm sorry not to have written: being so far away and having so much to do has prompted me to be economical with letters for the moment. What we are to one another remains unchanged.

Yours truly,

H.

FROM ISAAK VON SINCLAIR

Homburg vor der Höhe, 30 June 1802

Dear Hölderlin,

As terrible as the news I have to give you is, I cannot leave to chance what the succor of friendship is too slight to counter. And also I am better fitted for it since a similar fate has struck me, quite unexpectedly, which has wounded me to the depths of my heart. The noble object of your love is no longer, but yours she was, and if it is more terrible to lose it, it is more hurtful not to be regarded as worthy of love. That is your fate, this mine. I have no comfort to give you that is better than what you have yourself. You believed in immortality while she was still alive, you will surely believe in it more than before, now that the life of your love has parted from what passes away. And what is greater or more noble than a heart that survives beyond its world and that, from early on, is brought by fate into that seriousness of feeling in which alone life, peace and eternity are vouchsafed to us. I send you courage with an unshaken heart. Without all fear as I am, I can speak the truth out of love.

On the 22nd of this month S. G. died, from measles, on the tenth day of her sickness. Her children had it with her and came through safely. In the winter just gone she had had a dangerous cough that weakened her lungs. She remained the same right until the end. Her death was like her life.

It moved me deeply and I am crying as I write this. Since your separation I had not seen any more of her, and I thought it unworthy to ask after a being who lived the unchanging life of the gods. The news was all the more unexpected for that reason, but I received it into a heart all the purer and it is as someone not unworthy of her that I speak to you.

Since you left me I have suffered many strokes of fate. I have become calmer and colder, and I can promise you that you will be able to find peace on the breast of your friend. You know all my flaws, I hope that none of them will create a misunderstanding between us any more. So I invite you to come to me and to remain with me as long as I am here. The possible occurrences that would alter my situation we shall consider and decide together, and if fate should decree it we shall go its ways as a loyal pair. At the moment I can readily spare 200 fl. a year—that I can give to you, and free lodgings and all that goes with it. Do not take this as a mere plea but also as my advice, in so far as I can advise you without knowing your situation, since it may be the case that you can find the peace and quiet you need there. Let me know what you decide. I can also come to you in Bordeaux, if you like, and pick you up.

Our friend Ebel sends his greetings, he has been in Frankfurt since January. He was with SG. during her illness, and her comfort in her last hours.

Yours,

Sinclair

FROM ISAAK VON SINCLAIR

Homburg v. d. H., 20 July 1802

My letter to you I had enclosed with one to Landauer. He has written to me in the meantime that you are back from Bordeaux and in Nürtingen. Since then I've waited for letters from you and it unsettles me not to receive any. You are now closer to me than ever and I hope now to see and have more of you. If you like I can come and pick you up. Circumstances prevent me from coming to you now.

Yours,

Sinclair

FROM ISAAK VON SINCLAIR

Homburg v. d. H., 7 November 1802

[*Praising a poem of Pindaric sweep that H. had sent him. Singles out the golden arrows of love.—Made a journey through Swabia to Regensburg, but so speedily that he was not able to visit H.*] Our cause has not yet been decided, and we could not stay in Regensburg any longer since we had no more hope of success than before. The winter that keeps us apart will quickly pass. But you would give me great pleasure if you did not leave me without something from you during this time and sent me a few of your poems. [*Horn, who is in Regensburg, will write to H. shortly.*]

242. TO CASIMIR ULRICH BÖHLENDORFF

[Nürtingen, mid-November 1802]

My dear friend,

I have not written to you for a long time, have since been in France and seen the sad solitary earth, the shepherds of southern France and individual beauties, men and women, who grew up in the fear of patriotic doubt and of hunger.

The violent element, the fire of the sky, and the quiet of the people, their life in the open and their straitenedness and contentment, stirred me continually, and as one says of heroes I can probably say of myself: that Apollo has struck me.

In the regions that border on the Vendée the wild, warlike quality interested me, the purely male, where the life-light is immediate in the eyes and limbs and which, feeling death, feels a kind of virtuosity and satisfies its thirst for knowledge.

The athleticism of people in the south, in the ruins of the ancient spirit, made me better acquainted with the true essence of the Greeks; I got to know their nature and their wisdom, their bodies, the way they grew up in their climate and the rules by which they protected their exuberant genius from the violence of the element.

This determined their popularity, their manner of receiving foreign natures and of communicating with them, this is the source of their peculiar individuality that appears alive in as much as supreme understanding in the Greek sense is the power of reflection, and we may grasp this if we learn to grasp the heroic body of the Greeks; this is tenderness, like our own popularity.

Seeing the antiquities left me with an impression that has helped me understand not only the Greeks themselves but all that is highest in art, which even where movement and the phenomenalization of concepts and of every aspect of serious meaning is at its height still keeps every part in place, entire and true to itself, so that sureness, in this sense, is the supreme kind of sign.

After many shocks and commotions of soul I needed to find a firm footing, for a while, and I am now living in my hometown.

Nature in these parts also takes hold of me more powerfully the more I study it. Storms, not just in their greatest manifestation, but seen as power and figure, among the other forms of the sky, the effect of the light, shaping nationally and as principle and destiny, so that something is holy to us, the intensity of its coming and going, the characteristicness of the woods and the coincidence in one region of different characters of nature, so that all the holy places of the earth are together in one place, and the philosophic light at my window, they are now my joy. May I keep in mind how I have come to where I am now!

My dear friend, I think that we will not annotate the poets up to our time, but that song will take on a quite different character and that we've had little success because since the Greeks we are the first to sing nationally and naturally again, with actual originality.

Make sure you write to me soon. I need your pure tones. Psyche among friends, the formation of thoughts in conversations and letters, is vital for artists. Otherwise we have none for ourselves; but they belong to the holy image we are shaping. Take good care of yourself.

Yours,

H.

FROM CASIMIR ULRICH BÖHLENDORFF

Berlin, 2 December 1802

[Sends thanks for Hölderlin's letter and welcomes the homecomer back to his native land.—Asks for contributions for his next journal. He intends next time to be even more careful about limiting his selection.]

FROM ISAAK VON SINCLAIR

[Homburg, early December 1802]

Frau von Kalb asks me tell you that she has received very good news in relation to her financial affairs that you will also be glad to hear.—[*Fr. v. Kalb advises him to offer his* Sophocles *to* Göschen *in Leipzig or* Frommann *in Jena. She also intends to write to Prof.* Mehmel *in Erlangen, asking him to find a publisher for him there.*]

FROM ISAAK VON SINCLAIR

Homburg, 6 February 1803

[*H.'s letter gave him a great deal of pleasure. He has taken his poem to the Landgrave who received it with much pleasure and thanks and is looking forward to seeing him here.*] As soon as the harsh weather is over I count on your coming here, with the spring.

Yesterday *Böhlendorff* wrote to me to say that he had spoken with the bookseller *Fröhlich* in *Berlin* about your translation of Sophocles and that he seemed not uninclined to enter into a contract to publish it, once he had seen it. Might you then send *Boehlendorff* the *Sophocles*, at least the first volume: whatever else you might have ready he also wanted to find a publisher for. But it had to happen soon because he was intending to leave B. before long, for the Courland or for Göttingen. His address is: To Herr *Boehlend.*, Secretary, in *Berlin*, to be left at *Unger's* bookshop.

[*Then writes full of praise for a poem that H. had sent him.*] The passage about the Last Supper and the disciples moved me; but the end reminded me of our difference of opinion.

Frau v. Kalb sends her best regards. Also because of her it will be lovely for me if you come: her lively mind requires more than one opponent, and with the education she has it is never a waste of time, as in her company nothing is ever lost.

I didn't tell you before that on my way through *Heidenheim* I happened to meet *Enslin* which was a real surprise to him. I was taken right back to Jena again, and I was pleased to find him not without substance and with the same beliefs. He spoke of you with great warmth.

FROM CHRISTIAN LANDAUER

Stuttgart, 8 February 1803

A few days ago I received the enclosed letter for you, dear *Hölderlin*.

What are you up to? Probably you are working all day long and half the night and that's why you give no news of yourself and never visit me any more. I confess, my friend, it often pains me when I think that your friends no longer seem to mean anything to you, since you don't think it worth troubling to find out how they are. It would give me great pleasure if you would soon decide to visit me—at least for a few days. *Scheffauer* is in the middle of making a fine monument out of clay—over life-size—for the late heir to the throne of Baden.

Look after yourself, dear Hölderlin, and think at least from time to time of

your

C. Landauer

243. TO FRIEDRICH WILMANS

Nürtingen, near Stuttgart, 28 September 1803

Excellent and highly esteemed Sir,

I am very grateful to you for having taken such a kind interest in the translation of the Sophocles tragedies.

As I have not yet heard anything from my friend Schelling, who had undertaken to approach the theater in Weimar, I prefer to follow the safer course of taking advantage of your kind offer.

I am quite happy with the first volume's not appearing until the spring book fair, especially as I have plenty of material to preface the tragedies with an introduction that I shall probably be able to complete later in the autumn.

Greek art is foreign to us because of the national convenience and bias it has always relied on, and I hope to present it to the public in a more lively manner than usual by bringing out further the oriental element it has denied and correcting its artistic bias wherever it occurs.

I shall always be grateful to you for having sent your kind letter when you did because you have given me liberty to express myself at a point when I can write more out of a sense of nature and more for my own country than usual.

I remain, Sir, with true esteem,

your most obedient servant

Friedrich Hölderlin

244. TO FRIEDRICH WILMANS

Nürtingen, near Stuttgart, 8 December 1803

Esteemed Sir,

Forgive me for the delay in sending the manuscripts of the Sophocles tragedies. I wanted, as I had a better view of the whole, to change a few things in the translation and the notes. The language in the *Antigone* did not seem lively enough. The notes did not express sufficiently my convictions about Greek art or the meaning of the plays. Even now I am still not satisfied with them. If you think it appropriate, I should like to send you a specially written introduction to the tragedies of Sophocles in the next six months or whenever else might be suitable.

I'll look out some short poems for an almanac from among my papers straight after sending off this manuscript. I have a few things you might like.

I haven't yet written to Schelling. But will do later this week.

If you should find it awkward to send the edition of these tragedies to Goethe or the Weimar theater be so kind as to let me know. As I am personally acquainted with Herr von Goethe it will not be out of place for me to send it myself.

Later this winter I also intend to send you individual lyric poems of some length, 3 or 4 folio pages, each poem to be printed separately because they will deal directly with our country and the times.

I have been very glad of your kind encouragement. To have come into contact with you is for me a truly fortunate turn of events.

Your devoted servant,

Friedrich Hölderlin

245. TO FRIEDRICH WILMANS

Nürtingen, near Stuttgart, December 1803

Esteemed Sir,

Thank you for having taken the trouble of sending me a sample of the print of the Sophocles tragedies. I think that with letters like these it is easier for the eyes to find the meaning, since with overpointed letters one is easily tempted just to look at the type.

The physical beauty of the printing does not seem to lose anything because of it, not to me at least. It makes the lines stand more firmly balanced.

I am in the middle of going through a few Night Poems for your almanac. But I wanted to reply to your letter directly to prevent any sense of frustration from coming into our relationship.

It is a joy to sacrifice oneself to the reader and to enter with him into the narrow limits of our still childlike culture.

In my view love poems are always a weary flight, for we are still no further forward now, despite the difference of materials. The high and pure rejoicing of songs on our land and times is another thing altogether.

The prophetic quality of the *Messias* and of certain odes is an exception.

I am very eager to know how you will react to the sample of several longer lyric poems. I hope to send them to you in January; and if your judgment of this experiment is the same as mine it will probably be possible for them to appear in time for the spring book fair.

The introduction to the tragedies of Sophocles I intend to write separately, at the latest in time for the autumn fair; it will then be for you to decide, esteemed Sir, whether you want to make use of it or not.

I hope to send you soon an answer from Schelling.

I will try to find some subscribers in Stuttgart for the edition of the *Views* you have been so kind to send me a prospectus of. I am acquainted with a number of people there who might buy such works and could recommend them to others.

With all my regards, dear friend, and until a further sign of my devotion,

Hölderlin

FROM FRIEDRICH WILMANS

[Frankfurt, 3 January 1804]

[Prof. Voigt, his friend, sends him greetings.—Wilmans has already undertaken to publish the Sophocles; but seeks to postpone the printing—of the introduction.]

FROM FRIEDRICH WILMANS

[Frankfurt, 28 January 1804]

[Thanks him for the poems he has sent in for his almanac. He will shortly be sending him the advance sheets for the Sophocles.—Before the fair he would be hard put to find a home for the longer poems in his printing house. But straight after the fair he would get on with printing them.]

246. TO LEO VON SECKENDORF

Nürtingen, 12 March 1804

My dear friend,

I recently tried to visit you, but could not find your house. So I am fulfilling the duty that necessitated this visit in writing, and send you the prospectus of some picturesque views of the Rhine; possibly you could subscribe, and find other subscribers. The Prince has already shown an interest. I am eager to see how they will turn out—whether they will be pure and simple renderings from nature, so that on both sides nothing extraneous and uncharacteristic is included and the earth achieves a good balance with the sky, and such that the light, which defines the particular proportions of this balance, is not oblique and deceptively attractive. A great deal probably depends on the angle within the work of art and on the frame surrounding it.

The antiquities in Paris in particular have given me a genuine interest in art, so that I should like to study it more.

I would also ask you to take an interest in a translation of mine of the tragedies of Sophocles that has been accepted by the same publisher, Herr Wilmans in Frankfurt, and will come out at Easter.

Fable, the poetic view of history, and the architectonics of the sky preoccupy me above all at the moment, especially the national and its difference from the Greek.

I have gained a general sense of the various fates of the heroes, knights and princes—how they serve fate or relate to it in a more ambiguous manner.

I really should like to see you in Stuttgart sometime and have conversation with you. I truly value having as learned and humane a man as you among us. I have written as much to Herr von Sinclair.

I think there is a lot more I have to say to you. The study of our country, of its conditions and estates, is unending and at a very early stage.

That the good time may not become empty of spirit, and that we may find ourselves and one another again!

I think of the days of simplicity and quiet that may come. If the enemies of our country trouble us, a courage has been preserved, to defend against this other that does not quite belong to us. With humble regards,

Hölderlin

247. TO FRIEDRICH WILMANS

Nürtingen, near Stuttgart, 2 April 1804

Esteemed friend,

I have gone through the printer's errors in the *Oedipus*.

I almost preferred the raw print, probably because in this typography the traits that mark the solid aspect of the letters hold their own so well in relation to the modifying traits, and this was even more noticeable in the raw print than in the filed version. The inventor is often bashful toward his public, and his mannered courtesies then cause him to lose all trace of individuality, especially the solidity characteristic of this typography. That being said, refining the typography in this way is more of an apparent loss than a real one.

Once it is better known perhaps you will use the raw form of the first printing and leave it as it is, or give it a touch with the file.

I say this to show you how well I understand the quality of your work. And this oversevere use of the file only detracts from the solidity at first sight; if one sits with the pages set straight before one, or at a pure angle to them, the more solid traits appear clearly.

I only await the copies to send to Herr von Goethe and Herr von Schiller and to a few others who might be interested.

I should like to send a special copy to the Princess of Homburg. I do not know if you want to select special paper for it.

I am certain I have written in the direction of eccentric enthusiasm and thus reached Greek simplicity; I hope to continue to stick to this principle, even if that means exposing more boldly what was forbidden to the original poet, precisely by going in the direction of eccentric enthusiasm.

I look forward to sending you something very soon on which I place a particular value at the moment.

It is my wish that the ideas and points of contact that have brought this book into circulation may come into contact as quickly as possible.

Goodbye for the time being, my dear Wilmans.

Your friend,

Hölderlin

FROM FRIEDRICH WILMANS

Frankfurt, 14 April 1804

Esteemed Sir & friend,

Tomorrow at daybreak I set off to *Leipzig* for the fair—and an hour ago the 2nd vol. of the *Sophocles* was finished and thank heavens is already on its way to Leipzig.—

In haste, as you can imagine, I'm sending you 6 copies on vellum and 6 copies on ordinary paper as your complimentary copies for you to distribute to your friends.

If you need any more for this purpose you are very welcome.

With all the good will in the world it is not possible for me at present to enclose the honorarium, but as soon as I return from *Leipzig* it will happen without delay, you can depend upon it.

Unfortunately there are many misprints in the first part, but I consider it necessary not to append them—partly time is too short for this, partly the tiniest portion of readers will notice. You won't be blamed for them, rather the printers. If you desire to have them noted, please send me a list covering both volumes, which I shall have printed in the Jena *Literatur-Zeitung.*

The great hurry I am in only allows me to further assure you of my admiration

Fr. Wilmans

248. TO PRINCESS AUGUSTE OF HESSE-HOMBURG

[Nürtingen, April/May 1804]

[*Begins:*] Your Highness. I am sending you the first volume of my translation of Sophocles's tragedies. [*In it he speaks of the greatness of the ancients, but also of the*] unfathomably greater divinity of our sacred religion in its originality, [*and of the value of comparing ancient conditions with our own.*]

FROM FRIEDRICH WILMANS

Frankfurt, 27 May 1804

*[Both volumes of the Sophocles have appeared; Wilmans sends the
honorarium (222 fl. 45 x. for 2 parts or 13 1/2 sheets at 1 1/2 carolins).]*

FROM HIS MOTHER

Nürtingen, 29 October 1805

Dear beloved Son,

although I am not so fortunate to receive upon my repeated request
even a few lines from you my dear still I cannot refrain from assuring
you from time to time of our enduring love & remembrances of you.
how very much it would please and cheer me if you would only write
to me once again to say that you still love your dear family & think
of us. Perhaps I have unwittingly, & unwillingly, given you cause to be
offended that you are taking it out on me so harshly, just be so kind &
tell me so, I will attempt to make up for it. or if you should be lacking
for anything in the way of linen or articles of clothing, write and tell
me or ask your landlord to write to me. I am very pleased that, as the
gracious Frau von Bröck writes in her letter to me, you have such a
kindly disposed landlord. who looks after you so tenderly. you my dear
son will also appreciate this, & be grateful for all the particular favors
and attentions that your noble friend & benefactor Herr von Sincklär
shows you. as also his gracious lady mother. & the persons who tend to
you.

In particular though I implore you not to neglect your duties
toward our dear God & father in heaven. on this earth we can attain
no greater happiness than if we stand in our dear God's grace. this is
what we must strive for with all seriousness, so that we shall find one
another again where there is no more separation.

I'm sending you with this a jerkin & 4 pairs of stockings & 1 pair
of gloves as proof of my love & remembrance. but I ask you to please
be sure to wear the woolen stockings. Our good lord be praised, I can
send you the news that so far we—as also your dear brother & sister-

in-law in Zwiefalten—have been spared the distress & disturbance of war. & I thank dear God too that Homburg so far as I know has remained unaffected by the war. May God have mercy on us & and our country & grant us & all people sweet peace again.

Along with fond wishes from all of us & the plea that you will soon do me the pleasure of writing again, I close with the assurance that I remain as ever

your

faithful M. Gock

TÜBINGEN, 1806–1843

249. TO HIS MOTHER

[Tübingen, 15 September 1812]

Esteemed Mother,

I have the honor of vouching for the fact that the letter I received from you did not fail to give me great pleasure. Your excellent remarks have done me a great deal of good, and the gratitude I owe you is added to the admiration of your excellent sentiments. Your kind heart and your useful admonitions are never without pleasing expression, while also being useful to me. The article of clothing you sent with it will also do me very well. I must hurry. I should permit myself to add several other points, that is, how such exhortations to orderly conduct on my part will, I hope, be effective and agreeable to you. I have the honor of calling myself

your most devoted son

Hölderlin

250. TO HIS MOTHER

Dearest Mother

I'm seizing the opportunity most kindly granted me by Herr Zimmer to turn toward you in my thoughts and once again to entertain you

with earnests of my devotion and the sincerity of my attachment to
you. Your kindness, long so evident and clear to me, the continuance of
your tenderness and your moral influence, which is of such benefit to
me, are to me objects of veneration that float before my eyes whether
I seek to strengthen in myself the respect owing to you or whether
I consider what sort of remembrance I owe you, excellent Mother!
If I cannot be as entertaining as you are to me it comes from the
negative aspect of precisely the devotion I have the honor of showing
you. My sympathy toward you has not yet ceased; the endurance
of your motherly kindness is equaled by the unchangingness of my
remembrance of you, esteemed Mother. The days that pass without
detriment to your health, and with the certainty of your heart to be
pleasing to God, are still dear to me, and the hours I have spent in
your presence unforgettable, as it seems to me. I hope, and have every
confidence, that you will always be very well and find contentment in
this world. I have the honor of presenting my compliments and am

your

most obedient son

Hölderlin

251. TO HIS MOTHER

[Tübingen, 2 March 1813]

Herr Zimmer allows me to add my compliments. I commend myself
to your kind remembrance. Should you be able, dearest Mother, to give
me the pleasure of a letter again soon, it will find a grateful heart.

252. TO HIS MOTHER

Esteemed Mother,

I'm answering your kind letter with a contented heart and out of the
sympathy I owe your existence, your health and your continuance in this
life. When you instruct me, when you encourage me to orderly conduct,

virtue and religion, the gentleness of such a kind mother, the familiar and the unfamiliar in such respected proportion, is as useful to me as a book can be and beneficial to my soul as higher teachings. The naturalness of your pious and virtuous soul no doubt bears better comparisons than the one I have just made; I count on your Christian forgiveness, dearest Mother, and on my strivings to perfect and improve myself more and more. My faculty for communication is restricted to expressions of my attachment to you until my soul has gained in sentiments to the extent that it can impart them in words and be of interest to you. I take the liberty of commending myself in all obedience to your motherly heart and your habitual excellence. I believe that diligence and habitual progress in what is good cannot easily fail to attain a good goal. I send my compliments, esteemed Mother, and am in sincerity

your

obedient son

Hölderlin

253. TO HIS MOTHER

My esteemed Mother,

I count myself fortunate in having so many opportunities to show you my devotion by expressing my sentiments in letter writing. I believe it is possible to say that good sentiments, expressed in words, are not in vain, because the heart depends among other things on inner precepts that lie in the nature of man and which, in as far as they are Christian, are of interest for their constancy and beneficence. Man seems readily accustomed to reliability, to a greater purity that seems to conform with his inclination. This inner being also seems rich in powers, as it can, beyond this, contribute to the assuaging of the human heart and to the formation of the powers of the human heart. The divine, of the sort that man is receptive to, is wonderfully bestowed upon the more natural efforts a man makes. I ask forgiveness for having imparted myself to you in this unconsidered way. To occupy oneself with oneself is a vocation that, however serious it may appear, has the spirit of man to help it and, on account of the disposition of the human heart, can contribute to gentleness in human life and in doing so to higher receptivity. I must ask once again for forgiveness as I break off. I am with sincerest devotion

your

obedient son

Hölderlin

254. TO HIS MOTHER

My esteemed Mother,

I continue to want to entertain you with my letters, and to answer your kind missive. I cannot stop venerating you, and acknowledging your kindness toward me and tenderness in admonition. How right you are to remind me that I must not lose my reverence for Herr Zimmer and endeavor more and more to cultivate virtue and decent manners. Your kind letters are also proof to me of your enduring good health. I commend myself to your further kindness, my esteemed Mother, and am with heartfelt admiration

your

obedient son

Hölderlin

255. TO HIS MOTHER

My dearest Mother,

I thank you with all my heart for the recent expressions of your lasting kindness. These past days I have not been quite well, but am better again now. How you are yourself concerns me all the more and so too

I am all the more pleased when I think that you are well. Are you still happy to be living in Nürtingen, and is being there still conducive to your health, so dear to me?

That I can say so little to entertain you comes from the fact that I occupy myself so much with the sentiments I owe you. What concerns you otherwise, for me, in that regard, is your well-being, the repose of your excellent soul, and the way your soul partakes of this life. I shall endeavor to speak to you of this to the extent that I owe it to you. I have the honor to assure you of my utmost esteem and respect, and am

your

obedient son

Hölderlin

256. TO HIS MOTHER

My esteemed Mother,

I think that I am not a burden to you with the repetition of letters like these. Your tenderness and excellent kindness quicken my devotion into gratefulness, and gratefulness is a virtue. I think of the time I spent with you with much gratitude, my esteemed mother. Your example full of virtue will always remain unforgettable to me from afar and cheer me to follow your instructions and to imitate such a virtuous example. I add the profession of my sincere devotion and am

your

most obedient son

Hölderlin

My compliments to my dearest sister.

257. TO HIS MOTHER

My esteemed Lady Mother,

Here I am writing you a letter again. I don't know whether you have replied to the one I wrote last. I suppose that it has been answered. Do not, with the kindness that is yours, hold this assertion against me. I send you the sincerest wishes for your good health. Maintain me in your kind remembrance, and be assured that I am in truth

your

most obedient son

Hölderlin

258. TO HIS MOTHER

Esteemed Mother,

I am glad that you are in good health and that things are well with you in all respects. The good news you gave me of yourself pleased me. I have resolved to take ever truer interest in your well-being. Please give my compliments to my dear and highly cherished sister. I have not yet thanked her for the visits she had the kindness to pay me here. I am

your

most obedient son

Hölderlin

259. TO HIS MOTHER

Dearest Mother,

I cannot say otherwise than that I find myself most grateful in my soul for your exceptional, kindly pronouncements and such clear earnests of your goodness.

I shall just have to seek to earn this by good behavior and enduring respect toward persons who set me principles and whose principles I believe in.

To express myself has been granted me so little in life since in my youth I liked to occupy myself with books and thereafter distanced myself from you. What, despite this sort of confession, always remained, was a heartfelt belief in your excellent heart and in the seriousness of your motherly instructions.

Your example, your exhortations to honor a higher being, have indeed always been of use to me, so that what is in itself venerable about such objects of the spirit is also strengthened by your interwovenness in this life.

And thus I commend myself to you the more comforted in spirit and am

your

obedient son

Friederich Hölderlin

260. TO HIS MOTHER

Esteemed Madam,

I cannot thank you enough for your kindly missive. I find always the signs of your noble heart and strive to follow the gentle exhortations you see fit to convey.

I must also thank you with all my heart for what you enclosed and sent on to me.

You will have passed the holidays contentedly.

I hope, given the utterance so kindly made on your side, as far and as soon as I have got beyond the feelings that I owe you, to be able to write you a proper long letter too.

Be assured of my heartfelt interest in your precious health, well-being and contentedness of spirit and in the continuance of the same.

May I ask you to give my humble compliments to all your relatives.

I have the honor of being with utmost devotion

your

most obedient

Hölderlin

261. TO HIS MOTHER

[Tübingen, 18 April 1815]

My esteemed Mother,

If my letters have not heretofore been able to please you entirely, then the frequent demonstration of such attentions can show the well-meaning efforts behind them. It is often the case that practice may also take on this shape. What brings people together is practice in habit, in attitudes and relations moving closer together in the connections of humanity. Moreover there are other such closer attitudes: recognition, religion, and the feeling of committing relations. I commend myself most humbly to the continuance of your kindness, and am

your

most obedient son

Hölderlin

262. TO HIS MOTHER

My esteemed Mother,

Thank you very much indeed for what you sent. What you wrote me gave me a great deal of pleasure. People have to maintain themselves in goodness by exhortations, as is your duty, and by their way of presenting their compliments, as befits me.

I repeat what I have expressed and am

your

most obedient son

Hölderlin

263. TO HIS MOTHER

My esteemed Mother,

I am once more setting about writing you a letter. What I have usually written to you, you will remember, and I have written you almost identical utterances. I hope that you may always be very well. I commend myself in all obedience and am

your

obedient son

Hölderlin

264. TO HIS MOTHER

Dearest Mother,

I am giving myself the pleasure of writing you, as many times previously, another letter. I repeat the sentiments, and the attestation of the same, that I have made before. I wish you a very many good things always. Your health, so precious to me, will, in accordance with my hopes and my wishes, be ever more perfect and appropriate to your state. Remain well disposed toward me, dearest Mother, and grant me the continuance of your kindness and your benevolence. I commend myself to you in all obedience, and am

your

obedient son

Hölderlin

265. TO HIS MOTHER

My esteemed Mother,

That I am allowed to take this opportunity of writing to you is far from disagreeable to me. After all, it is the compliments of my being, so dependent on you, and the attempts to open my devoted soul to your continuing kindness that I should like to assure you of in the content of these letters, which are certainly not written without devotion. Do not take exception to my breaking off so soon. I remain

your

most obedient son

Hölderlin

266. TO HIS MOTHER

My esteemed Mother,

I have the honor of writing you a letter once again. The manifold kindnesses you have shown me in life give me cause to thank you, and every kind of courtesy I have to show you goes some way toward serving as a testimony of the same. Farewell, it was an honor to be able to write to you once again. I am

your

most obedient son

Hölderlin

267. TO HIS MOTHER

My esteemed Lady Mother,

I give you my most obedient thanks for the letters I have received from you, and assure you that it is an honor for me to give you from time to time the assurance of my devotion. Spend the time contentedly, as is my wish. I commend myself to you in all obedience and am

your

obedient son

Hölderlin

268. TO HIS MOTHER

My most esteemed Mother,

I am taking the liberty, with this note, of advertising to you my continuing gratitude. Be convinced of the devotion of my sentiments. The continuance of inner conviction that contributes to virtue is no small observation. For that matter I am unchanging in my obligations and convictions. I am with devotion

your

obedient son

Hölderlin

269. TO HIS MOTHER

Esteemed Lady Mother,

I ask you not to hold it against me that I am always burdening you with letters that are very short. To testify to how one is minded and the concern one has for others that one honors, and how people's lives pass by, this way of communicating is so constituted that one is bound to excuse oneself in this way. I close my letter once again, and am

your

most obedient son

Hölderlin

270. TO HIS MOTHER

My dearest Mother,

Because Herr Zimmer kindly allows me to write as well, I am doing so, if I may. I commend myself to your kindness. I think I can say that you will not abandon me. I hope to see you soon. I am with all my heart

your

obedient son

Hölderlin

271. TO HIS MOTHER

Esteemed Mother,

I am taking the liberty of writing you a letter, as has almost become a habit by now. I shall be delighted if you are in good health. It gives me pleasure to write of the sentiments I have written about in the past. I commend myself to you in all obedience and am

your

obedient son

Hölderlin

272. TO HIS MOTHER

My esteemed Mother,

Here I am writing to you again. The repetition of what one has written is not always an unnecessary state of affairs. It is founded in the nature of the matter that if one is exhorting oneself to good and saying something serious to oneself it will not be taken amiss if one says the same as before and does not always come up with something out of the ordinary. I will content myself with that. I commend myself to you in all obedience and am

your

obedient son

Hölderlin

273. TO HIS MOTHER

My esteemed Lady Mother,

It is a pleasure for me to make use of your kind permission by continuing my correspondence with you in this way. If you are well, that delights me to an astonishing degree. I shall however soon have to break off again. I must content myself with having given you news of my well-being. I commend myself to your kindness and favor and am

your

most humbly obedient son

Hölderlin

274. TO HIS MOTHER

Dearest Mother,

I thank you most obediently for what you have sent. Do not hold it against me that, as you have convinced me is the case, I continue to be a nuisance to you in this way. If it can at all be said, I should like to attest to you how much I wish to make up for all your concern for me and your goodness. Beyond that, I wish you good health, dearest Mother, and a peaceful life and am

your

most obedient son

Hölderlin

275. TO HIS MOTHER

My esteemed Mother,

I am taking the liberty of writing to you once more. What I have told you before I repeat with the sentiments you already know to be mine. I wish you well in every way. I break off once more, and ask your forgiveness.

I commend myself to you in all obedience, and am

your

obedient son

Hölderlin

276. TO HIS MOTHER

My esteemed Lady Mother,

The excellent Mrs. Zimmer reminds me that I should not neglect to attend to you with a letter and so testify to the continuance of my devotion to you. And the obligations people owe one another manifest themselves above all in such devotion, that of a son toward his mother. Human relationships have such rules, and following these rules and frequent practice of them means that the rules, to that extent, seem less hard and better suited to the heart. Make do with this sign of my constant devotion. I am

your

obedient son

Hölderlin

277. TO HIS MOTHER

My esteemed Mother,

I am writing to you, as far as I'm able to say something that is not disagreeable to you. Your well-being and your state of mind and heart are a matter of concern to me, as always. If you can be content with them you will be doing me a favor, you know how I am, with my entreaties and bothering you the way I do. I am

your

obedient son

Hölderlin

278. TO HIS MOTHER

Dearest Mother,

I am assured that my efforts to earn your satisfaction mean that the kindness that has always characterized your attitude toward me is unceasing. I must already close. Rest assured that I am with unending respect

your

obedient son

Hölderlin

279. TO HIS MOTHER

My esteemed Mother,

I just want to write you this letter. The news I have received from you makes me glad. I can tell you there is no better news for me than the sort that tells me that you are well. I must break off. I am

your

most obedient son

Hölderlin

280. TO HIS MOTHER

Esteemed Mother,

I am writing you this letter as a sign of my disposition as it usually presents itself in such conditions. It will give me great pleasure if I can always tell myself this, how my manner, well attested and known to you, of making myself understood to the people that concern me has brought itself into your remembrance. I am

your

obedient son

Hölderlin

281. TO HIS MOTHER

Esteemed Mother,

I thank you for the letter I have received. From what you have written me I can be assured that you are in good health and that you are living a satisfied and contented life. If you meant to tell me how I should comport myself toward you, my answer is that I strive unalteringly to remain on good terms with you.

I am

your

most obedient son

Hölderlin

282. TO HIS MOTHER

My esteemed Mother,

I do not want to miss out on writing you a letter. As delightful as presence is, still a sign from the soul, a sign not in itself alive, is of great benefit to human beings. Little as an excellence of the soul, such as kindness, or communication from the heart, or virtuous reminding, ever seems to get its due, still the expression of receptivity is also something for life and its appearance. Not only forthright communication, but expression and feeling are a form of that which is moral, a part of the world of the spirit and appearance. As there is body and soul, so there is also the soul and its outward expression. That is, man must express himself, do good out of merit, carry out good actions, but man must not just act on reality, he must also act on the soul. The moral world which entails the abstract seems to explain this. Make do with these utterances and continue to bless with your favor, my esteemed Mother

your

obedient son

Hölderlin

283. TO HIS MOTHER

My esteemed Mother,

I'm writing to you once again. Be so kind as to receive this letter
as you have my other letters and to preserve me in good memory. I
commend my innermost self to you, in devotion, and am

your

most obedient son

Hölderlin

284. TO HIS MOTHER

My honored Lady Mother,

I am writing to you in accordance, so I believe, with your instructions
and as it is appropriate for me to follow them. If you have news you
can transmit them to me.

I remain

your

most obedient son

Hölderlin

285. TO HIS MOTHER

My esteemed Mother,

I am writing you a letter this time as well as I can. Your health will
always be a matter of particular concern to me. It will always make
me glad if you are in good health and remain so. The connection with

you will always be dear to me. Grant me in the future also your favor and kindness. I am breaking off once more. I commend myself to your continuing love and am

your

most obedient son

Hölderlin

286. TO HIS MOTHER

My esteemed Mother,

Always I have to assure you how much your kindness and your native good temperament elicit my thanks and my endeavors to follow you on the path of virtue. Whoever can encourage others toward virtue and bring them further along that path is happy too, because he sees how his example promotes goodness and brings it about in the hearts of others. Happiness is happy in itself, but the contemplation of it is also happy, and also the hope of finding oneself supported in good works by others. Make do with these few words. I remain

your

most obedient son

Hölderlin

287. TO HIS MOTHER

Dearest Mother,

I have had the pleasure of receiving several letters from you. Your kindness in letting me have news of you convinces me that, as well as one can, one must be ready to appreciate this means of remaining in relative remembrance. I have intended to reply to your messages with these sentiments. I give you my humblest thanks for what you have sent. I remain

your

most obedient son

Hölderlin

288. TO HIS MOTHER

My esteemed Lady Mother,

I am taking the liberty of writing you a letter as so often before. The few lines with which I endeavor to express my respect will, I hope, not be disagreeable to you, as I am assured of your enduring kindness. Be so kind as to preserve good and enduring memories of me. I am taking the liberty of ending my letter. I commend myself to you, and am

your

obedient son

Hölderlin

289. TO HIS MOTHER

Esteemed Mother,

I have the honor of wanting to write to you once again. The letters you have written me have always given me great pleasure. I thank you for the kindness you have shown me in them. I must close once again. I assure you of my deepest respect and am

your

most obedient son

Hölderlin

290. TO HIS MOTHER

My esteemed Mother,

I have the honor of writing you a letter once more. That you are well is always a joy to me, and that you remember me in kindness is an opportunity for me to express veritable gratitude. Your letters I have taken as a testimony of kindness and true continuingness of such qualities of the heart as I, for my part, have given you signs of. I commend myself to you and am

your

most obedient son

Hölderlin

291. TO HIS MOTHER

Best of mothers!

I endeavor to cause you as little displeasure as possible and for that reason write as often as I can. I am glad if you are in good health and if I can put my sentiments toward you such that the debt I owe you and my conviction of your worth are visible. My wish is that you will always continue to recognize how good you are, and I remain

your

obedient son

Hölderlin

292. TO HIS MOTHER

Dearest Mother,

I am answering the letter you recently wrote. Make do with the little I can write you. You can be assured that I shall not cease to be true to the sentiments which I have tried to express in your honor. Believe me, the gratitude for what you have shown me in the way of goodness in life is no different. I am

your

most obedient son

Hölderlin

293. TO HIS MOTHER

My esteemed Mother,

I am once again taking the liberty of bothering you by writing a letter. It gives me great pleasure if things are going well for you and you find yourself in good health. The news I receive from you is for that reason pleasant and cheering. I commend myself to you in all obedience, and am with true respect

your

obedient son

Hölderlin

294. TO HIS MOTHER

My esteemed Mother,

Thank you very much indeed for your kind letter.

It is for me a double joy to see you so near and to have received a sign from your hands.

You will in the meantime have been doing very well. I take it my sister is well. Best of compliments to my dear Friz. And Heinrike.

I hope very soon to find much joy with you, commend myself to you and to my sister, and have the honor of being

your

loyal son

Hölderlin

For the trousers my humblest thanks.

295. TO HIS MOTHER

My dearest Mother,

I shall perhaps take the liberty of paying you my respects and visiting you. Especially should my stay be of a longer duration, I would ask you not quite to take me as a guest but to make do with whatever arrangements I might find to stay elsewhere. I am with true respect

your

most obedient son

Hölderlin

296. TO HIS MOTHER

Esteemed Mother,

I will always gladly write to you, as you will know, if I have the usual feelings of how I have come to be what I am, familiar to you, such that my necessary and natural inclination to make myself understood is as it must be. Write plenty to me always that I shall then be obliged to reply to with due courtesy. I remain

your

obedient son

Hölderlin

297. TO HIS MOTHER

Esteemed Mother,

I have not written to you for a long time. It pleased me that in your last kind letter you were moved to write to me of the contentedness of your life, which you have more reason to be happy with than not. I present you with thanks for the generous news you were eager to give me of your well-being and your peacefulness and am

your

most obedient son

Hölderlin

298. TO HIS MOTHER

Dearest Mother,

I must ask you to take upon yourself what I was obliged to say to you, and to inquire into it. I have been obliged to say certain things to you with the clarity you ordain, things you sought to apply to me. I must tell you that it is not possible to assume the feeling required by what you take to be the case. I remain

your

most obedient son

Hölderlin

299. TO HIS MOTHER

Dearest Mother,

You won't take it ill if I write you a letter again. I endeavor not to fall short in proving the devotion owing to you. I must break off once more. I remain, in attestation of my proper feelings,

your

most obedient son

Hölderlin

300. TO HIS MOTHER

My esteemed Mother,

My letter writing will not always mean a great deal to you as I have to say what I say, as far as possible, in few words, and as I now have no other way of saying. I take the liberty of asking you to look after me, as usual, with all your kindness, and not to doubt the good sentiments due to you. I am

your

obedient son

Hölderlin

301. TO HIS MOTHER

My esteemed Mother,

Forgive me if in its devotion to you my heart should look for words to seek to demonstrate its thoroughness and devotedness. I do not think my conceptions of you are very far wrong in respect of your virtuousness and kindness. But I should like to know in what ways I must exert myself to be worthy of that kindness, that virtuousness. As Providence has brought me thus far, I hope perhaps to continue my life without dangers and utter doubt. I remain

your

most obedient son

Hölderlin

302. TO HIS MOTHER

[Tübingen, November 1825]

My esteemed Mother,

It seems to me that it is a long time since I wrote to you last. In the calmness that is my own I count on your being well, and am glad that you have sometimes with so much kindness cheered me with news of your well-being. My dear sister is I trust also well? She can be assured of precisely those wishes that I have expressed to you. I close my letter once again, and am

your

most obedient son

Hölderlin

303. TO HIS MOTHER

Dearest Mother,

One day soon I must probably, so far as the grace of the Pope allows it, even pay you a visit. That these visits should not be troubled, I am touching in writing on a more credible or more incredible matter, the seemingly repeated talks, that is, about my legacy.

Be so kind as to gather all this together.

Your

truly obedient son

Hölderlin

304. TO HIS MOTHER

My esteemed Mother,

The sign of your good disposition and kindness toward me has, I hope, brought about true gratitude in me. Your charitableness will also in no part go without its rewards, if I think that every virtue tends to look for its sum in the whole, and that virtue in general does not always oppose harmony. As long as God grants me life, I shall always go out of my way not to call on your kindness and assistance overly to my advantage, and to become all the more grateful by seeking to earn your approval and by not lacking in sentiments toward you.

That you, as I may suppose, have spent some contented days, is a joy to me in itself. I commend myself to you and to all yours, and remain

your

most obedient son

Hölderlin

305. TO HIS MOTHER

My esteemed Lady Mother,

I am writing you a letter once more. I always have many good wishes for you. The sentiments with which I wish these things must be appropriate to them. Goodness and well-being are important matters that one does not willingly do without when one considers what is best for human beings. I take the liberty of breaking off once more. I am

your

most obedient son

Hölderlin

306. TO HIS MOTHER

My esteemed Lady Mother,

I give you my most obedient thanks for what you have sent and continue to impart myself to you and to prove to you the devotion of my heart. I beg you never to forget me entirely, most esteemed Mother, as you show yourself to be so kind toward me, and have always in the order of your excellent life been inclined to show kindness toward me.

You will be unforgettable to me because of the respect I owe you. With the sincerest expression of my devotion and admiration I am

your

most obedient son

Hölderlin

307. TO HIS MOTHER

With the permission of the most kind Mr. Zimmer I take the liberty of sending my humblest respects, and am

your

most obedient son

Hölderlin

308. TO HIS MOTHER

Likewise I have the honor of sending my humblest respects, and remain

your

most obedient son

Hölderlin

309. TO HIS MOTHER

Forgive me, dearest Mother, if I should be unable to make myself quite understood to *you*.

I repeat with all politeness what I have been able to have the honor of saying to you. Speaking as a scholar, I beg God in his goodness to help you in everything, and to help me.

Look after me. Time is exactly literal, and all-merciful.

I remain

your

most obedient son

Friedrich Hölderlin

310. TO HIS SISTER

My esteemed sister,

I thank you warmly for also, like our good mother, being willing to take so much interest in me and to give me the pleasure of such an excellent letter. You are alone at home; you have all the more opportunity to give yourself over to the peace of heart and mind that is your particular virtue, and the return of our dear esteemed mother recalls to you all your fondness for her. It would please me very much to see you again one day in Nürtingen; it pleases me deeply that you find yourself in this agreeable habitation and can attend to your health, which is so dear to me, and to the cheerful serenity of your soul. If you ever want to go to the kind trouble of addressing me a letter in the future, I shall be sure to summon up due gratitude and show you my appreciation. Mr. Zimmer's instructive company and cheering kindness toward me is of a great help to me. I commend myself to your sisterly love and am

your

most obediently devoted brother

Hölderlin

311. TO HIS SISTER

Dearest Sister,

I am giving myself, although I have received no letter from you, the honor of writing to you. It is always a pleasure to have inquired after your well-being and to have given the proofs of my devotion. I have the honor of giving you assurances of my enduring respect and am

your

most devoted brother

Hölderlin

312. TO HIS SISTER

Dearest Sister,

In addressing you thus I show you my gratitude that you still see fit to send letters inquiring after me, asserting to me the continuance of your kindness and of your sisterly benevolence. Your well-being is what leads to my sympathy, and your assertions of goodness I strive to acknowledge with sincere thanks. I must close. I am with veritable devotion

your

most obedient brother

Hölderlin

313. TO HIS SISTER

Dearest Sister,

I give you my most devoted thanks that you have written to me once again and with the assurances of your kindness have summoned up in me the true respect I owe you. The news you give me of your well-being is welcome and pleasing.

Be so kind to honor me with your benevolence in future and rest assured that I am with true reverence

your most devoted

brother

Hölderlin

314. TO HIS SISTER

Dearest Sister,

It is a true honor for me to write to you too on this occasion. The letters I have written to our mother I have always written with the desire of being able to say to you how much I truly appreciate you, and how I do not cease to strive to remain worthy of you. I intend to close this letter with the assurance that with sincere respect I am and remain

your

loyal brother

Hölderlin

315. TO HIS SISTER

[Tübingen, 1829]

Dearest Sister,

It is a true honor for me to write to you and to assure you that your kind letter gave me great pleasure.—Your expressions of kindness have always been of value to me. If you reply to me when it is convenient, the letter will be as valuable to me as the letters in the past. I have the honor of assuring you of my true devotion, and am

your

admiring brother

Hölderlin

316. TO HIS BROTHER

[Tübingen, 23 March 1823]

Dearest Brother,

You will be gratified to see that I am writing you a letter. I am convinced that you believe it is a true pleasure for me to know that you are well and that you are in good health. Even if I only write you very little, take this letter as a sign of my attentiveness. I see that I must close. I commend myself to your benevolent memory and am

your

appreciative brother

Hölderlin

FROM HIS BROTHER

Stuttgart, 25 July 1826

Dearest brother,

I consider it my duty as a brother to send over to you a copy of your excellent *Poems* which recently came out with the *Cotta* press. I had been hoping from one day to the next to bring it over to you myself, but unfortunately some urgent business affairs have held me up all this time and I regret that for this reason the handing over has been somewhat delayed. It will give me deep pleasure if it is agreeable to you to see that this collection has at last come about, carefully selected in your name by your admirers & friends.

A notable Prussian officer, Herr *v. Diest* in *Berlin*, whose father lived in Frankfurt and was probably a friend of yours, was the first mover behind it, I too thought I owed it to you, my dear brother, to ask the poets *Kerner*, *Schwab* and *Uhland* for their assistance with the editing, and they took on the task as a true labor of love.

So now the fruits of your excellent poems have been preserved for posterity, and your memory will always be honored in them by every sensitive and educated person.

What I have been able to contribute, is little, and barely worth thanking me for given what I owe you for the fraternal love you showed me in former times.

The honorarium that *Cotta* is paying for the poems & the 2nd edition of your *Hyperion* has been sent as your property to our dear mother in *Nürtingen*, who will make such use of it as *you* see fit.

On several occasions I have paid you a visit, dear brother, at your dear landlord's, Herr Zimmer's, but you will perhaps no longer have a clear memory of it.

I hope to visit you before the summer is out, as far as my many duties at work allow it. Perhaps it will be possible for my dear wife and my two children, *Carl* & *Ida*, who have long wished to see their uncle, to accompany me.

In the meantime I beg you to receive the assurance of my unalterable love & respect with which I am as ever

your

loyal brother

Carl

LETTERS

TÜBINGEN, 1788–1793

25. TO LOUISE NAST. Tübingen, December 1788

FROM LOUISE NAST. Maulbronn, early January 1789

26. TO LOUISE NAST. Tübingen, mid-January 1788

FROM LOUISE NAST. Maulbronn, 19 January 1789

FROM CHRISTIAN LUDWIG NEUFFER. Stuttgart, 21–24 March 1789

FROM LOUISE NAST. Maulbronn, March/April 1789

27. TO LOUISE NAST. Tübingen, March/April 1789

FROM IMMANUEL NAST. Leonberg, 17 April 1789

28. TO HIS MOTHER. Tübingen, April/May 1789

29. TO HIS MOTHER. Tübingen, ~ May 1789

30. TO CHRISTIAN LUDWIG NEUFFER. Nürtingen, perhaps September 1789

31. TO HIS MOTHER. Tübingen, before 25 November 1789

32. TO CHRISTIAN LUDWIG NEUFFER. Nürtingen, December 1789

FROM RUDOLF MAGENAU. Tübingen, December 1789

33. TO HIS MOTHER. Tübingen, January 1790

34. TO HIS MOTHER. Tübingen, second half of June 1790

35. TO HIS MOTHER. Tübingen, mid-August 1790

36. TO HIS MOTHER. Tübingen, late August 1790

FROM CHRISTIAN LUDWIG NEUFFER. Stuttgart, 24 October 1790

37. TO CHRISTIAN LUDWIG NEUFFER. Tübingen, 8 November 1790

38. TO HIS SISTER. Tübingen, 16 November 1790

39. TO HIS SISTER. Tübingen, late November 1790

40. TO HIS SISTER. Tübingen, 7 December 1790

41. TO HIS SISTER. Tübingen, mid-December 1790

42. TO HIS MOTHER. Tübingen, 7 February 1791

43. TO HIS MOTHER. Tübingen, 14 February 1791

44. TO HIS SISTER. Tübingen, March 1791

45. TO HIS SISTER. Tübingen, end of March 1791

46. TO HIS MOTHER. Tübingen, early April 1791

47. TO HIS MOTHER. Tübingen, mid-June 1791

48. TO HIS MOTHER. Tübingen, November 1791

49. TO CHRISTIAN LUDWIG NEUFFER. Tübingen, 28 November 1791

50. TO HIS SISTER. Tübingen, early December 1791

51. TO HIS SISTER. Tübingen, early March 1792

FROM RUDOLF MAGENAU. Markgröningen, 6 March 1792

52. TO CHRISTIAN LUDWIG NEUFFER. Tübingen, second half of April 1792

FROM RUDOLF MAGENAU. Markgröningen, 3 June 1792
53. TO HIS SISTER. Tübingen, 19/20 June 1792
54. TO HIS SISTER. Tübingen, late August/early September 1792
55. TO HIS MOTHER. Tübingen, ~ 10 September 1792
56. TO CHRISTIAN LUDWIG NEUFFER. Tübingen, after 14
   September 1792
57. TO HIS MOTHER. Tübingen, second half of November 1792
58. TO CHRISTIAN LUDWIG NEUFFER. Tübingen, May 1793
59. TO HIS BROTHER. Tübingen, early July 1793
60. TO HIS BROTHER. Tübingen, mid-July 1793
FROM CHRISTIAN LUDWIG NEUFFER. Stuttgart, 20 July 1793
61. TO CHRISTIAN LUDWIG NEUFFER. Tübingen, 21/23 July 1793
62. TO HIS BROTHER. Tübingen, second half of July 1793
63. TO HIS BROTHER. Tübingen, mid-August 1793
FROM CHRISTIAN LUDWIG NEUFFER. Stuttgart, 20 August 1793
64. TO HIS MOTHER. Tübingen, August 1793
65. TO HIS MOTHER. Tübingen, late August or early September 1793
FROM GOTTHOLD FRIEDRICH STÄUDLIN. Stuttgart, 4 September
   1793
66. TO HIS BROTHER. Tübingen, first half of September 1793
67. TO HIS MOTHER. Tübingen, mid-September 1793
68. TO CHRISTIAN LUDWIG NEUFFER. Nürtingen, early October 1793
69. TO CHRISTIAN LUDWIG NEUFFER. Tübingen, ~ 20 October 1793

WALTERSHAUSEN, JENA, NÜRTINGEN, 1793–1795

70. TO HIS MOTHER. Coburg, 26 December 1793
71. TO STÄUDLIN AND NEUFFER. Waltershausen, 30 December 1793
72. TO HIS MOTHER. Waltershausen, 3 January 1794
73. TO HIS SISTER. Waltershausen, 16 January 1794
74. TO HIS MOTHER. Waltershausen, 23 January 1794
75. TO HIS GRANDMOTHER. Waltershausen, 25 February 1794
76. TO FRIEDRICH SCHILLER. Waltershausen, ~ 20 March 1794
77. TO CHRISTIAN LUDWIG NEUFFER. Waltershausen, early April 1794
78. TO HIS MOTHER. Waltershausen, ~ 5 April 1794
79. TO CHRISTIAN LUDWIG NEUFFER. Waltershausen, mid-April 1794
80. TO HIS MOTHER. Waltershausen, 20 April 1794
81. TO HIS BROTHER. Waltershausen, 21 May 1794
FROM CHRISTIAN LUDWIG NEUFFER. Stuttgart, 3 June 1794

82. TO CHRISTIAN MATTHÄUS THEODOR BREUNLIN.
   Völkershausen, 8 June 1794

83. TO HIS MOTHER. Waltershausen, 1 July 1794

84. TO CHRISTIAN LUDWIG NEUFFER. Waltershausen, second week
   of July 1794

85. TO GEORG WILHELM FRIEDRICH HEGEL. Waltershausen, 10
   July 1794

86. TO HIS MOTHER. Waltershausen, 30 July 1794

FROM CHRISTIAN LUDWIG NEUFFER. Stuttgart, 16 August 1794

87. TO HIS BROTHER. Waltershausen, 21 August 1794

88. TO CHRISTIAN LUDWIG NEUFFER. Waltershausen, 25 August 1794

89. TO CHRISTIAN LUDWIG NEUFFER. Waltershausen, 10 October 1794

90. TO CHRISTIAN LUDWIG NEUFFER. Jena, November 1794

91. TO HIS MOTHER. Jena, 17 November 1794

FROM FRIEDRICH SCHILLER. Jena, December 1794

92. TO HIS MOTHER. Jena, 26 December 1794

93. TO HIS MOTHER. Jena, 16 January 1795

94. TO CHRISTIAN LUDWIG NEUFFER. Jena, 19 January 1795

95. TO GEORG WILHELM FRIEDRICH HEGEL. Jena, 26 January 1795

FROM CHRISTIAN LUDWIG NEUFFER. Stuttgart, 26 January 1795

FROM CHRISTIAN LUDWIG NEUFFER. Stuttgart, 5 February 1795

FROM HIS BROTHER. Nürtingen, 6 February 1795

96. TO HIS MOTHER. Jena, 22 February 1795

FROM HIS SISTER. Blaubeuren, 1 March 1795

97. TO HIS MOTHER. Jena, 12 March 1795

98. TO HIS BROTHER. Jena, 13 April 1795

99. TO HIS SISTER. Jena, 20 April 1795

100. TO CHRISTIAN LUDWIG NEUFFER. Jena, 28 April 1795

101. TO CHRISTIAN LUDWIG NEUFFER. Jena, 8 May 1795

FROM HIS SISTER. Blaubeuren, 9 May 1795

102. TO HIS MOTHER. Jena, 22 May 1795

103. TO FRIEDRICH SCHILLER. Nürtingen, 23 July 1795

104. TO JOHANN GOTTFRIED EBEL. Nürtingen, 2 September 1795

105. TO FRIEDRICH SCHILLER. Nürtingen, 4 September 1795

106. TO CHRISTIAN LUDWIG NEUFFER. Nürtingen, October 1795

107. TO JOHANN GOTTFRIED EBEL. Nürtingen, 9 November 1795

108. TO GEORG WILHELM FRIEDRICH HEGEL. Stuttgart, 25
   November 1795

FRANKFURT, 1796–1798

FROM FRIEDRICH SCHILLER. Jena, 24 November 1796
133. TO JOHANN GOTTFRIED EBEL. Frankfurt, 10 January 1797
134. TO HIS BROTHER. Frankfurt, 10 January 1797
135. TO HIS MOTHER. Frankfurt, 30 January 1797
136. TO HIS BROTHER. Frankfurt, 4 February 1797
137. TO CHRISTIAN LUDWIG NEUFFER. Frankfurt, 16 February 1797
138. TO HIS SISTER. Frankfurt, 17 February 1797
FROM CHRISTIAN LUDWIG NEUFFER. Stuttgart, 18 April 1797
139. TO HIS SISTER. Frankfurt, April 1797
140. TO FRIEDRICH SCHILLER. Frankfurt, 20 June 1797
141. TO CHRISTIAN LUDWIG NEUFFER. Frankfurt, 10 July 1797
142. TO HIS MOTHER. Frankfurt, 10 July 1797
143. TO HIS BROTHER. Frankfurt, ~ August 1797
144. TO HIS MOTHER. Frankfurt, ~ August 1797
145. TO FRIEDRICH SCHILLER. Frankfurt, mid-August 1797
146. TO HIS BROTHER. Frankfurt, ~ 20 September 1797
147. TO HIS SISTER. Frankfurt, late September 1797
FROM SIEGFRIED SCHMID. Mannheim, 19 October 1797
148. TO HIS BROTHER. Frankfurt, 2 November 1797
FROM SIEGFRIED SCHMID. Basel, early November 1797
149. TO HIS MOTHER. Frankfurt, November 1797
150. TO HIS BROTHER. Frankfurt, ~ November 1797
FROM HIS BROTHER. Markgröningen, 1 January 1798
151. TO HIS MOTHER. Frankfurt, early January 1798
152. TO CHRISTIAN MATTHÄUS THEODOR BREUNLIN. Frankfurt,
    10 January 1798
153. TO HIS BROTHER. Frankfurt, 12 February 1798, posted 14 March
154. TO HIS MOTHER. Frankfurt, 10 March 1798
155. TO CHRISTIAN LUDWIG NEUFFER. Frankfurt, in March 1798
156. TO HIS MOTHER. Frankfurt, 7 April 1798
157. TO HIS SISTER. Frankfurt, mid-April 1798
158. TO HIS MOTHER. Frankfurt, mid-April 1798
159. TO CHRISTIAN LUDWIG NEUFFER. Frankfurt, June 1798
160. TO FRIEDRICH SCHILLER. Frankfurt, 30 June 1798
161. TO HIS MOTHER. Frankfurt, 4 July 1798
162. TO HIS SISTER. Frankfurt, 4 July 1798
163. TO HIS BROTHER. Frankfurt, 4 July 1798
164. TO CHRISTIAN LUDWIG NEUFFER. Frankfurt, August 1798
FROM HIS SISTER. Blaubeuren, 13 August 1798

FROM SIEGFRIED SCHMID. Basel, late summer 1798
165. TO HIS MOTHER. Frankfurt, 1 September 1798
FROM SIEGFRIED SCHMID. Basel, 23 September 1798

HOMBURG, 1798–1800

FROM HENRI GONTARD. Frankfurt, 27 September 1798
FROM SUSETTE GONTARD. Frankfurt, ~ 25 September – 5 October
  1798
166. TO HIS MOTHER. Homburg, 10 October 1798
FROM SUSETTE GONTARD. Frankfurt, perhaps 31 October 1798
167. TO HIS MOTHER. Homburg, 12 November 1798
168. TO CHRISTIAN LUDWIG NEUFFER. Homburg, 12 November 1798
FROM ISAAK VON SINCLAIR. Rastatt, November 1798
169. TO HIS MOTHER. Rastatt, 28 November 1798
170. TO HIS BROTHER. Rastatt, 28 November 1798
FROM HIS BROTHER. Markgröningen, early December 1798
FROM SUSETTE GONTARD. Frankfurt, perhaps 5 and 6 December 1798
171. TO HIS MOTHER. Homburg, 11 December 1798
172. TO ISAAK VON SINCLAIR. Homburg, 24 December 1798
173. TO HIS BROTHER. Homburg, New Year's Eve/1 January 1799
174. TO HIS MOTHER. Homburg, January 1799
FROM SUSETTE GONTARD. Frankfurt, January 1799
FROM ISAAK VON SINCLAIR. Rastatt, 8 February 1799
175. TO HIS SISTER. Homburg, late February/early March 1799
176. TO HIS MOTHER. Homburg, early March 1799
FROM SUSETTE GONTARD. Frankfurt, after 4 March 1799
177. TO SUSETTE GONTARD, Homburg, Spring 1799
FROM SIEGFRIED SCHMID. Basel, 29 March 1799
FROM SUSETTE GONTARD. Frankfurt, 12 March – 4 April 1799
178. TO HIS MOTHER. Homburg, ~ 25 March and 18 April 1799
FROM SUSETTE GONTARD. Frankfurt, 9 May 1799
FROM SIEGFRIED SCHMID. Basel, 13 and 22 May 1799
179. TO CHRISTIAN LUDWIG NEUFFER. Homburg, 4 June 1799
180. TO HIS BROTHER. Homburg, 4 June 1799
FROM SIEGFRIED SCHMID. Zürich, 12 June 1799
FROM JOHANN FRIEDRICH STEINKOPF. Stuttgart, 13 June 1799
181. TO HIS MOTHER. Homburg, 18 June 1799

FROM SUSETTE GONTARD. Frankfurt, 2–7 November 1799
FROM JOHANN GOTTFRIED EBEL. Paris, November 1799
201. TO HIS MOTHER. Homburg, 16 November 1799
202. TO HIS SISTER. Homburg, 16 November 1799
203. TO JOHANN GOTTFRIED EBEL. Homburg, ~ mid-November 1799
FROM PRINCESS AUGUSTE OF HESSE-HOMBURG. Homburg, after
28 November 1799
204. TO CHRISTIAN LUDWIG NEUFFER. Homburg, 4 December 1799
FROM SUSETTE GONTARD. Frankfurt, before 5 December 1799
FROM SIEGFRIED SCHMID. Tuttlingen, 19 December 1799
FROM JOHANN FRIEDRICH STEINKOPF. Stuttgart, 12 January 1800
205. TO HIS MOTHER. Homburg, 29 January 1800
FROM SUSETTE GONTARD. Frankfurt, 31 January – 6 February 1800
FROM FRIEDRICH EMERICH. Mainz, 4 March 1800
FROM SUSETTE GONTARD. Frankfurt, 5 March 1800
206. TO FRIEDRICH EMERICH. Homburg, perhaps March 1800
FROM HIS BROTHER. Markgröningen, 8 March 1800
FROM SUSETTE GONTARD. Frankfurt, 15 March 1800
207. TO HIS SISTER. Homburg, 19 March 1800
FROM SUSETTE GONTARD. Frankfurt, 7 May 1800
208. TO HIS MOTHER. Homburg, 23 May 1800

STUTTGART, HAUPTWIL, NÜRTINGEN, BORDEAUX, HOMBURG, 1800–1806

209. TO HIS MOTHER. Stuttgart, end of June 1800
210. TO HIS MOTHER. Stuttgart, after 15 July 1800
211. TO HIS MOTHER. Stuttgart, late July 1800
212. TO HIS BROTHER. Stuttgart, ~ August 1800
213. TO HIS SISTER. Stuttgart, ~ September 1800
214. TO THE DUKE OF WÜRTTEMBERG. Stuttgart, September 1800
FROM KARL PHILIPP CONZ. Ludwigsburg, 4 October 1800
215. TO HIS SISTER. Stuttgart, late October 1800
216. TO HIS SISTER. Stuttgart, mid-November 1800
FROM JOHANN BERNHARD VERMEHREN. Jena, 28 November 1800
217. TO GOTTLIEB ERNST AUGUST MEHMEL. Stuttgart, November/
December 1800
218. TO HIS SISTER, Stuttgart, Autumn 1800

219. TO HIS SISTER. Stuttgart, beginning of December 1800
220. TO HIS SISTER. Stuttgart, 11 December 1800
FROM KARL PHILIPP CONZ. Ludwigsburg, 14 December 1800
221. TO HIS SISTER. Stuttgart, ~ 18 December 1800
FROM ANTON VON GONZENBACH. Hauptwil, 18 December 1800
222. TO HIS MOTHER. Stuttgart, just before Christmas 1800
223. TO HIS BROTHER. Nürtingen, late December 1800/early January 1801
224. TO HIS FAMILY. Stuttgart, beginning of January 1801
225. TO ANTON VON GONZENBACH. Stuttgart, ~ 6 January 1801
226. TO HIS SISTER. Stuttgart, ~ 9 January 1801
227. TO HIS FAMILY. Constance, 14 January 1801
FROM SIEGFRIED SCHMID. Friedberg, 15 January 1801
FROM JOHANN GOTTLIEB SÜSKIND. Tübingen, 22 January 1801
228. TO HIS MOTHER. Hauptwil, 24 January 1801
FROM SIEGFRIED SCHMID. Friedberg, 3 February 1801
229. TO CHRISTIAN LANDAUER. Hauptwil, February 1801
FROM SIEGFRIED SCHMID. Friedberg, 22 February 1801
230. TO HIS SISTER. Hauptwil, 23 February 1801
FROM JOHANN BERNHARD VERMEHREN. Jena, 27 February 1801
231. TO HIS BROTHER. Hauptwil, ~ mid-March 1801
232. TO CHRISTIAN LANDAUER. Hauptwil, toward the end of March 1801
FROM ANTON VON GONZENBACH. Hauptwil, 11 April 1801
233. TO AN UNKNOWN ADDRESSEE. Nürtingen, perhaps April 1801
FROM JOHANN BERNHARD VERMEHREN. Jena, 4 May 1801
FROM SIEGFRIED SCHMID. Friedberg, 8 May 1801
FROM CHARLOTTE VON KALB. Mainz, 15 May 1801
234. TO FRIEDRICH SCHILLER. Nürtingen, 2 June 1801
235. TO IMMANUEL NIETHAMMER. Nürtingen, 23 June 1801
FROM WILHELM FRIEDRICH ELSÄSSER. Stuttgart, 26 June 1801
FROM SIEGFRIED SCHMID. Friedberg, 6 July 1801
FROM SIEGFRIED SCHMID. Friedberg, 31 July 1801
FROM LUDWIG FERDINAND HUBER. Stuttgart, 6 August 1801
FROM CHRISTIAN LANDAUER. Stuttgart, 22 October 1801
236. TO THE FAMILY. Stuttgart, ~ October/November 1801
237. TO HIS BROTHER. Nürtingen, 4 December 1801
238. TO CASIMIR ULRICH BÖHLENDORFF. Nürtingen, 4 December 1801

239. TO HIS MOTHER. Lyon, 9 January 1802
240. TO HIS MOTHER. Bordeaux, 28 January 1802
241. TO HIS MOTHER. Bordeaux, Good Friday 1802
FROM ISAAK VON SINCLAIR. Homburg, 30 June 1802
FROM ISAAK VON SINCLAIR. Homburg, 20 July 1802
FROM ISAAK VON SINCLAIR. Homburg, 7 November 1802
242. TO CASIMIR ULRICH BÖHLENDORFF. Nürtingen, mid-November 1802
FROM CASIMIR ULRICH BÖHLENDORFF. Berlin, 2 December 1802
FROM ISAAK VON SINCLAIR. Homburg, early December 1802
FROM ISAAK VON SINCLAIR. Homburg, 6 February 1803
FROM CHRISTIAN LANDAUER. Stuttgart, 8 February 1803
243. TO FRIEDRICH WILMANS. Nürtingen, 28 September 1803
244. TO FRIEDRICH WILMANS. Nürtingen, 8 December 1803
245. TO FRIEDRICH WILMANS. Nürtingen, December 1803
FROM FRIEDRICH WILMANS. Frankfurt, 3 January 1804
FROM FRIEDRICH WILMANS. Frankfurt, 28 January 1804
246. TO LEO VON SECKENDORF. Nürtingen, 12 March 1804
247. TO FRIEDRICH WILMANS. Nürtingen, 2 April 1804
FROM FRIEDRICH WILMANS. Frankfurt, 14 April 1804
248. TO PRINCESS AUGUSTE OF HESSE-HOMBURG. Nürtingen, April/May 1804
FROM FRIEDRICH WILMANS. Frankfurt, 27 May 1804
FROM HIS MOTHER. Nürtingen, 29 October 1805

TÜBINGEN, 1806–1843

249–309. TO HIS MOTHER. 1812–1828
310–315. TO HIS SISTER.
316. TO HIS BROTHER. Tübingen, 23 March 1823
FROM HIS BROTHER. Stuttgart, 25 July 1826

CORRESPONDENTS WITH BIOGRAPHICAL NOTES

Böhlendorff, Casimir Ulrich (1775–1825), born in Mitau in the Courland (now Jelgava in Latvia), from 1794 studied law at Jena, where he joined a revolutionary group (the Society of Free Men) and probably first met Hölderlin and Sinclair. He joined Hölderlin and others in Homburg in 1799. In Switzerland he witnessed the French establish the Helvetic Republic in 1798 and wrote an account of it: *History of the Helvetic Revolution* (1802). He published two plays, *Ugolino Gherardesca* and *Fernando*, the first of which Goethe, to whom he had sent it, gave a scathing review. He returned to Courland a disappointed man in 1803 or 1804 and eventually took his own life.

Breunlin, Christian (or possibly **Christoph**) **Matthäus Theodor** (1752–1800), Hölderlin's brother-in-law, married Heinrike Hölderlin on 9 October 1792. Since 1785 he had been a teacher in Blaubeuren. He lost his first wife (with whom he had a son, Christian, in 1788) in 1791.

Breunlin, Heinrike, see Hölderlin, (Maria Eleonora) Heinrike.

Conz, Carl Philipp (1762–1827), repetitor at the Stift from 1789 to 1791 and a Hellenist, he had a strong influence on Hölderlin there, kept in touch with him, and was one of the first to try to collect and publish his work. Hölderlin approached him to contribute to his planned journal. In 1804 he was made professor of poetry and rhetoric at Tübingen, and published extensively. He also wrote a nice review of Hölderlin's novel *Hyperion*—see Letter 148.

Cotta, Johann Friedrich (1764–1832), one of the most prestigious publishers of his time, whose authors included Schiller, Goethe, Jean Paul, Fichte, and Schelling. He published the two volumes of *Hyperion* in 1797 and 1799.

Ebel, Johann Gottfried (1764–1830), doctor, naturalist, and writer. Hölderlin met him in Heidelberg in 1795 on his way back home from Jena, and not long afterward Ebel found him his second post as private tutor in Frankfurt. A good friend of the Gontard family, he was drawn to revolutionary Paris in 1796 and despite being disappointed by what he saw there stayed until 1802, when he attended to Susette Gontard on her deathbed. He wrote several successful books on Switzerland (where he lived permanently from 1810) that had some influence on Hölderlin.

Elsässer, Wilhelm Friedrich (1771–1855), at the Stift from 1789 to 1794, friendly with Conz. From Ludwigsburg, he became a pastor.

Emerich, Friedrich Joseph (1773–1802), a lawyer in Wetzlar and supporter of the French Revolution. When the French took Wetzlar in 1796 he joined their army and then worked in the administration of Mainz. Hölderlin probably met him in summer 1799, and helped him publish some of his poems. In 1801 he resigned from his position in Mainz and wrote out of disappointment at the discrepancy between the revolutionary ideals and the political reality a number of articles highly critical of the French, which resulted in his being dispatched over the Rhine. Not long afterward he died in Würzburg.

Goethe, Johann Wolfgang (1749–1832), the dominant literary figure of his time in all genres, became known throughout Europe for his *Sufferings of Young Werther* (1774). Hölderlin met him in 1794 in Schiller's house in Jena and came up in his correspondence with Schiller in summer 1797. He was a minister at the Weimar court and director of the theater there. After a final meeting with Hölderlin in August 1797 in Frankfurt, Goethe described him to Schiller as "rather weighed down and ailing, but genuinely endearing and with a modest, even anxious candor" (letter to Schiller, 23 August 1797). He regarded him as in Schiller's debt and advised him to write "small poems." Letter 186, a request for contributions to the planned journal, may be addressed to him.

Gok, Johanna Christiana (1748–1828), Hölderlin's mother. Her first husband, Hölderlin's father, died in 1772, and her second, wine merchant and mayor of Nürtingen, in 1779. Her father was a parish priest, and her mother lived with her during most of Hölderlin's childhood, and beyond. We have more of Hölderlin's letters to her than to anyone else, but only one of hers to him has survived.

Gok, Karl Christoph Friedrich (1776–1849), Hölderlin's half-brother. Unlike Hölderlin, his mother did not allow him to study, which is reflected in the often pedagogical tone of Hölderlin's letters to him. He became a successful civil servant.

Gontard, Henri (1787–1816), eldest child of Susette and Jakob Gontard and Hölderlin's pupil in Frankfurt from January 1796 to September 1798.

Gontard, Susette (1769–1802), the mother of Hölderlin's charge in Frankfurt. She and Hölderlin fell in love soon after he arrived in her household in 1796. She married her husband, Jakob Gontard (whose motto was "Les affaires avant tout"), in 1786. Her grace and beauty struck others beside Hölderlin, who in his poetry addressed her as Diotima. She died of German measles caught from her children.

Gonzenbach, Anton von (1748–1819), a magistrate and Hölderlin's employer in Hauptwil. His wealth came from the linen trade. Hölderlin's duties were to teach his two youngest children, Barbara Julia and Augusta Dorothea, and perhaps others also.

Hegel, Georg Wilhelm Friedrich (1770–1831), the philosopher, born the same year as Hölderlin and at the Stift with him 1788–93. The other main period of exchange was 1797 and 1798, when they were tutors in Frankfurt together. Some letters to him written from Jena have not survived, but their real influence on each other took place in conversation. Together with Schelling, they invented German idealism. Hegel addressed his only substantial poem, "Eleusis," to Hölderlin in 1796.

Hesse-Homburg, Princess Auguste of (1776–1871), later, by marriage, also Hereditary Grand Duchess of Mecklenburg-Schwerin. Hölderlin probably met her in Homburg in October 1798. She was a passionate reader of *Hyperion* and strongly attracted to its author. He dedicated the poems "Gesang des Deutschen" and "To the Princess Auguste of Homburg" to her, as well as his translations of Sophocles. The first letter to Böhlendorff survives in a copy in Sinclair's hand found among her papers. Probably in 1804, during his second period in Homburg, she gave him a piano. In a letter to her sister Marianne written in December 1816 she reports that Hölderlin has "gone mad" ("ist ein Narr geworden").

Heyn, Johanna Rosina, *née* Sutor (1725–1802), Hölderlin's grandmother on his mother's side, daughter and wife of churchmen, and a widow since 1772. From 1779 she lived mostly with Hölderlin's mother and so was closely involved in his upbringing. She was devout, and seems not to have had a particularly close relationship with her grandson.

Hölderlin, (Maria Eleonora) Heinrike (1772–1850), Hölderlin's sister, he called her Rike. Married Christian Matthäus Theodor Breunlin in 1792 and lived in Blaubeuren, returning with her three children—Christian, from Breunlin's first marriage, and Heinrike and Fritz—to live with her mother in Nürtingen after her husband's death in 1800. Only a few fragments of her letters to Hölderlin have survived.

Huber, Ludwig Ferdinand (1764–1804), from 1798 worked for the publisher Cotta as editor at the *Allgemeine Zeitung* in Stuttgart and also of the *Taschenbuch für Damen* (= *Damenkalender*) and the *Vierteljährliche Unterhaltungen*, where Hölderlin's poem "Der Archipelagus" appeared in 1804.

Jung, Franz Wilhelm (1757–1833), a radical democrat and friend of Sinclair's and Ebel's, his translation of Ossian, which Hölderlin had read and approved of in manuscript, appeared in 1808. From 1786 at the court of Homburg and a friend of the Landgrave, he fell out with him in 1794 because of his republican sympathies. In 1798 he went to Mainz and joined the French administration as police commissaire, leaving in disappointment in 1802 and moving to Frankfurt in 1806, then in 1814 back to Mainz, where he did much to encourage the arts.

Kalb, Charlotte von (1761–1843), *née* Marschalk von Ostheim, unhappily married to Major Heinrich von Kalb from 1783. Acquainted with several well-known writers of her day, including Schiller, with whom she had an affair after they met in 1784. It was through Schiller that Hölderlin got the position as tutor to her son Fritz in Waltershausen in late 1793. Some of her writings were published after her death, including her correspondence with Jean Paul.

Köstlin, Nathanael (1744–1826), deacon or "helper" (second pastor) in Nürtingen from 1775, later first pastor (*Dekan*) in Pfullingen and Urach. An uncle by marriage to Schelling, who as a boy spent two years or so in his household while attending the same school as Hölderlin—their friendship dates from then. Gave Hölderlin private tuition daily in the years leading up to his move to Denkendorf and was for a time his mentor. A representative of Württemberg Pietism, he had studied at the Tübingen Stift.

Landauer, Christian (1769–1845), known to Hölderlin via Neuffer, became a good friend during trips to Frankfurt, where his work as a draper often brought him. A democrat, he was convivial and fond of music, which made the months Hölderlin spent in his house in Stuttgart in the second half of 1800 one of the calmest and most productive periods of his life. Hölderlin addresses him in several poems.

Magenau, Rudolf (1767–1846), born in Markgröningen, followed the same educational path (Denkendorf, Maulbronn, Tübingen) as Hölderlin, overlapping with him at the Stift. A firm friend of his and Neuffer's in Tübingen, they soon lost touch afterward. Magenau married into a living in 1794, published unremarkable poems in 1795 and 1805, and later became a collector of ballads. Hölderlin's letters to him are all lost.

Majer, Johann Friedrich Ludwig (1742–1817), Hölderlin's uncle, married to his mother's sister Maria Friederike (1752–1816) and pastor in Löchgau. He had three daughters and a son, Ludwig (Louis), who accompanied Hölderlin to Frankfurt in 1795, on his way to Jena.

Mehmel, Gottlieb Ernst August (1761–1840), professor of philosophy at Erlangen and, together with Johann Georg Meusel, editor of the *Erlanger Litteratur-Zeitung*.

Muhrbeck, Friedrich Philipp Albert (1775–1827), studied philosophy at Greifswald, where his father was a professor. In 1796 he went to Jena, drawn by Fichte. A close friend of Böhlendorff's, with him he spent much of 1799 in Homburg with Hölderlin and Sinclair, having met them in Rastatt.

Nast, Immanuel Gottlieb (1769–1829), a clerk in Leonberg, west of Stuttgart, when Hölderlin knew him. Though gifted, his parents' circumstances did not allow him to study. He was Hölderlin's closest friend and main correspondent until the move to Tübingen in 1788, when their friendship petered out, but long after, in August 1828, he visited Hölderlin in the so-called tower.

Nast, Louise Philippine (1768–1839), Hölderlin's first love, a cousin of his friend Immanuel Nast. She was the daughter of the manager of the estate at the *Kloster* in Maulbronn, and their relationship began soon after Hölderlin's arrival there. They became engaged in 1788, but he broke off the relationship soon after going to Tübingen.

Neuffer, Christian Ludwig (1769–1839), at the Stift in 1786–91, where with Hölderlin and Rudolf Magenau he formed a poets' club. He then took the normal route and became a priest in various parishes, first at the orphanage in Stuttgart, and ending up in Ulm. His mother was thought to be Greek. He wrote conventional poems and translated Virgil's *Aeneid*. The friendship faded around 1800, but he is perhaps Hölderlin's most important correspondent.

Niethammer, Friedrich Immanuel (1766–1848), coincided briefly with Hölderlin in the Stift and went on to study in Jena, where in 1793 he became a professor of philosophy. In 1795 he founded the *Philosophisches Journal*, from 1797 coedited with Fichte. He was well known for his open house—in a diary entry of summer 1795 he records that Hölderlin, Fichte, and Novalis met together there and spoke "of religion and of revelation."

Schelling, Friedrich Wilhelm Joseph (1775–1854), the philosopher, knew Hölderlin in Nürtingen, where they were at school together, and came to the Stift in 1790. He was so precocious that the gap of five years between him and Hölderlin (and Hegel) was not apparent. He met Hölderlin for important talks in 1795 and 1796, and was visited by him in 1803, when he seems to have offered to approach the theater in Weimar about his translations of Sophocles.

Schiller, Friedrich (1759–1805), the dramatist, poet, philosopher, revered by Hölderlin from boyhood and like him a Swabian. Hölderlin met him in 1793 and got his first job as a private tutor in Waltershausen through him. In Jena Schiller took him under his wing, publishing poems and an early fragment of *Hyperion* in his journals—*Neue Thalia, Die Horen, Musen-Almanach*—and finding him a publisher for the complete *Hyperion*. But Hölderlin found his presence too much to bear and seems to have left Jena in part to escape it.

Schmid, Siegfried (1774–1859), son of a merchant and mayor of Friedberg, he studied theology in Gießen and then Jena (1792–95), where he met Sinclair. Hölderlin got to know him through Sinclair in October 1797 at what seems to have been their only meeting, when he was on his way to a house tutoring job in Basel. Briefly a protégé of Schiller's, in 1799 Schmid joined the Austrian army and led a restless life in and out of the military. He wrote plays, on one of which, *Die Heroine* (1801), Hölderlin, at his request, wrote a review (*Essays and Letters*, 312–15). Hölderlin dedicated his elegy "Stuttgart" to him, but none of his letters to Schmid have survived.

Seckendorf, Leo von (1775–1809), studied law in Tübingen, where he met Hölderlin in 1792, then in Jena, where he was among the radical political groupings and knew Sinclair. Became a diplomat in Württemberg and like Hölderlin was implicated when Sinclair was denounced for plotting to assassinate the Elector of Württemberg in 1805. He wrote himself, and published several of Hölderlin's major poems in his *Musenalmanach* in 1807 and 1808, including "Patmos," "The Rhine," and "Remembrance." Died fighting for the Austrians.

Sinclair, Isaak von (1775–1815), was acquainted with Hölderlin in Tübingen, and they became close friends in Jena and lived together for a few months. Sinclair was sent down from Jena in October 1795 for political activity, and maintained links with revolutionary groups even after entering into the service of the Landgrave of Hesse-Homburg. This eventually led to his being accused of plotting against the Elector of Württemberg in 1805. His hope was to establish the ideals of revolutionary France in Germany. Twice he provided vital support for Hölderlin in Homburg: in 1798–1800 after the split with the Gontard household, and in 1804–6 when at his own expense he arranged for him a sinecure as librarian at the court. He also wrote, and took part in the wars of liberation against

Napoleon in 1814. The major poem "The Rhine" is dedicated to him. Almost the entire correspondence between Hölderlin and Sinclair, which was substantial, has been lost.

Stäudlin, Gotthold Friedrich (1758–1796), the "beloved predecessor," Swabian man of letters who edited various literary journals and published some of Hölderlin's earliest poems. Hölderlin knew him from 1789, dedicated a poem to him, and was introduced by him to Matthisson and Schiller. Banished from Württemberg in 1793 for openly supporting the French Revolution, he drowned himself in the Rhine.

Steinkopf, Johann Friedrich (1771–1852), a minor publisher from Stuttgart with whom Hölderlin proposed to edit his journal *Iduna*, which failed due to lack of support from well-known writers. Steinkopf published Neuffer's two poetic "albums" (anthologies of new verse), and carried on publishing books of mostly local interest, as well as keeping a bookshop, until 1840. Schiller, advising Hölderlin not to go ahead with the journal in August 1799, refers to Steinkopf as an "insignificant beginner of a publisher."

Süskind, Johann Gottlieb (1773–1838), at the Stift from 1790, in the same year as Schelling. Thereafter house tutor and then *Repetent* in the Stift (1800); married a sister of Steinkopf in 1805 who in 1812 published his *Handbuch der Naturlehre* (*Handbook of Naturalism*). Pastor in Löchgau from 1817.

Vermehren, Johann Bernhard (1774–1803), from Lübeck, taught in Jena and an acolyte of Friedrich Schlegel's. He edited a *Musen-Almanach* for the years 1802 and 1803, in which Hölderlin's elegy "Menons Klagen um Diotima" appeared, spread over both issues. Died of consumption.

Wilmans, Friedrich (1764–1830), publisher of Hölderlin's Sophocles translations and of the "Night Poems." He published many of the German Romantics besides (including Friedrich Schlegel's journal *Europa*), as well as E. T. A Hoffmann's last work, *Meister Floh*, and Jean Paul. He began in his hometown, Bremen, moving to Frankfurt in 1802.

NOTES

At the end of the notes to each letter that letter's number in the "Große Stuttgarter Ausgabe" (Friedrich Hölderlin, *Sämtliche Werke*, edited by Friedrich Beissner and Adolf Beck, 8 vols., Stuttgart, 1943–85) is given, prefixed by a capital B. The letters, edited by Beck, are to be found in volume 6, with the letters to Hölderlin in volume 7. Beck's work of elucidation and commentary was immense, and it mostly stands, though later editors have clarified some details and occasionally altered the sequence. I have also used the "Frankfurt" edition, edited by D. E. Sattler and others from 1975 onward; the two volumes containing the correspondence are 18 and 19 (published in 1993 and 2007). The notes also give the number in that edition, prefixed with a capital S. In both cases, an asterisk denotes the separate numbering used for the letters *to* Hölderlin, which in the present edition are inserted without numbers. In addition, I have made use of the edition by Michael Knaupp, *Sämtliche Werke und Briefe*, 3 vols. (Munich: Hanser, 1992–93), and of the Italian edition by the late Luigi Reitani: *Prose, teatro e lettere* (Milan: Mondadori, 2019). The volumes of the intermittently appearing *Hölderlin Texturen*, published by the Hölderlin-Gesellschaft, are an invaluable source of biographical and other information, greatly enriching our knowledge of the context in which Hölderlin lived and wrote, and contain frequent comments on the letters. They are cited as *Texturen*, followed by volume and page number, usually without giving the names of individual contributors.

Reference is sometimes made to the bilingual edition of Hölderlin's *Poems and Fragments*, translated by Michael Hamburger, 4th ed. (London: Anvil, 2004), and for poems not found there, and occasionally in other cases, to *Selected Poetry*, translated by David Constantine (Hexham: Bloodaxe, 2018). For the essays, readers are referred to *Essays and Letters*, translated by Jeremy Adler and Charlie Louth (London: Penguin, 2009), which contains (almost) the complete essays but only a selection of the correspondence.

There is frequent mention of money in the letters. It is almost impossible to arrive at precise equivalents for the sums involved, but writing to his mother on 29 January 1800 Hölderlin reckons, probably with a good deal of optimism, that he could live for a year on five hundred florins. A florin he sometimes calls a *Gulden*, which I have translated as guilder, and he abbreviates it to fl. A florin was made up of sixty *Kreuzer* (cr. or x.). A carolin was worth eleven florins, as was a Napoleonic louis d'or.

The letters from Susette Gontard are translated by David Constantine.

DENKENDORF AND MAULBRONN, 1785–1788

1. TO NATHANAEL KÖSTLIN. Denkendorf, November 1785

A letter marked by the earnestness of Württemberg Pietism. H had been at the *Klosterschule* (convent school) in Denkendorf on the outskirts of Stuttgart since October 1784. It was a few miles north of his hometown of Nürtingen, where Köstlin was deacon or second pastor. **my father**: H lost his real father at the age of two, and his stepfather at nine. **pleasing to my fellow humans, but not to God**: remembering perhaps "We ought to obey God rather than men" (Acts 5:29). **prudent and wise**: in German more obviously in allusion to Matthew 10:16: "be ye therefore wise as serpents, and harmless as doves."
B1, S1

2. TO HIS MOTHER. Denkendorf, shortly before Christmas 1785

Mamma: the form of address Hölderlin uses for his mother until just after taking up his first job as house tutor in January 1794. **St John the Evangelist's Day**: 27 December. The "talk" he held on this day, effectively a short sermon given to his fellow pupils, has survived. His text was Hebrews 1. **Deacon**: Nathanael Köstlin. **Klemm**: Jeremias Friedrich (1766–1848), son of the first pastor (*Dekan*) in Nürtingen; he wrote in H's album on 4 August 1785. **Bilfinger**: Rudolf Ferdinand Friedrich (1769–1816), son of H's godfather Carl Friedrich Bilfinger (1744–1796); also put his name in H's album on 4 August 1785. **Grandmother**: Johanna Rosina Heyn, a widow—see list of correspondents. **something to distract you**: not clear what this is. **Harpprecht**: probably Valentin Christian Heinrich (1762–

1840), the Harpprechts being long-standing family friends. *Brittisches Museum*: presumably the journal *Brittisches Museum für die Deutschen*, edited by Johann Joachim Eschenburg from 1777 to 1780.
B2, S2

3. TO IMMANUEL NAST. Maulbronn, at the beginning of 1787

In October 1786 H had moved to the upper Klosterschule in Maulbronn, where Nast's uncle was administrator. Nast's name appears in H's album on 6 December 1786. **as far as the Cape**: it seems that Nast's unpromising situation led him to consider signing up for the regiment that Duke Karl Eugen of Württemberg was raising as mercenaries for the Dutch East India Company to protect its colonial interests in South Africa. **the Brutus and Caesar music**: presumably the setting composed by Johann Rudolf Zumsteeg in 1782 for Karl's song in Act IV, Scene 5 of Schiller's play *The Robbers*. **the Stuttgart *académiciens***: pupils at the Karl Eugen school in Stuttgart. **Schiller**: Friedrich (1759–1805), hugely admired by H in his youth and a fellow Swabian. **piano**: which H had been playing since the age of ten, continuing all his life. **Amalia**: another character from *The Robbers* and in particular her song in Act III, Scene 1. **Hesler**: Ernst Friedrich (1771–1822), in H's year, carried on like him to Tübingen but broke off his studies of theology and went to study law in Jena where H came across him again.
B3, S3

4. TO IMMANUEL NAST. Maulbronn, January 1787

Bilfinger: Christian Ludwig (1770–1850), from a different branch of the Bilfinger family from the one mentioned in Letter 2. A friend since childhood, after abandoning his theological training for the law he pursued a successful career as a diplomat. **My flute**: which by all accounts he played very well. **Efferenn**: Johann Jacob (1770–1824). **your aunt**: Nast was a nephew of the *Kloster* assistant (*Famulus*). **to the Cape**: see previous letter and note.
B4, S4

5. TO IMMANUEL NAST. Maulbronn, January/February 1787

somebody else: probably Louise Nast, Immanuel's cousin. H kept his relationship with her secret for a good year. See also the beginning of this

letter. **Did I not learn as a boy**: recalling among other things the deaths of his father and stepfather.
B5, S5

6. TO IMMANUEL NAST. Maulbronn, 18 February 1787

L Nast — : the initial could be read as *I* for Immanuel or *L* for Louise, and the possessive "your" also appears to be in the feminine ("deine"). **B—r**: might be read as Bilfinger or as Brecht, mentioned again at the end of the letter, but the possessive is again feminine. This is Heinrike Friederike Brecht (born 1770), daughter of the steward at the *Kloster*. **your Amadis**: Nast must have lent H a copy of Christoph Martin Wieland's comical poem *Der neue Amadis* (1771). **the great singer of the** *Messiah*: that is, Friedrich Gottlieb Klopstock (1724–1803), a very important writer for H; he introduced Greek meter into German verse. His principal work, *Der Messias*, appeared in its first form in 1773. **Ahasuerus**: referring to Christian Friedrich Daniel Schubart's "lyrical rhapsody" *Der ewige Jude* (1783). *Fiesko* **and** *Kabale & Liebe*: further plays by Schiller. **Louise**: blending Louise Nast and Luise the character in *Kabale und Liebe*, renouncing her love in Act I, Scene 3. **my friend Hiemer**: Franz Karl (1768–1822), then at school in Stuttgart, and son of the parson in Oberboihingen, near Nürtingen. In 1792 he made one of the few likenesses of H, in pastels. See Letter 16. **Brutus and Caesar**: see Letter 3 and note. **Miss Heinrike Nast**: a cousin of Immanuel's and Louise's from Leonberg, born 1767. For her wedding on 24 February 1789 H wrote his first published poem, which despite that has not survived. **Miss Brecht**: see above.
B6, S6

7. TO IMMANUEL NAST. Maulbronn, beginning of March 1787

Beck puts this a year later, but 1787 seems more likely. **my mystical letters**: probably referring to the playful code of the previous letter and possibly another now lost. *examen solenne*: an annual exam.
B19, S7

8. TO IMMANUEL NAST. Maulbronn, mid-March 1787

Put later by Beck. **Ossian**: in 1765 James Macpherson published *The Works of Ossian*, which purported to be translations from the poems of the legendary Gaelic warrior-poet Ossian and were partly based on exist-

ing Gaelic ballads. In Germany these were quickly translated (including by Goethe in *Werther* (1774)), and H owned *Ossians und Sineds Lieder*, by Michael Denis (1784), a hexameter version. The poems were vastly popular in the late eighteenth century and Ossian was sometimes called "the Homer of the North." See also Letter 184. **Cona . . . Morven**: respectively, Ossian's beloved river (the original Gaelic name for the Coe), and the name for Scotland. **Engelsberg**: a hill overlooking Leonberg. *académicien*: Hiemer. **at the curate's**: at Christian Ludwig Nast's (1763–1847), a brother of Louise and curate at the *Kloster*. Bilfinger fancied their sister, Wilhelmine. **the pantaleon**: a "large dulcimer" (*OED*), precursor of the piano, invented by Pantaleon Hebenstreit in 1690.
B12, S8

9. TO IMMANUEL NAST. Maulbronn, 26 March 1787

A request that Nast should visit him in Nürtingen during the Easter holidays. **Märklin**: Jeremias Wilhelm (1770–1820), the son of an apothecary and in H's year at Maulbronn.
B7, S9

10. TO IMMANUEL NAST. Maulbronn, mid-April 1787

It's done now: it seems Nast did not oblige by making the visit urged in the previous letter. *Kabale und Liebe*: Schiller's play, which H probably lent him with Letter 6. **Brutus and Caesar**: see Letter 3 and note. **Wieland's *Merkur***: the magazine *Der Teutsche Merkur*, edited by Christoph Martin Wieland between 1773 and 1789.
B8, S10

11. TO HIS MOTHER. Maulbronn, second half of April 1787

Sattler puts this in August. Reitani points out that it is the only letter written on the same paper as Letter 4 and puts it earlier. The first of several letters in which H's doubts about his vocation as pastor emerge, and the tension between them and his desire to please his mother. **the parson from Diefenbach**: Wilhelm Friedrich Moser (1752–1801). **one of the Camerers**: thought to be Gottlieb Friedrich Camerer (1766–1807). **the good man**: Johann Friedrich Hölderlin (1736–1811), one of H's godfathers and cousin of his father's, married to a Camerer, and pastor in Poppenweiler, a village to the north of Stuttgart. **Prelate**: in charge of the

Kloster—at the time, Johann Christoph Weinland (1729–1788). **my ser-mon**: not preserved. **Carl**: H's half-brother Karl Gok, then ten years old.
B9, S13

12. TO HIS MOTHER. Maulbronn, May/June 1787

Friz: that is, Fritz—Hölderlin. **Rise up**: parody of a recent poem by Christian Friedrich Daniel Schubart (1739–1791) who from 1777 to 1787 was incarcerated by Duke Karl Eugen for his support of the radical cause. **Rike**: H's sister Heinrike Hölderlin. **the chant**: (*Chor*) a short devotion held daily in the morning and late afternoon which the pupils took turns to lead.
B10, S11

13. TO IMMANUEL NAST. Maulbronn, summer 1787

splendid painting: presumably the "lovely Apollo" mentioned in the postscript to this letter.
B11, S12

14. TO IMMANUEL NAST. Maulbronn, late October 1787

your departure for foreign parts: see Letter 3 and note. **your honorable girl**: Heinrike Friederike Brecht.
B13, S14

15. TO IMMANUEL NAST. Maulbronn, November 1787

Another's dear lips: Louise Nast's. **your splendid girl**: Brecht. **H—**: Hiemer. **my Pfeffel**: a book, it's not known which, by Gottlieb Konrad Pfeffel (1736–1809), a poet from Colmar.
B14, S15

16. TO IMMANUEL NAST. Maulbronn, November 1787

our critic's tripod: as the Delphic priestess Pythia delivered her oracle from a tripod. **Trenk**: the hero of Hiemer's poem is probably Franz von der Trenck (1711–1749), leader of a paramilitary troop of mercenaries. **your good cousin**: Christian Reinhard Nast (born 1765).
B15, S16

17. TO HIS SISTER AND BROTHER. Maulbronn, New Year 1788

B16, S17

18. TO HIS MOTHER. Maulbronn, early February 1788

the Duke's birthday: Karl Eugen of Württemberg was sixty on February 11th.
B17, S18

19. TO HIS MOTHER. Maulbronn, mid-February 1788

Beck suggests 17th or 18th as the date. **my poem**: in honor of the Duke's birthday—it has not survived. **the wine**: asked for in the previous letter. **Rotaker**: Ferdinand Wilhelm Friedrich (1770–1830), fellow pupil, son of the parson in Hausen, regularly at the bottom of the class and in trouble. His father's letter has not survived. **at Wohlhaupter's**: instrument-maker in Nürtingen. **Unterland**: here, the area around Ludwigsburg where H had relatives in Markgröningen and Löchgau. **arrangements**: to return home for Easter. **Renz**: Karl Christoph (1770–1829), always top of the class and highly regarded by his peers (Schelling put him forward for a chair at Tübingen in 1813), he stayed on the normal path and became a clergyman. **Hiemer**: Philipp Jakob, younger brother of the other Hiemer who was at school in Stuttgart.
B18, S19

20. TO HIS MOTHER. Maulbronn, ~ 11 March 1788

once before: the family had visited their relatives in the Unterland in April 1780 and did so again this year. **the Tuesday after Palm Sunday**: fell on March 18th. **Schwiebertingen**: Schwieberdingen, near Ludwigsburg, where H would wait at the inn.
B20, S20

21. TO IMMANUEL NAST. Maulbronn, end of April 1788

my aunt's death-bed: Friederike Juliane Volmar (1741–1788) died on April 18th. **Gröningen**: Markgröningen (as often). **my lamented father**: Heinrich Friedrich Hölderlin (1736–1772), died when H was two (not

three). **My poems**: H would soon put together the pick of his poems in the so-called *Marbach Quarto Notebook*. He had sent some probably to his new friend Rudolf Magenau, who delivered his verdict on July 10th (see his letter). **Pfeffel**: see Letter 15 and note. **Brutus and Caesar**: see Letter 3 and note.
B21, S22

22. TO LOUISE NAST. Maulbronn, end of April 1788

Don Carlos: Schiller's play appeared in book form in 1787. **Schubart**: just released. Whether H did send in poems for his *Chronik* is not known.
B22, S21

23. TO HIS MOTHER. Maulbronn, ~ 10 June 1788

Letter and accompanying account (sent in two instalments) of a journey to Speyer on 2-6 June, the first time H travelled outside Württemberg and the first time he saw the Rhine. The letter with the expenses is hurriedly written, but the account is neat and on better paper. **Blum**: Johann Friedrich (1759–1843), on whose invitation H made the journey having met him at his uncle Ernst Ludwig Volmar's in Markgröningen at Easter. Blum was from Speyer and was there with Ernestine Friederike Volmar, to whom he had just got engaged, to introduce her to his family. She was the daughter of Ernst Ludwig Volmar, *Oberamtmann* (district administrator) in Markgröningen, and in 1793 Blum would follow him in that office. Later, in 1797, H's brother Karl Gok would enter into his service as a clerk. **Pfalz**: that is, the Palatinate, which H could see stretched out before him from the heights above Knittlingen, on the edge of Württemberg. The Bishopric of Speyer was the main ecclesiastical territory in the Palatinate. **Bretheim**: now Bretten. **Bruchsaal**: Bruchsal was the residence of the prince-bishops of Speyer. H's dislike for it probably reveals some anti-Catholic prejudice. **Frau Blum**: Sophie Margarethe (born 1738), widowed mother of Johann Friedrich Blum. She lived with her daughter and her husband Johann Adam Mayer (born 1756), a deacon at the Protestant church in Speyer. **Rike**: Ernestine Friederike Volmar, Blum's fiancée and H's cousin. **the Solitude**: a rococo palace near Stuttgart built by Duke Karl Eugen in the 1760s. **The new bridge**: built 1786-1788 and (like the castle) prominent in H's poem "Heidelberg"

(written 1798–1800). **National Theatre at Mannheim**: H saw *The Ensign* by Friedrich Ludwig Schröder, but Schiller's *Robbers* had premièred there in 1782. **staple-house**: a kind of warehouse, later the town hall. **Count of Styrom**: probably Count Ferdinand of Limburg-Styrum (1701–1791), a captain in the French army during the Seven Years' War. Not in fact a brother of the bishop of Bruchsal but a cousin of his father's. **Dillenius**: David Immanuel (born 1735), inspector of salt mines in Mannheim and uncle of Jeremias Wilhelm Märklin. **Okkersheim**: Oggersheim, the Electress's summer residence. **the same pub**: *Zum Viehhof,* where Schiller spent seven weeks in autumn 1782, hiding from the Duke of Württemberg. **Frankenthal**: the main manufacturing center in the Palatinate. **Boßler's music shop**: Heinrich Philipp Karl Boßler was a publisher of sheet music, the first to print Beethoven's works. He died in 1812. **the Gran**: probably a variant of Kran, a crane (derrick). **Rhine**: the river had already made an impression when H first encountered it on his way to Speyer. Here it deepens, and perhaps lays the ground for the fundamental importance of rivers in H's poetry. **Mrs Vogt**: Justine R. Gottlieb Vogt, *née* Nicolai (born 1755), a distant relation on his mother's side.
B23, S23-25

FROM RUDOLF MAGENAU. Tübingen, 10 July 1788

H had sent Magenau a sheaf of poems. Where these have survived they are not always in the versions discussed here. But H seems on the whole not to have taken much heed of Magenau's points. **"The Soul"**: H's poem "Die Unsterblichkeit der Seele" (Immortality of the Soul). **Conz**: see List of Correspondents. **the gentlemen in Berlin**: above all Friedrich Nicolai, chief exponent of Enlightenment criticism at the time. **"Hero"**: a poem based on Ovid's *Heroides.* Much later (1799), H translated half of the eighteenth poem into rhythmed prose. **Städelin**: Christoph Städele (1744–1811), involved in Schubart's *Chronik.* **"The Song of the Swede"**: this poem has not survived. **Longinus**: Magenau's copy of *On the Sublime,* now ascribed to Pseudo-Longinus. **room**: in the Stift, where H would soon move. ***experire et vide!***: see for yourself (Latin). **Eberhard**: Johann August (1739–1809), friend of Lessing and teacher of Schleiermacher. His book *Über das Melodrama* had just appeared. **Mohr**: Eberhardt Heinrich (1769–1831), in H's year from Denkendorf on.
*B4, *S1

24. TO IMMANUEL NAST. Maulbronn, ~ 6 September 1788

The last of the surviving letters to Nast. **Elsner**: Johann Christoph Friedrich (1770–1806), from Höfingen. **Landbek**: Johann Jonathan Christian (born 1763), soon gave up painting. **yesterday I finished something**: could be the poem "Am Tage der Freundschaftsfeier" (On the Day of the Celebrating of Friendship), or perhaps the Marbach quarto notebook, in which H made fair copies of most of his poems from the past four years before leaving Maulbronn, or his translation of the first two books of Homer's *Iliad*.
B24, S26

TÜBINGEN, 1788–1793

25. TO LOUISE NAST. Tübingen, December 1788

The dating of this letter is far from certain. Beck originally put it later but corrected this in an addendum which remains speculative. Knaupp hesitantly suggests late January 1789, Sattler mid-December 1788. **your last dear letter**: which has not survived. **the very first**: which has also not survived. **Miss Weber**: like the two names that follow, nothing is known about her.
B30, S27

FROM LOUISE NAST. Maulbronn, early January 1789

your dear letter: lost. **L—**: Leonberg.
*B6, *S3

26. TO LOUISE NAST. Tübingen, mid-January 1788

separation: caused by H's move to Tübingen. **your dream**: recounted in the previous letter. **sweet Heinrike**: Heinrike Nast, shortly to be married. **Miss Käufel**: either Friederike (born 1772) or Regina (born 1774), daughters of a churchman's widow in Maulbronn.
B25, S28

FROM LOUISE NAST. Maulbronn, 19 January 1789

The omissions in this letter indicate a coyness about the intensity of the writer's feelings. **your silhouette**: probably the likeness sent with Letter 25, though it could be another. Silhouettes were highly fashionable in Germany at the time. **Commerelle**: a feminized form of the surname Commerell. Nothing is known about this friend. **lake**: by Maulbronn.
*B7, *S4

FROM CHRISTIAN LUDWIG NEUFFER. Stuttgart, 21–24 March 1789

The first part of this letter is missing. Neuffer had been given leave to go home for Easter early. *Messias*: Klopstock's chief work, *The Messiah*, with which H was already well familiar—see Letter 6. It is an epic in twenty cantos. Schubart was known to read from it with brio. **the professor**: i.e., Schubart. **Stäudlin**: Gotthold Friedrich (1758–1796), see List of Correspondents. **visitor**: H paid Schubart a visit at the end of the Easter holidays when he also met Stäudlin. **sisters**: one of them, Rosine Stäudlin (1767–1795), later became engaged to Neuffer but died of tuberculosis; another, Lotte (c. 1770–1830), visited H in the tower in 1828. *lectoris ordinari*: (Latin) "appointed reader" (aloud, as in a monastery). The manuscript has "ornari," a slip of the pen. **Haselmeier**: not known. **"Eugen"**: no trace of this has been found. [**"Um Mitternacht"**]: this poem of fifteen rhyming quatrains, "At Midnight," dated 12 July 1785, has been omitted. **yours**: lost.
*B8, *S5

FROM LOUISE NAST. Maulbronn, March/April 1789

Of uncertain date and placed earlier by Sattler. **B.**: Bilfinger. **Mene**: for her sister Wilhelmine (also "Mine" below). **m—'s**: man's. In a lost communication H seems to have conveyed his mother's approval of their union.
*B10, *S2

27. TO LOUISE NAST. Tübingen, March/April 1789

The date is not certain, but probably two letters have been lost between this and Louise's above. Exactly what led H to break off the engagement

so suddenly is unclear, but his mention of ambition in this letter certainly refers to his ambitions as a poet, the subject of a number of poems from now and earlier. Louise Nast seems not to have been as accepting of the "new external footing" as the letter suggests.
B31, S30

FROM IMMANUEL NAST. Leonberg, 17 April 1789

Probably the first letter since H and Louise Nast's stay in Leonberg in autumn 1788. Nast knows nothing of the end of their engagement. H may not have replied—certainly their extant correspondence ends here. **L.:** Louise. **2 silhouettes:** presumably of Louise and Wilhelmine, the latter's to be passed on to Bilfinger (who also left his girlfriend not long after arriving in Tübingen). **Christian:** not certain, but perhaps Johann Christian Nast (born 1771), son of Immanuel's uncle Johannes Nast (1722–1807). **M.:** probably Maulbronn and so to Louise's father. **B.:** Heinrike Brecht. **Burk:** Eberhard Wilhelm Gottfried (1769–c. 1850), at the Stift, from Leonberg, later a clergyman. **foot:** mentioned also in Letter 31. **Linde & Karl:** not known. **Bleibel:** probably Georg Friedrich (born 1766), he worked in the *Kloster*'s offices. *Pfleghof:* a "Pfleghof" was an administrative building attached to a monastery, representing its affairs in another town—that in Illingen was attached to Maulbronn. **in *bona caritate*:** (Latin) "in sweet love." **area round Illingen:** presumably as a landscape painting.
*B9, *S6

28. TO HIS MOTHER. Tübingen, April/May 1789

Written in some agitation, with several words apparently left out. **my behaviour:** not clear, but perhaps to do with the break-up with Louise. **dearest Mamma:** the latter word is missing, but Beck inserts it as "urgently needed." **at peace & content:** the corresponding words are missing but are needed for the sense. **turned down:** i.e., refused permission to attend the spring festival in Nürtingen, first recorded in 1602 and still celebrated today.
B26, S31

29. TO HIS MOTHER. Tübingen, ~ May 1789

Rheinwald: the Rheinwald family was an influential one in Urach, but we don't know exactly which member is being referred to here. **Hegel:**

see List of Correspondents. **Märklin**: Jakob Friedrich (1771–1841), son of a merchant in Stuttgart, later professor at the Stift and then prelate in Heilbronn. Like Hegel, with whom he remained friends, he entered the Stift from the Gymnasium illustre in Stuttgart, pushing H down from sixth to eighth place. **a person**: that is, Louise Nast. **Bilfinger**: what had happened is not known. Perhaps not H's friend Bilfinger but a member of the Nürtingen branch of the family. **Seiffert**: properly Karl Felix Seyffer (1762–1822), who had just become professor of mathematics and astronomy in Göttingen and was later in charge of the Munich observatory. His family was connected to H's.
B32, S32

30. TO CHRISTIAN LUDWIG NEUFFER. Nürtingen, perhaps September 1789

The date is disputed. Beck puts it much later, around Easter 1793. Sattler proposes a date in late September 1789, going by the reference to Christiane Bardili below. **Come to me here**: Neuffer did so at the end of the month. The urgency is probably to do with H's doubts about pursuing his ecclesiastical career. **Gentner**: Carl Christoph Friedrich (1767–1824), at the Stift since 1785, then a clergyman. He married H's second cousin Karoline Blöst in 1799 (see Letter 171 and notes). **Counselor Bilfinger**: H's godfather Carl Friedrich. Stäudlin's day job was as a lawyer. **Miss Lebret**: first mention of Marie Elisabethe (Elise) LeBret (1774–1839), daughter of the chancellor of the university, with whom H was in a long and complicated relationship from the autumn of 1790. **Miss Bardili**: Christiane Luise (1769–1848), a childhood friend of H's from Markgröningen, was in Stuttgart at her sister's (wife of Counselor Jäger) to conceal her pregnancy. She was married on 24 November 1789. Sattler thinks the "enclosed letter" may have contained a (lost) epithalamium.
B56, S33

31. TO HIS MOTHER. Tübingen, before 25 November 1789

The first page of this letter is missing, perhaps discarded by H's mother because of the vehemence of his complaints about conditions in the Stift. They will in any case have formed the background to his desire to quit his theological studies. The atmosphere at the Stift had become particularly repressive after a visit from the Duke of Württemberg on November 5th, which was itself an attempt to assert order over the students' enthusiasm for the French Revolution. **permission**: the end of a sentence explaining

that H had requested a day's absence. In the event he hurt his foot just before leaving and stayed away for four weeks. **mistreatment**: among other things, H is perhaps thinking of the six hours of incarceration he was given on November 16th for having knocked the hat off a Tübingen townsman who had failed to doff it in greeting (as was required). This incident can be taken as a sign of the bad state H was in but also gives us a glimpse of his (entirely standard) sense of entitlement. **my late father**: H's father studied jurisprudence at Tübingen, though his son cannot have remembered him saying such words. **little song**: the rhyming lines "So lieb wie Schwabens Mägdelein"/"So sweet as Swabia's maidens." **what you sent**: probably money. On November 22nd his mother sent him two florins and forty-five kreuzer.
B27, S34

32. TO CHRISTIAN LUDWIG NEUFFER. Nürtingen, December 1789

unpleasantnesses: H was unhappy at the Stift and thinking of switching to law. **granted leave to travel**: by the authorities at the Stift. **a little song**: the one mentioned in the previous letter. **hymn to Columbus**: lost, though much later H returned to the theme; see "Kolomb"/"Colombo," written after 1802. **collection of old German legends**: *History of the Countess Thekla von Thurn, or Scenes from the Thirty Years War* (Frankfurt and Leipzig, 1789), not by Gottfried August Bürger (1747–1794) but by Christiane Benedikte Eugenie Naubert. **Gustavus**: Gustavus Adolphus, king of Sweden from 1611 till his death in 1632, was the subject of several poems by H at this time. He took part in the Thirty Years' War on the Protestant side. **beloved predecessor**: (in the sense of "model") Stäudlin. **M. Hoffman**: Carl Theophil (born 1768), an acquaintance at the Stift; the M. is for *Magister*, the degree which H was also to acquire in autumn 1790. **guardroom**: *Ritterstube*, one of the heated rooms at the Stift, shared with about ten other students. **Potatoes**: not common at the time in Swabia. The food in the Stift often needed supplementing.
B28, S35

FROM RUDOLF MAGENAU. Tübingen, December 1789

Master *Genius*: probably referring to Neuffer. **Holz**: H's nickname. **May heaven**: inaccurate quotation from Goethe. **Vive la Mariage!**: Long live

marriage! The jokes at the end, of which the wrong gender for "mariage" may or may not be part, are now obscure. Neuffer's name is written by Magenau. T.: probably stands for "testatur"; i.e., "witnessed by."
*B11, *S7

33. TO HIS MOTHER. Tübingen, January 1790

Mother: and not Mamma, which is how H otherwise addresses her in these early letters. Part of the submission to her will which this letter represents. **black coat**: required to preach in. From the autumn, preaching would form part of his ecclesiastical training, after two years of philosophy. **Vischer**: Benjamin Theodor Fischer (1769–1846), from Nürtingen, in the year above. **what you sent**: two small sums of money are noted in his mother's records. **Frau Schwab**: the wife of the Tübingen apothecary Johann Heinrich Schwab. **Miss F.**: unknown. **Bilfinger**: who in September 1789 had done what H was contemplating—left the Stift to study jurisprudence.
B29, S36

34. TO HIS MOTHER, Tübingen, second half of June 1790

What you have sent: five florins. **Rümelin**: Johann Christian Benjamin (1769–1821), thrown out of the Stift on June 15th for bad behavior. A symptom of the repressions brought in in the wake of the French Revolution. **candidature**: for the title of *Magister*, normally achieved after two years. This required the preparation of two dissertations. H's were "History of the Fine Arts among the Greeks" and "Parallels between Solomon's *Proverbs* and Hesiod's *Works and Days*." **Reutlingen**: town near Tübingen, where H's sister was evidently staying.
B33, S37

35. TO HIS MOTHER. Tübingen, mid-August 1790

what you sent: since July, sixty-nine florins, of which eleven for books and fifty for clothing. **Fischer**: written as Vischer in Letter 33. **carolin**: worth eleven florins. **Professor Bök**: August Friedrich (1739–1815), professor of philosophy, rhetoric, and poetry since 1775. Part of the exam involved defending and discussing a dissertation written by one of the professors. H, together with Hegel and others, was set Bök's *De limite officiorum*

humanorum seposita animorum immortalitate (On the limit of human duties with regard to the immortality of souls). **theses**: each professor in the faculty of philosophy prepared a number of theses (exam questions), which all candidates had then to spend the morning defending. **Camerer**: probably Clemens Christoph (1766–1826), from Reutlingen (later mayor there), whom H (and indeed Heinrike herself) would have liked to see married to his sister.
B34, S38

36. TO HIS MOTHER. Tübingen, late August 1790

Scheelhaß: Ulrich Balthasar Stephan von Schelhas (1742–1836), from Esslingen, a distant relation. H's mother had gone to approach him (successfully) for a grant to help cover her son's costs at university. Various family foundations provided financial assistance for students at Tübingen. **dissertation**: that is, the one by Bök mentioned in the notes to the previous letter. It was normal to send out copies as a way of announcing the title of *Magister*. **next week**: the exams took place in the first two weeks of September. **study of philosophy**: by now this probably includes Kant. **my silhouette**: one of H "as magister" survives. See the reproduction in *Hölderlin: Eine Chronik in Text und Bild*, ed. by Adolf Beck and Paul Raabe (Frankfurt am Main: Insel, 1970), 163. **Practical Logic**: probably either Johann Melchior Gottlieb Beseke's *Versuch einer Praktischen Logik, oder einer Anweisung den gesunden Verstand recht zu gebrauchen* (Leipzig, 1786) or Peter Villaume's *Practische Logik für junge Leute die nicht studiren wollen* (Berlin and Liban, 1787), both Enlightenment manuals intended for popular use.
B34a, S39

FROM CHRISTIAN LUDWIG NEUFFER. Stuttgart, 24 October 1790

at Weber's: each student at the Stift had an individual tutor, a repetitor (*Repetent*). In H's case this was Christian Friedrich Weber (1764–1831), the Stift's librarian since 1788, who later spent time in Jena. Neuffer's father, as the secretary of the consistorial board overseeing ecclesiastical affairs in Württemberg, had some influence in the matter. **Helvétius**: which book by Claude Adrien Helvétius (1715–1771, French atheist, materialist and freemason) this was is unknown. His main work is *De l'esprit* (1758). **L. St.'s**: Lotte Stäudlin's. **Nannette**: not known.
*B12, *S8

37. TO CHRISTIAN LUDWIG NEUFFER. Tübingen, 8 November 1790

Neuffer was at home in Stuttgart on sick leave. ***Video meliora . . .*** : "I see the better way and approve it, and take the worse" (Ovid, *Metamorphoses*, book 7, 20–21). **her**: Elise LeBret. **Perpetual ebb and flow**: referring to his moods. **"my better self is willing"**: in allusion to the poem "Elegy" by Gottfried August Bürger—"mein beßres Selbst ist willig." **Hymn to Truth**: an early version of the "Hymne an die Göttin der Harmonie"/"Hymn to the Goddess of Harmony," which shows the influence of the philosopher Gottfried Wilhelm Leibniz (1646–1716). **Hymn to Immortality**: Neuffer published a version of this as late as 1832. **Maro**: i.e., Virgil. Neuffer had embarked on a translation of the *Aeneid* in the original meter which eventually appeared in 1816 and, reworked, 1830. **"Vixi"**: (Latin) "I have lived" (Horace, *Odes*, book 3, 29). **Reuß's poem on Abel's departure**: in October 1790 Jakob Friedrich Abel (1751-1829) became professor of logic and metaphysics in Tübingen, moving from the Karlsschule in Stuttgart. The poem has survived, but the identity of Reuß is uncertain. **Kind, Magenau, Breitschwerd, Wieland**: various friends of Neuffer's, in his year. **Stäudlin's almanac**: the *Musenalmanach fürs Jahr 1792*, which eventually contained H's first published poems: "Hymne an die Muse," "Hymne an die Freiheit," "Hymne an die Göttin der Harmonie" and "Meine Genesung." **Visitation**: ironically referring to Duke Karl Eugen's visit on November 8th (dating the letter).
B35, S40

38. TO HIS SISTER. Tübingen, 16 November 1790

fair: this usually fell on the Tuesday after St Martin's, which in 1790 was November 16th. **My repetitor**: Weber. See the notes to Neuffer's letter of October 24, 1790. **Breier**: Karl Friedrich Wilhelm Breyer (1771–1818), later became a historian influenced by Schelling, who was a cousin of his. His uncle was Köstlin. H will have known him from Nürtingen. **Schelling**: see List of Correspondents. He had entered the Stift that autumn, aged only fifteen. **dear Carl**: the occasion is not known, but Karl had just embarked on his administrative career (at the age of fourteen).
B36, S41

39. TO HIS SISTER. Tübingen, late November 1790

von Vellenberg: Philipp Emanuel von Fellenberg (1771–1844), studied jurisprudence in Tübingen from November 1790 to the following summer.

Later he founded an educational institute near Berne, which inspired Goethe's imagining of a similar institution in his novel *Wilhelm Meister's Journeyman Years* (1829). **Miss Vischer**: almost certainly Marie Friederike Fischer (1770–1810), a young cousin of H's mother. **Kammerer**: probably the Camerer mentioned in Letter 35.
B37, S42

40. TO HIS SISTER. Tübingen, 7 December 1790

Klüpfel: August Friedrich (1769–1841). **chancellor**: Johann Friedrich LeBret (1732–1807), Elise's father. Theologian and historian, accompanied Duke Karl Eugen several times on journeys to Italy. **my essay**: lost.
B38, S43

41. TO HIS SISTER. Tübingen, mid-December 1790

Klein: who this is is not known. **Eßlingen**: see the first note to Letter 36. **Conz**: see List of Correspondents. In summer 1790 Conz held a class on the tragedies of Euripides. **Maier**: Johann Friedrich Ludwig Majer (born 1776), a son of H's uncle in Löchgau. He had just entered Denkendorf, would spend a year at the Stift, and went to study in Jena in 1796. See Letter 112.
B39, S44

42. TO HIS MOTHER. Tübingen, 7 February 1791

the tomfoolery: in a lost letter. **preaching again**: students with their *Magister* had to take turns to preach at lunch, which came round about every six weeks. **monitor**: "Oekonomus"—the oldest students took turns to oversee the kitchen and canteen and in that capacity were known as "oeconomi."
B40, S45

43. TO HIS MOTHER. Tübingen, 14 February 1791

I'll come later this month: in the event he made the journey early in March. **sermon**: lost, but a draft of a similar sermon from about this time survives. **a fierce opponent**: such as Kant in the *Critique of Pure Reason* (1781); this letter shows clear evidence that Hölderlin is reading Kant. **Spinoza**: Baruch de (1632–1677), the Dutch philosopher. H read, and perhaps owned a copy of, Friedrich Heinrich Jacobi's influential book

Über die Lehre des Spinoza (1785/1789). Some excerpts from this in his hand survive. He perhaps also, like Schelling, consulted Spinoza's works in the library at Tübingen. **miracles**: H seems here to be following, or at any rate agreeing with, the teachings of Gottlob Christian Storr, whose lectures he attended. For Storr, Christ's miracles are decisive, for the reasons set out in the letter and also in the draft sermon mentioned above. **pastor in Löchgau**: H's uncle was promoted to this position (from deacon/second pastor) on February 22nd following the death of his predecessor on the 3rd. **what you have sent me**: ten florins.
B41, S46

44. TO HIS SISTER. Tübingen, March 1791

the deacon's eye: who this is, or where H's sister had been, is not known. **The good doctor**: Camerer (a doctor of law). **what she sent**: seven florins, on March 9th.
B42, S47

45. TO HIS SISTER. Tübingen, end of March 1791

Joseph's brothers: referring to the Biblical Joseph at Genesis 37:19.
B43, S48

46. TO HIS MOTHER. Tübingen, early April 1791

This letter concerns the preparations for a walking tour of Switzerland, on which he set off later in the month. **Miss Gok**: an undetermined relative of H's stepfather. **at the Schwabs'**: the household of the Tübingen apothecary. **Privy Counselor**: Johann Christoph Schwab (1743–1821), professor of logic and metaphysics at the Karlsschule in Stuttgart and the Duke's secretary; brother of the apothecary and father of the poet Gustav Schwab, who in 1826, with Ludwig Uhland, put together the first collection of H's poems. **Hiller**: Christian Friedrich (1769–1817), whom H knew from Maulbronn, studied medicine then theology at Tübingen. Inspired by the ideals of the French Revolution he planned to emigrate to America but later became a teacher. H's poems "Kanton Schweiz" (1791) and "An Hiller" (1793) are dedicated to him. **Memminger**: Friedrich August (born 1770), studied medicine at Tübingen and then practiced in his hometown of Reutlingen. **Schaffhausen**: H's route took him via Schaffhausen and Winterthur to Zürich. From there they went over the Haggen pass to Lake Lucerne. H was back home in early May. **Mrs Ziegler**: This must be the widow of Hieronymus Ziegler, director of the hospital in Nürtingen. She had come with the house when H's stepfather bought it in 1774 and so lived on the same premises as his mother. **Dean Klemm**: Jakob Friedrich (1733–1793), *Dekan* (first pastor) in Nürtingen. **Chancellor**: LeBret. It was usual to gather letters of recommendation and visit well-known people on the way. In Zürich they called on Lavater (April 19th), who wrote "NB" by H's name in his visitors' book. B44, S49

47. TO HIS MOTHER. Tübingen, mid-June 1791

cousins: probably the daughters of H's uncle Majer in Löchgau. **knight errant**: referring to the Swiss journey. **piece of news**: his mother must have relayed something of Louise Nast's marriage plans. She did not in fact marry until 1794. **my ambition**: as in his last letter to Louise Nast (Letter 27), not spelled out. But in September H would inscribe his mother a copy of Stäudlin's *Musenalmanach fürs Jahr 1792*, which contained his first published poems, with the words: "Let me, dearest Mother, dedicate the little you will find here by me to you. They are youthful efforts. Even if this kind of poetry were better suited to our epoch they would fare badly with our readers, men and women. But one day perhaps something better! Then I shall proudly and gratefully say: this is thanks to my mother—to how she brought me up, to her lasting love as a mother, to the friendship she bears me. M. Hölderlin." **wine money**: instead of having wine at table, students at the Stift could take the equivalent in cash. **grant**: probably another instalment of the money from Esslingen (see Letter 36 and note). B45, S50

48. TO HIS MOTHER. Tübingen, November 1791

Sattler places this later, in January 1792. **Grüzman**: Christian Philipp (1770–1848), a fellow student from Nürtingen. **what you sent**: his mother's records note two small sendings of money in November. B46, S53

49. TO CHRISTIAN LUDWIG NEUFFER. Tübingen, 28 November 1791

Neuffer and Magenau had both left the Stift in September. H had visited them in Stuttgart earlier in the autumn. **My girl**: Elise LeBret. **love and**

friendship: variation on Goethe, *Iphigenie auf Tauris*, lines 2, 665–66, quoted by H more than once. In the correct form, he had written the words in Hegel's album earlier that year, and they come again in his letter to his brother of 2 June 1796 (Letter 122): "Love and pleasure are the wings for great actions." **"Hymn to Humanity"**: published in Stäudlin's *Poetische Blumenlese fürs Jahr 1793*, with a motto from Rousseau's *Contrat social*. **Jean-Jacques**: i.e., Jean-Jacques Rousseau (1712–1778). **Uhland**: Ludwig Joseph (1722–1803), superintendent at the Stift and the administrator of a bursary Neuffer qualifies for. *Saltus dithyrambicus!*: (Latin) "dithyrambic leap." **Swabian Almanac**: Stäudlin's *Musenalmanach*, with several poems by H.
B47, S51

50. TO HIS SISTER. Tübingen, early December 1791

Written between 5 and 10 December. **fire**: on December 3rd. **convent**: i.e., the Stift, which H here refers to as a "Kloster." **Frenchman**: the Stift took a few students from the county of Montbéliard, which until 1801 was part of Württemberg. **Proctor**: (*Prokurator*), or procurator, the financial manager of the Stift. **the latest sending**: three florins. **Miss Kühn**: not known. **Miss Nast**: seems to be no more than a rumor.
B48, S52

51. TO HIS SISTER. Tübingen, early March 1792

Written not long after a trip home to Nürtingen. **Christlieb**: Wilhelm Christian Gottfried (born 1772), at the Stift, had visited H in Nürtingen. **statutes**: under pressure from Duke Karl Eugen, the statutes governing life in the Stift were being reformed, the main intention being to control the liberal instincts released under the influence of the French Revolution. **by the time I can expect to serve as a clergyman**: had he taken this path, H would not have expected to be called to a parish for at least another ten years. **Prince Wilhelm**: Friedrich Wilhelm Karl of Württemberg (1754–1816), succeeded his (Catholic) father in 1797, becoming head of the Church at the same time. As Friedrich I, he became the first king of Württemberg in 1806, with Napoleon's help. **Georgii**: Eberhard Friedrich (1757–1830), a member of the Consistory or ecclesiastical authority governing the Stift.
B49, S54

FROM RUDOLF MAGENAU. Markgröningen, 6 March 1792

captive: probably a (lost) letter. **woes in love**: with Elise LeBret. **Thümmel's Travels**: Moritz August von Thümmel (1738–1817), whose *Reise in die mittäglichen Provinzen von Frankreich* (1791–1805; Travels in the Southern Provinces of France), relates an escape to rural happiness in the South of France, Margot being the name of his innkeeper's niece. **Conrad**: King Conrad III of Germany (1093–1152). **Caverac**: or Caveirac, Thümmel's idyllic refuge in his *Travels*. **a hymn**: "Hymne an die Freundschaft"/"Hymn to Friendship." **burning of Troy**: a reference to the new statutes mentioned in the previous letter. *parturiunt*: in allusion to line 139 of Horace's *Ars poetica*—"parturiunt montes, nascetur ridiculus mus" (the mountains groan, and give birth to a ridiculous mouse). ***impavidum feriunt ruinae***: the full quotation from Horace's *Odes*, book 3, 3 goes "si fractus inlabatur orbis, | impavidum ferient ruinae" (if the shattered world fell in, | the undaunted man would be struck by the debris). *B13, *S12

52. TO CHRISTIAN LUDWIG NEUFFER. Tübingen, second half of April 1792

Sattler puts this much later, at the end of August, but the opening seems written out of fresh memories of a visit to Stuttgart at Easter, which fell on April 8th. **the graceful figure**: "die holde Gestalt," not Elise LeBret, but an unknown person H seems to have met in Stuttgart. **Wergo**: Panagiot (1767–1843), born in Constantinople as the son of a Greek merchant and since March settled in Stuttgart as a cotton trader. H will have met him through Neuffer. **Caffro**: Gioseffo (1766–1808), or Giuseppe Caffaro, virtuoso oboist and cor anglais player. **the good doctor**: Stäudlin, who was able to remove the offending word before the poem appeared in his *Poetische Blumenlese fürs Jahr 1793*. B50, S56

FROM RUDOLF MAGENAU. Markgröningen, 3 June 1792

Goethe's words: in the first letter of *The Sorrows of Young Werther* (1774). **Caroline Olnhausen**: born 1774. **novelist**: apparently the first trace of H's plans for *Hyperion*. **Thalia**: one of the nine Muses. **little work**: it appeared anonymously in Augsburg in 1793. **gnome of Sachsenheim**: "Klopferle" ("knocker"), a friendly imp from Swabian folklore. **Crassus**: perhaps a mistake for Varus, since it was he who was defeated by Hermann (Arminius). *B14, *S13

53. TO HIS SISTER. Tübingen, 19/20 June 1792

France and the Austrians: on April 20th, France declared war on Austria, who had recently formed the First Coalition with Prussia (joined by England in 1793). **Elben's paper**: the *Schwäbische Merkur*, edited by Christian Gottfried Elben (1754–1829). The news was indeed wrong. **Lukner**: Nikolaus (1722–1794, guillotined), a veteran of the Seven Years' War in which he fought on the Prussian side, the commander of the French army in Alsace. **Lafayette**: Marie-Joseph de Motier (1757–1834), famous for his exploits in the American Revolutionary War, since 1789 a member of the National Assembly in France and head of the army in the Ardennes. Would soon switch to the Austrian side as the situation in Paris radicalized. **Miss Stäudlin**: probably Lotte. **my month's break**: this happened from July 27th. **Prof. Flatt**: Johann Friedrich (1759–1821), professor of philosophy and theology at Tübingen. **what you have sent**: five florins, thirty kreuzer.
B51, S55

54. TO HIS SISTER. Tübingen, late August/early September 1792

At the end of August Heinrike Hölderlin became engaged to Christian Matthäus Theodor Breunlin (1752–1800), teacher at the *Klosterschule* in Blaubeuren. See List of Correspondents. **did not stay**: for the engagement party.
B52, S57

55. TO HIS MOTHER. Tübingen, ~ 10 September 1792

without dear Rike: away in Stuttgart. **2 lads at home**: H is looking ahead to the period he will spend at home between leaving the Stift in September 1793 and taking his exams in December. **Camerer**: whom H seems to think more of than of Breunlin. **uncle**: Majer in Löchgau. **Rapp**: Heinrich (1761–1832). **money**: two fl., forty-five cr., on 6th September.
B53, S58

56. TO CHRISTIAN LUDWIG NEUFFER. Tübingen, after 14 September 1792

letter: an enclosed one, for the "graceful figure" mentioned in Letter 52 whom H had probably seen again in August. **the prophet Nahum**: see the Old Testament book of Nahum (3:12) on the ruin of Nineveh. **Autenrieth**: Christian Friedrich, in H's year, had left the Stift in April to study in Stuttgart and had died on September 14th. **Schubart in his grave**: Schubart had died on October 10, 1791. According to the "dreadful story," in the evening after his burial a clamor from underground made the gravedigger bring him up again. On opening the coffin Schubart was found on his front, his nails scratched bloody but dead. **Miss Breier**: possibly Auguste Breyer (1770–1806), fiancée of Georg Kerner (1770–1812) who had gone to Paris to follow events. Possibly, therefore, she is the "graceful figure" (Sattler thinks so), her engagement would explain why H can hope for no more than friendship. But this is very uncertain. **Hymn to Boldness**: "Dem Genius der Kühnheit"/"To the Spirit of Boldness," published in its final version in 1795 in Schiller's *Neue Thalia*.
B54, S59

57. TO HIS MOTHER. Tübingen, second half of November 1792

the fire's in the roof: i.e., it's too late. **war**: on October 21st, the French under Custine had conquered Mainz, making further invasion of southern Germany likely. On November 19th, the National Convention in Paris issued a decree offering its support to all nations that wanted to be free. **sweet and right**: remembering Horace's "dulce et decorum est pro patria mori" (*Odes*, book 3, 2). **victory at Mons**: on November 6th the French defeated the Austrian army at Jemappes.
B55, S60

58. TO CHRISTIAN LUDWIG NEUFFER. Tübingen, May 1793

Miss Hafner: Christiane Eleonore (born 1772), had broken off the relationship with Neuffer in November 1792. **Rößlin**: Christoph Heinrich (1767–1831), in the same year as Neuffer, married Hafner in 1804. **better path**: referring to Rosine Stäudlin. **without form and void . . .**: combining Genesis 1:2 and Psalms 32:4. **queen of my heart**: Elise LeBret. *Si magna licet componere parvis*: inversion of line 176 from Virgil's *Georgics*

IV: "si parva licet componere magnis" (if it is permissible to compare small things with great). **my Greeks**: in particular Plato at this time. **Kant's school**: H owned copies of the *Critique of Pure Reason* and of the *Critique of Judgement*. The pairing of Greek literature and Kant recurs several times—see especially Letter 85 (to Hegel, 10 July 1794): "Kant and the Greeks are virtually all I read." His final report from the Stift also picks out this conjunction and couples it with the cultivation of "litterarum elegantiorum" (belles lettres). **fragment of my novel**: from a very early version that has not survived. **dear doctor**: Stäudlin.
B57, S61

59. TO HIS BROTHER. Tübingen, early July 1793

Extract and summary by Schlesier. **Cotta**: Christoph Friedrich (1758–1838), an older brother of the famous publisher Johann Friedrich. He went to Strasbourg as an enthusiast for the Revolution in July 1791, took French citizenship, and edited a political journal there. **14th of July**: the storming of the Bastille on 14 July 1789 was not in fact celebrated with especial pomp in 1793. But a possibly apocryphal story relates that students from the Stift, including H, Hegel, and Schelling, observed the anniversary by erecting a Tree of Liberty. **future journal**: a plan to replace Stäudlin's *Chronik*, which came to nothing. The material H had ready for it was probably (from) the first version of *Hyperion*. **debts**: H's accumulated owings by the end of his time in Tübingen were paid off with a payment of 157 florins on 1st November.
B58, S63

60. TO HIS BROTHER. Tübingen, mid-July 1793

Summary by Schlesier.
B59, S64

FROM CHRISTIAN LUDWIG NEUFFER. Stuttgart, 20 July 1793

Urania's heavenly gardens: some sort of amalgam of the garden of the Hesperides, Urania as one of the Muses, and Aphrodite Urania. **one girl**: Lotte Stäudlin. **Mathison**: Friedrich Matthisson (1761–1831), poet—see next letter.
*B15, *S15

61. TO CHRISTIAN LUDWIG NEUFFER. Tübingen, 21/23 July 1793

An immediate and exact response to the previous letter. It was preceded by a (lost) letter to Stäudlin sending the early "fragment of a fragment" of *Hyperion*, the poem "To the Spirit of Boldness" and perhaps also "Griechenland"/"Greece," which is dedicated to Stäudlin and close to the evocation of Greece in this letter. For a translation of this poem see *Selected Poetry*, 19–20. **Ilissos**: river near Athens, setting for Plato's *Phaedrus*. **beginning of the world**: thinking of Plato's *Timaeus*. **banquet**: alluding to Plato's *Symposium*. **in which at present I live & move**: in allusion to Acts 17:28: "For in him we live, and move, and have our being." **the person you do not name**: (probably) Lotte Stäudlin. **if posterity**: this florid sentence repeats almost verbatim words of Neuffer's. **your hymn**: "Die Hoffnung" (Hope), published in 1795 in the same journal (*Urania*) as H's "Griechenland." **that unforgettable afternoon**: on June 27, 1793, when in Tübingen H read his hymn "Dem Genius der Kühnheit"/"To the Spirit of Boldness" to Neuffer, Stäudlin, and Matthisson, who flung himself into H's arms in enthusiasm and admiration. Matthisson was quite a well-known poet, travelling through Swabia at the time. **my Hesiod**: requested in the previous letter.
B60, S66

62. TO HIS BROTHER. Tübingen, second half of July 1793

Extract and partial summary by Schlesier. This letter makes H's attitude to the French Revolution clear: like many in Germany he was against the extremists but for its originating ideals. **Marat**: Jean Paul (1743–1793), a Jacobin behind the September Massacres, assassinated by Charlotte Corday on July 13th. **Brissot**: Jacques Pierre (1754–1793), leader of the (more moderate) Girondists, guillotined (as H fears) on 31st October. **confession**: of his debts.
B61, S65

63. TO HIS BROTHER. Tübingen, mid-August 1793

Summary and extract by Schlesier. **Hemsterhuis**: Franz (1721–1790), Dutch Neoplatonic philosopher whose influence is palpable in *Hyperion*. H seems to have sent him the first volume of his selected works in German, which appeared in 1782 with an important essay by Herder. **Machiavelli**: Niccolò (1469–1527) and his chief work *The Prince*. **Schiller**: had come to Heilbronn, and so back onto Württembergian territory for

this first time since his flight in 1782, on August 8th. A month later he moved on to Ludwigsburg.
B62, S69

FROM CHRISTIAN LUDWIG NEUFFER. Stuttgart, 20 August 1793

song of joy: Magenau in his memoirs remembers an evening in the garden of the Lamb Inn in Tübingen when the three friends sang "all the songs of joy one after another," finishing with Schiller's "Lied an die Freude." **Stäudlin's journal**: this in reply to H's question in Letter 61. **abroad**: i.e., to journals outside Württemberg. **Voß's and Bürger's almanacs**: see Letter 68 and note.
*B16, *S16

64. TO HIS MOTHER. Tübingen, August 1793

In the lost letter to which this replies, his mother had obviously assented to H's plans to seek a position as a house-tutor once his exams were over rather than serving as a *Vikar* (~ curate) in Württemberg while waiting for a call to a parish of his own. **the sum**: H's inheritance from his father, managed by his mother. **Neither Jena nor Switzerland**: as possible destinations as house-tutor. **Blaubeuren**: where H's sister now lived since her marriage. He would go only in November. **Mr Majer**: Christian Benjamin (1755–1801), a brother of H's uncle in Löchgau, had lost his job after getting into financial difficulties. In the German, he is referred to as "Herr Keller," where "Keller" (literally "cellarer") is probably the name of his job, here indicating a kind of financial administrator.
B63, S67

65. TO HIS MOTHER. Tübingen, late August or early September 1793

Uncle Majer: in a lost letter H must have suggested he would visit his relatives in Löchgau. **my dear sister's circumstances**: she gave birth on September 17th in Blaubeuren. **my Jena plans**: Jena was nearing its heyday as the most stimulating and progressive university in Germany. **Consistory**: on completing their exams, graduates from the Stift remained beholden to the ecclesiastical authorities of Württemberg (the Consistory) and were expected to become curates as the next step toward becoming pastors. Any divergence from that path needed approval, on the pain of reimbursing the cost of their studies, and the usual course for the best

students wishing to avoid or put off becoming a clergyman was to work as a house-tutor.
B64, S68

FROM GOTTHOLD FRIEDRICH STÄUDLIN. Stuttgart, 4 September 1793

Extract and summary by Schlesier. A reply to the lost letter with which H had sent the *Hyperion* fragment and a number of poems. **an accomplished poem**: which has apparently not survived.
*B17, *S17

66. TO HIS BROTHER. Tübingen, first half of September 1793

Sattler places this letter earlier, in July. An important early statement of H's hopes and ambitions. **new acquaintance**: presumably Matthisson, whose poems Karl had asked for. **something else**: Schiller's *Don Carlos* (1787). The passage referred to is a famous expression of Enlightenment ideals. The page number indicates that H had the first edition or a local reprint.
B65, S62

67. TO HIS MOTHER. Tübingen, mid-September 1793

Seits: Wilhelm Friedrich Seiz (1768–1836) had left the Stift in 1792 and taken a post as house tutor in Switzerland. By 1804 he was a pastor in Leonberg. **in Jena**: keen to go to Jena, H had learnt from Hegel that Schiller was looking for a house tutor for Charlotte von Kalb in Waltershausen, which he thought was close to Jena. In the event it was a much smaller and remoter Waltershausen (see notes to Letter 71). The post was first offered to Hegel, but when he turned it down H asked Stäudlin to put in a word for him with Schiller, which he did on 20th September.
B66, S70

68. TO CHRISTIAN LUDWIG NEUFFER. Nürtingen, early October 1793

The first letter to Neuffer since Letter 61. **my curiosity**: as to the fate of Stäudlin's new journal. **Bürger's and Voß's almanacs**: the *Göttinger Musenalmanach für 1794*, edited by Karl Reinhard (who had taken over from Bürger) carried three poems by Neuffer. The *Musen-Almanach für 1794* edited by the poet and translator Johann Heinrich Voß (1751–1826) had

none. **our exams**: the consistorial exams in Stuttgart, which took place on 6th December. **Guadet, Vergniaud, Brissot etc**: all Girondists soon to be guillotined.
B67, S72

69. TO CHRISTIAN LUDWIG NEUFFER. Tübingen, ~ 20 October 1793

a poem: "Das Schicksal"/"Fate." **post as house-tutor**: after interviewing him, Schiller had recommended H for the post in a letter of 1st October, but he only heard back at the beginning of November.
B68, S73

WALTERSHAUSEN, JENA, NÜRTINGEN, 1793–1795

70. TO HIS MOTHER. Coburg, 26 December 1793

H left Nürtingen on foot to Stuttgart, in about the middle of December, and then took the coach to Nuremberg on 20th. From there he travelled on to Erlangen, Bamberg, and Coburg, arriving in Waltershausen on 28th. It seems that he also went back to Nuremberg from Erlangen and spent the night of the 25th there, something the date of this letter conceals, since he actually arrived in Coburg on 27th.
B69, S74

71. TO GOTTHOLD FRIEDRICH STÄUDLIN AND CHRISTIAN LUDWIG NEUFFER. Waltershausen, 30 December 1793

The Waltershausen in question is a village in the Grabfeld region, on the border between present-day Bavaria and Thuringia, not to be confused with the town of Waltershausen near Gotha (which was closer to Jena). **Ludwig**: Ludwig Albrecht Schubart (1765–1811), son of the poet, editor of the *Englische Blätter* (republishing items from English journals) and secretary of the Prussian legation in Nuremberg. **Prof. Ammon**: Christoph Friedrich (1766–1850), professor of theology and philosophy at Erlangen, well-known as a preacher, a Kantian theologian. **a German version of St Antoine**: on 19th December, not long before H's arrival, there had been protests in Nuremberg over rising prices. H compares this to a popular revolt against the monarchy in Paris in 1750, regarded

as anticipating the French Revolution. **Major von Kalb**: Heinrich (1752–1806). **woman-friend**: Wilhelmine Marianne Kirms (1772–1840), who had joined Charlotte von Kalb as a lady companion in autumn 1792 having separated from her husband. **my future pupil**: Fritz von Kalb (1784–1852). **still in Jena**: Charlotte von Kalb had gone there in September and did not return until March 1794. **the house-tutor**: his name was Münch—Charlotte von Kalb had neglected to inform her husband of H's arrival. **poem to Fate**: "Das Schicksal." **parson and administrator**: probably the same person, rather than two—Johann Friedrich Nenninger (1760–1828), also a local historian and theologically a rationalist.
B70, S75

72. TO HIS MOTHER. Waltershausen, 3 January 1794

Frau von Kalb: Charlotte (1761–1843), not very happily married since 1783, she began a liaison with Schiller in 1784 which lasted several years. She also knew Goethe, had a correspondence with Jean Paul, and was generally well connected in the literary world. **Neckar**: the river of H's home, flowing through Tübingen, Nürtingen, Stuttgart, and Lauffen. **Court Councilor in Nürtingen**: Carl Friedrich Bilfinger, H's godfather (see notes to Letter 2). **Book club**: such clubs or "cabinets" were widespread at the time and key to the dissemination of Enlightenment ideas. That in Nuremberg was set up in 1787. **Son of the physician Jäger**: Karl Christoph Friedrich Jäger (1773–1828), son of the Duke's physician Christian Friedrich Jäger (1739–1808).
B71, S76

73. TO HIS SISTER. Waltershausen, 16 January 1794

widow: Wilhelmine Kirms. Her estranged husband had died on 7 February 1793. **The latest book by Kant**: *Die Religion innerhalb der Grenzen der bloßen Vernunft* (*Religion within the Boundaries of Mere Reason*), 1793. **Peace by Easter**: this assurance was premature.
B72, S77

74. TO HIS MOTHER. Waltershausen, 23 January 1794

over the Rhine: in December the French armies had occupied all the territory on the Rhine's left bank but did not cross over in 1794. **Troll**: not known. **Kleinmann**: perhaps Samuel Christoph Friedrich (1771–1854),

later pastor of Bönnigheim. **Herr von Wellwart's in Birkenfeld**: Birkenfeld, near Königshofen, was the home of a Franconian branch of a well-known Swabian family, the von Wöllwarths.
B73, S78

75. TO HIS GRANDMOTHER. Waltershausen, 25 February 1794

Written to his grandmother, Johanna Rosina Heyn, but then sent to his mother, so dual-purpose. **Friemar**: a village north-east of Gotha and in 1712 the birthplace of Johann Andreas Heyn, H's grandfather, who married his grandmother in 1744 and died in 1772. The family still had relatives there, but H seems not to have made the journey. **Mount the pulpit**: as required by the Consistory, even after graduation. **Löchgau**: his grandmother seems to be at her second daughter's, as often. **Louis**: his cousin Ludwig, now at Maulbronn (see Letter 41 and note).
B74, S79

76. TO FRIEDRICH SCHILLER. Waltershausen, ~ 20 March 1794

In a moment: refers to H's first meeting with Schiller, in Ludwigsburg in September 1793. **All he needs to know**: a draft parenthesis for the end of this sentence makes the Kantian provenance of H's ideas particularly clear: "(and will then be receptive to an example of selfishness denied, and so to the negative principle of morality *in concreto*)." As in the letter to Ebel of 2 September 1795, to which this can be usefully compared, the other main influence on these pedagogical thoughts is Rousseau. **For a week**: Charlotte von Kalb had returned from Jena in the middle of March. **chance**: what this was, or what H did to forego it, is not clear. **Some verses**: the poem "Das Schicksal"/"Fate," which Schiller did publish in his magazine (*Neue*) *Thalia* in November 1794. H calls it "a relic of my youth" though he in fact only finished it in Waltershausen. **M. Hölderlin**: H signs with his title, *Magister*.
B76, S80

77. TO CHRISTIAN LUDWIG NEUFFER. Waltershausen, early April 1794

something dearer: a reference to Rosine Stäudlin. **Your Virgil**: Neuffer's translation of the *Aeneid*—see Letter 37 and notes. **The opposite case**: H makes it himself in the famous penultimate letter of *Hyperion*. **my novel**: he had gone back to work on it and a (new and surviving) "Fragment

of *Hyperion*" appeared in Schiller's *Neue Thalia* at the end of the year. **Selma**: i.e., Rosine Stäudlin (Neuffer's name for her comes from Klopstock). The poem "Freundeswunsch" was sent with H's next letter. **the Einsiedlerin**: "An Neuffer" was indeed published in the Zürich magazine *Die Einsiedlerin aus den Alpen* before the year was out. **Magenau**: his friends were taken aback by Magenau's decision to marry into a vacant living in Niederstotzingen, near Ulm. It seems that H wrote to Magenau at about this time.
B75, S81

78. TO HIS MOTHER. Waltershausen, ~ 5 April 1794

Herder: Johann Gottfried (1744–1803), the philosopher, theologian, and anthropologist, was also the head of the Church in Weimar. The plans H outlines here seem to have had very little to go on. **Goethe**: see List of Correspondents. **Wieland**: Christoph Martin (1733–1813), a notable writer and man of letters of the day. **Journey to Nuremberg**: whether (and why) this took place is not known. **Duke of Meiningen**: Georg (1761–1803), the local noble, whom Charlotte von Kalb had known since childhood. **Take up arms as a volunteer**: there was pressure to do so in Württemberg since the French had occupied the Palatinate in December 1793, but it soon subsided. **Markgröningen**: Karl Gok eventually became a clerk there in 1797.
B78, S82

79. TO CHRISTIAN LUDWIG NEUFFER. Waltershausen, mid-April 1794

song for your Selma: the poem "Freundeswunsch," promised in Letter 77. **Bürger's Song of Songs**: Bürger's poem "Das hohe Lied von der Einzigen" (Song of Songs for the One and Only) ends by celebrating his own poem as a "spiritual Adonis." Adonis, darling of Aphrodite, meant here as an emblem of beauty. **Schiller is said to be sick?**: in several letters from Stuttgart at this time Schiller laments his poor health. **Poem to Fate**: see Letter 76 and note. **Region of the abstract**: H is probably thinking, among other things, of his so-called Tübingen hymns, addressed to abstract entities like Truth, Liberty, and Friendship. See the important letter to Neuffer of 12 November 1798 (Letter 168). **Schiller's treatise on Grace and Dignity**: *Über Anmut und Würde* was published in the *Neue Thalia* in 1793 and at the same time in book form.
B77, S83

80. TO HIS MOTHER. Waltershausen, 20 April 1794

20th April was Easter Day. Either H has got the date wrong or the letter was written in two goes, since near the middle he refers back to Easter Monday. Though Sattler seems to suggest that "20" has been corrected to "22." **Change in my situation**: the letter his mother enclosed evidently proposed a parish post.
B79, S84

81. TO HIS BROTHER. Waltershausen, 21 May 1794

Working on something now: his novel, *Hyperion*. *Thalia*: Schiller's magazine published H's "Fragment of *Hyperion*" and the poems "Das Schicksal"/"Fate," "Dem Genius der Kühnheit"/"To the Genius of Bold-ness," and "Griechenland"/"Greece" in this period. *Urania*: edited by Johann Ludwig Ewald (1748–1822), contained a different version of "Griechenland." *Flora*: a magazine published by Cotta—did not contain anything by H until 1801.
B80, S85

FROM CHRISTIAN LUDWIG NEUFFER. Stuttgart, 3 June 1794

A fragment transcribed by Schlesier. **poem to Gotthold**: the poem "Grie-chenland," dedicated to Stäudlin. For the other poems mentioned, see the two preceding letters to Neuffer (Letters 77 and 79). **Selma**: i.e., Rosine Stäudlin. Her father died on 21 May 1794. **hymns**: Neuffer means the "Tübingen hymns"—see notes to Letter 79. *Conz's* **Museum**: the short-lived journal *Museum für die griechische und römische Litteratur* (1794–1795) contains nothing by H.
*B19, *S19

82. TO CHRISTIAN MATTHÄUS THEODOR BREUNLIN.
Völkershausen, 8 June 1794

Völkershausen, a village near the borders between Thuringia, Hesse, and Bavaria, is now part of the town of Vacha. It was not far from Waltershausen and the home of Charlotte von Kalb's uncle Dietrich Philipp August von Stein, according to Schiller a "libertine of the first order." **a little excursion**: H was a good walker. This trip is also men-tioned in later letters. Fulda was about twenty-five miles away, over the hills. **Herder's *Letters for Humanity***: nothing of H's appeared in Herder's *Briefe zur Beförderung der Humanität*, published in Riga 1793–1797 and in fact written entirely by Herder. For the other journals see notes to Letter 81. **my nephew**: the Christian mentioned below, Breunlin's son from his first marriage, five at the time. **one of Major von Kalb's daughters**: Edda (1790–1874). **Your little one**: H's niece Heinrike, born 17 September 1793. B81, S86

83. TO HIS MOTHER. Waltershausen, 1 July 1794

The first frank rebuttal of an attempt to get H to settle down in Swabia; presumably his mother had transmitted an opportunity of taking a living. **the reason**: i.e., the trip to Völkershausen and the foot journey from there. **Miss L.**: Elise LeBret, who seems not to have given up on H. It sounds as if the offer of a parish and her reappearance are connected—her father, as chancellor of the university, would have had some influence on conferring benefices in the university's gift. **if indeed a decision of some sort**: the clause is incomplete, or suddenly halted (aposiopesis). B82, S87

84. TO CHRISTIAN LUDWIG NEUFFER. Waltershausen, second week of July 1794

blow: the death of Rosine's father, communicated in Neuffer's letter of 3 June 1794. **Herder's *Tithon and Aurora***: appeared in his *Zerstreute Blätter* in 1792. ***Catiline***: Neuffer's translation of Sallust was eventually published in 1819. **Kant's aesthetics**: i.e., the *Critique of Judgement* (1790). **my poem to Boldness**: "Dem Genius der Kühnheit" appeared in Schiller's *Neue Thalia* in 1795. **Fräulein Hegel**: Hegel's sister Christiane Luise (1773–1832). **Hesler**: an old friend, see Letter 3. B83, S89

85. TO GEORG WILHELM FRIEDRICH HEGEL. Waltershausen, 10 July 1794

"Kingdom of God!": for the new world of divine immanence the friends hoped for. Hegel uses the same words in a letter to Schelling in January 1795. **trait**: Beck glosses the German word here ("Zug") as "striving," which must therefore be possible. But the idea of a recognizable feature

seems clearly present, and it finds an echo in Hegel's poem "Eleusis" where Hegel imagines the friends looking for visible signs of one another's constancy to their ideals. **lakes and Alps**: since autumn 1793 Hegel had had a job as house tutor in Bern. **your good fortune**: Hegel had turned down the job in Waltershausen. **Frau von Berlepsch**: Emilie von Berlepsch (1757–1830), wrote verse (*Sommerstunden*, 1794). **Baggesen**: Jens Immanuel (1764–1826), Danish writer with connections to Schiller. **the latter**: Hesler was by now in Jena and had already published three plays. H would catch up with him in Jena. **Mögling**: Friedrich Heinrich Wolfgang (1771–1813), at the Stift, and now also a house tutor in Bern; see H to Schiller, August 1797 (Letter 145). **enclosed sheet**: not known what this is or anything about the affair H goes on to describe.
B84, S88

86. TO HIS MOTHER. Waltershausen, 30 July 1794

war: the French troops would soon be back in the Palatinate and so, despite H's assurances, close to Württemberg. **travelling again**: whether he did is not known. **letters *you enclose for me***: from Elise LeBret.
B85, S90

FROM CHRISTIAN LUDWIG NEUFFER. Stuttgart, 16 August 1794

Extract and summary by Schlesier. Reply to Letter 84. *Röschen*: Rosine Stäudlin would die on 25 April 1795.
*B20, *S19

87. TO HIS BROTHER. Waltershausen, 21 August 1794

to act out of duty: the emphasis on duty shows the influence of Kant. **enlightenment that is clear as mud**: precisely not an indictment of the Enlightenment as such but of reductive tendencies that made it incompatible with belief in God or necessarily involved in the mastery of nature. **Do not cast your pearls**: Matthew 7:6. **enclosed letter**: that announced in Letter 86. It spoke highly of H. **H., B., G. etc.**: of these, H. might be Hiemer, B. Bilfinger. **Robespierre**: Maximilien (1758–1794), guillotined on 28th July, bringing an end to the Terror. H's approval—general in Germany—is another sign of his moderate sympathies.
B86, S91

88. TO CHRISTIAN LUDWIG NEUFFER. Waltershausen, 25 August 1794

A reply to Neuffer's letter of 16th August announcing that his fiancée Rosine Stäudlin was going toward her grave.
B87, S92

89. TO CHRISTIAN LUDWIG NEUFFER. Waltershausen, 10 October 1794

estate: Dankenfeld, where presumably the whole family was staying. **in the *Thalia***: the issue containing the "Fragment of *Hyperion*" appeared in November, together with the poem "Das Schicksal"/"Fate." **play on the death of Socrates**: not carried out, and work on *Hyperion* went on into 1798. ***Academy***: *Akademie der schönen Redekünste*, a review begun by Bürger. None of the three journals mentioned had poems by H. **an essay on *aesthetic ideas***: apparently not written. **the Kantian analysis**: in the *Critique of Judgement* (1790). **"Grace and Dignity"**: "Über Anmut und Würde" (1793). **the Kantian borderline**: that between the phenomenon and the noumenon. **my poem to the genius of youth**: this was reworked into "Der Gott der Jugend"/"The God of Youth" and appeared in Schiller's *Musen-Almanach* in 1796. **Gotthold**: Stäudlin.
B88, S93

90. TO CHRISTIAN LUDWIG NEUFFER. Jena, November 1794

A gap has been left for the date in November but no figure inserted. The letter was almost certainly written after 9th November (see below). **proximity of truly great minds**: Jena was the center of German intellectual life at the time—the key figures for H are named in this letter. But it was also, as the letter itself suggests, a focus for politically minded students keen to convert the ideas of modern philosophy into practice. **Wieland's collected works**: the first volume had just appeared. Wieland was then at the height of his fame. **Fichte**: Johann Gottlieb (1762–1814), had been made professor of philosophy at Jena in the summer (as successor to Karl Leonhard Reinhold, an important expositor of Kant) and was in the ascendant. H had already begun reading him in Waltershausen and immediately went to his lectures. Fichte's chief work, the *Grundlage der gesamten Wissenschaftslehre* (*Foundations of a Total Theory of Knowledge*) began to appear in summer 1794 (Charlotte von Kalb immediately got copies of the sexto-decimo "Handschrift für seine Zuhörer" sent to Waltershausen), followed by the *Vorlesungen über die Bestimmung des Gelehrten* (*Lectures*

on the Vocation of the Scholar) in the autumn. His ideas, especially the emphasis on action, reverberate in this letter. In particular, the formulations suggest that H was present at Fichte's lecture "Über die Pflichten des Gelehrten" (On the Duties of the Scholar), which was given on November 9th (*Texturen* 2, 107). **at Schiller's**: Schiller was living in Jena since returning from Swabia in May 1794. His close association with Goethe was just beginning. **Meyer**: Johann Heinrich (1760–1832), a painter in the classical manner summoned to Weimar by Goethe. **Professors' Club**: a circle, mostly of academics, which met once a week; Goethe sometimes went and students could too. *Goethe*: Johann Wolfgang (1749–1832), overwhelmingly the dominant writer of the time and just down the road in Weimar. **Niethammer**: see List of Correspondents. H knew him from the Stift. **in Voigt's garden**: now Zwätzengasse 9.
B89, S94

91. TO HIS MOTHER. Jena, 17 November 1794

Friemar: where H had family—see Letter 75 with note. **Heyn**: his mother's maiden name. **were it not for the thought**: a thought prompted by Fichte. **Coadjutor Dalberg**: Karl Theodor von Dalberg (1744–1817), governor of Erfurt and coadjutor (first assistant and named successor) to the elector of Mainz, becoming elector himself in 1802. Friend of Schiller's. **I live in a garden**: these lodgings—Zwätzengasse 9—where H lived with his pupil Fritz von Kalb, were obtained via Schiller, who had previously lived there himself and passed them on to Wilhelm von Humboldt. **my landlord**: Johann Gottfried Voigt, who took over the reading club in 1788. **Paulus**: Heinrich Eberhard Gottlob (1761–1851), from Swabia, professor of oriental languages and of exegesis at Jena, later in Würzburg and Heidelberg.
B90, S95

FROM FRIEDRICH SCHILLER. Jena, December 1794

a small piece of work: "Dem Genius der Kühnheit"/"To the Spirit of Boldness"—see Letter 56 and later references.

92. TO HIS MOTHER. Jena, 26 December 1794

Nuremberg: what he might have been planning to do there is not known but perhaps it involved Schubart (see Letter 71 and note). In April 1795 Charlotte von Kalb sent him a letter there, so clearly the plans were serious.

In any case, he didn't go, but only to Weimar. **Camerer**: Johann Caspar (1772–1847), son of the pastor in Sondelfingen, near Reutlingen, and known to H from Tübingen where he studied medicine 1789–1794. One of H's closest friends in Jena, where he matriculated in May 1794—see Letter 138 for a brief account of their life together there. From 1796, he practiced as a doctor in Blaubeuren, marrying a friend of H's sister's, Katharina Sibylla Fehleisen. **I'll write to you again from Weimar**: this seems not to have happened. **I almost forgot an important point**: this is written on a separate sheet. **Nekarshausen**: Neckarshausen, downriver from Nürtingen and in that diocese. **when I am thirty**: by about this time, or a bit later, H could expect to be appointed to a parish by the Consistory, as opposed to a less official route (see next note). **the position of a petitioner**: H had no intention of becoming a pastor, but here he argues against receiving a parish through patronage. **my friend in T.**: Elise LeBret in Tübingen. Perhaps, as in Letter 83, the question of Neckarshausen was prompted by her. **the enclosed letter**: presumably for Elise LeBret.
B91, S97

93. TO HIS MOTHER. Jena, 16 January 1795

H had left Jena in the last days of December, for Weimar, and returned just before 14th January, an independent man. In a letter to Schiller written on that day, Charlotte von Kalb, who had relieved him of his duties in the kindest way, wrote that he was "a wheel that spins very fast." **the difficulties**: it seems that these sometimes exceeded his patience and that he probably resorted to beating his pupil. **pastor in Waltershausen**: Nenninger. **a vice**: masturbation, generally considered so at the time. **a piece of work**: *Hyperion*. **She means to write to you**: her letter, from January 17th, survives. It was perhaps written at H's request and in any case does much to reassure his mother and make her understand the importance of his decision to return to Jena. According to this letter, he wanted a post at the university. **give classes here**: this would have entailed taking further exams. *Fichte's house*: nowadays the "Romantikerhaus," Unterm Markt 12a. Which side of it H lived is not known.
B92, S98

94. TO CHRISTIAN LUDWIG NEUFFER. Jena, 19 January 1795

History of Mankind: Herder's famous *Ideen zur Philosophie der Geschichte der Menschheit* (*Ideas for a Philosophy of the History of Mankind*) was published in four parts, 1784–1791. **Club**: the Professors' Club—see Letter 90. **Wilhelm Meister**: the first volume of Goethe's novel *Wilhelm Meister's Apprenticeship*, containing the first two books, appeared at Christmas 1794. The episodes mentioned come at the end of book 1 and in the second chapter of book 2. **Fichte's lecture in the evenings**: this took place between 6 p.m. and 7 p.m., "a sort of introduction to transcendental philosophy" (in Fichte's words) based on Ernst Platner's *Philosophische Aphorismen* (1776 and 1782). **part of your *Aeneid***: the first part of book 7. See Letter 37 and note. **Horae**: the first issue of *Die Horen* appeared toward the end of January and quickly became the leading journal of the time. **the Nisus and Euryalus episode**: Neuffer's version of this (from book 9 of the *Aeneid*) was published in Conz's *Museum* in 1794. H later translated part of the same episode himself. **Voß**: famous for his great translations of Homer, he was now working on the *Aeneid* (published 1799). **some poems for Schiller's future almanac**: Schiller's *Musen-Almanache* for 1796 and 1797 each contain a poem of Neuffer's. **Woltmann**: Karl Ludwig (1770–1817). **my Tübingen affairs**: refers to H's difficult relationship with Elise LeBret. **a friend in the house**: Wilhelmine Kirms, who had left Waltershausen when H was in Weimar. In mid-July 1795 she gave birth to a daughter, Louise Agnese, who died fourteen months later of smallpox. It seems likely that H was the father. B93, S99

95. TO GEORG WILHELM FRIEDRICH HEGEL. Jena, 26 January 1795

H wrote to Hegel at least once from Jena before this. The letter is damaged, hence missing text. **Fichte's speculative pages**: see Letter 90 and note; "speculative" implies "theoretical" or "non-empirical." **dogmatism**: used in the Kantian sense to indicate thinking that is not conditioned by experience and claims direct knowledge of the nature of things. Fichte's attempt to "get beyond the fact of consciousness *theoretically*" would be an instance of that. **his absolute *I* (= Spinoza's substance)**: by "substance" Spinoza means "that which is in itself, and is conceived through itself" (*Ethics*, book 1, definition 3). Fichte himself makes the connexion in the *Wisssenschaftslehre* but rejects Spinoza as a dogmatist because he simply claims the necessity of substance. At this stage in his deliberations, H is effectively diagnosing a similar problem in Fichte's thought. H's handwriting distinguishes between the "absolute *I*" and the empirical I by giving the first a capital letter. **the first parts**: i.e., of the *Wissenschaftslehre*. **Fichte confirms**: this probably means "in person, now that I am in Jena." It seems possible that H's objections had some influence

on the further development of Fichte's work (see *Texturen* 2, 110–14). In the missing part of the letter (about five lines) H probably modified his judgment, based on further reading and listening. **His examination**: the German words here are partly surmised ("Seine Auseinandersezung" from "dersezung") due to the torn page. **reciprocal determination of the *I* and the *Not-I***: expounding this is how Fichte gets beyond the difficulty identified by H. **striving**: this forms the focus of the third part of the *Wissenschaftslehre*—see Letter 98. **the antinomies**: in the *Critique of Pure Reason* Kant deals with four contradictions that cannot be resolved by pure reason alone, such as whether the universe is finite or infinite (first antimony). As H says, he solves them all by ascribing a purpose to nature. **the ideal education of the people**: a major preoccupation of *Hyperion* and prompted or encouraged by Schiller, the first part of whose *Briefe über die äthetische Erziehung des Menschen* (*On the Aesthetic Education of Man*) had just appeared in the inaugural number of *Die Horen*. In both works the notion of education is set against that of revolution.
B94, S100

FROM CHRISTIAN LUDWIG NEUFFER. Stuttgart, 26 January 1795

Extract by Schlesier. **your *Hyperion***: the "Fragment of *Hyperion*" that had appeared in the *Neue Thalia* in November 1794.
*B22, *S21

FROM CHRISTIAN LUDWIG NEUFFER. Stuttgart, 5 February 1795

Extract and summary by Schlesier. **Griesinger**: Georg Friedrich (1734–1828). **Chair in Literature at Tübingen**: Schiller received such an offer at this time and turned it down. Abel had been his teacher in the Karlsschule.
*B23, *S22

FROM HIS BROTHER. Nürtingen, 6 February 1795

Extract and summary by Schlesier.
*B24, *S23

96. TO HIS MOTHER. Jena, 22 February 1795

Partly preserved by Schlesier. There is some confusion about the date, which may be 12th February. **Your last letter**: has not survived, but H's

mother had obviously given his Jena plans her blessing. **my letter before last**: Letter 92. **the times we're going through**: a reference to the war (France had conquered Holland), though why they may have helped justify his course of action is not clear. **new journal**: nothing of H's appeared in *Die Horen* until 1797. **The book**: *Hyperion*. **Counselor Brun**: Constantin (1746–1836), director of the Royal East India Company in Copenhagen and husband of the poet Friederike Brun. **hopes**: these seem to be of gaining a lecturing position in Jena. ***what I shall receive from you one day***: referring to the legacy left him by his father. **seven to ten carolins**: she sent 100 florins on 30th March, the first sending since he had left home. **Meiningen**: Meiningen is where Wilhelmine Kirms had been since leaving Waltershausen at about the end of the year. **Kammerer**: Johann Caspar Camerer (see Letter 92 and note).
B95, S101

FROM HIS SISTER. Blaubeuren, 1 March 1795

Extract preserved in a letter by Fritz Breunlin, H's nephew. **your dear portrait**: the pastel likeness done by Hiemer in 1792, which H gave to his sister on her wedding day.
*B25, *S24

97. TO HIS MOTHER. Jena, 12 March 1795

Cotta in Tübingen: See List of Correspondents. Schiller wrote to him on 9th March suggesting that he take on *Hyperion*, which was agreed on 20th March. **the offer**: of a chair at Tübingen, which Schiller turned down.
B96, S102

98. TO HIS BROTHER. Jena, 13 April 1795

a human being should always act . . . : Kant's "categorical imperative" (in the *Critique of Practical Reason*), but H makes it more personal by calling it the "sacred unalterable law of [one"s] being." **"There is in human beings . . .** : not a quotation from Fichte, but a summary of his thinking in the third part of the *Wissenschaftslehre* probably based on lecture notes since it had only just been published. The exposition here refines the point against Fichte made to Hegel (in Letter 95). ***Philosophical Journal***: his *Philosophisches Journal einer Gesellschaft Teutscher Gelehrten* began appearing in March and from 1797 was coedited with Fichte. It did not in

the end contain anything by H. See letter to Niethammer of 24 February 1796 (Letter 118). **examination**: to that end H matriculated at Jena on 15 May 1795 but left shortly afterward.
B97, S103

99. TO HIS SISTER. Jena, 20 April 1795

Letter torn at the end. **journey on foot**: he probably made this journey at the end of March or beginning of April. **Roßbach**: in 1757 Frederick the Great's troops defeated the French army augmented by the Imperial Army of the Holy Roman Empire in a battle during the Seven Years' War. **Lüzen**: where in 1632 Gustavus Adolphus succumbed to Wallenstein's troops. H had addressed a hymn to him years before (see Letter 32). **Prince**: Leopold Friedrich Franz von Anhalt-Dessau (1740–1817). **orphanage and educational institute**: a well-known institution founded by August Hermann Francke (1663–1727) in the late seventeenth century on Pietistic principles. **new churchyard**: laid out in 1787 in neoclassical style for Christians of all confessions. **gardens of the Luisium & Wörlitz**: created by Prince Leopold, the architect Friedrich Wilhelm von Erdmannsdorf (1736–1800) and the gardener Johann Friedrich Eyserbeck (1734–1818), they were widely admired for their English style and for their allusiveness. **Prof. Heydenreich**: Karl Heinrich (1764–1801), professor of philosophy in Leipzig. **Göschen**: Georg Joachim (1752–1828), alongside Cotta the most important publisher of the time, with Klopstock, Wieland, Goethe, and Schiller among his authors. **Demoiselle Fehleisen**: a friend of his sister's (see Letter 92). **summerhouse**: this probably lay on the slopes of the Hausberg on the other side of the Saale River. H almost certainly shared it with his friend Sinclair (see List of Correspondents).
B98, S104

100. TO CHRISTIAN LUDWIG NEUFFER. Jena, 28 April 1795

Goethe: Goethe was in Jena from 29 March to 2 May 1795. **Heyne**: Christian Gottlob (1729–1812), professor of classical philology at Göttingen and founder of modern textual criticism, he had responded favorably to extracts from Neuffer's *Virgil*. **Ovid's Phaethon**: *Metamorphoses*, book 2, lines 1–366, where Phaethon loses control of the chariots of the sun. Schiller then declined to take it, and H later felt the task had been a

waste of his time. In his other translations he generally kept close to the metrical form of the originals. **100 fl.**: in fact Cotta had merely promised this (ungenerous) sum, paying in full only on publication of *Hyperion*'s first volume in 1797.
B99, S105

101. TO CHRISTIAN LUDWIG NEUFFER. Jena, 8 May 1795

Neuffer's fiancée Rosine Stäudlin died of consumption on 25 April 1795.
B100, S106

FROM HIS SISTER. Blaubeuren, 9 May 1795

We missed you: at Easter (April 5th). **portrait**: by Hiemer—see the previous letter from his sister, 1 March 1795.
*B26, *S25

102. TO HIS MOTHER. Jena, 22 May 1795

so long to reply: it seems that the letter of 16 January 1795 (Letter 93) was the last time H had written. **a house-tutoring job**: no more is known about this. **my friend**: probably Sinclair.
B101, S107

103. TO FRIEDRICH SCHILLER. Nürtingen, 23 July 1795

H had suddenly left Jena at the end of May 1795, exactly why is not clear, and was living at home with his mother. **the enclosed**: the translation of the Phaethon episode from Ovid's *Metamorphoses* mentioned in Letter 100.
B102, S108

104. TO JOHANN GOTTFRIED EBEL. Nürtingen, 2 September 1795

the rest of my journey: having met Ebel in Heidelberg on about 13th June on his way from Jena, H continued home to Nürtingen. **the uncommon people**: referring to the Gontard family in Frankfurt. Ebel knew them and had presented H with the prospect of working for them. This letter makes the case. **cruel failure of my efforts**: in Waltershausen and Jena with Fritz

von Kalb. (**rational in the strict sense**): H means in Kant's sense. **Rousseau:** H is quoting from Rousseau's novel *Julie ou La Nouvelle Héloïse* (1761), part 5, letter 3: "The first and most important form of education is to render the child apt to be brought up." The whole of H's elaborations here is developed in dialogue with Rousseau, especially his book *Émile ou De l'éducation* (1762). **Livy:** the Roman historian was not thought well-suited for children by Rousseau. **Plutarch:** his Parallel Lives was a favorite eighteenth-century source for teaching about the classical world and was recommended by Rousseau. **maps:** one of several indications of H's interest in maps—see Letter 190. **a young scholar:** H is thinking of Hegel. **M. Fr. Hölderlin:** as in the letter to Schiller of 20 March 1794, which also sets out a program of education, H uses his academic title, *Magister*.
B103, S109

105. TO FRIEDRICH SCHILLER. Nürtingen, 4 September 1795

contributions: probably the poems "Der Gott der Jugend"/"The God of Youth" and "An die Natur"/"To Nature" of which Schiller took only the first for his *Muses' Almanac* for 1796. *res nullius*: term from Roman law—"nobody's thing," common property, there for anyone's taking. **the idea of an infinite progress in philosophy**: see the letter to Niethammer, 24 February 1796 (Letter 118). **intellectual intuition**: a term (*intellektuelle/intellectuale Anschauung*) used by Fichte and Schelling among others. For H it is the faculty by which the unity of subject and object can be grasped. **"warm themselves on ice"**: quotation from Goethe's novel *Wilhelm Meister's Apprenticeship* (1795). **In October**: in fact he only started at the Gontards' at the end of the year.
B104, S110

106. TO CHRISTIAN LUDWIG NEUFFER. Nürtingen, October 1795

situation: another post as house tutor for Friedrich Jakob Ströhlin (1743–1802), a teacher of classical languages and French at the Gymnasium illustre in Stuttgart and earlier a house tutor in Bordeaux. A friend of Neuffer's and distant relation of H's, he was the intermediary for H's posting to Bordeaux in 1802. **enclosed letter**: probably from Ebel revealing a delay in the arrangements in Frankfurt. **The relationship**: with Elise LeBret. **offer**: an employment of some sort; no more is known. **Schiller's poem

in the *Horen*: "Das Reich der Schatten" (The Realm of the Shades), an early version of "Das Ideal und das Leben" (Ideals and Life), published in the *Horen* in the September number. **I spoke of it**: during his (therefore recent) journey to the Unterland. **my speculative *pro* and *contra***: presumably referring to the thinking outlined in the previous letter. **Prof. Ströhlin**: see first note to this letter.
B105, S111

107. TO JOHANN GOTTFRIED EBEL. Nürtingen, 9 November 1795

another job as tutor in Stuttgart: see the previous letter. **Sinclair**: see List of Correspondents. Now in Homburg, not far from Frankfurt. It was probably through Sinclair that H met Ebel. **this invisible church militant**: the idea of a community of the like-minded as precursor to the kingdom of God on earth. Rooted in Pietism, it had been secularized by Kant and Herder, among others. In late January 1795 Hegel wrote to Schelling: "Reason and freedom remain our watchword, and our meeting point the invisible church." **an apostle**: Paul—see 1 Thessalonians 4:15 and the end of the next letter.
B106, S112

108. TO GEORG WILHELM FRIEDRICH HEGEL. Stuttgart, 25 November 1795

H was in Stuttgart for about a week from November 21st. Several other letters to Hegel between this and Letter 95 (January 1795) must have existed. H had been hoping to fix up jobs for both of them as house tutors in Frankfurt. **repetitorship**: at the Stift in Tübingen—the best former students were eligible to become such tutors. **my former foolishness**: he means his relationship with Elise LeBret. **the Tübingen gravediggers**: the dogmatic theologians they had been taught by. **travel grant**: made available to talented graduates to study at a university elsewhere. **Renz**: did indeed become a repetitor in 1797, turned down the offer of a chair in 1799, and in 1803 became a pastor in Lauffen. **Fichte is in Jena again**: he had been forced to leave after disputes with the student bodies boiled over but returned in October. **Sinclair**: known to Hegel from Tübingen.
B107, S113

109. TO CHRISTIAN LUDWIG NEUFFER. Nürtingen, early December 1795

Seits: Seiz, now back from Switzerland, also interested in a tutoring post in Frankfurt. **gentlemen in Stuttgart**: i.e., the Consistory. *impatiens limae*: "fed up with the file," i.e., unwilling to work up his poems. **the requirements of Herr Stähle**: nothing is known but he is perhaps the tailor. **Landauer**: see List of Correspondents. The first mention of this important friend. **the promised elegy**: if this is a classical elegy then this is the first mention of the form in H. Schiller had published his poem "Elegie" (later reworked into "Der Spaziergang") in the October issue of the *Horen*. Just possibly a first attempt at what became "Der Wanderer"/ "The Traveller."
B108, S114

110. TO JOHANN GOTTFRIED EBEL. Nürtingen, 7 December 1795

your kind invitation: to take up the house tutorship with the Gontards. H did not leave for Frankfurt until after Christmas. **lodgings**: H didn't live at the Gontards' initially, and Ebel found him a room at an inn (the *City of Mainz*).
B109, S115

111. TO CHRISTIAN LUDWIG NEUFFER. Nürtingen, after 7 December 1795

leaving for Frankfurt: having at last heard from Frankfurt. In fact he did not leave until after Christmas.
B110, S116

112. TO FRIEDRICH IMMANUEL NIETHAMMER. Löchgau, 22 December 1795

My friend and cousin, Majer from Löchgau: Ludwig/Louis—H probably left Nürtingen on 15th December, went to Stuttgart for a few days, and then spent Christmas with his relatives in Löchgau, setting off from there with his cousin on 26th. The latter then continued to Jena, presumably switching from theology to philosophy. **Schelling**: H had also seen him in July or August. He seems to be referring to Schelling's *Philosophische Briefe über Dogmatismus und Kriticismus*, the first four letters of which

had just appeared in Niethammer's *Philosophisches Journal*, revising his slightly earlier work *Vom Ich als Princip der Philosophie oder über das Unbedingte im menschlichen Wissen* (1795).
B111, S117

FRANKFURT, 1796–1798

113. TO HIS MOTHER, Frankfurt. 30 December 1795

my situation here: H arrived in Frankfurt to take up his new job as house tutor on 28th December, put up at first at an inn, and then met the family on 31st. **Our cousin**: Ludwig Majer, whom H accompanied as far as Frankfurt on his journey to Jena. *City of Mainz*: the pub he was staying in while his accommodation in the Gontard house was being made ready.
B112, S118

114. TO JOHANN FRIEDRICH LUDWIG MAJER. Frankfurt, 31 December 1795

my friend: that is, his cousin Ludwig, son of the addressee. **my future pupil**: Henry Gontard (1787–1816), eight years old at this point. **my former pupil**: Fritz von Kalb. **two venerable mothers**: presumably H's aunt and grandmother, the latter of whom divided her time between her daughters in Löchgau and Nürtingen.
B113, S119

115. TO HIS BROTHER. Frankfurt, 11 January 1796

very interesting people: H had made use of a few spare days to nip to Homburg. There he probably met Franz Wilhelm Jung (see Letter 199 and List of Correspondents) and Philipp Jakob Leutwein (1763–1800), pastor in Homburg, friends of Sinclair's.
B114, S120

116. TO CHRISTIAN LUDWIG NEUFFER. Frankfurt, 15 January 1796

Counselor Jung: see List of Correspondents. H had just met him in Homburg, but Neuffer had come to know him during a visit to Stuttgart in 1794.
B115, S121

117. TO HIS BROTHER. Frankfurt, 11 February 1796

in bad times: referring to the period after returning home from Jena. *Deus nobis haec otia fecit*: "A god gave us this peace" (Virgil, *Eclogues* 1, line 6), words spoken by the herdsman Tityrus. **further plans**: H was hoping to find his brother a post in Frankfurt since he was unhappy as a clerk in Nürtingen. The plans came to nothing. **court in Berlin**: Sinclair abandoned these plans on the death of his stepfather in an accident in March 1796. **philosophical letters**: on this see the next letter. **news about my novel**: H had sent part of *Hyperion* to Cotta in December. In May he was asked to rework and shorten it. **Schiller sent me anything**: he was waiting for the *Musen-Almanach für das Jahr 1796*, for which he had sent Schiller several poems. **Fripon**: probably a dog.
B116, S122

118. TO FRIEDRICH IMMANUEL NIETHAMMER. Frankfurt, 24 February 1796

the essays: the *New Letters on the Aesthetic Education of Man* H talks about later in this letter, promised to Niethammer for his *Philosophisches Journal*. The title indicates a revision of and challenge to Schiller, whose *On the Aesthetic Education of Man* had been published in 1795, also as a series of letters. **Reinhold**: Karl Leonhard (1758–1823), Fichte's predecessor as professor of philosophy in Jena, he moved to Kiel in 1794 for financial reasons. Important popularizer of Kant. The pairing of Kant and Reinhold here perhaps indicates a turning away from Fichte. **theoretically, through intellectual intuition**: if we compare this to the closely related letter to Schiller (Letter 105) we see that "theoretically" is being used in a different sense, analogously in fact to "aesthetically" in the earlier letter. It seems that H is using it with its etymological meaning of "looking" in mind (θεωρία). **from philosophy to poetry and religion**: indicating, as in *Hyperion*, a distrust of philosophy's ability to solve its questions on its own. The thoughts here are developed in all that remains of this project, the draft "Fragment of Philosophical Letters" (or "On Religion"). See *Essays and Letters*, 234–39. **Schelling**: see the note to the last letter to Niethammer (Letter 112). By "new convictions" H means Schelling's thinking in the *Philosophical Letters on Dogmatism and Critical Philosophy* he had just published in Niethammer's journal, which

he thinks a better course than that taken in *Of the I as a Principle of Philosophy*.
B117, S123

119. TO CHRISTIAN LUDWIG NEUFFER. Frankfurt, March 1796

perpetual ebb and flow: the same words as in one his first letters to Neuffer in November 1790 (Letter 37). **the permanent itself**: H wrote "*der Unvergängliche*" here where "*das Unvergängliche*" (neuter) would be expected. Unless it's a slip of the pen it must mean God. The translation hedges its bets. **the sweet creature**: probably Wilhelmine von Tessin (1778–1806), a pupil at a school Neuffer set up for a while in Stuttgart. Letters between them survive, but she married another in November 1796. **not to take Phaethon**: the translation from Ovid, which Schiller had commissioned—see Letter 100 and note. **Schiller's *Almanac***: the *Musen-Almanach für das Jahr 1796* contained one poem by H, "Der Gott der Jugend"/"The God of Youth," as well as a poem by Neuffer. The poem "An die Natur"/"To Nature," which H had sent him in the autumn, Schiller initially earmarked for the *Horen* but then dropped it on Humboldt's advice.
B118, S125

120. TO HIS BROTHER. Frankfurt, March 1796

Copy and summary by Schlesier. ***cacumina rerum***: (Latin) "the summits of things." Kant's system also only comes on to (aesthetic) judgment having first found a way through the "labyrinth" of reason.
B119, S124

121. TO JOHANN FRIEDRICH COTTA. Frankfurt, 15 May 1796

The letter to which this responds is lost, but H is thought to have sent Cotta a version of *Hyperion* in December 1795. His resolve to rework it resulted, much later than envisaged here, in the first volume of the final version, which returns to the letter form abandoned since the "Fragment of *Hyperion*" that appeared in the *Neue Thalia*. This first volume was finished at about the end of 1796 and published at Easter 1797. **a clean Roman font**: most German books at the time were printed in Gothic

script. Cotta agreed, and *Hyperion* was printed in Walbaum-Antiqua. **Plutarch**: H had subscribed to the Plutarch edition by Johann Georg Hutten, which began to appear with Cotta in 1791.
B120, S126

122. TO HIS BROTHER. Frankfurt, 2 June 1796

"Love and pleasure are the wings of great doings": from Goethe's classical play *Iphigenia in Tauris* (1787). H wrote the same words into Hegel's album on 12 February 1791. **true thoroughness**: the thoughts of this paragraph are Kantian; see in particular *Critique of Judgement*, section 76. **that you go to a university**: this plan too (see Letter 117) came to nothing, probably because of opposition from their mother, but it shows how much H wanted to make up for his brother's disadvantaged position in the family. **your friend H.**: not known. **He sorrows, as we do**: this seems to refer to contemporary events. On 21st May, Austria had broken the armistice agreed with the French on 1 January 1796, and hostilities resumed on 1st June. *Natural Right*: the *Grundlage des Naturrechts nach Principien der Wissenschaftslehre* (*Basis of Natural Right according to Principles of the Theory of Knowledge*), the first part of which appeared in March 1796. **the printing of my book**: in fact the first volume of *Hyperion* appeared only in April 1797 (see previous letter).
B121, S127

123. TO HIS BROTHER. Frankfurt, June/July 1796

Begun toward the end of June, with an addition on 10th July (H wrote June but this is certainly a slip, as Beck has shown). **I cannot possibly believe**: this probably in response to a letter from his brother announcing just that. **retreat from Wetzlar**: this began on 7th July, the French having crossed the Rhine at Strasbourg on 24th June and penetrated deep into German territory. Frankfurt was overrun by French troops on 14th July. **for Hamburg**: Susette Gontard's hometown. In the event they went no further than Kassel. The "whole family" included the Gontards' four children, Susette Gontard's mother-in-law, and Marie Rätzer, governess to the three daughters. **the French are in Württemberg**: true, and they took Stuttgart on 18th July.
B122, S129

124. TO CHRISTIAN LUDWIG NEUFFER. Frankfurt, June/July 1796

As with the last letter, the body was written at the end of June and the postscript on 10th July but wrongly dated June. A letter with many echoes of *Hyperion*. **a being in the world**: Susette Gontard (see List of Correspondents). This is the first clear mention of the love for her. **for Hamburg**: see note to previous letter.
B123, S128

125. TO FRIEDRICH SCHILLER. Kassel, 24 July 1796

The troupe had arrived in Kassel (H writes Cassel) on 13th or 14th July and stayed there. **a short contribution**: the poems "An die Unerkannte"/"To the Unknown Woman," "An Herkules"/"To Hercules," "Diotima," and "An die klugen Ratgeber"/"To those who Think they Know Best," which came too late for Schiller's *Musen-Almanach für das Jahr 1797*. **in flight**: French troops occupied Frankfurt on 14th July.
B124, B130

126. TO HIS BROTHER. Kassel, 6 August 1796

great events: French troops had entered Stuttgart on 18th July and overrun most of Swabia, but Nürtingen, where H's mother was, was not much affected. **the Greek thunderbolts**: in allusion to the second Persian war (480–479 BC). **General Saint-Cyr**: Laurent de Gouvion (1764–1830), later marshal of the Empire. Blaubeuren in fact saw no action. **Condé's monstrous lot**: the Prince de Condé (1736–1818), who had fled France in 1789, fought alongside the Austrians with an army of mercenaries notorious for their brutality. **Heinse**: Wilhelm (1749–1803), author of the novels *Ardinghello und die glückseligen Inseln* (1787) and *Hildegard von Hohenthal* (1795–1796) and librarian to the elector of Mainz, came to Kassel in flight from the French armies. A friend of the Gontard family, H dedicated his great elegy "Brot und Wein"/"Bread and Wine" to him. **King of Prussia**: Friedrich Wilhelm II (1744–1797) visited the landgrave Wilhelm IX of Hesse-Kassel on 3rd August. **Augarten**: now the Karlsaue. **Weisser Stein**: now the Wilhelmshöhe. **statues in the museum**: the Museum Fridericianum in Kassel contained many copies of classical statues and some original pieces. Heinse, an expert, would have been a good guide. The picture gallery contained works by Rubens and Rembrandt among many others and was one of the most significant collections of the time. B125, S131

FROM GEORG WILHELM FRIEDRICH HEGEL. Tschugg, August 1796

Draft. The form is a kind of free verse, mostly iambic, very loosely "Greek" in that the ultimate source for long unrhymed poems of varying line length, quite widely followed at the time in Germany, was Pindar. It seems likely that this poem was written in response to a lost letter from H sent "at the beginning of summer" and mentioned in Letter 128. It gave details of the "extremely advantageous position" in the Gogel household in Frankfurt, which Hegel duly took up in January 1797. Hegel had been a house tutor in Bern and Tschugg since leaving Tübingen in autumn 1793. It is possible that a fair copy of "Eleusis" was sent to H, but he never mentions it, nor is there any other trace of it. He may have seen the poem after Hegel joined him in Frankfurt, or never known anything about it. It represents part of the conversation between H, Hegel, and Schelling, which can also be followed in the so-called "Systemprogramm" (see "The Oldest Programme for a System of German Idealism" in *Essays and Letters*, 341–42) and in H's essay fragment on religion (see "Fragment of Philosophical Letters" in *Essays and Letters*, 234–39, a text also known as "On Religion"). All three texts were written in broadly the same period, around 1796. **Eleusis**: the site of the Eleusinian mysteries in ancient Greece, sacred to Demeter/Ceres. The main source for our knowledge of the mysteries is the *Homeric Hymn to Demeter*, which was discovered only in 1777 in Moscow, provoking widespread fascination in Germany in the following years. It is probable that Hegel's interest in the mysteries is connected to this discovery. In the *Phenomenology of Spirit* (1807) he returns to "the ancient Eleusinian mysteries of Ceres and Bacchus" in a context that shows some affinity to H's poem "Bread and Wine" (see Hegel, *Phänomenologie des Geistes*, ed. Wessels and Clairmont [Hamburg: Meiner, 1988], 77). **hopes of seeing you again**: this anticipated reunion (in Frankfurt) also opens and closes Hegel's letter of November. **the old alliance**: in Letter 84 H reminds Hegel of their parting in Tübingen with the words "Kingdom of God," standing for all their hopes for the future. [**my senses drift . . . with form—**]: these lines are crossed out in the manuscript. They are the point at which Hegel attempts what is otherwise forbidden in the poem, the direct articulation of the experience of pantheistic union with the absolute. **Ceres**: the Roman name for

Demeter. The fertility rites associated with her represent a religion of the earth which Hegel is implicitly setting against Christian spiritualism. **But your halls have fallen silent**: this desolating absence resembles that in H's elegy "Bread and Wine": "But the thrones, where are they? Where are the temples . . ." (*Poems and Fragments*, 323).
*B121

127. TO HIS BROTHER. Frankfurt, 13 October 1796

Frankfurt was freed of French troops on September 8th, but H and his party returned only at the end of the month. **Boeotia**: mountainous region in Greece the ancient Athenians regarded as uncultivated. **spa town**: Bad Driburg, where they spent about a month from 11th August after a two-day journey from Kassel. **Arminius**: chief of a Teutonic tribe who drove the Roman governor Varus out of south Germany in 9 AD, the subject of *Hermanns Schlacht* (*Arminius' Battle*, 1767), a drama by F. G. Klopstock (1724–1803). H owned a 1777 reprint. **the woods near Hahrd**: see the poem "Der Winkel von Hahrdt"/"The Nook at Hardt" (*Poems and Fragments*, 458/459). **the proposal I made**: to help pay for Karl to study at Jena. **fair**: the Frankfurt Autumn Fair (Messe) had been one of the largest in Europe but was beginning to be overshadowed by that in Leipzig.
B126, S132

128. TO GEORG WILHELM FRIEDRICH HEGEL. Frankfurt, 24 October 1796

You remember: the letter mentioned here has not survived but Hegel's poem "Eleusis" was perhaps written in response to it. **Herr Gogel**: Johann Noë (1758–1825), a friend and distant relative of the Gontards, a successful wine merchant with a significant art collection. Hegel took up the post in January 1797 and stayed until the end of 1800. **two good boys of 9 or 10**: these were Johann Matthias (1786–1849) and Johann Noë (1788–1865), sons of Gogel's older brother who had died in 1793. **one of the finest houses in Frankfurt**: the Gogel house was the very grand *Zur Goldenen Kette*, on the Roßmarkt. **Frau Gogel**: Margaretha Sibylla, *née* Koch. **repetitor in Tübingen**: it seems Hegel was considering this (see Letter 108) but he came to Frankfurt instead. **the main sum**: 400 florins was also what H got at the Gontards.
B127, S133

FROM GEORG WILHELM FRIEDRICH HEGEL. Tschugg, November 1796

From the first half of November, a prompt reply to the preceding letter. **embracing you**: as also anticipated in "Eleusis."
*B27, *S27

129. TO GEORG WILHELM FRIEDRICH HEGEL. Frankfurt, 20 November 1796

Bern: the family Hegel was working for in Switzerland divided its time between Tschugg and Bern. **2 girls**: these were Gogel's sickly daughter Sara Charlotte (1788–1805) and his niece Margaretha Wilhelmina (1785–1849). **What you say about leading and guiding**: there is nothing about this in the previous letter, to which this is a direct reply, but as it only exists in a transcription by C. T. Schwab we can assume that the corresponding words were part of the complete letter.
B128, S134

130. TO FRIEDRICH SCHILLER. Frankfurt, 20 November 1796

total silence: Schiller had not replied to H's letters since the flight from Jena in May 1795, but he answered this one immediately. **the unhappy verses**: see notes to Letter 125. **every slightest sign**: the attention to "signs" is typical of the letters to Schiller. **You also wrote me once**: this was probably in the (lost) letter mentioned in Letter 89.
B129, S135

131. TO HIS MOTHER. Frankfurt, 20 November 1796

teaching post: it seems that H had been offered a post at the grammar school (*Lateinschule*) in Nürtingen. **occupations which by nature and habit have become an indispensable need**: the first outright declaration to his mother of his need to write, though still not fully explicit.
B130, S136

132. TO HIS BROTHER. Frankfurt, November 1796

The space for the date has been left empty, but this is the letter announced in the preceding one. **whole wisdom of life**: this corresponds to the epi-

graph from Ignatius of Loyola affixed to *Hyperion*: *Non coerceri maximo, contineri minimo, divinum est* (Not to be constrained by the greatest things, to be contained by the smallest things, is divine). **Fichte's *Natural Right***: see Letter 122 and note. **My *Hyperion***: only the first volume appeared in April 1797. **two Swabian almanacs**: Stäudlin's *Musenalmanach fürs Jahr 1792* and *Poetische Blumenlese fürs Jahr 1793*, which contained most of the Tübingen hymns. H seems not to have reworked them.
B131, S137

FROM FRIEDRICH SCHILLER. Jena, 24 November 1796

Written in immediate reply to Letter 130. **Your most recent poems**: see notes to Letter 125. H had asked for them back in Letter 130. **add my comments to them**: as H had requested. **poem to Diotima**: i.e., the version of "Diotima" sent with Letter 125. Diotima was H's poetic name (from Plato's *Symposium*) for Susette Gontard. **Moses and the prophets**: Luke 16:29.
*B28, *S28

133. TO JOHANN GOTTFRIED EBEL. Frankfurt, 10 January 1797

Written in response to a disillusioned letter written in October 1796 from Paris (lost), where Ebel had gone in September out of enthusiasm for the French Revolution. **fermentation and dissolution**: H later took up the thought of this sentence in his essay-fragment "Das untergehende Vaterland . . ."/ "The declining fatherland . . ." (*Essays and Letters*, 271–76). It was how he saw his times. **one good soul in particular**: Margarethe Gontard (1769–1814), Susette Gontard's sister-in-law. The attraction was mutual, but the Gontard family opposed the match on social and perhaps political grounds. **Since I started this letter**: it is written in at least two sittings, which seems quite often to have been the case with H's letters. **someone else who might suit you**: Ebel must have been looking for a tutor on someone's behalf, perhaps in Paris.
B132, S138

134. TO HIS BROTHER. Frankfurt, 10 January 1797

B.: Johann Friedrich Blum, on whose invitation the young H made his journey to Speyer (see Letter 23). Karl would soon move to Markgrönin-

gen, where Blum was *Oberamtmann* (district administrator), to take up a civil service job under his direction. **splendid discipline**: one sign of H's interest in mathematics is his use of the term "Kalkul" in his discussion of tragedy in his *Notes to Sophocles* (*Essays and Letters*, 317). Jeremy Adler has suggested that this could be translated as "calculus." See also Letter 140. **journey to Frankfurt**: Karl visited at Easter.
B133, S139

135. TO HIS MOTHER. Frankfurt, 30 January 1797

the offer in question: another proposal to take a parish, which as the next letter reveals would have involved "marrying in." The confidence with which H rejects it is notable.
B134, S140

136. TO HIS BROTHER. Frankfurt, 4 February 1797

Extract and summary by Schlesier.
B135, S141

137. TO CHRISTIAN LUDWIG NEUFFER. Frankfurt, 16 February 1797

a world of joys: referring of course to his love for Susette Gontard. **a poem**: a reworked version in seven twelve-line stanzas of the "Diotima" sent to Schiller in July 1796. **song**: the poem "Sonnenuntergang im Walde" (Sunset in the Woods). **Hegel**: in Frankfurt since mid-January. **"Whom the gods love . . .**: perhaps a quotation from an early, lost version of *Hyperion*.
B136, S142

138. TO HIS SISTER. Frankfurt, 17 February 1797

Camerer: i.e., Johann Caspar. The spelling later in the letter, "Kammerer," shows how fluid the writing of names was at the time. **your friend**: Katharina Sibylla Fehleisen. **the reasons I gave**: in Letter 135.
B137, S143

FROM CHRISTIAN LUDWIG NEUFFER. Stuttgart, 18 April 1797

Extract and summary by Schlesier. *the beautiful poem*: "Diotima," sent with Letter 137. Neuffer also calls this a "song" at the end of the extract.

Lang's almanac: the *Taschenbuch für häusliche und gesellschaftliche Freuden*, edited by Friedrich Carl Lang (1766–1822) from 1796. The 1797 number had three old poems by H, "An eine Rose," "An Neuffer," and "Freundeswunsch," which Neuffer had sent in.
*B29, *S29

139. TO HIS SISTER. Frankfurt, April 1797

Written in the last days of the month. **accompanied our brother**: Karl was in Frankfurt over Easter, leaving on 20th April. **the hills around Homburg**: the Taunus range. **Mainz**: mainly due to Prussian bombardment, the city was in a pitiful state in 1797 and occupied by over thirteen thousand soldiers of the Imperial Army. **Prof. Vogt**: Nikolaus (1756–1836), since 1784 professor of universal history in Mainz but fled the city in 1792 as it was taken by French troops and went to Switzerland, returning in 1796. From 1798 he was in Frankfurt. A friend of Georg Forster's, Sömmerring's, and Heinse's, he succeeded the latter as librarian and inspector of galleries to the Elector in Aschaffenburg in 1803. **the republicans**: H's ironic distance is notable compared to his former enthusiasm. Against the background of Napoleon's successful campaign in Italy, French troops under the command of General Hoche had crossed the Rhine and came right up to the gates of Frankfurt. **a courier from Bonaparte**: bringing news of the armistice which Napoleon had imposed on the Austrians in Leoben on 18 April. This was a preliminary to the Treaty of Campo Formio, which ended the First War of Coalition. **General Hoche**: Louis Lazare (1768–1797). He died of tuberculosis in Wetzlar. **Nied**: the Nidda, a tributary of the Main to the northwest of Frankfurt. **a house in the country**: this is almost certainly the Adlerflychtscher Hof north of Frankfurt, though firm evidence that this is the place the Gontards used as their summer residence only exists for 1799 and 1800. **a book with the title *Hyperion***: the first volume had just appeared. H received ten copies.
B138, S144

140. TO FRIEDRICH SCHILLER, Frankfurt, June 20, 1797

why it is harder to bring nature to its proper expression: thoughts that seeded the essay-fragment "Der Gesichtspunct aus dem wir das Altertum anzusehen haben"/"The Standpoint from which we should consider Antiquity" (probably 1799, see *Essays and Letters*, 246–47). **positively**: like Hegel, H uses the word "positive" to designate the nominal, the given,

the merely formal. An opposite relation would be a dialectic, or in H's language a "living" one. **You took an interest in the book**: printing the "Fragment of *Hyperion*" in the *Neue Thalia* and then recommending it to Cotta. **the enclosed poems**: "An den Aether"/"To the Ether" and "Der Wanderer"/"The Traveller," and perhaps "Die Eichbäume"/"The Oak Trees" too. The first appeared in the *Musen-Almanach* for 1798, the other two in the *Horen*. **the poems that came too late last year**: see Letter 125 and note.
B139, S145

141. TO CHRISTIAN LUDWIG NEUFFER. Frankfurt, 10 July 1797

Replying to Neuffer's letter of 18 April 1797. **torn apart by love and hate**: perhaps softened slightly, but also complicated, if this is a reminiscence of Catullus's famous couplet "Odi et amo." 10th July, the date of this and the next letter, Marie Rätzer's wedding was held in the Gontards' house, bringing her time as governess to an end. That H had the leisure to write two letters suggests he was not invited, making his status as a servant palpable. He may also have been thinking that such a union was impossible for him or perhaps he had had an argument with Susette or her husband. **Lang's almanac**: see Neuffer's letter of 18 April 1797 and the note.
B140, S147

142. TO HIS MOTHER. Frankfurt, 10 July 1797

a new house to rent: H's mother had sold the Schweizerhof, the property belonging to her second husband, in 1795 but continued to live there. She moved into rented accommodation in the market square (now Kirchstraße 17) in early 1798. **ill-fated Nürtingen**: because her husband had died there. Blaubeuren was where her daughter lived and Löchgau her sister. **my cousin**: Ludwig Majer, who seems not to be turning out well in Jena. **my good acquaintances**: nothing is known.
B141, S146

143. TO HIS BROTHER. Frankfurt, ~ August 1797

The letter only exists in a transcription by Schlesier and the date is uncertain. On 22nd August H visited Goethe in Frankfurt and as no mention is made of this it was probably written before. **earned me great praise**:

it's not known what this refers to, but as yet there had been no reviews. **plan for a tragedy**: presumably the first mention of H's unfinished play, *Der Tod des Empedokles*/*The Death of Empedocles*. Specifically, this may refer to the "Frankfurt Plan," which was written in one of Henry Gontard's exercise books. **"The Traveler"**: "Der Wanderer," first version—see *Poems and Fragments*, 302/303. **something by me**: "An den Aether"/"To the Ether."
B142, S150

144. TO HIS MOTHER. Frankfurt, ~ August 1797

Probably very close in date to the previous letter. **a reason to write to me**: not clear what this is, but probably the request H says he can satisfy at the end of the letter. **Blum**: Karl had taken up his post in Markgröningen under the direction of Blum after Easter. **my relationship with Schiller**: these remarks are based on a lost letter that Schiller noted as having been sent on 28 July 1797—see the next letter, which is H's reply. **go to Geneva**: nothing came of this. **Fehleisen**: Carl Friedrich (1773–1797), whom H knew from the Stift, had drowned in Lake Bienne/Biel in Switzerland in July. His sister Katharina Sibylla was married to H's friend Camerer.
B143, S148

145. TO FRIEDRICH SCHILLER. Frankfurt, mid-August 1797

This letter could be slightly earlier than the previous two. Schiller noted its reception for 24th August, so it was perhaps written on about 18th. **your letter**: which Schiller sent on 28 July 1797. Among other things, it included the news that Goethe would shortly be coming to Frankfurt. H paid him a visit on August 22nd. **the metaphysical mood**: it seems very likely that the thoughts in this paragraph respond to Schiller's advice in the lost letter, accepting but also resisting it. **the new translation of *Kabale und Liebe***: Schiller's second play—*The Minister*, translated by M. G. Lewis (London, 1797). That's "Monk" Lewis. **Mögling**: he had gone to London on the occasion of the prince of Württemberg's marriage to Princess Charlotte, daughter of George III. **"The Traveler" ... "To the Ether"**: see Letter 140, in which these two poems were enclosed. Schiller passed them to Goethe for his opinion and on 28th June Goethe replied broadly approving of them ("both poems have good ingredients for a poet but which do not make a poet on their own"), and suggesting that they

could be printed in the journals H names here. **"Those who Think they Know Best"**: in the revised version (see Letter 125) "Der Jüngling an die klugen Ratgeber"—neither this nor "Diotima" were accepted. Schiller may have thought the first rather close to the bone.
B144, S149

146. TO HIS BROTHER. Frankfurt, ~ 20 September 1797

Copy and digest by Schlesier. *children*: the Gontard children, whom Karl knew from his stay in the house at Easter. **in the garden**: that is (probably) at the Adlerflychtscher Hof outside the city walls (see Letter 139 and note). **Neuffer did visit me**: with Landauer in the middle of September to coincide with the fair.
B145, S151

147. TO HIS SISTER. Frankfurt, late September 1797

an expectant mother: on 22 December 1797, Heinrike gave birth to her second child, Friedrich. **a journey**: the journey to Geneva with Henry, which didn't happen. **Elchingen**: where there is a Benedictine monastery. **Wiblingen**: also near Ulm, the site of a Benedictine convent. **once after a boat trip**: this occasion is also remembered in a later draft fragment for a poem to his sister.
B146, S152

FROM SIEGFRIED SCHMID. Mannheim, 19 October 1797

Digest and extracts by Schlesier. **two hours with you in Frankfurt**: probably their only meeting, just before this letter was written.
*B30, *S30

148. TO HIS BROTHER. Frankfurt, 2 November 1797

"To the Ether": the *Musen-Almanach* for 1798 came out on 2nd October. H's part in the anonymous attribution is unclear. **kind response to my *Hyperion***: probably also transmitted by Neuffer. Conz's favorable review of the book did not appear until 1801. **The poets who only play**: quoted (from memory) from Klopstock's *Die deutsche Gelehrtenrepublik* (*The Intellectual Republic of Germany*, 1774). **Dr. Sömmering**: Samuel

Thomas (1755–1830), a famous anatomist with connections to Goethe and the Humboldt brothers, professor of anatomy, surgery, and physiology at the University of Mainz from 1784 where he associated with Heinse and Georg Forster, in Frankfurt since 1792, where he frequented the Gontard household (his wife was a close friend of Susette Gontard's). **even if not in name**: Karl being a son of their mother's second marriage.
B147, S153-1

FROM SIEGFRIED SCHMID. Basel, early November 1797

The first part of the letter is lost. The fragment begins in the middle of a review of the contents of Schiller's *Musen-Almanach* for 1798. The first part probably dealt with Goethe's and Schiller's ballads and H's "An den Aether," and Schmid is now referring to poems by August Wilhelm Schlegel. **Sophie *Mereau***: see Letter 159 and note. **Fried. Brun**: (Friederike, 1765–1835), poet and travel-writer. **K.**: Heinrich Keller (1771–1832), sculptor and poet in Rome. *Mantissa*: "an addition of comparatively small importance" (*OED*). Schmid is referring to his own four poems. **Have I understood you correctly?**: as this question shows, the thoughts here pick up thoughts from the conversation with H in October. *Dextrae Deus adsit!*: "may God be at my right hand." ***Hermann und Dorothea***: Goethe's hexameter idyll in nine cantos had just appeared. **Dull and all too pitiful**: this poem appeared in a reworked version in Schmid's *Phantasien* (1803).
*B31, *S31

149. TO HIS MOTHER. Frankfurt, November 1797

constant visits, celebrations: these will primarily have been Marie Rätzer's wedding and a long visit by Susette Gontard's brother and his wife who were keen on society. **I'm sending you**: things probably bought at the autumn fair.
B148, S154

150. TO HIS BROTHER. Frankfurt, ~ November 1797

This is a postscript which has parted company from its letter because Karl sent it on to his mother to reassure her, as H wished. It is printed separately by Beck and the editions that follow him, on the assumption that the parent letter is lost, but even Sattler, who takes it as a postscript

to Letter 148, prints it after the letter to H's mother above. For that reason it is also separate here, though it indeed seems likely that it belongs to Letter 148, and that this though written on 2 November was left lying for some time. **my last letter**: this seems clearly to be Letter 149 and Karl's reply on 1 January 1798 shows that H was right to be worried.
B149, S153-2

FROM HIS BROTHER. Markgröningen, 1 January 1798

Reply to Letter 148 with its postscript Letter 150, which got held up in the post. *a letter to his mother*: Letter 149. **drama**: *Empedokles*.
*S32, *B32

151. TO HIS MOTHER. Frankfurt, early January 1798

unconditionally: there follows in the manuscript a scribbled-out sentence, which for all that is not illegible: "Such a form of contentedness would be no better than if I were to remain where I was when the coachman had thrown me off the coach into the road." **their child**: Rike had given birth to her second son, Friedrich (Fritz), on 22nd December. **dissonances**: for the rather unusual "Mistöne"; but see from the end of *Hyperion*: "Like quarrels between lovers, so are the dissonances (*Dissonanzen*) of the world. Reconciliation dwells within strife and all that is divided comes together again."
B150, S155

152. TO CHRISTIAN MATTHÄUS THEODOR BREUNLIN. Frankfurt, 10 January 1798

The recipient is H's brother-in-law, the occasion the birth of the Breunlins' second child (see notes to previous letter). **in whom we live and have our being**: cf. Acts 17:18: "In him we live, and move, and have our being." **we and the Father are one**: cf. John 10:30: "I and my Father are one."
B151, S156

153. TO HIS BROTHER. Frankfurt, 12 February 1798, posted 14 March

Preserved only in a transcript by Schlesier. Later parts of the letter perhaps added in March before posting. **parliamentary writings**: among H's

books at his death was *Über das Petitionsrecht der Wirtembergischen Land-stände* (*On the Right of Petition of the Estates of Württemberg*, 1797), which may have belonged to Karl. This and whatever else he had he perhaps lent to Hegel, who began writing a political pamphlet on Württemberg at this time. The context was the summoning of the Diet of Württemberg to con-sider the payment of war debts imposed by the French. **The letters**: Elise LeBret had apparently requested that her letters to H be returned—what follows refers to her. **unspeakably painful experiences**: perhaps refers to the unverified but not implausible story concerning Wilhelmine Kirms, recounted in the notes to the letter to Neuffer of 19 January 1795 (Letter 94). **Cisrhenanians**: the inhabitants of the left bank of the Rhine, occupied by the French. Early in 1798 towns in these areas, starting with Mainz, begun to acquire their own republican administrations.
B152, S157

154. TO HIS MOTHER. Frankfurt, 10 March 1798

journey to Switzerland: first mentioned in Letter 144 and never made. **troubles in those parts**: following uprisings inspired by the French Rev-olution France intervened, taking Bern on 5th March. This led to the proclamation of the Helvetian Republic on 12th April. **how the hair-net is put on**: these instructions relate to the hairnet sent with Letter 149; clearly the fashion was yet to reach Blaubeuren.
B153, S159

155. TO CHRISTIAN LUDWIG NEUFFER. Frankfurt, in March 1798

Herr Schinz: Wilhelm (1776–1836), the son of a pastor from Seengen in the Aargau, inheriting the position from his father in 1806. Related to the Schultheß family in Zürich and probably acquainted with Klopstock through them, he was also related to Lavater. It is likely that the con-nection came via Susette Gontard, who knew Klopstock from Hamburg.
B154, S158

156. TO HIS MOTHER. Frankfurt, 7 April 1798

7 April 1798 was Easter Saturday, and so in the period H had been hoping to visit his family. **troubles in Württemberg**: as touched on in previous letters, the reforms put forward by the Diet had met stiff opposition from

the new duke of Württemberg, causing revolutionary stirrings encouraged by the recent founding of the Helvetian Republic. **Rastatt**: in Baden, the location of a congress begun in November 1797 and lasting until April 1799. Its object was to negotiate the consequences of the treaty of Campo Formio and in particular the compensation of German princes who had ceded territory on the left bank of the Rhine. H accompanied his friend Sinclair to the congress in late 1798. **the Lord gives to his beloved in their sleep**: Psalm 127:2 ("so he giveth his beloved sleep" in the AV, "seinen Freunden gibt ers schlafend" in Luther). **the pulpit, which I have no wish to mount**: for the first time H comes clean to his mother about this, though he is gentler with her in later letters. **the fair**: the Easter fair in Frankfurt.
B155, S160

157. TO HIS SISTER. Frankfurt, mid-April 1798

in case of a change of circumstance: H is clearly readying himself for a break with the Gontard household, something he is more candid about to his sister than to his mother.
B156, S161

158. TO HIS MOTHER. Frankfurt, mid-April 1798

the other two: he had written to both his sister (Letter 157) and his brother, but the letter to Karl has not survived.
B157, S162

159. TO CHRISTIAN LUDWIG NEUFFER. Frankfurt, June 1798

your last letter: presumably just received and lost. **Heigelin**: either Johann Eberhard (1734–1812), the president of the guild of goldsmiths in Stuttgart or one of his sons. The younger of these, Johann Christian Hermann Heigelin (1773–1833), had recently established himself as a merchant in Frankfurt. **my contribution to your almanac**: Neuffer's *Taschenbuch für Frauenzimmer von Bildung* for 1799 contained fourteen poems by H, some of which Neuffer had already and some of which H only sent in August (with Letter 164). **enclosed letter**: (lost). **Frau Mereau**: the writer Sophie Mereau (1770–1806), renowned for her beauty and free living. Since 1793 she had been married to the law professor Ernst Karl Mereau, but in

1801 she got a divorce and in 1803 married the Romantic poet Clemens Brentano. The rumors of an affair with H have left no trace besides this letter. Neuffer will have wanted H to ask her to contribute to his *Taschenbuch*. **your almanac did not have my approval**: this was presumably how Neuffer had interpreted H's silence.
B158, S163

160. TO FRIEDRICH SCHILLER. Frankfurt, 30 June 1798

Schiller noted receipt of the letter on 6th August—possibly June in the date line is a slip of the pen for July (this is assumed by Sattler); or perhaps H failed to send the letter at once. Schiller did not reply. **a few poems**: "Dem Sonnengott"/"To the Sun-God," "Vanini," "Der Mensch"/"Man," "Sokrates und Alcibiades," "An unsre großen Dichter"/"To Our Great Poets," of which only the last two, the shortest poems, were included in Schiller's *Musen-Almanach* for 1799 (see *Poems and Fragments*, 100/101, 114/115, 116/117, 105/106, 107/108).
B159, S167

161. TO HIS MOTHER. Frankfurt, 4 July 1798

District Administrator: Blum (see Letter 23 and note).
B160, S164

162. TO HIS SISTER. Frankfurt, 4 July 1798

Miss My-bride-to-be: H's jocular name for his niece; see the end of Letter 157. **Dr Veiel**: Johann Gottlob (born 1772), having studied law became mayor of Blaubeuren. The remark on his "good taste" refers to his future wife.
B161, S166

163. TO HIS BROTHER. Frankfurt, 4 July 1798

period of fermentation: one of H's favorite metaphors of transition, with the implication of clarification to come; used in *Hyperion* and elsewhere and found also in Novalis and Hegel. **My character Alabanda**: what follows is from an earlier version of *Hyperion* than the published one. **And Hyperion says**: in a letter to Diotima, same wording as in the published

novel. **the children**: the Gontard children whom Karl had met on his visit to Frankfurt.
B162, S165

164. TO CHRISTIAN LUDWIG NEUFFER. Frankfurt, August 1798

my bits and pieces: poems sent to Neuffer earlier in the summer (with Letter 159) for his *Taschenbuch für Frauenzimmer von Bildung* for 1799, now complemented by the "few more little poems" mentioned at the end of this letter, some of which appeared only in Neuffer's *Taschenbuch* for the following year. θειον: "divine element," probably borrowed from Plato. **what I promised**: he had promised a longer poem.
B163, S168

FROM HIS SISTER. Blaubeuren, 13 August 1798

Fragment quoted by Fritz Breunlin in a letter to C. T. Schwab of 17 June 1870. Probably from a reply to Letter 162. **My Friz**: H's godson, named after him and born 22 December 1797. **portrait**: see the letter from his sister of 9 May 1795.
*B33, *S33

FROM SIEGFRIED SCHMID. Basel, late summer 1798

The end of an otherwise lost letter.
*B34, *S34

165. TO HIS MOTHER. Frankfurt, 1 September 1798

Schott: Andreas Heinrich (1758–1831), sublibrarian in the university library in Tübingen since 1784, had been appointed to the chair in logic and metaphysics in preference to Schelling (who was then offered a chair at Jena). **The Harter story**: Johann Heinrich Samuel Harter (1766–1823), at the time a curate in Enzweihingen, had been at the Stift and had republican leanings. In the summer of 1798 he was arrested under suspicion of having falsified the ducal seal and signature. H's mother had apparently brought this up in a letter.
B164, S169

FROM SIEGFRIED SCHMID. Basel, 23 September 1798

Transcript by Schlesier, who notes at the end that the rest is lost. **deeply thought and with sharp distinctions**: probably referring to remarks in lost letters from H.
*B35, *S35

HOMBURG, 1798–1800

FROM HENRI GONTARD. Frankfurt, 27 September 1798

This poignant letter was written just after H's sudden departure from the Gontard household (the exact date is not known). Henri was eleven. **Hölder**: it seems the children used both forms (Hölder and Holder, see further into the letter) to address H. **at Herr Hegel's**: Hegel was a house tutor in the Gogel family nearby, friends and relatives of the Gontards. **Herr Hänisch**: house tutor with Franz Gontard, a brother of Jakob Gontard's. **Jette**: the eldest of Henri's three younger sisters. **Posselt's *Annals***: *Europäische Annalen*, a political monthly edited by Ernst Ludwig Posselt (1763–1804) since 1795.
*B36, *S37

FROM SUSETTE GONTARD. Frankfurt, ~ 25 September–5 October 1798

Like most of SG's letters to H, this one was written in segments, probably on 25th and 28th September and 3rd and 5th October. **the Feldberg**: highest peak (879 metres) of the Taunus Mountains, clearly visible from Frankfurt, to the west of Bad Homburg where H was now lodging. **Then *Henry* had your letter**: H's reply to Henri's letter of 27 September 1798 is lost. **to send *Henry* to H.**: to Hegel. **Send me *Hipperion* if you already have a copy**: the first volume of *Hyperion* had appeared in April 1797. The copy for Susette bore the dedication: "The influence of noble-natured people is as necessary to the artist as daylight is to the plant, and just as daylight finds itself in the plant not as it is itself but only in the varied earthly play of colours, so noble-natured people do not find themselves, but rather scattered traces of their excellence, in the manifold shapes and devices of the artist." Susette's request implies H had already finished work

on the second volume, which did not appear until November 1799, but it seems likely that he finalized it in Homburg. **Often I have regretted**: it seems from Henry's letter that Gontard did not know H had left. **via S . . .**: Sinclair. **So, if you agree, we'll make this arrangement . . .** : with thwartings and alterations this became their arrangement for meeting. **Friday morning**: probably 5 October 1798. *Wilhelmine* **will stay with** *M*: the housekeeper, Wilhelmine Schott, and Male (Amalie), SG's youngest daughter, then aged six.
*B37, *S36

166. TO HIS MOTHER. Homburg, 10 October 1798

My book has had a certain amount of success at court: *Hyperion* and its author made a deep impression on Auguste von Hesse-Homburg in particular—see her letter to him (after 28 November 1799), and the List of Correspondents. Later H dedicated his translations of Sophocles to her. She was the daughter of the Landgrave (Prince) Friedrich V of Hesse-Homburg (1748–1820), dedicatee of "Patmos." At the time, their residence was being used to billet French military staff. **present events**: referring to the fragile political situation following the Treaty of Campo Formio. Frankfurt, close to the new French frontier, was particularly exposed. **Herr Gontard**: the manuscript shows that H first began writing "Gontard" without the form of address, before crossing it out and starting again. **we parted on polite terms**: this account smooths things over for his mother's benefit.
B165, S170

FROM SUSETTE GONTARD. Frankfurt, perhaps 31 October 1798

The date is Sattler's suggestion. It could be later. **You know the sign**: not clear which. Perhaps agreed in the next lost letter? They devised several to indicate was the coast clear or not. See, for example, the section dated 4 April below.
*B39, *S38

167. TO HIS MOTHER. Homburg, 12 November 1798

Rastadt: see note to Letter 156 (to his mother, 12 April 1798). H spent about two weeks in Rastatt from about 21st November, partly no doubt to put some distance between him and Frankfurt. **Neuenbürg**: on the edge of

the Black Forest, roughly halfway between Rastatt and Stuttgart. Neither this trip nor the one home took place. **the District Administrator**: Blum.
B166, S172

168. TO CHRISTIAN LUDWIG NEUFFER. Homburg, 12 November 1798

my tragedy: *Der Tod des Empedokles/The Death of Empedocles*, which H worked on throughout his time in Homburg but never finished. **your almanac**: see notes to Letter 159. **Life in poetry**: these important thoughts are at the center of H's preoccupations in Homburg, including his poetics of tones. **Brutus**: in Shakespeare's *Julius Caesar*.
B167, S171

FROM ISAAK VON SINCLAIR. Rastatt, November 1798

Excerpt by Schlesier. *Muhrbeck*: see List of Correspondents. *Zwilling*: Jacob (1776–1809), a Homburg friend of Sinclair's and an officer in the imperial cavalry, he was killed in the Battle of Wagram. H had known him since the year before.
*B54, see *S42

169. TO HIS MOTHER. Rastatt, 28 November 1798

Gutscher: Jakob Friedrich (1760–1834), the author of several writings on the constitution of Württemberg. In Rastatt not part of the official legation from Württemberg but of a delegation representing the estates. **What I am working on now**: his tragedy *Empedokles*.
B168, S173

170. TO HIS BROTHER. Rastatt, 28 November 1798

Morbek: Muhrbeck; see List of Correspondents. *Horn*: Fritz (1772–1844), like Muhrbeck attached to the revolutionary groups in Jena. Met H again in 1802 in Regensburg. *von Pommer-Esche*: Johann Arnold Joachim (1774–1814), secretary of the legation from Swedish Pomerania. **Councilor Schenk**: Johann Heinrich (1748–1813), Jacobi's secretary as well as friend. **Jacobi**: Friedrich Heinrich (1743–1819), man of letters and non-systematic philosopher, author of *Über die Lehre des Spinoza* (1785/1789). **R.**: not known. **Gutscher**: see note to previous letter.
B169, S174

FROM HIS BROTHER. Markgröningen, early December 1798

Fragment. H replies with Letter 173, giving some indication of the contents of the lost part. Whose opinions are being relayed when the fragment starts is not known. **Conz**: see List of Correspondents. Possibly, the opinions are his. **the letter our dear mother sent me to enclose for you**: lost, but the next letter is written in reply to it. **our dear friend** *Sinclair*: Karl had met him during his visit to Frankfurt in April 1797.
*B55, *S39

FROM SUSETTE GONTARD. Frankfurt, perhaps 5 and 6 December 1798

The date is uncertain, 5 and 6 December is Sattler's guess. **My letter**: lost.
*B38, *S40

171. TO HIS MOTHER. Homburg, 11 December 1798

among my relatives: meaning here the family of the pastor Johann Adam Blöst, who had died on 19 November 1798, in Klingenberg am Neckar, near Heilbronn. His wife was a sister of H's grandmother, and their daughter, Marie Eberhardine, would marry Karl Gok in 1804. **the proposed post**: with the von Gemmingen family in Heilbronn, north of Stuttgart, an offer transmitted via the Blösts. **opinion of my heart**: a significant and recurring phrase—see especially the poem "Andenken"/"Remembrance," lines 33–34: "zu sagen/Des Herzens Meinung" ("to speak/The heart's opinion"). **all that was and is and will be**: alluding to Revelations 1:4: "which is, and which was, and which is to come." **Karoline**: a further daughter of Blöst, she had just married the Gentner to whom H sends congratulations in the postscript. **Gentner**: see note to Letter 30.
B170, S175

172. TO ISAAK VON SINCLAIR. Homburg, 24 December 1798

Fragment. This letter is close in tone and subject to the essays H was writing at the time. Sinclair was still in Rastatt. **your letters**: only the fragment excerpted by Schlesier above has survived. **Pommer-Esche**: see note to Letter 170. **Diogenes Laertius**: wrote in the third century AD his *Lives and Opinions of the Famous Philosophers*, H's main source for *Empedokles*. **the transient and changeful nature of human thoughts and**

systems: compare Keats to J. H. Reynolds, 3 May 1818: "A mighty providence subdues the mightiest Minds to the service of the time being, whether it be in human Knowledge or Religion."
B171, S176

173. TO HIS BROTHER, Homburg, New Year's Eve/1 January 1799

Fragment—the beginning of this long letter is missing. **a humorous little essay**: "Teutsches Dichterkorps oder Chor" ("The German band or chorus of poets"), which appeared anonymously on 19 December 1798. **philosophical and political reading matter**: the essay just mentioned notes that that the "transcendental speculation of critical philosophy" on the one hand and "politics" on the other put poetry at a great disadvantage. *glebae addicti*: properly *glebae adscripti*, "bound to the sod," a legal term for the status of certain peasants. **the good-hearted Dutch painter**: if he has a particular artist in mind it's not known whom. **Thales and Solon**: the linking of these two fifth-century Greeks, the natural philosopher and the legislator, derives from Diogenes Laertius whom H was in the middle of reading; in fact they were unconnected. **So much has already been said about the influence of the arts on the education of man**: especially by Schiller in *On the Aesthetic Education of Man*; the remarks on "play" in the next sentence seem to be directed at thoughts in this work. **the verses**: "Meiner verehrungswürdigen Großmutter"/"To my honoured grandmother." **my little poems**: probably the epigrammatic odes that appeared in Neuffer's *Taschenbuch* for 1799. **homo sum . . .**: "I am human and think nothing human foreign to me," from the Roman playwright Terence's *The Self-Tormentor*.
B172, S177

174. TO HIS MOTHER. Homburg, January 1799

religion: much in this letter touches on the themes of the unfinished essay "On Religion" (also known as "Fragment of Philosophical Letters") H probably wrote in 1799. **him, that lives**: alluding to Revelations 1:18—"I am he that liveth." **Christ says**: Mark 16:16. **Gellert**: Christian Fürchtegott (1715–1769), a popular writer of didactic poems, became professor of moral philosophy in Leipzig in 1745. **the book I'm writing now**: *Empedokles*.
B173, S178

FROM SUSETTE GONTARD. Frankfurt, January 1799

Sattler suggests January 2nd. **The long dreaded visitors have arrived**:
SG's friend and former governess of her girls, Marie Rätzer (now Rüdt),
with husband and baby. They stayed till the middle of February. All visits,
even of people she was fond of, were more or less distressing since they
complicated her arrangements with H. **my brother**: Henry Borkenstein
(1773–1828), wine dealer. **H.**: Hegel.
*B40, *S41

FROM ISAAK VON SINCLAIR. Rastatt, 8 February 1799

Summary and extract by Schlesier. **Agis**: Agis was the name of several
Spartan kings. Whether H really began such a work is uncertain. Perhaps
Empedokles is meant.
*B56, *S42

175. TO HIS SISTER. Homburg, late February/early March 1799

Probably sent only in April (see postscript). **The new war**: the second War
of Coalition was declared on 12 March 1799, but could be seen coming
from the middle of February. On 1st March French troops under General
Jourdan crossed the Rhine at Strasbourg, whereupon the Austrians headed
into south-west Germany. **Veiel**: see Letter 162 and note. **Kammerer**:
Johann Caspar Camerer (see Letter 92 and note). **Morbek**: Muhrbeck.
B174, S180

176. TO HIS MOTHER. Homburg, early March 1799

Fragment; the last part of the letter is lost. **accident**: nothing is known
about this. **a good source**: probably Sinclair. **the war**: see note to last letter.
changes: as H knew from Sinclair and was perhaps more nearly involved in
(see end of letter), groupings of reform-minded republicans in Württemberg
had hopes of founding a Swabian republic with the help of the French.
B175, S179

FROM SUSETTE GONTARD. Frankfurt, after 4 March 1799

Sattler's dating; perhaps earlier. **the upheavals that may be approaching
us**: alluding above all to the coming war (see note to Letter 175). **I wish**

for his own good he would get away from here: aged twelve, Henry was soon sent away to Hanau for his further education. H mentions this in a letter to his mother from Homburg, 29 January 1800 (Letter 205). **Herr Hadermann**: Konrad Ludwig (1770–1846). He had been Henry's tutor before H was appointed.
*B41, *S43

177. TO SUSETTE GONTARD. Homburg, Spring 1799

Sattler's dating is "before 11 March," but it could be later. The beginning of a draft. H's actual letters to SG are lost. The four extant fragments are drafts that may contain precisely what H did not dare say. Possibly, this fragment is not addressed to SG at all but belongs with *Hyperion* or to a poem.
B176, S181

FROM SIEGFRIED SCHMID. Basel, 29 March 1799

Extracts and summary by Schlesier. ***Cotta has told him***: if so, nothing came of it. ***proposal in Berlin***: explained further in Schmid's letter of 12 June 1799. ***H.'s visit***: H had visited the Schmid home in Friedberg. Nothing more is known. **your picture**: presumably promised by H.
*B57, *S45

FROM SUSETTE GONTARD. Frankfurt, 12 March–4 April 4, 1799

Fragmentary. **a little French novel**: neither this nor "the picture" (below) has been identified. **your mother**: Susanne Borkenstein, *neé* Bruguier (1741–1793). **I shall not even be able to imagine where you live**: if H moves away, as she has suggested he should, to find employment and further his career as a writer. **M. la Fontaine**: August Heinrich Julius Lafontaine (1758–1831), prolific writer of light fiction living in Berlin. **holidays**: Easter was March 24th. **our church**: that is, it belonged to the Gontard family. **I was trying to make a plan**: see the segment of 4 April. **our garden**: a separate one which belonged to SG's mother-in-law. She says more about it in later letters.
*B42, *S44

178. TO HIS MOTHER. Homburg, ~ 25 March and 18 April 1799

the letter you will now have received: i.e., Letter 176. **my book**: meaning *Empedokles*. **a passage from the Jena literary magazine**: the review,

which appeared in the *Allgemeine Literatur-Zeitung* on 2 March 1799, was written by August Wilhelm Schlegel, the most important and influential critic of the time. **Hillmar and Siegmar**: pseudonyms of H and Neuffer respectively. **Reinhard**: Karl Friedrich (1761–1837), a Swabian who had been at the Stift, joined the French Revolution as a house tutor in Bordeaux and became ambassador to the French Republic in Hamburg in 1795 before being transferred to Florence in 1798. **a couple of my poems**: these were "An die Deutschen"/"To the Germans" and "An die Parzen"/"To the Fates," the latter containing the allusion to *Empedokles*; see *Poems and Fragments*, 96–97, 70–71. **Morbek**: Muhrbeck. **news of the war**: on 25 March 1799 Austrian troops defeated the French in Stockach and drove them back over the Rhine.
B177, S182

FROM SUSETTE GONTARD. Frankfurt, 9 May 1799

Begun in April, all missing before this fragment. **Weidenhof**: the inn H stayed at on the Zeil in Frankfurt when he came to see SG.
*B43, *S46

FROM SIEGFRIED SCHMID. Basel, 13 and 22 May 1799

a kind of legacy: this was a collection of Schmid's poems. H did what he could to get it published, offering it to Johann Friedrich Steinkopf on 23 August 1799 (Letter 192). **positions taken up by the armies**: Basel was in the middle of the left flank of the French army. A way through to the Austrians became possible when they broke through to Zürich on 5th June.
*B58, *S47

179. TO CHRISTIAN LUDWIG NEUFFER. Homburg, 4 June 1799

a few contributions: for Neuffer's *Taschenbuch für Frauenzimmer von Bildung* for 1800, his "second son." **a few things by people I know here**: as emerges in subsequent letters, H sent poems by Emerich and Böhlendorff (see List of Correspondents). **a monthly poetry journal**: H later considered calling the journal *Iduna*—it was a project that didn't in the end come off. **Steinkopf**: see List of Correspondents. ***Death of Empedocles***: the

title of the second version, which was probably not as far on as suggested here and was never finished. **On the *Iliad*, particularly the character of Achilles**: see the essay-fragments "Achilles (1) & (2)," "A Word on the Iliad," and "On the Different Modes of Poetic Composition" in *Essays and Letters*. **the different kinds of poetry**: see the essay-fragment mentioned in the last note. **Heinse**: see notes to Letter 126. **Heydenreich**: see notes to Letter 99. **Bouterwek**: Friedrich (1766–1828), professor of philosophy and aesthetics in Göttingen, author of the novel *Graf Donamar* (1791–1793), which was an influence on *Hyperion*. **Matthisson**: see notes to Letter 61. **Conz**: see List of Correspondents. **Schmid**: see List of Correspondents. **the *Horae***: Schiller's journal *Die Horen*, which had recently stopped appearing and was a model for H's own project. **the promised essays**: probably never written.
B178, S183

180. TO HIS BROTHER. Homburg, 4 June 1799

The thoughts in this letter, which should possibly be dated 14 June 1799, give an idea of what H had in mind for his journal and are close to some of the theoretical prose he did write in Homburg, especially to "The Standpoint from which we should consider Antiquity." **creative impulse**: for "Bildungstrieb," a word originally introduced as a biological term by J. F. Blumenbach in 1780 and adopted by Kant and then Schiller. It might also be translated as "formative drive," and "Bildung" also contains the idea of education as well as creativity and formation. H uses the term frequently in 1799 and it is central to the thinking behind his journal project. **an aesthetic church**: i.e., a community bound by aesthetic values in the Kantian sense, relating to the apprehension of art and nature. Cf. the "invisible church militant" mentioned in the letter to Ebel of 9 November 1795 (Letter 107). **a passage from my tragedy**: from the second version of *Empedokles*, lines 397–430, with some slight differences of wording.
B179, S184

FROM SIEGFRIED SCHMID. Zürich, 12 June 1799

Summary and partial transcription by Schlesier. ***Archduke Karl***: (1771–1847), third son of Leopold II and commander of the Austrian forces. **rather more than a usual cadet**: given his education and age. ***his***

posthuma: the "legacy" of poems Schmid sent with his last letter. *Heinrich Frölich*: Heinrich Fröhlich (d. 1806), the publisher of the Romantic journal the *Athenäum*.
*B59, *S48

FROM JOHANN FRIEDRICH STEINKOPF. Stuttgart, 13 June 1799

Summary and extracts by Schlesier. *a letter to Neuffer*: Letter 179, which Neuffer must have acted on immediately. **names**: for more on those listed see the Index and/or List of Correspondents. *almanac*: Neuffer's *Taschenbuch für Frauenzimmer for 1800*. **The essay on Solon**: in Letter 179 H had proposed pieces on "Thales and Solon and Plato." **very short narrative or novel about Emilie**: H took this up and wrote an uncharacteristic but not uninteresting idyll, "Emilie vor ihrem Brauttag."
*B60, *S49

181. TO HIS MOTHER. Homburg, 18 June 1799

my second father: Johann Christoph Gok died in 1779 when H was almost nine. **the 100 fl.**: offered in the spring (see Letter 178) and sent (in fact 133 florins) on August 19, 1799, the first sending since 1795. It came out of the interest on the legacy left for him by his father.
B180, S186

182. TO JOHANN FRIEDRICH STEINKOPF. Homburg, 18 June 1799

Copy and digest by Schlesier. Prompt reply to Steinkopf's letter of 13 June 1799. *project*: the "monthly poetry journal" announced in the letter to Neuffer of 4 June 1799. Steinkopf was to be the publisher. *popularity*: H is responding to the request made by Steinkopf and steering it into something more congenial. **the same thing has recently been attempted**: by the brothers August Wilhelm and Friedrich Schlegel in their journal *Athenäum*, which began appearing in 1798. The criticisms which follow apply to them. H himself is aiming for more balance. **its due as a product of nature**: the same words are used in the prospectus (see below). **Iduna**: in Norse myth the keeper of the magic apples that preserved the youth of the gods. She was a goddess, married to Bragi, god of poetry. H may have known of the myth from a dialogue by Herder, *Iduna or the Apple of Youth*, published in Schiller's *Horae* in 1796. There does not appear to be an earlier journal with this title. It would in any case have

been an odd reason to pick the title. **prospectus**: see the fragment of this that survives—"From a draft of the Journal Plan," in *Essays and Letters*, 245. Its rejection of "affectedly mischievous saltos and curios" is again a jab at the Schlegels. **my tragedy**: *Empedokles*, which was to appear in the journal. ***"Emilie"***: see notes to letter to Neuffer of 3 July 1799 (Letter 184). ***a few other poems***: see the letter to Neuffer written in the second half of July (Letter 191). ***a young poet***: probably Emerich, but perhaps Schmid or Böhlendorff (see List of Correspondents).
B181, S185

183. TO SUSETTE GONTARD. Homburg, ~ late June 1799

Fragmentary draft, copied by Schlesier. The date is uncertain: I follow the German editions in placing it here, toward the end of June, but late August is also possible. Luigi Reitani in his Italian edition not only prefers the later date but regards this draft as belonging with Letter 194, forming the later sections of that letter (for his reasoning, see pp. 1669–72 of his edition). **firewood**: behind this word lies the Greek ὕλη, which means wood, firewood, but also matter. The combination of matter and spirit (through and in poetry) is a focus of the essay "When the poet is once in command of the spirit . . ." (*Essays and Letters*, 277–98). With the general thought of this passage compare Keats to J. H. Reynolds, 19 February 1818: "Man should not dispute or assert but whisper results to his neighbour, and thus by every germ of Spirit sucking the Sap from the mould ethereal every human might become great, and Humanity instead of being a wide heath of Furze and Briars with here and there a remote Oak or Pine, would become a grand democracy of Forest Trees." **"The French have been beaten in Italy again"**: the French suffered three defeats in Italy that year, at Cassano (27th April), by the Trebbia (17–19th June), and at Novi (15th August), setbacks for the republican cause. Which of the latter defeats Muhrbeck is referring to determines the date of the letter.
B182, S187

184. TO CHRISTIAN LUDWIG NEUFFER. Homburg, 3 July 1799

what I promised: the idyll "Emilie vor ihrem Brauttag"/"Emilie before her Bridal Day," which H had written at Steinkopf"s request. **Jung**: see List of Correspondents; now living in Mainz. Nothing is known about H's journey. **Ossian**: Jung's translation appeared in 1808. **commentary**: apparently envisaged by H himself, perhaps in the manner of his later "Pindar

Fragments." **the poetic genre**: i.e., the idyll. **the strictest of all poetic forms**: H's reflections on tragedy continued in several of the Homburg essays, in *Empedokles*, and in his later work on Sophocles. **your comedy**: about which nothing is known. **another young poet**: Emerich, whose poems H took an interest in—see List of Correspondents. **Bölendorf**: see List of Correspondents.
B183, S189

FROM JOHANN FRIEDRICH STEINKOPF. Stuttgart, 5 July 1799

Summary and extracts by Schlesier. **Humboldt**: Wilhelm von (1767–1835), philosopher, linguist, diplomat. **Falk**: Johann Daniel (1768–1826), writer and philanthropist. **Meisner**: August Gottlieb Meißner (1753–1807), a writer of novellas. *Iduna*: H's projected journal—see Letter 182 and notes.
*B61, *S51

185. TO FRIEDRICH SCHILLER. Homburg, 5 July 1799

Schiller noted reception only on 17th July. The letter was perhaps taken to Jena by Böhlendorff who went there in the middle of the month. Schiller did not reply until 24 August. **a humanist journal**: using the word Steinkopf had advised. **My publisher joins his request to mine**: Steinkopf wrote to Schiller himself on 27th July. **M. Hölderlin**: M. for *Magister*.
B184, S190

FROM SUSETTE GONTARD. Frankfurt, ~ 3–6 July 1799

The beginning, perhaps a double page, is lost. **Tasso**: Goethe's play *Torquato Tasso*, first published 1790, examines the necessarily uneasy relationship between poetry and the social order. **3 July**: she wrote June but must have meant July. *S . . .*: Margaretha Elisabeth Sömmerring, artistically gifted close friend of SG, died a few months before her on 11 January 1802. **Thursday morning**: presumably 4th July.
*B44, *S50

186. TO JOHANN WOLFGANG GOETHE (?). Homburg, early July 1799

Sattler supposes 5th July. Survives only as a copy and part-digest by Schlesier. Incomplete draft. Beck doubts whether any such letter was actually sent, and Goethe may not be the addressee at all though it is certainly possible (considered by Schlesier and assumed in the German editions). B187, S191

187. TO FRIEDRICH WILHELM JOSEPH SCHELLING. Homburg, early July 1799

Draft. Schelling's reply on 12 August 1799, with its mention of August Wilhelm Schlegel and Sophie Mereau, shows that the letter he received from H was not identical to this draft. The wording is very close to that in the next letter and must be of similar date (6 July). **Since we last met I have followed your affairs and your fame**: perhaps the first contact with Schelling since their meeting in April 1796. He was now a professor in Jena and had made a name for himself with two major publications: *Ideen zu einer Philosophie der Natur* (1797) and *Von der Weltseele* (1798). **theoretical concerns**: the word H uses is "Wissenschaft." **in an aorgic state, will tend to become organic**: *aorgisch* and *organisch* are an important pair of terms in H's thinking at this time and are used extensively in connexion with *Empedokles* and also later in his notes on Sophocles's *Antigone*. Deriving perhaps from the speculative branch of Württemberg Pietism, they denote the opposition between the unbound, unorganized, formless energy of nature (*aorgisch*) and the organized and organizing, shaping principle of art and spirit (*organisch*). In *Von der Weltseele*, Schelling also uses the terms in a slightly different form (*anorgisch/organisch*) and it is likely that H (who avoids them in the similar letter to Ebel) is seeking to remind him of their shared concerns and perhaps of an earlier conversation in which the words had come up.
B186, S192

188. TO JOHANN GOTTFRIED EBEL. Homburg, 6 July 1799

This letter was published only in 1999 and is therefore not in Beck's edition. There are many overlaps with the letter to Schelling above. **the harmonic exchange of its tones**: as elaborated in H's tone-theory (see *Essays and Letters*, 302–10). **Your depiction of the mountain inhabitants of Switzerland**: the first volume of Ebel's *Schilderung der Gebirgsvölker der Schweiz* had appeared in 1798. **Herr von Humboldt**: Wilhelm von Humboldt had returned to live in Paris in 1797 having been there on and off since 1789. He left on a journey to Spain in September and was probably never made aware of H's request.
S193

189. TO HIS MOTHER. Homburg, 8 July 1799

those verses: "An die Parzen"/"To the Fates," which appeared in Neuffer's *Taschenbuch für Frauenzimmer von Bildung* for 1799 and which H probably sent with Letter 178. It begins "One summer only grant me . . ." **God sends rain**: Matthew 5:45—"for he maketh his sun to rise on the evil and on the good, and sendeth rain on the just and on the unjust." **the letter to my dear sister**: Letter 190. **the money**: see Letter 181 and note. B185, S195

190. TO HIS SISTER. Homburg, July 1799

Referred to in the previous letter and perhaps written the same day. **your letter**: lost. **without drawing too much attention to myself**: once within the borders of Württemberg, without an identifiable job, H would become exposed to pressure from the ecclesiastical authorities to enter the clergy. **a wild friend**: probably Sinclair. B188, S194

FROM CHRISTIAN LUDWIG NEUFFER AND JOHANN FRIEDRICH STEINKOPF. Stuttgart, 9 July 1799

Extract and summary by Schlesier. In reply to Letter 184, which included "Emilie." **talking with Schiller**: this picks up after a fashion on remarks in H's letter. Neuffer met Schiller during his return to Württemberg in 1793–1794. **Goethe's elegies**: principally the *Römische Elegien* (1795). **Emilie's letters**: that is, "Emilie vor ihrem Brauttag," which consists of four letters in verse. *a younger poet*: Emerich. *Märklin*: Jakob Friedrich, see Letter 29 and note. *Süßkind*: see List of Correspondents. *Pfister*: Johann Christian (1772–1835), at Denkendorf and Maulbronn 1786–1790, and at the Stift 1790–1795 where he was a close friend of Schelling's. *The Batavian envoy*: Paulus Hubert Andrian Jan Strick van Linschoten (1769–1819), envoy of the Dutch Republic in Stuttgart. *Voß's* **Luise**: Johann Heinrich Voß (1751–1826), the famous translator of Homer, also wrote this verse idyll (1795 in its final form), which views contemporary German life through a classicizing lens. *Goethe's* **Hermann**: *Hermann und Dorothea*, an idyll in hexameters, partly inspired by *Luise* and published in 1797. *B62, *S52

FROM KARL PHILIPP CONZ. Ludwigsburg, 19 July 1799

Summary and extract by Schlesier.
*B63, *S53

191. TO CHRISTIAN LUDWIG NEUFFER. Homburg, second half of
July 1799

Reply to the letter from Neuffer/Steinkopf of 9 July 1799. **some poems**:
for his *Taschenbuch für Frauenzimmer von Bildung auf das Jahr 1800*.
Apart from "Emilie," the poems by H in this almanac not already sent
last year are "Die Launischen"/"The Capricious Ones," "Der Tod fürs
Vaterland"/"Death for One's Country," "Stimme des Volks"/"Voice of
the People," "Sonnenuntergang"/"Sunset," "Der Zeitgeist"/"Spirit of the
Times," and "Die scheinheiligen Dichter"/"The Sanctimonious Poets" (for
two of these, see *Poems and Fragments*, 98/99 and 102/103). **a *story***: this
in response to the request in the letter of 9 July. H seems to have been
ready to embark on this for the sake of his journal but never did. **his
last letter**: of 5 July 1799. **Matthison**: Friedrich Matthisson (1761–1831),
poet, known to H since 1793. **little epos**: an idyll in Voß's manner, *Der
Tag auf dem Lande* (*A Day in the Country*), which appeared anonymously
in 1801. **Landauer**: see List of Correspondents. **Bilfinger**: an old school-
friend; see notes to Letter 4. Whether he was the author of the poem has
not been ascertained. **noble friend**: Strick van Linschoten, mentioned
in Neuffer's letter. When H met him in Frankfurt is not known, but he
moved in republican circles. **the tones do not vary enough**: as they ought
to according to the theory H was elaborating at the time. Neuffer took one
poem by Emerich (probably the one H reworked) and one by Böhlendorff.
B189, S196

FROM FRIEDRICH WILHELM JOSEPH SCHELLING. Jena, 12 August
1799

Extracts and summary by Schlesier. Reply to Letter 187. **Frankfurt**: they
met there in April 1796. ***delighted to take part***: that is, in H's ill-fated
journal. ***a few lectures***: Schelling was lecturing on the "System of Tran-
scendental Idealism," which touches on the themes mentioned and was
published as a book in 1800. ***Schlegel***: August Wilhelm, whose journal
was the *Athenäum*. **the *word* humanism**: this is the word (according to

Schlesier's digest, *humanistisch*) H had introduced to his exposition of the journal's aims on Steinkopf's urging. Herder published his *Briefe zur Beförderung der Humanität* in ten volumes in 1793–1797.
*B64, *S55

192. TO JOHANN FRIEDRICH STEINKOPF. Homburg, 23 August 1799

Extract and summary by Schlesier. Late reply to Steinkopf's letters of 5 and of 9 July 1799 (the postscript), whose own reply is lost. **Konz**: see Conz's letter of 19 July 1799. **Neeb**: Johann (1767–1843), professor of philosophy in Mainz, whom H had probably met via Jung. He had published in Niethammer's *Philosophisches Journal*. Among his other writings: *Reason against Reason; or, A Justification of Faith* (1797). **Schlegel**: August Wilhelm, as reported by Schelling. **Humboldt**: see note to Letter 188. **Lafontaine**: Steinkopf was keen to have him, but there is no sign H contacted him. **Schiller**: the doubts were confirmed in the next letter. **Haug**: Friedrich (1761–1829), a school friend of Schiller's, librarian at the court in Stuttgart, and well-known as the author of satirical epigrams. H included his name among those he wished to send a copy of his Sophocles translations in 1804. **a young poet**: Siegfried Schmid. Steinkopf didn't bite.
B190, S197

FROM FRIEDRICH SCHILLER. Jena, 24 August 1799

Transcription by Schlesier, also preserved in a copy by Friedrich Haug.
*B65, *S56

193. TO HIS MOTHER. Homburg, 27 August 1799

the fourth I've written: on this letter his mother has written "but I received only 2 of them." **send me the money**: according to her records she had sent 133 florins on 19th August, which arrived on 4th September.
B191, S198

194. TO SUSETTE GONTARD. Homburg, late August or early September 1799

Incomplete draft, in a transcription by Gustav Schlesier who notes that the draft breaks off at the end. **a place where I can support myself by giving lectures**: H is thinking principally of Jena.

B195, S199

195. TO HIS MOTHER. Homburg, 3 September 1799

in present circumstances: referring to the ongoing war. **sizeable sum**: 133 florins (see notes to previous letter). **my good brother-in-law**: who was seriously ill and died on 2 March 1800. **Blaubeuren**: Blaubeuren, where his sister lived, was closer to the fighting but remained untouched. B192, S200

196. TO HIS MOTHER. Homburg, 4 September 1799

Ostertag: Wilhelm Friedrich (1768–1845), parson in Wolfenhausen, known to H from the Stift, he married Elise LeBret in October 1799. **taxes**: as the Duke of Württemberg was part of the Second Coalition against the French, extra taxes became inevitable. **peace**: temporary peace came not until the Treaty of Lunéville on 9 February 1801. **worry about the Consistory**: having left his employment, H was technically now liable to be called to serve as *Vikar* (~ curate) in a parish in Württemberg. B193, S201

FROM SUSETTE GONTARD. Frankfurt, ~ 8 August–5 September 1799

S. . . . : the Sömmerrings husband and wife. He (Samuel Thomas, 1755–1830) was a well-known anatomist and doctor. His book *On the Organ of the Soul* appeared in 1796. H wrote two epigrams concerning his work. He attended SG in her final illness. **your first visit to the house**: the Gontards' town house, Zum Weißen Hirsch, in Frankfurt. See SG's first letter, where she suggests he might safely visit. **here in the house**: their house in the country, the Adlerflychtscher Hof. **your journal**: the planned *Iduna*, which as he reports to her with some bitterness (Letter 194) was foundering due to the lack of support from the established writers he approached. **my little journey**: 19–29 July 1799 ("a week later" than originally planned). She travelled with her brother's wife, Eugenie Elisabeth Radde, and Gunda Brentano who was not the "youngest" but the second of the Brentano girls. **Tischbein**: Johann Heinrich Wilhelm (1751–1829), the painter, Goethe's friend in Rome, director of the Naples Academy. He had returned to Germany only a few months before SG met him. **your own observations on Homer . . .** : H intended them for *Iduna* but made only a few sketches (see *Essays and Letters*, 248–53), which he abandoned when the whole

project foundered. **an old and dear friend from Hamburg**: not identified. **Wieland's estate**: Oßmannstedt, close to Weimar. *la Roche*: Sophie von La Roche (1731–1807), novelist, friend of Wieland, she was visiting him with her granddaughter Sophie Brentano. **Mme *Merau***: Sophie Mereau.
*B45, *S54

197. TO FRIEDRICH SCHILLER. Homburg, first half of September 1799

Incomplete draft. The clean and certainly not identical copy actually sent to Schiller—in reply to his from 24 August—arrived on 20th September. It received no answer. **some time ago**: probably in a letter from summer 1797 which has not survived. *Robbers*: *Die Räuber* (1781), Schiller's first play; the "scene by the Danube" is act III, scene 2. *Fiesko*: Schiller's second play (1783). *Don Carlos*: Schiller's fourth play (1787). **who for their part**: this last section, sketchily written in different ink at the bottom of the page, refers to the other writers H had hoped to win for his journal. B194, S202

FROM SIEGFRIED SCHMID. Kappel in the Toggenburg, 10 September 1799

Extracts and summary by Schlesier. **Zwilling**: see notes to Sinclair's letter of November 1798. **Schiller's *Wallenstein***: this trilogy of plays appeared in June 1800. *the publication of his poems*: Schmid is referring to the manuscript of his own poems he hoped H would find a publisher for. *B66, *S57

FROM JOHANN FRIEDRICH STEINKOPF. Stuttgart, 18 September 1799

Summary and extract by Schlesier. *Their letters crossed*: and both have disappeared. H's was dated 12 August, as mentioned a few lines later. *letter of 23rd August*: Letter 192. *speculation*: i.e., philosophical writing. **a heavyweight**: the word Steinkopf uses is "Matador"; who he is referring to is not known. *Haug*: Friedrich Haug, see notes to Letter 192.
*B67, *S59

FROM FRIEDRICH MUHRBECK. Jena, September 1799

The (fragmentary) original of this and the next letter, which may in fact form one, disappeared from the municipal library of Homburg during

the American occupation at the end of the war. *principes rationes phil. artis*: "The Principles of Aesthetics" ("Grundsätze der Kunstphilosophie"), a series of lectures Schelling gave in the winter semester. **Schlegel**: August Wilhelm, who that winter lectured on Greek and Latin literary history.
*B68, *S58

FROM FRIEDRICH MUHRBECK. Jena, September 1799

See notes to previous letter. **his lectures on transcendental philosophy**: during the summer semester, which that year went on until about 20th September, Schelling gave lectures on "The System of Transcendental Idealism." In its book form, which appeared in 1800 (*System des transzendentalen Idealismus*), the thoughts on history alluded to later in this letter occur toward the end. This is a version of the triadic thinking familiar from H's own work and in many of his contemporaries'.
*B69, *S58:4

FROM SUSETTE GONTARD. Frankfurt, October 1799

Sattler dates this to 2nd October. *Hipperion*: the second volume, due to appear soon. See Letter 200 and SG's November letter. **the great upheavals in Hamburg**: many bankruptcies, caused not by the wars but by speculators.
*B46, *S60

198. TO HIS MOTHER. Homburg, 8 October 1799

The account of his dealings with Steinkopf here makes the journal-project seem securer than it was but also indicates that H must have agreed to the idea of a coeditor. Several letters between H and his publisher have not survived. **I expect a reply any day**: Schiller did not of course reply. **Don't send the money**: this request came too late, and H's mother sent 100 guilders on 10th October, via Neuffer. See H's letter to Neuffer of 4 December 1799 (Letter 204).
B197, S203

FROM CASIMIR ULRICH BÖHLENDORFF. Jena, 24 October 1799

Digest and transcription by Schlesier. *Schwarzburg*: a castle overlooking the Schwarza river, about twenty-five miles from Jena and meeting-place

for the Society of Free Men. **I have given it**: that is, the first volume of *Hyperion*; the second was about to appear. **Goethe**: he wrote only the first canto of a planned epic on Achilles, and the idea of a long poem on nature, based on Lucretius's *De rerum naturae*, came to nothing. He read Schelling's *Ideen zu einer Philosophie der Natur* in 1798 and was in Jena from mid-September to mid-October 1799 where he met with Schelling frequently. **Schlegel's lectures**: see notes to the first letter from Muhrbeck of September 1799. **Italian Letters**: Böhlendorff made a journey through Northern Italy in 1797, which he wrote up in a series of letters published in Friedrich Wilmans's *Taschenbuch auf 1803*. He had left them in Homburg for his friends to read. **Gries**: Johann Dietrich (1775–1842), the first part of whose translation of Tasso's *Gerusalemme liberata* appeared in 1800. From Hamburg, he came to Jena in 1795 (after H's departure) and was part of the Society of Free Men.
*B70, *S61

FROM SUSETTE GONTARD. Frankfurt, 31 October 1799

My feeling that you would mistake today's date: the arrangement was the first Thursday of the month. **Don't go back where you fled from**: that is Jena and Weimar. SG seems jealous of, possibly, Charlotte von Kalb, or may be harking back to H's affair in Waltershausen with Wilhelmine Kirms during his first employment as house-tutor in 1794–1795. Perhaps though she is just wary of Schiller's effect on H. **no such experience again**: that is, unpleasantness from Jacob Gontard.
*B47, *S62

199. TO FRANZ WILHELM JUNG. Homburg, October/November 1799

Summary and transcription by Schlesier. **Saxony**: i.e., for Jena.
B196, S208

200. TO SUSETTE GONTARD. Homburg, early November 1799

Incomplete draft, transcribed by Schlesier. Schlesier notes, on the back of the sheet, some slightly misquoted lines from Klopstock which Sattler thinks H was considering using as a dedication in SG's copy of the second volume of *Hyperion*: "To be pure in heart / That is the highest, / What the wise thought up / The wiser did." **Here is *Hyperion***: the second volume,

which appeared at the end of October. SG's copy has survived and bears the dedication "For whom else but you." **Diotima**: the name given to SG in H's poems and also in the novel. **Your illness, your letter**: referring to SG's last letter (October 31st), which includes details of a fever and the words: "without you my life is wilting and slowly dying."
B198, S204

FROM SUSETTE GONTARD. Frankfurt, 2–7 November 1799

S. . .: Margaretha Elisabeth Sömmerring. **Z. . .**: Ludwig Zeerleder (1772–1840), financier and man of feeling, he was in Frankfurt a good deal in 1793–1794 and fell in love with SG. He copied out for her the "Fragment" of H's *Hyperion*, which appeared in Schiller's literary periodical *Thalia* in November 1794. **B. . .**: probably a member of the Brevillier family. **his country**: that is, Switzerland. **You had a book in your hand**: the second volume of *Hyperion*.
*B48, *S63

FROM JOHANN GOTTFRIED EBEL. Paris, November 1799

Summary and transcription by Schlesier. A late reply to Letter 188. **Humboldt**: Wilhelm, who had been in Paris and whom Steinkopf wanted as a contributor to the journal. **galleries**: which by then contained among other things the classical works Napoleon had plundered in Italy.
*B71, *S64

201. TO HIS MOTHER. Homburg, 16 November 1799

journey: probably to daughter and family in Blaubeuren. **what you have sent**: see note to Letter 198. **Bonaparte made a sort of dictator**: (18 Brumaire)—though it sounds negative H may either be distancing himself from the term or using it in the Roman sense of a consul assuming total powers to bridge a crisis.
B199, S205

202. TO HIS SISTER. Homburg, 16 November 1799

Veiel: see note to Letter 162. **the worries for your dear husband**: the recovery did not last.
B200, S206

203. TO JOHANN GOTTFRIED EBEL. Homburg, ~ mid-November 1799

Incomplete draft transcribed by Schlesier. Written in direct reply to Ebel's letter from Paris earlier in the month. **my literary enterprise**: that is, the soon-to-be-abandoned journal.
B201, S207

FROM PRINCESS AUGUSTE OF HESSE-HOMBURG. Homburg, after November 28, 1799

gifts: for her twenty-third birthday on 28th November, H had sent the poems "Der Prinzessin Auguste von Homburg" and "Gesang des Deutschen" together with the second volume of *Hyperion* (see *Poems and Fragments*, 150–53 and 160–65). **song**: the ode "Der Prinzessin Auguste von Homburg."
*B73, *S65

204. TO CHRISTIAN LUDWIG NEUFFER. Homburg, 4 December 1799

Probably the last letter to Neuffer. They saw one another in Stuttgart in 1800 but had less and less in common. **your poem**: one of several in Neuffer's *Taschenbuch für Frauenzimmer von Bildung* for 1800, which he had just sent and which also contained several poems by H. **the death of your good mother**: she had died on 13 January 1799. **the inconvenient change in your job**: following the death of the pastor under whom he had been serving as *Vikar* at the orphanage in Stuttgart, Neuffer had been obliged to take on extra duties. **a journey at the Consistory's expense**: this would have been for some kind of educational journey, to help bridge the wait for a parish. **the sure, thoroughly purposeful and considered progression of ancient works of art**: the same thought recurs in the "Notes on the *Oedipus*" (*Essays and Letters*, 317) and underlies the poetological essays H was writing in Homburg at this time. **unthinking remarks about poetry**: made in Neuffer's letter of 9 July 1799. **Only let a god**: perhaps echoing a famous line from the end of Goethe's play *Torquato Tasso* (1790): "A god has let me say how I suffer." **the letter to our friend Steinkopf**: probably enclosed, and lost. **the 100 florins**: from H's mother, sent via Neuffer (see Letter 198).
B202, S209

FROM SUSETTE GONTARD. Frankfurt, before 5 December 1799

Sattler's dating, 5th December being the first Thursday of the month.
Z. . . : Zeerleder; see notes to SG's last letter. **my aversion to your being in *Jena*:** see SG's letter of 31 October 1799, which this passage hardly clarifies.
*B49, *S66

FROM SIEGFRIED SCHMID. Tuttlingen, 19 December 1799

Summary and excerpt by Schlesier. ***his poems*:** H had sent them to Steinkopf with Letter 192 and Steinkopf returns them in the following letter.
*B72, *S67

FROM JOHANN FRIEDRICH STEINKOPF. Stuttgart, 12 January 1800

Summary by Schlesier. ***his two letters*:** both lost. ***two manuscripts*:** that by Jung was his Ossian translation. ***Landauer*:** see List of Correspondents. He had just set off on a trip to Frankfurt.
*B74, *S68

205. TO HIS MOTHER. Homburg, 29 January 1800

Fragment: copy and part-digest by Schlesier. The missing part of the letter seems to have dealt with his mother's urging him to take up a post of some kind in Württemberg, perhaps a teaching post. He was in any case considering moving to Stuttgart, which he eventually did in June. **400 fl. from my bookseller:** Steinkopf's last letter, which only survives in the briefest of summaries, must have raised hopes of launching the journal again. No doubt H is putting a better shine on his prospects than they really had. **against embarking on such a course:** referring to the matter dealt with in the missing part of the letter. This is the sixth time since 1794 that H has fended off his mother's attempts to get him into a steady job. **a friend in the imperial army:** presumably Jacob Zwilling. **Gontard:** Johann Heinrich (1736–1799). **Dear Henry:** Susette Gontard's son and H's pupil in Frankfurt.
B204, S210

FROM SUSETTE GONTARD. Frankfurt, 31 January–6 February 1800

Friday 30 January: Sattler points out that Friday was in fact the 31st. **compatriots of yours**: among them probably Christian Landauer, H's close friend, protector and confidant. **our beloved Cassel**: in the summer of 1795 Kassel was one stopping place en route to Bad Driburg, out of harm's way as the French advanced on Frankfurt. The journey confirmed them in their love. **further away from me than that**: than Swabia, Nürtingen, where his family are. **Z. . . .** : Zeerleder.
*B50, *S69

FROM FRIEDRICH EMERICH. Mainz, 4 March 1800

Summary by Schlesier. As an official in Mainz Emerich uses the Revolutionary Calendar. ***2nd part of* Hyperion**: which had appeared in the autumn of the previous year. ***verdict on the Germans***: in the penultimate letter of the novel, the so-called *Scheltrede*. ***like Böhlendorff***: this is probably an insertion of Schlesier's who had seen letters from Böhlendorff now lost. The expectation of a "third part" will derive from the novel's closing words, "More soon."
*B75, *S70

FROM SUSETTE GONTARD. Frankfurt, 5 March 1800

The first sheet is missing. On the back of the second H later drafted a poem that begins "Was ist der Menschen Leben . . ." ("What is the life of men . . ."; see *Poems and Fragments*, 612/613). **He will move into your rooms**: not clear who this is. **my relatives**: her brother and his wife. **another change in our family**: the imminent death of her mother-in-law. See her next letter.
*B51, *S71

206. TO FRIEDRICH EMERICH. Homburg, perhaps March 1800

Incomplete draft. The date is uncertain: Beck and Sattler connect it to the letter from Emerich of 4 March 1800, but Schlesier's summary is so brief there is little to go on. Reitani places it earlier (November 1799), perhaps with good reason. **publishing your poems**: these seem to have

been published in 1799. They were reviewed in summer 1800. **We cold Northerners**: anticipates thoughts in the first letter to Böhlendorff (Letter 238, 4 December 1801). **a true penitent**: seems to refer to H's advocacy of "artistic sense" over "genius." **if I appear to be angry**: i.e., in making the criticisms in this letter.
B206, S211

FROM HIS BROTHER. Markgröningen, 8 March 1800

Summary by Schlesier. *Prof. Bräunlen*: Breunlin died on March 2nd—see Letter 207. *Requests him to come home*: if H did so, then not till Easter (13th April).
*B76, *S72

FROM SUSETTE GONTARD. Frankfurt, 15 March 1800

Susanna Maria Gontard, born 1735, died on 14th March.
*B52, *S73

207. TO HIS SISTER. Homburg, 19 March 1800

the loss of your husband: on 2nd March. **all things are good**: cf. from the poem "Patmos" (line 88): "alles ist gut" ("everything is good").
B205, S212

FROM SUSETTE GONTARD. Frankfurt, 7 May 1800

This final letter, four sides, is written hastily and nervously in pencil, the last half-dozen lines barely legible from folding and refolding. **the garden on the Main**: recently inherited from Gontard's mother. **out here**: to the Adlerflychtscher Hof, the family's summer residence. **Z. . .**: Zeerleder.
*B53, *S74

208. TO HIS MOTHER. Homburg, 23 May 1800

the news: the French, under Moreau, had again crossed the Rhine on 25 April 1800 and advanced through Württemberg as far as Ulm. **my lodgings**: at Landauer's. **abroad**: i.e., outside Württemberg, though H's

next job was in fact in Switzerland. **additional occupations**: private lessons. **merchant from Frankfurt**: nothing more is known about this. **Herr Kling**: a draper, business friend of Landauer's. According to her records, H's mother sent the money on 1st June.
B207, S213

STUTTGART, HAUPTWIL, NÜRTINGEN, BORDEAUX, HOMBURG, 1800–1806

209. TO HIS MOTHER. Stuttgart, end of June 1800

H had left Homburg in June 1800, gone first to his mother's in Nürtingen (where since the death of her husband in March his sister and her children also lived), then to Landauer's in Stuttgart. **my friend's house**: Landauer's house, where H was a paying guest, stood in the middle of Stuttgart. **expenses**: his mother sent twenty-five florins on 15th July and a further twenty-five florins expressly for the desk on 26th August. **a little poem**: only notes for a poem to H's sister exist. **peace**: H's hopes were based on the news of Napoleon's victory at Marengo on 14 June 1800, but this led only to a ceasefire.
B208, S214

210. TO HIS MOTHER. Stuttgart, after 15 July 1800

to thank you: for the money requested in the last letter. **Gutscher**: see note to Letter 169. **Registrar Frisch**: Johann Georg (1763–1836), a bookkeeper, rather than registrar, for the Church council. Like H he lived at Landauer's. He may be the "young man" H announces he is giving lessons to in the previous letter, though as he is considerably older than H this must be uncertain.
B209, S215

211. TO HIS MOTHER. Stuttgart, late July 1800

Transcription and summary by Schlesier. He notes that the letter is from July, but how it fits with the preceding letter is uncertain. **visit to Reutlingen**: whom H intended to visit is not known.
B210, S216

212. TO HIS BROTHER. Stuttgart, ~ August 1800

Fragment of an unfinished letter. **Bookkeeper Frisch**: see note to Letter 210. He seems to have offered the prospect of a new job, Karl being unhappy in Markgröningen. See the next letter. **this fine and splendid time**: this would seem to refer to the French victories in Italy and southern Germany. **old sufferings**: perhaps a covert, or even not-so-covert reference to Susette Gontard, though the letter was probably not sent in this form.
B213, S217

213. TO HIS SISTER. Stuttgart, ~ September 1800

Probably written in September, perhaps early October. **his new post**: Karl took up a new post in Lichtenstern, near Löwenstein, sometime in September 1800. **full of praise and gratitude**: H's mother had given Karl 232 florins "on his departure from Markgröningen & for clothing."
B214, S218

214. TO THE DUKE OF WÜRTTEMBERG. Stuttgart, September 1800

A draft summarized by Schlesier. The request, to be allowed to reside in Württemberg without being obliged to take on a parish, was approved on 10th October. *the educator of his children*: this claim seems not, or only very partially, to have been true.
B211, S219

FROM KARL PHILIPP CONZ. Ludwigsburg, 4 October 1800

Summary by Schlesier. The second volume of *Hyperion* had appeared more than a year before. The review in the *Tübingsche gelehrte Anzeigen* which appeared on 12 January 1801 was probably by Conz.
*B77, *S75

215. TO HIS SISTER. Stuttgart, late October 1800

the Sunday after next: on the strength of this opening sentence and of reports of fine weather in the local paper for 23–27 October, Sattler assumes the letter was written on Saturday, 25th October. His mother's

records show that H made a brief visit to Nürtingen on Sunday, 9th November. **the peace**: it came, briefly, with the Peace of Lunéville in February 1801. **mothers**: i.e., mother and grandmother.
B216, S220

216. TO HIS SISTER. Stuttgart, mid-November 1800

Sattler's guess is 15th November, the Saturday after the visit home on 9th. **your friend**: nothing is known about this friend in Stuttgart.
B217, S221

FROM JOHANN BERNHARD VERMEHREN. Jena, 28 November 1800

The letter is addressed to H as the "author of *Hyperion*." **their almanacs**: the final *Muses' Almanacs* edited by Voß and by Schiller were both for 1800. **nine sisters**: the Muses. **Kosegarten**: Ludwig Gotthard (1758–1818), fashionable lyric poet then in a living in Rügen, later professor in Greifswald. For the other names, see the index. **contributions**: in spring 1801 H sent the elegy "Menons Klagen um Diotima" / "Menon's Lament for Diotima" and the Sapphic ode "Unter den Alpen gesungn" / "Sung beneath the Alps" (*Poems and Fragments*, 292–301 and 228–31).
*B78, *S77

217. TO GOTTLIEB ERNST AUGUST MEHMEL. Stuttgart, November/ December 1800

Incomplete draft (previously thought to be addressed to Christian Gottfried Schütz: see notes to Letter 235). The probable date is end of November. **your kind invitation**: the letter is written in reply to a printed invitation to work as a reviewer for the *Erlanger Litteratur-Zeitung*, of which Mehmel was one of the editors. H's copy has not survived but that sent to A. W. Schlegel on 15th November carried a postscript by Mehmel and it seems plausible that H's did too. **The rules I commit myself to**: the invitation contained four "principles" reviewers were expected to adhere to. **The intense study of the Greeks**: while in Homburg H did a word-for-word translation of most of Pindar's Olympian and Pythian odes and made a particular study of tragedy. **the words *want*, *ought* and**

can: together with other phrases at the end here, these pick up terms in the editors' guidelines.
B203, S222

218. TO HIS SISTER. Stuttgart, Autumn 1800

Date uncertain, perhaps late November or early December, but Beck puts it earlier. **nothing from Switzerland**: forced to begin searching for another source of income but also perhaps attracted by Switzerland, H was again looking out for a post as house tutor. He had approached Conz: see Conz's letter of 14 December 1800. Conz's enquiries led to a proposal, but by then H had negotiated the post in Hauptwil he took up in the New Year. **faith, hope and charity**: cf. I Corinthians 13:13. **I have lived!**: Horace, *Odes* book 3, 29 ("vixi": see Letter 37). **Mrs Landauer**: Johanna Margarete Louise, *née* Heigelin.
B215, S224

219. TO HIS SISTER. Stuttgart, beginning of December 1800

Summary by Schlesier, who notes "doubtless December 1800." *a family in Switzerland*: the Gonzenbach family in Hauptwil (Thurgau). The son of the family, Emanuel von Gonzenbach (born 1778), had been charged with finding a tutor for his younger sisters. *where the place is situated*: H knew the region from his tour of Switzerland in 1791. *30 louis*: a smaller sum than he had received in Frankfurt.
B218, S223

220. TO HIS SISTER. Stuttgart, 11 December 1800

the unexpected visitor: Emanuel von Gonzenbach. **a few louis d'or for the journey**: she gave him thirty-three florins. **Landauer's birthday**: H wrote a poem for the occasion, "To Landauer."
B219, S225

FROM KARL PHILIPP CONZ. Ludwigsburg, 14 December 1800

Summary by Schlesier. Seems to be the reply to a lost letter from H. It arrived too late, as H had just accepted the post in Hauptwil. *Kerner*: Georg

(1770–1812), secretary to Reinhard. **Reinhard**: see notes to Letter 178. He had recently moved from Florence to Berne. **a wealthy manufacturer**: this was Johann Caspar Zellweger (1768–1855). **Salomon Geßner**: (1730–1788), a well-known painter and writer of idylls. **Archipelagus**: "The Archipelago" (*Poems and Fragments*, 272–91). H had lent Conz the manuscript.
*B79, *S78

221. TO HIS SISTER. Stuttgart, ~ 18 December 1800

back here for at least a day's visit: after spending Christmas with his family in Nürtingen, H returned to Stuttgart for about five days before leaving for Hauptwil. **money our kind mother sent**: her list records fifteen florins sent on 10th December. **bill for board and lodging**: H's mother sent a further 136 florins at the end of the year.
B220, S226

FROM ANTON VON GONZENBACH. Hauptwil, 18 December 1800

Brief summary by Schlesier. Addressed to H at Landauer's.
*B80, *S79

222. TO HIS MOTHER. Stuttgart, just before Christmas 1800

Summary by Schlesier. Written on receipt of the letter from Gonzenbach.
B221, S227

223. TO HIS BROTHER. Nürtingen, late December 1800/early January 1801

our time is at hand: a variation on Christ's words at Matthew 26:18 ("my time is at hand"). **the peace that is forming now**: after the armistice at Steyr on 25th December, Austria agreed to negotiations for peace which began at Lunéville on 2nd January 1801. At this point France seemed to have subdued all its enemies and there were widespread hopes of a new order in Europe which H combines with utopian longings for renewal. **common spirit**: *Gemeingeist*, could be translated by "public spirit" but it has religious as well as political connotations: in a late variant to "Der Einzige"/"The Only One" H uses the word for Dionysus.
B222, S228

224. TO HIS FAMILY. Stuttgart, beginning of January 1801

Written on 6th January or a day or two before. **a bit tired**: from Nürtingen
to Stuttgart was about four hours' walk. **until Saturday**: 10th January.
B223, S229

225. TO ANTON VON GONZENBACH. Stuttgart, ~ 6 January 1801

Draft with many crossings out. **your son**: Emanuel—see notes to Letter
220.
B224, S230

226. TO HIS SISTER. Stuttgart, ~ 9 January 1801

B225, S231

227. TO HIS FAMILY. Constance, 14 January 1801

Summary by Schlesier.
B226, S232

FROM SIEGFRIED SCHMID. Friedberg, 15 January 1801

Summary and extract by Schlesier. **drama**: *Die Heroine, oder zarter Sinn
und Heldenstärke* (Frankfurt, 1801). H wrote a review as requested (*Essays
and Letters*, 312–15) but it was not printed. The "earlier" play is mentioned
in other letters from Schmid. **Huber**: see List of Correspondents.
*B81, *S80

FROM JOHANN GOTTLIEB SÜSKIND. Tübingen, 22 January 1801

Excerpt and summary by Schlesier. Schlesier gives the initials "F. G."
or "T. G.," but probably "J. G." is meant: Johann Gottlieb rather than
the older brother Friedrich Gottlieb. **the review of your** *Hyperion*:
probably by Conz, this appeared in the *Tübingsche Gelehrte Anzei-
gen* for 12 January 1801. **Schoell**: not identified. *just before he left*: for
Hauptwil.
*B82, *S81

228. TO HIS MOTHER. Hauptwil, 24 January 1801

H arrived in Hauptwil, near St. Gallen in Switzerland, in mid-January to take up his third post as tutor in the house of Anton von Gonzenbach. **large family**: Anton and Ursula Gonzenbach had three sons and six daughters. H taught the two youngest daughters, Barbara Julia (1786–1831) and Augusta Dorothea (1787–1868), and possibly others. **the oldest**: Georg Leonhard (1772–1808), involved in running the business. **what I owe you**: meaning the thirty-three florins H's mother had given him for the journey. **Fräulein Schwab**: nothing definite known, but perhaps the daughter of the Tübingen apothecary Johann Heinrich Schwab, later married to Immanuel Nast.
B227, S233

FROM SIEGFRIED SCHMID. Friedberg, 3 February 1801

Prompt reply to a lost letter from Hauptwil. **the poem**: i.e., the drama *Die Heroine*, mentioned in Schmid's last letter. **professorship**: Schmid was hoping to get a chair in oratory and poetry in Gießen, but nothing came of it. **the seven peaks in the Toggenburg**: including the Säntis, prominent from Hauptwil.
*B83, *S82

229. TO CHRISTIAN LANDAUER. Hauptwil, February 1801

Written in two parts, the first before news of the Peace of Lunéville (9 February 1801) arrived in Hauptwil, the second on about 23rd February. **a wondrous legend**: H is probably thinking of Hesiod's *Theogony* which relates the birth of the mountains from Gaia. Similar thoughts go into the great elegy "Heimkunft"/"Homecoming," written on H's return from Switzerland (*Poems and Fragments*, 330–37). **My dear friend**: the letter seems to be resumed here. **the peace**: the negotiations begun in January resulted on 9th February 1801 in the Peace of Lunéville, concluded between France and the Holy Roman Empire. Despite its fragility, it resonates far into H's writing from now on, in particular in "Friedensfeier"/"Celebration of Peace" (*Poems and Fragments*, 522–33). **Boreas**: the north wind. **the ladies**: Landauer's mother and wife.
B229, S234

FROM SIEGFRIED SCHMID. Friedberg, 22 February 1801

Summary and extract by Schlesier. *the drama mentioned above*: i.e., in Schmid's last letter. **to comply with the language of journalism**: which H's review (see notes to Schmid's letter of 15 January 1801) can hardly be said to do.
*B84, *S83

230. TO HIS SISTER. Hauptwil, 23 February 1801

Like Letter 229, written in two parts, the date being added on completion to what was mainly written in mid-February. **the negotiated peace**: Lunéville, news of which would have reached Hauptwil by mid-February. **these splendid peaks**: see the beginning of "Heimkunft"/"Homecoming" and "Unter den Alpen gesungen"/"Sung beneath the Alps" (*Poems and Fragments*, 330–37 and 228–31). **what I owe her**: see notes to Letter 229.
B228, S235

FROM JOHANN BERNHARD VERMEHREN. Jena, 27 February 1801

Summary by Schlesier. See the earlier letter from Vermehren (28 November 1800).
*B85, *S84

231. TO HIS BROTHER. Hauptwil, ~ mid-March 1801

Sattler speculates that the letter may have been written on 20th March, H's thirty-first birthday. **in faith and in sight**: alluding to 2 Corinthians 5:7: "For we walk by faith, not by sight." **a *sign* of the soul**: by "sign" H means physical presence, external aspect. In his poetic thinking in the Homburg essays "sign" is related to "ground": the ground expresses itself in a sign which is always different, even opposed to it. **A *Deo principium***: "The beginning is from God," perhaps derived from "Ab Iove principium" in Virgil's *Eclogues* (3, 60) where it applies to poetry.
B231, S236

232. TO CHRISTIAN LANDAUER. Hauptwil, toward the end of March 1801

your second letter: lost, like the first. **if you go to Frankfurt, think of me**: the fair, which Landauer visited every year, was due to start on April 6th. Landauer knew about H's love for Susette Gontard and as a friend of the family was able to pass on news.
B230, S237

FROM ANTON VON GONZENBACH. Hauptwil, 11 April 1801

Two days later, Gonzenbach also wrote a brief reference, which like the letter gives no indication of anything untoward having happened to force H's departure from Hauptwil: "At the request of Magister Hölderlin I hereby certify that this gentleman has as the tutor of my children earned my entire esteem, and I only regret that the unforeseen turn that things have taken is parting us so soon.—I shall lose in him a valued friend, and it is my wish that the happiest of futures and uninterrupted contentment shall always be his." H seems to have left Hauptwil by the middle of the month, bound for Nürtingen.
*B86, *S85

233. TO AN UNKNOWN ADDRESSEE. Nürtingen, perhaps April 1801

Fragmentary draft, stranded among work on the elegies "Heimkunft"/ "Homecoming" and "Der Gang aufs Land"/"A Walk into the Country" (*Selected Poetry*, 88–89). "Heimkunft" was written only after the return from Hauptwil. Sattler suggests Huber as the recipient without saying why.
B212, S238

FROM JOHANN BERNHARD VERMEHREN. Jena, 4 May 1801

Summary and extracts by Schlesier. Sent to Hauptwil, which H had by then left. **the poems he has received**: including "Unter den Alpen gesungen" and "Menons Klagen um Diotima." **the elegies**: Vermehren means "Menons Klagen um Diotima," which is in nine strophes. He printed it over two years of his *Musen-Almanach*, cutting up what is a single elegy.

Tieck: Ludwig (1773–1853), the Romantic writer, published a *Poetisches Journal* in 1800 which then folded. H's great poem "Der Archipelagus" eventually appeared in 1804 in Huber's *Vierteljährliche Unterhaltungen*.
*B87, *S87

FROM SIEGFRIED SCHMID. Friedberg, 8 May 1801

your lovely last letter: the letter suggests that Schmid received several from Hauptwil, all sadly lost. **professorship**: which Schmid was half-hoping to get in Gießen—see his letter of 3 February 1801.
*B88, *S88

FROM CHARLOTTE VON KALB. Mainz, 15 May 1801

back in Franconia: i.e., in Waltershausen where H had his first job as tutor.
*B89, *S89

234. TO FRIEDRICH SCHILLER. Nürtingen, 2 June 1801

The last letter to Schiller, left unanswered like the previous one of September 1799 (Letter 197). Schiller noted reception on 16th September. It was addressed to him in Jena, though he had moved to Weimar in December 1799. **the great clarity these writers have is a consequence of their abundance of spirit**: this anticipates the thoughts of the first letter to Böhlendorff (Letter 238).
B232, S239

235. TO IMMANUEL NIETHAMMER. Nürtingen, 23 June 1801

Survives in a copy by J. L. Döderlein. Having waited in vain for a reply from Schiller, it looks as if H turned to Niethammer instead. This letter seems also to have gone unanswered. **silence**: probably they had not been in touch since H's last letter of 24 February 1796 (Letter 187). The "philosophical letters" mentioned there were never completed. **Schütz**: Christian Gottfried (1747–1832), editor of the influential *Allgemeine Literatur-Zeitung* and professor of classics at Jena. **Tennemann**: Wilhelm Gottlieb (1761–1819), professor of philosophy at Jena. His chief work

was a *Geschichte der Philosophie* in twelve volumes (*History of Philosophy*, 1798–1819); also a translator of Hume and Locke.
B233, S240

FROM WILHELM FRIEDRICH ELSÄSSER. Stuttgart, 26 June 1801

A note preserved in a copy by Schlesier. **your *Agis***: cf. Sinclair's letter of 8 February 1799. Here it is probably a copy of Plutarch's *Life of Agis* that is meant.
*B90, *S90

FROM SIEGFRIED SCHMID. Friedberg, 6 July 1801

Fragment transcribed by Schlesier. **Bartz:** Christian Jakob, had studied in Jena from 1797. **editor:** Schütz (see notes to Letter 235). **Huber:** see List of Correspondents.
*B91, *S91

FROM SIEGFRIED SCHMID. Friedberg, 31 July 1801

Fragment transcribed by Schlesier. **my last letter**: either the letter above, in which case Schmid sent H's review back with it, or a lost letter between this and the last.
*B92, *S92

FROM LUDWIG FERDINAND HUBER. Stuttgart, 6 August 1801

Summary by Schlesier. ***publication of his poems***: there are notes in Cotta's ledger of plans to publish H's poems on terms identical to those given here, but nothing came of them. *1 old louis d'or*: worth about nine guilders. **Damenkalender**: nothing of H's appeared here, but "Der Wanderer" appeared in Cotta's journal *Flora* in 1801 and four further substantial poems—"Heimkunft," "Die Wanderung," "Dichterberuf," and "Stimme des Volks"—in *Flora* in 1802. These are noted in Cotta's ledger as "sample poems" for the projected collection. See *Poems and Fragments*, 330–37, 482–89, 232–37, 238–43.
*B93, *S93

FROM CHRISTIAN LANDAUER. Stuttgart, 22 October 1801

Prof. Ströhlin: see notes to Letter 106. H went to Stuttgart the day he received this letter. **Bordeaux**: this is the first mention of H's last tutoring job, for which he set off at the end of the year. **dispensed from preaching**: officially, H was engaged in Bordeaux as "private tutor and preacher in a German Protestant household" (see Letter 238). **a sermon**: nothing known.
*B94, *S94

236. TO THE FAMILY. Stuttgart, ~ October/November 1801

The original is lost. In the first publication by C. T. Schwab (1846) the date is given as "probably November 1801." It is likely the letter was written on a short visit to Landauer's in Stuttgart where H had gone in response to his letter above. It is also possible that it is from the year before, referring not to the prospect of Bordeaux but of Hauptwil.
B234, S241

237. TO HIS BROTHER. Nürtingen, 4 December 1801

B235, S242

238. TO CASIMIR ULRICH BÖHLENDORFF. Nürtingen, 4 December 1801

Survives in a copy in Sinclair's hand found in the papers of Princess Auguste of Hesse-Homburg in Schwerin—an indication of the importance in which this letter was held by H's contemporaries. **Your *Fernando***: the play *Fernando oder die Kunstweihe. Eine dramatische Idylle* (1802), which Böhlendorff had dispatched on receiving a lost letter sent by H from Hauptwil. Böhlendorff's play is dedicated to Muhrbeck and was published by Friedrich Wilmans, later the publisher of H's Sophocles translations. **what we are born with**: the word H uses is "das Nationelle," used in the sense of "innate." In his new understanding, the Greeks and the Germans, the ancients and the moderns, are born with opposing origins or natures, and for that reason imitation of the Greeks in the neoclassical sense is wrongheaded. As epitomized in their burial rites,

the Greeks are fiery (associated by H with passion, the sky, formlessness) whereas the moderns are earthy (associated with clarity, sobriety, form). The aim of culture, though, is a balance, to be achieved by the moderns in a way diametrically opposed to the Greeks, by tending toward fire. Homer achieved this balance by appropriating "occidental" plasticity, and H praises Böhlendorff for combining "precision" and "warmth" in his play. *Junonian sobriety*: Juno was famous for her stately beauty; she represents here plastic form. **Apollonian realm**: Apollo was among other things the sun god ("heavenly fire"). **living craft and proportion**: the balance. The word here translated by "craft," *Geschick*, can also mean propriety, in the sense of the "sacred propriety with which they [the Greeks] *had* to proceed in dealings with the gods" (Letter 217 to Mehmel). It can also mean "fate," but this meaning seems to be secondary here. **the Greeks are indispensable to us**: because they allow us to experience in the foreign clarity of their art our own original nature. **a more epic treatment**: one which brings out occidental sobriety. **fear and pity**: according to Aristotle's *Poetics* the emotions through which tragedy produces catharsis. **Jupiter**: the supreme god, made palpable by tragedy. **your Spain**: where *Fernando* is mostly set. **"with a calm hand . . .**: freely citing Goethe's poem "Grenzen der Menschheit"/"Limits of humankind." **this sign**: i.e., lightning ("heavenly fire"). **Tantalus**: son of Zeus who in Greek mythology was allowed to eat with the gods but offended them and was cast into the underworld to suffer eternal "tantalization."
B236, S243

239. TO HIS MOTHER. Lyon, 9 January 1802

H probably left Nürtingen on about 10th December, going via Stuttgart to Strasbourg (arriving 15th) where he was detained by the authorities until the end of the month. **flooding**: the river Saône was prone to break its banks. **Tomorrow I set off for Bordeaux**: the journey remained complicated and he arrived only on 28th January. **the route via Lyon**: the reasons for taking this unusual and much more difficult route are not certain, but it seems possible that contrary to what he tells his mother here H chose it himself, hoping to see Napoleon who was due in Lyon where he had summoned a meeting of the Italian deputies of the Cisalpine Republic. The passport issued on 9th January permitted him to stay four days in the city, so it is quite likely that H did see Napoleon, who arrived on 11th,

no doubt with great pomp. **Karl will be in Nürtingen**: he took up a new post there at the beginning of the year.
B237, S244

240. TO HIS MOTHER. Bordeaux, 28 January 1802

Written immediately on arrival in Bordeaux. **my new situation**: H's new job was in the household of the wine-merchant and consul for Hamburg Daniel Christoph Meyer (1751–1818) and his wife Henriette Andrieu de St André (1753–1833) who was born in San Domingo. They were very well to do and had a grand house in the middle of the city. H lived not in that house but nearby among Lutherans of which there was a large community in Bordeaux. He had four or five girls to teach. **walking**: H covered most of the 350-odd miles from Lyon to Bordeaux on foot, the exact route is not known.
B238, S245

241. TO HIS MOTHER, Bordeaux, Good Friday 1802

Good Friday fell on 16th April. It seems likely that this is the first letter home since the last, and these are perhaps the only letters written from Bordeaux (see the end of this letter). Schlesier, who also copies the letter, notes at the end H's address: "chez Mons: Gauthier et Compagnie à Bordeaux." **our now blessed grandmother**: she had died in Nürtingen on 14 February 1802. **Things here could hardly be better**: and yet on May 10th, H received his passport for the journey home and on June 7th was issued with a visa in Strasbourg.
B239, S246

FROM ISAAK VON SINCLAIR. Homburg, 30 June 1802

Survives in partial copies by Christoph Theodor Schwab and Schlesier. H had written Sinclair a lost letter on 11 December 1801, just before his departure for Bordeaux, but seemingly nothing since then. The present letter was sent to Landauer in Stuttgart for forwarding to Bordeaux, where Sinclair took H still to be. In fact, having passed through Strasbourg on 7th June, H probably arrived in Stuttgart about the middle of the month (Michael Franz thinks 10th or 11th), in a wild and possibly deranged state,

presumably staying at Landauer's. On July 3rd, Landauer wrote to Karl Gok saying that H's condition "was gradually becoming more peaceful." Sinclair's letter then arrived, either while H was still in Stuttgart, in which case it may have provoked a sudden flight home, or just after he had already gone back to Nürtingen. It seems likely that H first learnt of Susette Gontard's death (22nd June) from this letter, but this is not certain. **a similar fate**: not known what this is. **Ebel**: Ebel had returned from Paris in January 1802 and was the doctor attending Susette Gontard on her sickbed.
*B95, *S96

FROM ISAAK VON SINCLAIR. Homburg, 20 July 1802

Survives in a copy by Schlesier. Sinclair wrote to H's mother on the same day, enclosing this. H replied with a letter of August 2nd that is lost. **My letter to you**: i.e., his previous letter, of 30 June.
*B96, *S97

FROM ISAAK VON SINCLAIR. Homburg, 7 November 1802

Summary and extract by Schlesier, who notes that the letter was sent to H in Nürtingen. H replied in a lost letter of 22 November 1802. *a poem of Pindaric sweep*: probably "Die Wanderung"/"The Journey," which had just appeared in *Flora*. It speaks of "loving arrows" rather than of "golden arrows of love." **Regensburg**: H had been in Regensburg in late September/early October with Sinclair, who was there to represent the duchy of Hesse-Homburg at the negotiations following the Peace of Lunéville. There he got to know the Landgrave of Homburg, to whom he would soon dedicate the hymn "Patmos." The Landgrave hoped to extend his territories (the "cause"). **winter**: Sinclair was intending to get H to Homburg in the spring, though he did not go until June. *Horn*: see note to Letter 170. H had met him again in Regensburg and from Nürtingen sent him the manuscript of his Sophocles translations. Horn was to approach the publisher Unger in Berlin but had no luck. He may however have engineered the eventual agreement with Wilmans.
*B97, *S98

242. TO CASIMIR ULRICH BÖHLENDORFF. Nürtingen, mid-November 1802

Found among H's papers, and so probably the draft for the letter to which Böhlendorff replied on December 2nd. Though it is not certain this writing

is addressed to Böhlendorff it is widely accepted as such. The thinking in the first letter to Böhlendorff, the tension between formlessness and form, is evident here too in the descriptions, but it has become less theoretical and more matter of lived experience, a threat. **the fear of patriotic doubt and of hunger**: referring to the tribulations and divisions endured by the population of rural France during the Revolution. **the fire of the sky**: one of several phrases shared with the first letter to Böhlendorff. **as one says of heroes**: as, for example, of Patroclus or Oedipus. **the Vendée**: in this region, which H will have travelled through on his return from Bordeaux, there were notable uprisings, brutally quashed, by movements loyal to the monarchy. **virtuosity**: the second section of the "Notes on the *Antigone*" also speaks of Antigone's "virtuosity" as she faces death. There are many correspondences between this letter and H's notes to his Sophocles translations. **popularity**: (*Popularität*) possibly glossed in the following phrase ("their manner of receiving foreign natures . . ."), or else meaning "what defines them as a people." **tenderness**: (*Zärtlichkeit*) also in the sense of "sensitiveness to impression" (OED). **the antiquities**: in Paris (see Letter 246 to Seckendorf, 12 March 1804), where Napoleon had brought trophies from Italy and Egypt. H's journey home from Bordeaux almost certainly went via Paris. **the coincidence in one region of different characters of nature, so that all the holy places of the earth are together in one place**: see lines 20–21 of "Vom Abgrund nemlich . . ."/"For from the abyss . . .": "And there I am/All things at once" (*Poems and Fragments*, 678/679). The landscape around Nürtingen is transitional, mixing northern and southern vegetation. **annotate**: (*commentiren*) the sense being "imitate."
B240, S247

FROM CASIMIR ULRICH BÖHLENDORFF. Berlin, 2 December 1802

Summary by Schlesier, who notes that the letter was enclosed in the following letter from Sinclair. **Berlin**: Böhlendorff had been there since May 1802 as secretary to Karl Ludwig Woltmann. *Hölderlin's letter*: almost certainly Letter 242. *journal*: the *Poetisches Taschenbuch* (1803) has nothing by H in it.
*B98, *S99

FROM ISAAK VON SINCLAIR. Homburg, early December 1802

Extract and summary by Schlesier. **Frau von Kalb**: Charlotte von Kalb was living with Sinclair's mother in Homburg. The good news about her

finances, which had been ruined by speculations made by her brother-in-law, turned out to be misleading. **Sophocles**: H's translations of *Oedipus* and *Antigone* were eventually published by Wilmans. There is no archival trace of approaches Charlotte von Kalb may have made to the publishers mentioned, nor of a letter to Mehmel.
*B99, *S100

FROM ISAAK VON SINCLAIR. Homburg, 6 February 1803

Summary and extracts by Schlesier. **H.'s letter**: lost. **his poem**: "Patmos," dedicated to the Landgrave of Hesse-Homburg and given to him on his fifty-fifth birthday on 30 January 1803 (in *Poems and Fragments*, 550–65). **B.**: Berlin. **passage about the Last Supper and the disciples**: "Patmos," lines 78–107 (Schlesier makes this sound like a different poem from the one given to the Landgrave but that cannot be). **difference of opinion**: not ascertainable. **Enslin**: Johann Karl (1773–1826), doctor in Heidenheim, from Tübingen, studied in Jena 1794–1796.
*B100, *S101

FROM CHRISTIAN LANDAUER. Stuttgart, 8 February 1803

the enclosed letter: not preserved. **Scheffauer**: Philipp Jakob (1756–1808), sculptor in Stuttgart, friend and brother-in-law of Landauer's, known to H since 1800, perhaps longer. **monument**: for Karl Ludwig of Baden, who died in 1801 in Sweden; part of the "Gothic Tower" in the Erbprinzengarten in Karlsruhe.
*B101, *S102

243. TO FRIEDRICH WILMANS. Nürtingen, 28 September 1803

the translation of the Sophocles tragedies: H's translations of *Oedipus the King* and *Antigone* were published by Wilmans in 1804 (*Die Trauerspiele des Sophokles*). He intended to do more. **Schelling**: H had visited him in June 1803 in Murrhardt, probably chiefly with the aim of soliciting his help in finding a publisher for his Sophocles. In a letter to Hegel of 11 July 1803, Schelling recounts the visit: he was appalled by his appearances and state of mind and wondered whether Hegel might be able to look after him in Jena. It seems unlikely that Schelling ever approached the

Weimar theatre. **spring book fair**: in Leipzig (*Jubilatemesse*). Both volumes appeared in time for the fair in 1804. **an introduction**: mentioned in the next two letters also but sadly (it seems) never written. On the other hand we have the "Notes" (see next letter). **national convenience**: for "-konvenienz" H first wrote "-karakter." **the oriental element**: "heavenly fire" as opposed to the "occidental," modern element (see first letter to Böhlendorff). **artistic bias**: H's odd word is *Kunstfehler* (literally, "art-error"), the process through which the Greeks corrected their inborn tendency toward fire, which H now thinks of as having been overdone, at least from a modern perspective. The first letter to Böhlendorff provides a sort of commentary. (The modern sense of *Kunstfehler* is "professional error," but this was introduced only in 1870.)
B241, S248

244. TO FRIEDRICH WILMANS. Nürtingen, 8 December 1803

A note on the back of the previous letter, in Wilmans's hand, suggests he sent a chasing letter on 19th November, to which this responds. **lively enough**: i.e., it did not bring out the "oriental element" enough (see previous letter). Several layers of work are evident in the translation of *Antigone*. **notes**: the famous "Anmerkungen" H appended to each of the two plays—in English in *Essays and Letters*, 317–32, and in *Selected Poetry*, 312–17 and 367–73. **short poems for an almanac**: Wilmans had asked (presumably in the lost letter of 19th November) for poems for an annual he was editing, *Taschenbuch. Der Liebe und Freundschaft gewidmet*. H sent the "Night Poems" mentioned in the next letter. **Schelling**: see notes to the previous letter. Whether H wrote is not known. **individual lyric poems of some length**: (some of) the hymns, mentioned again in the following two letters to Wilmans; see especially "Friedensfeier"/"Celebration of Peace" with its prefatory note which was clearly ready for publication (*Poems and Fragments*, 522–33).
B242, S249

245. TO FRIEDRICH WILMANS. Nürtingen, December 1803

Written in late December, in reply to a lost letter from Wilmans whose dispatch is noted on the back of the previous letter as 19th December and which accompanied a galley proof of (part of) the Sophocles translations.

letters like these: H's Sophocles was printed in a modern Latin typeface (Walbaum-Antiqua) rather than Gothic script. **Night Poems**: this is usually taken to be the *Nachtgesänge*, nine poems which belong together: "Chiron," "Tränen"/"Tears," "An die Hoffnung"/"To Hope," "Vulkan"/"Vulcan," "Blödigkeit"/"Timidness," "Ganymed"/"Ganymede," "Hälfte des Lebens"/"Half of Life," "Lebensalter"/"Ages of Life," "Der Winkel von Hahrdt"/"The Nook at Hardt" (all in *Poems and Fragments*). They appeared in Wilmans's annual in 1804, under the simple title "Poems." **songs on our land and times**: H's phrase is "vaterländische Gesänge," which it would be misleading to translate more literally as "patriotic hymns": "vaterländisch" for H means something like "relating to present European possibilities," but in the first instance his "Vaterland" was Württemberg. He is imagining poems that deal with the times and understand those times as fundamentally different from ancient Greece. To be read alongside both letters to Böhlendorff (Letters 238 and 242). **the *Messias* and [. . .] certain odes**: by Klopstock, who had died earlier in the year. His work is taken to be an "exception" to the general drift of German poetry. ***Views***: *Malerische Ansichten des Rheins von Mainz bis Düsseldorf* (*Picturesque Views of the Rhine from Mainz to Düsseldorf*), published by Wilmans. See Letter 246, to Seckendorf.
B243, S250

FROM FRIEDRICH WILMANS. Frankfurt, 3 January 1804

Summary by Schlesier, who gives the date 3 June 1803. On the back of Letter 245 Wilmans noted the date of his reply: "3 Jan 1804," and Sattler convincingly claims that this is a summary of that reply, Schlesier having misread "Jun" for "Jan," and Wilmans having erroneously written "1803" for "1804" at the beginning of the new year. The curt summary seems to suit the later dating better, but does not quite rule out the earlier date. ***Prof. Voigt***: Nikolaus Vogt—see note to Letter 139.
*B102, *S103

FROM FRIEDRICH WILMANS. Frankfurt, 28 January 1804

Summary by Schlesier. ***poems***: the *Nachtgesänge*. ***longer poems***: some of the hymns mentioned earlier, perhaps also the elegies; the plan to publish them was not realized.
*B103, *S104

246. TO LEO VON SECKENDORF. Nürtingen, 12 March 1804

your house: in Stuttgart. **prospectus**: for *Picturesque Views of the Rhine from Mainz to Düsseldorf* (see Letter 245). This was a three-volume work with thirty-two "views" of the Rhine as copperplate engravings, intended to show the beauty of the region. The prospectus is dated 1 May 1803 and comes with a sample plate showing the area around the "Mäuseturm" near Bingen. H's following remarks relate to this. **Prince**: the Elector Friedrich of Württemberg. **angle**: ("Winkel"), presumably meaning the perspective. **antiquities in Paris**: cf. Letter 242. H probably passed through Paris on his way back from Bordeaux. **Fable**: used in the sense of "myth"; see H's notes "On the Fable of the Ancients" (*Essays and Letters*, 333). **enemies of our mother country**: probably H is thinking of the elector of Württemberg and his conservative supporters at the court, who were adopting a more and more absolutist stance at this time.
B244, S251

247. TO FRIEDRICH WILMANS. Nürtingen, 2 April 1804

Printer's errors: both volumes were plagued by misprints. A list of errata for *Oedipus* in H's hand survives with forty-one items, some of which are revisions rather than corrections. It wasn't printed. **raw print**: the sample pages Wilmans sent in December 1803 seem to have been printed with a thicker layer of ink, accentuating the shapes of the letters. **copies**: Wilmans sent twelve copies on 14th April. In his list of those to receive copies (see next letter) Schiller's name is missing. **Princess of Homburg**: the translation was dedicated to her. **in the direction of eccentric enthusiasm**: the first letter to Böhlendorff offers a framework for understanding this difficult sentence: "eccentric enthusiasm" is another term for the native Greek tendency, as opposed to occidental "sobriety." In his work as translator of Sophocles, which he hoped to continue, H has brought out "what was forbidden to the original poet" by going toward this Greek pole and away from his native pole, which is the direction he had explained to Böhlendorff that modern writers had to go in. H wrote "gegen die exzentrische Begeisterung," which could also mean "*against* eccentric enthusiasm," but it is hard to make sense of the words if they are taken in this way. **sending you something**: the long poems mentioned in earlier letters to Wilmans.
B245, S252

FROM FRIEDRICH WILMANS. Frankfurt, 14 April 1804

Esteemed Sir & friend: beneath this H wrote, presumably as a savage rejoinder to the formal address: "but exposed to the rabble like no other." **complimentary copies**: down the left-hand side of the letters H has written a list of names, presumably of those to whom he intended to send copies. The names are: Seckendorf, Haug, Hegel, Goethe, Bahnmaier, Schmid, Heinse, Hartmann, Matthisson, Schelling, Le Pique, and Sinclair. Additional notes suggest he intended to send a copy of the elegy "Stuttgart" to Schmid, of "Bread and Wine" to Heinse, and of the hymn "The Only One" to Sinclair—they are the dedicatees of these three poems. Bahnmaier is Jonathan Friedrich (1774–1841), probably known to H from the Stift, but it is not clear why he figures here. Hartmann is probably Ferdinand (1774–1842)—a painter in Stuttgart H will have known via Neuffer or Landauer—or one of his brothers. Le Pique is Johann Philipp (1776–1815), probably known to H from Jena where he studied theology 1792–1796. **a list**: whether H drew one up for the *Antigone* as well is not known, but nothing appeared in the *Literatur-Zeitung* or anywhere else. *B104, *S105

248. TO PRINCESS AUGUSTE OF HESSE-HOMBURG. Nürtingen, April/May 1804

Summary and excerpts by Schlesier who notes that the original was an incomplete draft. **the first volume of my translation**: it bore the printed dedication: "TO THE PRINCESS AUGUSTE OF HESSE-HOMBURG. You encouraged me years ago by writing to me so kindly, and in the meantime I have left you without a response. Now, since with us a poet is obliged to take up other work for the benefit of himself or of others, I have chosen this occupation because it is bound up in what are foreign but also solid and historical laws. My further wish, if there is time, is to sing of the ancestors of our princes and their seats and the angels of our sacred country. Hölderlin." By the encouragement, he means the brief letter she sent on 28 November 1799. B246, S254

FROM FRIEDRICH WILMANS. Frankfurt, 27 May 1804

Summary by Schlesier. *the honorarium*: on March 28th H's mother had asked Wilmans to deduct an amount owing for books. *B105, *S106

FROM HIS MOTHER. Nürtingen, 29 October 1805

The only surviving letter to H from his mother. Since June 1804 he had been living in Homburg where Sinclair had fetched him to a sinecure as court librarian. **landlord**: H lodged at first with the clockmaker Calame in Dorotheenstraße 34, near Sinclair's. Later he had to move to the saddler Lattner's in Haingasse 8. **Frau von Bröck**: Auguste Wilhelmine von Proeck (died 1815), Sinclair's "gracious lady mother." **Zwiefalten**: H's brother had moved to Zwiefalten an der Donau to a new post in 1803 and married Marie Eberhardine Blöst (1773–1853) in 1804. **distress & disturbance of war**: the War of the Third Coalition broke out in 1805. Napoleon and his troops swept through southern Germany, taking Ulm in October, Vienna in November, and routing the allies at the Battle of Austerlitz in December.
*B106, *S107

TÜBINGEN, 1806–1843

Mostly, it seems, at his host Ernst Zimmer's prompting, H wrote sixty-eight surviving letters or notes from the "tower" in Tübingen, almost all to his mother (who died in 1828). He had been discharged from Autenrieth's clinic in Tübingen in May 1807. The letters cannot be dated at all accurately, with the exception of three which are postmarked, two to which H's nephew Fritz Breunlin affixed the month/year of reception, and the single letter from Tübingen to his brother, which is reliably dated by Gustav Schlesier. The chronological order of the body of the letters is also uncertain. Most of the letters were numbered 1–60: the first three numbers, in ink, in the mother's hand, but the others in pencil and a different hand. There is no clear evidence that this sequence was meant to be chronological, but most editions take it as their order, usually with the working assumption (tacit in Beck's edition) that it is chronological. The only editor to diverge in a serious way from this sequence is Luigi Reitani, who also published an article justifying the decisions guiding his arrangement in *Prose, teatro e lettere*, while emphasizing their "fragile basis" ("Zur Anordnung der "Turm"-Briefe Hölderlins," *Hölderlin-Jahrbuch* 42 [2020–2021]). He attempts a rough chronology using watermarks and a few other indications, but the datings he proposes are capacious. (The most frequent indication is "between 1813 and 1828.") Sattler, in the Frankfurt Edition, treats the sequence as chronological (with two adjustments) and following but not acknowledging the work of Gregor Wittkop in his documentation of H's Tübingen years (*Hölderlin: Der Pflegsohn: Texte und Dokumente 1806-1843*) assumes that the letters were sent with Zimmer's quarterly bills, going so far as to propose precise dates for each letter. As Reitani observes, these do not entirely fit with the few known dates we do have. However, as the watermarks do not appear to offer conclusive evidence, and as taking the handwritten numbering as broadly chronological seems not entirely wayward, it is followed here. Like the German editions, but unlike Reitani, I also separate out the letters to H's mother and those to his sister and brother. The notes sometimes mention alternative findings, but do not attempt to assign dates where no information exists. They give the handwritten numbers where present.

249. TO HIS MOTHER. Tübingen, 15 September 1812

The date is that of the postmark.
No. 1
B247, S255

250. TO HIS MOTHER

Zimmer: Ernst Friedrich (1772–1838), was a joiner and cabinet-maker from Tübingen who in 1807 became the owner of Bursagasse 6, the house by the Neckar, built into the town walls, where H was taken in as a lodger in May 1807. His workshop was on the ground floor. With his wife Marie Elisabetha he had five children of which two daughters and a son survived. The youngest, Lotte (1813–1879), was closely involved in looking after H, especially after Zimmer's death.
No. 2
B248, S256

251. TO HIS MOTHER. Tübingen, 2 March 1813

Added at the bottom of a dated (and postmarked) letter from Zimmer to H's mother. The closing words run: "I asked Hölderlin whether he would not like to write as well, it seems though that he has no desire to at the moment." Hence the brief postscript.
B249, S258

252. TO HIS MOTHER

No. 3
B250, S260

253. TO HIS MOTHER

No. 4 (the first number not in his mother's hand)
B251, S261

254. TO HIS MOTHER

No. 5
B252, S262

255. TO HIS MOTHER

No. 6
B253, S263

256. TO HIS MOTHER

No. 7
B254, S264

257. TO HIS MOTHER

No. 8
B255, S265

258. TO HIS MOTHER

No. 9
B256, S266

259. TO HIS MOTHER

One of two letters to his mother (the other being Letter 309) which H signs with his full name (here with an extra *e*).
No. 10
B257, S267

260. TO HIS MOTHER

holidays: probably referring to Christmas. Both Sattler and Reitani put this letter early in the year, albeit not the same one (1815 and 1814 respectively).
No. 11
B258, S268

261. TO HIS MOTHER. Tübingen, 18 April 1815

Date as postmark.
No. 12
B259, S269

262. TO HIS MOTHER

No. 13
B260, S270

263. TO HIS MOTHER

No. 14
B261, S271

264. TO HIS MOTHER

No. 15
B262, S272

265. TO HIS MOTHER

No. 16
B263, S273

266. TO HIS MOTHER

No. 17
B264, S274

267. TO HIS MOTHER

No. 18
B265, S275

268. TO HIS MOTHER

No. 19
B266, S276

269. TO HIS MOTHER

No. 20
B267, S277

270. TO HIS MOTHER

No. 21
B268, S278

271. TO HIS MOTHER

No. 22
B269, S279

272. TO HIS MOTHER

No. 23
B270, S280

273. TO HIS MOTHER

No. 24
B271, S281

274. TO HIS MOTHER

No. 25
B272, S282

275. TO HIS MOTHER

No. 26
B273, S283

276. TO HIS MOTHER

Mrs Zimmer: Marie Elisabetha, *née* Gfrörer (1774–1849).
No. 27
B274, S284

277. TO HIS MOTHER

No. 28
B275, S285

278. TO HIS MOTHER

No. 29
B276, S286

279. TO HIS MOTHER

No. 30
B277, S287

280. TO HIS MOTHER

No. 31
B278, S288

281. TO HIS MOTHER

No. 32
B279, S289

282. TO HIS MOTHER

No. 33
B280, S, 290

283. TO HIS MOTHER

No. 34
B281, S291

284. TO HIS MOTHER

No. 35
B282, S292

285. TO HIS MOTHER

No. 36
B283, S293

286. TO HIS MOTHER

No. 37
B284, S294

287. TO HIS MOTHER

No. 38
B285, S295

288. TO HIS MOTHER

No. 39
B286, S296

289. TO HIS MOTHER

No. 40
B287, S297

290. TO HIS MOTHER

No. 41
B288, S298

291. TO HIS MOTHER

No. 42
B289, S299

292. TO HIS MOTHER

No. 43
B290, S301

293. TO HIS MOTHER

No. 44
B291, S302

294. TO HIS MOTHER

Friz and **Heinrike**: H's nephew and niece.
No. 45
B292, S303

295. TO HIS MOTHER

This letter was sent "per Express" and the address, written by Zimmer, is smudged. So it was perhaps dispatched in a hurry, possibly in alarm at H's intentions of paying his mother a visit. The previous letter possibly also envisages a visit, as does much more clearly Letter 303.
No. 46
B293, S304

296. TO HIS MOTHER

No. 47
B294, S305

297. TO HIS MOTHER

No. 48
B295, S306

298. TO HIS MOTHER

An unusual letter, in that it upbraids his mother, seemingly in response to a specific matter. Beck notes that the agitation is perhaps visible in the handwriting. The watermark is the same as for Letter 261 (18 April 1815) and Reitani presumes a date between 1815 and 1817. Sattler (without particular evidence) assumes November 1824, which tallies with Wittkop's dating.
No. 49
B296, S307

299. TO HIS MOTHER

No. 50
B297, S308

300. TO HIS MOTHER

No. 51
B298, S309

301. TO HIS MOTHER

No. 52
B299, S310

302. TO HIS MOTHER. Tübingen, November 1825

Date in pencil in Fritz Breunlin's hand. Breunlin took over H's mother's account books in the same year. Reitani thinks this may be H's last letter to his mother.
No. 53
B300, S311

303. TO HIS MOTHER

my legacy: that is, the money left to him by his father, parsimoniously administrated by his mother. This is the only place in which H raises any sort of claim to it.

No. 54
B301, S312

304. TO HIS MOTHER

No. 55
B302, S313

305. TO HIS MOTHER

No. 56
B303, S314

306. TO HIS MOTHER

No. 57
B304, S315

307. TO HIS MOTHER

Sattler gives an early date for this and for the next letter, but Reitani sees
no grounds for dating this postscript to a letter of Zimmer's more precisely
than between 1807 and 1828.
No. 59
B305, S257

308. TO HIS MOTHER

A postscript cut off from a letter of Zimmer's.
No. 60
B306, S259

309. TO HIS MOTHER

Usually treated as H's last letter to his mother, though Reitani doubts it
and presumes on no real evidence a date between 1813 and 1815. Together
with Letter 259 the only one of these late letters H signed with his full
name (in the manuscript followed by a comma).
B307, S316

310. TO HIS SISTER

Sattler assumes that all H's letters to his sister were written after their mother passed away on 17th February 1828, in which case the mention of her "return" here ("Zurükkunft") would have to be an odd reference to her death. It's more likely this letter was sent some time before—Reitani suggests late 1812. **alone at home**: probably a reference to Heinrike Breunlin's widowed state; otherwise to their mother's death.
No. 58 (the only letter to H's sister with one of these penciled numbers, which itself makes it less likely that it was written after Frau Gok's death).
B308, S317

311. TO HIS SISTER

It seems likely, and is generally assumed, that this and subsequent letters were written after the death of the mother (but see note to next letter).
B309, S321

312. TO HIS SISTER

Reitani thinks this letter may have been written between 1813 and 1815.
B310, S320

313. TO HIS SISTER

B311, S318

314. TO HIS SISTER

This letter and the next turned up in America in 1963.
B311a, S322

315. TO HIS SISTER. Tübingen, 1829

His sister has added in pencil: "In the year 1829."
B311b, S319

316. TO HIS BROTHER. Tübingen, 23 March 1823

Transcript by Schlesier. The letter was enclosed with one from Zimmer to H's mother, noting that H recently seemed "as if woken from a long dream." The date is that of Zimmer's letter.
B312, S300

FROM HIS BROTHER. Stuttgart, 25 July 1826

copy of your excellent *Poems*: the 1826 edition of H's *Gedichte*, of which H's brother had received thirty copies. Schwab and Uhland did the actual editing, anonymously. ***Diest***: Heinrich von (1791–1824), a lieutenant in the Prussian army, who began gathering materials for the edition with the support of Princess Auguste von Hesse-Homburg and her sister Marianne. ***Kerner***: Justinus (1786–1862), a poet, but also a doctor who looked after H while he was in Autenrieth's clinic in Tübingen. ***Schwab***: Gustav (1792–1850), poet, father of C. T. Schwab. At the Stift, and later a pastor in Gomaringen. He published an influential version of the Greek myths. ***Uhland***: Ludwig (1787–1862), a well-known poet of the so-called Swabian School and also an active politician. **2nd edition of your *Hyperion***: this had been published by Cotta in 1822. **visit**: of one of these visits H's brother told Kerner that H "looked good for his age and was very friendly and quiet."
*B107, *S108

SELECTED READING

Editions

Sämtliche Werke. Edited by Friedrich Beissner and Adolf Beck. 8 vols. Stuttgart: Kohlhammer, 1943–85 = "Große Stuttgarter Ausgabe" [letters in volumes VI and (letters to Hölderlin) VII/1].

Sämtliche Werke. Edited by D. E. Sattler et al., 20 vols. Frankfurt: Stroemfeld/Roter Stern, 1975–2008 = "Frankfurter Hölderlin-Ausgabe" [letters in volumes XVIII and XIX].

Sämtliche Werke, Briefe und Dokumente in zeitlicher Folge. Edited by Dietrich Sattler. 12 vols. Munich: Luchterhand, 2004 = "Bremer Ausgabe" [seeks to put all the writings and documents in chronological order].

Sämtliche Werke und Briefe. Edited by Michael Knaupp. 3 vols. Munich: Hanser, 1992–93 [judicious reading edition that takes the earlier volumes of Sattler's edition into account].

Sämtliche Werke und Briefe. Edited by Jochen Schmidt. 3 vols. Frankfurt: Deutscher Klassiker Verlag, 1992–94 [follows the Stuttgart edition, extensive notes on the poems].

Translations

Poems and Fragments. Translated by Michael Hamburger. 4th ed. London: Anvil, 2004 [includes German text].

Selected Poetry. Translated by David Constantine. Hexham: Bloodaxe, 2018 [includes Hölderlin's Sophocles complete, no German].

Hyperion, or the Hermit in Greece. Translated by Howard Gaskill. Cambridge: Open Book, 2019.

The Death of Empedocles: A Mourning Play. Translated by David Farrell Krell. Albany: State University of New York Press, 2008 [includes the essays associated with *Empedokles*].

Essays and Letters. Translated by Jeremy Adler and Charlie Louth. London: Penguin, 2009 [contains 120 letters and the complete essays].

The Poet's Vocation: Selections from Letters by Hölderlin, Rimbaud, and Hart Crane. Translated by William Burford and Christopher Middleton. Austin: University of Texas, 1968 [the first translation of thirteen of Hölderlin's letters (sometimes extracts) into English, by Christopher Middleton].

The Recalcitrant Art: Diotima's Letters to Hölderlin and Related Missives. Translated by Douglas F. Kenney and Sabine Menner-Bettscheid. Albany: State University of New York Press, 2000.

Oeuvres. Edited by Philippe Jaccottet, Bibliothèque de la Pléiade. Paris: Gallimard, 1967 [letters translated by Denise Naville].

Prose, teatro e lettere. Edited by Luigi Reitani. Milan: Mondadori, 2019 [letters translated by Andreina Lavagetto].

Resources

Hölderlin: Eine Chronik in Text und Bild. Edited by Adolf Beck and Paul Raabe. Frankfurt am Main: Insel, 1970.

Hölderlin: Der Pflegsohn: Texte und Dokumente, 1806—mit den neu entdeckten Nürtinger Pflegschaftsakten. Edited by Gregor Wittkop. Stuttgart: Metzler, 1993 [contains all the documents relating to the second half of Hölderlin's life].

Hölderlin-Handbuch: Leben—Werk—Wirkung. Edited by Johann Kreuzer. Stuttgart: Metzler, 2002, 2020 [including section on Hölderlin's letters by Christiane Löhr].

Hölderlin Texturen. Edited by Michael Franz, Ulrich Gaier, Valérie Lawitschka, et al. Tübingen: Hölderlin-Gesellschaft [fascinating biographical, intellectual, and political context: eight volumes published, further volumes planned]:
    1.1 *"Alle meine Hofnungen": Lauffen, Nürtingen, Denkendorf, Maulbronn, 1770–1788* (2003)
    1.2 *"Alle meine Hofnungen": Tübingen, 1788–1793* (2017)
    2 *Das "Jenaische Project": Wintersemester, 1794/95* (1995)
    3 *"Gestalten der Welt": Frankfurt, 1796–1798* (1996)
    4 *"Wo sind jetzt Dichter?": Homburg, Stuttgart, 1798–1800* (2002)
    5 *"Unter den Alpen gesungen": Hölderlin als Hauslehrer in Hauptwil* (2008)
    6.1 *"Offen die Fenster des Himmels": Nürtingen, Homburg, 1802–1806, Lebensstationen und Werke* (2024)
    6.2 *"Und freigelassen der Nachtgeist": Nürtingen, Homburg, 1802–1806, Interpretationen* (2024)

Der Brief—Ereignis und Objekt. Edited by Anne Bohnenkamp and Waltraud Wiethölter. Frankfurt: Stroemfeld, 2008.

General on Hölderlin

Bertaux, Pierre. *Friedrich Hölderlin*. Frankfurt am Main: Suhrkamp, 1981.

Constantine, David. *Hölderlin*. Oxford: Clarendon, 1988.

Hayden-Roy, Priscilla A. *"Sparta et Martha": Pfarramt und Heirat in der Lebensplanung Hölderlins und in seinem Umfeld*. Ostfildern: Thorbecke, 2010.

Martens, Gunter. *Friedrich Hölderlin*. Reinbek bei Hamburg: Rowohlt, 1996.

The Solid Letter: Readings of Friedrich Hölderlin. Edited by Aris Fioretos. Stanford: Stanford University Press, 1999 [includes an extensive bibliography of work on Hölderlin in English].

On Hölderlin's Letters

Raabe, Paul. *Die Briefe Hölderlins: Studien zur Entwicklung und Persönlichkeit des Dichters*. Stuttgart: Metzler, 1963.

Szondi, Peter. "Der Brief an Böhlendorff vom 4. Dezember 1801." In *Hölderlin-Studien: Mit einem Traktat über philologische Erkenntnis*. Frankfurt am Main: Suhrkamp, 1970.

Louth, Charlie. "The Question of Influence: Hölderlin's Dealings with Pindar and Schiller." *Modern Language Review* 95, no. 4 (October 2000): 1038–52.

Hölderlin-Jahrbuch 34 (2004–5) [special issue on "Hölderlins Briefe und die Briefkultur um 1800"].

Studia theodisca—Hölderliniana II (2016) [special issue on Hölderlin's letters, essays in German and Italian].

Index

Correspondents are asterisked; more information about them can be found in the List of Correspondents (pp. 573–80). In entries for correspondents, page numbers of letters to them are given in bold and letters from them in bold and italics. Names are generally given in what is now their standard form, though some alternatives are noted. In the letters themselves the original spellings are preferred. The notes (pp. 581–704) are only indexed selectively and usually not when findable from the main reference.